WHY SURVIVE?

BEING OLD IN AMERICA

Books by Robert N. Butler, M.D.

WHY SURVIVE? BEING OLD IN AMERICA

AGING AND MENTAL HEALTH (WITH MYRNA I. LEWIS)

HUMAN AGING (CO-AUTHOR)

WHY SURVIVE?

BEING OLD IN AMERICA

Robert N. Butler, M.D.

HARPER & ROW, PUBLISHERS

New York, Evanston, San Francisco, London

Acknowledgment is gratefully made for permission to reprint the following material under copyright:

Lines from "East Coker" in *Four Quartets* from *Collected Poems, 1909–1962* by T. S. Eliot. Copyright, 1943, by T. S. Eliot; copyright, 1971, by Esme Valerie Eliot. Reprinted by permission of Harcourt Brace Jovanovich, Inc., and Faber and Faber Ltd.

Lines from "The Nursing Home" by Ralph Robin, from *Southern Humanities Review* 7:4 (Fall, 1973), page 420.

Appendixes A, B and C, from *Aging and Mental Health* by Robert N. Butler and Myrna I. Lewis. St. Louis: The C. V. Mosby Company, 1973.

Designed by Janice Stern

Library of Congress Cataloging in Publication Data

Butler, Robert N
  Why survive?
  Bibliography: p.
  Includes index.
    1. Aged—United States. 2. Old age assistance—United States. I. Title.
HQ1064.U5B87 1975   301.43′5′0973   73-4066
ISBN 0-06-010591-7

75 76 77 78 79 10 9 8 7 6 5 4 3 2 1

To my children

Christine, Carole, Cynthia

my hope for a long and

satisfying life for them

CONTENTS

A PERSONAL NOTE

What leads a physician to gerontology? A psychiatrist? A young practitioner did not find in his medical or clinical training in the 1950s—any more than today—much knowledge, sympathy or understanding of the mental and physical needs of the elderly; but my childhood compelled this interest.

My grandparents reared me from infancy. My parents separated shortly after my birth, and when I was eleven months old, my mother brought me to live with her parents in Vineland, New Jersey, where my grandfather, then in his seventies, was a gentleman chicken farmer. I remember his blue overalls, his lined face and abundant white hair. He was my close friend and my teacher. Together we rose at 4 A.M. each day to feed chickens, candle eggs, grow oats and tend to the sick chickens in the "hospital" at one end of the chicken house. He would tell me of his younger days in Oklahoma and I would listen eagerly.

He disappeared suddenly when I was seven. I came back from a visit to a neighbor and he was gone. It made no sense. My grandmother said he went to visit relatives in Oklahoma—but he had not told me anything about the trip. With time, I realized I was never going to see him again. Dismay turned to fright and then to grief. I knew before they told me that he was dead.

Why? Why had he died? Why did people die? There was no talk, no funeral, only a "protective" silence that was more confusing than shared sorrow. I felt my silent way through a child's questions and a child's answers. Mostly, of course, I wanted to bring him back. Surely someone could arrange it. Everyone ought to live forever. No, that clearly would make for too many problems: old people would accumulate in hordes and the world would be packed so tight there would be no room for babies.

Well, what about a commission to decide who should live and who should die? My grandfather would undoubtedly qualify for resurrection and continued life—but could I be certain the commission would recognize his special worth? Would there be cheating? Would there be mistakes? This did not appear to be a satisfactory answer either.

It was Dr. Rose, our elderly white-haired family physician, who led me to a solution; I had cherished him for his reassuring presence and care through my serious bout with scarlet fever. If Dr. Rose had been there with the right medicine, I would certainly have had my grandfather with me longer. To be a doctor was clearly the answer. For the first time my anxiety eased.

If love of my grandfather and old Dr. Rose brought me to medicine, it was my grandmother in the years that followed who showed me the strength and endurance of the elderly. This was during the Depression. We lost the farm. She and I were soon on relief, eating government-surplus foods out of cans with stigmatizing white labels. Grandmother found work in a sewing room run by the WPA, and I sold newspapers and fixed bicycles for ten cents an hour. We moved into a hotel. When I was eleven, it burned to the ground with all our possessions. We started again. And what I remember even more than the hardships of those years was my grandmother's triumphant spirit and determination. Experiencing at first hand an older person's struggle to survive, I was myself helped to survive as well.

If this book informs, illuminates, angers and guides its readers, I shall have repaid some of the debt I owe.

ROBERT N. BUTLER

PREFACE

Old age in America is often a tragedy. Few of us like to consider it because it reminds us of our own mortality. It demands our energy and resources, it frightens us with illness and deformity, it is an affront to a culture with a passion for youth and productive capacity. We are so preoccupied with defending ourselves from the reality of death that we ignore the fact that human beings are alive until they are actually dead. At best, the living old are treated as if they were already half dead. And, because we primarily associate old age with dying, we have not yet emotionally absorbed the fact that medical and public-health advances now make it possible for millions of older people to be reasonably healthy.

Ten percent of the American population, or more than 20 million people, are now over 65 years of age. By the year 2000, this figure could increase to 25 percent. Paradoxically, the extended average life expectancy (which has risen from 47 years in 1900 to 71 years in 1970) has reduced the already limited social status of the old. Old people are commonplace among us rather than unusual. Longevity is no longer viewed with awe and envy now that it has been mass-produced through medical science. The old are people caught in a cultural time lag—suddenly there are large numbers of them and no one knows quite what to do. In each succeeding decade the proportion of elderly to young in the population increases. Anticipated breakthroughs in major killers like cancer and heart disease may swell the ranks of the old even more.

But is it all worth it? The truth is that we cannot promise a decent existence for those elderly now alive. We cannot house them, employ them or even feed them adequately. The American attitudes toward the old are contradictory. We pay lip service to the idealized images of beloved and tranquil grandparents, wise elders, white-haired patriarchs and matriarchs. But the opposite image disparages the elderly, seeing age as decay, decrepitude, a disgusting and undignified dependency. Our national social policies mirror these conflicts. We talk earnestly about our "senior citizens," but we do not provide enough for them to eat. We become angry with them for being burdens, yet we take for granted the standard of living that their previous work has made possible for us. Neglect is the treatment of choice, with medicine failing to care for their physical needs, mental-health personnel ignoring their emotional problems, communities neglecting to fill their social expectations. In America, childhood is romanticized, youth is idolized, middle age does the work, wields the power and pays the bills, and old age, its days empty of purpose, gets little or nothing for what it has already done. The old are in the way, an ironic example of public-health progress and medical technology creating a huge group of people for whom survival is possible but satisfaction in living elusive.

There have been many societies in which the old tended to give up their portion of vital resources to enable the young to survive and prosper and to ensure the continued existence of the social group. At times older persons have been forced into a position of sacrifice; at other times they voluntarily bestowed resources on the young out of empathy and generosity. Social policies like this can be likened to what military doctors call "battlefield triage"—those wounded who are in the worst condition (the old) are left unaided since resources can be more efficiently used to help the less seriously wounded (the young). But in our time need we sacrifice one age group for another? And do we indeed give to the young what we have denied the old? There are enormous numbers of malnourished children in the United States. One out of every four children under 18 grows up in poverty. Two-thirds of the nation's children receive inadequate medical care. Older people have begun to reach their own conclusions. Nelson Cruikshank, president of the National Council of Senior Citizens, acknowledges the concern of older people for children: "We as grandparents recognize our obligation to assure today's young boys and girls the fullest opportunity possible to mature as able-bodied citizens." But he adds: "We know, however, that a nation as rich as ours—with a gross national product amounting to more than a trillion dollars a year—can afford to rescue [both] young and old from the miserable life of the forgotten poor."

Misunderstandings, inaccurate assumptions and stereotypes abound in the public mind: most elderly are infirm and live in rest homes, hospitals or with their children; they are emotionally disengaged and bored with life; "senility" is inevitable and pervasive; they are unproductive and resistant to change. Few of these assumptions have been adequately tested, but what clinical work and research have been done refute many such myths.

This book portrays realistically the experience of older people in the United States today. An emotional appeal is not my primary intention. I am concerned, rather, with an appeal to rationality and an examination of public policy toward the elderly. Do our present social and economic policies make sense for old people? Do they make sense for our national well-being?

In my own twenty years of work with older people as a physician, researcher, psychiatrist and participant in community and public affairs, I have been forced to go beyond the traditional confines of medicine to look at cultural attitudes and economic circumstances. The sense of well-being, the physical and mental health, and the level of adjustment of the old are profoundly affected by societal attitudes, prejudice and poverty.

As this book went to press in early 1975, the situation of the average older person was becoming increasingly desperate. In the past year food prices had risen 15 percent, fuel a monstrous 45 percent, housing 12 percent, health costs 50 percent—with no end in sight. Anxiety among all age groups was pervasive. Being old in America has become more difficult than ever. At the highest levels of government, there is talk of cutting social programs, and the Social Security program is being attacked; nor are there any immediate or imaginative programs in the making to mitigate the anomalous combination of inflation and recession.

I have chosen to make heavy use of statistics rather than to rely on generalized case illustrations. *Why Survive?* is meant to be a useful source and resource book for some years to come. The particular statistics I cite will change rapidly, but they are significant because the general truths they illustrate are unfortunately likely to persist. The bases of my data are public policy and research material, professional literature and my own professional and personal experience.

I am concerned also with solutions. How does a nation alter its own cultural sensibility toward the old? I have offered my own and other people's solutions in this book, presenting ideal as well as more realistic possibilities. But I also hope others who have not previously considered these issues may be stimulated to formulate and experiment with their own solutions, especially the elderly themselves. Our ultimate goal is a national policy on aging of which we can be proud.

When we talk about old age, each of us is talking about his or her own future. We must ask ourselves if we are willing to settle for mere survival when so much more is possible.

Chapter 1

THE TRAGEDY OF
OLD AGE IN AMERICA

What is it like to be old in the United States? What will our own lives be like when we are old? Americans find it difficult to think about old age until they are propelled into the midst of it by their own aging and that of relatives and friends. Aging is the neglected stepchild of the human life cycle. Though we have begun to examine the socially taboo subjects of dying and death, we have leaped over that long period of time preceding death known as old age. In truth, it is easier to manage the problem of death than the problem of living as an old person. Death is a dramatic, one-time crisis while old age is a day-by-day and year-by-year confrontation with powerful external and internal forces, a bittersweet coming to terms with one's own personality and one's life.

Those of us who are not old barricade ourselves from discussions of old age by declaring the subject morbid, boring or in poor taste. Optimism and euphemism are other common devices. People will speak of looking forward to their "retirement years." The elderly are described respectfully as "senior citizens," "golden agers," "our elders," and one hears of old people who are considered inspirations and examples of how to "age well" or "gracefully." There is the popularly accepted opinion that Social Security and pensions provide a comfortable and reliable flow of funds so the elderly have few financial worries. Medicare has lulled the population into reassuring itself that the once terrible financial burdens of late-life illnesses are now eradicated. Advertisements and travel folders show relaxed, happy, well-dressed older people enjoying recreation, travel and their grandchildren. If they are no longer living in the old family home, they are pictured as delighted residents of retirement communities with names like Leisure World and Sun City, with lots of grass, clean air and fun. This is the American ideal of the "golden years" toward which millions of citizens are expectantly toiling through their workdays.

But this is not the full story. A second theme runs through the popular view of old age. Our colloquialisms reveal a great deal: once you are old you are "fading fast," "over the hill," "out to pasture," "down the drain," "finished," "out of date," an "old crock," "fogy," "geezer" or "biddy." One hears children saying they are afraid to get old, middle-aged people declaring they want to die after they have passed their prime, and numbers of old people wishing they were dead.

What can we possibly conclude from these discrepant points of view? Our popular attitudes could be summed up as a combination of wishful thinking and stark terror. We base our feelings on primitive fears, prejudice and stereotypes rather than on knowledge and insight. In reality, the way one experiences old age is contingent upon physical health, personality, earlier-life experiences, the actual circumstances of late-life events (in what order they occur, how they occur, when they occur) and the social supports one receives: adequate finances, shelter, medical care, social roles, religious support, recreation. All of these are crucial and interconnected elements which together determine the quality of late life.

Old age is neither inherently miserable nor inherently sublime—like every stage of life it has problems, joys, fears and potentials. The process of aging and eventual death must ultimately be accepted as the natural progression of the life cycle, the old completing their prescribed life spans and making way for the young. Much that is unique in old age in fact derives from the reality of aging and the imminence of death. The old must clarify and find use for what they have attained in a lifetime of learning and adapting; they must conserve strength and resources where necessary and adjust creatively to those changes and losses that occur as part of the aging experience. The elderly have the potential for qualities of human reflection and observation which can only come from having lived an entire life span. There is a lifetime accumulation of personality and experience which is available to be used and enjoyed.

But what are an individual's chances for a "good" old age in America, with satisfying final years and a dignified death? Unfortunately, none too good. For many elderly Americans old age is a tragedy, a period of quiet despair, deprivation, desolation and muted rage. This can be a consequence of the kind of life a person has led in younger years and the problems in his or her relationships with others. There are also inevitable personal and physical losses to be sustained, some of which can become overwhelming and unbearable. All of this is the individual factor, the existential element. But old age is frequently a tragedy even when the early years have been fulfilling and people seemingly have everything going for them. Herein lies what I consider to be the genuine tragedy of old age in America—we have shaped a society which is extremely harsh to live in when one is old. The tragedy of old age is not the fact that each of us must grow old and die but that the process of doing so has been made unnecessarily and at times excruciatingly painful, humiliating, debilitating and isolating through insensitivity, ignorance and poverty. The potentials for satisfactions and even triumphs in late life are real and vastly underexplored. For the most part the elderly struggle to exist in an inhospitable world.

Are things *really* that bad? Let's begin by looking at the basic daily requirements for survival. Poverty or drastically lowered income and old age go hand in hand. People who are poor all their lives remain poor as they grow old. Most of us realize this. What we do not realize is that these poor are joined by multitudes of people who become poor only after growing older. When Social Security becomes the sole or primary income, it means subsistence-level life styles for many, and recent increases do not keep up with soaring costs of living. Private pension plans often do not pay off, and pension payments that do come in are not tied to inflationary decreases in buying power. Savings can be wiped out by a single unexpected catastrophe. In January, 1971, half of the elderly, or over 10 million people, lived on less than $75 a week, or $10 per day. Most lived on far less. Even the relatively well-off are not assured of an income that will support them:

> Rose Anderson was 90 years old, wispy and frail. She lived in a room filled with yellowed newspapers, magazines and books; it was filthy. There were cockroaches. There was an ugly permeating stench. She was too weary to clean. She gave her energy to caring for her canary.
>
> She had been the wife of a prominent physician but she had the "misfortune" of living to a ripe old age and outliving both the $300,000 her husband had carefully provided for her and her only child, a son, who died at the age of 57 when she was 76. She had given over some of her money to support her daughter-in-law and grandchildren. But most of it went for her own extensive medical expenses. She ended up living on welfare.

It has been estimated that at least 30 percent of the elderly live in substandard housing. Many more must deprive themselves of essentials to keep their homes in repair:

> Seventy-three-year-old Emil Pines was picked up by the police wandering along Market Street in San Francisco. He was mentally confused and unable to remember his name and address. After a medical examination it was determined that he had not eaten for several days and was dehydrated. Food and liquids were immediately prescribed and shortly thereafter his mind cleared. He remembered that he had used his pension check to pay for emergency house repairs and had not had enough left for food that month.

The American dream promised older people that if they worked hard enough all their lives, things would turn out well for them. Today's elderly were brought up to believe in pride, self-reliance and independence. Many are tough, determined individuals who manage to survive against adversity. But even the tough ones reach a point where help should be available to them:

> Now 81, Joseph Bartlett could look back on a long and useful life. He was living in a dusty Oklahoma town where he had lived since leaving farming and becoming a barber. He had been present at the opening of Indian Territory to white settlers and during the later oil boom. He had lost his wife and his only son ten years before. Since he had been self-employed he had no Social Security and was forced to turn to welfare. He was without transportation in the rural village. There were no social services, and medical care was inaccessible. His close friends and family had died, and he was too proud to ask other townspeople for the help he needed. He admitted to living in pain for a number of years but declared he would never burden anyone—"I will make do for myself."

Age discrimination in employment is unrestrained, with arbitrary retirement practices and bias against hiring older people for available jobs. Social Security penalizes the old by reducing their income checks as soon as they earn more than $2,400 a year. Job-training programs don't want the elderly (or the middle-aged, for that matter), so there is no opportunity to learn new skills. Employers rarely make concessions for the possible physical limitations of otherwise valuable older employees, and instead they are fired, retired or forced to resign.

It is obvious that the old get sick more frequently and more severely than the young, and 86 percent have chronic health problems of varying degree. These health problems, while significant, are largely treatable and for the most part do not impair the capacity to work. Medicare pays for only 45 percent of older people's health expenses; the balance must come from their own incomes and savings, or from Medicaid, which requires a humiliating means test. A serious illness can mean instant poverty. Drugs prescribed outside of hospitals, hearing aids, glasses, dental care and podiatry are not covered at all under Medicare. There is prejudice against the old by doctors and other medical personnel who don't like to bother with them. Psychiatrists and mental-health personnel typically assume that the mental problems of the old are untreatable. Psychoanalysts, the elite of the psychiatric profession, rarely accept them as patients. Medical schools and other teaching institutions find them "uninteresting." Voluntary hospitals are well known for dumping the "Medicare patient" into municipal hospitals; municipal hospitals in turn funnel them into nursing homes, mental hospitals and chronic-disease institutions without the adequate diagnostic and treatment effort which might enable them to return home. Persons who do remain at home while in ill health have serious difficulties in getting social, medical and psychiatric services brought directly to them:

> Professor Frank Minkoff, a 70-year-old Russian immigrant with a university degree in engineering, was still teaching mathematics at an evening school. He was unmarried, the only member of his family in the United States, and lived in an apartment crammed with books. Suddenly he became confused and disoriented. He was frightened and refused to leave his room. Concerned neighbors quickly called a doctor, who expressed his unwillingness to make a home visit, saying, "There is nothing I can do. He needs to be in a nursing home or a mental institution." The neighbors were unconvinced, remembering Mr. M.'s earlier good functioning. They pleaded with the doctor and, under pressure, he angrily complied and visited the home. While there he again repeated his conviction that Mr. M. needed "custodial" care. Mr. M. was coherent enough to refuse, saying he would never voluntarily go to a nursing home or mental hospital. He did agree to be admitted to a medical hospital. Admission took place and studies resulted in the diagnosis "reversible brain syndrome due to acute viral infection." Mr. M. was successfully treated and released to his home in good condition in less than a week.

Many others are not so fortunate. Afflicted with reversible conditions of all kinds, they are frequently labeled "senile" and sent to institutions for the rest of their lives.

Problems large and small confront the elderly. They are easy targets for crime in the streets and in their homes. Because of loneliness, confusion, hearing and visual difficulties they are prime victims of dishonest door-to-door salesmen and fraudulent advertising, and buy defective hearing aids, dance lessons, useless "Medicare insurance supplements," and quack health remedies. Persons crippled by arthritis or strokes are yelled at by impatient bus drivers for their slowness in climbing on and off buses. Traffic lights turn red before they can get across the street. Revolving doors move too quickly. Subways usually have no elevators or escalators.

Old women fare worse than old men. Women have an average life expectancy of seven years longer than men and tend to marry men older than themselves; so two-thirds (six million) of all older women are widows.*

---

* Twenty percent of American women are widows by 60, 50 percent by 65, 66⅔ percent by 75.

When widowed they do not have the same social prerogatives as older men to date and marry those who are younger. As a result, they are likely to end up alone—an ironic turn of events when one remembers that most of them were raised from childhood to consider marriage the only acceptable state. The income levels of older working women are generally lower than those of men; many never worked outside the home until their children were grown and then only at unskilled, low-paying jobs. Others who worked all their lives typically received low wages, with lower Social Security and private retirement benefits as a result. Until 1973, housewives who were widowed received only 82.5 percent of their husbands' Social Security benefits even though they were full-time homemakers.

Black, Mexican-American and American Indian elderly all have a lower life expectancy than whites, due to their socioeconomic disadvantages. Although the life expectancy of 67.5 years for white men remained the same from 1960 to 1968, the life expectancy for black men *declined* a full year during that time (from 61.1 to 60.0). Blacks of all ages make up 11 percent of the total United States population, but they constitute only 7.8 percent of the elderly. The life expectancy for Mexican-Americans is estimated at 57 years, and for American Indians at 44 years. Most do not live long enough to be eligible for the benefits of Social Security and Medicare. Poverty is the norm. Scant attention is paid to their particular cultural interests and heritage.

Asian-American elderly (Chinese, Japanese, Korean, Filipino and Samoan) are victims of a public impression that they are independently cared for by their families and therefore do not need help. However, patterns of immigration by Asian-Americans to this country, the cultural barriers, language problems and discrimination they have faced have all taken a toll of their elderly and their families.* This is particularly true of older Chinese men, who were not allowed to bring their wives and families with them to the United States or to intermarry.

MYTHS AND STEREOTYPES ABOUT THE OLD

In addition to dealing with the difficulties of physical and economic survival, older people are affected by the multitude of myths and stereotypes surrounding old age:

> An older person thinks and moves slowly. He does not think as he used to or as creatively. He is bound to himself and to his past and

---

* One recommendation of the 1971 White House Conference on Aging was for fully crediting toward Social Security and other benefits the accumulated time spent by Japanese-Americans in United States "relocation" camps during World War II.

can no longer change or grow. He can learn neither well nor swiftly and, even if he could, he would not wish to. Tied to his personal traditions and growing conservatism, he dislikes innovations and is not disposed to new ideas. Not only can he not move forward, he often moves backward. He enters a second childhood, caught up in increasing egocentricity and demanding more from his environment than he is willing to give to it. Sometimes he becomes an intensification of himself, a caricature of a lifelong personality. He becomes irritable and cantankerous, yet shallow and enfeebled. He lives in his past; he is behind the times. He is aimless and wandering of mind, reminiscing and garrulous. Indeed, he is a study in decline, the picture of mental and physical failure. He has lost and cannot replace friends, spouse, job, status, power, influence, income. He is often stricken by diseases which, in turn, restrict his movement, his enjoyment of food, the pleasures of well-being. He has lost his desire and capacity for sex. His body shrinks, and so too does the flow of blood to his brain. His mind does not utilize oxygen and sugar at the same rate as formerly. Feeble, uninteresting, he awaits his death, a burden to society, to his family and to himself.

In its essentials, this view I have sketched approximates the picture of old age held by many Americans. As in all clichés, stereotypes and myths there are bits of truth. But many of the current views of old age represent confusions, misunderstandings or simply a lack of knowledge about old age. Others may be completely inaccurate or biased, reflecting prejudice or outright hostility. Certain prevalent myths need closer examination.

THE MYTH OF "AGING"

The idea of chronological aging (measuring one's age by the number of years one has lived) is a kind of myth. It is clear that there are great differences in the rates of physiological, chronological, psychological and social aging within the person and from person to person. In fact, physiological indicators show a greater range from the mean in old age than in any other age group, and this is true of personality as well. Older people actually become more diverse rather than more similar with advancing years. There are extraordinarily "young" 80-year-olds as well as "old" 80-year-olds. Chronological age, therefore, is a convenient but imprecise indicator of physical, mental and emotional status. For the purposes of this book old age may be considered to commence at the conventionally accepted point of 65.

We do know that organic brain damage can create such extensive intellectual impairment that people of all types and personalities may become dull-eyed, blank-faced and unresponsive. Massive destruction of the brain and body has a "leveling" effect which can produce increasing homogeneity among the elderly. But most older people do not suffer impairment of this magnitude during the greater part of their later life.

THE MYTH OF UNPRODUCTIVITY

Many believe the old to be unproductive. But in the absence of diseases and social adversities, old people tend to remain productive and actively involved in life. There are dazzling examples like octogenarians Georgia O'Keeffe continuing to paint and Pope John XXIII revitalizing his church, and septuagenarians Duke Ellington composing and working his hectic concert schedule and Golda Meir acting as her country's vigorous Prime Minister. Substantial numbers of people become unusually creative for the first time in old age, when exceptional and inborn talents may be discovered and expressed. What is most pertinent to our discussion here, however, is the fact that many old people continue to contribute usefully to their families and community in a variety of ways, including active employment. The 1971 Bureau of Labor Statistics figures show 1,780,000 people over 65 working full time and 1,257,000 part time. Since society and business practice do not encourage the continued employment of the elderly, it is obvious that many more would work if jobs were available.

When productive incapacity develops, it can be traced more directly to a variety of losses, diseases or circumstances than to that mysterious process called aging. Even then, in spite of the presence of severe handicaps, activity and involvement are often maintained.

THE MYTH OF DISENGAGEMENT

This is related to the previous myth and holds that older people prefer to disengage from life, to withdraw into themselves, choosing to live alone or perhaps only with their peers. Ironically, some gerontologists themselves hold these views. One study, *Growing Old: The Process of Disengagement,* presents the theory that mutual separation of the aged person from his society is a natural part of the aging experience. There is no evidence to support this generalization. Disengagement is only one of many patterns of reaction to old age.

THE MYTH OF INFLEXIBILITY

The ability to change and adapt has little to do with one's age and more to do with one's lifelong character. But even this statement has to be qualified.

One is not necessarily destined to maintain one's character in earlier life permanently. True, the endurance, the strength and the stability in human character structure are remarkable and protective. But most, if not all, people change and remain open to change throughout the course of life, right up to its termination. The old notion, whether ascribed to Pope Alexander VI or Sigmund Freud, that character is laid down in final form by the fifth year of life can be confidently refuted. Change is the hallmark of living. The notion that older people become less responsive to innovation and change because of age is not supported by scientific studies of healthy older people living in the community or by everyday observations and clinical psychiatric experience.

A related cliché is that political conservatism increases with age. If one's options are constricted by job discrimination, reduced or fixed income and runaway inflation, as older people's are, one may become conservative out of economic necessity rather than out of qualities innate in the psyche. Thus an older person may vote against the creation of better schools or an expansion of social services for tax reasons. His property—his home—may be his only equity, and his income is likely to be too low to weather increased taxes. A perfectly sensible self-interest rather than "conservatism" is at work here. Naturally, conservatives do exist among the elderly, but so do liberals, radicals and moderates. Once again diversity rather than homogeneity is the norm.

THE MYTH OF "SENILITY"

The notion that old people are senile, showing forgetfulness, confusional episodes and reduced attention, is widely accepted. "Senility" is a popularized layman's term used by doctors and the public alike to categorize the behavior of the old. Some of what is called senile is the result of brain damage. But anxiety and depression are also frequently lumped within the same category of senility, even though they are treatable and often reversible. Old people, like young people, experience a full range of emotions, including anxiety, grief, depression and paranoid states. It is all too easy to blame age and brain damage when accounting for the mental problems and emotional concerns of later life.

Drug tranquilization is another frequent, misdiagnosed and potentially reversible cause of so-called senility. Malnutrition and unrecognized physical illnesses, such as congestive heart failure, may produce "senile behavior" by reducing the supply of blood, oxygen and food to the brain. Alcoholism, often associated with bereavement, is another cause. Because it has been so convenient to dismiss all these manifestations by lumping them together under an improper and inaccurate diagnostic label, the elderly often do not receive the benefits of decent diagnosis and treatment.

Actual irreversible brain damage,* of course, is not a myth, and two major conditions create mental disorders. One is cerebral arteriosclerosis (hardening of the arteries of the brain); the other, unfortunately referred to as senile brain disease, is due to a mysterious dissolution of brain cells. Such conditions account for some 50 percent of the cases of major mental disorders in old age, and the symptoms connected with these conditions are the ones that form the basis for what has come to be known as senility. But, as I wish to emphasize again, similar symptoms can be found in a number of other conditions which *are* reversible through proper treatment.

THE MYTH OF SERENITY

In contrast to the previous myths, which view the elderly in a negative light, the myth of serenity portrays old age as a kind of adult fairyland. Now at last comes a time of relative peace and serenity when people can relax and enjoy the fruits of their labors after the storms of active life are over. Advertising slogans, television and romantic fiction foster the myth. Visions of carefree, cookie-baking grandmothers and rocking-chair grandfathers are cherished by younger generations. But, in fact, older persons experience more stresses than any other age group, and these stresses are often devastating. The strength of the aged to endure crisis is remarkable, and tranquillity is an unlikely as well as inappropriate response under these circumstances. Depression, anxiety, psychosomatic illnesses, paranoia, garrulousness and irritability are some of the internal reactions to external stresses.

Depressive reactions are particularly widespread in late life. To the more blatant psychotic depressions and the depressions associated with organic brain diseases must be added the everyday depressions that stem from long physical illness or chronic discomfort, from grief, despair and loneliness, and from an inevitably lowered self-esteem that comes from diminished social and personal status.

Grief is a frequent companion of old age—grief for one's own losses and for the ultimate loss of one's self. Apathy and emptiness are a common sequel to the initial shock and sadness that come with the deaths of close

---

* Human beings react in varying ways to brain disease just as they do to other serious threats to their persons. They may become anxious, rigid, depressed and hypochondriacal. (Hypochondriasis comprises bodily symptoms or fear of diseases that are not due to physical changes but to emotional concerns. They are no less real simply because they do not have a physical origin.) These reactions can be ameliorated by sensitive, humane concern, talk and understanding even though the underlying physical process cannot be reversed. Therefore, even the irreversible brain syndromes require proper diagnosis and treatment of their emotional consequences.

friends and relatives. Physical disease and social isolation can follow bereavement.

Anxiety is another common feature. There is much to be anxious about; poverty, loneliness and illness head the list. Anxiety may manifest itself in many forms: rigid patterns of thinking and behaving, helplessness, manipulative behavior, restlessness and suspiciousness, sometimes to the point of paranoid states.*

Anger and even rage may be seen:

> Mary Mack, 73, left her doctor's office irritable, depressed and untreated. She was angry at the doctor's inattention. She charged that he simply regarded her as a complainer and did not take the necessary time to examine her carefully. She had received the same response from other doctors. Meanwhile her doctor entered the diagnosis in his file: hypochondriasis with chronic depression. No treatment was given. The prognosis was evidently considered hopeless.

> John Barber, an elderly black man, spent all his life working hard at low wages for his employers. When he was retired he literally went on strike. He refused to do anything. He would sit all day on his front porch, using his family as the substitute victim of his years of pent-up anger. He had always been seen as mild mannered. Now he could afford to let himself go into rages and describe in vicious detail what he was going to do to people. A social worker viewing his behavior declared to his family that he was "psychotic." But Mr. Barber was not insane; he was angry.

AGEISM—THE PREJUDICE AGAINST THE ELDERLY

The stereotyping and myths surrounding old age can be explained in part by lack of knowledge and by insufficient contact with a wide variety of older people. But there is another powerful factor operating—a deep and profound prejudice against the elderly which is found to some degree in all of us. In thinking about how to describe this, I coined the word "ageism"†
in 1968:

---

* No less a thinker than Aristotle failed to distinguish between the intrinsic features of aging and the reaction of the elderly to their lives. He considered cowardice, resentment, vindictiveness and what he called "senile avarice" to be intrinsic to late life. Cicero took a warmer and more positive view of old age. He understood, for example, "If old men are morose, troubled, fretful and hard to please . . . these are faults of character and not of age." So he explained in his essay "*De Senectute.*"

† I first publicly described my notion of ageism at the time of stormy opposition to the purchase of a high-rise in northwest Washington for public housing for the elderly.[1] (Numbered notes follow Appendixes, page 447.) I also developed it in observing the social and economic impact of the extended life span.[2] Ageism is a

Ageism can be seen as a process of systematic stereotyping of and discrimination against people because they are old, just as racism and sexism accomplish this with skin color and gender. Old people are categorized as senile, rigid in thought and manner, old-fashioned in morality and skills. . . . Ageism allows the younger generations to see older people as different from themselves; thus they subtly cease to identify with their elders as human beings.[4]

Ageism makes it easier to ignore the frequently poor social and economic plight of older people. We can avoid dealing with the reality that our productivity-minded society has little use for nonproducers—in this case those who have reached an arbitrarily defined retirement age. We can also avoid, for a time at least, reminders of the personal reality of our own aging and death.

Ageism is manifested in a wide range of phenomena, both on individual and institutional levels—stereotypes and myths, outright disdain and dislike, or simply subtle avoidance of contact; discriminatory practices in housing, employment and services of all kinds; epithets, cartoons and jokes. At times ageism becomes an expedient method by which society promotes viewpoints about the aged in order to relieve itself of responsibility toward them. At other times ageism serves a highly personal objective, protecting younger (usually middle-aged) individuals—often at high emotional cost—from thinking about things they fear (aging, illness, death).

The media illustrate the extremes to which negative attitudes toward the old can lead:

August 29, 1970

Mr. Douglas J. Stewart in *The New Republic* (Vol. 163, No. 8-9) advocated that all persons lose their vote after retirement, or at the age of 70, or at 55 when moving to another state.

Mr. Stewart, 37 years old at the time, was an associate professor of classics at Brandeis University. Perhaps one should allow for the possibility that he was speaking tongue in cheek, implying that the old are already effectively disenfranchised. But there can be no doubt about the serious-mindedness of the following proposal:

From Livermore, California, in what was described as an imaginative Rand Corporation study, a report entitled "The Post Attack Population of

---

broader concept than "gerontophobia," the classic fear of old age. Gerontophobia refers to a rarer "unreasonable fear and/or irrational hatred of older people whereas ageism is a much more comprehensive and useful concept."[3]

the United States"[5] suggested methods the United States should initiate with regard to old people, chronic invalids, and the insane in the event of nuclear war. The famous think tank said survivors of a nuclear war "would be better off without . . . old and feeble members." The author, Ira S. Lowry, stated that after a nuclear war, policy makers would be presented with a difficult problem because "the working members of the society would insist on transferring some part of their personal advantages to members of their families who were not directly contributing to output." The report continues by saying,

Policy makers would presumably have to draw the line somewhere, however, in making such concessions and those most likely to suffer are people with little or no productive potential; old people, chronic invalids and the insane. Old people suffer the special disadvantage of being easily identified as a group and, therefore, subject to categorical treatment. . . . In a literate community, the elderly do not even serve their prehistoric function as repositories of traditional wisdoms . . . the amount of care and attention necessary to sustain life increases with age. . . . In this sense, at least, a community under stress would be better off without its old and feeble members. . . .[6]

The easiest way to implement a morally repugnant but socially beneficial policy is by inaction. Under stress, the managers of post-attack society would most likely resolve their problems by failing to make any special provision for the special needs of the elderly, the insane, and the chronically ill. Instead of Medicare for persons under 65, for example, we might have Medicare for persons under 15. Instead of pensions, we might have family allowances. To be sure, the government would not be able—nor would it be likely to try—to prevent the relatives and friends of old people from helping them; but overall the share of the elderly in the national product would certainly drop.[7]

Lowry, an economist and demographer, was quoted in a telephone conversation to Roger Rapaport of the Washington *Star* as follows: "The AEC (Atomic Energy Commission) told me that they were very satisfied with the final product." Extreme though this may sound, the abandonment of older people in time of crises is obviously not unthinkable.

Ageism, like all prejudices, influences the self view and behavior of its victims. The elderly tend to adopt negative definitions of themselves and to perpetuate the very stereotypes directed against them, thereby reinforcing society's beliefs. As one older woman describes it:

Part of the neglect [of old people] can be attributed to the attitudes of the senior citizen himself. Rather than face the fact that being old is just another stage in the external aging process and being thankful that he has been blessed to reach this pinnacle in life, he has chosen to contemplate his plight with resignation, and even in some instances with disgust and frustration. This defeatist attitude has been adopted by society in general. We are now trying to reverse this trend.[8]

The elderly's part in eliciting the kind of response which they receive from the young and from society at large is often a subtle but powerful factor in the public's generally disparaging views of them. They collaborate with their ostracizers. Some individuals act "senile"; others may deny their true feelings in an attempt to "age graciously" and obtain the approval which is otherwise denied them. Psychologist Margaret Thaler Singer observed similarities between the Rorschach test findings in members of a National Institute of Mental Health sample of aged volunteers who were resigned in the face of aging and those in American GI prisoners of war who collaborated with their captors in Korea.

Other self-sabotaging behavior can be a refusal to identify oneself as elderly at all. One sees older persons who affect the dress and behavior patterns of the young, pretending like Peter Pan that they have never grown up. Older women can be seen engaging in sad, frantic attempts to appear young, as if this would ensure appreciation and acceptance in the eyes of others.

A significant minority of older people conceal their age from themselves as well as from others. In a study of 1,700 elderly persons, Taves and Hansen[9] found that one-sixth thought of themselves as old between the ages of 54 and 69, one-third between the ages of 70 and 79, and only 40 percent by age 80 and over. About one person in seven said they never thought of themselves as old.

In a study by Tuckman and Lorge[10] that queried over 1,000 persons from 20 to 80, those under 30 classified themselves as young, and of those between 30 and 60, most classified themselves as middle-aged. At age 60 only a small proportion classified themselves as old, and at age 80 slightly over half called themselves old. A small percentage of the 80-year-olds persisted in describing themselves as young.

Of course, considering oneself "young" is not simply a prejudice or a delusion.[11] Healthy older people do feel strong and vigorous, much as they did in their earlier days. The problem comes when this good feeling is called "youth" rather than "health," thus tying it to chronological age instead of to physical and mental well-being.

Lack of empathy is a further reaction by the elderly to their experiences in the larger culture. Out of emotional self-protection, many healthy, prosperous, well-educated old people feel no identification with or protectiveness toward the poor elderly. A lack of compassion is of course not unique to the aged, but it has a special irony here—with the advent of catastrophic illnesses or the exhaustion of resources that goes with a long life, they too run a high risk of finding themselves among the poor, facing similar indifference from their wealthier peers.

Older people are not always victims, passive and fated by their environment. They, too, initiate direct actions and stimulate responses. They may exploit their age and its accompanying challenges to gain something they want or need, perhaps to their own detriment (e.g., by demanding services from others and thus allowing their own skills to atrophy). Exploitation can backfire; excessive requests to others by an older person may be met at first, but as requests increase they are felt as demands—and may indeed be demands. Younger people who attempt to deal with a demanding older person may find themselves going through successive cycles of rage, guilt and overprotectiveness without realizing they are being manipulated. In addition to his "age," the older person may exploit his diseases and his impairments, capitalizing upon his alleged helplessness. Invalids of all ages do this, but older people can more easily take on the appearance of frailty when others would not be allowed this behavior. Manipulation by older people is best recognized for what it is—a valuable clue that there is energy available which should be redirected toward greater benefit for themselves and others.

It must also be remembered that the old can have many prejudices against the young. These may be a result of their attractiveness, vigor and sexual prowess. Older people may be troubled by the extraordinary changes that they see in the world around them and blame the younger generation. They may be angry at the brevity of life and begrudge someone the fresh chance of living out a life span which they have already completed.

Angry and ambivalent feelings flow, too, between the old and the middle-aged, who are caught up in the problems unique to their age and position within the life cycle. The middle-aged bear the heaviest personal and social responsibilities since they are called upon to help support—individually and collectively—both ends of the life cycle: the nurture and education of their young and the financial, emotional and physical care of the old. Many have not been prepared for their heavy responsibilities and are surprised and overwhelmed by them. Frequently these responsibilities trap them in their careers or life styles until the children grow up or their parents die. A common reaction is anger at both the young and the old. The effects of financial pressures are seen primarily in the middle and lower economic classes. But the middle-aged of all classes are inclined to be ambivalent toward the young and old since both age groups remind them of their own waning youth. In addition—with reason—they fear technological or professional obsolescence as they see what has happened to their elders and feel the pressure of youth pushing its way toward their position in society. Furthermore, their responsibilities are likely to increase in the future as more and more of their parents and grandparents live longer life spans.

THE ELDERLY POPULATION EXPLOSION

There are now well over twenty million people over 65 years of age in the United States, comprising 10 percent of the population.* A population explosion of older people has been under way for a number of decades, and the elderly are now the fastest-growing group in the United States. Between 1960 and 1970 the aging increased by 21 percent, compared with an 18 percent increase among those under 65.

Older people have become a highly visible phenomenon only since the nineteenth century; before then relatively few people were long lived. In 1900 only three million, or 4 percent of the population, were 65 and older. Influenza, pneumonia, tuberculosis, typhoid and paratyphoid fever, diphtheria and scarlet fever were major killers, causing high death rates all along the life cycle. Increased life expectancy followed medical advances in the prevention and treatment of these diseases, as well as generally improved public-health measures, particularly in sanitation. Lowered rates of infant and maternal mortality enabled larger numbers of people to reach old age, and once there, new drugs and medical techniques allowed many old people to survive once-fatal illnesses.

The average life expectancy at the turn of the century was 47 years; now it is 70.4 years. A boy born today can expect to live to 66.8 years; a girl to age 74.3. Half of all older people (ten million) are over 73; 1,000,-000 elderly are 85 and over; and the 1970 census reports 106,441 centenarians (over 100 years old).

Every day 1,000 people reach 65; each year 365,000. More than 70 percent of the 65-and-over age group in 1970 entered that category after 1959. With new medical discoveries, an improved health-care delivery system and the presently declining birth rate, it is possible that the elderly will make up one-quarter of the total population by the year 2000. Major medical advances in the control of cancer or heart and vascular diseases could increase the average life expectancy by ten or even fifteen years. Discovery of deterrents to the basic causes of aging would cause even more profound repercussions. The presence of so many elderly, and the potential of so many more, has been a puzzlement to gerontologists, public-health ex-

---

* Two of every ten Americans are now between 45 and 65. This is 20 percent of the population, or 42 million people.

perts and demographers, who don't know whether to regard it as "the aging problem" or a human triumph over disease. What is clear is that it will result in enormous changes in every part of society.

Changes will therefore occur in our definition of the aging process itself. Much of what we think of as aging today is actually disease and illness, and not a part of fundamental physical aging. This includes many of the physical, mental and emotional conditions seen in older people. The major diseases of late life may become preventable or at least treatable. The mental depressions of late life and the acute brain syndromes are already treatable and reversible. The removal of pathogenic elements—excessive sun exposure and cigarette smoking (both are causes of skin wrinkles), air pollution and others—may slow down the physical appearances of deterioration. Even genetic traits responsible for such changes as graying and loss of hair may eventually be controllable. What is in the future if acute and chronic disease states are identified and largely eliminated, undesirable genetic traits mainly nullified and pathogenic environmental conditions alleviated? We should see for the first time that flow of human life from birth through death truly called aging. Aging refers to patterns of late-life changes which are eventually seen in all persons but which vary in rate and degree. Although human beings will never be able to live indefinitely, they can live much longer and more comfortably, mostly free from the violent ravages of disease, with perhaps a gradual and fairly predictable decline toward eventual death.

The physical health of the majority of the elderly is already better than is generally believed. Eighty-one percent of those over 65 are fully ambulatory and move about independently on their own. Ninety-five percent live in the community; at any one time only 5 percent are in nursing homes, chronic-disease hospitals and other institutions—a startling fact when one thinks of the popular image of the old "dumped" en masse into institutions by their families because they have become enfeebled.

Our view of who is old and when aging happens will also change. It is becoming more common to find retired people in their sixties and seventies who have living parents in the eighties and nineties. Sometimes it is the 80-year-old who is taking care of the 60-year-old! Chronological age is an inaccurate measure of how old one is because aging as we presently experience it occurs unevenly—one may be at very different "ages" at one and the same time in terms of mental capacity, physical health, endurance, creativity and emotions. Society has arbitrarily chosen ages 60–65 as the beginning of late life (borrowing the idea from Bismarck's social legislation in Germany in the 1880s) primarily for the purpose of determining a point for retirement and eligibility for services and financial entitlements for the elderly. This social definition has had its legitimate uses but also its abuses. Not everyone is ready to retire at 60 or 65. Older people do not appreciate the "social" definition of old age encroaching into every corner of their lives, rigidly stamping them with a uniform label regardless of condition or functioning. Gerontologists divide old age into early old age, 65 to 74 years, and advanced old age, 75 and above. A much more flexible view, which took actual capacities into account, would be more realistic.

STUDYING THE OLD

We have put precious little work and research into examining the last phase of life. What research has been done has concentrated primarily on studies of the 5 percent of elderly who are in institutions. The few research studies on the healthy aged living in the community have produced exciting new looks at the possibilities and problems of this age group.[12] But on the whole medicine and the behavioral sciences seem to have shared society's negative views of old age and have quite consistently presented *decline* as the key concept of late life, with *neglect* forming the major treatment technique and research response.

Why study the elderly? Why spend research money on old people when there are compelling priorities for other age groups, particularly the young? In the first place, life cannot be carved up into bits and pieces—what affects one age group affects another. To illustrate this on the biological level, it is well known that carcinoma in the breast of a woman has a much more fulminating malignant course if it occurs in young women than in old. Leukemia, another form of cancer, tends to be more chronic in the old and more acute in the young. Diabetes is much more severe in childhood than in the aged. Why? Is there something we can learn about disease processes in the old that may help both them and those who are younger? Many of the diseases occurring in old age do not begin there. Arteriosclerosis, a major cause of much morbidity and mortality (affecting such major organs as the kidney, the heart and the brain), begins early in life. If we are to stop it, it must be studied, prevented and treated in its earliest phases. Stroke, typically thought of as occurring in late life, also kills the young in significant numbers.

In the psychological sphere, too, our understanding of emotions like grief can gain enormously from the study of the old, in whom grief occurs with such frequency and profundity. This is true of a whole variety of human reactions to stress, as well as to the normal events in late life. The natural history of human character and its disorders can only really be studied in the old. The degree to which change and improvement in mental diseases and emotional illnesses occur, the nature of survival characteristics, and successful modes of adaptation, among other matters, are natural subjects for study in those who have lived an entire life span.

Ultimately interest must focus on clarifying the complex, interwoven elements necessary to produce and support physical and mental health up to the very end of life rather than our present preoccupation with "curing" ills after they develop. Understanding what interferes with healthy development throughout the life cycle gives us a chance to prevent problems, instead of rushing frantically and often futilely to solve them after they occur. Life is a continuing process from birth until death and it seems strange that it so seldom occurs to us to study life as a whole.

Finally, from a philosophic view, a greater understanding and control over the diseases and difficulties of later life would hopefully make old age less frightening and more acceptable as a truly valuable last phase of life. The relief of human suffering has merit in itself, but it also releases human beings from the fears and defenses they build up around it.

WHOSE RESPONSIBILITY ARE THEY?

Are older Americans entitled to decent income, health, housing, transportation and opportunities for employment as well as to social status and participation in society? Who should see to it that they get them? Why can't they manage their lives themselves? The struggle to decide on the place of the old in a culture has been familiar throughout history. Cultural attitudes have ranged from veneration, protectiveness, and sentimentality to derogation, rejection, pity and abandonment. William Graham Sumner, in his *Folkways*, published in 1907, wrote in a section, "Mores of Respect or Contempt for the Aged":

. . . [There are] two sets of mores as to the aged: (1) in one set of mores the teaching, and usages, inculcate conventional respect for the aged who are therefore arbitrarily preserved for their wisdom and counsel, perhaps also sometimes out of affection and sympathy; (2) in the other set of mores the aged are regarded as societal burdens which waste the strength of the society, already inadequate for its tasks. Therefore, they are forced to die, either by their own hands or those of their relatives. It is very far from being true that the first of these policies is practiced higher up in civilization than those who practice the second. The people in lower civilizations profit more by the counsel from the aged than those in higher civilizations and are educated by this experience to respect and value the aged.

Older Americans of today—indeed the old people in any society—contributed to the growth of the society in which younger people live. One might assume that they would have a justifiable expectation of sharing in what is referred to as America's affluence. All of us, whatever our age, are now contributing taxes and services to our nation and are collectively preparing for our own old age. What will the future bring for us? Will anyone help us if we cannot adequately help ourselves?

There are people who believe that the responsibility for one's old age can and should be assumed by the individual alone. They hold that improvidence is the major cause of an impoverished old age and agree with the nineteenth-century Social Darwinist, Herbert Spencer:

Pervading all nature we may see at work a stern discipline, which is a little cruel that it may be very kind. . . . The poverty of the incapable, the distresses that come upon the imprudent, the starvation of the idle, and the shouldering aside of the weak by the strong . . . are the decrees of a large, far-seeing benevolence. . . . Similarly, we must call spurious philanthropists who, to prevent a present misery, would entail greater misery upon future generations. All defenders of a poor-law must be classed among them. . . . Blind to the fact that under the natural order of things society is constantly excreting its unhealthy, imbecile, slow, vacillating, faithless members, those unthinking, though well-meaning, men advocate an interference which not only stops the purifying process but even increases the vitiation.[13]

Such a harsh view fails to take into account the life circumstances and historical conditions of today's older Americans. Americans born in the 1900s found themselves, in the prime of their earning years, trapped in the massive Depression of the 1930s. Many lost jobs, homes, savings and their morale.

By the 1960s, when they were retiring, inflation eroded their fixed incomes to an alarming degree. Economic forces, not improvidence, have placed today's elderly in their predicament.

The Depression of the 1930s convinced many rugged individualists that forces beyond the control of the individual could bring widespread devastation and poverty. A legislative landmark of Roosevelt's New Deal was the inauguration of Social Security in 1935, a consequence of many pressures that included the Townsend movement;* perhaps the final impetus came from the need to have the old retire in order to provide employment for the young. Thus, years after most Western European industrial nations had introduced it, the United States made its decision for the collective insur-

---

* A movement representing older persons and led by Dr. Francis Townsend, a retired physician.

ance-policy form of income maintenance for the disabled and retired. Eighty-five cents ($0.85) of every federal dollar now expended annually for programs for the elderly derive from Social Security trust funds to which we all contribute—as did the majority of the present elderly themselves in their working days.

Social Security, Medicare and federal housing programs have helped to gain for the elderly *some* income security, *some* health care and *some* housing. But the task has not been finished and the efforts do not match the needs. The chapters that follow offer a portrait of old age in America as it actually is, and some recommendations for what can be done to make it more than mere survival.

Chapter 2

HOW TO GROW OLD AND POOR
IN AN AFFLUENT SOCIETY

In our image of affluent America we tend to think of poverty as isolated in self-contained "pockets," rather than in terms of the dry statistics that tell us that up to one-fifth of our nation are poor, and that one-fifth of the poor are citizens over 65 years of age. In our mind's eye the poor are black ghetto children playing in the streets, or "welfare mothers," or a formal front-stoop portrait of a white family in Appalachia. We are less likely to see the old as poor because they are literally less visible. They rarely make newsworthy scandals in the daily papers or models for the posters of the United Givers' Funds. They escape notice by staying in their homes, locked in by timidity, illness and disability, lack of money, poor transportation and fear of crime. Some have been left behind in rural backwaters after the young reached out for work in the city or life in the suburb. Others are lost even to the Census Bureau, when they hole up in "hotels" or boardinghouses, or even wander, transiently, from town to town. A few are tucked away in institutions, their aloneness safely hidden from view.

Many we don't see because we don't care to look. One research group describes what can happen:

If too many of them frequented a cafeteria where food was low in cost and where it was possible to sit for a long time over a cup of coffee and a roll, younger people began to go elsewhere to eat, repelled by the sight of arthritic hands carefully counting out coins, dragging feet, and clothes unkempt or clumsily restyled. All too often even a friendly proprietor was obliged to change the rule or close his restaurant. Then the customers disappeared, to hot dog stands or to the hot plate in a furnished room.[1]

A vast number of older people in America are poor by government definition.* Many more are economically deprived by anybody's definition.

---

* The facts and figures of poverty in America do change, although not remarkably. A few dollars may inch someone above the official poverty threshold, but is he —or more likely she—no longer really poor? This chapter was completed in July,

In 1970 one in every four older persons had *less* income than the official, very conservative poverty estimate based on the government's own emergency food budget.[2] By 1972, with the passage of significantly increased Social Security benefits, there was a reduction in the number of the "officially" poor. Nonetheless, a minimum of 3 to 3.6 million older Americans remain poor by government standards. Millions more barely manage to survive.* Moreover, virulent inflation erodes new benefits.†

Over half of our elderly population live in deprivation. I am not speaking of lacking money enough to visit one's grandchildren, keep chilled drinks in the refrigerator or buy a subscription to the local newspaper. I mean lacking food, essential drugs, a telephone in the house to call for help in emergencies. Some take desperate measures to make ends meet:

> A 69-year-old widow was apprehended while trying to steal a 25-cent can of soup in a supermarket in Miami Beach with its opulent waterfront hotels. Shoplifting is seen as a necessity by some old people. This widow had $114 each month to live on in 1971.

The problem of *relative deprivation* cannot be ignored either. The daily ordeal that so many of the aged experience occurs in the context of an affluent society. Bare economic survival erodes the body and spirit even when it is the common condition. It is the more painful and humiliating in a country where the needed resources are not scarce but merely distributed unevenly; where the top fifth of the population has over 40 percent of the wealth and the bottom fifth less than 5 percent;[3] where the average aged family lives on half of what it had in earlier years. This country grosses almost a trillion dollars a year and spends only 4.2 percent of it toward aiding the old. With much smaller resources at their disposal, Britain and

---

1973. It was possible to take the 1972 and 1973 Social Security legislation somewhat into account. I could not bring all the material in this chapter completely up to the *same* date since not all data necessary to complete analyses were available. The changing poverty statistics depend upon fluctuating prices, inflation, employment, property taxes, savings, the value of the dollar, and other factors as well as Social Security.

Lenore Epstein Bixby, Herman Brotman, Margaret Gordon, Michael Harrington, Juanita M. Kreps, James N. Morgan, Jack Ossofsky, Mollie Orshansky, James H. Schulz, Ben B. Seligman, Harold L. Sheppard are among those who have contributed much to an understanding of the economics and the poverty of the elderly in America.

* The 1970 poverty threshold for a single person was $1,852; for a couple, $2,328. The 1972 figures were $1,940 and $2,520 respectively; 1973: $2,100 and $2,650 respectively. Poverty-index increases are based on the Consumer Price Index (CPI) and do not reflect changes in the nation's standard of living.

In the language of official government poverty indices the near poor are those whose income is below 125 percent of the poverty index.

† The first six months of 1973, for example, saw further skyrocketing inflation in food, rents and other necessities. Food prices alone went up 12 percent.

France spend 6.7 and 7 percent of their respective gross national products on their elderly. The denial of an active part in the social life of a nation or in a fair share of its benefits increases the feeling of isolation, fear and deprivation.

THE TOTAL INCOME PICTURE

To understand the poverty of older Americans in an affluent society we need to see how the old currently are supported and the difficulties they experience. Those 65 and older as a group receive their aggregate income as follows:

TABLE 1

Percent of Income	Income Source
46	Retirement benefits (Social Security, 34%; public pensions, 7%; private pensions, 5%)
29	Earnings from employment
15	Income from assets
4	Public assistance
3	Veterans' benefits
3	Other (contributions from family, etc.)[4]

THE OLD GROW POOR

Two crucial and distressing facts about poverty and old age are clear. First, although the numbers of those in poverty in other age groups are said to be decreasing, there has been an increase in both the number and the proportion of aged poor. The U.S. Senate Special Committee on Aging, using the conservative government-established poverty threshold, reported that in 1969 there were approximately 4.8 million people aged 65 and older who were living in poverty, almost 200,000 more than in 1968. In this same period, said the committee, poverty declined by 1.2 million for all other age groups.

Second, the elderly are the fastest-growing poverty group. This is new poverty, not simply the poverty transmitted from generation to generation within the same family. Independently of previous means and previous socioeconomic status, one may be thrown into poverty for the first time in old age. Catastrophic diseases, or the sheer cutback of income in retirement, may create instant poverty where none previously existed.

In fact, *many—-I think most—elderly poor have become poor after be-*

coming old. What does it mean in the lives of retired persons to receive a total pension income from both public and private sources of one-quarter to one-half or less of their average preretirement earnings?

> Mrs. Woods: an old lady with a lightly made, stately body, carried with pride and some pain. Her beautifully wrinkled skin was almost translucent, showing her high cheekbones.
>
> She would be pretty if not for the worried strain in the voice, face and hands, the shifting feet, distant eyes. A successful lawyer's wife, she had always been able to live in comfortable circumstances but was now under increasing financial pressure. She had outlived her savings.
>
> When her lawyer makes a visit she puts on the violet and blue print dress. She does not change her flat brown shoes. She pins her hair in a soft white knot in back. The lawyer was the family attorney for years. He comes to receive her endorsed checks and pay her bills. He makes out a check to the realty company for rent, and two other checks, one for the housekeeper who comes once a week, the other for food. He continues to help her now, when she is on public assistance of $92 per month.

Why should Mrs. Woods's last years have become mired in the struggle to survive? She is not the exceptional case—her situation is commonplace among the old.

WHAT IS POVERTY?

The words "poor," "poverty" and "relative deprivation" have become so commonplace that they have lost all reality. Anyone who reads newspapers is apt to be familiar with the images of the outstretched hands of some of the six million starving, homeless refugees fleeing from East Pakistan, or of the distended stomachs and empty expressions of malnourished children in our own rural backwaters or city streets. If one keeps these painful images in mind, it becomes tempting to imagine that less dramatic poverty is "only relative," and therefore less worthy of concern.

How does one arrive at a realistic idea of what constitutes poverty in old age? The official government estimate of poverty,* that is, the amount of income necessary to meet essential needs, is based on the Department of Agriculture's Economy Food Plan for emergency use, designed to keep

---

* The Council of Economic Advisers provided the first "official" estimates of the numerical extent of poverty in its January, 1964, "Economic Report of the President." They chose $3,000-per-year income for a family of four as the dividing line.

a healthy person alive and functioning reasonably for thirty days. Since the average family spends approximately one-third of its income on food, government economists multiplied this amount for food by three to obtain the total minimal budget that one could possibly live on; those with less are considered poor. In 1973, for an individual this was an income of $2,100 a year or less. The 1973 weighted average for a two-person older family was $2,640.

What if we take a less biological view of poverty and consider more than brute survival by examining the lot of the aged in terms of America's standard of living? The Retired Couple's Budgets of the Department of Labor estimate what a "modest but adequate" standard of living would cost, rather than an emergency budget. These budgets are detailed listings of items and quantities to meet the normal needs of an urban retired couple as judged adequate by the staff of the Bureau of Labor Statistics (BLS), which intermittently revises them.

The "experts"—economists, statisticians and social-science analysts—develop these hypothetical budgets for a hypothetical standard of living, assuming an existing inventory of clothes, furniture, appliances and so on. The retired couple is defined as a husband, age 60 or over, and his wife, who are self-supporting, living independently in their home, in reasonably good health and able to take care of themselves. More recently the Bureau of Labor Statistics has designed two additional Retired Couple Budgets, one at a somewhat lower standard of living and the other at a higher standard. "All three budgets provide for the maintenance of health and allow normal participation in community life, taking into account social and conventional as well as physiological needs." So say the government experts—but is this the case?

DO THE OLD NEED LESS?

The total Intermediate Budget for the Retired Couple, calculated in 1971,* was $4,776.† Let's look at what that detailed budget allows. The

---

* Some of the figures given here for specific items such as a pet or haircut, rather than general categories such as food or recreation, are from 1967 calculations. Budgets updated since 1967 have been limited in detail and based on the Consumer Price Index rather than actually pricing the contents of the budgets in the marketplace. The intermediate was pegged at $4,776 (the lower at $3,319 and the higher at $7,443).

† No budget has been developed for the single aged person, but unattached older people were much worse off economically than their married counterparts. The BLS estimates that the costs for one person are approximately 55 percent of the costs for a retired couple. Personal communication, Helen H. Lamale, Chief, Division of Living Conditions Studies, Bureau of Labor Statistics, U.S. Department of Labor, November 16, 1971.

staff concluded that $24 per week was adequate for groceries. (An elderly couple was allotted a little over $3 per meal plus tip in a restaurant once every week.) Housing averaged $139 per month, including household repairs and furnishings. For example, 1 percent of a sofa could be purchased every year. In the way of clothes, every year 7 percent of a topcoat was allowed for a man, one and one-fourth of a street dress for a woman, one house dress, two-thirds of a bra, etc. The husband was allowed 15.3 haircuts a year and his wife 1.7. For each person, one-fifth of an eye examination for glasses was allowed and one-half pair of glasses. Needless to say, it is not possible to live statistically.

America advertises and fantasizes old age as a period of leisure, travels and hobbies, but the recreation allotment in 1971 was $91 a year for both the husband and wife. No allowance was made for visits with children, travel away from home or vacation costs. The retired couple was allotted $5.30 a year to provide for a pet animal, which is for many people their major solace in loneliness, and often an aid to safety as well. Traditional American virtues have emphasized providence, but no money was allotted for savings.

The Retired Couple's Budgets in themselves tell us something about popular conceptions about the old "needing less." The Bureau of Labor Statistics has developed a whole set of budgets to describe a modest but adequate income for different family compositions. To compare the itemized accounts of these budgets for retired and younger couples with those for the four-person family is informative. One might expect housing, transportation and certain other costs to be greater for the larger younger family and some personal-care costs to be higher for the older family, which is, indeed, reflected in the budgets. But the reasoning behind the appreciably smaller clothes allowances for the adults in the older family or for home furnishings or gifts and contributions is less understandable. In the intermediate budget,* for example, the retired man was allowed $94 for clothing, the younger man $204. The older woman was given $100 for all clothing, and the younger wife $211.† Should we automatically assume that retired men and women are going to be leading drab and inactive lives? The older family was allotted $231 for gifts and contributions, the younger family $270. Yet the older couple might well have children and grandchildren to make gifts to, as well as churches and special causes to which to contribute.

---

* Only 1967 figures are available for the specific comparisons that follow.

† A case could be argued that younger active men and women wear their clothes out more quickly, but unfortunately inadequate money for clothing only reinforces the likelihood of forced inactivity by older people embarrassed by their appearance.

Retirement budgets are calculated on the assumption that the older couple have already accumulated much of what they will need for the rest of their lives. This is asking a lot of the healthy, potentially active older couple who may have twenty or more years ahead of them—if not the hundred years it would take to save the 1 percent a year allotment toward a new sofa! Are the elderly expected to keep their appliances and furniture in better shape than the rest of the population in our economy of planned obsolescence? Are they expected to care less for the satisfaction of wearing something new on those special occasions when they go out? What do we know about the spending patterns of older people?

In studies of consumer expenditures high-income families—whether younger or older—tend to show similar expenditure patterns.[5] In other words, if older couples have the money, they are as interested in recreation, clothes and a pleasant home environment as anyone of any age. *The reason old people spend less is that they have less to spend.*[6]

To put these two government estimates—the poverty line and the modest but adequate budgets—into perspective, let us note that economist Leon Keyserling considers those who are above the poverty line but below the Bureau of Labor Statistics budget to be living "in deprivation."[7] In terms of elderly couples and individuals the following are the poverty "definitions" and "guidelines" available at the time of the 1971 White House Conference on Aging:

TABLE 2

Organizations Which Have Defined Poverty	Point Below Which Poverty Occurs	
	Couple	Individual
Official poverty level, 1970	$2,328	$1,852
Retired Couple's Budget (Bureau of Labor Statistics, 1971) Intermediate Budget		
"Modest but Adequate"	4,776	2,627*
Higher Budget	7,443	4,094
National Welfare Rights Organization, 1971	**	2,250
Chairman, National Caucus on Black Aged, 1971	9,000	6,000

* Estimated as 55 percent of couple.
** No "guideline" available.

Hobart Jackson, chairman of the National Caucus on the Black Aged, affirms that an adequate income is the chief need of the elderly. He sets a minimum floor of $6,000 for a single old person and $9,000 for an aging couple. Jackson's figures are much more realistic than the official guidelines. They begin to approximate the median income of Americans regardless of age. The National Council of Senior Citizens, however, only supports the recommendation of the 1971 White House Conference on Aging for approximately $4,500 a year per couple, which was less than the 1970 Retired Couple's Intermediate Budget. Official 1967 analyses of the Retired Couple's Budgets against actual income levels, completed by the Bureau of Labor Statistics, found that 56 percent of all older couples had less income than even this "modest but adequate" budget!

Estimates of government agencies and private organizations—other than the National Caucus—run low because of conceptions of "political realities." In other words, requests and estimates are determined by what politicians feel have a chance of being approved by Congress, or the President, or an appropriate state official, rather than by what is needed. Government agencies also feel pressures to minimize the estimate of need. Increasingly, mild reform proposals become no more than mere ritual, a tinkering with the lives of the old.

What would it cost to provide a better standard of living? The National Welfare Rights Organization estimated in 1971 that to bring all Americans up to their minimal budget estimates ($6,500 for a family of four, $2,500 for a single person) would cost between $30 and $50 billion. Other agencies and organizations have offered similar estimates. To support all age groups decently will cost a lot of money; it cannot be done cheaply. As a people we either want to direct our resources in this direction or we do not.

THE WIDOW'S MITE

Widows, single women and members of minority groups are particularly disadvantaged economically. As one leading economist, Dr. Juanita Kreps, views it, "The older woman is the poorest in society today."[8] In 1970, 51 percent of elderly women living alone fell below the poverty line. As we noted in Chapter 1, one reason for the poverty among older women is that more women than men become widowed because they tend to marry men older than themselves and outlive males by an average of seven years.

Since 1973, with the change in Social Security law, widows (and dependent widowers) now receive 100 percent of the spouse's Social Security benefits instead of the 82½ percent that worsened the widow's economic plight before then. But other retirement programs remain prejudicial. Under the federal retirement system, for example, the survivor of a retiree gets only 55 percent of the retirement benefits received before the retiree's death. The wife who in a very real way helps in the support of her husband and family with the care of the home, food and children during working years is not supported in turn upon her husband's death.

The 1972 change in the Social Security law meant that nearly 3.8 million persons (widows and dependent widowers) would receive an additional $1.1 billion in benefits. An estimated 200,000 persons would be "removed" from official poverty. But note what this means in actual dollars—benefits for the average widow were increased $18 per month, from $138 in 1972 to $156 in 1973. That's not much!

Today's thirty million working wives will be in a better position when widowed than the present generation of widows. As Dr. Kreps points out, however, if women continue to earn less than men their retirement benefits will be proportionately smaller. Women's life opportunities have been restricted throughout the life cycle by sex-role conditioning, inequitable salary levels and prejudice, and this continues on into old age with pension benefits. Job discrimination early in life adversely affects an older woman's options. Department of Labor statistics show that a woman's median income is substantially lower in all major fields of employment.[9] In the labor force as a whole, 60 percent of women working full time the year round earn less than $5,000 annually, compared with 20 percent of the men. Only 3 percent of women earn more than $10,000, compared with 28 percent of men. On the average, women earn 58 percent of the income earned by their male counterparts.

These statistics, of course, refer to working women. The Department of Labor estimates that another 32.5 million women are not "working" because of home responsibilities. These women, mostly married, will be especially dependent on their spouses' retirement benefits. As they age, many will be forced increasingly to turn to the state for help.

MULTIPLE JEOPARDY

Minority-group elderly live in multiple jeopardy because of the effects of both racism and ageism. Blacks, Chicanos, Puerto Ricans and Chinese are among the minorities whose old age is often marked by grim poverty. It is frequently said that we have very little useful data about the relevancy of race to aging. But we know the overall truth: to be old is bad enough; to be old and not white is even more terrible. The likelihood of being poor, reports the Senate Special Committee on Aging, is twice as great for elderly minority groups as for the white population, and four times as great as for our total population at all ages.

America's one million elderly blacks continue to face discrimination and most live in poverty.

> For them life has meant the slum, the public aid roll, the second-hand store and the empty table. They have lived through six decades of inadequate medical care and have survived the ravages of discrimination, poor education, slum conditions, and unemployment. . . .
>
> Seven of ten elderly black Americans have incomes below $3,000 per year and half of them less than $2,000 per year.[10]

In absolute numbers more whites than blacks are elderly poor (85 percent of the total elderly poor are white, 15 percent black). Black poverty, however, is more profound than white poverty. The percentage of aged blacks living in poverty is twice that of aged whites. Forty-seven percent of all aged black females have incomes under $1,000. In rural areas two out of three aged blacks fall below the poverty line.[11] Furthermore, elderly blacks tend to have more people dependent on them than do the white elderly.

More elderly black people live with younger people than do white elderly: 28 percent of them live in families with a young head of household compared to 8.9 percent for all elderly regardless of race. There are many reasons why a larger percentage of black elderly live with their children: the importance of the role of grandmother because the mother works or is away; the need for the sharing of income within a family, including the older person's Social Security and public-assistance payments; and the respect and sense of responsibility, said to exist more strongly in black households, in caring for and protecting one's parents, particularly the aged mother.

Those older blacks who do not live with relatives are in a much more disadvantaged economic situation: 75 percent of all elderly blacks living alone fall below the poverty line, and Project FIND reported that of black widows an amazing 85 percent were living in poverty, with another 5 percent on the borderline. These are depressing facts indeed for an affluent society.

The impacts of racism upon aging are reflected in life expectancies at time of birth, which in turn affect retirement benefits. Robert Hill has emphasized that the average life expectancy of black males has actually declined by a year over the 1960–70 decade. Among males, nonwhite death rates were higher than those of whites through age 84, with a reversal occurring beyond that age. Nonwhite female death rates were higher than white through age 74.

Poverty is widespread among minority groups, and even the traditional kinship support of the family is broken down when the family as a whole is impoverished or the needs of the elderly outstrip the family's ability to help. Even East Asian–American elderly, usually thought of as much better off financially than other minority racial groups, experience the late-life consequences of lifetimes of discrimination.

The American Indian elderly suffer from a much lower life expectancy than blacks or whites; their average length of life is estimated at 44 years, so comparatively few survive to old age. Mexican-American elderly fare little better; for example, in Colorado their life span is 56.7 years compared to 67.5 for other Colorado residents.

In view of these differential life expectancies a number of people, including Dr. Jacqueline Johnson Jackson of Duke University and Dr. Inabel Lindsay, former dean of social work at Howard University, have called for the enactment of legislative changes in existing Social Security policies. There is a need to reflect differences in racial life expectancies by lowering the minimum age-eligibility requirements for beneficiary status for old age, survivors, disability and health insurance. This holds true for other pensions as well, since few elderly blacks live long enough to collect benefits.

THE RURAL ELDERLY POOR

Rural older people tend to be poor in part because self-employed farmers or agricultural workers were not covered by Social Security until recently. Few have private pension plans. Rural communities suffer from a shrinking tax base and an increasing scarcity of services when young people migrate to cities. The rural elderly are left with the task of maintaining their communities and services. A shortage of employment further hampers them in their attempts to supplement their income.

MYTHS ABOUT POVERTY

We need to examine the myths about income that underlie the plight of the elderly.

THE MYTH OF IMPROVIDENCE

Many Americans tend to believe that poverty among the old is their own fault, attributable to their failure to prepare adequately for economic security. Consider, however, the hypothetical John McCabe,* born in 1900 and living his primary earning years during the Depression between 1929

---

* He is typical of older Americans; the median age of those over 65 is about 74.

and 1939—in which, at its height, 25 percent of the work force was unemployed. Between his twenty-ninth and thirty-ninth years his situation was greatly affected by the economic status of the nation. He, like the rest of today's elderly, bore the brunt of the Great Depression—as they have borne the brunt of the inflation of the 1960s and 1970s. Moreover, since retirement occurs much earlier now than formerly (the average man leaves the work force at 57*) and is increasingly compulsory, McCabe will have had to finance an extended retirement period. He has roughly 14 years in "retirement" if he dies at the average age of 71. (The longer one lives, of course, the more one has the chance of outliving private pension benefits and exhausting savings.)

McCabe entered the army or the work force in 1917. He would have been in the work force approximately 40 years. During those 40 years he would have had to earn enough not only for his immediate purposes but for his future needs in his old age. In addition, he would have had to provide for his wife, who probably will outlive him. He most likely helped support his own parents, who would not have been covered by Social Security. He started contributing to the Social Security fund at 35 in 1935.

It would have been difficult for McCabe to accumulate any savings during the Depression in his prime years, or in the inflation of his so-called golden years. Like other retirees, he is dependent on a fixed income from Social Security and possibly (but unlikely) a private pension now being radically eroded by the rising cost of living. Between 1948 and today the value of the dollar has fallen catastrophically. What was worth 100 cents then was only worth 57.6 cents by 1972.† Virtually half of the dollar's purchasing power was gone. Whatever McCabe had saved between 48 and 72 years of age, and whatever plans he had made, were profoundly affected by that erosion.

The pointing finger of "improvidence" becomes a cruel gesture to this man, who was told—when he was in his thirties—that only by spending every penny would he help remobilize the economy; unfair to a man with the burden of supporting both young and the old in his family during his peak middle years; misdirected onto a man living in a technology of planned obsolescence.

As a final indignity, the same people who claim old poor people have been improvident may accuse them of hiding their assets. But about 40 percent of single older citizens have total assets of less than $1,000.

---

* Calculations producing this low average age of retirement include illness and unemployment as well as arbitrary or compulsory retirement rules.
† Of the 42.4-cent loss, 19.4 cents occurred between 1965 and 1972, the period of escalation of the Vietnam war.

THE MYTH OF AVAILABLE JOBS FOR THE ELDERLY

Against overwhelming odds almost one-third of the income of older people still comes from current earnings. This income is derived largely from part-time, unskilled and low-paid jobs such as janitor, night watchman and babysitter. Employment is often concealed "bootleg" work to avoid income taxes and Social Security penalties that could nullify any financial benefits of working.

Age discrimination, unemployment levels and arbitrary forced retirement drastically reduce the incomes of the elderly.* (The problem of employment in America goes beyond the elderly, of course, with youth, women, minorities and workers over 45 particularly subject to underemployment and unemployment. We have also failed to develop successful techniques for the great transitions: from military to peacetime industries, from goods to services. Obviously these problems have affected the old age of the elderly of today and will affect those of tomorrow.)

THE MYTH OF ADEQUATE SOCIAL SECURITY

Social Security keeps more than twelve million persons of all ages out of poverty as officially defined. It is the source of 50 percent of the income of nearly 66 percent of retired single workers and 50 percent of elderly couples. It is essentially the sole source of support for some 30 percent of retired workers and 14 percent of elderly couples. In absolute numbers, for more than two million of the twenty million aged, Social Security is the *only* source of income.[12]

Nonetheless Social Security has not eliminated poverty in old age. Along with other forms of income maintenance, such as private pensions and the emergent "guaranteed annual income," it is under skeptical scrutiny. In January, 1973, the U.S. Senate Special Committee on Aging began a series of hearings on the "Future Directions of Social Security."[13] There are major problems with the concepts *and* the benefit levels of all kinds of income maintenance in old age, including Social Security, which I shall discuss later.

WHAT ABOUT THE WAR AGAINST POVERTY?

One wonders what happened in the Office of Economic Opportunity (OEO), which was the one agency supposed to be concerned primarily with poverty. What did OEO ever do for older people? During 1965 and 1966

---

* These problems will be dealt with in Chapters 4 and 13.

there were arguments as to whether the aged poor would be a prime target group or simply a minor concern of the agency. In the end, budgeting outlays for the aged in the OEO through 1966 ran 2 percent of the total. This was against the Congress's mandate in 1965 that directed OEO to consider special programs for the aged "wherever possible." In its early days, the only program to which OEO gave any priority was the Medicare Alert Program,* in which older people were given temporary jobs at $1.25 per hour in order to let other older people know of the benefits available under Medicare. One of the few other OEO programs for the aged poor was the Foster Grandparent Program,† which allowed older people to help neglected, institutionalized, or mentally retarded children. It was a very successful but very modest program.

In some measure the cost-benefit philosophy that was popular among many federal agencies contributed to a negative attitude toward the old; the elderly were felt to be a very poor investment. Indeed, this was the point of view that Sargent Shriver, then OEO director, seemed to take when he spoke before a Senate subcommittee. He felt that there was little that could be done for older people, that they had low educational levels and poor health, and could not compete for jobs.[14]

. . . It seems to be extremely difficult to find efficient, economical ways of actually helping the very elderly poor to get out of poverty. Congress already has a magnificent record through the Social Security Administration, through the proposed Medicare bill, and through other programs, for bringing effective help to the aged, but when you get to the problem of how do you actually help the aged to help themselves to get out of poverty it is more difficult.

It was not clear from what Shriver said why, if Congress had such a "magnificent record," there was so much poverty.

Since those first years of OEO, the allocation for special programs for older persons has increased somewhat, and several new service programs have begun. From the OEO's Office of Special Programs the following fund pattern was given for specific programs,[15] collectively called Senior Opportunities for Services (SOS):‡

(Requested)	1968	1969	1970	1971	1972
(Millions)	$2.8	$6.4	$6.8	$8	$8

* This model could be employed to register older people for the guaranteed federal income floor, SSI.
† Now part of ACTION.
‡ Created in 1967 under amendments to the Economic Opportunity Act.

SOS is an appropriate acronym if one considers the enormity of the problems of old people and the short time available to them before death. But these yearly budget increases have been modest to the point of tokenism and light-years away from eradicating poverty among the elderly.

In addition to specific programs for the elderly, older persons have been served by Neighborhood Health and Legal Services, Emergency Food and Medical programs and others. One of the more creative programs was Operation FIND,* which employed 320 older persons as canvassers and reached more than 50,000 older persons. The objective was to find the friendless, isolated, needy and disabled to determine needs and to direct them to services.

THE IMPACT OF POOR SERVICES

We should be concerned not with income alone but with the *means* by which society provides for a decent old age. If we assured older people certain essential *public* and *social* services, such as transportation, adequate medical care, decent public housing, and rent subsidies, being "poor" would take on a different meaning; it would be less cruel and terrifying. But in fact, our country does not provide or provides inadequately such essential services. Government-backed medical insurance and public housing are still controversial and poorly implemented concepts in the United States, decades after they have become commonplace throughout Western Europe.

Neither money alone without services nor services provided under "means tests" without adequate income are desirable. Older people would prefer to be able to pay all their taxes, to pay full fare on transportation, to be able to afford an occasional movie. They don't really want to depend upon tax abatement, reduced transportation fares, food stamps, golden-age cards for the movies, Medicaid and Old Age Assistance. They should not be stigmatized by "special" cards and "benefits," nor be forced to hustle frantically to survive.

* Conducted by the National Council on the Aging under Jack Ossofsky.

Chapter 3

WHAT ABOUT MY PENSION?

How can the poverty of so many older Americans be eliminated? Primarily through retirement-benefit and income-maintenance systems, the subject of this chapter. In 1974 significant if modest national reforms were effected, assuring workers—under certain conditions and for the first time—that they would receive their pensions gained in private employment. But the lot of today's elderly has not been improved as a result.

And if workers of the future were somewhat heartened by private pension reform, they were treated to unnecessary and invalid scare stories about their Social Security. These appeared in newspapers and magazines of varying political viewpoints. *U.S. News and World Report*, the *Wall Street Journal* and the Washington *Post*, for example, carried articles about the coming crisis in Social Security, projecting bankruptcy as a result of a massive unfunded liability. Taxes would have to go up or benefits down. The declining birth rate would reduce the number of active workers compared to the growing number of retirees. The frightening inflation would also drain Social Security funds because of the cost-of-living escalator. Younger workers would probably rebel against increasing payroll taxes. Moreover, some high governmental figures spoke of the need to control (and presumably cut back) such "uncontrollable" programs as Social Security.

As I shall propose, major improvements in the Social Security system are clearly necessary. But panic is unjustified. Social Security remains one of the few instrumentalities of government that gives some measure of protection, however imperfect, against the inevitable vicissitudes of life.

SOCIAL SECURITY

Three different techniques of public support are operative in the United States; social insurance (Social Security), social assistance ("welfare"), and universal pensions (Supplemental Security Income). Social insurance is based on the general principle of insurance, where the pooling of resources balances the risks among large numbers of participants as well as over extended periods of time. Social assistance refers to the availability of benefits which are conditional on proof of need. Universal pensions are an unconditional minimum-income guarantee upon reaching a specified age.

Until we move to a different system of income maintenance the Social Security system continues to be the main source of pension income for most American retired workers. (As the table on page 24 indicates, only about 12 percent of retired workers are receiving private and public pension benefits, accounting for 5 percent of the aggregate income of older people.) The aim of the Social Security Act of 1935 was to provide a social-insurance program that would partially replace earnings from job income lost through retirement, disability or death. The United States was one of the last industrial nations to establish a contributory earnings-related system. Social Security began as a trust fund* made up exclusively of payments—"contributions"—provided equally by workers and their employers. There is some confusion as to whether Social Security should be considered strictly as an insurance plan or as a pension since it has elements of both. Social Security contributions are not saved and invested as insurance premiums are. Rather, they are paid out to today's beneficiaries. The Social Security Act is complex and has been amended many times. It now includes not only benefits for dependents, survivors and the disabled, but health insurance for the aged (Medicare).

Since 1973 the employee and employer have each contributed 5.85 percent† of a portion of the employee's wages or salary to the Social Security trust fund. Congress has increased this percentage over the years, to keep the fund solvent as outgoing Social Security payments have increased.‡ In 1973 the taxable income was raised to a maximum "base rate" of earnings of $10,800 a year and to $14,100 in 1975. Individuals earning more than this are not taxed beyond this amount nor are their benefits determined by income above this base rate.

Serious questions have been raised since the beginnings of Social Security about the adequacy of the concepts behind the system as well as the levels of benefits. For low-income or large families, a serious handicap is the "regressive" nature of the tax rate, which applies a uniform rate for covered

* There are now the Federal Old Age and Survivors Insurance trust and the Federal Disability Insurance trust funds, which totaled $32.5 billion as of December, 1970. These funds are used to pay benefits—usually, there is only enough reserve to pay one year's benefit—and administrative costs. They may not be used for any other purpose. In addition, there are the Medicare trust funds, including the Federal Hospital Insurance trust fund and the Federal Supplementary Medical Insurance trust fund. All these funds are invested in interest-bearing U.S. Government securities. The interest is sufficient to cover the administration of Social Security programs conducted by some 45,000 employees.

† Total: 11.7 percent. The employer contribution is regarded by some economists as a fiction since this "contribution" tends to keep wage levels down by roughly that equivalent.

‡ Six percent in 1978; 7.3 percent in 2011.

wages up to the "base rate." The Social Security payroll tax contrasts with the graduated or progressive income tax, in principle more clearly related to the ability to pay. Economists have varied in their views of the implications of the Social Security payroll tax. Some believe money is transferred largely from the lower middle class to the poor,[1] others from the poor to the middle class.[2] All agree that the rich don't lose. Those in low-income brackets or large families may pay more flat-rate Social Security payroll taxes than personal (somewhat graduated) income taxes. Social Security taxes, the fastest-growing taxes in America, are levied on employment income, without any modifications for people in poverty, and accounted for 4 percent of federal revenues in 1949 and 29 percent in 1973.*

Some Social Security experts, like former Social Security Commissioner Robert Ball, are afraid of putting an end to the trust-fund system altogether (as Milton Friedman and others have proposed) and replacing it completely by use of general federal tax revenues. They do favor the use of some tax dollars from the federal treasury, but they feel a separate trust fund is less susceptible to political whims. Some experts believe that contribution rates should be graduated—low for those in low-income brackets and higher as the income rises.

The Social Security system is further unfair in that it handicaps those who continue to work for wages past the age of eligibility—by a work penalty—though there is no reduction in benefits for those who receive additional income up to any amount from clipping stock and bond coupons or from insurance annuities or rents.

There are difficulties not only with the general concepts of Social Security but with the benefit levels. Present Social Security payments† do not even

---

* Strictly speaking the Social Security tax is a contribution, not a pure tax (the Federal Insurance Contribution Act—FICA), as people like Nelson Cruikshank, president of the National Council of Senior Citizens, emphasize. It is also an insurance premium, but, as Cruikshank says, "It's not as regressive as other insurance premiums." With life insurance you pay the same premium at a given age regardless of income. Nonetheless, in 1963 these Social Security payroll taxes raised 42 percent as much money as personal income taxes; in 1968, 58 percent; by 1973, 68 percent. Or, to express it in terms of percentage of federal budget receipts, Social Security payroll taxes accounted for 19 percent in 1963; 23 percent in 1968; and 29 percent in 1973. The maximum tax per employee has moved from $60 in 1949 to $1,544 in 1974. For an excellent discussion, see John A. Brittain, Brookings Institution economist, *Future Directions in Social Security*, Part 3, Hearings, U.S. Senate Special Committee on Aging, January 23, 1973. Washington, D.C.: U.S. Government Printing Office, 1973.

† Senator Frank Church led the Democratic forces in passing the 1972 20 percent increase in benefits, costing $5.5 billion per year. President Nixon signed the bill, saying, "It fails the test of fiscal responsibility by failing fully to finance its increase." But, he added (this being a presidential election year), "Older Americans need and deserve increased benefits." It must be noted that absolute benefit increases help most those with higher benefits to begin with.

approach minimum required support levels.* Today 27 million persons—about one in eight Americans of all ages—receive some sort of Social Security benefit; up to one-third of this group live below the poverty line. The minimum monthly benefits, $84.50 for a retired single person and $105 for a retired couple (1972 figures), really guaranteed only one thing: that the recipient who did not already have independent income would be dependent on welfare assistance through 1973 or upon the new Supplemental Security Income program (see pages 52–55) as of 1974. More than 10 percent of all those who get Social Security checks—2.8 million persons—receive the minimum benefit.†

What about the 90 percent who receive more than the minimum benefit? Even the average benefits which were paid in 1973—$161 for a single person, $270 for a couple and $137 for an aged widow‡—are inadequate for current living costs and, in effect, below the poverty line.§ The average $270 for a couple provides somewhat more than one-half of the U.S. Bureau of Labor Statistics meager "Modest but Adequate" Budget for retired couples in urban areas. (The Intermediate Budget *for 1971* called for $398 per month or $4,776 per year.)

The lower benefits for a married couple compared to two single beneficiaries has created further difficulties, as an April 5, 1971, *Time* article described:

There are thousands of elderly couples living out their lives in the sunny, ramshackle old-age ghettos of Florida or Arizona or Southern California. Widows and widowers, they come together for companionship, but frequently dare not marry because if they were a legal couple their Social Security payments would be reduced. So, often to the unaccustomed moralistic dismay of their children, the elderly go "unchurched" and endure the mailman's smirks.

To relieve at least this one indignity of old age, Connecticut Congressman Robert N. Steele has proposed what is now erringly called the "Steele Senility Sex Bill," which would allow the same Social Security payments to married and unmarried alike. Not all of the elderly sinners would rush to the church, of course. Says a cranky septuagenarian named Charlie, who has been living with a woman named Mary for five years in the seedy South Beach area of Miami: "I was burned once. I want to know what the hell a woman's like before I marry again."

* For example: the across-the-board Social Security rise doesn't help the elderly poor as much as persons with higher Social Security benefits to begin with.
† This percentage will decrease as more persons retire who have paid taxes long enough to get more substantial benefits.
‡ For comparison purposes the maximum benefits possible are $259 for a single worker and $389 for a couple.
§ The new Supplemental Security Income program beginning in 1974 assures a guaranteed annual income floor, also below the poverty threshold.

Congressman Claude Pepper (D.-Fla.) resolved part of this problem through legislation introduced in 1965 which prevents loss of certain Social Security benefits by reason of remarriage. (He also led the effort to amend the Railroad Retirement Act and the Civil Service Retirement Act for the same purpose.)

Another inequity in Social Security involves the manner in which husbands and wives are treated as separate taxable units, though not as separate recipients of benefits after retirement. This can cause them to pay much more into Social Security yet possibly receive less on retirement than would a retired man whose wife had not worked. Assume, for example, that a man will retire in the future with average monthly earnings for Social Security purposes of $650. He and his wife both will be 65 and can expect monthly benefits of $376.10. A second couple, both employed, also can plan to retire at 65. Each has covered earnings of $400 a month. However, they can expect combined monthly benefits of only $353.40. The first couple will receive more than the second, although they will have paid less in taxes.

Despite gaps and inequities, however, the 1972 Social Security legislation did significantly aid the economic plight of the elderly. The most obvious aid was the straight 20 percent raise in monthly benefits. Senator Frank Church said 1.4 million Social Security beneficiaries of all ages were raised from poverty* by his amendment. As we have seen, widows and dependent widowers were helped. Important also was the provision of an automatic escalator whenever the cost-of-living increase in any given year exceeds 3 percent. President Nixon joined the Democrats in putting his weight behind the escalator clause, to take effect January 1, 1975.† He applauded this "inflation-proof" feature, calling it "a major breakthrough for older Americans." (It is. However, since Social Security is only 34 percent of the total aggregate income of retirees, more than 50 percent of their income still remains unprotected against inflation.)

Furthermore, the retirement test regarding earnings was liberalized by raising to $2,400 per year the maximum amount that a beneficiary under age 72 may earn without loss of benefits. It has been estimated that 1.3 million workers under age 72 will be able to earn at least $420 more per year without losing benefits. This is, in truth, very little improvement! The

---

* This, of course, is poverty according to the conservative government definition based on brute survival. In such cases, a few dollars may take one out of "official" poverty but not out of authentic poverty.

† In June, 1973, with inflation increasing, Congress passed and the President signed a 5.6 percent cost-of-living increase in Social Security benefits effective June, 1974. In December, 1973, a two-step 11 percent increase was passed, securing an average monthly benefit of $186 for the individual and $310 for the couple by June, 1974. None of these increases kept pace with inflation, however.

elimination of the "means test" altogether would undoubtedly encourage many more older people to work.

There was a lowering of the age of computation for benefits for men from 65 to 62, the same as now exists for women. This helps the black aged to a degree, given their lower life expectancy and frequent death before reaching the age of eligibility. But for benefits to become a truly viable source of income for them and other nonwhite groups, the age levels need to be even lower or their life expectancies drastically improved.

Basic reform of Social Security benefits is dependent on political uncertainties of congressional action and thus is at the mercy of "higher"-priority items and consuming political exigencies. The fact that Congress has held the Social Security benefits to so low a level also reflects a resistance on the part of the middle-aged working constituency, who do not wish to carry an increased tax burden for what they feel is the support of other people's obligations. Such logic, understandable on the surface, is tragically misguided. In providing a common insurance program—or some form of income replacement and maintenance—we are merely assuring support of our citizens in circumstances of retirement and family tragedy or disruption *from which virtually no income or age group is excluded.* Out of about 27.8 million beneficiaries of Social Security, over one-fourth are the survivors of deceased workers as well as younger disabled workers and their dependents.* We tend to think that only the disabled or retired worker receives benefits, forgetting that the family of a disabled or retired person receives financial help as well. Middle-aged middle-class persons who feel they are being taxed to take care of down-and-out old-timers had better take a closer look at who the recipients of Social Security are.

Our country's economy expands as well as inflates. In addition to an escalator clause based on inflation there should be a second kind of expansionary escalator clause in which an individual receives money as a reflection of the continuing economic growth of the country, enabling him to partake of the gross national product. This exists in some European nations. Such an escalator would follow wages as well as prices. The reasoning is that the person now older and retired is, nonetheless, part of the work force which set in motion the economy that is now growing. If we regard ourselves as citizens, each with a stake in our country, then we have a right to a dividend—a continuing, annual dividend derived from greater produc-

---

* In 1969 the Social Security Administration reported that of 24,807,000 beneficiaries 15,686,000 were retired workers and dependents; 6,087,000 survivors of deceased workers; 2,392,000 disabled workers and dependents; 642,000 special age-72 beneficiaries. Social Security provides a kind of life-cycle insurance. For example, in August, 1969, one in eight beneficiaries was under 18.

tivity. All age groups should share in an improved standard of living.

Modern pension systems (including Social Security) are also techniques of deferred wages. That is, during our work life, we set aside a certain amount of money so that it may be available to us in the nonworking period of our life.* The current work force is also making a direct contribution toward the care of the retired, representing their debt to those who preceded them. The generations never really quite catch up with themselves. There are some actuarial calculations regarding the intergenerational aspects of financing that are hair-raising. For example, since over $300 billion are already committed and there are only some $30 billion in the trust funds, we must depend heavily upon the younger generation to pay for the older generation.[3]

Social Security payments were increased 15 percent in 1970, 10 percent in 1971 and 20 percent in 1972. This 45 percent increase really amounted to 51 percent compounded over the three years. However, the Consumer Price Index went up over 22 percent from 1968 to January, 1973. Thus the *effective* increase in Social Security amounted to 29 percent. Without the 1972 increase, therefore, the Social Security increases would have just barely kept up with inflation. Moreover, the inflation-ridden economy of 1973-4 wiped out much of the 1972 rise in benefits.

Another problem with the Social Security increases is that they tend to aid the poorest the least,† and in many cases they may actually lower income by changing benefit levels under Old Age Assistance or ending eligibility to Medicaid, food stamps and public housing. Veterans may lose certain of their service-connected benefits.

Another nightmarish example of the problems of income maintenance of retirees is the Federal Railroad Retirement system set up by Congress in 1937. The industry has shrunk. There are now about 600,000 members; at its peak there were 2 million. The active members are now assuming primary responsibility in assuring the pensions of the million retirees.

THE FEDERAL RETIREMENT SYSTEM—A GOOD MODEL?

The federal government is the largest employer in the world, employing about three million people. It has its own retirement system, started in 1920, financed by matching 7 percent (of gross income) payments made by the

---

* The Keogh Act of 1962 established this practice for the self-employed. This congressional act, providing a means for planning pensions for the self-employed, is named for its sponsor, former Representative Eugene J. Keogh (D.-N.Y.).

† Consider a 10 percent increase on $100 per month and $200 per month. In the first instance an additional $10 is available; in the second, $20. Proportions and absolute amounts are quite different from each other.

government and the employee. Federal retirements are based on years of service and the average earnings of the highest three years of service. While working for the government, federal employees are not included in Social Security. We might expect the federal retirement system to act as a model in providing adequately for those who have spent their working lives in its service, but let us examine the facts.

As the president of the National Association of Retired Federal Employees (NARFE) pointed out in 1971 testimony in Congress,* two-thirds of all federal retirees and their survivors receive less than $300 per month annuity. In other words, two-thirds of these retired families and individuals barely survive. Almost one-fourth of this group receive less than $100 a month. Half receive less than $200 a month.

Two questions come to mind when we think about these unbelievable figures. First, could the majority of these low-annuity retirees be "short-term" federal employees who spent only a few years of their working careers in federal service? And second, how many have other sources of income, particularly Social Security, from their work for other employers? The National Association of Retired Federal Employees, with a current membership of 153,000 (a small percentage of the more than 1,050,000 federal retirees), published in its retirement magazine a request for members with more than 15 years of service and monthly annuities of less than $350 to contact them. Only four months after their initial request they had received over 20,000 letters from retirees with 15 years or more of government service who receive less than $3,000 a year, or $250 monthly. What they found from their poll was that the poor among federal retirees were most often among long-term government workers who retired a number of years ago, when salaries were much lower and the retirement computation formula was much less liberal than it is today. The annuities they receive from a career of federal service simply do not provide them with adequate income to maintain a decent standard of living, especially in an inflationary economy. For example, one retiree reported a $209 annuity based on 45 years of service, and one with 54 years' service receives a mere $292. One couple with more than 50 years' service between them receive less than $250 a month.

Though federal retirees have received periodic cost-of-living increases since 1963,† these increases have little equalizing value in helping low-

---

* Statement by Thomas G. Walters, president of NARFE, before House Subcommittee on Retirement, Insurance and Health Benefits, Committee on Post Office and Civil Service, Congressman Jerome Waldie, chairman. June 23, 1971.

† The rises occur whenever the Consumer Price Index (CPI) increases by 3 percent for three consecutive months over the previous base month.

income annuitants to meet day-to-day living costs; they provide no substantial gain in buying power. What is needed is a significant increase in the low annuities, so that the cost-of-living increases would have a more realistic base.

We do not know what percentage of these retirees have other sources of income, from investment, work after retirement, etc. NARFE estimates that 30 to 33 percent of federal retirees also have some Social Security; it is most likely that a majority of the other two-thirds count the federal annuity as their sole source of retirement income.

I am not implying here that federal retirement benefits are inadequate across the board. Recent amendments to the Civil Service Retirement legislation have liberalized benefits for current employees and very recent retirees. It is those who retired some time ago who fare so poorly. Until the establishment of a truly suitable national guaranteed income, Congress should at the very least set a minimum Civil Service annuity along the lines provided in Social Security.

As with private pensions, the vesting rights* of federal employees are minimal to say the least.† In most cases, in order to be eligible for the annuity, which means a payment each month until the death of the retiree and his survivor, one must remain with the government for many years. For example, a person with thirty years of service would be eligible to draw benefits at 65. Those who have served the requisite number of years but are not of retirement age can either leave their contributions in the fund until age 62 or 65 and then receive payments, or withdraw their own contributions and receive no share of the government contribution.

Those who leave government service and have not worked an adequate number of years to be eligible for retirement can either leave their contribution plus the matching contribution from the government, or withdraw their own contribution at the time they leave the government service and receive none of the matching funds of government. These regulations are clearly legislated as an incentive for long-term government service which has many positive advantages. But the incentive has serious negative results too. It makes it psychologically difficult for the middle-aged who have spent ten or fifteen years, but not the twenty-five or thirty years necessary for maximal retirement benefits, to leave their jobs in government service if they are unhappy or wish to try something new. This system, which of course has its counterparts in the private sector, constrains the individual

* Cash equity or nonforfeitable right to future benefits.
† If one leaves government employment after service of up to one year one receives a refund of one's contribution; between one and five years of service one receives a refund plus interest computed at the rate of 3 percent compounded annually.

unnecessarily. The federal government should provide part-time work, flexible schedules and a negotiable retirement credit system. The latter means that the years that one has contributed to a government pension system would be added onto the years of contributions to other pension plans, so that all would add up to a decent retirement income at the end of an individual's working years.

There is also a great need for liberalization of benefits, especially for those who retired some time ago. Under present Civil Service retirement laws an employee, at retirement, is given the option to designate a survivor annuitant and provide for this survivorship benefit (i.e., that one's spouse receive benefits in the case of the retiree's death) by having a certain percentage of his annuity withheld monthly. At one time the cost of this reduction was as much as 25 percent, though liberalizations in the law over the years have decreased the amount for later retirees.

It should be repeated that under the federal employees retirement system a survivor, usually a widow, receives about 55 percent of the retiree's annuity upon his death. This is not true under Social Security, where the survivor now receives 100 percent of the retiree's benefit.

To summarize bluntly, the federal pension system is not an ideal model, courtesy of the world's number one employer.

MILITARY INJUSTICE

Military pensions are the oldest form of pensions granted by the U.S. government, going back to 1792 and the veterans of the American Revolution.

Our military are not well covered against disability and retirement. It is disgraceful that veterans, whether careerist or conscripted, should have to exist in poverty in old age. As of 1972 there were nearly a million career military personnel who had retired before 1958. They receive half of the pension of those retiring at the present time. The 1958 frozen rates do not allow for annual cost-of-living raises, and the overall result is penury. There has been a struggle by retired military groups to gain recomputation.

THANK GOD FOR PRIVATE PENSIONS?

There is a great delusion in American private business that the good and faithful worker is rewarded upon retirement. The following statement is closer to reality: "If you remain in good health and stay with the same company until you are 65 years old, and if the company is still in business, and if your department has not been abolished, and if you haven't been laid off for too long a period, and if there is enough money in the fund, and if that money has been prudently managed, you will get a pension."[4]

The problem with the private pension is not only too small a return, but the fact that so few workers who count on private pensions for their retirements end up receiving them. Over 35 million workers have private pension coverage under 34,000 separate plans. Until 1974 reform legislation, probably fewer than half would ever collect. But this pension reform did not help today's elderly. It will not significantly help American workers who are now over 50.

Congressional research and testimony resulting in the 1974 legislation brought out many dismaying facts. Ninety-two percent of workers who were enrolled in plans that required eleven or more years for eligibility did not qualify for benefits when they left their jobs, according to one Senate Labor Subcommittee study covering the 1950–70 period. At present there are about 16 million retired employees who collect some pension income.* The same study found the median monthly payment to be $99 and, for those who retired early on account of disability, less than $50. Private-pension payments in themselves are simply not enough to maintain a decent standard of living. This is often true even when there are Social Security payments to supplement the pensions.

The loss of pension rights is another major problem:

For 41 years Charles N. Evelyn worked for a Newark, New Jersey, chemical factory as a mechanic. As part of his compensation Evelyn was promised a pension of $100 a month when he retired at 65. At 63 Evelyn was laid off when the firm was acquired by a larger concern. Because he was not working for the company when he turned 65 Evelyn became ineligible for the pension he had counted on for years. "I never thought it could happen," says Evelyn, now 75 and subsisting on Social Security. "I thought the money was secure as a bank account."

(Washington *Post,* November 24, 1970)

Mr. Bernard Rouss testified before the Senate that he had worked for Columbia Gas from 1946 to 1969 except for three years when he was in the armed forces. He left in 1969 because the concern was relocating in another state. Since the company does not assign pension credits to employees until they reach the age of 45, he is not eligible for a pension from Columbia. (The company had been invited to testify at the hearing but declined.)

(*New York Times,* July 29, 1971)

Another witness, Mrs. Iris Kwek, who had spent 40 years as an office worker with the Anaconda American Brass Company, said she was being

---

* Most private pension plans do not provide survivor benefits, and those that do are inadequate. This contributes especially to the plight of older women.

terminated by the company involuntarily, and since the pension plan has no vesting provisions she will get nothing.[5]

(*New York Times*, July 29, 1971)

Such cases occur because the pension plans were poorly built to begin with and because pension funds remain one of the least-regulated financial institutions in the country. Though unions have collected millions of dollars through their pension funds, "only a tiny percentage of workers in medium to low-wage industries of all kinds ever receive retirement benefits under union pension plans."[6]

Growth in pension funds is a relatively recent development in the United States, although the first formal pension plan was established in this country in 1875 by the American Express Company. Employer provisions for retirement security remained a novel experiment in labor relations until World War II, when controls clamped a lid on wage and salary increases but not on fringe benefits such as pensions. With the help of a 1941 Supreme Court ruling allowing labor unions to negotiate pensions under collective bargaining laws, plus generous tax concessions as incentives, pension-fund assets grew from $7 billion in 1940 to $108 billion in 1960,* including funds run by companies, unions, insurance companies and state, local and federal governments.

Between 1961 and 1971 pension assets more than doubled to $240 billion, an amount equal to about one-third of the gross national product. This figure includes $34 billion in Social Security assets. Private-pension funds alone amount to about $137 billion and are made up of employers' and employees' contributions based on salary scale and length of employment. The money is the equivalent of one-eighth of all the savings held by individuals in checking and savings accounts, stocks, bonds and life-insurance policies. One out of ten shares traded on the New York Stock Exchange is owned by a pension fund.[7]

FEDERAL REGULATION

Private pensions have been "one of the largest reservoirs of unregulated wealth in the American economy."[8] Public policy had established tax savings for employers without appropriate surveillance. Starting a pension fund was relatively easy. To obtain favorable tax treatment the Internal Revenue Service required filing of a special form stating that the money would be

---

* Since 1940 retirement benefits have been growing faster than wages. See Gilbert Burcke, "That Ever-Expanding Pension Balloon," *Fortune*, October, 1971; pp. 100-103, 130.

used solely for the benefit of the employees and listing financial details. Only about 1,000 of some 115,000 such forms on file were examined by IRS agents each year, according to former IRS Commissioner Sheldon S. Cohen. However, the IRS looked over corporate pension plans when the companies were examined. Pension funds of companies and unions had to file annual statements with the Department of Labor, disclosing overall financial data but not individual investments. This was required by the Welfare and Pension Plans Disclosure Act of 1958. Unless pension-fund administrators violated criminal-embezzlement statutes, however, these requirements essentially constituted the extent of regulation of the pension industry.[9] There was no regulation of the operation of the plans, no provision for insurance of the funds and no guarantees for the covered workers.

Unlike bank accounts, pension funds were neither audited nor insured by outside agencies. Employers were not required to place enough money in the funds to cover benefits promised should the company become bankrupt or simply close its doors. If the company did dissolve, it was not liable for the obligations of its pension fund. This was true not only of a small marginal company but of big business as well.

In 1963, for example, some four thousand employees of Studebaker Corporation's South Bend, Indiana, plant found that their pensions amounted to little after the factory closed down. There was not enough money in the fund to pay benefits, although Studebaker had honored all its contract obligations. Men who had worked for the company for thirty and forty years got 15 percent of their promised pensions; many others received nothing.

Business interests such as the U.S. Chamber of Commerce argue that the tremendous growth of pension coverage would not have been possible under strict government regulation and that abuses have been minimal. They claim that more than one of every two American workers is now covered by a pension plan and some ten million persons receive benefits. Herman Brotman, knowledgeable statistician about conditions of the aged, puts these statistics in a more meaningful perspective: about 12 percent of the aged do receive some income from private pensions, but only 5 percent of all income of those 65 and over comes from private pensions.[10] The problem exists for white- as well as blue-collar workers. A notable example is the 125,000-member Council of Engineers and Scientists, whose membership was hard hit by massive layoffs in the aerospace industry in 1971.[11] As their jobs went so went their retirement money.

Because of the economic pinch that developed in 1969, Congressmen received hordes of letters about pension problems from their constituents and became increasingly aware of the subject. Senator Jacob Javits

(R.-N.Y.) reported that the subject of private pensions ran second only to Vietnam as a matter of constituent concern. A 1971 preliminary study by the Senate Committee on Labor and Public Welfare indicated that millions of workers contributing to pension plans never collect a cent in benefits. One Senate investigator said that the rate of disappointment is as high as nine out of ten in some industries.[12] Senator Harrison A. Williams (D.-N.J.) called the findings illustrative of the "nightmarish problems" older workers face in receiving adequate retirement income.

At least five major problems must be dealt with in any reform: the problem of "vesting"—cash equity or nonforfeitable benefits—in a pension system after a certain period of employment; the lack of insurance for the funds in case of bankruptcy or poor investment by the company; the lack of portability of pension credits, so that people are locked into one job for forty years in order to receive retirement benefits; the absence of cost-of-living escalators; and the failure to provide survivors' benefits.

VESTING AND PORTABILITY

Restrictive private-pension rules often denied benefits to workers unless they were employed by the same company for fifteen to twenty years and are still there at the age of 65 when they begin receiving benefits. Because of the many forfeitures by workers who leave, die or are fired before age 65, the employer can get away with lower contributions to the pension fund. The preliminary Senate study found that:

Fifty-one of the 87 plans in the study, with assets of $10 billion, provide no vesting at all or vesting only after at least 11 years of employment. In this group 92 percent of the 5.2 million workers since 1950 who left their jobs before retirement received nothing. Of the 6.9 million who were or are covered, only 253,118 or four percent had received any retirement benefits at the time of the survey.

The other 36 plans, with $6 billion in assets, required ten years or less for vesting, but even here, the study found, 73 percent of the 1.5 million workers who left early forfeited all their benefits. Of the 2.9 million workers covered by these plans since 1950 only 242,510 or eight percent had gotten any pension benefits.[13]

For fear of losing pensions many workers stay on in jobs they find boring or hate, to the disadvantage of all. On the other hand, the sweat and blood—the forfeitures—of the workers who leave their jobs early help pay for the pensions of those who stay.

FINANCIAL IRREGULARITIES

Through the years any number of financial irregularities have been uncovered in various pension funds, often the very large ones. One of the most publicized union-pension-fund "peculiarities" was the insistence of the United Mine Workers of America on keeping as much as $70 million from its pension and welfare fund (managed by "trustees" who employed friends and relatives of the union's officers) in an interest-free checking account at the National Bank of Washington, which is 75 percent owned by the union. One balance, according to congressional investigators, was $26 million, representing an annual loss of $1.3 million at simple 5 percent interest. Officials of the union said the practice was followed to keep the money readily available for a strike! In 1972 Federal Judge Gerhard Gesell required that the money be withdrawn from the National Bank of Washington, and he awarded $11.5 million in damages to retired and disabled United Mine Workers for losses suffered through the noninterest-bearing accounts.

Du Pont Company pensions may be revoked *after* retirement for "any activity which is harmful to the interest of the company." Former Republican Governor Russell Peterson of Delaware, previously an employee, decided to obtain written exception to protect himself should he act against Du Pont while in office.[14]

Some pension-fund administrators have made loans to themselves or to their companies out of the funds' capital, frequently under circumstances when the transactions would be too shaky for a traditional lender to approve them, or they engaged in other self-dealing. Many bankers and pension administrators believe pension funds that invest heavily in the stock of the fund's own company present opportunities for conflict of interest and place employees in double jeopardy: if the company goes bankrupt, the pension assets are worthless. Each year at least thirty thousand workers have lost out on pensions simply because their employers went bankrupt. By 1973, a Treasury Department report showed some 750,000 workers in this position.

CONTINUING BARGAINING AFTER RETIREMENT

To protect retired workers from the erosion of inflation, unions should be able to continue to bargain on their behalf. The National Labor Relations Board held that retirement benefits are a mandatory subject of bargaining because retired employees are still employees within the meaning of the act. However, the U.S. Sixth Circuit Court of Appeals reversed the NLRB decision in 1971. In December, 1971, ironically right after the White House Conference on Aging, the U.S. Supreme Court ruled six to one that unions do not have legal authority to require management to bargain on benefits for retired employees.[15] This decision is most unfortunate because it denies a crucial right to workers.

"WELFARE" AND GUARANTEED ANNUAL POVERTY

For those elderly who have no pensions or other resources or who need to supplement small incomes, Old Age Assistance, known as "welfare," has been the last resort. Nineteen seventy-two saw passage of a Supplemental Security Income (SSI) program, a nationally uniform system of benefits for the needy aged, blind and disabled, to begin January 1, 1974. It provides a guaranteed annual income, placing a floor under the income of all older Americans for the first time. But it remains unclear whether it will prove merely to be welfare under a new name, resulting in guaranteed annual poverty. The measure is supposed to reduce the inequities and red tape inherent in its predecessor, Old Age Assistance, a system of 1,152 varying state and local programs with different benefits, eligibility standards and rules. However, there is no assurance that some beneficiaries will not suffer losses of other benefits under SSI. One major issue is what constitutes income which affects entitlements to Medicaid (health care for the poor) and public housing. Another is the absence of a cost-of-living clause.

The Supplemental Security Income program is administered by the Social Security Administration and financed out of general tax revenues. Since the first $20 of Social Security or any other monthly income is disregarded in determining eligibility for SSI, the effect for those who receive exactly $20 a month was to insure $160 per person and $225 per couple effective July 1, 1974.* This means annual figures of $1,920 and $2,700 respectively —barely at the official poverty threshold, based on 1973 figures.

The program was estimated to save the states $1.5 billion in welfare payments and cost the federal treasury over $2 billion on an annual basis. It was believed that the SSI rolls of the retired would swell to over five million under this program. But federal, state and local governmental efforts to register people have lagged. There have been fatiguing trips to SSI offices, interminable eligibility studies and delayed checks.† Old people themselves are confused. The public retains its negative attitude toward welfare.

---

* In 1973, $10 was added to SSI payments, effective July 1, 1974. There is no cost-of-living escalator.

† By June, 1974, six months after the inauguration of the program, only one in eight of the newly eligible was receiving benefits.

WELFARE: IMAGE AND REALITY

People who get angry about welfare are not usually aware of exactly who the welfare recipients are. Fifteen and five-tenths percent of recipients have been old people whose chances of being able to work and function are severely compromised in our society. The permanently disabled and the blind make up 13 percent of recipients. Aid to Dependent Children accounts for 55 percent.[16] This adds up to over 83 percent. Members of these groups do not quite fit the stereotype of the shiftless, lazy, able-bodied person unwilling to work.

An important illustration of a notable switch from the welfare myth that "they're hungry because they're shiftless" was that of Senator Ernest F. Hollings (D.-S.C.). Senator Hollings held this view until January, 1968, when he visited a slum area of Charleston, South Carolina, at the invitation of a social worker, Sister Anthony.

Cold and wet, we moved from door to door, alley to alley. Before we had gone a block I was miserable. I saw what all America needs to see. The hungry are not able-bodied men, sitting around drunk and lazy on welfare. They are children. They are abandoned women, or the crippled, or the aged.

The average Old Age Assistance payment in 1969 was $70 a month, less than half the amount needed then to escape "poverty." The average benefits have varied enormously by state, ranging from more than $108 in California to only $38.40 in Mississippi.

Nearly two million older Americans were "on welfare" or Old Age Assistance in 1972. Three million more might have been eligible but were not receiving benefits for a variety of reasons. Pride is one of them, understandable in the historic context of lives that emphasized independence, achievement and thrift.

. . . decades' old pride is still apparent, for while more than 500,000 of the city's [New York City] elderly are reported below the official poverty level, only about 10 percent—or 54,000—have applied for available welfare aid.*

Pride is not the only reason, of course. Some older people became confused and uncertain when they faced the thicket of bureaucracy and the mountain of forms that had to be filled out. They often did not even know how to obtain welfare help. Further, red tape often required proof of birth, which may be very difficult for this age group. Eligibility require-

* "City's Elderly Fight Ailments and Economics to Survive," *New York Times,* June 30, 1969, p. 33.

ments varied from state to state. The conditions were often very demeaning. Many states, for example, placed liens on the property of public-assistance recipients or their relatives, from which the state was reimbursed upon the recipient's death for welfare payments made to him. For many older people, their homes are filled with memories and offer great emotional sustenance. Moreover, imagine the feeling of humiliation involved in welfare regulations that require an old person to sign a written statement that he or she owns absolutely nothing of real value—after a lifetime of work and thrift!

Many states required recipients to cash in any life-insurance policy worth more than $200. An insurance policy, however, is often one of the few tangible tokens through which an old person feels he has provided proper protection for his family, and for some it is the only assurance that they will not have a pauper's funeral.

Another major obstacle in applying for welfare was the responsible-relative clause required by many states.[17] This clause may require families to provide some financial assistance to an older family member. Such regulations were frequently not enforced, but they acted as a strong deterrent to application for Old Age Assistance (OAA).[18] I observed this in families where children and their elderly parents were not on good terms, or where the older individual felt the need to remain independent of his or her children. The old person did not want to demand assistance when it had not been offered; and he often did not wish to inform relatives of his financial plight. Seeing his children already financially burdened and desirous of better opportunities for his grandchildren, he often chose to remain quiet, and to struggle alone with extremely little rather than apply for assistance.

For the independent American who was brought up to have pride in his capacity, to lift himself up by the bootstraps and to pay his own way, for the American who lived by the "American Dream," the idea of going on welfare for the first time in late life was a terrible prospect. This dread was compounded by the harassing attitudes of welfare "intake" workers toward applicants for Old Age Assistance. William Bechill, the former and first Commissioner of Aging of the Administration on Aging in the Department of Health, Education, and Welfare, had visited numerous welfare agencies throughout the country during his service and was dismayed at the "harassment which inhibits Old Age Assistance enrollees." Thus, the fact that only about two million of perhaps five million eligible elderly poor have been on welfare is a crude statistical measure of the special pride and cruel harassment of older Americans. What indeed will happen under the new federalized system of benefits?

Shockingly, the recipients of both Social Security and old-age benefits lost income despite increases in Social Security benefits, because states made offsetting reductions in old-age welfare benefits. Legislation was effected in 1970, 1972 and 1973 to protect aged welfare recipients to some degree against such reductions in the future, and to help secure for them the full amount of Social Security increases without penalty.

Despite this, because of changed eligibility levels for Medicaid, food stamps and other benefits following the 20 percent 1972 increase, some Social Security beneficiaries continued to be less well off after the increase. In New York City, for example, when Social Security increases raised some elderly persons' incomes above eligibility levels for Medicaid and food stamps, they actually sustained a real financial loss.

The new program, Supplemental Security Income, is a major structural reform but it does continue what already existed—the condoning of poverty among the elderly by our national government. Through its own programs *the federal government continues to provide income at levels below the official poverty lines which the federal government itself established.*

THE UNITED STATES AND EUROPE

In most Western industrialized nations the idea of "social security" means the right to a job, fair pay, sufficient food, clothing and shelter, medical care and protection against poverty in old age because of disability or death of the breadwinner. Twenty-nine countries instituted social-security systems before we did and most of them provide more for their elderly than we do. The present British system of social security, the Beveridge Plan,[19] "from the cradle to the grave," provides standard pensions regardless of previous earnings, with contributions from the government, employers and employees. Great Britain spends 6.7 percent of its gross national product on the elderly. In West Germany people can receive social-security benefits at 65 even if they are still working. The American government makes no contribution to Social Security. All the moneys it disburses are collected from employers and employees. In other nations, the government also contributes through general tax revenues.

In the United States "social security" has a more restricted meaning. Its scope is narrower. All United States Social Security payments to the elderly in the 1960s amounted to no more than 4.2 percent of the gross national product. For the nations of the European Economic Community in the 1960s, the average ratio of social-security expenditure for the elderly to gross national product was approximately 14 percent; for the three Scandinavian countries it was around 12 to 13 percent, for Canada 9.9 percent. The United States percentage was barely above the level of Portugal.[20]

Even this comparison is conservative considering the greater availability in many European countries of social-welfare services—in addition to pension benefits—which older people receive.

There are, of course, many social and economic problems of old age which Europe and other nations of the world have not solved either. Since 1969 the United Nations has been looking into the economic and social problems of aging and retirement throughout the world. But the United States can already learn much that is right as well as wrong by comparing its policies and procedures with those of other nations. Specific solutions to specific problems in various countries—for example, the extensive home-maker services in Sweden—demonstrate feasibility; they are not simply utopian. Enormous as the problems are, concepts and methods are available which are not exploited. What is lacking is the decision by the American people to commit the necessary resources.

THINGS ARE LOOKING DOWN

Those presently middle-aged will not retain their political, economic and social positions forever. They too will grow old and, if present conditions continue, they too will be subject to poverty and despair. In fact, today's middle-aged are in for more trouble tomorrow than their parents experience today. Consider those retiring in the next decade and a half: it has been projected that almost 60 percent of those with pre-retirement earnings of $4,000 to $8,000 will receive pension income of less than half of those earnings.

A crucial new factor is the questionable trend toward a shortened number of working years and earlier retirement ages. While the average number of retirement years for a man is now fourteen, it is predicted that in the year 2000 the average man will have twenty-five years of retirement for which to save—unless there is a major change in public policy! And many more healthy men and women will be living to a ripe, if not pleasant, old age.

Statistics indicate that the economic status of the elderly has improved since the Depression. However, the economic plight of the elderly will worsen for those now middle-aged if current programs of income mainte-nance remain the same. Fundamental reform is required that goes far be-yond a few additional dollars for monthly Social Security payments or modestly improved health-care services. More Americans are spending more years in retirement, and the difference between the incomes of members of the labor force and those in retirement is widening. As a nation, what do we want for ourselves when we are old and what do we want for those who are old today?

WHAT TO DO?

Significant reforms in Social Security and private pensions are under intense discussion by policy makers, economists and Congress. The costs of establishing and maintaining decent income levels for older retired people are staggering. They may be better controlled by adopting a fundamental universal pension system rather than tinkering with patchwork reforms in Social Security and private pensions. The burden on workers aiding their elders and their future selves may be reduced by enhancing work opportunities for older people who have the competence, health and desire to take advantage of them.

Concern about the inflationary impact of a broadened system of income maintenance for retirees is realistic but must be evaluated in the context of many other forces that increase available currency and credit out of proportion to accessible goods and services. It can be argued, of course, that improved Social Security benefits are inflationary. However, can keeping the aged in poverty be justified as an anti-inflationary device?

SOCIAL SECURITY REFORMS

The growing burden of Social Security payroll taxes falls upon the middle- and lower-income workers while higher-income employees have been getting a *break* in their taxes. I concur with many economists* who believe that the wage base should be raised so that the total wages of most employees are subject to the Social Security tax and, at the same time, more closely related to their actual earnings.† At the very least the taxable base should promptly be raised to at least $15,000‡ and then expanded toward a graduated-income-tax approach. Thus, Social Security costs would be shifted to the general revenues of the federal government; and this shift could occur in stages, first to one-third of the total costs and then to two-thirds. The staging, over a three-year period, necessitates guidance by the Social Security Advisory Council.§

The final one-third of costs should continue to be supported through

---

* Among them Juanita Kreps, Leon Keyserling and Joseph Peckman.

† The wage base when first developed in 1935 was much less regressive than the current amount. Although that first wage base was only $3,000, over 90 percent of all workers during those years of Depression had their total wages covered by this maximum Social Security amount. In 1972, 68 million of the 94 million persons (some 72 percent) subject to the payroll tax made less than $9,000 per year.

‡ As recommended by the National Council of Senior Citizens and by former Social Security Commissioner Robert Ball.

§ The council should be expanded to include representatives of organizations for the elderly.

Social Security trust funds in order that the changed financing can retain in part the contributory features of the Social Security system, with payments by employers and employees. Social Security benefits are and should be determined by one's average earnings. But the change should help those with low incomes, through a greater government contribution at this level. There should be an exemption by choice from contributions for, say, the first $1,000 earned, to protect those with low income. Another advantage of this option would be to allow students, housewives and others to participate in a voluntary system. Contributions from employers, employees and general revenues are common in the financing of many systems in European nations. Women who carry out household and family duties should be eligible for Social Security. This is the case in France, for example. Former HEW Secretary Wilbur J. Cohen, among others, has argued for this proposal.

The so-called "retirement test" or "earnings test" of Social Security needs to be further liberalized or eliminated. As it now stands it provides for reductions in the benefits of individuals who exceed certain earnings limitations. Each beneficiary under age 72 (except disabled workers or disabled children of retired, disabled or deceased workers) may earn $2,400 per year without any reduction in OASDI benefits.* If a beneficiary exceeds this limit his benefits are reduced by $1 for every $2 of annual earnings.

The proponents of the retirement test explain that the purpose of Social Security benefits is to furnish only a partial replacement of earnings which are lost to a family because of death, disability or retirement in old age. It is argued, further, that repeal of this provision without reduction of other benefits would add substantial costs to the program.† It has been estimated (using 1970 figures) that elimination of the retirement test would add approximately 1.9 million beneficiaries to the Social Security rolls and would increase the cost of the system about $2.6 billion in the first year. If the system is to be kept on an actuarially sound basis, an additional 33 percent in both the employees' and employers' contributions would be required in all future years. The 1972 liberalization meant 1.2 million persons would receive $856 million in additional benefits.

* There is a loophole that too few retirees know about. One can receive benefits for any month in which earnings are not over $200 even if the total year's earnings exceed the $2,400 limit. Thus one could earn $800 monthly during the Christmas selling months of November and December and $200 per month the other ten months, for a total of $3,600 without penalty in the other months.

† The National Council of Senior Citizens favors maintaining the earnings test. Their position is that the costs could be better spent helping needy aged, including those who cannot work because of medical illness. However, there is no assurance that such an amount of money would be spent for such purposes. The National Council may have another motivation for its position since it depends upon labor-union support. There is concern over rises in Social Security taxes on younger union workers, who may begin to rebel against such taxes.

Those who would eliminate the "retirement test" believe that payments are due as a matter of right. This, they argue, is consistent with the "insurance" concept of the system: benefits are related to the wages of the employee contributor and should be payable without an income test. Moreover, it is stressed, the provision causes inequities in a great number of individual cases where the individual has need to work for more income than Social Security benefits can provide. Furthermore, in practice the test is complicated and difficult for the ordinary person to understand. Often a retiree will lose benefits because he was not aware of the intricate formulas involved. I have been impressed by the amount of anger the work "penalty" arouses, the destruction of incentive and the indignity of "bootleg" work that it forces upon some.

PRIVATE-PENSION REFORMS

Consumer advocates Ralph Nader and Karen Ferguson have suggested that the pension system be changed so that employees choose their own fund.[21] These funds would be private, competitive, independent, financial organizations outside companies or unions, and regulated by the Securities and Exchange Commission. Under the Nader plan employers would continue to receive a tax deduction for contributions made toward their workers' retirement. But the employee would be able to choose his own plan. He would immediately acquire a vested interest in the fund. The money could be withdrawn only at retirement or disability, but the employee would retain the right to transfer his money to another fund if he chose. Nader's group insists that such a plan would not cost the employer significantly more. They view such a reform as equalizing the distribution of the existing pension funds, not as a panacea for income maintenance of the aged.

Numerous bills and recommendations concerning reform of pension plans have floated through the halls of Congress every session, ranging from mild reform, such as the 1970 recommendation of the President's Task Force on Aging and the 1972 legislative initiatives of the Nixon administration, to the more far-reaching bills of Senators Javits and Williams and the proposal of Ralph Nader introduced as a bill in the Senate by Senator Philip A. Hart (D.-Mich.) in 1973.

The role and potential of the private-pension system received searching inquiry by the President's Task Force on Aging (1970).[22] Two major recommendations evolved: First, an independent pension commission should be established to engage in activities that would result in the fullest protection of employee rights. Second, the President should direct the commission to enlist the help of the financial community in designating a portable voluntary pension system as a companion to the Social Security system.

The Nixon administration's plan was a voluntary pension scheme. Workers would be encouraged to save $1,500 a year or 20 percent of their income, whichever was less, for retirement. This money would be deducted from a worker's taxable income. (This is similar to the Keogh Plan tax write-off available to the self-employed—doctors, lawyers and others— since 1962.) A voluntary pension system (such as exists in other nations) which encourages individual providence and supplements a basic income program is certainly desirable, though it should not be thought of as a solution in itself. The Nixon administration also offered only minimal reforms on vesting in its plan, and essentially nothing on portability and protection of pension funds.

In an attempt to remedy pension shortcomings and provide needed "landmark" reforms, Senators Javits and Williams introduced the Retirement Income Security for Employees Act of 1972. The two Senators have said, "The first expectations . . . of many American workers have failed to materialize, and they are left with insecurity at that twilight stage of their lives." Their bill was the product of a comprehensive two-year study, undertaken by the Senate's Labor Subcommittee, of the private-pension-plan system in the United States.

A bipartisan coalition of Senators, all members of the subcommittee's parent Labor and Public Welfare Committee, had co-sponsored the bill with hopes of raising the private-pension system to "partnership status with our basic federal Social Security System." The measure would have set up an Office of Pension and Welfare Plan Administration within the Department of Labor; established minimum funding standards of pension plans to ensure that all pension liabilities incurred by the plan would be funded over a forty-year period; authorized the Secretary of Labor to grant variances from funding requirements for qualifying plans under certain circumstances; set up a federal insurance program;* and instituted a voluntary program for portability through a central fund, whereby employees might transfer vested credits from one employer to another. The bill prescribed minimum vesting requirements, whereby an employee, after eight years of service, would acquire a vested nonforfeitable right to 30 percent of pension benefits; each year thereafter he would vest an additional 10 percent; and at the end of fifteen years he would have vested rights of 100 percent.

Businessmen—especially pension-fund managers—worried over the proposals of Javits, Williams and others, particularly those involving early

---

* Similar to the Federal Deposit Insurance Corporation (FDIC) which protects bank deposits.

vesting rights. It has been predicted that pension costs could go up from 5 to 15 percent for many companies if the Javits-Williams bill was passed. For some industries, particularly those with high employee turnover—such as the textile industry—it is claimed that the extra cost could go as high as 20 percent and drive them out of business.

The fact is that the majority of private pension plans are designed to retain employees by denying them any retirement benefits if they leave after five or ten years,* and are actually computed on the basis that many of those currently members of a plan will, in fact, leave and forfeit their benefits. In other words, management and the employee contribute less than would be necessary if every member actually received his retirement benefits, because it is known, in practice, that the fund will have to pay off only a small fraction of the members enlisted in the plan.

Although the Republican Task Force proposal, the later 1972 Javits-Williams bill and the Nader-Hart proposal differed in important ways, all three agreed on the immediate need to impose minimum standards for vesting, pension insurance and certain fiduciary responsibilities of managers of pension assets. This was quite a coalition—across parties, across interests, across ideologies. Such agreement is rare and speaks to the overwhelming recognition of need.

On Labor Day, 1974, President Ford signed the Employee Retirement Income Security (Pension Reform) Act of 1974, which, broadly speaking, guarantees that employees promised pension benefits after working for an employer a given number of years will actually be paid. It represents seven years of hard work and controversy. Senators Williams, Javits and Lloyd Bentsen (D.-Tex.) carried the battle.

Although the Act is not a landmark legislative achievement,† it marks a significant, if modest, reform that will help the future elderly and be the basis for further improvements.‡ It covers less than half of American workers in the private sector. The Act has nothing to do with the dollar amount of a benefit. It provides three alternative schemes but not mandatory portable credit—which is particularly disadvantageous to women, who tend to have shorter job tenure. Vesting will not begin until age 25 (although the bulk of blue- and gray-collar workers begin full-time work at 16, 17 and 18),

---

* While employers may wish to tie employees to their companies or unions, the economy as a whole is stronger when workers are free to move. Report of economist James H. Schulz, then of the University of New Hampshire, Senate Special Committee on Aging, January, 1970.

† See the severe criticism of Merton C. Bernstein, "Pension Reform: Insult Added to Injury," Washington *Post,* April 7, 1974; and the answer of Senator Bentsen, "Protecting the Worker: A More Hopeful View," Washington *Post,* April 14, 1974.

‡ An Office of Employee Benefits Security was established in the Department of Labor to answer questions and deal with complaints.

and this is likely to discourage firms from hiring older workers. It requires at least 50 percent survivor's benefits, but not 100 percent, as does Social Security. Pension plans remain voluntary, so some unions and companies (especially those facing economic uncertainties) will not create such plans or may drop those they have. (Existing plans must comply with the terms of the Act by January 1, 1976.) There is no arrangement for cost-of-living increases. It requires funding and uniform fiduciary and disclosure standards. The Pension Benefit Guarantee Corporation, created by the Act, will insure a worker against loss of his entitlement up to $750 a month. This insurance does not apply to profit-sharing plans. The Act also liberalized the Keogh programs.

Merton Bernstein, an authority on pensions and author of *The Future of Private Pensions* (1964), argued that the Javits-Williams bill should be scrapped and the billions now paid for private pension plans should be funneled into the Social Security system. The tax advantages of some $4 billion a year[23] granted to private-pension funds would then be available for Social Security. In addition, unfortunately, private pensions are not compulsory; Social Security is.

Nelson McClung, formerly economist for the Joint Economic Committee, also recommended that private pension plans all be integrated into an expanded Social Security system. The myriad forms of pensions, funds and programs should be combined, reducing administrative expenses and present chaos. But it would have to be a different kind of Social Security from the one we have at present.

How much income do we want the elderly—and ultimately ourselves—to have upon retirement?

Suppose the pension income of Americans now retired was suddenly elevated to 50 percent of their final wage. The total cost would probably amount to $60 billion, or about 10 to 12 percent of the nation's current payroll. If pensions were raised to 75 percent of final pay, the payroll deduction for everybody would be 15 to 18 percent.[24]

This is expensive but it would solve a host of problems for all of us, and our families as we grow old. In Europe most pensioners receive 50 to 70 percent of their previous take-home pay.* In America the average retiree gets 25 to 50 percent of his maximum or terminal salary or wage.

The necessity for a national, compulsory system is manifold—to ensure security in old age, to reduce administrative costs and to eliminate impossible

---

* Many European nations have automatic pension adjustments reflecting changes in both prices and productivity.

burdens upon some employers, including states and municipalities. For instance, New York City municipal employees—policemen, civil servants, transit workers, etc.—can retire after twenty years, which means that many leave at 40 or 45 and draw pensions for 30 or 35 years. Taxpayers from states and cities with such programs can ill afford the massive costs. It is inefficient to have a hodgepodge of various programs, and prohibitively expensive to private businesses* as well as local and state governmental employers.

So that the American people do not grow poor as they grow old in our affluent society a universal pension system should be established. It should incorporate under one umbrella all private and public pension plans, including Social Security. Benefit levels should depend on the length and level of lifetime work-related earnings—that is, "contributions"—in turn a function of a graduated income tax. There should be immediate 100 percent vesting and mandatory portability. Funds should be fully insured to afford total protection. There should be survivor benefits. There should be two escalators: one related to the cost of living,† the other reflecting a share in the nation's productivity. Retirement income would then conform to the current standard of living. The costs would be great but not beyond our capacity, with two-thirds of the financing coming from general federal tax revenues and one-third from trust funds.

All this is, of course, an ideal program. In reality, however, Americans may choose or be forced by the present economic system to continue to chance growing poor as they grow old.

* Private businesses bear the risk of trying to estimate long-range investment returns, probable salary and wage increases, likely retirement ages, employee turnover, disability and mortality.

† The Gerontological Society announced support of the concept of constant purchasing power bonds as one means of providing a hedge against inflation. See, also, U.S. Senate Special Committee on Aging, *A Constant Purchasing Power Bond: A Proposal for Protecting Retirement Income*, which was published in 1961!

Chapter 4

THE RIGHT TO WORK

The right to work is basic to the right to survive. Work, denied to older people by practice and by attitudes, is often needed to earn a living and provide personal satisfaction.

> The oldest volunteer for the National Institute of Mental Health study of human aging was a 92-year-old man who complained, "I want a job and no one will hire me." Samuel Morris was a vest maker and vests went out with the advent of World War II because of fabric shortages. By the time vests came back he was in his eighties and no one would hire him. He detested having "nothing to do." He lived with his daughter, herself in her sixties, and she didn't like him working in the kitchen and around the house.

Samuel Morris did not take his case of age discrimination in employment to court but other older people are beginning to do so. There have been legal suits against mandatory retirement. In 1959 the Appellate Court of the State of Illinois ruled that a man could not be forced to retire because he was 70. The court said that "common law has never held that a person attaining 70 has absolutely lost his status in being a man and, as a matter of law, has become a disabled shell of his former self so that he was deemed incapable of performing the functions he has been performing for 69 years."

THE WASTE OF HUMAN EXPERIENCE

Man thinks of himself as wise and distinguished from other animals by his capacities for forethought, language and symbolic thinking, and for the transmission of culture. And yet we have failed to create and maintain conditions which bring these capacities to their fulfillment. Those qualities which are especially associated with middle and later life—experience, accumulated skills, knowledge, judgment, wisdom and perspective—are discarded just when they are coming to fruition in human beings.

Each year as thousands of people are encouraged or forced to retire, their skills, knowledge and wisdom are lost and their opportunities to instruct, teach, consult or advise, listen and reflect, as well as to work, are cut off.

Sixty-nine-year-old philosopher Paul Weiss talked animatedly about his $1 million suit against Fordham University, charging age bias.[1] This vital and vitalizing teacher had been offered the $100,000-per-year Albert Schweitzer chair—one of a number of state-financed professorships at various universities in New York—but then was denied it on the basis of his age.

Weiss was strong-voiced, cheerful, ebullient, altogether impressive. Author of sixteen books, including *Man's Freedom* in 1950, he was teaching at Catholic University in 1970, following his retirement as Sterling Professor of philosophy at Yale.

Weiss felt that Fordham* was illegally denying him the prestigious chair. He charged in U.S. District Court that Fordham's action was discriminatory and violated federal and state law as well as constitutional rights. The suit alleged that the Older Americans Act of 1965 states it is the responsibility "of the governments of the United States and the several states and their political subdivisions to assist our older people to secure equal opportunity to the full and free enjoyment of . . . employment with no discriminatory personnel practices because of age."

Weiss pointed out ironically that the chair was named for the famous Dr. Schweitzer, "many of whose major achievements came after he was older than the plaintiff." Schweitzer died at 90 in 1965. ". . . America will never be of age until it knows how to make most use of its people—no matter what their color, sex or years," wrote Weiss.[2] In the complaint the professor was described as in "excellent" physical health. "He walks eight miles every day, swims and does various calisthenics. His mental condition is also beyond question excellent."

In reviewing the case U.S. District Court Judge Harold R. Tyler, Jr., dismissed all statutory motions; that is, any aspects of the case directly related to statutes or laws enacted by legislative bodies. Moreover, he dismissed the constitutional claim that age discrimination is not in keeping with the U.S. Constitution. He stated that despite advances in our knowledge of aging it is nonetheless clear that abilities

---

* Fordham itself had a mandatory retirement age of 70.

diminish with aging and that age is not discriminatory because it cuts across all categories of race, religion and sex!

The judgment was appealed unsuccessfully, but it marked an important step toward legal redress.

The constitutionality of denial of work through mandatory retirement or refusal to hire is questionable,[3] and we can expect more court battles on the subject.* In an era when people made their own products and were their own bosses, they used to work until they were disabled or died. To have some control over production, as farmers or craftsmen, protected old people from mandatory age-invoked idleness. Today this is still the case for the self-employed, who also have some control over the work they do—lawyers, physicians and the like; they continue to be protected and are apt to work to the end. But this does not help the 73 million Americans of all ages—80 percent of all those who work—who are in the hire of others.

Older people begin to face age discrimination as early as age 45, even if highly qualified. Many are mustered out of the work force at an automatic cutoff age, usually 65, and told to "enjoy" a retirement that often locks them into poverty as well as idleness. They are denied the right to work and, thus, one important ingredient in the right to survive. They are restricted in the control of their own lives because they are captives of their economic history—first depression, now inflation—and their previous thrift is meaningless, for life savings are gobbled up by the caprice of the marketplace. The price of retirement leisure is the loss of one-fourth to one-half of their income. People who may have truly loved to work feel empty and useless when their jobs are stripped away. Others who would welcome retirement† if they could afford it must spend their energies in

---

* It has long been the policy of the American Medical Association to favor voluntary retirement and to oppose enforced retirement keyed to any chronological age. The AMA joined as *amicus curiae* in a suit filed in federal court by Martin Weisbrod, an attorney with the U.S. Department of Housing and Urban Development. Weisbrod brought the suit in December, 1972, two months before reaching age 70 and mandatory retirement, declaring that the civil service provision forcing him to retire is unconstitutional. "I'm not built for retirement. I don't want to sit on a park bench," the plaintiff told *Time* magazine. Although this case involves federal employment standards, legal decisions will influence private employment as well.

† There is no doubt that many look forward to retirement, and even seek early retirement on the premise that they want to enjoy life while they are physically able. Unions and industry supported the movement to early retirement, beginning in the 1950s. "The number of mandatory retirement plans seems to increase in direct proportion to our efforts to defeat them," said Norman Sprague, economist with the National Council on the Aging. By 1974, with roaring inflation, some reversal of this trend was evident because the provisions of many plans did not include cost-of-living clauses.

fighting to survive rather than enjoying the leisure they have looked forward to.

Older people are not the only losers in all of this. We as a nation are deprived of their very real skills and experience; a whole generation of people trained in every conceivable occupation is suddenly cut off from us. Retirement and age discrimination cause a tremendous waste of human resources.

More than half of all people over 65 are physically able to work and a great many more could work if jobs were modified to fit their physical condition. Employers don't want to invest in the training of older workers even though studies show that they often have better work records than the young, with less absenteeism, greater stability, a steadier rate of production and higher-quality work.

The popular public view is that older Americans are retired in the name of efficiency . . .

Modern-day private industry has set the pace when it comes to retirement. The great majority of industrial organizations make retirement mandatory, generally at age sixty-five. The reason is that greater efficiency means better profits.

> Former Senator Jack Miller (R.-Iowa)
> June 14, 1971

. . . and in order to provide jobs for younger workers through union rules and agreements. But are older workers less efficient? And is it just to sacrifice one age group for the benefit of another? Indeed, can younger workers shoulder the consequences that follow from a large unproductive population of retired persons?

One of the paradoxical consequences of arbitrary retirement is inflation, for one of retirement's major effects is to increase the supply of money without producing additional goods and services. In addition, with an increasing proportion of older people to young in the population, the cost of financing the care of the retired falls ever more heavily upon the middle-aged and young. The U.S. Census Bureau predicts that the United States may attain a stationary population by 2037 if fertility continues to fall.[4] We could then have as much as 15 percent of our population over 65. This means that the "dependency ratio"—the ratio of nonworkers to workers—will be very high indeed. If there are breakthroughs in medicine and science that affect longevity, the number of retired could soar astronomically. How long before younger workers rebel at the reality of having to support so many elders? How soon will it become totally impossible for them to do so? The time is fast approaching when work for those over 65 must become a viable option, not just for their own personal survival and satisfaction, but to keep the national dependency ratio at tolerable levels. If we are to be able to afford a decent standard of living for those who are too sick or incapacitated to work and for those who freely choose the option to retire, we shall have to find ways of employing the many older people who can and want to work.*

AGEISM IN EMPLOYMENT

Since the turn of the century with the transition from an agricultural to an industrial urban population, the number of older workers has been progressively reduced, especially males. In 1900 close to two-thirds of older men were still working, but today this has been reduced to one-fourth.† Interestingly, women over 65 participate somewhat more than at the turn of the century; and there has been an increase, for example, from 8 percent of the older female population working in 1900 to 10 percent in 1970. In 1972 only about 16 percent of all persons over 65 were known to be in the labor force.

Many forces conspire to hamper the older person in finding work: the Social Security ceiling on earnings, which says that only a small amount may be earned, after which the Social Security check will be reduced; educational and technological obsolescence, with little chance for retraining; increasing possibilities of physical limitations; and direct age discrimination in employment through arbitrary retirement and the bias against promoting or hiring older workers. During cutbacks in employment, mass layoffs, plant shutdowns and company relocations the worker over 45 is far less likely to find a new job than a younger worker. Employers are all too glad to let them go since older workers often command higher salaries by reason of seniority, and a younger worker can be brought into a job at less pay. When all of this is put together it amounts to discrimination or ageism.

Not only are fewer older people in the work force, but many of those who do work are restricted to low earnings in part-time jobs and in heavy agriculture and domestic work. Older job seekers are especially vulnerable

---

* "We are loading the retirement system with enormous burdens. . . . To encourage retirement at age 55 (for example) this nation has got to be crazy," stated Ewan Clague, former Commissioner of the U.S. Bureau of Labor Statistics. Quoted in "The Early Retirement Ethic" by William Chapman, Washington *Post*, March 25, 1973.

† The validity of this comparison may be somewhat questionable since the older population in 1900 (because of lower life expectancy) was younger in years than the present-day older population.

to exploitation because their urgent need pushes them into whatever is available—often unpleasant, even risky and physically difficult jobs. Rarely is work shaped to fit their physical abilities or handicaps.

Unemployment is another crucial issue. An older worker is defined as anyone over 45, and age discrimination in employment begins early. In 1971 older workers accounted for 21 percent of the total unemployment in the United States. Unemployment for persons 45 and older rose from 596,000 to 1,062,000, an increase of approximately 76 percent, between January, 1969, and February, 1971, according to a 1971 report of the U.S. Senate Committee on Labor and Public Welfare.*

Succeeding years have not improved the 1969-71 situation. Moreover, once unemployed, older workers usually remain without work for longer periods than other age groups.[5] In addition, "mature workers" tend to be underemployed, their full abilities underutilized and they are forced to accept pay cuts or forgo increases as alternatives to losing their jobs.

Official unemployment rates are low for people over 60, but this is quite misleading. Older persons often become understandably discouraged in seeking jobs. If they stop looking for work for four weeks, they are no longer counted in the work force. Even more than those over 45, the over-60-year-olds who are classified in the labor market as unemployed remain unemployed longer than younger people. In addition, retirement clearly hides much unemployment. Early claims for Social Security often reflect urgent need, and thus Social Security has become for some people unemployment compensation—certainly not its original purpose.

Minority groups especially suffer from work discrimination in old age as they have throughout life. Ageism combines with racism to victimize blacks, Mexican-Americans, Chinese and other minority groups. For example, black aged men participate in the labor force in the same proportions as whites but they earn less, do harder physical work and are in poorer health. (Remember that their life expectancy is 7½ years less than that of white males.) Black elderly women are more apt to work than white women because of their greater need to support themselves. Like black men, they earn less, usually in domestic and service work. Retirement by choice is less of an option because blacks' retirement benefits are often meager, in line with previous low earnings. Indeed, there may be no benefits at all. When they are forced to stop working, usually because

---

* A Senate Labor and Public Welfare Committee report in 1970 suggested that "the critical period in work lives of adults occurs during their late forties and early fifties. For this age group several discernible trends become evident: joblessness begins to rise, duration of unemployment increases sharply, labor force participation declines, and poverty increases. . . . Yet mature workers are underrepresented in existing manpower and training programs."

of poor health, they must turn disproportionately to Supplementary Security Income as the only income source available to them.

RETIREMENT AS A BIAS AGAINST THE OLD

Retirement itself is a form of age bias, for there are no scientific data to support arbitrary retirement on the basis of chronological age. Retirement has emerged over the last two centuries as a new development and, in some respects, as a stage (albeit somewhat artificial) of the life cycle. Given present tendencies, Americans may soon spend up to one-third of their lives in retirement.

The concept of retirement as an opportunity for leisure was first implemented on a broad scale in the latter part of the nineteenth century when social legislation in Germany was enacted to provide income during late life. Retirement is, of course, a much more complicated issue than simply insuring income for the old. It involves social and economic factors which include the desire to keep jobs available for younger people who are supporting growing families. It recognizes as well the fact that there are many older people who are indeed not capable any longer of carrying out their jobs successfully.

But what presumably began as an essentially humanitarian, if complicated, social policy has become for many people a formidable burden. There are increasing numbers of older people in good physical and mental health who would like to continue to work. But about 50 percent of American workers are now employed in companies with compulsory retirement policies. Flexible, individualized retirement is uncommon. Even where formal age-mandated retirement does not exist, various pressures coerce the older worker to retire. He (or she) may be subjected to subtle hints to leave, or to blunt attacks upon his ability. Poor health may force a decision for early retirement. Sometimes financial incentives, "bonuses," are offered to induce retirement, and the underlying atmosphere is like the army joke—volunteer or else.

Retirement tends to be precipitate. People are simply mustered out, sometimes with a gold watch, more often with no ceremony at all. Phased or gradual retirement is rare. Seminars and counseling to prepare the retiree are infrequent. The truth quite simply is that Americans are ill prepared by their culture, education and past experience to enter the increasingly lengthened period of retirement. The federal government itself has served as a poor model to industry and business in the way it handles employee retirement.

CIVIL SERVICE RETIREMENT

The federal government's retirement practices reflect the ambivalences seen throughout the culture toward older people and employment. A booklet prepared for older workers by the Manpower Administration of the Department of Labor reads:

You want to be useful. In many jobs the very qualities that come with age are bonuses. . . . You have experience, skill and stability, and the good judgment that has come with a lifetime of work. You're conscientious, loyal, hard-working because you want to make good. Our Nation can't afford to waste valuable manpower. There are too many jobs that need doing.[6]

Wise words, yet the federal government practices age discrimination directly and retires arbitrarily rather than on an individual basis. According to the Labor Department pamphlet "the federal government evaluates each job applicant on the basis of ability, not age. . . . There is no maximum age for federal jobs." But it goes on to contradict itself, saying: *"Persons under 70 can qualify for regular appointments* [italics mine], while persons over 70 can receive only temporary appointments subject to renewal."

Federal employees are strongly pressured to retire early through various incentives or bonuses, even when they prefer to continue working.[7] An example is the liberalizing of retirement rules for Civil Service employees who lose their jobs through defense spending cuts or other government reductions in force. They may retire if they have completed 25 years of service or are at least age 50 with 20 years of service; whereas the usual minimum age for Civil Service retirement is age 55 with 30 years of service.

There have been efforts—so far unsuccessful—to impose maximum age limits on federal jobs.

In 1972, the House of Representatives unexpectedly defeated a measure which would have allowed the President to set maximum age limits for entry into any or all of the 1500 job occupations which compose the federal work force, when age is found to be a "bona fide occupational qualification reasonably necessary to the performance of the duties of the position." The Nixon Administration–backed bill was attacked as a further aggravation of the problems faced by middle-aged and older workers in finding jobs and as another abdication of congressional responsibility to the executive branch.

Congressman Herman Badillo (D.-N.Y.), one of the many who opposed the bill, stated that "present medical examinations for entry into the federal service are ample safeguards to determine conclusively whether an applicant can properly perform on the job." He warned his colleagues of the "tremendous potential for misuse" if other agencies or officials were in a position to "invoke arbitrary legal maximum age requirements to deny free access to all jobs of professionally and physically qualified applicants."[8]

MILITARY RETIREMENT

The military arm of the federal government can retire its members after 20 years service,* operating arbitrarily with length of service as the criterion. Retirement may be accomplished under humiliating circumstances, as in the discharge of officers who are "passed over twice" in evaluation for promotions. In recent years the Department of Defense has developed a referral program, Transitional Manpower Programs, in the office of the Assistant Secretary of Defense to help ease the transition to civilian life. There have been the beginnings of a valuable literature on the impact of retirement on servicemen and their officers.

THE RETIREMENT SYNDROME

There is much mythology built into the notion of an emotional and physical condition known as the "retirement syndrome," characterized by anxiety and depression. People who retire do not automatically develop declining mental and physical health. What social-science studies we have indicate such generalizations to be a fallacy.[9] Yet there are clinical indications that some individuals are badly affected.† Men and women who are otherwise perfectly healthy sometimes develop headaches, gastrointestinal symptoms, oversleeping, irritability, nervousness and lethargy in connection with retirement. These conditions may even manifest themselves before retirement takes place; they can heighten with the confusion of roles, activities and changes in the structure of one's life that develops at the time of retirement; they worsen if one does not find a satisfactory life style and work supplements after retirement. Without the customary defensive value of work, old emotional conflicts may re-emerge, especially if one has been a "workaholic"—addicted to work. Without purpose, a sense of inadequacy can evolve; and apathy and inertia—and what some have called "senile" behavior—may follow unless the condition is prevented or reversed.

---

* Military retirees are principally able-bodied men in their forties who retired after twenty years of active service. In 1970, seven hundred fifty thousand persons received retirement pay from the U.S. government.

† Reconciliation of clinical experience and social-science data tends to be difficult since individuals experiencing difficulty are often buried in the larger generalized social-science data.

The emotional impact of retirement is a function of economics, temperament, health care, vigor, range of interests, all those factors that can affect individuals whatever their age.

> Effects of retirement can come long after retirement. A 73-year-old skilled worker dreamed at night of work. He reported depressed feelings in response to varied stresses during his life; none of these states was severe. Retired for four years, he finds himself discontented, wishing he had more interests, hobbies, etc. His planning both for old age and for the future was incomplete; he is fatalistic regarding the future. He feels that his retirement was forced but it was ostensibly voluntary; i.e., he wanted "to give younger men a chance." He now regrets his decision.

Even the professional, managerial-executive and academic persons for whom intellectual activity is paramount often have great difficulty in adjusting to retirement despite the long-held assumption that intellectual resources and interests would be protective. Not having a concrete field of action, an arena for decision making, may be one explanation for these difficulties.

People can become upset because they did not conceive of, let alone prepare for, retirement:

> A 66-year-old man who was recently retired had been diagnosed as having a chronic brain syndrome associated with cerebral arteriosclerosis. He was driving the successor to his high business position frantic by his constant phone calls, giving advice, checking on details, etc. concerning not only past events of work but those of the present and future as well. He deeply resented and resisted hospitalization, but his doctor and family insisted. He was hospitalized for four months during which he received intensive psychotherapy four times a week in addition to family conferences. He not only gained some insight into the psychological significance of work to him and into his great difficulties in adjustment to his retirement but was also encouraged to find a utilitarian outlet for his financial talent. He became voluntary treasurer of a charitable organization and continued to do well in the community for some three years before his death of causes unrelated to his previous psychotic depressive reaction.

In 1971, 105,000 federal workers who could have retired chose not to do so.* Gordon F. Streib and Clement J. Schneider found that "both

---

* In the United Auto Workers, skilled workers opt to a lesser extent for retirement than do unskilled workers even though the pensions are higher.

men and women of higher income levels, higher educational attainments, and higher levels of occupational structure tend to work longer than their counterparts with lower socioeconomic status."

On the other hand, some groups of people holding tedious, assembly-line or heavy-labor jobs can't retire fast enough.[10] Retirees from these groups, not surprisingly, show some improvement, not decline, in health as a result of retirement. But this again illustrates how difficult it is to generalize from either the clinical or the social-science perspective. What becomes clear is the need for continuing research which studies in detail various categories of people not only in terms of social-economic classes and occupations, but also in terms of differing life styles and psychological motivations.

An indication of how a number of older people feel about work can be found in the fact that older-age employment services (e.g., Over-60 Clubs) are overloaded with applications. Some old people need the money because Social Security or pension checks won't stretch far enough, and some want to get out of the house and away from their families. Many want simply to be needed and useful.

It must be noted that money can be one of the major pleasures resulting from work.[11] In fact Frances Carp has cast doubt on the facile assumption that voluntary work *per se* enhances mental well-being.[12] In our money-oriented society at least, paid work has a "powerful positive impact on happiness, self-esteem and relationships with other people." Freud wrote: ". . . work bind[s] the individual more closely to reality . . . [and] the human community."[13]

Since work is an important element in the attainment and maintenance of human satisfaction, we can expect disorders to occur in the often blank retirement period, with its absence of structure, no work or social calendar and no definite place to go. When the Italian physician Bernardino Ramazzini published his treatise on occupational disorders in 1700[14] he could not have anticipated that another class of disorders, nonoccupational disorders, might be observed 250 years later.

RETIREMENT AS AN INTERNATIONAL CONCERN

Retirement is a "luxury" enjoyed only in Western societies where life expectancy has increased. The United Nations indicated interest in retirement in 1969 by setting up a staff study of retirement around the world. In 1972 the UN Secretary General and staff issued a report on old age, stating: "The long-range overall picture is of a world with an aging population. This poses a new challenge—with social and economic considerations not yet understood." There are now 200 million people over 65 in the world, 24 million more than in 1965. The UN report continues: "Most countries won't be able to afford, culturally, psychologically or financially, to go on supporting such large dependent populations without serious social changes," and it suggests the raising of retirement ages.*

Individual nations have begun to reverse the trend toward early retirement. Sweden has provided incentives against retirement and raised the retirement age to 67.† Compulsory retirement is under question in Great Britain, the Soviet Union and other nations where zero population growth obtains or is approaching, causing shortages in the work force. In Japan the labor force increased at a rapid annual rate of 29 percent until the mid-1900s but then the birth rate began to fall and since 1955 it has dropped to one percent per year.[15] The older worker, as a result, is perceived as a valuable resource. There is irony in the way older people are welcomed back into the work force when a nation needs them, as Japan, the U.S.S.R. and others are doing today and as the United States did in World War II.

The Soviet Union's attitudes toward retirement provide an interesting illustration of the use of the older worker when labor shortages occur. The Soviet population past retirement age (60 for men, 55 for women) has virtually doubled in the past three decades.[16] The over-60 population in Russia was 11.8 percent in 1970. Projections for 1980 point to an over-60 population of 44 million—about 16 percent of the total! State pensions are now the major source of income for over 40 million retired men and women—about one in every six citizens of the U.S.S.R.‡ At the same time there exists a chronic labor shortage.

A 1956 Soviet law had increased old-age pensions and thereby encouraged retirement; so, to offset this trend, legislation was enacted in 1964 to provide substantial incentives to continue working after retirement. Persons who remain on the job usually get full payment of their pensions in addition to regular wages, and the result has been a vastly increased pensioner participation in the labor force. By 1972 about 53 percent of men past age 60, including almost 3 percent of 80-year-olds, were still actively working.

---

* The UN report also recognizes that "certainly, the strongly competitive societies in which too much emphasis is given to an individual's productive work and achievement, in which inactivity is suspect and leisure highly commercialized, are not congenial environments in which to grow old."

† In the United States the 1972 Social Security amendments have a potential "sleeper"—a provision for an increase in Social Security benefits of one percent for each year after 65 and before 72 a person *delays* retirement!

‡ Many are only recently covered by social security. For example, collective farmers have been included in the national social-security plan only since 1964.

Soviet women, however, tend to retire at age 55 in order to be available for child care and housework for their families. Three-generation families in which young wives and mothers are expected to work cause many elderly women to take advantage of old-age pensions to work in the home.

PERSISTENT PRODUCTIVITY AND CREATIVITY IN OLD AGE

Negative contemporary views about productivity and creativity in old age provide grist for those who draw dismal conclusions about the abilities of old people to work—and certainly contribute to present-day restrictions upon their right to work. It is quite extraordinary, therefore, that in spite of mandatory retirement and age discrimination elderly people manage to acquire about one-third of their aggregate income through work. What could they do if they were not systematically inhibited by their culture? They have been found to be as productive as, or more productive than, younger people. In point of fact, studies from the 1940s to the present document the continuing high efficiency of older workers as well as their reliability, low turnover and low absenteeism.[17] Critics then ask, "Yes, but what about their creativity, their capacity for new ideas, their ability to produce something fresh and different?"

Some studies have concluded that creativity declines with chronological aging. Nevertheless, the universal validity of the presumed relation between aging and loss of creativity is questionable, and innumerable instances of persistent creativity in late life contradict this widely shared belief. Drawing upon history, Sophocles, Michelangelo, Titian, Tintoretto, Cervantes, Voltaire, Goethe, Tennyson, Humboldt, Franck, Hugo, Verdi, Tolstoy, Shaw and Freud are among the classic examples of creative individuals who remained creative into their old age. In our own time we have witnessed the important contributions of many elderly men and women in the professions, sciences, arts, theatre and politics:

What next for Rubinstein? Arthur Rubinstein concluded his massive series of ten piano recitals last night in Carnegie Hall. But they were more than piano recitals. They were an attitude toward life—the expression of a civilized man who, in creating and recreating beauty throughout his life, has refused to grow old.

This great musician will be with us, one knows, for many more years. He is, after all, only 72 and seems to be able to outplay, outenjoy, outrun and outlast any of his younger colleagues. Now that he has given ten New York recitals in one season, what next? The complete works of Chopin and Liszt and Beethoven, with Kalliwoda, Ries, Kalkbrenner and Moscheles thrown in? Who knows? Nothing would occasion any surprise where Arthur Rubinstein is involved.

—Editorial, *New York Times*
December 11, 1961

Almost a decade and a half later Rubinstein is still performing for sold-out concert audiences.

In a superb example of late-life creativity Benjamin Dugger, arbitrarily retired science professor, was hired by the Lederle Laboratories, where at 72 years of age he discovered the life-saving antibiotic Aureomycin. The profits from the sale of this contribution to medicine amply repaid this pharmaceutical company for its enlightened personnel policy.

Of course, simply citing instances of persistent creativity does not prove or disprove a relationship between aging and creativity but it does provide intriguing background for the investigation of such relationships. In his book *Age and Achievement* (1953), psychologist Harvey C. Lehman presents "evidence that any stereotyped conception of later maturity is quite untenable . . . this chapter [entitled "Older Thinkers and Great Achievements"] sets forth brief biographical notes regarding an appreciable number of individuals who did notable creative work late in life—in some instances their most important work."[18]

Extending Lehman's thinking I have developed the following examples of older individuals who produced significant work late in life:

1. *Comprehensive reconstructions of a lifetime of study and reflection*: Galileo's *Dialoghi delle nuove scienze*; written at age 72, in which he recapitulated the results of his early experiments and mature meditations on the principles of mechanics.
2. *Continuing Development of Material*: The melodies which are the bases of Elgar's "Wand of Youth Suites" were composed when the composer was 12. When he was 72, sixty years later, he discovered the pieces among his juvenilia and reworked them.
3. *Cosmology*: Alexander Humboldt produced a 2-volume masterwork, *Kosmos*, at age 76–78; a second 2 volumes at ages 87–89; still another volume was published posthumously.
4. *Lexicography*: Maximilien Paul Émile Littré completed his *Dictionnaire de la Langue Française* (begun 20 years before) at age 62.
5. *History*: George Bancroft (1800–91), in late-life revisions of his historical writings, "sought to correct the mistakes of earlier editions, to profit by newly acquired information, and to reduce the floridity of much of his earlier writing."
6. *Life Cycle*: At 74 Pierre Joseph Van Bendel began the study of the reduction of the chromosome number of egg cells to half that in body cells.

He found that chromosomes have a genetic continuity throughout the life cycle.

William Harvey at age 72 in his *Exercitationes de Generatione Animalium* showed that the embryo developed from the egg by the process of "epigenesis."

7. *Psychology*: Franz Brentano completed *Sinnespsychologie* at age 69.

Sigmund Freud continued to contribute new ideas and observations, summarize and revise until his death. He did this despite extensive cancer of the mouth which developed at age 67 and plagued him until his death at age 88.

8. *Geriatrics*: Pierre Brisseau at age 74 was the first to demonstrate by dissection the clouded lens in cataract.

Sir John Floyer wrote the first treatise of the diseases of old age, *Medicina Geronomica*, at 75.

Benjamin Franklin invented bifocal lenses at age 78 when his eyes had flattened and he needed two pair of spectacles, one for far sight and one for near.

Friedrich Hoffman at age 71 described "senility" as a disease, not inevitable to aging.

Fritz Verzar. The 1966 International Congress of Gerontology in Vienna paid honor to Dr. Fritz Verzar[19] for whom a *Festschrift* was edited by Nathan Shock. Shock wrote in his preface to Dr. Verzar on his 80th birthday: "Experimental Gerontology represents a second career of Dr. Verzar, a scientist with many recognized accomplishments in the field of physiology." In 1952, pioneer of gerontology V. Korenchevsky visited the then 66-year-old Verzar at Basel and sparked his interest in the biology of aging. In 1956, upon retirement, Verzar moved his rat colony into a new laboratory and began his work in gerontology. He established the Institut für Experimentals Gerontologie. Verzar was the author of 18 books and monographs and 473 papers. Five of the books and 44 of the papers were completed after he became 66 years of age.

9. *Memoirs*: François René de Chateaubriand wrote *Mémoires d'Outre-tombe* (*Memoirs from Beyond the Tomb*) between 65 and 80 years of age.

10. *Maintenance of Life, Rejuvenation*: Giovanni Colle provided the first definite description of blood transfusion at 70.

It is crucial to bear in mind that creativity in old age does not occur simply in the famous. It is common in everyday life—particularly in the absence of disease and social adversity. Creative older people are seen as lively individuals who are resourceful and adaptive, actively involved with their families and community, contributing in myriads of ways, in voluntary as well as paid roles.

We have much still to learn about how time or chronological aging relates to creativity.* Lehman suggests that (with some notable excep-

---

* An example of early work in this area is that of Brinkman, a German scholar who published a study in 1925 concerning the late work of great painters who continued to be productive in old age. He found their styles showed tendencies toward introspection, clarification and universality.

tions) the contributions of later maturity are likely to differ from the contributions of early youth. Persistent creativity and new creativity appearing for the first time in old age should be further clarified and documented. Biographies and historical-personality studies would be valuable evidence, the behavioral student's parallel to the historian's "oral history."

Since 1962 I have been studying persons in middle and later life (over 50) who have distinguished themselves in their careers and in national life.[20] I have collected memoirs* on tape through extensive interviewing,[21] exploring for insights into the nature of creativity and its vicissitudes over the course of the life cycle, and into the psychological nature of middle and later life. I have been deeply impressed with the continuing capacity of older people to change, and I am struck by the boredom nurtured by fixed identities. One sees the active searching for new dimensions of the personality.

Others involved with the aged remark on these same qualities. The late Rabbi Abraham Heschel said at the 1961 White House Conference on Aging:

Our work for the advanced in years is handicapped by our clinging to the dogmatic belief in the *immutability* of man. We conceive of his inner life as a closed system, as an automatic, unilinear, irreversible process which cannot be altered, and of old age as a *stage of stagnation* into which a person enters with his habits, follies, and prejudices. To be good to the old is to cater to their prejudices and eccentricities.

May I suggest that man's potential for change and growth is much greater than we are willing to admit and that old age be regarded not as the age of stagnation but as the *age of opportunities* for inner growth?

The years of old age may enable us to attain the high values we failed to sense, the insights we have missed, the wisdom we ignored. They are indeed formative years, rich in possibilities to unlearn the follies of a lifetime, to see through inbred self-deceptions, to deepen understanding and compassion, to widen the horizon of honesty, to refine the sense of fairness.

What are the kinds of work which should be available to nurture the natural capacities of the elderly? Which work capacities are uniquely suited to the age-specific qualities of old age?

* I prefer the term "memoir" rather than "oral history" because the focus is upon memory and reconstruction, and the term "memoir" more pointedly describes the raw nature of the data. In addition, "oral history," like "oral tradition," suggests something spoken and individual, whereas the interview memoir involves a second person—the interviewer—who, regardless of his efforts at maintaining his neutrality, cannot help influencing the nature of the process. Unlike standard biographies and autobiographies, these influences between the interviewer and the memoirist are open to examination so long as the tapes are maintained. Imagine if we had tapes of James Boswell on (that is, *with*) Dr. Samuel Johnson.

LATE-LIFE WORK CAPACITIES

Because of the personality characteristics which tend to flower in late life, both as a result of a lifetime of experience and as a consequence of actually being old, the elderly tend to show natural inclinations for certain kinds of work. Teaching, counseling and the preservation of crafts; sponsoring and encouraging the young; serving in judicial and administrative roles; commenting on political and social events from a lifetime perspective; safeguarding of heritage through historical records, memoirs and the protection of historical objects; and conserving of natural resources as a legacy to the young are some of the most prominent predilections.

These represent tendencies, not inevitabilities, and the old should not be stereotypically associated *only* with these activities. We must respect the desire of older people who wish to continue the same careers and interests they had in their youth as well as those who want to escape to totally new work identities in every conceivable direction. But many of the elderly do gravitate to the activities listed above as a way of expressing the concerns and interests of late life, and they would like work opportunities to reflect these directions.

The following represent a sample of the work interests of older people along with some of the ways in which work opportunities have been or could be located or created:

TEACHING

There is little reason why professional teachers should be retired wholesale on the basis of age. The present "oversupply" of teachers is questionable since many children are inadequately taught, many schools are understaffed, and education itself could be expanded from children and youth to reach people of all ages, including the elderly. Remedial teaching of children in basic skills is needed. I have observed the despair of excellent older teachers forced into unwanted retirement even when the schools from which they have retired needed their services. A more sensible solution would be the creation of more teaching opportunities, together with individual evaluation of the teaching capacities and wishes of older teachers. Persons not wanting to work full time could serve part time as teachers' assistants or preceptors, working in workshops, small seminars, and laboratories after the regular teacher has lectured. They might evaluate or mark papers, work with children with problems, handle recesses and offer special courses.

Some enterprising older people have invented schools of their own:

> Seventy-year-old famed pilot Lt. Col. George Hutchinson runs "Kiddie Kollege," an innovative nursery school in Ruxton, Maryland, a Baltimore suburb. (Hutchinson was originally the leader of the "Flying Hutchinsons" who helped promote aviation in the early 1930s.)

Others help perpetuate branches of learning which might otherwise wane:

> I asked a 75-year-old professor of civil engineering what his years of experience had taught him to transmit to his students. He replied that interest in the fundamentals of engineering must be kept alive; for example . . . "ordinary engineering camps now have reduced the number of surveying courses to a bare minimum. . . . Only a few engineering schools . . . are really giving anything approaching adequate survey instruction and none of it is as much as I got back in my day. . . . The students say, 'Oh, why do I have to do this survey work?' I try to impress on them that if you are a design man and you are going to be a construction man, etc., you are going to be absolutely at the mercy of the survey crews unless you know what the survey thing is all about. They can ruin you in nothing flat."

Retired college professors can take advantage of clearinghouses developed to help place them in new jobs. The Retired Professors Registry is a joint employment project of the Association of American Colleges and the American Association of University Professors. The American Association of Emeriti also has employment as one of its objectives.

Colleges founded and run by the elderly are another possibility. Hastings College of Law of the University of California has been a most successful program for older professors.[22] In 1940, partly because of the wartime teacher shortage, Hastings began employing emeritus professors. In 1948 it introduced a new procedure and a novel form of discrimination—only professors over 65 would be employed! The result was a star-studded faculty, and in 1957 the mean age of the faculty was 73. The famous retired Harvard law professor, Roscoe Pound, wrote to the dean of Hastings College: "I am inclined to think you have the strongest law faculty in the country."

Other professions might well follow suit. There are, for example, physicians who have taught long and well in medical schools or have held administrative and policy-making positions who would like to continue their work but have been retired with the designation of emeritus. Were they to form schools or group practices together they might contribute immeasurably toward fulfilling the need for a greater number of doctors and paramedical workers. In 1970 Dr. Joseph Moldaver, retired faculty member at Columbia University College of Physicians and Surgeons, set up an organization of physicians subject to mandatory retirement from active staffs. The Service of Senior Medical Consultants is comprised of retired professors available for consultations and clinical conferences at non-university affiliated hospitals needing teaching staff. Moldaver began his program with a grant from the National Institutes of Health.

Many major cities have special qualities which lend themselves to utilization of their retired professionals. In Washington, D.C., schools of diplomacy, foreign affairs and languages could be assembled with faculties of older and retired men and women who have distinguished themselves in these fields. What a unique opportunity this would be not only for those wishing to enter such careers but for those working in allied areas, such as international law, linguistics, journalism. An experimental and novel school combining the best of the Hastings experiment with the concept of New York City's New School for Social Research* would be exciting in many places, including the nation's capital.

The educational and cultural resources of developing "new towns" could derive from the contributions of retired persons. Funds should be made available from the Office of Education and the Administration on Aging within the Department of Health, Education and Welfare to organize and run teaching programs. Retired persons as well as younger people seeking degrees might join the student body.

HISTORY

Older people are a major source of historical information.† Only recently, tape-recorded oral history has emerged as one method of collecting information. By 1972 there were 700 centers for oral history in

---

* The New School for Social Research was founded in 1919 as a small center for adult education. It has evolved into a university maintaining a "major commitment to meeting the intellectual and cultural needs of adults." The Institute for Retired Professionals was created within the New School in 1962 to meet the needs of those who have retired.

† The anthropologist Margaret Clark has written, "The aged are certainly no strangers to anthropologists—we have relied on the knowledge, memories and insights of elderly informants for much of the data that we have collected. If it were not for the accumulated experiences and recollections of the elders in preliterate societies, we would know much less than we do about human custom and the varieties of culture."

47 states and several foreign lands.* It would be extremely valuable to have a Division of Memoirs within the National Archives to support the collection of the memoirs of both distinguished Americans and people from every walk of life about historically important aspects of American life. The recollections of the elders of various racial and ethnic groups should be preserved.

COUNSELING

Counseling of those who are younger about many aspects of their lives —education, emotional problems, religious concerns and the like—used to be the major way in which knowledge and help were transmitted from generation to generation. It is still valid despite notions that the old are obsolete, that the young can only learn from each other or teach themselves, and that more efficient methods of counsel have been found. There is no substitute for human warmth and lifetime experience.

It seems sad that we have come so far from our past as to require experiments to demonstrate the worth of counseling from one's elders. Even sadder is the fact that so few studies and counseling programs are taking place. Margaret J. Rioch[23] conceived the idea that carefully selected "mature" people could be taught to do formal mental-health counseling with patients, and she demonstrated this by using the experience-developed skills of middle-aged women. The same use could be made of older people in many different areas.

CRAFTSMANSHIP

Craftsmanship should be preserved. Organizations such as the Cumberland Mountain Crafts Association should be aided by federal funds in order to support older craftsmen in their work and their training of the young. The National Trust for Historic Preservation has called for a national training for building crafts of the seventeenth, eighteenth and nineteenth centuries "before they vanish along with their current and aging practitioners." There are many dying arts. By 1966, for example,

---

* Even Columbia University, a pioneer in oral history, did not save all its tape recordings until recently—imagine if the reminiscences of Abraham Lincoln were destroyed and the tape reused for reasons of economy—and the methods have been extremely limited from the point of view of the psychiatrist, sociologist or psychologist. For instance, there is no comparability of data from one oral history to another and the life histories do not follow any kind of orderly study of life development. There have been few efforts to cross-validate by collecting material from different participants and observers at the same events, etc. Graduate students who serve as interviewers in many oral history programs are seldom trained in interviewing skills.

there were only about a hundred engrossers (who copy documents by hand in a large, often ornate, script) left in the United States, men whose art had survived the impact of the linotype and the printer.

Aged craftsmen could teach workshops in schools and senior centers. Glass blowing, quilt making and countless other arts could be propagated. The craftsmanship movement has been and could be further stimulated through the annual Festival of American Folklife sponsored by the Smithsonian Institution since 1966. America has seen a major revitalization of interest in crafts recently, and the elderly are a great resource for this knowledge.*

PRIVATE ENTERPRISE

Companies which make the effort to employ older workers have found the elderly to be a useful employee resource.

> The 51-year-old president of Texas Refinery (a roofing-supplies manufacturer) A. M. Page, says, "Good salesmen, like good wines, get better with age." He finds the highest sales are achieved by those over 60. He has a group of older salesmen called the "Sizzling Sixty" Club. The average age of its members is 70 and their earnings range from $6,000 to $10,000 annually.

General Motors, Bankers Trust Company of New York and Woodward and Lothrop, a department-store chain based in Washington, D.C., are among companies hiring retirees. The department store's personnel man states:

> [We] began appealing to senior citizens groups in Washington a few years ago after a sizable radio, newspaper and direct mail employment campaign failed to turn up enough qualified younger people to fill the firm's temporary vacancies. We found hundreds of qualified elderly persons eager to put in a few hours a day.

Obviously, the opening-up of these firms to older and retired employees is a welcome sign; however, one must be aware of the possibilities of exploitation. Some companies know they can obtain older people at low salaries, without fringe benefits, on a part-time basis for kinds of work which younger people are reluctant to do.

---

* Eliot Wigginton has edited a fine series of memoirs of older people living in the Georgia Appalachians, *The Foxfire Book* and *Foxfire 2* (Garden City, New York: Anchor Books, 1972 and 1973). There are descriptions of hog dressing, log-cabin building, mountain crafts and foods, basket making, soap making, fruit preserving, etc.

. . . Corporate personnel chiefs are finding that oldsters form a ready and willing labor pool for a wide variety of part-time, temporary or hard-to-fill jobs that even in a time of high unemployment still exceed the number of workers willing or qualified to accept them. And retirees, many of them feeling the pinch of inflation and many others just plain sick of sitting at home staring at the walls, are responding to the new demand with alacrity.[24]

But the *Wall Street Journal* also reported that older workers may face discrimination in trying to obtain the same benefits and working conditions as those who are younger.

Placement agencies designed particularly for older people are beginning to appear, "Over-60" employment services are now found in some cities. There are specialized services for certain types of people, such as "Plus-40" and "Plus-50" placement agencies for executives. The diversified Philadelphia concern the Colonial Penn Corporation, has established Mature Temps, an employment agency specializing in the employment of retirees, and it makes money.

SELF-ENTERPRISE

Forty-one out of every 100 people over 65 who are working are self-employed. Of these 876,000 self-employed old people, 531,000 are in nonagricultural occupations and 338,000 are in agriculture. Many old people are self-employed as real-estate agents, income-tax preparers, answering-service operators, seamstresses, typists, gardeners, caterers, craftsmen, carpenters, repairmen, babysitters, small shop and restaurant owners and farmers. Many more capable older people could be encouraged to enter self-employment.[25] A few become successful beyond their wildest imaginings:

Colonel Harlan Sanders, of Kentucky Fried Chicken fame, made his first million at age 73. A former gas station operator and restaurateur, Sanders was penniless when he retired at 65.

With his first Social Security check for $105 he embarked on a promotion campaign for his recipe for fried chicken. Eight years later he sold the American and Canadian rights to the recipe for $4 million. "I went from rags to riches," he recalls.[26]

THE OPTION TO WORK

What has been done in the United States to provide jobs for older people who want to work and social roles for those wishing to remain active during their retirement? What has been done to eliminate ageism in employment? What educational programs have been introduced to reduce obsolescence of skills? What changes have been undertaken in our factories both to make work more attractive and to fit work to the worker's limitations? What has been done to facilitate the movement toward a society that emphasizes humane and public services? What can unions do in all of this?

ATTEMPTS TO END AGEISM IN EMPLOYMENT

In 1965 the U.S. Labor Department issued a report on older workers (named the Wirtz Report after the then Secretary of Labor, W. Willard Wirtz), calling for a clear, unequivocal national policy against age discrimination in employment.[27] Among the report's findings was the fact that in the thirty states without laws against age discrimination most job openings were closed to applicants over 55, and one-quarter to applicants over 45. The report was prepared under a directive of the Civil Rights Act of 1964. The report urged "a new system of continuing educational opportunity." Workers over 45 might earn credits toward "educational sabbaticals." Financing would derive from a system of contributory insurance.

Age discrimination in employment is directly related to unemployment. The Age Discrimination in Employment Act of 1967, in part an outgrowth of the Wirtz Report, is administered by the Department of Labor's Wage and Hour Division in 350 offices throughout the nation. This act has not been enforced adequately and *applies only to persons under 65.* People over 65 are totally unprotected by law although some individual and class legal efforts are attempting to challenge this.

> Hailed by Labor Department officials as a "landmark in our efforts to eliminate arbitrary age discrimination and myths about the capabilities of middle-aged and older workers," a 1971 U.S. Court of Appeals ruling has ordered back wages for a 47-year-old woman who was refused employment on the basis of age.
>
> Charges were first filed in 1969 after a Labor Department investigation revealed that the employer, First Federal Savings and Loan Association of Broward County, Florida, had noted on the woman's job application that she was "too old for teller." First Federal claimed its personnel interviewer had considered the job too strenuous for the woman because she was overweight; the Labor Department, however, alleged the woman was turned down because of her age, since the

bank had considered hiring a younger girl of the same height but weighing twenty pounds more. The appeals court upheld the Labor Department's contention, stating, "It is clear that [First Federal's] physical structure standard was applied in an unequal manner to the detriment of older applicants."

And in another case:

Twenty-nine former employees of Pan-American Airways, Inc. were awarded $250,000 damages in a suit under the Age Discrimination in Employment Act (ADEA) in U.S. District Court in Miami in 1973.

And another:

The largest age discrimination settlement, amounting to $2 million, ever awarded occurred in 1974. The Standard Oil Company of California agreed to pay 160 former employees individual awards ranging from $10,000 to more than $50,000. The consent decree also called for the reinstatement of 120 of the employees. The workers were all found to have been terminated simply because of age. They included area sales representatives, engineers and assistant station managers.

Typical ways in which employers avoid hiring the older person are to declare that he or she is "overqualified," "unskilled," less in need of a job compared to a younger applicant, or less reliable and flexible. Most of this is false and evasive and the problems of qualifications could easily be remedied, for example, by training programs which accept the person over 50 years of age.

Through the efforts of Senator Lloyd Bentsen (D.-Tex.), the Age Discrimination in Employment Act was made more comprehensive in 1974, covering governmental workers on the federal, state and local levels. It should be extended beyond 65, and Senator Hiram Fong (R.-Hawaii) introduced appropriate legislation in 1974. There must also be greater enforcement of existing laws; in 1971, for example, there were 2,500 lawsuits filed, but only 80 suits taken to court. This will require increases in funds.

Vocational evaluation and counseling are critical first steps in job placement. The U.S. Employment Service (USES) has made disappointing and feeble efforts to place older workers, and pressure should be placed upon USES and its various offices to do a better job. There are Federal Job Information Centers in various cities which give advice and information on federal job opportunities; more older people should be made aware of them.

CONTINUING EDUCATION AND TRAINING

Continuing education and retraining have rarely been undertaken to reduce the obsolescence of human skills. Yet education, the continuing acquisition of new knowledge and skills, is frequently the key to continuing work. When we think of education we tend to think only of young people. A few schools have developed continuing education in middle and later life, especially for women. Virginia Senders has written of the Minnesota Plan for the Continuing Education of Women, "Our program is one small step toward the broad goal of the full and appropriate utilization of human talents and resources."[28] Rabbi Heschel, in an address delivered at the 1961 White House Conference on Aging, "To Grow in Wisdom,"[29] urged education for the elderly. He considers old age "a major challenge to the inner life," and proposes that old-age homes not only have directors of recreation but also a "director of learning in charge of intellectual activities." And further, "What the nation needs is senior universities, universities for the advanced in years where wise men should teach the potentially wise, where the purpose of learning is not a career, but where the purpose of learning is learning itself."

Education for the elderly should include:

1. Education for education's sake—inner satisfaction.
2. Education for retirement—instructional, e.g., pre-retirement seminars.
3. Education for post-retirement—instructional e.g., through senior centers.
4. Education for societal utilization—special training, job retraining.

How might continued opportunities for learning through adult-education programs be made available in the American education system? There are age limits for acquisition of degrees—that is, age discrimination in education —in many colleges and universities. Given the opportunity, many people in middle and later life would avail themselves of educational opportunities. Adult education and extension facilities have grown considerably since World War II but much more is needed. About 40 percent of all colleges and universities now offer courses that adults may take without necessarily working for a degree. Only a few colleges and universities—among them, Queens, Fordham, Brooklyn, Syracuse, Oklahoma and Ohio State—offer special programs in which older students can seek a degree; and a few give courses free of charge to the elderly. Although adult education in one form or another does seem to be growing in the United States, nothing quite approaches the development of the Third Age College, a new division of the French University of Toulouse, which had some 1,000 retired persons as students in 1974.*

Existent agencies, such as the U.S. Office of Education and the U.S. Employment Service should participate more actively in educational programming in later life.

In addition, certain stark realities have to be faced concerning today's elderly. Some three million of twenty million older Americans are functionally illiterate. For the remainder a minimal education is the norm. At the time of this writing, the average urban person over 65 has had eight years of education, rural elderly have even less. This scanty education contributes not only to his technical and intellectual obsolescence insofar as his participation in the work force is concerned, but also may hamper him in using his leisure meaningfully in the best sense of leisure—as an active, contemplative and participatory utilization of one's experience in one's society. Now that formal education of our children is compulsory, the older people of tomorrow will presumably be considerably better educated. But much more could be done to educate further the elderly of today.

What about the criticism that the knowledge the old do have is "outmoded"? Advances of all kinds, especially technological, have been so rapid that the knowledge of the professional or scientific person may indeed be outdated by mid-life. Here only retraining programs can help; e.g., physicians taking refresher courses. We create "old fogies" if we continue to dispose of "non-reusable" human beings rather than to recycle people through retraining.

A relatively small proportion of the nation's training and retraining efforts has focused upon people 45 and older in spite of their high percentage among the long-term unemployed. In programs available for all age groups—such as those under the Manpower Development and Training Act —middle-aged and older individuals rarely exceeded 10 percent of the total numbers of enrollees during the fiscal year 1969, for example. Even in Operation Mainstream, with its emphasis on the aged, persons 45 and over comprised only 58 percent of all enrollees.

The 1970 Employment Security Amendments (Public Law 19–373) established "extended benefits" during periods of high unemployment for those whose regular unemployment-compensation entitlement has been exhausted. But financial benefits are not enough. Retraining should be available to the unemployed, many of whom are workers over 40. Most important are necessary vocational guidance, retraining and job placement.

* There have been some experiments in multigenerational living at Syracuse University and Fairlawn College in Bellingham, Washington, in the United States.

Provisions for a "mid-career service" were included in the Employment and Manpower Act of 1970, which was vetoed by the President. These provisions would have provided training,* retraining, counseling, and other needed services for middle-aged and older workers.

FITTING JOBS TO PEOPLE

Job requirements and criteria of skills should be adapted to life-cycle characteristics. The U.S.S.R. has explored certain aspects of the physiology of work and job adaptation and Professor Ross McFarland of Harvard has done this in the United States.[31] As people change through life jobs should be fitted to them rather than trying to force the person to fit the job. Dexterity, neuromuscular coordination and endurance change. These factors need not be deterrents to continued useful employment if work is arranged to take such realities into account and thus humanize our present grimly mechanistic view of labor.

"Lowered efficiency" is theoretically at odds with maximum productivity, but jobs and persons can be more effectively matched. Payment on a piecework basis, for example, can help finance "lowered efficiency" workers.† Increased opportunities for less-efficient or handicapped older workers also reduce the financial burden on the middle-aged. But financial considerations are only one of the incentives that can be used to encourage the less efficient to continue or return to work. We must be prepared to adopt a more realistic principle of *total social efficiency*,[32] which can encompass a "lowered efficiency" without overall penalty as long as it benefits people and the environment.

Obviously there are conflicts in priorities and value systems here. A humanized view of work is not compatible with rigid cost-benefit analyses of production. This is an extremely important dilemma that requires diligent research and imaginative social policy. Eli Ginzberg,[33] Columbia University professor of economics, regarded by many as one of the fathers of modern human-resource study, points out that even Adam Smith put human resources at the center of concern. Too often today the production of goods and the return on investments occupy center stage rather than the worker.

PROTECTION AGAINST PLANT AND INDUSTRY SHUTDOWN

The loss of jobs through shutdowns of plants or businesses or cutbacks in entire industries can be a grave blow at any age. But it is especially devastat-

---

* "Industrial gerontology" is a specialty that has developed to carry out research and action programs in the field of older worker employment and retirement. There have been significant studies and efforts in training adult workers.[30]
† One must of course guard against the exploitative possibilities in piecework.

ing to older workers for whom the job market is steadily shrinking even under the best of circumstances. The government and the automobile and steel industries make some early pension provisions. But other alternatives are possible, as illustrated in the following account:

In 1963 the Studebaker Corporation announced the end of automobile production in its South Bend, Indiana, facilities. The company plant shutdown affected nearly 10 percent of the area's total work force of ninety thousand people. More than half of those laid off were over 50 years of age. Seniority rules are only partly protective, for plant shutdowns, relocations and mergers do not spare older workers.

The initial impact on workers was vividly described by one observer:

We have come to realize that nothing erodes the older worker's personality more than enforced idleness. Nothing attacks human dignity and self-respect more tragically than joblessness. There is no meaningful measure of discouragement or the sense of personal failure; no way to trace the consequences in terms of the medical care that he and his family do not get; the drop in his family's day-by-day living standard; the slow attrition of skill and knowledge; the loss of status in the community; and the loss of faith in a social and economic order that indefinitely denies him the opportunity to do useful work.

The impact of unemployment can change an older adult from a social and economic asset to a liability. In all too many instances, out of a sense of frustration and repeated failure, he eventually ceases to actively seek employment. Soon he is no longer represented in the statistical computations which record the unemployed.[34]

Fortunately, the entire community rallied together with state and federal agencies, producing the successful Project ABLE (Ability Based on Long Experience), an experimental action and demonstration program supported through the Department of Labor's Office of Manpower, Automation and Training. The project demonstrated that large numbers of unemployed older workers could be returned to productive employment through mobilization of the community, individual counseling, job development and opportunities. Some workers were hired by new companies to work in the old plants. Some got jobs using their auto-industry-related skills. Others were trained for computer work—for example, as a key-punch operator. South Bend itself recovered financially from what had seemed to be a hopelessly devastating blow to its economy.[35]

REVITALIZATION OF THE UNIONS

The union movement is hardly a movement of social responsibility any longer, doing little for those presently low on the socioeconomic ladder—

the poor, the minority workers, and the elderly. "They collaborate with employers to maintain the status quo," said Herbert Hill, national labor director of the National Association for the Advancement of Colored People (NAACP).[36] Of the 80 million Americans in the United States work force 20 million—one in four—are union members who earn $3 to $5 per hour. Thus they do not number the poor people of America among their ranks nor do they necessarily sympathize with them.

Walter Reuther successfully fought for a guaranteed annual wage for assembly-line workers and company-paid pensions for those who were "too old to work and too young to die," a slogan he coined in the 1950 fight for funded pensions. He negotiated an early-retirement plan by which a worker may retire at 60 with $400 per month. This was a major achievement then, but times have changed. Sixty-year-olds are younger and healthier in the 1970s than in 1950. The wisdom of early and arbitrary retirement is more questionable now. Skills need not be allowed to obsolesce. The unions have not re-evaluated the fundamental value of retirement to workers and society or sought to resolve the dilemma of jobs for the young *and* productive lives for the older worker.

Moreover, the unions should be working toward basic reform in work patterns so that workers do not become bored or apathetic, especially if they have worked in the same job for years. For example, many auto workers, despite higher-than-average pay, are not happy in their jobs. Absenteeism, slowdowns, and sabotage are among the means they use to fight the boredom and repetitiveness of the assembly line. There is no individual recognition, sense of personal fulfillment or acquisition of new knowledge and skill.

Some employers (the Polaroid Corporation is an example) have endeavored to undertake job rotation as a basic policy. "Job enlargement" refers to efforts to engage more deeply the interest of workers in a job by expanding it in contrast with the traditional assembly-line, piecemeal approach. So far, however, there have only been modest efforts in industry to make work more meaningful for those older (and younger) workers who are trapped in jobs stultifying to mind and emotion.

A MORE FLEXIBLE RETIREMENT

Ideally, retirement should be an option based upon the individual's needs and wishes and upon an evaluation of his physical and emotional capacities to function. It is often argued that individualized retirement creates painful situations in which the employer must tell the employee when his competence is waning. But consider the painful effects of our present system on far greater numbers of people. There are certainly dignified and thoughtful ways to handle individual evaluations, which could result in humane and sensible agreement between employer and employee. This requires personnel trained in specific procedures of appraisal and decision.

We have a useful example in physicians, lawyers, judges and elected officials who are generally not restricted by mandatory retirement ages and often do not elect voluntary retirement for personal and financial reasons until late in life, if at all. They represent a unique group in terms of older persons who work. In studying them we may gain new insights into less rigid and more individualized (but hopefully reliable) methods of determining ages of retirement.

With respect to the judiciary, a pioneering system came into being as a result of the interruption of a California murder trial for four days because an older judge vanished on an alcoholic binge. This led Chief Justice Phil S. Gibson to undertake a study on the basis of which he pressed for a state constitutional amendment which would give the California Supreme Court full power to remove unfit judges at all judicial levels, including its own. The amendment was approved by three to one in a 1960 election. A nine-member commission—composed of five judges, two lawyers, and two laymen—was established to evaluate judicial qualifications. Focus is on alleged disability and misconduct. The commission has the power to subpoena medical records and order medical examinations. Twenty-five states have followed California's example. The very fact of the existence of commissions has been useful in encouraging judges to evaluate their competence on their own.

One inducement to voluntary retirement is decent retirement benefits, and they were increased for judges in California. As a result of both larger benefits and direct removal from office, the number of judges over 70 was reduced from eighty to six between 1959 and 1965. On the other hand, court loads are heavy and there is a need to avail ourselves of capable judges. The law which provides for retirement of federal judges at 70 also enables them to continue their services as senior judges. This increases the number of judges available for duty as long as they remain physically and mentally fit.[37]

How applicable would such mechanisms be to other fields? And how successful are they within these judicial systems? Obviously further innovative exploration and evaluation are necessary.

Physicians do not tend to retire. Some should; more should not. The decision depends upon their specialty and competence. Obviously surgeons need to be monitored because of the complex physical/mental demands of their work. If group practice increases, it should be possible for group members to help assay a colleague and utilize the older person's experience, if not his direct activity. In 1971 there were 25,000 doctors over 65 in active practice and 6,000 of them were over 75. Twenty-five percent of all practicing medical doctors and doctors of osteopathy are between 50 and 65. There are some externally imposed pressures on older doctors to retire when it may not be useful or desirable to lose their skills—for example, if they are refused malpractice insurance or forced to pay such high premiums that part-time practice is not economically feasible. Moreover, other doctors may stop referring patients to them, and the older doctor's remaining patients may become reluctant to see him simply because of his age. When the doctor is clearly competent, this is a tragic waste. We need an objective and more individual system of determining competence and capacities. Scientifically controlled studies of samples of the 25,000 doctors over 65 who are in private practice could prove very valuable.

GOVERNMENT WORK PROGRAMS FOR THE ELDERLY

Until such time as private enterprise changes its age-discriminatory policies, public employment will have to play a major role in providing jobs for the elderly who desire, need and have the competence to work. The government will need to be "the employer of last resort" in the face of technological and other unemployment since private industry is unlikely to absorb the older worker in the near future. But, beyond that, the government should become "the employer of first resort" in taking leadership on behalf of elderly workers and creating new service-related jobs.[38]

Public employment can help accomplish the many tasks that are not now being done in our society, especially human and personal services such as home health care and the maintenance of the environment. Public employment can also be shaped to the special characteristics of those unemployed who have few skills or little experience.

PROGRAMS FOR LOW-INCOME ELDERLY

The Emergency Employment Act of 1971, stimulated by the recession of 1970–71 employment, provided nearly 150,000 public-service jobs for workers of all ages. The law would seem to assure that persons over 45 will be adequately represented in new public-service-employment programs, but so far this has not proved to be the case.

A number of programs of limited scope already exist for persons over 60 years of age with incomes below the OEO (Office of Economic Opportunity) guidelines. Salaries are equivalent to the federal minimum wage.

1. Foster Grandparents

The Foster Grandparent Program was begun under the Office of Economic Opportunity as an older-worker program within the Community Action Program.* It recruits, trains and employs elderly persons (60 and above) who are below the poverty line to serve neglected and deprived children who lack close personal relationships with adults. Some of these children may be mentally retarded, physically handicapped or emotionally disturbed, in or out of institutions.

The day-care forum at the White House Conference on Children in 1970 recommended 50,000 additional child-care workers each year for the next decade. A substantial number of those could be trained Foster Grandparents. In 1970 there were an estimated 40,000 "latch-key" children, whose mothers work and who are left unattended in the daytime.† But so far, there have been at most 4,400 foster grandparents.

2. SOS (*Senior Opportunities for Services Programs*)

Sponsored by OEO, the SOS programs provide services to older people in nutrition, consumer education, outreach programs, employment opportunities, referral and the like. Staffing at SOS, both paid and volunteer, is intended to include as many older workers as possible.

3. Operation Mainstream

Operation Mainstream is run by the Department of Labor for the chronically unemployed and includes the Green Thumb program for men, Green Light program for women, Senior AIDES and Senior Community Service Aides.

Green Thumb. Rural America is the home of several million low-income old people. In 1965 the National Farmers Union began sponsoring an active program, Green Thumb, to provide job opportunities for old people who live in rural pockets of poverty. The Farmers Union obtained a grant from the U.S. Department of Labor's Bureau of Works provided by an amendment of the Economic Opportunity Act of 1964. Other state and local agencies and the universities also contribute in a matching arrangement. This program operates in only seventeen states.

---

* It originated from Project TLC of the National Council on the Aging.
† The word "latch-key" comes from the practice of putting keys to their houses on strings around the children's necks so they can let themselves in or out of their empty homes.

Green Thumbers, men aged 55 and older,* plant trees and sod, build new parks and rebuild old ones, create rest areas, reconstruct historical sites and beautify highways. They have reconstructed Indian burial mounds in Minnesota, developed overlooks and vistas along the highways, carried out such conservation projects as ditching and planting, and refurbished picnic areas. They may also receive two weeks' training as landscapers, gardeners, nurserymen and highway maintenance men and have been hired by landscape companies.

Green Thumb employs about 3,000 persons, usually retired persons, who receive the federal minimum wage of $1.60 (through 1972) per hour, working eight hours daily for three days a week. Thus in 1972 they earned $12.80 daily or $38.40 weekly. A Green Thumb brochure overenthusiastically declares: "It helps them not with a handout but with a chance to earn a decent way of life." This is hardly the case. Men can work all year and barely reach the Social Security limit! In addition, they are not eligible to work as Green Thumbers unless their income is below $1,500 per year. Those farmers who entered the Social Security system late receive small pension benefits and thus fall within this income range.

Green Thumb is vaguely comparable to the Civilian Conservation Corps (CCC) of the New Deal years. For example, Pocahontas State Park near Richmond, Virginia, was one of Virginia's state parks created by CCC labor. Now Green Thumbers work there creating nature trails and planting trees. It would be harsh to call the Green Thumb program the "geriatric CCC," and unfair also to fail to commend the leadership and good intentions of its director, Blue Carstenson, and others. The usefulness of the work clearly helps some older people psychologically and financially and serves in a minimal way to preserve our environment. But Green Thumb is a very small program, operating on a $9 million budget in 1972.

Green Light. Green Light started in 1969 when older women began serving as aides in community service and outreach programs to help the handicapped, the sick elderly and shut-ins. They also work as aides in libraries, schools and day-care centers. Green Light exists in 11 states and as of 1972 there were only 290 jobs allotted per year.

Senior AIDES and Senior Community Service Aides. Senior AIDES and Senior Community Service Aides are engaged in such activities as home-making and health assistance, nutrition, institutional care, home repair, child care and social-service administration. The National Council on the Aging and the National Council of Senior Citizens have conducted successful programs using low-income elderly (55 and over); and the Senior AIDES

---

* The oldest has been 94. The average age is 68.

(Alert, Industrious, Dedicated, Energetic, Service) program of the NCOA and NCSC was originally supported by a $2 million grant from the Department of Labor.

All these government programs are at present token programs,[39] essentially geriatric WPAs* with catchy acronyms.† In 1974, for example, the National Council employed only 2,040 aides in 34 areas in 25 states. They are not substitutes for full-scale employment efforts and should be incorporated into major legislated programs such as those Senator Harrison A. Williams (D.-N.J.) has tried to effect for some time.

He first introduced legislation to establish an Older Americans Community Service Program within the Administration on Aging in 1967. The bill would have set up a program to "match a desire to serve with an opportunity to serve." He offered it as Title VI of the Older Americans Act. The bill would have made it possible to pay each participant up to $1,500 per year.

His bill read, in part, that "the Congress hereby finds and declares:

(1) that there are millions of Americans aged sixty and over who are forced into idleness and inactivity by unemployment, compulsory retirement policies, or lack of opportunities for meaningful community service projects;

(2) that certain grave consequences of such enforced idleness are impaired morale and physical, mental, and psychological health among members of this age group who are forced to endure frustration, feeling of futility, loss of self-respect;

(3) that another consequence of such enforced idleness is inadequate incomes for this age group, many of whom receive pensions and other retirement incomes which are totally inadequate, and others of whom have not yet reached ages of eligibility for such pensions;

(4) that there are needs in every community and area of the Nation which are not now being met, not because of the lack of manpower to meet those needs, but rather because of the lack of adequate arrangements for utilizing available manpower to meet them;

(5) that individuals aged sixty or over are capable and qualified to perform services which would meet many of those needs and that there is an important potential national asset in the talents, abilities, experience, training and energy of Americans in that age group who have been forced into unwanted inactivity; and

(6) that providing this age group with opportunities for services will better

---

* The WPA was the acronym for the New Deal agency the Works Progress Administration, founded in 1935 to provide work for needy persons on public-works projects.

† Consider: SWAP (Senior Workers Action Program) in Akron, Ohio, and Project WORK (Wanted Older Residents with Knowledge) in Long Beach, California.

their morale, will benefit their physical, mental and psychological health, can, in many cases, provide them with needed income supplementation and will be a means of providing services needed by all age groups which are not now being provided.

One consequence of Senator Williams's efforts is a modest voluntary program, Retired Senior Volunteer Program (RSVP), with minimal funding, a very small step toward the necessary goal of the Williams bill.

I offered testimony in support of Williams's bill and urged leadership by the elderly themselves:

Older retired people should be sought to lead projected community service programs by their placement in key policy-making and administrative positions within the proposed National Community Senior Service Corps (as an amendment of the Older Americans Act of 1965). Such positions should be defined as they would be for anyone holding such critical posts irrespective of age. Selection should be rigorous, training in community organization and action should be provided, and salary and fringe benefits should be comparable to similar positions held by the non-retired. In short, the leadership of the National Community Senior Service Corps should not imply second-rate status. Nor should the general membership of the Corps become regarded as "second-class" or as "cheap labor." It is essential that the Corps be a success and those conditions which will promote success are similar to those which operate in any organization comprising any other age group within the life cycle.[40]

VOLUNTEER PROGRAMS

There are some government programs which provide opportunities for elderly volunteers.

RSVP (Retired Senior Volunteer Program)

The model for RSVP was SERVE (Serve and Enrich Retirement by Volunteer Service). SERVE was sponsored by the Community Service Society of New York City and partially financed by a grant under the Older Americans Act.

Now part of ACTION, RSVP funds volunteer programs in public and nonprofit institutions. Its volunteers are reimbursed for travel and meal expenses. Funds for RSVP were held up by the Nixon administration in 1970 and 1971 and as a result the program has barely begun. It was projected to have some 25,000 volunteers.

SCORE (Service Corps of Retired Executives)

Small business enterprises throughout the United States have been aided by the Service Corps of Retired Executives (SCORE), which was established in 1964 by Eugene P. Foley, then head of the Small Business Administration (SBA), to help small businessmen liable to failure through faulty management. The idea was orignated in 1950 by Maurice du Pont Lee, a retired businessman of Wilmington, Delaware. The SBA lends money to small companies. When and if they fail, taxpayers lose. Foley believed they could benefit from the experience available in the reservoir of retired executive business talent.

To be eligible for help a firm must have no more than 25 employees, a qualification that includes about 95 percent of the 4.8 million American businesses. It is assumed that such small firms cannot afford the high fees ($250 per day and more) of management consultants. Individuals considering starting a business alone may also utilize the services of SCORE consultants. SCORE executives advise businessmen how to conduct inventories, order stock, keep records, arrange loans and carry out promotion of products. The consultants serve without fee for the first 90 days but are reimbursed for travel expenses in the amount of $5 for a visit within twenty-five miles. By 1970 more than 37,000 small businesses had received assistance.

SCORE is organized in self-governing chapters across the nation. By 1970 there were 3,300 SCORE men and 184 active chapters. SCORE has been placed under ACTION though it is still administered by the SBA.

Peace Corps

Reflecting prevailing stereotypes concerning the elderly, the American emphasis upon youth, and the views of President John F. Kennedy and Peace Corps Director Sargent Shriver, the Peace Corps unfortunately began as a youth corps in 1961. The idea of utilizing the services of people over 65 in the Peace Corps has been slow in developing. Elderly Peace Corpsmen find special welcome and respect in those other cultures where old age is valued so differently than in ours. They have much to offer: an old-line sanitation engineer, for example, could administrate the improvement of sanitation in a Peruvian village with skills he gained in his early career when conditions in our country were comparable to the primitive conditions of underdeveloped countries.

Disease risk among older participants is a legitimate concern, but the

Peace Corps experience has shown that it has been overestimated. There was some shift toward the use of older people in the Peace Corps under the administration of President Nixon and former ACTION director Joseph H. Blatchford.[41] In his initial appearance before the House Foreign Affairs Committee in July, 1969, Blatchford said there were increasing demands for Peace Corpsmen who were experienced carpenters, machinists, electricians, management officials, accountants and farmers. By 1971 persons over 60 years of age made up only 1.1 percent of the corps's total of some 8,000 volunteers and only 265 had served since its inception. In 1972 about 70 Peace Corpsmen over 60 were serving around the world; this represents a substantial increase.

VISTA (Volunteers in Service to America)

VISTA has been called the domestic Peace Corps. It is a component of ACTION. It was one of the major antipoverty programs (although total VISTA membership is only 4,000) established by the Economic Opportunity Act of 1964 to provide an opportunity for men and women from all walks of life and all age groups to join in the "war on poverty." Youth was given less emphasis than in the Peace Corps.

Volunteers have worked in education, health, vocational counseling, recreation, conservation, sanitary construction and community services. They receive subsistence allowances to cover housing, food and clothing, and $75 monthly for personal needs. (An additional $50 per month is accumulated and paid on completion of service.) Medical care is provided. From its inception through 1972, a total of 3,075 of its volunteers have been over 50.

IESC (International Executive Service Corps)

IESC is an independent organization started in 1964 to help business in underdeveloped nations. By 1970 some 400 projects in 33 nations had been undertaken by business executives, many, but not all of them, retired. It is supported by government and nongovernment funds.

TOWARD A SERVICE SOCIETY

It is simply not true that there is not enough work to do in the United States. Politicians, economists, employers and unionists propose earlier and earlier retirement as a quick solution to employment problems, yet this creates more troubles than it solves. The truth is that our need for goods and services requires an expanded work force.

As America moves toward population control the need for utilizing the capabilities of old people and for building new skills will grow. A major shift in the economy toward a service society is an inevitable feature of future American life. The term "service society" refers to skills in governmental, human and personal services and the maintenance and repair of products rather than skills needed in manufacture. The health industry is a prime example of a service industry and will soon be the country's largest industry in terms of both manpower and money expended. (It is now third-largest, next to construction.) Government, too, is a service industry and by 1975 one in seven persons will be employees at some level of government—federal, state or municipal. By 1980, two-thirds of the labor force will be employed in the services sector.

All kinds of services, public, quasi-public and private, become possible if we move out of the confines of our rigid thinking about work patterns. Some economists and critics, whether they call themselves liberals or conservatives, tend to deride as "make-work" the training and hiring programs for positive and constructive service jobs like school aides, social-worker aides, paraprofessional medical workers, fire and police department service employees, workers in conservation and ecology. The same criticism is not directed toward the manufacture of sixteen different kinds of colored facial tissues, the design of different-shaped potato chips or the manufacture of more and more ingenious but hardly essential electric coffeemakers, because these are profitable to company owners. We are already in need of a wide spectrum of services in many fields: in the health industry alone there are 125 different skilled occupations which require manpower. Many more services could be instituted if we began to think creatively about what the needs of our society are—and are going to be in the near future.

We need to determine those needs (and pleasures) within society which are not being met, or which have not yet been thought of and developed, but which the elderly could fulfill. It would be of practical value to ascertain how many elderly people there are now unemployed who meet the following criteria: (1) adequate mental and physical health;[42] (2) occupational competence; and (3) desire to return to work.* We do not know.

Once we have a determination of available elderly people and of unmet societal needs we could begin to develop plans to match resources and needs in a mutually useful and satisfactory manner. Legal issues (such as legislated retirement ages), economic factors (such as Social Security earnings limitations) and social attitudes operate against rational solutions

---

* I do not wish to imply that elderly people must meet a strict criterion of physical and mental health in order to represent a valuable human resource. Those with varying degrees of impairment can continue to function in many important ways.

reached through logistical matching. Here public education, as well as social and political action mobilizing opinion toward legislative change, are required.

In summary, we must develop flexible retirement systems with adequate financial support. Arbitrary arrangements must end. Active pressure is important; class-action suits should be brought against employers for violation of equal-employment provisions on the basis of age discrimination. The goal of full employment should be facilitated by continuing lifelong education and by expansion of work through greater emphasis on services and innovative job creation. So long as work and money remain central to human dignity and, indeed, survival in America, they should never be denied anyone of any age.

Just as every able and willing person should be able to work regardless of his age, so also those who elect retirement from their regular occupations should live in a society that provides a wide variety of roles with substance and purpose. These should be available on full-time and part-time bases, either voluntary or paid. The special characteristics of old people should be utilized in matching skills with needs. There should be either a National Senior Service Corps for this purpose or old people should function within a comprehensive National Service Program for people of all ages.

To go even further, might it not be possible to consider arranging our fundamental work-and-money patterns and eliminate retirement as it is currently practiced? Why not redistribute education, work and leisure throughout the life cycle instead of concentrating those activities into three distinct periods: early life, middle life and old age? Chapter 13 will discuss these far-reaching possibilities further.

Chapter 5

NO PLACE TO LIVE

A PLACE TO CALL HOME

In human terms the issue of housing for older people is far more than simply providing a roof over their heads. When we talk about housing we are really addressing the concept of "home" and what this means to the elderly. The place where one lives is often profoundly connected with who one is and how one expresses this sense of self. Home is where all individuals feel most comfortable to be themselves, to drop social façades. Many older people also associate home with autonomy and control, for them it is sometimes the only place where they can feel certain of their surroundings, free from the control and restraints of others. Home is an expression of one's personality through furnishings, decorations, memorabilia, ambience, plants, pets. It is a familiar place in what may be a changing and unsteady outer world. Ties to the past are maintained through personal possessions, household routines learned and carried out through the years, and through the memories surrounding these very personal expressions of one's self and the selves of family and friends. For an older person to have a home of his or her own is to have the opportunity to socialize, to give and receive invitations, to have privacy with chosen companions and to be alone when this is desired.

The details of what constitutes "home" are different for each person. It can primarily mean the four walls surrounding one, or the things that make one feel at home—flowers, pets, possessions. Home can include the people with whom one lives in close contact, whether they be spouse, children, other relatives, friends or the neighbors. A specific neighborhood, the proximity to certain shopping areas, even the larger community or city can produce powerful feelings of "home." Therefore, home is whatever the concept of home means to each individual.

An older person may strongly resist the thought of having to leave his own home, particularly if this means a move to totally strange surroundings or, worse, an institution. Some insist upon remaining in their homes "at all costs" to their physical security.

Mrs. Salley Gruen, a 78-year-old woman holds tenaciously on to her home, which is now rat infested and dilapidated, in the inner-city slum area of Washington, D.C. Once robust and attractive, she has become thin and sallow and has to make financial choices among food on her table, prescription drugs for her ailments, and payments of her property taxes, which have been increasing in recent years. She can no longer afford repairs for her deteriorating home. She has no electricity, no heat, no water. In order to stay warm she has closed off most of the house except for one downstairs room. In the coldest days of winter she stays at the houses of her few surviving friends. Water collects in the basement. She lives by candlelight since the electricity was cut off.

She has been referred to a protective-services program by the Board of Unsanitary Condemnation. The referral slip states that she is resistant to moving and that she is undoubtedly "senile" or "crazy." She is a "stubborn old lady," states a city official who examined her situation. "Her home is wretched and must be eliminated."

Mrs. G. and her husband had worked long and hard to own their home, which she now possesses "free and clear." Her husband died ten years ago and she is living on his minimal Social Security, which, together with some babysitting money, gives her an income of $94 per month. On that $94 she cannot move to a better location, nor does she want to. The City will have to force her out by condemning her property.

Many factors produce such tenaciousness: pride, a desire for freedom and independence, a need to be in contact with familiar people, places and things, and anxiety about change and the unknown, which can be especially frightening in old age. There may realistically be so little money that moving is impossible without asking for assistance—which the elderly may be loath to do. The idea of home ownership is deeply ingrained in this generation of older people, of whom 69 percent are home owners. Many cannot easily accept the idea of renting or the communal living inherent in institutions, both of which they view as a loss of dignity and personal liberty.

There are actual physical and emotional dangers involved in uprooting older people from familiar surroundings. Many studies have shown that moves, particularly abrupt moves, result in increased illness and death in the elderly. This problem can be alleviated somewhat by preparing the person carefully and making the move in a gradual, thoughtful manner; but the threat of increased morbidity and mortality remains. Resettling in an unfamiliar new home has its own physical perils—the older person may forget which way to turn at night on the way to the bathroom and fall, and there is the stress of learning about a whole new environment, which can lead to exhaustion and depression. There are hazards in a strange home for the hard of hearing, those with poor eyesight, or shaky balance and physical weakness, and for the mildly mentally confused. Older persons often realize these potential difficulties instinctively, adding yet another motivation for their wish to remain in their own homes as long as possible.

One can of course overly romanticize the importance of home. There are certainly cases in which living situations convey no sense of home in the traditional sense. There are those older people who do not feel "at home" where they presently are. The in-law situation is classic, where a parent moves in with a son or daughter and everyone winds up unhappy. Of course these arrangements can also work out satisfactorily, but in a significant number the older person feels he is a burden and the children concur.

Others dislike their living conditions because some change has occurred and they are eager to move somewhere else—even to an institution:

> Harry Marshall cared for his wife while she was dying of cancer of the breast. Then he fell apart. He was unable to grieve openly, but he often drank himself senseless. He didn't pay his bills or manage his affairs. He drifted the streets and was badly beaten up once; the gold watch his father had given him was taken. He didn't want to return home, where he found the memories too painful. He asked to be put away—anywhere!

There are old people who live in shelter that is truly unlivable—cheap "retirement hotels," skimpy boardinghouses, bare rooms. There are others who literally have no place at all to live, no fixed residence. They drift from park bench to doorways, to subway, bus and train stations, to "bowery" missions, surviving on their wits and luck.

> Frail, gray and tangle-haired Mary Gunston lost her husband a year before, leaving her penniless. She was on a lengthy waiting list for public housing. She was evicted from the small apartment she had shared with her husband; her belongings were strewn on the curb. She sat helplessly while people brazenly carted off her furniture and household objects. She stayed in a city park for seven months, even during the winter. She wrapped old newspapers around her body beneath four sweaters and three skirts. Her few possessions, mainly pictures, were contained in a black bag with drawstrings, kept in the hollow of a tree. The park police periodically chased her out and she systematically returned.

The Washington *Post*, September 1, 1973, ran a story about an elderly black man with the headline "Elderly N.Y. Inventor, Evicted, Lives in Street":

Solomon Harper, 78, is an inventor, a World War I veteran, a former researcher for the federal government and a former member of the mayor's Central Harlem Urban Committee.

He is also broke and he has no place to sleep at night.

The 1920 graduate of the New York Electrical School, who has studied at Berkeley, Syracuse University and Pratt Institute, was evicted from his apartment last April.

Since that time, he said at a news conference, he has been living on the subways and in the streets.

It is rash to make quick judgments about what home means to people and what kinds of housing would be appropriate. Home is extraordinarily significant to most persons, but each person may define home differently. How can housing choices be provided to meet individual needs? What can be done to help the elderly remain in their homes if they wish to and are able to? When should a move be considered? Who makes the decision? What if the older person refuses to move? These are some of the questions that must be considered along with the very explicit challenge of providing a decent physical structure which older people can afford.

HOUSING THE ELDERLY

In my rounds in the nation's capital I came upon an old man living in a windowless closet so small he could not stretch his ancient stained mattress to its full length. This lonely, arthritic old man, who had no family, had originally rented an entire room in a deteriorated slum building. Suddenly the rent was increased and he could no longer afford to remain. He appealed to the landlord, who agreed to rent him the closet. Admittedly this is an extreme example, but it is by no means unique. How many other older people live in substandard and inhumane housing?

The 1970 census did not collect data regarding substandard housing because it was decided that the term "substandard" was too "subjective," and the government was reluctant to develop objective measures of inadequate housing. Thus we must rely upon the 1960 census statistics, which showed that about 30 percent of the elderly (compared to about 25 percent of the population as a whole) lived in housing that was dilapidated, deteriorating* or lacking some facilities.[1] If we keep to this estimate of 30 percent, we can calculate that in 1972 some 6 million elderly people were living in approximately 2.8 million substandard apartments or homes! This means that some 30 percent of the housing of older people had no inside flush toilets, some 40 percent no bath or shower with hot water, and some 54 percent minimal heat in winter.

The housing problems of the aged are much more severe than is commonly recognized. Housing consumes one-third of the budget of an elderly couple, according to the Department of Labor's Bureau of Labor Statistics (BLS.† Those who own their own houses face great difficulties maintaining them, for the home may be their only equity. They often lack money to pay for necessary repairs, services and property taxes. Many are forced to give up their homes. Those who remain find that neighborhoods, particularly in the inner city, can change rapidly, leaving the old person trapped in his own home in unfamiliar, unsupportive and often dangerous surroundings. Alternatives are scant. There is a limited availability of low-income housing. Retirement villages may be too expensive or psychologically and physically unsuitable.

Many older people—especially those with no living relatives—must reside in boarding homes, third-rate hotels, trailer parks and single room occupancy units.

Seven out of every ten older Americans live with a spouse or with their children or other relatives. The remainder live alone or with nonrelatives. Because of a shorter life expectancy most older men live with their spouses and perhaps other family members, while only one-third of older women do so.

Although the black elderly often live under extremely impoverished conditions (more so than whites)

both in numbers and percent white aged exceeded the blacks in being without housing altogether. One reason for this may reflect greater adherence to an "extended family" concept among blacks than whites, the black elderly being more often accepted as members of the household. Another reason may be purely economic. The elderly black may be able to make a meager contribution to the family income through a small Social Security benefit or public assistance.[2]

---

* "Dilapidation" is a state of not being habitable. "Deterioration" means that a dwelling has not yet quite reached dilapidation but is substandard.

† According to the Bureau of Labor Statistics, the cost of living for the elderly is significantly greater in metropolitan areas than in smaller cities. Geographically the Northeast is most expensive, followed by the West, the North-Central region and finally the South.

The housing situation of other racial groups is varied but generally inadequate. We know that many Chinese and Filipino men live alone in poverty-stricken circumstances. The Japanese elderly receive more family support because they were allowed to immigrate to the United States in families. Spanish-speaking and American Indian elderly live in housing that reflects their long history of impoverishment in America.

The largest concentrations of older Americans are found in the agricultural Midwest, in New England and in Florida. The majority (60.8 percent) of aged blacks reside in the South. California, New York, Pennsylvania and Illinois each has more than a million older people. New York alone has nearly two million old people. Sixty percent of old people are in urban areas, 33 percent in the center cities, 40 percent in nonmetropolitan areas (only 5 percent on farms, the rest in towns).* Older people represent a fairly stable population, moving less frequently and not as far as the young.

Both the federal government and private housing enterprise have failed to provide sufficient reasonably priced housing for the elderly. Public housing is inadequate in amount and quality. Necessary services are fragmented or nonexistent. Some elderly are too poor to afford public housing and others, of course, are poor yet have too much income to qualify for either public housing or housing originally developed for the low-middle-income elderly. Minority-group elderly are ignored to a large extent. As Hobart Jackson, chairman of the National Caucus of the Black Aged, stated in 1972, "Of the federally subsidized housing projects for the aged, only 3 percent are black. Only 1 percent of the black elderly are in integrated housing. In other words, two-thirds of that 3 percent are in primarily black-run facilities."

WHERE THE ELDERLY LIVE

THE ELDERLY HOME OWNER

Sixty-nine percent (or 13.2 million) of older people own their own homes with the mortgages paid off. This does not necessarily assure them the prerogatives generally associated with home ownership: namely, substantial equity, low housing costs in relation to income, and sufficient capital assets to move to a new location if desired.

---

* However, suburbs and their inhabitants are growing older. By 1990 the people whose need for shelter stimulated the post–World War II housing boom will be elderly. Then new problems will arise. For example, most suburbs now have poor public transportation, and in many places not even sidewalks. Old people may become even more isolated in suburbia than they presently are in the city.

1. The Problem of Low Equity

In 1967, thirteen percent of the aged home owners had a net equity of between $1,000 and $4,999, 26 percent had between $5,000 and $9,999, and altogether 48 percent had a net equity of less than $25,000. Thus, although older home owners can live rent free, they are at a disadvantage if they wish to sell and move elsewhere. Many older people find themselves trapped in their homes, unable to find available or alternative living arrangements at reasonable prices in a suitable locale.

Economics professor Yung-Ping Chen has suggested one solution, namely the combination of home sale and annuity purchase. In effect the older person would give up his house at death in exchange for a lifetime of income and the use of his house. Another plan is that offered by former HEW Secretary Wilbur J. Cohen, who recommended a U.S. government corporation that can rent, renovate or sell the residential property of older people. Cohen proposed:

The corporation could purchase the home of an aged person who was ill and pay the aged person a monthly annuity which might enable him to meet extraordinary medical or nursing home costs.

Or the corporation could pay for remodeling the large home of an aged person and make it possible for one or more additional aged persons to live there, thus making it financially feasible for all the aged to have a comfortable residence at a reasonable rental.[3]

2. Utility and Maintenance Costs

The older person's home was usually purchased thirty or forty years ago and often has deteriorated physically. Repairs, utility and maintenance costs tend to outstrip the capacity of the elderly person to pay for them. These costs have risen dramatically—as much as 35 percent between 1963 and 1971. This is catastrophic to anyone living on a fixed income. In addition to dealing with financial problems, how does an older person cope physically with all the ordinary problems of homes—carpenter ants, termites, wornout switches, clogged drains and downspouts, or flooded basements?

3. Property Taxes

The typical urban household spends approximately 3.4 percent of its income for property taxes, but elderly home owners frequently find the burden much more substantial. Their taxes average 8.1 percent of their retirement income, but can go as high as 20 to 40 percent. Property taxes averaging $1,500 annually on modest homes are not uncommon, and one can quickly see what this does to a modest retirement budget. In major American cities in the United States the vast majority of aged property owners can expect to pay $300 at the very least for property taxes. Fortunately, by 1973 twenty-five states offered a minimal break on property taxes to older home owners. But those remain crushing to elderly fixed-income home owners. President Nixon said at the 1971 White House Conference on Aging, "The same house which has been a symbol of their independence becomes the cause of their impoverishment."

The research report of the National Commission on Urban Problems in 1968 observed that property taxes as they are presently levied burden the poor more than the wealthy and discourage maintenance of decent housing. Inequitable tax rates hit home owners hard, while large corporate owners of land, real estate and minerals pay less than their fair share. The International Association of Assessing Officers, the National League of Cities, the National Council of Mayors and other municipal groups have been examining inequities in land assessment and property taxes.* The property tax as a taxing device is actually one of the best ways to equalize income and wealth but only if it taxes the value of properties fairly.[4]

Property taxes currently provide 40 percent of all state and local government revenue. Seven-eighths of the locally collected tax revenues for the support of local governments come from property taxes. One of the dilemmas for the old is the fact that funds for public education of children in a community derive in large part from property taxes. The elderly (and to some degree the middle-aged), whose children are long grown, resist rises in school funding costs through property taxes or bond issues. One then sees the old and young pitted against each other—as when, for example, old people voted down school loans in Youngstown, Ohio, leading to brief school closings in 1969. Close examination indicates that the vote was dictated by their pocketbooks rather than "political conservatism," just as the votes of citizens of all other groups are influenced by financial considerations.† The old feel legitimately that their limited incomes should not be further burdened by paying for the education of the young.

If through congressional legislation the federal government were to make a larger contribution to local education, this would relieve local property

---

* Monthly mortgage payments to banks usually include money for local taxes which actually need not be paid until the end of the year. In the meantime, the banks are making money on home owners' money. Class-action cases by home owners are in order. See "Agenda for Activism" in Chapter 11.

† Indeed, in Seal Beach, California, more-affluent older residents have voted in favor of school loans.

owners and greatly help the elderly.* Of course, the amount of relief would depend upon the extent to which much-needed overall federal income-tax reform eliminates the tax loopholes, capital gains and depletion allowances that have reduced potential revenues, and establishes a more straight-line graduated income tax.

President Nixon saw revenue sharing as one means of providing property-tax relief, as stated in his Message to Congress, March 23, 1972. Governor Marvin Mandel (D.-Md.) has taken that approach on behalf of elderly homeowners.

4. Age Discrimination Through Mortgage Regulation

For those elderly who wish to purchase a new home there is age discrimination in obtaining a mortgage. As one example, in 1971 "Fannie Mae" (the Federal National Mortgage Association), a quasi-public† agency that buys and sells home mortgages in the resale or secondary market, laid down guidelines considered discriminatory against minority groups, women and the elderly. Mortgage lenders were instructed that loans generally should not be made in cases where the age of the borrower plus the term of the loan exceeds 80 years.[5] No alternatives, such as forms of mortgage insurance, were recommended.

5. Welfare Liens on Private Property

Some states require that old people sign over their homes to the state welfare departments if they require Old Age Assistance. They can continue to live in their homes, but once the welfare recipient dies the state gains title to the property. The welfare departments in four southern states (North and South Carolina, Virginia and Florida) constitute collectively "the largest slumlords in the south," according to a 1970 report of the Southern Regional Council, as a result of acquisition of property in this manner. Other states have similar arrangements. The main effect of lien laws is that thousands of older people are discouraged from applying for public assistance because they cannot tolerate the thought of losing control of their property. In addition, for those who do sign liens the incentive for keeping the property in good repair is lessened since it cannot be passed on to heirs.

The actual financial recovery by public welfare under the lien system

* There would, of course, have to be protections guaranteed to local school districts to reduce the possibility of federal control over education.

† Fannie Mae determines the level of its mortgage purchases without having to make its case to the Office of Management and Budget.

is not substantial because of the deteriorated condition of much of the property. If the property is not sold within legal intervals that range from six months to perhaps two or three years it is disposed of at auction, usually at bargain prices. It cannot be rented or leased during the period of waiting for buyers.

THE ELDERLY RENTER

The elderly renter faces enormous problems resulting from a fixed income in the face of steadily rising rents. The problem of rental costs and of age discrimination is well illustrated by New York's elderly population faced with rent decontrol in 1971.[6] There are some one million older people in New York City, which is 13 percent of the city's population. Seventy percent of these old people rent. Many are widows living alone in SRO ("single room occupancy") units; many live in walkups and must climb four or five flights of stairs. New York City's elderly population represents the largest single group of citizens in the United States living on fixed incomes. A vast majority live at or near the poverty level. About half of the households headed by persons 65 and over have a yearly income of less than $3,000, and one-third have incomes of $2,000 a year or less.

In July of 1971 New York's new rent-decontrol law came into being. Under this law the landlord can increase the rent whenever a tenant moves. Immediately after the law went into effect the Office of Rent Control received many complaints by older people of harassment and lack of services from landlords who wanted them to move. The Office for the Aging in New York City, headed by Alice M. Brophy, tried to help older people deal with intimidation but they were limited in what they could do.

The 1972 increase in Social Security payments raised the fear that landlords all over the United States would raise rents for elderly persons and thus reap profits at the expense of the old. In the past there were complaints (but no definitive data) which indicated that this had happened whenever raises in Social Security benefits occurred. Upon the advice of Dr. Arthur S. Flemming, Special Adviser to the President, the Nixon administration introduced the "rent watch" by way of the Cost of Living Council.* With the 20 percent increase in Social Security going into effect in October of 1972 the "rent watch" was to monitor any potential increase which would offset the Social Security benefit. But the "watch" faded out and federal rent controls were ended in January, 1973.

When and if there is federal, state or local property-tax relief for older

---

* Then-Director Donald Rumsfeld said between 4 and 7 million of the 28 million Social Security beneficiaries live in rental units under Price Commission regulations.

home owners, there should also be tax rent refunds to provide comparable relief for elderly renters.

Tenant Activism

Increasingly, tenants have organized to negotiate rents and conditions of tenancy with their landlords. The power of landlords to raise rents and to evict has been under confrontation and court pressure since the late 1960s. Low-income and, more recently, middle-income tenants and the retired on fixed incomes have been active on a limited but national basis.

> Washington, D.C., residents General and Mrs. Geoffrey O'Flynn, both 82 years of age, were among 80 tenants, 65 percent of whom are retired and living on fixed incomes, who protested rent increases of 17 to 30 percent in March of 1970. They put equivalent amounts into an escrow account and did not pay their landlord. The latter served termination notices, demanding that the protestors "remove from and quit the premises." But none of the tenants left. The settlement was successfully negotiated through a compromise.

For the middle class and the elderly to undertake rent strikes in American cities prior to 1970 would have been considered quite remarkable.[7] But they have been learning from the example of others.[8] A significant minority of the tenants represented by the militant National Tenants Organization in Washington, D.C.,* for example, are middle-class and/or elderly.

As a consequence of tenant efforts in New York State, landlords are now legally required to keep rent security deposits made by tenants in interest-bearing accounts and to pay accumulated interest to tenants once a year. A 1971 decision in the U.S. Court of Appeals in the District of Columbia upheld the right of the striking tenants to put their rents in escrow while housing-code violations by their landlords were being settled in court.

In 1971 the Department of Housing and Urban Development issued the nation's first set of rules covering tenants' lease and complaint rights for the benefit of three million residents of publicly subsidized housing.† A tenant, for example, could no longer be evicted without a special hearing. Landlord-tenant codes of a model nature have been proposed as federal law.

As a result of increasing tenant activism, tenants have become members of the boards of city housing authorities. Older people have developed advisory committees related to decision making on the acquisition of housing

---

* The National Tenants Organization (NTO) was formed in 1969 in Washington, D.C. Its impetus came from the 1963 Harlem rent strikes led by the Reverend Jesse Gray and by the development of tenants' unions in Chicago in 1966.

† The federal government as the largest landlord in the nation has not set proper standards for tenancy and is increasingly itself the target of tenant groups.

and the provision of services. Tenants have increasingly played a part in direct management. But these efforts protect only a small number of the elderly. Tenant activism has a long way to go to ensure a real balance of power between tenants and landlords. In the meantime, elderly renters remain especially vulnerable to landlords.

The Condominium Squeeze

Conversion of rental-apartment residencies to condominiums has caused great difficulties for many elderly, especially those in lower- and middle-income brackets. They can't afford the high down payments to buy the units they may have lived in for decades. Eviction notices provide little time. It is difficult and expensive to move. Rents for comparable homes are usually higher. The owners of the condominium buildings find conversion profitable. They don't have to engage in court battles over rent increases. They no longer need pay rising maintenance costs. Conversions are attractive if the structure and utilities system are sound and the purchaser can afford the investment and the upkeep. Laws to regulate the conversion of rental units into condominiums have been weak and late. Ninety-to-120-day notices are of little help. Indigent, handicapped and older people should be offered the option of continuing rental leases regardless of conversion.

TOO POOR FOR PUBLIC HOUSING

Most Americans think of public housing in connection with tenants without any private source of income, when in fact it is a program for low-income people, a somewhat higher group economically. This is an important distinction. Federal public housing is administered on the local level by local housing authorities pursuant to HUD policy consistent with the Housing Act of 1937. It is financed by federal funds. Some states and municipalities have also created public housing. Insofar as the federal program is concerned, Senator Edward Brooke's (R.-Mass.) amendment to the 1969 Housing Act provided that people would not have to pay more than 25 percent of their income for public housing and for some publicly assisted or subsidized housing. But many people, including old people, are too poor even for public housing despite the Brooke amendment.* They require direct aid with respect to rent.

* There are always those who fall between the cracks—too rich and too poor for public services including housing. Income eligibility for nearly one million units of public housing ranges from roughly $4,500 to $9,800. Some eight million American families make less than the minimum. Nineteen million families fall within the income range.

In turn, public-housing authorities do not have adequate income, particularly when they must depend upon their tenants, many of whom are too poor to pay more than minimal rents, for their costs. The idea of raising the upper limit of income eligibility and permitting tenants to remain in public housing despite increases in their incomes would allow for a greater income mix in public housing. But, with escalating costs of maintenance, personnel, supplies and equipment, such raises in eligibility limits and in rents would still be unable to cover costs. There is a great need for operating subsidies for public authorities.

In 1972 lack of maintenance funds for public housing reached a nationwide crisis level, which especially affected the elderly. Some public-housing authorities were forced to evict those behind in rents and to raise rents, resulting in deeper inroads into fixed incomes and the 20 percent Social Security increase. Thus the government was giving with one hand through Social Security increases and taking away with the other by raising rents.

Public-housing rents currently cover only about 60 percent of operating and routine maintenance costs. Nineteen seventy-two HUD regulations required that rents paid by tenants of new public-housing projects must cover 85 percent of the general maintenance and operating costs of these projects. Since rents from public housing are based on a figure of 25 percent of the families' income, the poorest families have to be excluded. The greatest impact will be felt by the poor elderly residents who have no hope of increasing their income; and also by large poor families.

In addition to maintenance problems, public housing is not being built fast enough to accommodate all those who need it. Three million Americans live in public facilities, or 3 out of every 200, but in 1971, a typical year for the past decade, only 32,300 public-housing units were begun compared with more than 2 million housing units by private developers or builders. In 1973 the building of public housing was frozen for an indefinite period. Political support for publicly financed renewal of business districts is always easier to come by than public support for the building of public housing or the scattering of housing more uniformly throughout the city.

About 38 percent of available public housing has been designated for the elderly.* As of the end of 1970, however, only about 18 percent was actually occupied by older people. In 1971 former Commissioner of Public Housing Marie C. McGuire made clear the continuing housing needs of old people:

---

* Under the 1956 Housing Act the nation's first development specifically devised for the elderly was built in Somerville, Massachusetts. Victoria Plaza in San Antonio, Texas, was built under Marie C. McGuire in 1960. The selection of its residents was evaluated in a study by Dr. Frances Carp.[9]

"I would place it [quota for housing by HUD] at not less than 20 percent of the total dollars suggested for all housing . . . the only way we can achieve equity."[10] We do not know what happens to the many older people awaiting entrance into public housing or enough about the conditions under which they live as they endure their final years. We do know that once they get into public housing the maintenance is often so poor that they live with rats and roaches, no heat in the wintertime, broken pipes and fear of crime. (Older people themselves usually take good care of their housing and, therefore, all things being equal, public housing for the elderly shows less deterioration than that occupied primarily by families or younger people.) The federal government, the nation's largest landlord, is actually a slumlord, hardly setting a good standard for other landlords. The reasons for the slum conditions are manifold and the problems real—local control* and absence of national standards, inadequate operating and maintenance funds, poor site locations, and lack of protection against vandalism. Public housing tends to turn into ghettos. It would be desirable to have housing allowances and scattered rather than concentrated public housing, in order that old people and others needing public-housing assistance could live throughout various available housing areas. Public-housing design is often unaesthetic, and stigmatizing as well as impractical. For instance, the notorious Pruitt-Igoe project in St. Louis was so inhuman that it had to be completely demolished within 20 years after it was built.

THE RURAL ELDERLY

Two-thirds of the nation's substandard housing is to be found in small towns and villages.† There is often no plumbing or electricity. When the freeze fell on HUD in January, 1973, rural housing programs were deeply affected; especially hurt were the low-income elderly.

There were six million farms in the United States in 1940 and only three million thirty years later. According to the Census Bureau the number of farmers across the nation dropped 35 percent between 1954 and 1969. Older people become part of the problem of rural poverty. When they are no longer able to work they often have to leave the land and housing even though it has been a part of their lives. They may have very little to show as a monument to a lifetime of hard labor.‡

---

* Two million eight hundred thousand tenants in public housing pay rent to 1,900 local autonomous housing authorities.

† In 1970 and 1971 there was an important series of hearings on "Older Americans in Rural Areas" conducted by the U.S. Senate Special Committee on Aging.

‡ It is interesting that old people with some but not extensive means would actually do well to retire to small towns, where they could live reasonably, pleasantly

The rural elderly may no longer live in rural areas unless those areas are redeveloped. Migration from the farms to the city has followed upon the fact that the "smaller marginal farms ceased to operate when their owners retired or died."[11] Agri-business has taken over in the upper-central Midwestern states—Minnesota, North and South Dakota, and upper New England states such as Maine, New Hampshire and Vermont.

RETIREMENT COMMUNITIES—ARE THEY GHETTOS?

Many spontaneous, unplanned retirement communities like St. Petersburg and Miami Beach, Florida, grew like Topsy. The easy climate and low costs of housing and food were appealing. One-fourth of St. Petersburg's population is old. The city fathers originally encouraged the coming of the retirees; more recently they have been trying to reduce if not eradicate the image of St. Petersburg as a retirement community and have even thought of removing the sidewalk benches as one way of lowering the visibility of the older population. South Beach below Miami evolved quite differently, but attracted its older residents for the same reasons. The Miami Beach boom of huge hotels left other housing at South Beach available for the less affluent and the poor elderly. In 1972 40,000 people lived there, almost entirely European-born Jews. They are separated from glittering Miami Beach by Lincoln Road—and by a considerable income difference. The average annual income of the South Beach population was $2,460 in 1967. Services of all kinds are not well organized or plentiful in unplanned communities, and evolve in a helter-skelter fashion.

Planned retirement communities which have emerged since the fifties and sixties have been controversial. Some developers have been exploitative. There are those who feel strongly that old people should not be walled off in sequestered worlds, even if comfortable, but rather remain a part of the mainstream of life.[12] The issue may be best resolved in the more humane concept of the right of choice. Older people have the right to a wide range of possible alternatives, one of which is the retirement community.

It costs a minimum of $6,000 a year for a single person and $8,000 for a couple (1973 figures) to live in an average retirement community. This is beyond the financial ability of most retirees since the median income of older couples is $5,500.

Jurisdictions find retirement communities appealing because higher-density development populated by families with children results in high

---

and cheaply in what decent housing is available there. It would also be helpful to the economic base of the small town.

demand for costly services, particularly schools. Communities of older adults provide decent tax returns to the jurisdiction with minimal provision of services.

There is no question, as government sociologist Clark Tibbitts says, that some older people "appear to find satisfaction in these planned [i.e., retirement] villages and apartment complexes because they enjoy the companionship of others of the same stage of life with whom they find common interests." Children under 15 are usually banned. University of Southern California investigator Maurice Hamovitch found that older people he studied do like to be with other older people; they want segregation. He was, of course, studying those who were already in retirement villages. "Some say they feel guilty in their former communities, seeing young people rush around to go to work. But now that they are in a retirement community they want to go out and play golf." It does seem likely that some of the interest in retirement communities is also a defensive counterreaction to the negative attitudes in American society toward elderly people as well as to their own considerable fear of urban crime.

Hamovitch's studies also found some anti-Semitism and racism among elderly residents.[13] Salesmen of one retirement village said there were two things residents didn't have to worry about, "colored people and mosquitoes."[14] Other prevalent attitudes are patriotism and nostalgia. There is deep sentiment about the past. Many of the names used in these communities are expressive of such feelings—a restaurant in Sun City, Arizona, for example, is called Memory Lane.

In terms of geographic location, retirement to the sunshine states is synonymous with the retirement-village movement and it often appeals to the more affluent and adventurous elderly. In general, though, old people are the least mobile of the age groups in American society.* Retirement overseas is theoretically appealing, and a number of Americans have gone to Mexico. But retiring abroad, while adventuresome, may be more difficult for the elderly than for young people because of problems of health care, transportation and other necessities. Moreover, the declining value of the dollar has been devastating to the lives of many overseas retirees.

There have been very critical descriptions of retirement communities. Calvin Trillin described the Del E. Webb Development Corporation's creation of Sun City near Phoenix, Arizona, in 1960: "[The] Sun City formula for happiness . . . is roughly that happiness equals activity plus friendliness."[15] He observes that the activities director and the public-relations men stationed in Sun City seem to divide their time about equally in trying to

---

* In the year that ended March, 1971, 8.7 percent (1.7 million) older people moved from one residence to another. Only 1.4 percent, however, moved across a state line.

make the residents happy and telling them how happy they are. Members of the Webb marketing department know a great deal about the people who live in Sun City, and especially those who might be induced to live there. For example, "the foreign born are difficult to lure to Sun City no matter where they live, apparently because they still maintain the custom of having the old people remain with their families." Sun City appears to find this an archaic, primitive view.

The California builder Ross W. Cortese developed Rossmoor Leisure Worlds in California, New Jersey and Maryland. The individual gets a forty-year mortgage insured by the FHA and has single "easy" monthly payments, which amortize the home mortgage, cover the principal, interest, taxes, insurance, maintenance, use of all community facilities, and 80 percent of some health coverage. The lower-limit age group accepted is 50 years. In some respects these retirement communities have the character of a vacation resort, offering swimming, golfing, riding and hobby shops. But the houses do provide architectural aids for older people, such as helper bars in baths and a gradual rise on stairs, and by and large they are much more attractive than any of the suburban subdivisions available for the middle class. Residents have been able to build equity and get their money back if they decide to move. They can bequeath their titles. The colonies stress in their advertising the problems of crime and violence in the world outside, and the good value offered, pointing out the tight-money situation with the high cost of financing, and the major inflationary trends of the economy. They note the presence of security guards to stop unwanted door-to-door salesmen and solicitors as well as intruders and teenage gangs. As Wolf von Eckhardt has said, "Selling a complete and attractive community is better business than selling only housing."[16]

The general American private housing business has rarely been willing to move in the direction of age-integrated communities. The Levitt Development Corporation featured a full-page advertisement with a picture of children and text that read:

Allow us to introduce the species we know as children.
You'll find both parents and children at Palm Coast and that should tell you something about our community and what it will be like. You see, Palm Coast isn't really a retirement community.[17]

But Palm Coast is an exception. Old-timers are rarely found in other Levitt towns.

Life-care residences or housing projects for the old are another form of segregation, which on the continuum of housing need may make some sense when they provide comprehensive care up to the end of life. Founders' or entrance fees range from $10,000 to $57,000* (in effect, the tenant's share of the building cost of the project). Monthly costs run from $240 to $595. In 1965, in one such life-care housing project, $22,000 was the founder's fee to provide a life lease on a two-room ground-level apartment, with air conditioning, wall-to-wall carpeting and drapes, together with lifetime medical care. In addition there was a $230 per person monthly maintenance fee which would cover food in the central dining room, heat, electricity, local phone service, linen, laundry and weekly maid service. Upon death the founder's fee would become the property of the sponsor of the community. The resident had up to one year after entry to decide if he wished to leave and receive a refund of his founder's fee, less 2 percent per month. Profit-making companies develop and run life-care projects like this for various church groups.

In summing up the movement toward retirement communities, it does not seem valid to generalize about whether old people do best with people of all age groups or only with their own age group. It depends very much on the individual. Robert Fulton of the University of Minnesota has said, "The retirement city movement is another strategy [of society] to cope with death. It in fact segregates and isolates those most likely to die, allowing us to avoid [facing the fact] of death almost entirely."[18] Fulton believes that nursing homes, rest homes, hospitals for the chronically ill and retirement communities in Florida and Arizona are "sort of elephant graveyards" where old people wait until they die. This is too global a condemnation, since retirement communities do serve as a useful option to those elderly who prefer them. It is my own conviction, however, that in an increasingly open society, where the old are accepted and welcomed, many will prefer to remain integrated with people of other age groups, just as with different social classes, ethnic groups and races. But this conviction, while perhaps ideally a part of long-range public policy, should not be used to subvert the individual decision of those older persons who choose retirement-community living.

MOBILE HOMES—STOPGAPS OR PERMANENT SHELTER?

The Nixon administration stated in April of 1970 that the nation's housing goals—set at 26 million new units between 1968 and 1978—could be met only if they also included the production of four million mobile homes.[19] The counting of mobile homes represented a sharp departure from

---

* Fee systems that require turning over all of one's assets still exist but are much less common than in the past.

past practices. When Congress first set the housing goal in 1968 it did not anticipate relying on new mobile homes to meet the target. But the production of low-cost mobile homes—the average price is about $6,000—has skyrocketed, stimulated by the increasing cost and the dwindling supply of regular homes. By 1970 mobile-home firms were manufacturing 450,000 units a year, more than four times the number they produced in the early 1960s. Most purchasers now use mobile homes as permanent residences by placing them in special parks. The 1969 Housing Act gave the Federal Housing Administration authority to guarantee loans on both new mobile-home purchases and land purchases for mobile-home parks.

It is difficult for most of us to escape the old mental image of the ugly trailer court of the 1930s and to see mobile housing as one variety of stable and aesthetic environment we find acceptable for our population. Trailer parks have been and often still are notorious for their tacky image and transient look. There are no national standards for mobile homes, and fire and safety hazards are real.

Those who live in mobile homes are living a special life style with a culture all its own.[20] Studies have shown that, despite being cramped for space, many people enjoy mobile-home life. Mobile-home owners apparently move no more frequently than the rest of the population, thus belying the image of transiency.

When one considers the perspective of the life cycle in thinking about housing, one observes that most mobile home owners are young married couples or retired people. These groups can least afford higher-priced homes and presumably—consciously or unconsciously—most do not plan to remain in mobile homes for long, the young expecting to move on, the elderly anticipating their deaths.

Mobile homes tend to depreciate at least 10 percent in value the first year and continue to depreciate to half their original value in eight years. Houses in stable neighborhoods, on the other hand, are more apt to appreciate. The total monthly costs of a mobile home tend to be higher than is generally realized.[21]

Mobile homes do not require repainting and other repairs, which makes it easier for older people to maintain them. They may be financed as one does automobiles, with 20 to 30 percent down and ten years to pay. Rents at mobile-home parks had been low, varying from $35 to $55 per month, but by 1972 they were spiraling.[22] There are no property taxes in most places, but one has to have a motor-vehicle license. By 1970 there were some 22,000 parks across the United States (with relatively few in the Northeast, where there has been resistance against such parks). Mobile homes are easy to build since they are free of local building codes and restrictive labor practices.* Prices are cheap, from $3,500 to $10,000 each. By 1970 some six million Americans, or 2.75 percent of the United States population, lived in mobile homes. The 1970 census showed that mobile homes accounted for an increasing share of rural housing; for example, from 1 to 6 percent in Georgia and 5 to 10 percent in Delaware. Mobile homes should not be accepted as a wide-scale housing alternative to more substantial homes.

HIGH-RISES

High-rises as well as mobile homes, as presently designed, are questionable as suitable and safe living quarters for older people. Too many residential high-rises have a "potential for catastrophe." The newest towering buildings are built around a central core, which concentrates elevators, heat and plumbing pipes, electrical wiring and air-conditioning ducts in a central shaft. If a fire occurs heat and smoke are drawn to the core and sucked up to other floors. Elevators and sometimes stairwells become unusable and, in fact, death traps. Some building codes emphasize the protection of structures over the protection of human life. In November, 1972, ten elderly persons died in an eleven-story modern "fire-resistive" Atlanta high-rise home for the aged. There was no sprinkler system, yet the building was in full compliance with local and state fire codes.

To date there are no national standards for high-rise buildings. Such standards should include ceiling-mounted automatic sprinkler systems, smoke-control devices, and systems designed to contain a fire at its point of origin. Construction and furnishings (such as carpeting, upholstery, curtains and plastic materials) must be evaluated for their flammability and the possibility of producing flammable gases or acrid killing smoke.[23]

COMMUNES

Several communes for the elderly have emerged in the United States. One of these is comprised of twelve active oldsters who live together in a mansion in Winter Park, Florida. Ranging in age from 71 to 94, they share the work and expenses in the old house in a communal arrangement. Their organization, called Share Home Association, came under court challenge because of neighborhood zoning problems, but after a visit to the commune the circuit court judge ruled in their favor.

It is impossible to predict whether the commune movement will attract increasing numbers of older people. Aside from the problems inherent in

---

* Mobile homes are the oldest industrialized type of housing in this country.

group living, communes made up entirely of older people would be faced with the physical and emotional stresses brought on by aging and eventual death of members. Age-integrated communes might be a more viable arrangement, with younger members to counterbalance the elderly. Communal life could be especially helpful to older women, so often widowed, lonely, frequently destitute and always vulnerable to crime.

WHY A HOUSING SHORTAGE?

Why is there a shortage of decent housing within the income levels of older people? The system of financing housing, which relies on private builders even for publicly subsidized housing and which encourages profiteering through depreciation allowances, tax and mortgage interest, and deductions for property owners, is one of the several causes of the housing shortage affecting people of all ages.* The deductibility of mortgage-interest payments and real-estate taxes from taxable income on federal returns amounts to $3.5 billion and $3.3 billion respectively, according to revised figures given to the Congressional Joint Committee on Internal Revenue Taxation by the U.S. Treasury in 1973. This $6.8 billion in lost federal tax revenues, if collected, could go a long way toward creating new housing or providing housing subsidies for the underprivileged, including the elderly.

Tax policies encourage landlords to put up as little cash as possible and mortgage their property heavily. The builder† tries to move fast, build quickly and sell early without any interest in long-range maintenance. Thus tax laws have encouraged landlord and builder speculation.[24]

There has been a basic failure in housing planning. One solution is offered in a 1972 statement on National Growth Policy by the American Institute of Architects (AIA). It came out strongly for public acquisition and preparation of land in advance of any development. The AIA's new concept for land utilization would have federal and state governments begin immediately to acquire one million acres of land within the centers of cities and in the metropolitan periphery. Appreciation over a thirty-year period would be enough to cover the original cost and a large proportion of the cost of preparing land for development.

The shortage of mortgage money off and on from 1966 has been another major factor in the housing scarcity. The problem of tight money relates to

---

* Since World War II building has been the nation's number-two industry, accounting for 10 percent of the GNP—and yet over 25 percent of Americans remain ill housed. (Food production is the number-one industry.)

† Realtors favor direct housing subsidies to help people in the private housing market. Builders prefer subsidies for new housing. Thus we see the complexities of competing profit-oriented interests.

the competition from a variety of sectors—business, consumers, even government—for credit.

Still another problem is that of restrictive trade unions. At a 1968 meeting with AFL-CIO President George Meany, HUD Secretary George Romney blamed the nation's failure to keep pace with its housing needs largely on high wage rates and restrictive work practices of the building-trades unions. Meany is said to have retorted that labor ranks fourth among the major costs of building—behind mortgage money, land and material, in that order.[25]

Many unions favor restrictive work practices that keep costs high when improved technology could lower them—two small examples are restricting the width of paint brushes and the refusal of carpenters to install prefabricated doors. There are rigid craft demarcation lines that slow down work and curb efficiency. But clearly blame can't be placed entirely on the unions. Construction-company management has been very slow to modernize the use of "systems building" to maximize production.* Mass-produced housing was proposed by Archibald MacLeish as early as 1932 in his book *Housing America.* The Nixon administration's HUD program Operation Breakthrough has been an effort to test industrialized, factory-built housing. This is an assembly-line production of "modular" sections of housing which are then transported to the building site and assembled. It differs greatly from conventional building techniques. Precasting, prefabrication and other aspects of mass production are useful for the making of component parts and for techniques of assembly. Large companies have been stimulated to new efforts by Operation Breakthrough. "Systems building," like tract development, can result in monotonous replication of housing, but at this point, sadly, the demands for immediate shelter would seem to supersede aesthetics.

Unstandardized building codes are an obstacle to our housing supply. Plumbing, carpentry and electrical requirements are so variable that it makes the manufacture of uniform items difficult and complicates the training of the plumbers, carpenters and electricians.

Zoning practices designed to preserve the status quo have discriminated against various social and racial groups. Zoning has also been used to restrict housing as well as facilities and services for the aged, including public housing, nursing homes and homes for the aging. Zoning has not been used directly against individual elderly home owners, but it has an indirect effect when it restricts density. High density is necessary to support services and low-income groups.

---

* It is interesting that the origin of the assembly-line techniques for housing started in Europe and not in the United States. The European assembly-line methods came into being in the aftermath of World War II bombs and shellfire.

Zoning was first introduced in the United States in 1916 (in New York City) to regulate land use. It was seen as a tool to implement planning and the orderly development of land but was a limited concept that tended to segregate industry, commerce and residence. Since then it has often been used as a method of protecting residential areas from "undesirables." In recent years, this includes the elderly in institutions.

In Washington, D.C., the Baptist Home for the Aging, even though composed almost exclusively of white residents, was turned down in its bid to expand its facility in a white neighborhood. Public housing moving into white northwest Washington, D.C., was met with community opposition that reflected negative attitudes not only toward the poor and black but toward the elderly.[26] A developer of long-care facilities whose future residents were persons with net worths of between $150,000 and $250,000 met the same kind of response.[27] Distaff House, a retirement home for the wives of army officers in Washington, D.C., was opposed. The National Council of Senior Citizens was fought in its efforts to build a special housing complex for the elderly in Montgomery County, Maryland, in 1971. Through zoning restrictions Arlington County, Virginia, remained (as of 1973) the only metropolitan jurisdiction in the United States without a nursing home or housing project for the elderly even though it has the highest percent of elderly persons in the Washington suburbs.

Zoning decisions are often made in secret. Hearings should be open and formal with sworn witnesses and cross-examination. Zoning boards which review requests for variances from zoning regulations have many deficiencies in their procedures. Because zoning has been so entangled in local politics, state governments have been moving to control local land-use policies. Hawaii created a State Land Use Commission in 1961. Since then California, Vermont, Maine and Massachusetts have legislated land-use regulation. Comprehensive state and local master planning and public accountability should replace local zoning politics.

In some states there have also been a few efforts to establish nonprofit community-controlled urban and suburban development corporations with the power to bypass the more obstructionistic zoning ordinances and building codes, in order to acquire and develop large masses of land for the common good.

WHAT HAS THE GOVERNMENT DONE ABOUT HOUSING?

The landmark federal legislation directed at meeting the national needs for housing and community development for older Americans began with the Housing Act of 1937, which established the low-rent public-housing program. The Housing Act of 1949 set the national goal of a "decent home and a suitable living environment for every American family." It also initiated the ill-fated urban-renewal program. The Housing Act of 1954 set up special Federal Housing Administration (FHA) insurance programs for private housing in urban-renewal areas, established the requirement of a workable program for community improvement, and launched the program of urban-planning grants. The Housing Act of 1961 initiated the FHA program of below-market interest-rate financing for housing for families of moderate income. The Housing and Urban Development Act of 1965 established a rent-supplement program for private housing for low-income families. The Demonstration Cities and Metropolitan Development Act of 1966 promoted a Model Cities program for comprehensive attacks on the problem of blight and deprivation in towns and cities. The Housing and Urban Development Act of 1968 was passed with impressive bipartisan support and was the most far-reaching measure to be enacted in the area of housing and community development. Among other things it expanded the programs of urban renewal, public housing, rent supplements and Model Cities.

Despite these legislative measures enacted over a period of three decades, actual progress has been inadequate. During the same period of time the nation's population has increased, its housing stock has deteriorated, cities have decayed and the demographic structure of the population has changed: the old, the poor and minority groups and particularly the blacks continue to live in cities and in rural pockets of poverty, while affluent and upwardly mobile ethnic groups have moved into the suburbs. Expanded federal highway systems and the FHA home-mortgage program, with its emphasis upon individual home ownership, have proved to be public-policy decisions which have had massive impact on the decay of the cities and expansion of suburbs.

Congress's housing program in 1949 mandated 135,000 low-rent public-housing units per year. Had that goal been met, by 1968 there would have been 2,575,000 such units. But instead only 667,249 units had been completed, according to the President's Commission on Urban Problems chaired by former Senator Paul Douglas (D.-Ill.).* Indeed, since the very beginning of government-supported public housing in 1939 the total number of units constructed had reached only about one million units by 1972.†

* The National Commission on Urban Problems was appointed in 1967 by President Lyndon B. Johnson, who called for the creation of a commission to generate "ideas and instruments for a revolutionary improvement in the quality of the American city."

† The two years which saw the greatest number of public-housing units produced came three years after the 1949 act, during the Eisenhower administration.

Congress continued to try to resolve the housing problem, in part spurred by the Douglas Commission. The 1968 Housing Act, with its ten-year goal of 26.5 million new housing units, was considered to be of landmark significance. Out of 25.5 million new units specified (the other 1 million are subsidized rehabilitations, and an additional 1.7 million nonsubsidized rehabilitations were not included in the overall figure), 13.5 million were to accommodate new family formations. Six million of these units were to be for low- and moderate-income families. Some 600,000 units were to be built each year.

Since one-fifth of the poor are elderly the Senate Special Committee on Aging* proposed 120,000 units per year for the elderly. At that rate, however, it would take over twenty years to replace inadequate units, and since actual building has been slower than called for, the present rate alters the figure to twenty-three years. Older people do not have twenty-three years to wait!

Indeed, government programs have actually resulted in a loss of available housing. The 1968 Douglas Commission wrote: "Government action through urban renewal, highway programs, demolitions and public housing centers, code enforcement and other programs have destroyed more housing for the poor than the government at all levels has built for them."

At any one time, the demand for housing is based on the number of net new family formations on the one hand and the number of units that leave the housing supply on the other.† By 1970 the number of net new family formations was moving along at an annual rate of about 1.3 million. In the same year the number of housing units that were deteriorating or destroyed ran between 600,000 and 700,000 units each year. Thus, the housing demand per year would run about 2 million units, exclusive of the previous accumulated housing deficit.

Senator Harrison A. Williams, Jr. (D.-N.J.), said in August of 1970:

It is a national disgrace that the United States is falling far behind other nations in providing better housing. Last year the United States built 7.69 new housing units per 1000 residents. By way of contrast, Sweden built 13.45 units per 1000. Japan built 11.89, the Soviet Union built 9.80, the Netherlands built 9.63, and France built 8.23.‡

---

* As well as the conferees at the 1971 White House Conference on Aging.

† Household formation gives one a sense of the way in which the life cycle interrelates with the environment. The baby boom is over; the marriage boom is on. Post–World War II babies are now married. Household formation which averaged about 900,000 per year in the sixties reached 1.3 million early in the 1970s. Housing for young families (apartments and moderate-priced homes) will be seen on the real-estate market for some time.

‡ A number of countries have made special arrangements for the elderly. For example, the Danish government requires that any housing development constructed

URBAN RENEWAL—THE DESTRUCTION OF HOUSING

A survey of urban renewal between 1949 and December 31, 1968, by the General Accounting Office showed that the government spent $7 billion but managed to cause a net loss of 315,000 housing units.[28] The same report demonstrates how the program was used against the poor minorities, essentially on behalf of the rich. For every unit that it put up, urban renewal tore down 3.5 units. In their place went high-rise apartment buildings for the affluent in the downtown areas. Between 1937 and 1968 only 650,000 units of low-income housing were built compared to over 10 million middle- and upper-class dwellings.

Urban renewal was meant to remove slums but it became a ruthless blitz. Neighborhoods were wiped out. Downtown demolition destroyed small businesses, many of which were run by older people, and lifeless, dull downtown areas filled with buildings that emptied at 5 P.M. were no attraction for people after a day's work.[29]

Typically, areas cleared for projects were made up of one-half to one-third elderly residents, and most of them were never rehoused in the ensuing construction of new buildings in their old neighborhoods. Many were forced to relocate elsewhere.

Joan Colebrook wrote movingly about urban renewal in the south end of Boston.[30] She observed "social workers trying to provide some moral support for impoverished and isolated older people who found themselves in the way of the bulldozers." She wrote of old people trying to survive in their rundown neighborhoods, amid abandoned and substandard housing, garbage-strewn empty lots and dimly lighted streets, the victims of muggings and purse snatchings. Personal accumulations of a lifetime were often thrown into the streets by city representatives if the elderly owner was away from home or hospitalized when urban renewal was about to begin. She discussed the effects of relocation on death and illness in the elderly. It is well known that the aged are "more vulnerable to the shocks and losses attendant on relocation."[31]

Benefits from the Uniform Relocation Assistance and Real Property Acquisition Policies Act of 1970, while a step forward, really do not provide adequately for the displaced. Individuals forced to move can collect only up to $300 in moving expenses. Displaced businessmen and farm owners can receive only between $2,500 and $10,000. Tenants who have

---

under either private or government auspices must reserve 10 percent of the total number of units for the elderly. Nonetheless, many other nations, just as we, have not solved the housing problem of their older population.

been displaced are eligible for $1,000 annually and limited rent supplements for four years. To encourage home ownership the legislation provides at least $2,000 down payment on a home for displaced individuals. These figures are not realistic in today's economy. More generous arrangements for relocation are necessary, with equitable financial reimbursement and adequate moving assistance.

THE 202 CONTROVERSY

Section 202 of the National Housing Act of 1959 authorized a program of direct loans from the federal government to nonprofit sponsors who desired to provide housing for the elderly and handicapped. Sponsoring religious and benevolent organizations could borrow up to 100 percent of project cost and repay the loan with 3 percent interest over fifty years.

A great deal of controversy emerged in the early 1970s over the Nixon administration's effort to phase out the Section 202 direct-loan program. Over a ten-year period only 45,000 units were built under the program, but many who utilized it were convinced that it was an economical way of obtaining good housing. Despite the relative success of the 202 program the Federal Housing Administration succeeded in phasing it out in 1969* and substituted instead Section 236 of the National Housing Act of 1968 (multifamily units), which requires sponsors to go to the private money market for capital and simply offers interest subsidy, on a sliding scale allowing the rate to be as little as 1 percent if a maximum number of limited-income tenants are to be housed there. The purpose of the change was to hold down immediate government outlays of funds, bring all department programs under one system and avoid competition with private enterprise. Under Section 236 the government pays all interest above 1 percent for the life of the mortgage, usually forty years. This is an enormously expensive program.

Senator Harrison A. Williams and his Special Committee on Aging fought the phasing-out of 202 in favor of 236. The committee was impressed by 1969 testimony of a St. Petersburg, Florida, housing consultant, Robert P. Renfrow. Renfrow projected that a $2.8 million project under way at Raleigh, North Carolina, for example, would cost the government $7 million under Section 236 but would cost $2.6 million under Section 202.

Section 236 is expensive in yet another way. There are a number of fees that must be paid to the FHA (including examination, inspection, financing,

---

* Congress did appropriate money to continue Section 202, but the administration did not use it.

brokerage fees) that were not paid under Section 202. Finally, there is revenue loss to the government, because tax shelters are provided for high-income people who invest in 236 housing. In effect, what happens is that, rather than lending money itself, the government pays people to invest in the housing that it presumably wants built.

The Reverend Richard L. Fullerton, an Atlanta housing consultant, called the 236 subsidy program a "gift to the mortgage bankers." Other complaints are that it provides quick profits for builders and investors and encourages poor construction. Rents tend to be as much as 30 percent higher for 236; local taxes were abated under nonprofit sponsorship of 202, whereas 236 private development is fully taxed.

Dr. M. Powell Lawton, an expert in the field of housing for the elderly, expressed before the Special Committee on Aging his concern on the organizational downgrading of policy voices for the elderly and the death blow to the highly successful 202 program. He stated:

"My conviction is that a specialized program for the elderly is necessary. It is based solely on the point of view that a disadvantaged group needs extra assistance in order to be raised to an equal level to favored groups. The elderly clearly are one such minority." Lawton also proposed "active equalization measures" to rectify the imbalance in racial composition in subsidized housing.[32]

The 1971 White House Conference on Aging, the Democratic members of the Senate Committee on Aging, the Chairman of the House Republican Task Force on Aging, Representative Robert Steele (R.-Conn.), religious organizations and many housing experts have recommended a return of Section 202. Due largely to the efforts of Representative Steele, a revised 202 program became law in 1974.

MODEL CITIES

The idea for Model Cities was conceived in 1966 after it became obvious that the Vietnam war would prevent any massive allocation of funds to rebuild cities. The Johnson administration decided that it would demonstrate in some cities how particularly deteriorating neighborhoods could be thoroughly renewed through a concentration of federal, local and private funds, services and facilities. These were to be locally administered. Residents of the neighborhoods themselves were to share in the decisions. As of January, 1970, fifty-eight cities had approved Model Cities programs; but then Commissioner of Aging John B. Martin pointed out that of 193 Model Cities applications reviewed originally, there were only two—those of

Seattle and Denver—that contained plans for meeting the problems of the aging. Martin stated:

> I am not necessarily advocating the establishment of a large number of new special age-segregated services for older people only. Instead I am asking for assurance that wherever there is a program for people, older people are included in its planning, in its detailed design, and in a fair share of its services and opportunities—not the least of which is an opportunity to serve.[33]

Over 400,000 persons aged 65 and over lived in the first 75 cities under the Model Cities program, and older persons in Model Cities target areas range from 10 to 50 percent of the population. Nonetheless, as Senate hearings reveal, the needs of the elderly in Model Cities are not being considered.[34]

THE CREATION OF NEW TOWNS

The concept of "new towns" refers to the planning and creation of complete communities where none existed before. The idea is not a new one. Plato, an early philosopher of new towns, and Leonardo da Vinci, who proposed a satellite community for Milan in 1484, were among the earliest thinkers about new communities. The utopian movement (as witness Sir Thomas More and Edward Bellamy) had close ties with the physical conceptions of new towns. It was not until this century, however, that new towns became a focused effort to resolve the problems of increasing population, industrialization and the decay of cities. They offer the promise of new housing forms to the elderly as well as all other age groups.

Modern city planning began with Ebenezer Howard and the garden-city movement. England's Welwyn and Letchworth were pioneer new towns. Many other countries in Europe have built new towns, and the Soviet Union has created some three hundred new towns since the Revolution. One of the most impressive new communities is Finland's Tapiola,* a nonprofit town. America's Radburn,† under Clarence Stein's direction, and the three government-sponsored Greenbelt towns of the Depression were early American contributions to planning concepts in new towns. Direct federal sponsorship of new communities began in 1917 to meet housing shortages near war industries; this was followed by World War II "bomber communities," such as Willow Run, Michigan, and later atomic-energy towns like Los Alamos, New Mexico.

---

* Tapiola was started in 1952 and geared for 20,000 inhabitants. Only 243 of its 670 acres are actually covered by homes and skyscraper apartment buildings.

† The Radburn concepts, for example, include the superblock, greenbelts, designed neighborhoods and the separation of people and cars through pedestrian pathways.

The New Communities Act (Title VII) of 1968 and 1970 created a major U.S. federal program to promote orderly growth for the projected national population increase through the formation of new towns. The act's regulations include provision for "the creation of a substantial number of jobs" and for services, education, health and recreation. Indeed, the total concept is of a social as well as physical community.*

One of the great contributions of New Communities Act money will be to help meet the massive costs of land acquisition, creation of an underground utilities, and the provision of necessary public facilities and services *before* there is adequate population to support them. Title VII may provide up to $50 million for a single community. Its loan guarantees constitute a potentially major step forward in new-town development. The first new town to receive Title VII money was Jonathan, Minnesota, near Minneapolis.†

The 1970 American Institute of Architects Report on Urban Growth Policy recommended the "creation of 100 new communities averaging 100,000 population each and ten communities of at least one million population" outside existing cities. New towns *inside* cities as well as outside of them could add much to the revitalization of cities, particularly if complemented by restoration of salvageable old neighborhoods—unlike the bulldozer approach of previous urban-renewal programs.

The integration of the elderly into new towns is still in the experimental stage. One new town which has been quite disappointing as far as the elderly are concerned is the difficult, controversial Fort Lincoln "new town in town" in Washington, D.C., where the first buildings, completed in 1970, were for the elderly. The elderly were left isolated, devoid of immediate social, medical and other services when further building was delayed. Fort Lincoln, which was the idea of President Johnson in 1968, was slowed down by the change of national administration, local political infighting, planning disputes and budgetary limits.

I have had the interesting experience of participating in a task force founded to implement a philosophy for a new town:

> A Prince George's County tobacco farmer who died in 1959 willed nearly a mile square of land for the benefit of retired clergymen in the

---

* One of the problems of the new towns has been the narrow socioeconomic band of residents. The Reston, Virginia, buyer, for example, has averaged between 30 and 40 years of age, is white, the head of the family with two children, and has an income of $17,000.

† Unfortunately, the limited amounts of money made available under Title VII, combined with inflation, so affected new-town development that in January, 1975, HUD shelved all pending applications. It will continue to help fund those new towns already in the federal program.

Washington Episcopal Diocese and his own parish. Rather than use the land only for retired clergy, the Bishop and his task force decided to create a new community emphasizing the life cycle as a whole and the achievement of social values.[35] Its residents would be of varied ages, races, socio-economic levels and religions. To take into account and to match the characteristics of people throughout the course of the life cycle, with appropriate social, institutional and environmental processes and arrangements is one of the major theoretical goals of this town.

Because of zero land cost and non-commercial goals, there would be greater opportunities to fulfill social purposes. Many technical developments such as the Radburn concept of minimizing vehicular interference would be utilized. Great emphasis would be placed upon a prosthetic and aesthetic environment which would maximize the safety, security and social intercourse among age groups. At the hub would be a multi-purpose conference center and hotel available for national and local organizations of a secular or religious nature and small research organizations who have long desired a meeting place with cultural amenities, library facilities, audio-visual aids and research resources.

All new towns should be self-sustaining to some degree; but not "islands." It is hoped that the conference center and libraries and health care and other programs will employ a sizable percentage of the population, including older people.

THE NIXON FREEZE

In January, 1973, the Nixon administration suddenly froze all subsidies for low- and middle-income housing construction, including public housing. It also ended the rent-supplement program that assisted the poor in obtaining better shelter. A moratorium was placed on new commitments for water and sewer grants, open-space grants and public-facility loans. As of July, 1973, the hold-down covered urban renewal, Model Cities and, indirectly, the development of new communities.

The administration did not offer immediate substitutes. It claimed revenue sharing would ultimately be the funding mechanism for urban renewal, water and sewer monies, and other elements of "community development." There were clearly things wrong with the New Deal, Fair Deal, Great Society programs, one being that they had never really been adequately financed. But there were also waste, corruption, ugliness and poor planing, all of which gave the administration ample rationalization for their stringency.

In 1974 Congress passed a $11.9 billion Housing and Community Development Act which is neither comprehensive nor innovative. It provides public housing and subsidy programs and $8.6 billion authorizing block grants over three years to communities to replace ten existing categorical programs such as urban renewal, Model Cities, open-space acquisition and sewage treatment plant development. Construction of senior-citizen centers and projects to remove architectural barriers are authorized. For those three years, no city is to receive less than it has been getting. With less federal control by way of specific revenue sharing, local governments would have greater flexibility. Funds would be allocated on the basis of population, overcrowding and poverty, with poverty doubly weighted.

This same act includes Congressman Steele's amendment that renewed the popular and successful 202 housing for the elderly program. Eight hundred million dollars ($800,000,000) in loans for developers of housing was authorized.

THE OLD CAN'T WAIT FOR HOUSING

What can be done *now* to meet the immediate and future housing needs of older Americans? Nearly all housing in the United States has been built with public assistance,* but the government has not been effective in providing shelter for those with low incomes, especially the elderly, minority groups and the poor. The old cannot wait. Clearly massive housing production is indicated.

Until the income-maintenance problem of the elderly has been solved, housing subsidies must be available.† The formula that a person must not pay more than 25 percent of his income for housing may need to be adjusted according to local socioeconomic conditions. In order to broaden choice, housing payments must not be tied to specific buildings. There must be control of some rents or else a wave of rent increases is likely to follow upon the inauguration of housing payments on a national basis. There should be national housing standards in order to reduce the possibility of shoddy construction designed to cash in on the massiveness of the program.

The existing housing supply could absorb some but not all of the elderly through the provision of direct money payments or through the direct provision of rent or housing subsidies. A rent-supplement program does exist in Section 236 of the 1968 Housing Act, under which monthly federal

---

* Essentially *all* housing built in the United States is publicly assisted, not merely that designated as "public housing." The federal government's program of subsidy occurs through income-tax deductions of interest rates and property taxes. (The deduction amounts involved actually exceed public-housing costs, both building and maintenance.)

† In 1973 a nationwide HUD experiment in grants was begun, involving 20,000 households with persons of all ages, in two- and three-year tests of the influences of direct grants for housing upon choice of living arrangements, the market, etc.

payments are paid to property owners on behalf of low-income tenants. Payments amount to the difference between 25 percent of the tenant's gross income and the FHA-approved rental for the unit.* In order to participate in a 236 rent-supplement program, the tenant's *assets* cannot exceed $5,000. Thus, someone with a small income but with assets worth more than $5,000 would not be able to take advantage of the program.

Another solution to the housing crisis for the elderly would be direct acquisition of existing housing by local housing authorities, which would mean an expansion of the HUD acquisition program. Special direct payments and loans to families for additions to their homes and other renovations would help.

All new multi-unit housing should have at least 10 percent of its units (based on the proportion of the elderly in the general population) available for older people. Such a stricture would apply also to single-family homes in new communities being built. In view of the high incidence of poverty among the elderly, all low-income housing should have at least 20 percent of its housing earmarked for old people.

Zoning difficulties must be dealt with. The creation of independent public-housing corporations (as in New York State) is one way to give the leverage necessary to have zoning dominated by human values rather than solely by profit-motivated business interests.

The heavy weight of property taxes must no longer fall disproportionately upon the elderly and other low and fixed-income groups. A first step is property-tax reductions based on income. But there must be basic national income and property tax reform.

People of all ages, the elderly among them, must exercise greater influence. "Neighborhood control" and tenant as well as home-owner activism, in addition to legal redress of grievances, are all-important steps.

Active housing-rehabilitation programs would help older people remain in their homes as well as maintain housing that may be old and beautiful and of special historic and ethnic character. The elderly need assistance with day-by-day maintenance and repairs as well as with major rehabilitation from time to time.

In some places home-repair programs carried out by the elderly themselves† have been set up for rehabilitation of the homes of the elderly poor. The creation of a National Community Service Corps (see Chapter 4) should include within it a national repair corps, which might be com-

---

* Mr. John Carter, 76, had an income of $130 a month. A fair rent on his apartment was established to be $100 a month. He had to pay $32.50, and $67.50 in rent supplement was paid by the 236 program.

† For example, in Patinsville, Kentucky, in 1971.

posed of persons of different ages who would provide special help in the repair and rehabilitation of housing for the elderly and disabled.

The interrelatedness of services with housing is another consideration. Marie McGuire, expert on housing for the elderly, emphasizes: "We certainly need to . . . have a variety of services for old people . . . so that the older person knows where to go in his community for services . . . hopefully as part of the fabric of the neighborhood just as the school is to the child."[36]

The older person cannot function in a vacuum. Like the younger person, the older person needs a network of services, including recreation, education and health care. Otherwise his chances of functioning independently in the community lessen. At least in part, the social, physical and psychological needs of older people must be met in their housing and immediate environment. The old need to participate in daily life and many avail themselves of every opportunity, likely or improbable, to do so. Public facilites like the Port Authority Bus Terminal in New York take on the function of "indoor parks" for the aged who congregate there, and there are outdoor parks famous for their gatherings of older people, such as Los Angeles' MacArthur Park (near old rundown hotels and rooming houses) and Lafayette Park. Old people congregate in bus terminals, at law courts and in other indoor public places, seeking protection from the weather and diversion in their daily lives. Surely more opportunities could be provided for them to enjoy nature, their neighborhoods and the comings and goings of life around them.*

Many other services could be built directly into housing for the old. Campuslike arrangements that offer a variety of services and facilities which take into account the changing characteristics and increasing disabilities of older people are especially practical. Each older person goes through an individual time gradient of change which requires corresponding changes in his environment, and it would be sensible to anticipate such changes with appropriate services and architectural supports.

Our national housing policy has been most remiss in the provision of services. For example, sections 202 and 236 of the Federal Housing Act did not permit nursing facilities in their projects. (This was changed in 236 in 1972.) Therefore, older people have had to move when nursing care became necessary. Moreover, Congress did not authorize funds for services, so HUD programs depend upon state and local provision of

---

* One such opportunity was created by the Office of Midtown Planning and Development in New York through the use of incentive ordinances which encourage private developers to include particular types of amenities for public use.

services, which are often unavailable. It was not until 1970 that the housing act finally authorized congregate meal-service facilities in public housing, closing a major gap. Tenancy for older people should always include medical, nursing and home care, education and recreation—a whole range of services.

Architectural design must be improved in housing for the elderly and in the public buildings which they use. If barriers to the access of the physically handicapped and infirm to buildings, homes and transportation were eliminated, it would be a sign of a changing national sensibility toward the realities of the old and disabled. A federal law requires that any building constructed in part or in whole from federal funds must be "architecturally barrier-free,"[37] that is, accessible to the handicapped. But, law or not, buildings with barriers continue to be built with federal funds. For example, builders save five cents a door on a volume basis by being allowed to continue building doors that are 22 to 24 inches in width, rather than building 36-inch doors which provide access for a wheelchair.

Building design should take account of new technology. Air conditioning is particularly valuable for old people who are so vulnerable to summer heat waves. Similarly, another technological advance, that of soundproofing, is important for maintaining "insulation without isolation" for older people.

Design features necessary for the aged include many that are valuable for people of all ages. Hand rails on stairs, electric-eye doors, nonskid floors, ramps, safety bars in bathrooms, sinks at proper heights, appropriate illumination and internal communication systems are useful to everyone. Children, pregnant women, the disabled and the handicapped of all ages —not just the elderly—would welcome such design features. But we have much more to learn about various aspects of our home. Alexander Kira, professor of architecture at Cornell, studied one room in the home, the bathroom, and gathered information of value to the old in terms of health and safety.[38] The same could be done for other rooms.

We also need more studies of human behavior in relation to the personal and social use of space, a subject which anthropologist Edward Hall has termed "Proxemics."[39] Studies of the relationships of physical design and behavior (such as sociability and communication) in the elderly are relatively rare.[40]

The lack of research on the relationship of our social institutions to physical design is notable. In the Department of Housing and Urban Development and elsewhere there should be a vast expansion of funds to rectify this. Research must especially examine man as he moves through the course of the life cycle. Housing ought to be planned to dovetail more effectively with life's successive stages: rearing of a family, the emptying of the nest, retirement and leisure, illness and disability.

Economic and technological advances must be implemented in meeting the housing needs of all Americans, including older Americans. The latter, of course, need instant housing, for they live within a limited time perspective. New economic programs and policies, particularly economic pluralism, with mixes of public and private monies, might prove effective where public efforts and private enterprise alone have failed. A truly adequate national housing policy, however, must take a longer time frame. Such a policy requires revitalization of cities and towns, creation of new communities, and awareness and planning for the changing demographic and age characteristics of people in the cities, suburbs and rural areas.

To help meet the objectives sketched, leadership is necessary within the Department of Housing and Urban Development. There should be an Assistant Secretary of Housing for the Aging. The needs of the elderly must be represented by an established visible component of the nation's housing agency. Only when and if the housing needs of the elderly have been met can they be included with the rest of the population rather than receive special attention.

Chapter 6

NO TIME TO WAIT

For all too long old people have had to wait endlessly for services essential to survival and to a decent and pleasurable old age. They need an effective network of facilities, programs and services to enable them to survive short-term crises and meet long-term needs. Without these supports many of them lose their capacity to live independently or semi-independently in their own homes. They wait through agonizing intervals for the doctor to visit, the homemaker to come, the hot noon meal to be delivered. Much too often they wait in vain, for the services may be totally unavailable. Then one more old person is forced to abandon his home for a nursing home, hospital or other facility, and society is burdened with another unnecessary bill for institutional care.

> The 75-year-old librarian, Henry Stein, retired and widowed, was determined to remain independent. He lived on a small income among the books and mementos in his densely cluttered apartment. He took long walks to the library and stores. He continued to write. One summer he caught cold and didn't eat well for a few days. His energy faded quickly. Somewhat confused because of poor nutrition, he forgot to shop and ran out of food. He failed to drink enough fluids. An acute brain syndrome followed, and he began to wander the streets aimlessly. People would find him and with the help of the police return him to his address. Several neighbors and the apartment manager attempted to seek help. They couldn't get a doctor to make a home visit. They were put on waiting lists by various agencies like homemakers and "meals on wheels." Meanwhile Mr. Stein could wait no longer. He had become totally incapable of caring for himself and was sent to a nursing home.

Old people need the same basic services as people of other ages—education, recreation, health care, tax assistance, social services, transportation and repairs for everything from shoes to houses. When illnesses strike, immediate home care is required. During recovery, special programs of physical, speech and other therapies may be mandatory. If alone, older people need telephone reassurance for security and contact with the outer world. To continue to live with one's family may require "respite" services —giving families occasional or systematic relief from arduous duties of caring for ill and disabled older members.

There are parts of the world where old people have less income than the American elderly, but this is compensated for by more services. Even poverty is less terrible and survival more possible when many forms of help are at hand. In the United States, government (federal, state and municipal), private nonprofit (voluntary) and commercial agencies provide services. Separately or collectively, these agencies have made some progress in the past decade but they have not been able to meet the needs of older people fully, effectively and promptly. The lack of money is one cause. A poor delivery system is another. Actually we already know how to keep people in the community but we have not really used this knowledge. We know what services older people need and that these needs are extensive. The financing and logistical problems are not insoluble. Further, when they are solved society will save money by preventing unnecessary institutionalization; and older people will have the humane benefits of choice and independence.

Now, however, services of all kinds for old people are fragmented, limited, discriminatory, inaccessible or nonexistent. When services are available their quality is questionable, and the key word, certainly, is "wait"—for one's turn or in line or on benches or at home. To get medical, social, home-care, legal, protective and recreational services old people must wait during specified times—most often the conventional office hours of nine to five on week days, since services are rarely available during evenings and weekends. We seem to assume that old people have all the time in the world to wait!

The denial of services on the basis of age is common among both governmental and voluntary agencies and reflects institutional ageism. Society seems to be saying, "They're old—they don't need much in the way of services. Don't waste resources on them. Or give them a little service now and then. That will keep them quiet and we'll have done enough." The absence of services is a fundamental indicator of a general unwillingness to provide for the disadvantaged of various ages and categories. Many of the old must become totally impoverished or so ill as to require hospitalization or institutionalization before they are regarded as "eligible" for even minimal services. They most certainly do not have the advantage of preventive services, the early diagnosis and treatment as well as routine services that would forestall the emergence of new problems and disabilities.

KINDS OF SERVICES NEEDED BY THE OLD

INFORMATION AND REFERRAL SERVICES

Centralized information and referral services for the elderly are especially needed so they and their families may know the nature and availability of specific services. People should be able to find out by phone whether they are eligible for a service, what the costs are, how to make appointments, where services are located, how to get there, and other simple but important facts. Skilled personnel should be able to assist the older caller (or his family) in deciding what help is appropriate and in gaining access for him by direct referral. They should also follow up, making home visits as necessary. They should be active advocates for the elderly.

Unfortunately, relatively few cities and localities have this essential resource. There is much lost motion. Since the late 1950s various agencies have begun offering limited information and referral, and local or state commissions on aging or advisory committees on aging have been of some help. Social services and human resources or welfare departments (the names vary in municipalities and states) usually have telephone information numbers. The 1,160 Social Security district and branch offices can provide certain information on services as can the approximately 200 family-service agencies in the United States. The local offices of the United States Department of Agriculture and the Office of Economic Opportunity are further potential sources for referral. The news media, radio and television should be playing a much more important role in the provision of information to the elderly than they have. The Federal Communications Commission should examine the frequency and adequacy with which different age groups are represented in public-service-broadcasting announcements devoted to information and referral.

HOME HEALTH SERVICES

Older people often need a wide range of services brought directly to their homes, from mental-health counseling to medical nursing; homemaking; home health, dental, protective, legal, nutritional and social services. Religious support, outpatient care, and physical, occupational and speech therapy should be available. Home care should be brought to the chronically ill, to those recuperating from hospitalization, to those who may be acutely ill but can be treated outside a hospital, and finally to all those older people who simply need some help from time to time to fill in the gaps left by declining functions and the loss of friends and relatives.

While writing a book on *Aging and Mental Health* we found in the chapter on home care that we went further than in any other chapter in describing what ideally should exist but in reality does not.[1] Just one example can be found in the homemaker–home health aides who are so crucial in keeping people at home and reducing institutionalization. The term "homemaker–home health aide" is used for one and the same person* although in some parts of the country different names are given—housekeeper, nurse's aide, etc.—and functions are divided. Homemaker–home health aides offer a wide range of services to people on either a short- or long-term basis. When assigned to home-health-aide duties they work under the supervision of nurses and take the patient's vital signs, apply simple dressings, give massage or provide physical therapy. They may be called upon to provide light cooking, housecleaning, patient hygiene and laundry. If working in a homemaker capacity they provide broader care of the home and other members of the family as well.

There is a serious shortage of homemaker–home health aides in the United States—an estimated 30,000 aides exist compared to an estimated need of 300,000. England with nearly 40 million population (one-fifth as large as the United States) has 60,000 persons serving as home helpers. Sweden with a population of 8 million has 35,000 (they're called samaritans).[2] Ethel Shanas studied home health services in five countries. In Britain and Denmark they were already well developed, while Israel and Poland, like the United States, were still developing such services.[3]

Brahna Trager, in her study for the U.S. Senate Special Committee on Aging, *Home Health Services in the United States*, in 1972, found that 54 percent of all American communities, including 99 with populations of more than 50,000, have no home-health-service agencies whatsoever. But even where agencies exist they may not be fully used. Provision has been made under both Parts A and B of Medicare† to provide 100 paid visits by a homemaker–home health aide per year. Doctors rarely authorize such care for their older patients, however, and when they do they sometimes have been faced with arbitrary retroactive denials of payment by Medicare, which has further discouraged use of the program. Less than 1 percent of Medicare expenditures went to home health care in 1971. The number of

---

* "Homemaker" describes the full range of homemaking activities available to people, while "home health aide" is a title used in Medicare regulations and describes a somewhat narrower definition of care, centered more around simple nursing and personal care.

† For a full discussion of Medicare (the government health insurance program for the elderly and disabled), see Chapter 7.

home health agencies participating in the Medicare insurance system has declined because participation has been made so difficult.*

Yet data strongly suggest that home care saves health dollars. In one study in Rochester, New York, it was found that of the 1,554 patients receiving home care in 1970, 653 (almost half) would have otherwise required hospitalization. The Associated Hospital Service (Blue Cross) of New York saved 113,000 hospital days on the first 5,000 patients admitted to home care.

Brahna Trager believes that "funding the developmental phases of home health services" is as essential to health care as is Congressional Hill-Burton funding of hospital building. In other words, as much attention needs to be paid to the development of home care as has been paid to the construction of hospitals and nursing homes in the American health-care system. A National Personal Care Corps should be created to provide adequate manpower and to help end the traditional jurisdictional disputes by educating jacks-of-all-trades. Members should have in-service training and open-ended career ladders.

Physicians' house calls are another home service sorely needed but unavailable to most of the elderly. From 1957-58 doctors made between 45 and 47 million calls, but in 1966-67 they made 27.3 million even though the population had risen. In 1972 fewer than half the doctors in the country still made house calls, whatever the age of the patient, and most of those practiced in rural areas. Doctors claim that it is rare that a house call is really justified, and that they can give better treatment in their office or, if it is a true emergency, at the hospital. But many older people find it very difficult to get to either office or hospital. Profit-making house-call organizations have been established in a few of the larger cities such as New York and Los Angeles, but fees are extremely high, ranging from $20 to $25 per call.

The geographical maldistribution as well as an actual shortage† of doctors further hampers services to the old. The National Health Service Corps is a unit within the Health Services and Mental Health Administration of the United States Public Health Service charged with carrying out the Emergency Health Personnel Act of 1970. This act authorizes the assignment of commissioned officers and Civil Service personnel to areas in the United States where health services are inadequate. There is no

---

* Two thousand three hundred and fifty home health agencies participated in June of 1970; one year later in June of 1971 there were only 2,256 participating home health agencies.

† The United States has only one physician for every 650 people compared, for instance, to one to 500 in Italy and one to 400 in Russia.

doubt that the inner-city elderly should qualify for such care. But such assignments have not been made.

Nursing has been and continues to be one of the very few professions which routinely offer home care. Public-health nurses working for city and county health departments and visiting nurses sponsored by the Visiting Nurse Association, a voluntary health organization, are the two general groups of nurses who make house calls. The elderly either receive services free if eligible or pay a fee adjusted to their income. Unfortunately there have never been enough nurses to care for the growing elderly population, and many nursing agencies are now cutting back on staff because of restrictive Medicare regulations, curtailment of Medicaid benefits and reduced voluntary financial support.

"Visiting dentists" are beginning to appear in some communities; but because dentistry is not covered under Medicare, payments are difficult. Home delivery of physical, occupational and speech therapy is partly reimbursable under Medicare, but use is severely limited by strict eligibility requirements.

Other home services which should be routinely provided to the old involve live-in or part-time companions, help in shopping and transportation, and direct aid to support or compensate for various disabilities (for example, help in handling wheelchairs and other medical appliances).

Day care is another seldom-available but invaluable method of caring for older people who want to continue to live in their homes. It is in fact more economical for a program to have a number of older people centered in one place during the day than to send personnel out to individual homes. Day care can give respite to families who may need to provide a place for an older family member while they work. Residential facilities should also be available to care temporarily for an older person so that his family can take vacations away from home.

Multipurpose senior centers located conveniently in a community could become cornerstones for many home services as well as an important extension of "home" itself. Hospitals can be major resources for home care but too often are not. Commercial nursing homes have not taken the initiative in building programs which include home care and day care in addition to the more usual residential care. Medicare and the insurance programs for the elderly encourage hospitalization rather than home care in their coverage. Thus only the very poor may be able to get some home-care services through welfare, while self-supporting elderly tend not to be able to afford them. Free care or care based on ability to pay is only sporadically available through United Fund organizations and charitable agencies. Federal funds for the rather weak existing programs of home health aides have been cut back in the 1970s.

NUTRITION SERVICES

The nutritional needs of the reasonably healthy elderly are really little different from those of younger people. They certainly need the same proteins, vitamins and minerals—perhaps in slightly smaller quantities, but even this is debatable. When they are less active they do need fewer calories, but it should be remembered they may be less active because they have not had an adequate energy level due to malnutrition and because they have not enjoyed stimulating activities. Old people, like young, retain the capacity to build new body tissues but only if they have adequately nutritious diets. Without such diets, poorly nourished people of all ages are a greater health risk. Reversible (though ultimately irreversible) organic brain syndromes can result from malnutrition and from hypovitaminosis. Resistance to many kinds of physical disease processes is lowered. Recovery from illness can take much longer if the body is poorly nourished. Mental disorders such as depressions are exacerbated or even caused by malnutrition.

Poor eating habits can be induced by psychological conditions—loneliness, grief, apathy, confusion. Physical disabilities can make shopping and cooking difficult. Fear of crime keeps some older people from going to the grocery store. But perhaps the most widespread problem is the need to scrimp on food because of an inadequate income. A Washington *Post* article of August 9, 1973, reports:

Supermarket managers have told me that many of the heaviest dog food buyers are not pet owners but the elderly poor who can't make it on fixed incomes or food stamps when they are lucky enough to have either. So they buy dog food, mix it with ketchup, sprinkle on some onions and make a meal of it.

Malnourishment can occur at any income level:

A 95-year-old retired corporation executive lived in an exclusive apartment complex. He had outlived friends and relatives. He had an income of over $900 a month and $300,000 in assets, yet he was starving to death. His memory had become hazy and he forgot his mealtimes. No one realized he was subsisting on a few sweets and tea.

The 1969 White House Conference on Food, Nutrition and Health expressed concern about malnutrition among the elderly, but like other

White House conferences its results have been meager.[4] The President's
1970 Task Force on Aging studied the nutritional needs of the elderly
and recommended certain guidelines for future programs:

In examining the incidence of malnutrition among the elderly the Task Force
concluded that insufficient income was only one of several causes. The lonely
older person who can afford an adequate diet but does not eat properly; the
older person who finds going to the store too great a burden; the older person
who is nutritionally ignorant; the chronically ill older person unable to prepare
a hot meal—all are part of the problem. The Task Force believes that
programs can be designed which not only provide adequate nutrition to older
persons, but equally important, combat their loneliness, channel them into the
community, educate them about proper nutrition, and afford some of them
an opportunity for paid community services.[5]

The task force urgently recommended that the President direct the
Administration on Aging and the Department of Agriculture to develop
a program of technical assistance and, when necessary, financial assistance to local groups so they can provide daily meals and group dining
to the many aged who need them; and to the homebound who require
"meals on wheels." Such programs would not only meet nutritional needs
but provide meaningful employment and voluntary service for the healthy
aged who are looking for work and are discriminated against in the job
market. Moreover, older people gain immeasurably from the social setting
of communal dining.

The Administration on Aging conducted thirty-two research demonstrations in nutrition projects for the aged between 1968 and 1971. These
"pilot programs" were considered very successful and helped advance
the passage of congressional legislation for a nutrition program for the
elderly. Senator Edward M. Kennedy (D.-Mass.) and Representative
Claude Pepper (D.-Fla.) sponsored the 1972 Nutrition Program for the
Elderly Act which provides low-cost nutritious meals at conveniently
located settings for older people (defined as 60 years and above) daily.
One hundred million dollars was to be available for the fiscal year 1973
and $150 million for fiscal year 1974. However, the program did not get
under way until fiscal year 1974. An estimated 250,000 older people
would benefit, but there are more than 5 million persons over 60 years
of age who would actually qualify for the program!

It is instructive to note that the federal government spent approximately
$180 million for nursing-home care under Medicare in 1970 and about $1.3
billion on such care under Medicaid. In contrast we see the still minuscule
provision for programs that might help patients to remain at home.

In the nutrition bill, money is provided only for food, not for equipment, so the sponsoring agency must still raise funds. This, of course, tends to favor the middle- and lower-middle class over the poor; it is much easier, for example, for middle-class churches to obtain funds than for churches serving the poorer black communities or inner-city elderly. Old people are encouraged to pay 50 cents daily for the program, but for many this is a hardship.

Most current and past food programs have been legislated by the House and Senate Agriculture Committees and administered under the Department of Agriculture. The House and Senate Agriculture Committees have consistently dragged their feet on all nutritional and food proposals unless they benefited certain special interests. Federal school lunches, for example, came into being after World War II chiefly as a means of dissipating farm surpluses.

The commodity food program, administered by the Department of Agriculture, has been inept:

The Department of Agriculture has evidenced virtually no awareness of the particular needs of older people. . . . The very acts of placing surplus commodity depots in locations most inaccessible to the relatively immobile urban aged; the packaging of such commodities in quantities unsuited to use by the single aged; the published food guides which few elderly can or feel inclined to read suggest some insensitivity to the needs of this major population group.[6]

On the other hand there is no doubt that the food-stamp program, initiated through a congressional act of 1964, has served many thousands of elderly persons denied access to an adequate diet without such assistance. By 1972 as many as 2.5 million older Americans were involved either in the food-stamp or the food-distribution program. These figures exaggerate the actual amounts and quality of additional food provided, but they indicate that a significant number of elderly received some benefit. Cost-of-living adjustments were annual until the summer of 1973; now they are semiannual. However, deficiencies in the program keep many older people from participating; there are often transportation problems in getting to and from sites where food stamps are sold, and they must wait on long lines, so discouraging, degrading and difficult for the elderly.

In a line along with a number of welfare mothers were a group of older people waiting for food stamps at 6:30 in the morning. The center opened at 8:15 A.M. By 9:20 A.M. the number of applications that could be accepted that day was closed, yet some eight or ten older people who had been waiting these three hours did not get signed up and their eligibility determined. They had already spent 40 cents one way on D.C. Transit to get to the food-stamp place, and now would have to return again.

Certification for food stamps is time consuming, repetitious and hardly appropriate for people whose incomes are relatively unchanging. The use of food stamps is stigmatizing and embarrassing. The stamps are slightly smaller than dollar bills and come in three colors—maroon, blue and orange—which flag each recipient at the grocery counter as a "poor" person.

During the summer of 1972, a political year, President Nixon launched Project FIND under the direction of Dr. Arthur S. Flemming. The purpose was to locate elderly people who were eligible for food stamps. Four and a half million dollars was reimbursed by the government to the American Red Cross for administrative costs. Information about the program was mailed out with Social Security checks. (Many black elderly and other minority elderly who were not eligible for Social Security were missed by both the mailing and the predominantly white Red Cross volunteers.) This effort was of decided help but many eligible people remained unfound.

In 1974 the Senate Select Committee on Nutrition and Human Needs reported that the rise in total spending for federal food programs between 1970 and 1974 was offset by inflation, and that only 27 percent of older people eligible for food stamps were receiving them.*

"Meals on wheels," the most widely known food program for the elderly, consists of one or two meals, usually a hot lunch and a cold supper, delivered directly to an older person's home on a daily basis. Home-delivered food programs were originated in London, England, during World War II to serve meals to those—the elderly, among them—who had been bombed out of their homes. In 1968, 12.5 million meals on wheels were delivered and nearly 6 million meals were served in lunch clubs for the elderly in Great Britain.

In the United States meals-on-wheels programs began to be established in the fifties and sixties. Many programs run largely by voluntary organizations independently or in association with federal support require that the

---

* It cannot be assumed that programs in existence are necessarily safe from cuts or dissolution. At the Christmas, 1974, season, President Ford announced that one of his budget-cutting proposals would include using his presidential authority to require food-stamp purchasers to pay a flat 30 percent of their income for whatever amount of stamps they used each month. (The previous average was 23 percent.) An estimated one million elderly poor would be forced out of the program by this executive order because their other fixed expenses would not leave them with 30 percent for stamp purchases.

person pay a minimum fee. A 1971 national survey disclosed the existence of only 349 meals-on-wheels programs, operated mainly by private groups and serving only 10,000 to 12,000 older persons, younger shut-ins and handicapped people—quite a contrast to England.

DRUG SERVICES

Drugs constitute the largest single medical expenditure which the elderly must meet almost entirely from their own pockets. Medicare does not cover out-of-hospital drug prescriptions. Thus those with chronic ailments who regularly need digitalis, antibiotics and other medicines are at a great disadvantage. Drug costs for the elderly are substantially greater than for younger persons. The elderly, constituting 10 percent of the population, use 25 percent of all drugs prescribed. Some organizations, such as the National Council of Senior Citizens and the American Association of Retired Persons, provide low-cost drug-prescription services. Group drug buying through cooperatives formed by the elderly is another possible way of countering high costs. Physicians could help the elderly save money by prescribing drugs on a generic rather than brand-name basis. The drug industry itself has done little to meet the financial problems of older people.

TRANSPORTATION

For older people to have the necessities of life—food, medical care, recreation and social activities—they must have access to an inexpensive, well-coordinated, barrier-free transportation system. They do not.

Transportation was one of the "sleeper issues" of the 1971 White House Conference on Aging. Previously no one had seemed quite willing to recognize the urgency of the problem. Old people who are often restricted to their homes by fear of street crime, illness, financial and physical limitations are further locked in by the inadequacies of so-called modern transportation. It is very hard to find assistance with one's baggage on trains, buses and subways. There are long walkways, steps and ramps. Stations are dirty and crowded. Signs and symbols are confusing. Terminology and abbreviations on tickets and other documents are inconsistent. Even to those who are not hard of hearing public-address announcements are often unintelligible. Public transportation routes may be inconvenient and time schedules irregular. The rural and to some extent the suburban elderly can become completely stranded because there are no public transport facilities. For those elderly who depend on walking for mobility, lack of sidewalks, high-speed traffic, absence of pedestrian crossings, poor street lighting and street crime present multiple hazards.

All the elderly should be assured of balanced, human-oriented methods of transportation—pedestrian and vehicular systems that are innovative, ranging from moving sidewalks and special subway elevators to innovations like demand-actuated, portal-to-portal public transportation.* Mass transportation is essential for the many elderly who have no access to automobile travel. In order to absorb operating costs through taxation and thus keep fares within reasonable limits, mass transportation should be either publicly owned or handled as a public utility. The 1964 Urban Mass Transit Assistance Act called for the participation of older people themselves in transportation planning, but they have had, in fact, very little to say. Instead of a balanced, coordinated mass-transit system, transportation has been dominated by the highway lobby.[8] Congressional legislation in 1973 did provide, for the first time and in a small way, for trust funds to be used for mass transit. And 1974 saw passage of the significant National Mass Transportation Act providing both operating subsidies and capital grants. We must have local mass transit, high-speed inter-city rail transportation, and water and air transportation that meets the needs of all age groups, with special attention to children, the elderly and the handicapped, who have physical problems in movement. Even now we could make more efficient use of the facilities that are available; 200,000 schoolbuses stand idle a good part of every day and during vacations.

Barrier-free design of transportation systems is a necessity for the elderly and the handicapped. Our current efforts in this direction are feeble indeed. Many elderly give up hope of using public transportation because of the fear of escalators, high bus steps and stiff exit doors. They cannot enter many public buildings because of high steps and the absence of a ramp. Many churches and synagogues are designed so that old people with respiratory or heart conditions cannot come to worship. Even newly designed transportation such as the Metro subway system in Washington, D.C., has had a struggle over the provision of elevators for the handicapped and elderly. Congress had not fully funded these facilities by 1973 despite its 1968 passage of the Architectural Barriers Act.

The little that has been done to assist the elderly has been in the form

---

* Demand-actuated, portal-to-portal "Dial-A-Bus" makes it unnecessary for old people to wait long on cold or hot street corners. The Administration on Aging has experimented with dial-a-bus systems in Chicago.[7] Regina, Saskatchewan, which has temperatures that can be as low as 20 degrees below zero, has a "telebus" system that has been remarkably successful. Cleveland, Ohio, has provided Medibuses to transport the elderly and the poor to medical-care facilities. Where the portal-to-portal system doesn't exist, bus stops should have roofs, a bench and telephone.

of direct financial assistance. There has been pressure for reduced fares similar to the pressure for tax rebates and reduced-price movie tickets. All of these efforts actually place older people in a second-class position. Ideally they should be assured the economic security which makes such "special" and therefore possibly humiliating arrangements unnecessary. But until adequate income maintenance is established, subsidization with reduced-fare programs for buses, subways, trains and planes is mandatory. By 1971 some 50 cities had established reduced fares for old people, usually set up during nonrush hours. National organizations such as the National Council of Senior Citizens and the National Council on the Aging favor federal subsidization of transportation for the elderly.*

A minority of the elderly rely on automobiles, and the possession of a driver's license is a key to freedom, independence and mobility. It is estimated that some 58 percent of older Americans still have their driver's licenses, and it can be a major psychological blow to lose one. Some older people, of course, never learned to drive at all and others have given up driving as a result of their own self-evaluation of their capacities. Of those who do drive, some do so at peril to themselves and others, while some have been unfairly taken off the roads because they could not get insurance or because of rigid rather than flexible tests for driver's licenses. Surprisingly, some studies show that older drivers have lower accident rates than younger drivers.[9]

What are needed are examinations that screen out older drivers who are dangerous because of disease and disabilities, while not penalizing people simply for being old. Reaction time, vision, hearing, judgment and health status should be assayed. Such a test battery should be compulsory on an annual basis after 45 and semiannually after 65. Driver improvement programs could help update driving habits learned many years ago.

Like the driving population as a whole, an estimated eight million elderly motorists would benefit from no-fault insurance legislation, but American trial lawyers†form a powerful lobby against this issue. Forty-four cents of every insurance-premium dollar goes for legal fees—a high cost indeed for the elderly. Massachusetts pioneered in no-fault insurance and the movement has spread to 23 other states. There is already proof

---

* In 1974, in West Virginia, the Office of Economic Opportunity established an experimental transportation-stamp program (modeled after food stamps).

† The American Trial Lawyers Association is the principal opponent of federal and state no-fault auto-insurance legislation. It solicited its 25,000 members for contributions of up to $1,000 each for American Trial Lawyers Association's "nationwide battle for the preservation of our adversary system of justice." It is estimated that lawyers would lose $1 billion per year with the creation of no-fault insurance.

that money is saved,* but the efforts to legislate national no-fault failed in 1972, 1973 and 1974 and only one state (Michigan) has enacted a no-fault law as strong as the proposed federal law.

It must be kept firmly in mind, however, that the majority of older people cannot depend on the automobile because of their physical and mental limitations and the high cost of purchase and maintenance of a car. For them public transportation is the essential element in avoiding isolation and maintaining their independence.

COMMUNICATION SERVICES (TELEPHONE, RADIO, TV, NEWSPAPERS)

The telephone is a lifeline, not a luxury, reducing the sense of isolation as well as the fear and reality of being unable to gain assistance in an emergency. The telephone can literally mean a longer life. There are reports of people without a phone having significantly higher death rates because they could not summon help or because they lost interest in living.† Six million older Americans do not have a phone, principally because of the cost.

Most elderly people have access to a radio or television set; many will sacrifice food, medicine and clothing to obtain them and keep them in repair.‡ The electronic media are the only source of entertainment for many isolated older people. Newspapers and magazines are additional communication necessities.

LEGAL SERVICES

Until 1968 no public or private legal program existed for older people. Yet poverty, mental depression, physical frailty and mental deterioration make older people particularly vulnerable to exploitation and needful of legal counsel. Public funds under OEO supported the Legal Research and Services for the Elderly of the National Council of Senior Citizens for four years under David Marlin. Some organized bar associations began to recognize the special needs of older people and founded exploratory

---

* The Massachusetts experience has shown that during the first nine months of 1971 bodily-injury claims dropped 48 percent from the same period of 1970, and the size of the average settlement fell from $419 to $165.

† Telephone reassurance services which check up on older people have been found to be quite useful. See Sondra K. Match, *Establishing Telephone Reassurance Services*, The National Council on the Aging, 1972.

‡ Because of the widespread possession of TVs, cable TV (CATV) has great potential in keeping homebound older people in contact with the outside world through special programs for their information and entertainment.

committees to examine these needs. But privately practicing lawyers have not made special efforts or reduced fees for older people.* The National Senior Citizens Law Center in Los Angeles was formed in 1972, and designed to be a national central resource in poverty law and law for the elderly.

For the past five years the importance of legal work on behalf of older people has been amply demonstrated in the areas of income, federal benefits such as Medicaid and Medicare, housing, hearing aids and many other issues. State legislative reform proceeded with the development of model statutes[10] for correcting consumer abuses, working toward uniformity and equity in property taxes, and other matters of direct value to the survival of older people. But 1974 saw congressional passage of the watered-down independent legal services corporation (run by a White House-appointed board) with no categorical assistance for older Americans. The debate among lawyers as to whether there are legal problems special and peculiar to the elderly had lessened. Ironically lawyers themselves may exploit the vulnerability of the old. Walter Newburgher, then 81 years old, president of the 250,000-member Congress of Senior Citizens of New York, notes a good example with respect to the element of death: "When older people have small claims . . . they are probably dead before they collect," because defense attorneys in aged-plaintiff cases can deliberately delay the case with this purpose in mind.

Guardianship and other forms of legal protection can become vitally important. There are older people who do not require institutionalization but who need help with everyday fiscal chores—handling Social Security checks,† paying the rent, buying necessary food and clothing, handling a checking account. They are easy prey for relatives or acquaintances who exploit their diminished competence. And they are very vulnerable to deliberate fraud.

Fraud in services to the elderly is a serious problem. For example, the burgeoning "loneliness industry" (computerized mating services, mating bars, elaborate travel cruises) that exploits the loneliness of people of all ages is a vast move beyond the old-time deceptive contracts of dance studios and other operations designed to bilk the innocent.

---

* Prepaid legal-services programs are only beginning to be available and these few remain out of the financial reach of most older people. The National Center for Legal Services in Washington, D.C., advises how these may be set up.

† In our Protective Services Project in the District of Columbia we found cases, for example, of older people living in rented rooms, starving and dehydrated, with piles of uncashed pension checks underneath the mattress. Yet these were individuals who would be able to function quite adequately in their homes with the aid of legal assistance and other services.

A conservatorship or public guardianship may prove an economical means of assisting older people in protecting their financial resources and allowing them to remain in their own homes as long as possible. In the case of the person with substantial financial assets, laws frequently provide for the appointment of a conservator of the estate. In some jurisdictions, such as the District of Columbia, when a person is unable by reason of advanced age, mental weakness (not amounting to unsoundness of mind), mental illness, or physical incapacity to take care of his property properly, the court upon petition or upon the sworn petition of one or more of his relatives may appoint a fit person to be conservator of his property. The conservator must be bonded, have the power to collect debts due and to adjust and settle debts owed. He may also be made responsible by the court for the personal welfare of the person. He is paid from the estate such an amount as the court approves, not to exceed 5 percent.

As a practical matter a private conservator is too expensive for a person of moderate or small means. Thus in some states, notably California and Illinois, there are laws providing for a public official or even a private social agency to act as public guardian of the estate of such disabled persons.* But there should be model programs put into effect in all states. There must be assurances of the probity of the guardian. Criteria must be established to decide on the applicability and appropriateness of conservatorships and public guardianships. Manifestations by the person of gross inability to manage his own affairs, the lack of responsible relatives or friends to undertake management, and the danger of exploitation are three good criteria. Of course it is crucial that such a legal arrangement not be taken lightly; it can be a crushing psychological blow to older people to be told that they are unable to manage their own affairs and to become totally dependent on another person, even, for example, for petty cash. Such a move should be made as a last resort after everything else has been tried to help the person remain self-sufficient but protected.

The American Law Institute and American Bar Association have prepared a model probate code which would treat the probate process (which legally establishes the validity of a will) as an administrative matter and not as an adversary proceeding. This would reduce costs. If adopted by the states, it would mean that when there is not disagreement, there would be swift distribution of the estate.

---

* The public guardian should be attached to the court or there should be some contracted arrangement with a nonprofit family agency in order to avoid the stigma of welfare. The agency should have a social worker, a lawyer, case aides, and a consultative staff including medical and psychiatric consultants, so that adequate evaluation can be made of the capacity of the older person to manage his or her own affairs.

Old people are often very wary of lawyers and uncertain of their rights. Congressman Herman Badillo (D.-N.Y.) has considered legislation setting up a corps of "circuit riding" lawyers who would travel to senior centers and nursing homes and other places where the elderly congregate, providing service in a more direct and less intimidating manner. As we have seen with other programs including housing, income and work, it is important to have special programs designed categorically for the elderly, since they otherwise tend to get lost in the shuffle or placed at the end of every waiting line and waiting list.

Since 1965 legal services for the poor have led to the creation of a whole new field of law. "Poverty lawyers" have won major cases and established significant precedents. Tenants, debtors and workers have all been aided. Governmental bureaucracies as well as free enterprise have been tested. During the Nixon administration there was a major weakening of the thrust of poverty law* but it remains a beginning in the evolution of protection for the poor. Since the elderly make up 20 percent of the poor, they have gained as tenants or debtors.† Class-action cases (cases where one plaintiff can represent a whole class of people) should represent problems relevant to the aged, including the use of age itself as an inappropriate and prejudicial criterion in determining eligibility for insurance, employment and credit.‡

Enforcement of existing legislation may stop short of the kind of fundamental reform necessary to protect the elderly and other disadvantaged groups adequately but it provides important steps. There should be clearly defined techniques for consumer representation before administrative agencies of the executive branches of the federal, state and local governments. Public hearings should always be held well before guidelines and regulations to implement legislation are established by governmental bureaucrats. There should be established and effective grievance mechanisms to hear complaints, and funds must be provided to cover litigation. Ultimately this should move us toward a "legicare" or "judicare," comparable to Medicare in intent but more effective in financing and implementation.

---

* In 1970 there were 850 Legal Services Program offices operating in 49 states, staffed by 2,200 lawyers and funded by the Office of Economic Opportunity for $53 million. These numbers, and the freedom of action allowed, decreased steadily during the Nixon administration.

† One telling example of the value of public-interest law on behalf of the elderly was the success of the Washington Research Project. It won the United Mine Workers case regarding the loss of their pension-fund monies that had been placed in non-interest-bearing accounts. (See Chapter 2.)

‡ A 1973 Supreme Court decision has unfortunately imposed stringent restrictions on class-action cases, for example requiring the individual to seek a minimum $10,000 in damages.

Lawyers, like every other group including doctors, protect their professional interests. It may therefore be anticipated that lawyer-legislators will be less than enthusiastic about developing a national insurance program providing free or low-cost legal services.

PROTECTIVE SERVICES

"Protective services" is the term used for a group of services given to a person who is so mentally deteriorated or disturbed as to be unable to manage his affairs in his own best interest, and who has no relative or friend able or willing to act on his behalf. It is a much broader concept than public guardianship in that social work, legal, medical, psychiatric, nursing, homemaking and home-health-aide services may be provided. Federal legislation under the 1962 Public Welfare Amendments to the Social Security Act permits local welfare offices to set up protective-service programs with a 75 to 25 percent federal-state financial match; in November, 1970, such services were mandated for inclusion in all state plans. Very few states, however, have actually established protective-service programs.

In most instances where protective services are called upon, the older person is a casualty by reason of his own problems. But deliberate victimization does occur and the exploiter may reside in or outside the family:*

> A 67-year-old woman, widowed eight years, was regularly beaten up by her 35-year-old unmarried son. She had turned her little money and her property over to the son. He stopped working. They subsisted on her $80-a-month Social Security check. She did some baby sitting to supplement the income.

> Mrs. James was 78 years old. She had retired from a government job and contributed her modest income to her son with whom she lived. But now he had been dead for two years. She and her daughter-in-law had many conflicts, and the daughter-in-law would become enraged and strike the older woman. She moved out and now lived in one dirty room. The neighborhood children called her a witch and tormented her physically and verbally.

These are two examples of what I have called the "battered old person syndrome," both cases where protective services would be an appropriate safeguard.

---

* Consequently one cannot always advocate maintaining the older person at home. There are, after all, no "standards" in private homes, and an older person may be vulnerable to mistreatment by neighbors or within his or her own family.

TAX SERVICES

Income-tax forms, confusing enough for the younger taxpayer to decipher, compound the difficult financial circumstances of the elderly. The U.S. Senate Special Committee on Aging reports that perhaps one-half of all retired persons receiving pensions or annuities pay more taxes than they should because they misunderstand the complicated and intricate provisions of the tax system.[11] The older person may have difficulty figuring out his retirement-income credit, for example. On the other hand, tax-preparation services can be both expensive and unreliable. In 1972 the Internal Revenue Service began to investigate commercial tax-preparation services which IRS Commissioner Johnnie M. Walters described as a "drain on the taxpayer." About 80 percent of the 1971 tax returns were prepared commercially. Simplification of forms would cut back the need to pay for preparation of tax returns.[12] Those elderly who need help should be given easy access to assistance from Internal Revenue Service staff as well as the assurance of reliable and reasonably priced commercial services. The American Association of Retired Persons–National Retired Teachers Association began operating a tax-aide program in 1968 in which retired persons are trained to help other older persons prepare their tax returns. Help through the mail would be a boon to housebound persons.

RECREATION

Despite the clamor about the rewards of retirement and the greater possibilities of leisure, the chance for older people to try out much-advertised recreational, entertainment and social activities is seriously reduced by high costs, the absence of decent transportation and inadequate health care. Few accommodations are especially designed for people with handicaps. It was not until 1972 that the Department of Interior's National Park Service produced a *National Park Guide for the Handicapped* to help the blind, deaf and those who are confined to wheelchairs or otherwise handicapped to enjoy the National Park System.

The few programs that reach out into the homes of older people do not offer escort and companionship services to parks, museums and theatres even though such activities could brighten the boredom of the restricted older person's life. Recreation and socialization decrease illness and give excitement and dignity to the later years. Doctors could probably write prescriptions for recreation and enjoyment just as they do for drugs—and with fewer adverse side effects. Recreation for the housebound requires the invention of new indoor sports and games.

PROBLEMS IN DELIVERY OF SERVICES

NOBODY IS OUT THERE

George Roby, chief of the Adult Services Division of the Social Services Administration in Washington, D.C., has described his experience with older people in a large urban community.[13]

I became quickly aware that there were few other people out there. Our aged are deserted. People who normally provide services and human contact have fled the scene. There are no more delivery boys to bring the groceries. "Friendly visitors"* from the church, the family doctor, even visits from close relatives such as children and grandchildren are few and far between. The social worker has discontinued the regular home visit and the public health nurse, bless her, is still out there but in fewer and fewer numbers. The "go to the home" services are almost nonexistent. Many old people are on waiting lists for two or more years. Many never survive the waiting list.

Roby describes the situation in the municipal government as well as private, nonprofit voluntary organizations:

In three years we have been able to recruit only two friendly visitors from this metropolitan area of two and a half million people who were willing to go into their client's home. . . . Our programs for the aging represent the meanest kind of tokenism. They dangle a carrot that can be nibbled at by too few of those in need. They are a smokescreen to hide a problem that communities will not face up to.

My own observations of the availability of services are similar. The elderly are as abandoned as ever. One should not be fooled by the public-relations efforts of various service programs; when it comes down to actual service the elderly are getting very little.

SHORT-SIGHTED SERVICE ORGANIZATIONS

All types of service organizations, whether voluntary nonprofit, governmental or commercial, have tended to neglect older people. Only one-third of all the voluntary nonprofit agencies of the United States can even claim to have special programs for the aged. Older people have had little influence upon these agencies, whose "accountability" derives largely from self-selected boards of trustees, even though 80 percent of their budgets

---

* A volunteer program of social visiting of the elderly and shut-ins.

comes from public donations. A substantial percentage of the dollars contributed to voluntary organizations through community drives (such as United Givers Funds and Community Chests) goes into overhead and administration, and what is left over is allocated to the actual provision of services. A minuscule amount of this goes to the elderly.

Nonprofit foundations also illustrate institutionalized ageism by seldom providing money for use on behalf of the elderly. In rare instances where funding has occurred, little of lasting value has resulted. The Ford Foundation supplied a $500,000 grant to the Family Service Association of America in 1959. Consultant Ollie A. Randall, a pioneering social worker in the field of aging, had hoped that the work accomplished by the Ford grant would lead to greater services to the aged by the family-service agencies throughout the country. But Randall has said, "The impact on the work of the family services agencies was, to my disappointment, not at all noticeable except in one or two spots where one would have expected it without the grant."[14]

Commercial providers such as businesses that provide nursing, companion and housekeeping service are no better and in some ways far worse than voluntary agencies. Since these are profit-making operations, accountability in the commercial service industries is largely confined to one or several owners or to a large number of stockholders. If the accountant says the company is in the red, the quality and quantity of services will diminish. As in any other business, decisions are made primarily on the basis of the debit sheet and the need for specific kinds of quality services becomes subordinated to profit and loss.

Where governmental services are at issue, the situation depends upon the nature of the legislation and the interplay between the federal government and the states. When programs such as Social Security and Medicare do not contain a "means test," the issue of national standards is a lesser one though there are still problems. But the situation becomes more complicated when it is a state-federal program such as Medicaid (Title XIX of the Social Security Act) which does require the test of income eligibility. States make the decision as to who is eligible and what standards will be enforced. As revenue sharing to the states from the federal government advances, stringent federal guidelines are obviously necessary. Important though local control may be, there must be a dynamic equilibrium in the struggle between federal guidelines and local power.

As noted earlier, other hindrances to governmental provision of services include varying age eligibilities, the responsible-relative clause, liens on homes, and the increasing reluctance of the middle class to pay for services which are usually available only to the poor. Universal government programs without income-eligibility limits would eliminate many of these obstacles although increased costs would result.

AMBIVALENT FEDERAL SERVICE PROGRAMS

In 1962 Congress enacted Public Welfare Amendments to the Social Security Act that provided 75 percent federal matching funds for state expenditures for social services and training activities. This little-noticed provision provided an "open-ended" financing possibility. The more states decided to spend, the more the federal government would be automatically obliged to spend. By 1972 this had become a multibillion-dollar program.[15] Services covered are broad and include "services to a family or any member thereof for the purpose of preserving, rehabilitating, reuniting, or strengthening the family, and such other services as will assist members of the family to attain or re-attain capability for maximum self support and personal independence." Not only could current welfare recipients be covered, but after 1965 borderline cases could be covered as well. The states were allowed to purchase services from public agencies and private agencies which had public support. With respect to older people, protective services for dependent persons, mental-health services, community health services and homemaker services were among the valuable programs that could be financed.

Those who were canny and knowledgeable soon ascertained the kinds of monies and services that were provided under the 1962, 1965 and 1967 changes in the Social Security Act.[16] For example, Title IV, Parts A and B, of the 1967 amendments and Titles I, X, XIV and XVI* have all been used to build social programs in the states.[17] In 1972 HEW Secretary Elliot L. Richardson called state requests "a virtual open-end raid on the federal treasury."[18]† Not all states caught on to the windfall immediately, but it was of interest that states with Republican governors, such as California, Illinois and New York, did act quickly. It was only after their states were well funded that the Nixon administration in 1971 and 1972 began to press for a ceiling on the open-ended financing provision. A ceiling was placed on the Social Security social-services provision up to $2.5 billion in 1972. Moreover, restriction was placed on the allocated federal matching dollars that could be spent on borderline cases (past or potential welfare recipients). This is a serious blow to the elderly.

---

* Social services for the adult categories were combined in a new Title VI of the Social Security Act by the amendments of 1972.

† There are ironies in the fact that money for social services is regarded as a trap door to the federal treasury but monies that subsidize either business or the aerospace industry are not.

The 1972 Federal Revenue Sharing Act did not make up for the losses brought about by the Social Services ceiling.* The elderly (and the poor) are among the eight priorities in general revenue sharing (along with public safety, environmental protection, reforestation, health, recreation, libraries and social services), but this will probably mean little for them in terms of special benefits. As an indication of the direction of future priorities, revenue sharing has rewarded growth.† Therefore the suburbs, which have the fewest old people and the fastest growth, have received the greatest share, and rural areas and central-city cores, where many older people live, have fared the worst.[19] As of 1974, only two-thirds of one percent of revenue-sharing funds were being spent for the elderly.‡

Other service monies for old people have also been limited. The intended 1972 expansion of programs for older people was curtailed by President Nixon's pocket veto, just before election, of the Older American Comprehensive Service Amendment. The President said the bill contained "a range of narrow categorical programs that would seriously interfere with our efforts to develop coordinated services for older persons." The catch in this reasoning is that special target-type programs are necessary for older people. Only after the elderly become a traditional focus of special concern can they be umbrellaed within more comprehensive types of programs. In 1973, the President signed a compromise bill, providing less money than Congress had originally authorized.

Because of the costs, many states have been slow to participate in various programs such as Medicaid, which provides funds in a federal-state match for health services for the poor. Virginia typifies the late starter, not beginning its program until July 1, 1969. Within six months it began to cut back its coverage of services. Its expenditures were still within the range of the appropriations, but enrollment was nearly 25 percent above original estimates and funds were insufficient to care for all of them. Similar experiences have caused other states to cut back their Medicaid programs.

Title III of the original 1965 Older Americans Act is a major source of federal monies to provide services. Funds are allotted to the states on the basis of their population of older people. The states in turn make grants to local public and private nonprofit agencies which provide serv-

---

* The five-year $30 billion program applies to 38,000 state and local governments; $2.65 billion was distributed in 1972, $5.6 billion in 1973.

† Revenue-sharing grants are based on a complex formula, important factors being the "tax effort" and per capita income of state and local governments.

‡ See William R. Hutton, "Study Reveals Revenue Sharing Is Neglecting Older Americans," *Senior Citizen News*, 4:1 (1974).

ices to and for old people. The actual amounts of money given have been insufficient.

In 1967 then HEW Secretary John W. Gardner fashioned a new federal agency called Social and Rehabilitation Services (SRS), which merged three existing agencies, including the Administration on Aging. One purpose was to "separate the administration of programs having to do with cash programs—that is, public-assistance payments—from the programs offering rehabilitation and social services."* Most public-welfare workers who had spent their time in the determination of eligibility were then freed to provide direct social services. However, some 90 percent of workers had not been educated to provide these services; they were not fully trained social workers. Moreover, special skills are needed to work with the elderly. So far, training has been desultory and resulting services have been hampered by lack of skilled staff.

THE COST TO THE ELDERLY

Services follow a predictable course. They are delivered the most to those who need them the least. Eligibility requirements stigmatize recipients and anger nonrecipients; yet if there are no eligibility limits the middle- and higher-income population tends to make the greatest use of services while the disadvantaged and undereducated poor get overlooked. When programs focus on the poor, one runs into a troublesome facet of the Protestant ethic which demands that "the deserving poor" be separated from the "undeserving." More than half of the poor are either over 65† or under 16, yet the image of the welfare recipient as a shiftless and lazy able-bodied adult persists as a major hindrance to provision of services.

The financing of public and private services should allow for eligibility independent of income, with a fee schedule that is scaled on the basis of income for those services which cannot feasibly be supplied free to all. A progressive fee schedule scaled upward as well as downward could correct the current situation where the poor usually pay proportionately more for services and the rich get bargain prices.

Private social and health agencies and some public agencies do charge fees according to a person's ability to pay. The Bureau of Labor Statistics

---

* Mary Elizabeth Switzer was the administrator.

†A 1960 study of characteristics of recipients of Old Age Assistance shows that they tend to be about four years older than the median age for the total population age 65 and over. Thus, they average 76.4. Two-thirds are women, largely widowed; three-fourths receive no contributions from children; 20 percent are confined to their homes; and 8 percent are bedfast or chairfast. And a majority, or about 55 percent, live in nonmetropolitan counties.

has suggested that its three budget levels—low, intermediate and high—provide guidelines for fee schedules. Given the conservative nature of the budgets, I would question the rigidity that is likely to follow. These budgets have not been influenced by the voice of the consumer—and certainly not by the elderly consumer—except through government studies of consumer expenditures.[20] They reflect what is, rather than what should be, and thus perpetuate current inequities.

SERVICES FOR MINORITY-GROUP ELDERLY

It is no news that various minority groups receive less adequate services than the majority groups in American life. American Indians—those who have survived in spite of the extraordinarily low life expectancy of the American Indian—receive the same paternalistic and inadequate services in old age that they received throughout life. Spanish and Asian-Americans suffer from the lack of a bicultural and bilingual approach to services as well as a generally poor living standard. It is a myth that Asian-American elderly are well taken care of:

This emasculating myth that discriminates against Asian-American elderly is that Asian-American aged do not have any problems, that Asian-Americans are able to take care of their own and that Asian-American aged do not need nor desire aid in any form. Such assertions which are generally accepted as valid by society are false . . . it is impossible for Asian-Americans to look only to their families for help.[21]

Racial minority groups do not have adequate opportunities to join the service professions as doctors, social workers and nurses.* Those providing services to the minority groups should have the assistance of interpreters and training with respect to language and culture when this is appropriate. The service provider must understand the differing patterns of behavior that affect the giving and receiving of service.

Somewhat unexpectedly, older Jews are a minority group who suffer from lack of services. The Jewish population has traditionally taken such initiative in the care of their old people that it is surprising to find extensive poverty among elderly Jews. In New York City alone it was estimated in 1971 that most of the city's 250,000 indigent Jews were over 65. Tropical retirement havens in California and Florida also house Jewish elderly poor.[22] In 1972 B'nai B'rith acted to involve its 500,000 members throughout the nation in volunteer personal services for the isolated Jewish elderly,

* Only 3 percent of American social workers are black, for example.

asserting that indifference to the plight of the elderly had contributed to the deterioration in Jewish family life.

A 1970 report on the use of grant funds under the Older Americans Act[23] proudly claims support of 130 different projects "addressed to solving problems of aging in American society." There is no evidence, however, that any of these projects dealt specifically with minority elderly. Organized interest in the plight of minority elderly and their lack of service began in the late 1960s[24] and is still in its formation stages.

CREDENTIALISM

Who gets served the most—the providers of service or those who are supposed to be served? There are many self-serving interests on the part of providers of services which interfere with the provision of quality care to people of all groups, including the elderly. Credentialism, sometimes called diplomaism,[25] is one. Credentialism is the requirement that people must have certain academic or professional degrees in order to provide certain services even though the performance of these services may not require that much training. We are seeing some reversal of this trend through the paraprofessional and new careers movements, which capitalize on the natural skills of people and incorporate them into various occupational categories. Such an emphasis admittedly requires careful thought and implementation since it involves a balancing of proper standards and natural skills. But it is well worth the effort when the result is many more competent people available to perform services.

Providers of service tend to be jealous of their prerogatives. Some psychiatrists, for example, feel themselves threatened by the increasing role of nonmedical workers in community mental health work. One psychiatrist said, "The end result of the egalitarian principle may be to debase psychiatrists and to promote paramedical team members to superior ranks."[26]

PEER CONTROL

Related to credentialism is peer control of licensing. Physicians, lawyers and druggists, for example, control their own local state licensing boards. The consumer-public has little or no representation. Representation of consumers at various points of the service system—education, licensing, accountability, financing—is desirable. Of course the question arises as to how consumers should be selected. How are they to render judgments concerning professional standards? How are professionals going to learn to profit from listening to consumers? We don't know all the answers yet because we are just beginning to try. "Consumerism" is a relatively recent movement and there are many problems—but none more serious than those created by providers who have taken advantage of the fact that they have been answerable largely to themselves.

SERVITUDE IN THE SERVICE INDUSTRY

The extent to which service is linked to servitude will diminish with better pay and greater opportunities for advancement through on-the-job training in the service industry. It is little wonder that morale in the service industry is low, particularly on the nonprofessional level. People who are competent, interested and psychologically suited to perform the many services needed by the old are understandably unwilling to work for the low salaries that are usually involved. Their wages represent a sort of "coerced philanthropy"—not quite but almost giving their services free. President Nixon once said that "scrubbing floors and emptying bedpans" has "just as much dignity as there is in any work to be done in this country —including my own."[27] This is patent nonsense. Emptying bedpans is distasteful work by anybody's standards and the only way to handle the situation fairly is either to distribute such work evenly to everyone or to compensate justly those who must perform these tasks. The Fair Labor Standards Act should be broadly applicable to service workers. The minimum wage should be more realistic. Even a $2-per-hour minimum wage would allow the wage earner, working forty hours per week, to earn only slightly more than a poverty-level income. Eighty dollars per week, or $4,160 per year, is hardly enough to provide for a family with, say, two growing children. Enforcement of the 1970 Occupational Safety and Health legislation, potentially so important to workers faced with occupational hazards and diseases, has hardly been rigorous. Fringe benefits, including health care and provision for old age, need improvement.

THE OLDER PERSON'S RESISTANCE

If problems in service organizations were solved there would still be "problems." The recipients of our ministrations do not always "cooperate" —and often out of wisdom! In the case of older people their independence may be at stake.

A 92-year-old woman living alone in a two-room apartment refused help. She was afraid that if she allowed anyone to take over her duties she would begin to lose her capacity to care for herself. She was clear

mentally and in reasonably good shape physically. The landlord wanted
her to get help in order to be sure her apartment was well maintained.
He suggested that perhaps she was ready "for an institution."

Many older people feel as this woman did. The first concession toward
accepting help is seen by them, and by others, as an omen that they are
becoming incapable of remaining in the community. It is very important
that those who provide services recognize this and collaborate with the
elderly in maintaining their sense of independence. Inducing dependency
or helplessness is one of the most dangerous aspects of work with older
persons. Margaret Blenkner[28] reported greater mortality among a group
receiving services than among a comparable population that did not. The
group being served seems to have read service as a sign that they were no
longer capable of operating effectively on their own. It can become a self-
fulfilling prophecy to be told you are declining and need help.

Much of the training for service occupations—doctors, nurses, lawyers,
homemakers—is oriented toward "doing for" rather than "collaborating
with." A nurse is trained to nurse. Her gratification comes from nursing.
It is very difficult for her to stand by and watch the older person painfully
feed himself or herself. Yet it is imperative that the provider of service
stimulate the older person to remain active and reduce opportunities for
the development of helplessness. One must be able to ease the obstacles
to survive without extinguishing the will to struggle to survive.

The resistance of older people to service can also reflect a realistic fear
of change. There may have been previously bad experiences with service
personnel or policies. Some older persons carry resistance to an extreme,
causing harm to themselves or others. A good façade or the appearance
of adequate functioning may be maintained long after incapacity has set
in. It is then the task of the skilled helper to judge as accurately as possible
the discrepancy between the older person's subjective view and his objective
reality. The older person's trust must be earned so that appropriate service
can be accepted.

Sometimes, too, older people reject help because of their deep responsibility toward others.

A 77-year-old woman took care of her mentally retarded brother
who was younger by five years, but she was now seriously ill and refusing hospitalization. She said she could not leave her brother whom
she had cared for since his teens. When she was married she brought
her brother along with her. Now he was 72. Their income was extremely
limited. The efforts of the case worker were directed toward expressing
to the older sister an appreciation of her great responsibility and how

well she had carried it out and appealing to her that it was necessary for her to accept the need for planning on behalf of her brother if for no other reason than the eventuality of her own death. It would help her to feel secure if her lifelong responsibility would continue to be met.

The resistance of older persons to services is sometimes matched by the providers' stubborn insistence on judging people by their age rather than their functioning. I saw one 103-year-old woman who was living quite successfully in public housing, but everyone who came in contact with her thought she should be in an institution simply because she was 103. She stuck to her principles and remained at home, where she eventually died peacefully.

The bureaucratic impulse to complete and close a case and put the files away is especially inappropriate when it comes to the elderly, because services for the elderly often need to continue until death. The "cases" of older people should be kept flexible, with the possibility of their returning for further help remaining open to the end of life. The point is that such openness and availability must not interfere with necessary and demonstrated independence.

REMEDIES TOWARD PROVIDING BETTER SERVICES

IN THE PUBLIC INTEREST

Arguments persist as to whether commercial, voluntary nonprofit or government-provided services are best. The profit motive is generally considered to be an important motivation in the provision of outstanding goods and services. But, given the present inadequacies of private enterprise services, from health-care delivery to tax assistance, it is difficult to sustain the notion that the desire for commercial profit *per se* leads to the larger social good. On the other hand, nonprofit organizations, whether in the private or the governmental sector, have not demonstrated great efficiency or, at times, even integrity. Indeed, voluntary and governmental agencies often are unaccountable for their activities; consider, for example, the voluntary, nonprofit hospital which, despite its tax-favored status and provision of congressionally allocated Hill-Burton monies, maintains discriminatory quotas for the care of the indigent, including the elderly.*

Special direct federal subsidies, indirect subsidies and tax rebates assist medical practice, nursing homes, public and private transportation and a

* See Chapter 7, "The Unfulfilled Prescription."

variety of service activities. These offer both justification and leverage for more explicit accountability of private profit and nonprofit organizations. Clearly there is a need for established standards of performance and for continuing surveillance of different services and institutions, whether they be governmental, profit or nonprofit, by all levels of government and by consumers.

Public policy should also favor the diversion of direct and indirect subsidies from commercial industries to nonprofit voluntary organizations. The intent of this suggestion is not to wipe out commercial enterprises but to enhance thriving competition. "Nonprofit" does not mean "not for profit," of course. There is no reason why nonprofit service organizations should not develop efficient organizations with returns which can be recycled into expanding social programs.

We also need new forms analogous to the public utility for delivering services. The utility is a business or public organization placed under government regulation because it provides an essential service or commodity such as water, energy and power (electricity, gas, light), transportation (airlines, trains, buses, trucking) and communications (telephone, telegraph, radio and television broadcasting). Ownership is influenced by the fact that franchises or permits must be obtained from governments. "Social utilities"—for the delivery of a different kind of essential service —would be a broadening of this concept, for they would concern themselves primarily with human services. Public welfare and public health, in particular, should receive prime emphasis. Like public utilities, there should be a regulation of ownership and profits. The question of commercial profits *per se* is not within the purview of this book, but human greed or profit as a primary motivation at the expense of the vulnerable sick and elderly certainly cannot be tolerated by anyone interested in their welfare.

PRACTICAL ECUMENISM

Secular sponsorship of programs for the elderly is not the only important area where improvement could occur. Clergymen of all faiths have been involved in the care of older people, but the quality of religious support thus far has been inconsistent. In spite of the fact that clergymen have been among the few professional groups that have cared directly for aging and dying persons, there are many examples of inadequate and inappropriate responses to the old. Religious homes for the aged include some of the worst as well as some of the best facilities. Each denomination has built its own little island of concern, isolated from everyone else's. Religious groups could benefit from pooling their personnel and resources for the greater good of all their elderly communicants. "Practical ecumenism" could allow churches and synagogues to protect their separate identities yet combine their assets in a planned effort to help the old.[29] One example is the cooperative buying of necessary supplies for homes for the aged in a community in order to cut costs sharply. Sharing skilled manpower such as social workers and doctors would increase the range of services each home could give. Other ventures might be the cooperative planning of a vital community program such as meals on wheels, or "friendly visitors."

SENIOR-CENTER MOVEMENT

The senior-center movement is an example of institutionalized provision of services designed especially for the elderly. The National Institute of Senior Centers was established by the National Council on the Aging in 1970. This institute followed the development of senior centers through the 1940s and 1950s. The first such center, the Hodson Center in New York City, was established in 1944, directed by pioneer Gertrude Landau. The first United Auto Workers center was set up in Detroit in 1951. In 1962 the National Council on the Aging published Jean Maxwell's *Centers for Old People*, documenting the senior-center movement. Title III programs under the Old Americans Act of 1965 aided senior centers and encouraged more community services.* In 1971 Representative John Brademas (D.-Ind.) introduced legislation to authorize construction of Multi-purpose Senior Citizen Community Centers. A revolving fund would be established to insure mortgages for such centers. But Brademas's effort has yet to see fulfillment.

At first senior centers provided recreation and social activities as their primary services—shows, parties, music, card games, group shopping and TV. But recent emphasis has included group-therapy discussion groups, information and referral services, medical assistance, residential-care programs, homemaker services and education.

The senior-center movement illustrates the continuing debate over the development of comprehensive versus categorical programs. Should the services needed by old people be assured within comprehensive programs for all people of all ages or should they be provided in specialized, age-segregated ways? Philosophically, socially and psychologically the integration of services is clearly the more desirable. But experience continues to demonstrate that old people get overlooked and underserved. Until there

* In some areas where these centers are located as many as 15 percent of the older population has participated in their programs. However, in general they do not yet reach significant proportions of the elderly population.[30]

is a finely honed change in the cultural sensibility, it seems essential to press for necessary, highly visible categorical programs.

REGISTRATION DRIVES

Many old people do not avail themselves of services to which they are entitled and to a surprising degree this is simply because it has been made difficult for them to sign up. It is arduous and expensive for them to travel to the right agency, find their way through the bureaucratic maze and understand the complexity and language of the forms. There have been successful registration drives which should serve as models for future efforts to see that older people receive the assistance and benefits they need and qualify for.

One effective major registration drive was Operation Medicare Alert undertaken by the National Council on the Aging. Medicare Alert, sponsored financially by the Social Security Administration, was a nationwide project conceived in 1966 for the purpose of signing up eligible candidates for Medicare. It employed 14,000 older poor people and 20,000 volunteers in 467 Community Action Agencies. These "outreach" workers knocked on doors in city slums and rural poverty areas. One by-product of the use of poor older people in these drives was to put money in their pockets and give them a sense of usefulness. Another advantage was the familiarity these "indigenous" workers had with their communities. Social Security Administration officials estimated that Medicare Alert helped over four million people sign up for Part B of Medicare, the portion concerned with payment of doctors' benefits.

Operation FIND (friendless, indigent, needy and disabled) has been an extension of the concept of reaching out and finding the poor, both to survey needs and to try to provide services. It too was sponsored by the National Council on the Aging and was supported financially through the Office of Economic Opportunity (OEO). Project FIND sought out elderly in low socioeconomic areas in twelve communities across the United States in 1967 and 1968; 52,203 old people were found to need services. Referrals were made for 28,079, and 19,391 received some kind of service. The remaining 24,124 were not referred at all because there was no available service! The report *The Golden Years—A Tarnished Myth* resulted from this work. It provides a vivid exposition of the tragedy of the old in America.

Richard A. Cloward and Frances F. Piven stated in 1966 that "adding all eligible persons to the welfare rolls would generate a financial crisis of such magnitude that the federal government would be pressured to respond with a plan for a guaranteed annual income." How federal, state and local governments will actually respond to the cumulative effect of these pressures is still in question, however, since a "backlash" against the elderly—as against the poor—is conceivable.

One of the aims of the National Welfare Rights Organization, led by the late Dr. George Wiley (who shared the view of Cloward and Piven), has been to educate poor people concerning their rights and entitlements and to register them for public assistance, Medicaid, food stamps and other entitlements.* But older people have not been included in the National Welfare Rights Organization, which has focused primarily on welfare mothers. In 1972 Wiley left the NWRO and devoted his time to building a "Movement for Economic Justice," which would have a broader base, representing the aged as well as welfare recipients, the unemployed and low-income workers. He believed NWRO should be a key element in the new movement. His tragic death in 1973 left the movement without his skilled and compassionate leadership.

It is surprising that, except for the National Council on the Aging, which built the model of Medicare Alert, none of the national organizations representing the aged have undertaken major registration drives.

TRAINING OF PERSONNEL

The training of service workers is another issue. Former Commissioner Martin has said, ". . . a third of a million professional and technical workers are employed in programs designed primarily or solely for older persons and . . . fewer than 10 to 20 percent of these people have had formal training for their work."[32]

Consultation and training from the various vocations and professions should be available to the police, churches and other institutions to deepen the knowledge of groups and institutions about older people and their needs.

Federalization of support and standards, the diversion of federal funds to nonprofit service organizations, registration drives, advocacy, class-action cases and training are various means for improving the quality of services to older Americans.

OLD PEOPLE HELPING THEMSELVES

Old people themselves can be a source of services to other older people through cooperatives and self-help organizations. It is unrealistic to con-

---

* Former HEW Secretary Elliot Richardson commented that if we implemented congressional programs for all eligible citizens we would have to double the federal budget—an additional $256 billion![31]

sider this to be more than an ancillary possibility, an "extra" potential source of help, but it has unexploited potential. An illustration is the "Good Neighbor" Family Aide Program that provides child care and companionship for the elderly, and at the same time employs older women to perform these services.

ADVOCACY

There is a great need for advocates for old people. Some already exist. There are churches that have lay commissions and special ministries to the aged. Cities and states have advisory committees and commissions. By 1965 most states had small units with responsibility for planning, coordinating and evaluating programs and making recommendations. In 1971 twenty state commissions on aging were independently responsible to governors. Nineteen more were placed within multipurpose departments such as human resources; and six others had varied special status. Massachusetts created a cabinet-level Department of Elder Affairs in 1971 to oversee all programs for the elderly. The new department has authority over such functions as income maintenance, disability assistance, licensing and inspection of nursing homes, rest homes and similar facilities, and the construction and administration of housing and transportation services for the elderly.

It is obvious that for advocacy to mean anything there must be accountability. The challenging of delivery systems must be balanced by constructive reactions from the challenged as well as sanctions to be imposed upon those who do not respond by improvements. An apparent example of "empty" advocacy was the 1971 White House Conference on Aging. Its pile of recommendations has produced too little in the way of change.

Old people themselves should have a major role in decisions that are made concerning the kind, quality and delivery of various services. It is imperative that they be represented on the boards of trustees of all of the organizations and agencies that have had or might potentially have services to offer them. They need to be educated and to educate others concerning their rights and entitlements.

THE RIGHT TO SERVICES

There should be class-action cases to establish an enforceable legal right to services. One basis for suits would be equality before the law, which finds its clearest constitutional embodiment in the Fourteenth Amendment:

All persons born or naturalized in the United States, and subject to the jurisdiction thereof, are citizens of the United States and of the State wherein they reside. No State shall make or enforce any law which shall abridge the privileges or immunities of citizens of the United States; nor shall any State deprive any person of life, liberty, or property without due process of law; nor deny to any person within its jurisdiction the equal protection of the laws.

Equal protection of the laws would seem to mean equal treatment with respect to public goods and services. Should older people by virtue of living under impoverished inner-city slum conditions or in rural poverty in Minnesota or Montana have insufficient fire protection, negligible police surveillance, poor sewer and water facilities, inadequate trash collection? One would be hard pressed to find constitutional justification for our present inequities.

Administrations and agencies have put forth demonstration projects to provide "seed money," which will presumably lead to the proliferation of major programs of service for older people. But the demonstration projects come and go, the same facts are proven over and over again, old people still wait. One hears with some regularity the clarion call for integrated, comprehensive rather than specialized services for the elderly. This reflects ageism, a way of dropping the elderly to the bottom of the barrel. Likewise, one hears that volunteers and voluntary agencies should take care of the elderly. This is a moribund proposition. Such a call has long been made and never effectively answered. It becomes a convenient dodge for municipal, state and federal governments to avoid providing the money and manpower necessary for the delivery of services. The provision of services costs money, and federal general tax revenues are the most realistic resource.

Chapter 7

THE UNFULFILLED PRESCRIPTION

MEDICAL NEEDS OF THE ELDERLY

The exciting aspect of medical care for the elderly is that much of what has long been considered to be aging is disease. Many of the ailments of the old are possibly preventable, probably retardable, and most certainly treatable. Medical knowledge and techniques are already available to ameliorate many of the illnesses of late life. Major breakthroughs in the treatment of cancer, stroke, and heart disease are anticipated in the not-very-distant future. The time may soon come when old age is marked by a gentle and predictable decline rather than the dreadful, painful onslaughts of disease and chronic disability which now haunt late life. With devastating illnesses mostly gone, elderly people would have the opportunity to live a very different kind of old age from that they now experience.

The bad news is that the majority of older people can't afford proper medical care; doctors and health personnel are not trained to deal with their unique problems; their medical conditions are not considered interesting to teaching institutions; and they are stereotyped as bothersome, cantankerous and complaining patients. Direct prejudices exist. Primitive health problems like malnutrition are widespread, partly because many older people are too poor to feed themselves properly, partly because loneliness, disability, depression or fear of crime may keep them from shopping for and cooking food. The close association between mental and physical health is largely ignored. The old are submitted to enormous emotional stresses and a low social position. Preventive medicine, and recognizing the complex interplay among physical, emotional and social factors, is set aside in favor of simplistic diagnoses of "senility" and prognoses of "chronic" or "irreversible."

The elderly account for one-fourth of the nation's health expenditures because of their greater need for medical services and their costlier illnesses. Older patients require more physician time, more frequent hospital admissions and longer stays in the hospital. They are the main users of long-term-care facilities and home-health agencies. They consume 25 percent of all drugs.

The leading causes of death for those 45 years of age and older are heart disease, cancer, stroke and accidents. But the care of chronic conditions, from mild aches and pains to long-term illness and disability, constitutes the bulk of the physical health problems of the elderly. About 86 percent (15.4 million) of people 65 and older, and 72 percent (28 million) of those from 45 to 64 are estimated to have one or more chronic conditions. High blood pressure, arthritis, diabetes, heart disease and arteriosclerosis are a few examples. Multiple ailments in the same individual are common.

On the other hand, acute and chronic health problems do not keep the majority of the elderly from being active and independent. As we have noted earlier, 95 percent of all people over 65 live in the community, with only 5 percent in institutions. Eighty-one percent are physically capable of getting around on their own with no assistance.

The availability of emergency care is vitally important in old age. Of the four leading causes of death, three of them—heart disease, stroke and accidents—often require emergency care.* Acute illnesses, whether they occur alone or are superimposed on chronic conditions, are usually more serious in the old because they may not have physical reserves with which to fight them. When acute conditions are not treated promptly they can result in chronic disability or unnecessary death.

Caring for the medical needs of older people requires knowledge of the special ways in which illnesses manifest themselves in this age group. For example, acute illnesses may not present the classic signs found in younger people, such as fever and an elevated blood count. Doctors and medical personnel must be carefully trained in the specific techniques of diagnosing and treating the older person. Unfortunately, as I shall describe more fully later, such teaching is rarely done in medical training institutions. As a result, the care of the elderly falls far short of adequate. Even the most obvious measures may not be taken to treat symptoms or the actual illnesses themselves, to instruct the old in preventive care, to reassure them about normal changes with age, or to offer support when they are dying.

There are several excellent books on geriatric medicine, such as those edited by Stieglitz, Cowdry and Rossman. They cover the wide spectrum of illnesses that affect the elderly and the special principles that should guide their care. It is not within the scope of this book to review the many conditions that strike older people. However, attention will be quite selectively given to a few examples of medical problems of older people that are often misdiagnosed, improperly treated or ignored.

The failure to diagnose and treat *reversible brain syndromes* is so un-

---

* "Emergentology" or emergency medicine is a growing specialty. The American College of Emergency Physicians began in 1969.

necessary and yet so widespread that I would caution families of older persons to question doctors involved in care about this. Reversible brain syndromes are characterized by fluctuating levels of awareness which may vary from mild confusion to stupor or active delirium. Hallucinations may be present, usually of the visual rather than auditory type. The patient is typically disoriented, mistaking one person for another, and other intellectual functions can also be impaired. Restlessness, unusual aggressiveness or a dazed expression may be noticed.

The causes can be malnutrition and anemia, congestive heart failure, infection, drugs, head trauma, alcohol, cerebrovascular accidents, dehydration, reactions to surgery and many others. If the patient does not immediately die (from accompanying physical diseases or exhaustion) and if treatment of the cause is quickly given, the chances for recovery are high, especially if there is no serious underlying physical problem. If reversible brain syndromes are not swiftly diagnosed and treated, however, they can become chronic and irreversible. Thus they represent a true medical emergency. Unfortunately many doctors dismiss the symptoms, assuming that the person is demonstrating typical confusion from chronic brain syndromes caused by hardening of the arteries or senile brain disease,[1] and fail to treat the patient.

Chronic brain disorder is, of course, a reality for numbers of older people, but it has become a wastebasket diagnosis applied whenever anyone starts "acting senile." Not only are reversible brain disorders misdiagnosed, but depression and anxiety can also cause the same symptoms and also will respond to treatment.[2] Serious physical diseases such as heart attacks or diabetic comas[3] may be undetected and thereby go untreated because they first present themselves as mental confusion and are diagnosed as chronic brain disorders.

"Stroke" is a lay term for destruction of parts of the brain. It is sometimes fatal. People may be left with paralyzed arms and legs and impaired speech. Active care and treatment are uncommon in the acute phase and vigorous rehabilitation programs are equally rare in the recovery phase. As many as 75 percent of stroke patients could learn to move about by themselves, either completely on their own or with the aid of crutches, canes, braces, walkers or wheelchairs. They could also relearn countless other activities. But typically these patients are given brief occupational and/or physical therapy and then are allowed to lapse back into inactivity. They seldom receive help in the difficult psychological adjustments required. Patient apathy and discouragement are reinforced by custodial, rather than active, supportive care.[4]

Older men and women tend to be concerned about their *sexual abilities*.

Men fear impotence, women fear loss of sexual acceptance after the menopause. Much of what is feared is a direct result of cultural attitudes toward the sexuality of the elderly. Older men become the butt of jokes for their interest in sex; older women are depicted as unattractive and uninteresting. In truth, sexual interest and activity are much more common in old age than is generally realized and an active sex life promotes sound physical and mental health. Masters and Johnson as well as others have reported that the two major requirements for enjoyable sexual activity until late in life (and this can mean the seventies, eighties or later) are reasonably good health and an interested and interesting partner.

It is therefore imperative that medical attention be given to any health problems that interfere with sexuality. Impotence in men can be caused by excessive drinking, medical and psychiatric disabilities, fear of failure, fatigue, boredom and misuse of drugs, including tranquilizers and anti-depressants.

Doctors need to be particularly well informed about the effects of prostate removal and heart disease on sexuality in men. There can be both realistic problems and unreasonable fears which need clarification.

Older men need information about normal changes in sexuality with age so these are not interpreted as signs of impairment.

From a psychosexual point of view, the male over 50 has to contend with one of the great fallacies of our culture. Every man in this group is arbitrarily identified by both public and professional alike as sexually impaired.[5]

Older women usually experience little sexual impairment as they age and should be able to continue normal sexual activities until late in life. Certain physical problems which can result from menopause, such as thinning of the vaginal walls, can be reduced or eliminated through sex-steroid replacement therapy. Fears of insanity, inevitable depression,[6] severe physical symptoms and defeminization accompanying the menopause are largely myths, but because women have been led to believe them, they may need support and accurate information from health professionals.

Sensory impairments are particularly important in old age, for they can contribute to mental symptoms (depression, anxiety and suspiciousness) and to accidents. Such incapacities often go undetected, are recognized late or are untreated. Hearing impairment is first noted in the higher frequencies past the age of 50. This is called presbycusis (old hearing).[7] In the 1964 national health survey significant hearing loss was found in over 29 percent of the 65-plus population. Hearing loss is more common than visual loss. The four most common causes of severe visual impairment of people over

65 are macular degeneration,* cataracts, glaucoma and diabetic reti-
nopathy.⁸ Ten percent (1.9 million) of the elderly population have some
impairment of vision.⁹ However, in studies of people over 100 years of
age only 5 percent were totally blind and 2 percent totally deaf.

The above illustrations are a small sampling of what remains to be done
in diagnoses and treatment of older people's medical problems. In addition,
health education and prevention of illness should be emphasized in late
life. The doctor should function as teacher (the original meaning of the word
"doctor"), by educating older people regarding the maintenance of health
through diet, exercise, relaxation, early detection and treatment of illness,
and other aspects of preventive medicine. Older people require knowledge
about their bodies as they change through time and in the presence of
diseases. Myths, ignorance and misinformation abound.

In general, the possibilities for good health in late life have become much
brighter in recent years and may soon improve even more dramatically.
But the reality of health care for the old is another story.

PHYSICIANS' SERVICES

MEDICINE'S DISINTEREST IN THE OLD

The medical profession and other health personnel share the culture's
negative attitudes toward the old. In a medical context this can take the
form of active avoidance and dislike, or a less obvious pattern of paternalism
and infantilism, pained tolerance or caretaking rather than aggressive,
positive forms of treatment.

How can such attitudes be accounted for in professions which are designed to serve the sick, regardless of their personal circumstances, including
age? I will discuss my own profession, medicine, since I can present an
insider's view. The attitudes of physicians toward the old are complicated by
personal, professional, bureaucratic and financial considerations. Physicians, like the lay public, are personally ambivalent and frightened by
aging and death.† Indeed, studies have shown that significant numbers of

---

* Macular degeneration affects the vital parts of the retina essential to vision.

† Sudnow, in his studies of both charity and private hospitals, demonstrated that
physicians are usually intentionally absent at the time of death of their patients.¹⁰
The not uncommon insensitivity of physicians toward older patients is graphically
described in *Episode: Report on the Accident Inside My Skull* (New York: Atheneum
Press, 1964) written by Eric Hodgins, the author of *Mr. Blandings Builds His Dream
House.* He described his own stroke, during which his physician of many years stand-
ing would refer to him in the third person as if, because he was paralyzed, he was
also insensate.

physicians experienced in childhood the death of an important person in their lives, which influenced their decision to enter medicine. But, more generally, doctors have incorporated the larger culture's fears, denial and avoidance of the whole issue of aging, dying and death. Many are only dimly conscious, if conscious at all, of these powerfully negative forces operating in their lives and work.

Professionally, physicians are uninterested in the aspect of medicine most crucial to the old: the care of chronic conditions. The great majority of the elderly have chronic health problems of one kind or another. American medicine takes an extremely narrow view of medical care, focusing on the diagnosis and treatment of acute illness. Paradoxically, this does not include acute exacerbations of chronic ailments. Dramatic conditions which respond to fast cures are exciting and quickly satisfying. Slower, less spectacular preventive medicine and chronic care are considered boring, tedious, uninteresting and unproductive. Since chronic conditions are by nature irreversible (though nonetheless treatable) doctors tend to view them with despair and even nihilism. There is almost a Peter Pan sense that medicine should be immediately gratifying and not spoiled by situations which defy the doctor's ability to "make it all better." Yet the medical care of the old is more complex than that of the young, involving many more elements. Inherent in this is a greater challenge to the perceptions and intellect of physicians— if they can avoid the beguilement of "fast return" medicine.

A genuine problem for physicians has been the quantity of paperwork, confusion and delay in billing Medicare, Medicaid and private insurance companies for older patients' care. This has led many doctors to refuse to accept such patients altogether while others set a limit on the number they will treat. Some doctors have had to hire extra staff to handle the paperwork. The delays and inequities must be carefully worked out cooperatively among doctors, government agencies and policy makers. But doctors have to accept their share of the responsibility in making medical care available to the old through the existing programs. It must be pointed out that the majority of doctors are making proportionately more money than ever before, partly as a result of Medicare.

The question of responsibility is larger than Medicare. Physicians may find the elderly to be undesirable patients because they live on fixed incomes and are unable to afford the drugs, diets, appliances, glasses and hearing aids their doctors prescribe for them. (These items are not covered by Medicare.) Treatment of the old is more time consuming—there is more history to take, their symptoms are more complicated, they may want to talk at length, they do not respond to treatment as quickly as the young. Furthermore, they present inconvenient demands. Many need home visits, care after office hours, and transportation to and from doctors' offices and clinics. All of this is bothersome to the doctor who wants to get on with those problems that fit more comfortably within his truncated definition of medicine.

One sees a curious philosophic priority evidenced by doctors when they discuss the care of the old. There may be talk of "dollars and cents investments" and a conviction that the old are not worth such investment of resources. "It's like throwing money away; after all, they aren't going to be around much longer. They've had their chance. Now the money should go elsewhere. Children, on the other hand, are an investment in the future." This is again the naïve and perhaps cynical American tendency to discard objects once they are unproductive or out of fashion. There is little sense of old age as the culmination of life, or of the individual life as a carefully accumulated assemblage of years and experience to be valued and supported up to the very moment of death. Of course there are socioeconomic realities of undeniable importance. There are not adequate medical resources for all. But it becomes a society's responsibility to find ways to provide for all of its members rather than to sacrifice one age group for another.

Even if basically unprejudiced to begin with, American doctors are introduced to ageism and stereotyping of the old when they receive their medical training. Among medical students and their professors a "crock" is an undesirable patient, usually a middle-aged woman or an older person with a multiplicity of complaints.[11] Describing an older person as having "serum porcelain levels" is an in-house joke, elaborating on the word "crock." To say that an older person is "super tentorial" means that his illness is imaginary or all in his mind. There are other derogatory terms—"fogy," "constitutional inadequate," "snag," "neuropath," "rounder," "shopper," "floater"—and also "crud" and "crap"! Starkly un-Hippocratic attitudes persist: "A lot of people come in here with their brains pickled in alcohol and you wonder sometimes if they're worth helping," said a young 1970 medical graduate in his internship at D.C. General Hospital.[12]

The following are memories of my own medical-school days:

> As a medical student at Columbia University I heard talk about "crocks" among the attending physicians and the young interns and residents which was contagious and infected the medical students. "Crocks" included stroke patients, who would be quickly sent to Bellevue. I can remember, too, the Group Clinic which was part of the training in the third year to give us an opportunity to see "real" illness —that is, organic illnesses unencumbered by emotional problems.

Patients were carefully screened and yet some of us estimated that up to 50 percent had psychological problems, often a very major component of their illnesses, all of which were ignored. In fact, it was just such experiences that interested me in psychiatry. I also recall the academic professors and attending physicians referring with clinical exactitude to "the serum potassium in the fourth bed on the right" in the ward—rather than Mr. Jones or Mrs. Smith. I was struck by the highly prejudicial references to "LMDs," local medical doctors, those out on the line in practice, who were denigrated by professors. Importance was placed on teaching and research rather than upon decent service and humane treatment.

Twenty years later these attitudes have yet to change noticeably. Medical education is largely to blame for the "negativism, defeatism, and professional antipathy" which characterize medical care for the aged, according to researchers at the Langley Porter Neuropsychiatric Institute who were studying medical students at the University of California.[13] "At no point in their medical education," the investigators said, "are students exposed to any systematic consideration of the nature of old people and their medical (or social) problems." These students share most of society's misconceptions about aging and are likely to discriminate against the aged in their medical practice.

Spence, Feigenbaum *et al.* continue:

It is far from comforting to find that senior medical students, after three years of socialization in a profession whose express ethic is one of non-discrimination and adherence to scientific evaluation of fact rather than unexamined prejudice, do not differ significantly from freshmen who lack this experience. . . . One is led to question the efficacy, at least in this dimension, of medical socialization.

Of course, the attitudes of students and doctors illustrated by the use of such terms as "crock" reflect deeply felt anxiety. It is essential that medical education help students understand their fears and why it is they use such terms.

In 1962 while at the National Institute of Mental Health I sent a direct-mail survey to deans of all medical schools and to all chairmen of departments of psychiatry. The 90 percent-plus response indicated that there was little interest in establishing special courses related to geriatric medicine, the principles of gerontology or aging, or chronic illness. There was no interest in creating a specialty in geriatric medicine, or endowing special chairs. Most deans felt that the subject was sufficiently covered within the existing curriculum. Eight years later, in 1970, Dr. Joseph T.

Freeman[14] noted that of 99 medical schools, 50 made no mention of the subject in any form. Furthermore, medical students have little knowledge of the humanities, anthropology and sociology, all of which profoundly affect the conception of health and actual health care itself. They know little about environmental conditions, especially poverty, as they affect their patients.*

The results of medical-school training are quickly seen when physicians begin their practices and are confronted by older patients. As a psychiatrist I routinely telephone all other doctors who are involved in the care of my older patients. I am interested in their appraisal of the patient's situation. One repeated characteristic is the tendency by even the most conscientious of physicians to write off old people as untreatable on the basis of "age" or "hardening of the arteries" or "senility." One hears pessimistic descriptions of "organic impairment," "irreversibility," "limited life expectancy," and patronizing phrases like "second childhood," "childish" and "childlike."

Some old people are able to challenge their doctors directly when they feel they are being written off:

> Mr. Morris was one of the volunteers for study at the National Institute of Health at the age of 92. He lived to be 102 years old. Near the end of his life he was having pain in his left leg and went to see his doctor. The doctor declared, "Sam, for Pete's sake, what do you expect at 102?" Sam retorted, "Look, my right leg is also 102 but it doesn't hurt a bit. Now explain that!"

A favorite assumption of doctors is that sexuality is unimportant in late life. Important symptoms can thereby be ignored:

> One doctor informed me thoroughly about the cardiac condition and hypochondriasis of a psychiatric patient of mine. He was ready to say goodbye when I asked about a disease (Peyronie's) which the doctor had mentioned in passing and which affected the man's sexual performance. "Oh that—oh well, he's too old for that to matter," said the doctor. But to this vigorous 69-year-old it did matter a great deal that he had a condition that prevented intercourse. To him it had greater psychological import than his other physical ailments.†

---

* When the Legal Services Program (in the Office of Economic Opportunity) was established in 1965, no law school in the country had courses in poverty law; today, more than a hundred do. Medical schools have not been as responsive as law schools to social change.

† Peyronie's disease, named after a French physician, is not as rare as previously believed. Its origin is obscure; its treatment nonspecific; it is characterized by a

An unfortunate result of medical pessimism about old age is that many elderly people and their families accept and echo their doctors' negativism, taking the view that nothing can be done—it's just old age.

THE INACCESSIBILITY OF DOCTORS

Many doctors work sixty hours a week or more. Yet, despite their toiling, outpatient medicine is largely invisible at night, on weekends and holidays. The old and the weak suffer most. They may not make it unaided through the night or until Monday morning. If they can get to emergency rooms, they must wait like everyone else, regardless of their wearied or weakened condition. Transportation expenses can be prohibitive. There may be no one who can accompany them.

Eight percent of the community-resident elderly are totally housebound. Many others are afraid to leave their homes, especially in the inner city, if they are weakened by illness. Some require stretcher or van service to get to the doctor, and these are usually unavailable.

House-call services are rare. Physicians are reluctant to take the time in view of the fee they could expect to collect. There is a fear of criminal attack in the inner city and low-income areas. In most cases doctors feel they can treat a patient better in an office or emergency room. There are exceptions:

> One New Jersey cardiovascular specialist takes his mobile office from one low-income housing project to another every Tuesday in a time when many doctors refuse to make home calls. Fifty-six, Dr. Huerta Neals has practiced privately in Jersey City for twenty-three years. In his view old people are "lost in the shuffle," and, "many old people die needlessly because they give up the idea of trying to get to a doctor. Depression sets in because they feel helpless." "It is disheartening to me to see older patients who have trouble with their breathing waiting for long periods of time in a clinic." Dr. Neals bought a used truck which he equipped with electro-cardiography, a unit for analyzing blood, and other medical equipment. "What I bring that is needed most is myself." He also makes house calls and has night office hours several days a week, which is not very common any more. He sees his patients regularly on a non-crisis basis instead of waiting until they're in trouble. He thoughtfully phones a day in advance of his visits. "These patients are vulnerable to a major reversal in their health with the slightest neglect from doctors."[15]

bowing of the penis and by pain during intercourse; and its emotional impact can be devastating. It may correct itself after several years' time.

Profit-making house-call organizations have been established in several large cities, with Medicare covering 80 percent of what is determined to be the customary and prevailing fee for a particular area. Home medical care is useful in catching emergency situations such as heart attacks in early stages, treating minor but painful ailments and providing an enormous sense of security to the older person who is unable to leave home for the treatment of aggravating but noncritical illnesses.

Walk-in clinics should be well distributed within easy walking distance of as many older people as possible. The New York State Hospitals Code authorized "walklinics" for New York in August, 1969.

THE DOCTOR SHORTAGE

There are not enough doctors and they are unevenly distributed. The American Medical Association, which long denied it, now acknowledges a doctor shortage. The 1971 estimated shortage was fifty thousand doctors. One of every fifty Americans has no access to a physician. Twenty percent of the newly licensed physicians in the United States are foreign trained,* and these are the doctors especially likely to see the poor and elderly. Problems with language and culture are frequent.†

A 1970 Carnegie Commission on Higher Education report[16] recommended that the nation produce more doctors by cutting the time required for a degree from four years to three. It also stressed patient care over research programs, increased numbers of doctors' assistants, more federal support for medical education and more women and minority-group members trained as doctors.‡

The health-care complex is the third-largest industry and the largest employer in the United States economy. Approximately 3.7 million persons were so employed in 1968, 4.5 million in 1974. Every person in the country is a potential consumer of this industry's services, and when sufficient pain and disability are present they have no choice but to buy. This generalization is especially true for the elderly.

In addition to doctor shortages there is a general health manpower shortage, as well as selective shortages particularly harmful to older people. More personnel with nursing skills are urgently needed for the old. In 1968 there were 680,000 registered nurses, 345,000 licensed practical nurses and 800,000 nursing aides, orderlies, attendants and home

---

* Some seven thousand foreign medical-school graduates are imported each year.
† Educational efforts to offset these problems could be sponsored by federal and state governments.
‡ Only 7 percent of doctors are women and 2 percent black.

health aides. These numbers are inadequate for the demand. In 1973 it was estimated that the United States needed 50,000 more registered nurses.

During the Vietnam War some 35,000 highly trained medical corpsmen from the armed forces were discharged annually. The Vietnam veteran has a knowledge of medicine that should be utilized for civilian purposes. Training, of course, is required. By 1970 some 40 schools in the United States had training programs for assistant physicians—called paramedics, clinical associates, or health practitioners. Physicians' assistants could help reduce the doctor shortage[17] by increasing the number of patients that doctors can see and relieving doctors of many routine responsibilities. Care, of course, must be taken that they do not become total substitutes for doctors, especially in impoverished rural and urban areas. Within the states, issues of licensure, control and malpractice have still not been worked out.

Still, as far as the aged are concerned it is not enough to cry "doctor shortage." If we had enough doctors, would they be interested in caring for the aged?* Would they have the necessary education? This will depend on the development of a new sensibility toward the old. One specialty which might become particularly amenable to a change in attitude is the new field of family medicine, replacing the dying profession of general practice. The family-doctor specialty was recognized by the American Medical Association in 1969. Twenty percent of all doctors are presently in general or family practice, including 61,000 general practitioners in the United States in 1970. The question of creating a geriatric specialty will be discussed later in this chapter.

DOCTORS' FEES

Doctors' fees are too high for many older people and, ironically, doctors' charges—and their incomes—have gone up since the inception of Medicare. When Medicare was passed in 1965 the physician's median net income was $28,960 but it jumped 11.1 percent in 1966 to $32,170. The average net income of physicians in 1969 (the latest year for which HEW has complete data) was $40,550, up 7.8 percent from the 1968 level.†

The Judicial Council of the AMA, the doctors' ruling body on ethical

---

* One practical solution is the monetary incentives used in England under the National Health Service. The general practitioner is paid an extra capitation fee for each old person he has on his list of patients.

† In the ten years from 1959-69 average hourly wages of workers in manufacturing rose at an annual rate of 3.7 percent, while earnings of doctors climbed 6.3 percent per year. The biggest leaps came after the enactment of Medicare. The gains were not solely due to higher fees. Increased productivity on the part of doctors and improved collection rates contributed.

matters, said in November, 1970, that too many physicians are casting aside humanitarian concerns and becoming preoccupied with the business side of medicine. Dr. Elmer G. Shelley of Florida, council chairman, referred to the age-old professional ideal of medical service to all whether able to pay or not. He stated, "The increase of collections by adding 1.5 percent interest per month to a bill of an honest patient, financially embarrassed because of inflationary trends, or the bill to some retired person living on a small pension is, in the opinion of the judicial council, not justifiable."

On the other hand, according to a survey by the magazine *Medical Economics,* most doctors are generous about the scope of benefits that should be included in a national health-insurance plan—including nursing-home and psychiatric care.[18] Most would prefer a fee-for-time reimbursement formula, however, rather than straight salary or fixed annual payment per patient (capitation).

Federal control is in the air—first by "fee profiles" and "percentiles" and probably soon by other means. From the beginning of Medicare, the Social Security Administration has not automatically paid whatever doctors have charged. Fee profiles refer to the computed picture of actual charges of individual physicians under Medicare. Percentiles refer to a statistically set level (e.g., 75 percent) of acceptable fees, depending upon the percentage of doctors (say 75 percent) charging least in the claimant's locale for the same service. The Price Commission ruled in 1972 that doctors may raise their fees, on the average, by no more than 2.5 percent a year and that any increase must be the result of higher costs. This was raised to 4 percent in 1973. Controls ended in 1974.

The Medicare law states that the government cannot attach controls to the billions of dollars going into hospital coffers and doctors' pockets:

Nothing in this title shall be construed to authorize any federal officer or employee to exercise any supervision or control over the practice of medicine or the manner in which medical services are provided or over the selection, tenure or compensation of any officer or employee of any institution, agency or person providing health services; or to exercise any supervision or control over the administration or operation of any such institution, agency or person.

The need to control costs will continue to be at the center of the national debate over health care in the 1970s. There are increasing signs from Capitol Hill that hospitals will eventually be regulated like public utilities if they want to share in federal funds, and that further controls will be placed on the doctors' fee-for-service charges and on the quality of their service.

PEER REVIEW

American doctors have been responding to public demands for control of the medical profession by advocating the concept of peer review. The House of Delegates of the AMA adopted the following definitions in 1971:

Peer Review: evaluation by practicing physicians of the quality and efficiency of services ordered or performed by other practicing physicians. Peer review is the all inclusive term for medical review efforts.

Utilization Review: evaluation of the efficient use of professional medical care services, procedures and facilities.

There is scant evidence that peer and utilization review mechanisms as measures of the performance of physicians and hospitals have had notable effects on the quality of health care. There is none to show that it has favorably affected the care of older patients.

Peer review as it is presently practiced is in fact, really record review. "Medical records can hide a heap of medical sin,"[19] observed one doctor, who urged the monitoring of actual work with patients rather than medical records. Samplings of patients should be evaluated by review doctors and the findings and conclusions recorded.

Peer review should not be under the exclusive influence of the local medical communities as in the Professional Standards Review Organizations established since 1972. Cost and quality control should be influenced by representatives of the consumers of hospital services and by other professionals, particularly sociologists, economists, nurses and social workers. At Massachusetts General Hospital nurses and social workers participate in evaluating patient care. Specialists on aging should be represented in the review of hospitals and physicians in treating Medicare patients.

About two hundred diagnoses and treatments account for 80 percent of all medical problems. Dr. Donald Harrington of the San Joaquin Foundation for Medical Care in Stockton, California, is developing the first national norms for medical care.

Dr. Alex Gerber, respected critic of his profession and professor of surgery of the University of Southern California Medical School, believes as I do that doctors cannot objectively judge other doctors. Patients should have mechanisms for grievance about doctors' attitudes, fees and medical skills. That medical self-supervision does not work well is asserted by the 1970 Nader report entitled *One Physician—One Life*. It declares that state licensure laws lack uniformity and fail to guarantee that physicians remain fit to practice. It noted that the quality of hospital-patient care is not directly policed by the Joint Commission on Accreditation of Hospitals (JCAH), which confines itself to inspection of the institutional "environment."

The Nader group recommended that Congress establish a national board of medicine to oversee the quality of all federally financed health-care programs. It further urged development of standardized patient record forms, national standards by which to judge physicians' and hospitals' performance, and specialized licensing standards with re-examination required for renewal.

HOSPITAL CARE

HOSPITAL TACTICS IN HANDLING THE ELDERLY

Older patients have difficulties when they need hospitalization unless they have a regular doctor and, generally speaking, a good-sized income. When they become ill, a significant number of them arrive at the emergency rooms of voluntary nonprofit and public hospitals to discover that they are not considered desirable patients. The long wait for care, called "hard-bench medicine," is typical in most emergency rooms for people of all ages. But certain hospital tactics are used particularly with the elderly, or at least have particular effect on them:

1. The Emergency-Room Hustle

One of the fastest ways to avoid dealing thoroughly with the problems of the older person is through the technique called "treatment and release." This means the doctor quickly examines a patient, decides nothing is drastically wrong and tells the patient to go home, perhaps to return on another day. Confused and disoriented persons may never return. And, if they do, their mental symptoms are often considered to be outside the province of medicine. Acute brain syndromes are overlooked; chronic brain syndromes are dismissed as "senility." Social problems and loneliness are ignored:

The old man walks with a cane and stutters. "Please, can I see a doctor, please, Miss," he begs the admissions attendant. Earlier in the evening he was examined by a doctor who could find nothing wrong with him.

"I haven't seen no doctor, I didn't see him," the man says. He is crying now.

"There it is, right here," the attendant says. "You were here at 7:35 P.M.

Treated and released, it says. You have an appointment for 10:00 A.M. tomorrow."

The man walks outside into the cold night air.[20]

2. *The Transfer*

Voluntary hospitals may refuse care to old people and transfer them to the overloaded and underfinanced public municipal hospital:*

> Two ambulance attendants wheel in a 77-year old woman whose forehead and chin are bandaged. She has apparently fallen down a flight of steps but remembers nothing about the accident.
>
> She has been transferred from the Washington Hospital Center which—following a quick examination—has refused to treat the woman further. She is financially ineligible for that private hospital's care.
>
> "This is the tenth one we've brought you from the Center today, baby," the ambulance driver tells the head nurse.
>
> "They have to take everybody's trash here," says the driver whose firm is under contract to D.C. General to handle transfers from other hospitals.
>
> "Some of these patients are too sick to transfer," adds the nurse who has worked in the D.C. General emergency room for more than four years.[22]

It strains credulity to know that in 1934 the American Medical Association adopted as a policy "the age-old professional idea of medical service to all whether able to pay or not," and to observe discriminatory practices like this today.

3. *The Shuttle*

This is a prolonged version of the transfer. A patient is moved from one place to another until someone gives in and admits him.

> An 86-year-old man, described as delirious and near coma from a kidney ailment, was shuttled between three D.C. hospitals Tuesday afternoon as doctors argued over who should take responsibility for his care. He finally ended up at St. Elizabeths Hospital for the mentally ill.[23]

In some cases patients conveniently die in the ambulance.

---

* According to the Hospital Planning Council of Metropolitan Chicago one thousand patients died because private hospitals turned them away or transferred them to Cook County Hospital in 1970. The average waiting time in the Cook County emergency room was two hours.[21]

4. The Quota System

Quotas are a time-honored method of excluding undesirables. As chairman of the D.C. Advisory Committee on Aging I wrote to a voluntary hospital in February, 1970, protesting the poor care of an 85-year-old woman received in its emergency room. The hospital replied that it is concerned with acute and not chronic care and that the patient was the "responsibility of the District of Columbia." Further,

In answer to your specific question regarding the policy of our hospital on the admission of Medicare and Medicaid patients, this hospital does not refuse emergency department care to any individual no matter what his ability to pay may be. This statement obviously also refers to Medicare and Medicaid beneficiaries. The hospital's outpatient clinics presently accept all patients within prescribed income levels, including all Medicaid patients and many Medicare patients and the number of such patients cared for in the outpatient setting is *limited only by the physical and staffing capabilities of these clinics.* In terms of admissions policy the hospital has no restriction on the number of Medicare and Medicaid patients admitted by members of the hospital's attending staff. However, from the hospital's beginnings the Board of Trustees has maintained that the *number of patients admitted* to the hospital in any one time without previously designated physicians *will not exceed 10 per cent of the hospitals' total bed count.* The sole intention of this policy is that an *adequate number of beds will be available to members of the hospital's attending staff. At times this policy can impose the limitation of a number of Medicare and Medicaid patients admitted to this hospital.* [All italics mine.]

5. Two-Class Medicine

Two-class medicine has traditionally referred to the differing quality of care given the rich and the poor. This concept may justifiably be extended to the divergent care given the young and the old. Hospitals may not set out deliberately to ostracize the aged and their needs. Instead, they can simply put them on a back burner. One way is through two-class medicine. Staff doctors (that is, interns and residents) treat the elderly poor, if they are treated at all. The patient may wait long hours for care. Voluntary hospitals take a very restricted view of their responsibilities to their city and its citizens. The public hospitals are overwhelmed. Many old people and poor people, white as well as members of various minority groups, are still the teaching material—and too often guinea pigs—for young interns and residents. Medicare and Medicaid were presumed to lead to a unitary class of medicine but they have not eradicated the double standard.

6. Shut the Door and Wait

The final indignity in hospitals is to isolate the old when they are dying. The doctors and nurses hope the patient will not inconveniently die on their shift. Visiting restrictions may keep family contacts limited. Young children are not allowed in at all. One of the greatest fears of older people is that of dying alone—and this is made almost inevitable by current hospital procedures.[24]

HOSPITAL-BED SPACE FOR THE OLD

The number of general hospital beds available—and empty—is increasing, yet older people are turned away when they should be admitted.* Emergency shelter and overnight care, prompt comprehensive diagnostic evaluation, care of chronic disease and intervening superimposed acute exacerbations, mental-health care and interim family and social services are among the hospital services needed by older people, in addition to the treatment for acute illnesses which most hospitals already offer.

The growing older population require especially trained units ready to appraise and treat them. Quality care similar to the hospital-based Oxford program of Lionel Z. Cosin would be desirable. Cosin's program treats the older patient as a whole person and starts with a comprehensive assessment of medical, psychiatric, social and community conditions. On the basis of these findings a plan is developed for the multidisciplinary treatment of each problem. This requires a team—the general physician or internist, social worker, psychiatrist and allied health-care workers— helping the patient and his family. There should be a program of physical and mental rehabilitation carried on by trained nurses, physiotherapists, occupational and speech therapists. There must be continuing assessment. All during contact with a patient, work with the hospital, family physician, family and community should be closely linked.

The provision of bed space for effective chronic-disease units and reception-diagnostic complexes could be accomplished simply by more effective utilization of existing space and pertinent remodeling. Major new construction may be unnecessary.† Comprehensive planning that co-

---

* Actually hospital bed occupancy has never been 100 percent. In 1960 it was 74.7 percent according to the American Hospital Association; in 1970, 78 percent; in 1971, 77 percent.

† In fact, hospital overbuilding may have already occurred. As of 1972 only fifteen states had laws empowering them to deny the construction of unneeded health facilities. The Hill-Burton program has been held partly responsible for overbuilding. However, since about 1970 this program has supported modernization of existing hospitals rather than new construction.

ordinates outreach supportive services operating from an institutional base could also be done on the basis of existing facilities. Patients suffering from chronic physical and mental illnesses and their exacerbations could move back and forth between the hospital and the community with a working alliance maintained among the patient and his family, existing community resources, and the institution.

It is practical and desirable to have identifiable chronic or long-term facilities physically connected with short-term general hospitals. Such facilities could be a separate adjacent building or special floors or parts of floors of general hospitals. The highly regarded Commission on Chronic Illness, which studied the problem in the early 1950s, concluded that total separation of acute and chronic care systems was ill advised for a variety of reasons. Such segregation has taken the chronic patient out of the mainstream of health-care delivery. It has reduced incentives for research and has led to neglect in the training of health practitioners. The integration of chronic care into general hospitals is in keeping with present and future needs of the growing population of older and chronically ill patients. Money will have to be spent training additional manpower. Physical renovation will be expensive. Ultimately, however, incorporating research, education and service regarding chronic diseases within the general care system will save health dollars. Disease prevention, earlier treatment and more efficient use of beds and staff for long-term care are among the benefits.

Emergency bed space is another problem. Emergency shelter is especially vital for the old to allow them a period of decision—thinking about what to do next. Old people arrive at hospitals for social reasons (evictions, fear of crime, malnutrition due to insufficient income) as well as medical and psychiatric ones. A brief admission with immediate treatment can supply a proper diagnostic workup, and an evaluation of that diagnosis by assessment of the results of treatment. It also gives shelter to the older person in time of stress and should provide contact with proper services to assist in whatever problem he has.

HOSPITAL STANDARDS

Another obstacle to decent health care for the elderly is the low standards of hospitals. The Joint Commission on the Accreditation of Hospitals,

---

Low maternity and pediatric censuses have also affected hospital use. Cutbacks in Medicaid, tightening-up on Medicare and the lapsing of health insurance on workers who have been laid off have contributed to reduced bed occupancy—but those are unfortunate causes that should be rectified.

the only body responsible for hospital accreditation in the United States (JCAH), does not provide public monitoring of Medicare patients receiving either medical or psychiatric care. There is no comprehensive approach to standard setting, outpatient care, staff-patient ratios, and the quality of overall hospital care.[25] Instead, JCAH Director John D. Porterfield states: "We attempt to evaluate the quality of supporting services such as nursing, housekeeping, and safety, and to require adequate clinical recordkeeping." Obviously JCAH deals with the peripheral issues rather than with direct patient needs and care.*

A class-action suit on behalf of all Medicare beneficiaries against the HEW Secretary in November, 1971, declared that San Francisco General Hospital and others across the nation are "operated under unsafe, unsanitary, and frequently inhumane conditions" to the detriment of elderly persons dependent upon such institutions for care. The complainant argued that this is partly because Congress declared that JCAH standards were adequate for Medicare certification of hospitals. The suit further argues that the standards are both inadequate and inadequately enforced. Among poor conditions cited specifically were the findings of maggots on a comatose patient; urine, stool and blood specimens stored with food; and a hospital with no fire drills in eight and a half years. It was recommended that JCAH should be accountable to the public or to the HEW Secretary. The charge was made that the Medicare law's delegation of authority to the JCAH without HEW guidelines, surveillance or judicial reviews deprives Medicare beneficiaries of "due process" and violates the first, second and fifth amendments to the Constitution. It is an unconditional delegation of governmental authority to a private body.

The Health Insurance Benefits Advisory Council (HIBAC)† made the same points in a 1967 report to Congress:

> There is reason for concern that JCAH standards are not applied with the frequency of inspection and the range of inspection skills necessary . . . [and] because of present statutory provisions, the JCAH standards in some could impose an undesirably low ceiling on the maximum level at which health and safety standards under Medicare may be set.

---

* "Although half the hospital expenditures in the country come from local, state and federal governments, and although hospitals receive large subsidies in the form of exemptions from taxes, there is no federal law requiring disclosure of hospital finance data or prohibiting conflicts of interest by hospital governing boards."[26] There should be federal guidelines for state regulation by commissions similar to public-utility commissions that regulate telephone and power companies. The American Hospital Association also backs this approach.

† The public advisory council on Medicare. Its influence has been shockingly downplayed by HEW.

Congress mooted the litigation through its 1972 Social Security Amendments which allow HEW to survey a selected sample of hospitals to validate JCAH findings and inform Congress annually. It remains to be seen whether this will work effectively.

HOSPITAL STAFFING

It is not possible to cite definite numbers of hospitals that are below standard in staffing since there are no surveys oriented specifically to direct patient care. However, there is little to indicate that older people are receiving quality inpatient care from health practitioners, whether doctors, nurses or aides. Few are well trained in the broad principles and special knowledge of chronic disease and geriatric health care.

An added problem is that of low wages for all levels of hospital staff. For example, physicians' wages in public hospitals are not competitive with private practice and academia, and the work is much more demanding. A shortage of doctors willing and qualified for work in public, state and municipal institutions has led to heavy utilization of foreign doctors, who provide the bulk of medical manpower. Many are poorly trained, have language problems and are not familiar with American culture.* Throughout the United States the staffing of public hospitals is inadequately monitored by the hospitals and municipal or state authorities. The following tragic example illustrates what can happen:

> Although unlicensed in Illinois, Dr. Richard Munoz-Valez received a permit to work at Elgin State Hospital outside Chicago. Although hired as a pathologist, he practiced "general medicine" in a geriatric unit where a number of deaths suggested some irregularities on his part.
>
> He was suspended in February 1972 after the state's attorney's office called in Dr. George LeRoy, professor of medicine at the University of Chicago, to review the deaths of 26 geriatric patients during the previous 18 months. Dr. LeRoy found no evidence of homicide, but described Dr. Munoz' use of drugs as "injudicious, irrational, or ignorant." One example: the prescription of antiarrhythmia agents without any knowledge or documentation of a rhythm disorder.
>
> The case is forcing the Illinois state administration to examine the status of some 400 doctors working in its mental hospital system, and the process by which these unlicensed doctors—almost all foreign born —are screened.[27]

---

* This should not be read as a universal indictment. There are, of course, gifted and able foreign-born and trained physicians.

Such a case is an extreme, of course, but it is sympotomatic of the kind of care the old have been led to expect.

HILL-BURTON REGULATIONS

Municipal hospitals and the nonprivate sections of voluntary hospitals are reluctant to serve the elderly, particularly if they are indigent.* The provision in the Hill-Burton hospital survey and construction act requiring grantee hospitals to provide a "reasonable volume" of free or reduced-cost services for the poor has been long ignored.† Consumer-oriented groups have filed class-action suits to compel hospitals and other institutions accepting Hill-Burton funds to provide a reasonable volume of services to persons unable to pay. Successful outcomes were achieved in New Orleans, Colorado, and Florida.

Nineteen seventy-three HEW regulations setting forth guidelines for Hill-Burton-aided hospitals and nursing homes provide three ways of qualifying for "presumptive compliance." A Hill-Burton facility may not deny admission and services to anyone unable to pay. It must provide free services at levels not less than 3 percent of its annual operating costs (excluding costs reimbursed under Medicare and Medicaid). It must declare it will provide free care equal to 10 percent of Hill-Burton assistance.

DRUGS

One hundred ninety-eight million prescriptions given to 19 million older Americans in 1966 (the last year for which figures are available) cost $772 million for 7,000 different drug products. Modern medicines have increased average life expectancy through significant progress in the treatment of acute diseases. Chronic diseases, such as diabetes and cardiac disease, have also been the targets of effective pharmaceutical agents. Further advances in the drug treatment of heart disease, cancer and other chronic illnesses are expected. Emotional problems—anxiety, severe agita-

---

* Private hospitals, generally speaking, take good care of the affluent older patient, just as they do the affluent of any age. The Washington Hospital Center is illustrative. It was built with congressional appropriations; one-third of its budget comes from federal funds. An excellent series, *The Hospital Business*, was written by Ronald Kessler in the Washington *Post*, October 29–November 8, 1972.

† The Hill-Burton Act was passed in 1946. This program makes grants and loans available to aid in the building and equipping of hospitals and other health facilities and provides technical and consultation services to assist health-facility sponsors. Since 1970 it has aided modernization of hospitals. Altogether, since its beginnings, some 60 percent of American hospitals have benefited.

tion, depression—may respond to the supportive treatment of tranquilizers and antidepressants in the context of other therapy. Thus the older population, living longer than ever before and with a greater number of physical and emotional diseases than the young, requires a higher proportion of drug usage.

Yet, despite the importance of drugs in the health care of older people, there are dangers, abuses and hardships involved in their use.

THE HIGH COST OF DRUGS

HEW's 1968 Task Force on Prescription Drugs conducted the most recent major study on the uses and costs of drugs for older people.[28] It found that "the burden of drug costs falls heavily on the elderly. . . . Many elderly men and women are now unable to meet these needs with their limited incomes, savings, or present insurance coverage. Their inability to afford the drugs they require may well be reflected in needless sickness and disability."* Yet Medicare does not yet cover out-of-hospital prescription drugs, the largest single personal expenditure the elderly must presently meet largely from their own resources.

Use of generic rather than brand names would save money for the older consumer. The task force found that 409 drugs were most frequently used by the elderly and accounted for 88 percent of their prescription drug costs in 1966. Those 409 drugs, 175 million prescriptions, cost $682 million at the retail level. Of the 409 drugs, 290 were still under patent, with no generic substitute available; 30 were available and actually dispensed under generic name; and 22 were available under generic name but not at any applicable saving over brand-name counterparts. But 67 drugs were obtainable under generic rather than brand names and purchase in this manner would result in a saving of $41.5 million to the elderly.†

The HEW drug task force recommended coverage of out-of-hospital prescription drugs under Medicare and urged controls on the cost and quality of drugs. It observed that "the exceptionally high rate of profit which generally marks the drug industry is not accompanied by any peculiar degree of risk or by any unique difficulties in obtaining capital growth." Former Commissioner James L. Goddard of the Food and Drug

---

* This is true even though drugs at discount prices can be obtained by way of national organizations of older people like the National Council of Senior Citizens and the American Association of Retired Persons.

† For example, Ciba's 1975 price to druggists for one thousand tablets (0.25 mg.) of Serpasil, a drug which lowers high blood pressure, is $39.50. The generic name for this drug is reserpine. Stayner Laboratories, whose name was chosen at random from a drug prices handbook used by all pharmacies, sells reserpine for $2.50 per thousand tablets.

Administration has said that if the drug establishment persists in its present course of making extremely high profits, Congress may well demand to know "why it should not be made into a public utility."[29]

DRUG SAFETY AND EFFECTIVENESS

Beginning in 1960, Cincinnati's William S. Merrell Company sold MER/29 as a medication to lower blood cholesterol and thus reduce the risk of heart attacks. MER/29 was the trade name for a synthetic hormone substitute, triparanol. A number of patients who used it developed baldness, impotence and blindness from an unusual form of cataract. The Food and Drug Administration, upon investigation, stated: "In applying for approval of MER/29 Merrell improperly withheld information already in its files that triparanol had caused cataracts in animals."[30] In court the company and its executives pleaded *nolo contendere* (no contest) and the drug was withdrawn from the market in 1962.[31]

Many other drugs need to be more fully tested. From 1966 to 1969 thirty panels formed by the National Academy of Sciences–National Research Council checked the effectiveness of nearly four thousand drug products marketed between 1938 and 1962,* and submitted reports to the Food and Drug Administration. Seven percent of drugs reviewed were found ineffective. The panels also became concerned that the hazards of long-term use of drugs such as steroids in arthritis patients "often outweigh the advantages of disease suppression." They questioned the possible effects of long-acting estrogens in stimulating cancer and long-acting vasodilators in producing angina—as well as many other time-bomb effects on people receiving drugs over extended periods.

The American Public Health Association and the National Council of Senior Citizens† sued the federal government in 1970 to compel it to enforce the law against dangerous and ineffective medicines. Bruce J. Terris of the Center for Law and Social Policy conducted the suit, which originated with Dr. Robert S. McCleery, a consultant to Ralph Nader's Center for Study of Responsive Law. The result was a legal decision to speed up the evaluation of ineffective drugs. In January, 1971, HEW declared it would not pay Medicare and Medicaid money for 512 drugs termed ineffective or only possibly effective by the FDA. The Veterans Administration, armed services and the Agency for International Develop-

---

* Required by the 1963 Kefauver-Harris amendments to the Food and Drug Act. The amendments followed the thalidomide disaster. In 1974, shockingly, the AMA voted to work to rescind these amendments.

† APHA is a century-old group with 25,000 members including 7,000 physicians. NCSC is an organization of about 3 million elderly persons.

ment had previously announced buying guidelines based on the same information.

After four and a half years of hearings on the drug industry, Senator Gaylord Nelson (D.-Wis.) has produced a proposed overhaul of the Federal Food, Drug and Cosmetic Act.* His forty-eight-page bill, presented as an omnibus amendment to that act, would require among other things the establishment of a national drug testing and evaluation center.

Safety features could be introduced easily into our present drug-dispensing methods. In Canada, Latin and South America and most of Europe the law requires manufacturers to label all medicines with brand name, ingredients and dosage as well as the purpose of the medicine, its side effects, full dosage range and expiration date if there is one. Until the United States has such laws doctors should instruct druggists to label prescriptions in full. This is valuable regardless of the patient's age, but especially so for old people who may have memory loss or confusion. If allergic or other untoward reactions occur, emergency care can be given even if the patient's original doctor or pharmacy cannot be contacted.

Drug packaging could also be designed for greater safety. One company, Eli Lilly and Company, launched a new safety coding system for capsules and tablets in 1966 (Indenti-code system). They did not patent the system so it could be adopted by other companies, but unfortunately little interest has been shown. Compact tablet or capsule dispensers, such as used for birth-control pills, could be useful as an aid to the memories of older people; it is easy for them to forget they have already taken a pill, or forget to take one.

PACIFICATION THROUGH DRUGS

A common and vivid memory for anyone who sees numbers of older people in nursing homes, mental hospitals and psychiatric wards is the image of overmedicated, zombie-like persons only dimly aware of the world around them. Since the advent of the psychoactive drugs in the 1950s, tranquilizers and antidepressants have become widely used in the care of older patients suffering from agitation, anxiety and depression. These drugs are frequently given as much for the tranquility of the institution as for the comfort of the patient. On an outpatient basis general practitioners and psychiatrists find psychoactive agents an all too easy answer for the many complicated physical and emotional reactions of late

---

* There is great need for reform. There has been a "well-traveled, two-way street" between the drug industry and Washington, described, for example, by Dr. Louis C. Lasagna in *The Doctors' Dilemma*, 1962. Mintz has called it FDA's "revolving door."[32]

life. It is much simpler to give a pill than to listen to complaints. Chemotherapy can often bring quick cessation of symptoms as the patient becomes benumbed and pacified.

Two tranquilizers, chlordiazepoxide (Librium) and diazepam (Valium) are among the ten most frequently dispensed drugs of all kinds. Tranquilizers represented about 8.5 percent of all drugs prescribed for elderly patients in 1966. Phenothiazines such as chlorpromazine (Thorazine) and thioridazine (Mellaril) are in particularly heavy use in institutions. The United States Senate Special Committee on Aging found that in the states of Illinois, Ohio and New Jersey in 1971, 35 to 40 percent of all prescriptions for elderly consumers under Medicaid (the federal-state health program for the needy) were tranquilizers and sedatives.

Often drugs represent the only form of treatment given to older persons. An overall treatment plan that includes attention to diet, physical and social activities, psychotherapy and correction of living problems may be totally ignored. Drug companies encourage the use of pills as cure-alls. Roche advertised Librax (its trade name for chlordiazepoxide, a minor tranquilizer and an anticholinergic agent) to control gastrointestinal hypermotility and spasm, with a picture of a forlorn-looking old woman and the caption:

Widowed and alone (with irritable colon syndrome). Loss of loved one. Loneliness. Job insecurity. The high correlation between stress factors in a patient's life and irritable colon syndrome is a matter of clinical experience.[33]

Nowhere was it suggested that the drug should be but one component of a comprehensive treatment including efforts to find new relationships, job security and a life with less stress.

Sandoz displayed an old woman characterized as "the collector" and added:

At 85 she's collected many things, a family who avoids her whenever possible, total dependence on strangers, restricted financial resources, limited mobility, and various physical symptoms—real or imagined. When her collection leads to anxiety or mixed anxiety-depression . . .[34]

For this miserable-looking female Sandoz recommended Mellaril, trade name for thioridazine, a major tranquilizer. Again no other professional care is even hinted at. Of course, it is the ultimate responsibility of doctors to use medications appropriately. But the easy availability and quick pacifying action of tranquilizers and antidepressants make them tempting substitutes for decent, humane attention through diagnosis and careful treatment.

IATROGENIC (DOCTOR-INDUCED) DISORDERS

"*Primum non nocere*"—"First, do no harm"—is a cardinal rule in medicine, but it is not always obeyed. Drugs are given far too readily with inadequate consideration for possible short- and long-term complications. An estimated one million Americans of all ages (probably an underestimate) suffer untoward drug reactions yearly. An estimated thirty thousand die annually. The added cost is between $1.1 billion and $2.1 billion.

"The artificial introduction of an organic compound that does not occur in nature, but is man-made and is nevertheless active in a living system, is very likely to be harmful. . . . All man-made compounds that are at all active biologically ought to be treated as we do drugs, or rather, as we should treat them—prudently, cautiously."[35] One remembers Voltaire's comment: "Doctors pour drugs of which they know little, to cure diseases of which they know less, into human beings of whom they know nothing."

There are "diseases that would not have occurred if sound therapeutic procedure had *not* been employed" (my italics).[36] Tranquilizers and hypnotics can cause chronic, irreversible brain conditions as in tardive dyskinesia, an affliction associated with prolonged use of phenothiazines. Steroids used in the treatment of arthritis can produce organic brain disorders as well as hypomania and/or depression.

Twelve of the twenty most common medications used in persons over sixty-five have a sedating effect, which can result in serious problems. Physical speed and coordination may be impaired, and actual death can occur from slowing-down of the body's functions. Fear and depression can strike older people on drugs, when they equate such slowing of their responses with failing health and dying.

Drug metabolism is not as effective in old age. Blood flow in the liver, the organ of drug metabolism, may be reduced and thus the rate of drug detoxification slowed. Moreover, older people have a lower general bodily metabolism rate, and this prolongs drug action. Kidney impairments slow excretion of drugs and their metabolic products. Drug effects in the old may also be prolonged by the accumulation of drugs in body fat. It is wise to administer all drugs with caution, and to begin with low dosages. Patients must be under continuous laboratory and clinical surveillance.

Physicians need a great deal more training and experience in the specifics of prescribing drugs for the elderly. Possible side effects and complications must be carefully explained to older patients to avoid misinterpretation of normal reactions or ignoring of important danger signals. Judicious use of drugs for ailments of old age can be enormously helpful, but it must be emphasized that many drugs tend to reinforce the normal slowing-down of responses and the sense of aging and depression and may contribute to or cause acute and chronic brain syndromes.

ELDERLY GUINEA PIGS

Medical experiments on institutionalized patients in medical and mental hospitals have become commonplace. The elderly, institutionalized more than any other age group, are vulnerable to studies that may be questionable or conducted without informed consent. To cite one example, two eminent physicians at the prestigious Sloan-Kettering Institute for Cancer Research —as part of a study on immunology—supervised the injection of live cancer cells under the skins of twenty-two "senile" and ailing patients at the Jewish Chronic Disease Hospital in Brooklyn without telling them that the cells were malignant. It was never formally established that any of the subsequent deaths of the elderly patients resulted directly from the injection, but the evidence was suspicious. The physicians were merely placed on probation for one year, and they stoutly defended their judgment in experimenting on unsuspecting elderly people.

The 1962 Harris-Kefauver amendments to the Food, Drug and Cosmetic Act required the "informed consent" of all persons in advance of receiving experimental drugs; but doctors were also given the right to determine whether it was in the "best interest" of patients to notify them of the nature of the experiment. It was argued, for example, that through such notification some patients might learn that they had cancer. The assumption was that secrecy was psychologically sound. Yet the patient has the right to know even when it hurts to know. This is as true of drugs as it is of the prognosis of diseases and operative risks.

DOCTORS AND DRUG COMPANIES

There is far too cozy a relationship between the drug industry and the medical profession. Doctors receive from the drug industry free gifts, drug samples, medical magazines and financial backing for professional meetings and conventions. Up to recently few saw this as a conflict of interest. But there have been signs of change. In 1969, for instance, more than a third of the second-year class at Harvard Medical School "cut an economic umbilical cord with the drug industry."[37] They piled gifts from a drug maker—percussion hammers, stethoscopes, tape measures, tuning forks and black vinyl bags—on a couch in a dormitory and called a press conference to explain that the gifts would be returned as a symbolic protest against "an unhealthy relationship" between the industry and the medical profession. The entire medical profession would do well to follow suit.

Doctors must act as a crucial part of the monitoring system for drug treatment and the drug industry. They are in a position to evaluate drugs clinically. They see the problems caused by high-priced drugs for fixed-income patients. They can use drugs as a supportive component of a well-thought-out treatment plan rather than a one-shot form of cure. But to be objective and responsive to their patients, it is imperative that they get their hands out of the cookie jar of gifts and favors from the drug industry and their local drug salesmen.

MEDICAL RESEARCH ON AGING

It should be self-evident that health care in old age requires continuing research and development. But the government has not committed itself to a level of research commensurate with the number of older persons in the population and the severity of their health problems.* For instance, less than one percent of the budget of the National Institutes of Health, the major research arm of the government, goes to studies on aging. Furthermore, current programs important to the understanding of chronic diseases and the aging process itself have been scaled down. The most striking example is the well-known Framingham Study, which has produced valuable research information yet has been under threat of premature extinction.

The Framingham Study of five thousand persons has been a classic of medicine, a prospective (that is, before the diseases appeared), longitudinal,† epidemiological study of heart and circulatory diseases. Both its findings and its methods are taught in nearly all American medical schools. It cost the nation only $6 million over twenty years. Dr. William B. Kannel, its director, has pointed out that the study results have been affirmed by similar results found in studies by the American Heart Association, which included six all-male population studies in different cities.

Yet in October, 1969, the National Heart and Lung Institute an-

---

* It is generally recognized in industry that at least 2 to 10 percent of the total operating budget should be put into research and development. Thus 10 percent of Medicare payments in, say, 1971 would mean $141 million!

† Longitudinal research in aging presents methodological difficulties. For example, when a sample is studied over time, how are intrinsic changes to be differentiated from those due to the environment? Greenhouse and Schaie, among others, have considered these problems.[38]

nounced it would phase out its direct support of the Framingham Heart Disease Epidemiology Study after the tenth round of regular biennial examinations. It would provide support at a reduced level until June, 1971, in order to provide the time required to complete processing and analyzing the data collected over a twenty-year period. This announcement brought a barrage of protest, since the Framingham Study had been a source of significant advances in medicine.

When the study began in 1950 there was considerable controversy about the relation to heart diseases of cholesterol, hypertension, obesity, physical activity and other factors. The study has provided "coronary risk profiles" which delineate the factors found to be related to heart disease. Popular myths were exploded. It was found, for example, contrary to prevailing medical belief, that the systolic blood pressure is no less a predictor than the diastolic.* The study also found, surprisingly, that even after years of smoking the cessation of smoking reverses the danger of heart attacks. Obesity is related only to fatal, not nonfatal, heart attacks. Much was learned about silent or unrecognized coronary attacks. Framingham was one of the few studies to include women, and a major finding was that they are not as vulnerable to heart disease as men. In all, twenty-two volumes of rich data about heart disease resulted from the research.

Stroke was also being studied, and during the study there were 153 documented cases of stroke, 75 of the victims women and 78 men. Unlike heart disease, women seem as vulnerable as men.

Dr. Kannel stated:

We don't think stroke is an inevitable consequence of aging. The most potent contributor to stroke in general and the ABI [atherothrombotic brain infarction] in particular is hypertension, including the asymptomatic kind. The key to the prevention of cerebro-vascular accidents would appear to be early detection and control of hypertension.[39]

The understanding of stroke would help the young as well as older people. Cerebrovascular diseases were responsible for nearly 6,000 deaths at ages under 45 in the United States in 1967.[40]

Dr. Kannel emphasized the possibilities of genetic studies and stressed the importance of long-term studies in contributing to the understanding of aging and chronic illness:

. . . do today's 30-year-olds have the same serum cholesterol values as 30-year-olds in 1950? (We have 40,000 frozen samples in storage and could

* The systolic blood pressure refers to the phase of heart contraction; the diastolic blood pressure refers to the phase of heart relaxation.

compare new cohorts age for age with our population for cholesterol and other components not destroyed by freezing.) Do men with high serum cholesterol values tend to have offspring with higher values? If progeny are classified by the father's attributes or vice versa, can predictions be made of their propensity to disease? . . .

Framingham's potential for studying stroke and other chronic disease, even problems associated with aging of a population, has been cited by some epidemiologists as grounds for continuing the study of our population. In another decade 3000 of the original group would be in the 60-plus ages. The yield of data on the evolution of chronic disease over 30 years could have been quite fruitful, we believe. However, the climate in which Framingham first flowered apparently has become inhospitable owing to an ice-age cold wave originating in Washington.

Other advocates also defended the continuation of the Framingham Study. Dr. Thomas R. Dawber wrote:

Medicine is under attack for allegedly not being sufficiently concerned with the prevention of disease. Many who should know better imply that a change in the method of delivery of medical care will solve the problem. Unless far more is known about the epidemiology of the chronic diseases, it is very unlikely that anything can be done about their prevention. It thus seems strange that at the very time a cry is being made for more prevention, a study that can provide much of the needed knowledge for this task is being eliminated.[41]

Following these protests, the Framingham Study has now, fortunately, been given significant reprieve. NIH research grants to Boston University have made it possible to follow the original population and to study, in particular, stroke, eye diseases (glaucoma and cataract) and the characteristics of cancer victims.

Healthy as well as sick older people should be studied from many perspectives. Disease must be distinguished from the effects of the aging process itself. The aim of research should not simply be the extension of life but improvement in the quality of life by the ensuring of vigorous years. It is difficult to estimate how close we are to medical breakthroughs, but probably within several decades there will be great gains in the prevention and treatment of cancer and heart disease. We must learn much more about how to make these added years part of the prime of life and not simply a longer waiting period before death. Fortunately, legislation establishing a National Institute on Aging was passed in 1974, though modestly funded.

PREVENTION OF ILLNESS

From 1961 to 1969 prevention accounted for only 4 percent of annual health-care expenditures. HEW Secretary Wilbur J. Cohen stated in 1968 that it was too soon to add preventive health-care services to Medicare benefits. He was concerned about the costs and effectiveness of annual physical checkups and comprehensive health screening programs.

Actually, controversy has developed as to the value of periodic health examinations. It is true that a certain amount of hypochondriasis can be wittingly or unwittingly encouraged by annual physical examinations or any other medical attention. But this should not rule out preventive care. Hypochondriasis is an emotional problem which must itself be treated. Expense is another issue. It is difficult to put a price value on the early detection of cancer or any other disease even if it saves only a few lives. But, even with strict cost-benefit analysis, there is evidence on the national level that preventive testing would save health money, in addition to preventing disability and death. Thirty-five hundred people are blinded by glaucoma each year. Three thousand of them would be spared if there were periodic tests. Nine thousand of fourteen thousand women who die of cervical cancer would be saved if all women over twenty had an annual Papanicolaou smear.

Two hundred thousand men and women die annually before they are sixty-five because of heart attacks. Prevention programs could have saved many of these lives. Atherosclerosis (a form of arteriosclerosis or hardening of the arteries that is characterized by the accumulation of fat deposits in the arterial walls), which is a leading cause of heart attacks, should be regarded as a "pediatric disease," with prophylaxis beginning early in life. Present evidence suggests, for example, that the lipid-rich diet of Americans, with chops, marbled steaks, butter, cheese and eggs, is contributory and should be revised.

Cirrhosis of the liver, which has been on the increase in recent years, is the fifth leading cause of death in the United States. It is responsible for more than half of the deaths in middle life, between the ages of 45 and 64. The bases for cirrhosis are not fully understood, but alcohol and diet are of paramount importance, and much could be done to prevent this disease. There are an estimated 23 million Americans suffering from hypertension, only half of whom are aware of it, and only half of these are receiving proper treatment. In 1972 at least 4.4 million Americans had diabetes, and 1.6 million of these were undetected cases.

Health education is another aspect of prevention, but it has been a hit-or-miss proposition. According to a Louis Harris survey conducted for the Blue Cross Association (the association of all 74 Blue Cross plans in the U.S.), 30 percent of their sample could not identify any of the "seven danger signals of cancer," 17 percent could identify one of the signs, and only 13 percent could identify four or more. Only one-half of the sample knew even one symptom of a heart attack or heart condition. The doctor was the most common source of health information, followed by television commercials, newspaper medical columns and medical news on television. Clearly, none of these resources is doing an adequate job of educating Americans of all ages about health and the prevention of illness or even the early detection of illness.

Sound health practices cannot begin in adult life, since by then much damage may already be done. Prevention should begin with prenatal and infant care, followed by good health practices and health education for the nation's 55 million schoolchildren. The physical and emotional environment, sanitation, level of stress, diet, rest, exercise and self-conscious control of harmful habits are elements of preventive care.

MEDICARE AND MEDICAID

HEALTH INSURANCE FOR THE AGED—HOSPITAL INSURANCE
(Popular name: Medicare—Part A)

This program provides hospital insurance protection for covered services to any person 65 or over who is entitled to Social Security or Railroad Retirement benefits. A dependent spouse 65 or over is also entitled to Medicare based on the worker's record. The covered protection in each benefit period includes hospital inpatient care, post-hospital extended care, and home health visits by nurses or other health workers from a participating home health agency. It does not include doctors' services.

Under Social Security, workers, their employers, and self-employed people pay a contribution based on earnings during their working years. At age 65, the portion of their contribution that has gone into a special Hospital Insurance Trust Fund guarantees that workers will have help in paying hospital bills.

HEALTH INSURANCE FOR THE AGED—SUPPLEMENTARY MEDICAL INSURANCE
(Popular name: Medicare—Part B)

Social Security's medical insurance program helps pay for doctor bills, outpatient hospital services, medical supplies and services, home health services, outpatient physical therapy, and other health care services.

Medical insurance is not financed through payroll deductions and is not based on earnings or period of work. As a voluntary supplemental extension of Medicare's hospital insurance protection, it helps pay for many of the costs of illness not covered by hospital insurance.

MEDICAL ASSISTANCE PROGRAM
(Popular name: Medicaid Title XIX)

This program provides grants to states to administer medical assistance programs that benefit: (1) the needy—all public assistance recipients in the federally aided categories (the aged, blind, disabled, and families with dependent children) and those who would qualify for that assistance under federal regulations; (2) at a state's option, the medically needy—people in the four groups mentioned above who have enough income or resources for daily needs but not for medical expenses; and (3) all children under 21 whose parents cannot afford medical care.

State plans must include at least seven basic services for the needy, and a similar but less extensive program for the medically needy. Family planning services may be included in both.

In 1970 old people paid an average of 57 percent of their health-care needs out of their own pockets or through private insurance. The remaining 43 percent was paid for by Medicare and Medicaid. Ironically, because of the rapidly rising costs of health care, the old are actually paying more in dollars now than they did before the advent of Medicare some few years ago. The average annual medical bill for persons 65 and older in fiscal 1972 was $982, compared to $147 for a youth under 19, and $358 for those 19 to 65.[42] Out-of-pocket uninsured expenditures for health care* dropped from more than one-half of the elderly's medical bill in 1966 (before Medicare and Medicaid) to about one-fourth of the total bill in 1971. But inflation and some increased use of services have actually put out-of-pocket per capita spending *$42 above* where it was—*$276 in 1972 compared to $234 in 1966!*

---

* Although old people make up 10 percent of the population they account for 25 percent of all health expenditures. It should be noted that medical expenses are not the same as health expenses. The latter are and should be greater since they include costs of prevention not covered in any present insurance program, including Medicare and Medicaid.

The federal budget reflects the dizzying inflation in health-care costs. Outlays in 1971 for federal health programs ballooned to $22.6 billion, of which $8.3 billion was for Medicare* and $3.2 billion for Medicaid.† This immense expenditure of money has not yet produced acceptable medical care nor has it properly protected the incomes of the old from the catastrophic effects of illness.

Medicare came into being in 1965 as a means of providing health insurance for older people.‡ Most Americans breathed a sigh of relief, feeling confident that basic health care for their families and themselves in old age was now assured. Unfortunately this was soon revealed to be far from the truth. The basic concept of Medicare's health insurance—to provide hospital and some nursing-home care (Medicare—Part A) and doctors' services (Medicare—Part B) for people over 65 under Social Security without a stigmatizing means test—was a sound and very important step forward. But crucial considerations were ignored.

Medicare was intended to serve the medical needs of the old, but it failed to consider their most pressing need—that of chronic care for long-term diseases and disabilities. Medicare is oriented toward short-term acute illnesses and accidents. Thus American medicine's peculiarly limited definition of medical care as acute care is reinforced by Medicare, which excludes payment for chronic care unless an acute exacerbation of the chronic condition occurs. At what point in recovery should Medicare stop paying the bills for the chronic patient? People need care as long as they are still sick or incapacitated. Medicare has set arbitrary limits on the length of time it will pay, and after that patients are on their own.

In spite of all these restrictions the nation spends more on chronic§ than

---

* For purposes of comparison, in 1967 Medicare expended only $3.4 billion.

† Next in line in the federal budget for various departmental health programs were Defense, $2.5 billion; Veterans, $2 billion; Environmental Protection Agency, $1.3 billion; and Federal Employees Health Insurance, $365 million.

‡ Peter A. Corning in his brief and excellent *The Evolution of Medicare from Idea to Law* (1969) describes the history of the idea of health insurance (an idea as old as the Greek city states) and the implementation of this idea. In modern history the first compulsory health-insurance program was enacted in Prussia in 1854. Theodore Roosevelt sponsored a health-insurance program in 1912 in the United States. The American Medical Association once supported national health insurance. It gained momentum after the Wagner-Murray-Dingell bill of 1939. President Franklin D. Roosevelt's 1944 state-of-the-union message outlines an "economic bill of rights," including "the right to adequate medical care and the opportunity to achieve and enjoy health." Finally, following the assassination of President John F. Kennedy, an age-limited national health insurance was propelled into enactment.

§ Of course, chronic illness is not limited to old age, although there is a very high correlation. Chronic illness includes chronic physical ailments and disabilities, long-term mental disease, mental retardation, blindness and deafness, neurological disorder, diabetes, cancer, arthritis and rheumatic diseases, and heart and circulatory disorders.

acute care. Of the $83.4 billion spent on health in 1972,* two-thirds of it was on chronic disease.† Much of this is custodial rather than active treatment, partly because chronic disease is not intriguing to those who operate or guide health-service and research institutions. Moreover, the health-care establishment is virtually deaf to consumers. Voluntary hospitals, even though they receive support from their community or federal money (e.g., Hill-Burton), are primarily answerable to their boards of trustees and attending physicians rather than to the community they serve. The right of consumers to participate in directing these institutions is being raised in legal battles over hospital accreditation and denial of care to low-income patients. The Medicare statute, though aimed at benefiting the old, gave the Social Security Administration a constituency of those with a vested interest in things as they are—doctors, hospitals and insurance companies.

Medicare has been deficient in other ways. It has supported physicians and other health personnel who are not properly trained to work effectively in the diagnosis, treatment and care of older people. Geriatric medicine has not yet been recognized as a specialty in the United States, although 40 percent of the average internist's patients are people 65 years old and above, with whom he spends 60 percent of his time.

Medicare and its companion program Medicaid, the medical-assistance program for the poor, have proved to be expensive means of aiding old people and the poor. They have pumped money into a system that inflated costs for all Americans. To avoid conflict with doctors and hospitals, federal money deliberately was not used as leverage for basic improvement and reform in the delivery of health care. Instead, Uncle Sam found himself stuffing money into the coffers of hospitals and the pockets of doctors to mollify the "losers" in the Medicare fight, that is, the American Medical and Hospital Associations.‡ Hospitals were reimbursed on a cost-plus basis, a method that encourages extravagance. Physicians were paid their "usual, customary and reasonable (UCR) fees," which they themselves set. There were no standards and controls regarding the quality or efficiency of the "care" rendered.

Skyrocketing health inflation resulted. Between 1965, when Medicare

---

* 7.4 percent of the gross national product.

† According to Dorothy Rice of the Social Security Administration, the percentage of money Americans spend on chronic health care as compared to the total amount they spend for health care was 53.4 percent for the year 1963. No figures are available for subsequent years; the study was a one-shot deal, itself a comment on our irrational health-care system.[43]

‡ Organized medicine, the American Medical Association, opposed Medicare despite the tremendous medical needs of older Americans. The AMA claimed that doctors would not turn away anyone in need, that the voluntary health-insurance system was adequate, that Medicare would destroy the sacred doctor-patient relationship.

began, and 1970, physicians' fees rose by 38.9 percent and hospital charges by 110 percent.* Everyone had to pay more. "By 1970 the average consumer—who is too young for Medicare and too 'rich' for Medicaid anyway —is worse off medically than he had been in 1964." The premiums and deductible fees that Medicare patients pay out of their own pockets have substantially increased since 1965. Each participant currently must pay a monthly premium of $6.30, almost double what it was originally.† In paying coverage for the doctors' bills the older person must pay the first $60 of such outpatient bills each year and the first $84‡ for each hospitalization under the deductible provision. Furthermore, he must bear 20 percent of outpatient doctors' services under a co-insurance requirement. "The aggregate of all these features imposes a crushing burden on persons with low fixed income," said the Group for the Advancement of Psychiatry in 1970.[45]

Consider the average single person who was a Social Security beneficiary in 1972. He was receiving $161 per month. The $6.30-a-month premium cost a total of $75.60 a year.§ If he paid $60 for his first outpatient visit

* Compared to a 27 percent rise in the Consumer Price Index. Hospital revenues rose post-Medicare. Hospital net income averaged $.90 per patient day from 1961 to 1965 compared to $2.36 in the Medicare period 1967 to 1969, according to the Social Security Administration. Doctors' bills actually account for 15 percent of medical costs, but the public feels that "since Medicare and Medicaid have come in doctors have just jumped their fees to take advantage of it," according to the Harris Survey (Washington *Post*, November 9, 1970). Each of 1,000 doctors received more than $25,000 from Medicare and Medicaid in 1968, much of it undoubtedly appropriate. Despite early allegations there has been little proven tax and other cheating, although some doctors, of course, have been dishonest.[44] What *is* striking is that doctors are making money in the program their professional organization so bitterly opposed.

Labor has also been unfairly blamed for soaring hospital costs. The wages of hospital workers, among the lowest in the nation, did rise 31 percent between 1966 and 1971 due to unionization and minimum-wage laws. Unionizing hospitals has brought their employees better income—and perhaps more dedicated care to patients. It is not surprising that hospital workers, paid peonage wages, had high turnovers. ". . . while many hospital workers are for the first time earning a living wage, their pay raises and fringe benefits are usually considerably less inflationary than the rate increases sought by Blue Cross," wrote Judith Randal ("Blue Cross's Unused Big Stick," Washington *Star*, June 11, 1970). Nonprofit hospitals are among the last bastions against unionization. The American Hospital Association is opposed. The National Labor Relations Act does not cover their employees.

† Once again the government has given with one hand and taken with the other: 1972 saw a 20 percent rise in Social Security benefits, but on July 1, 1973, Medicare Part B premiums were elevated a full 8.6 percent, from $5.80 a month to $6.30. On July 1, 1974, there was another jump to $6.70, a 6.4 percent boost.

‡ This has risen steadily from the $44 when Medicare became effective in 1965; in January, 1975, it was $96.

§ There have been proposals to eliminate Part B (Doctors' Benefits) Medicare premiums, which it is estimated would be equivalent to a 3 to 5 percent increase in Social Security benefits. One Nixon health program would have eliminated Part B Medicare costs for old people—but would have had them paying part of their hospitalization on the thirteenth instead of the sixty-first day. The old would be charged (the deductible he is responsible for), that would bring the yearly outgo to at least $135.60. This approaches the sum of one month's Social Security check. The individual might be eligible for a Medicaid supplement in most states. But many older people are too proud and independent to apply for Medicaid or other public assistance or are not aware that it is available.

According to the Health Insurance Institute about one-half of persons 65 and over (the relatively more affluent elderly) have some form of health insurance in addition to Medicare. But these policies do not adequately fill in the gaps, are expensive* and add to the red tape involved in financing care. When Blue Cross–Blue Shield began its special "65" program for older people in 1966 the premium rate was $6.80 monthly. By 1973 it was about double that.

Thus the deductible and co-insurance features of Medicare are barriers to care. They encourage delay in seeking help until an illness has intensified. There is no proof that such deductible and co-insurance features deter unnecessary use of health services, but there is evidence that they increase the eventual expense of treatment for the patient and for society by not supporting early care and preventive measures.

As costs began to rise, largely because of inflation generated by Medicare and Medicaid, benefit improvements in Medicare were minimized and benefits reduced while eligibility standards were raised in Medicaid. In New York City, for example, eligibility was changed and more than one million people were dropped from the Medicaid program between 1968 and 1969.

Physicians have become more and more selective about their patients, and people on Medicaid and Medicare often have found themselves unwelcome at private doctors' offices† and at private voluntary hospitals. Many doctors refused to lower their fees for the elderly with low incomes.‡ Thus

---

less when well and more when sick. It is hard to imagine how that would assuage anxiety about medical costs!

* Bankers Multiple Life Insurance Company of Chicago received $5,270,399 in premiums in 1969 but paid out only $2,248,273. The rest was "expenses." (In contrast, the interest alone of the Social Security trust funds covers the running expenses of the program.) These figures are from *Chilton's Spectator*, annual health-insurance review issue, September, 1970, as cited by Victor Cohn, "Drastic Changes Needed for Better National Health," Washington *Post*, March 29, 1971. Although in 1970 there were some 1,200 health-insurance plans of all kinds in the United States, the public could not possibly rate their equality. Many hard-sell plans are replete with exclusions and deductibles. They are very costly and provide little.

† Only 34.6 percent of New York City's 20,464 licensed physicians have participated in the Medicaid program and a few hundred of these handle more than half the cases. According to a 1973 AMA survey, over one-fourth of physicians "rarely or never" accept Medicare patients.

‡ Nineteen seventy-two levels of doctors' fees in New York City far exceed reimbursement allowances, and older people either had to pay the difference or depend on overcrowded, understaffed hospitals.[46]

older persons have been forced to rely on antiquated municipal facilities—hospitals and clinics—which are also uninterested in them despite the fact that federal programs were presumed to reduce two-class medicine for the rich and the poor.[47] Rather than opening doors, the Medicare and Medicaid programs have closed them. Instead of breaking down professional arrogance, they have reinforced it.

Academic medicine has been guilty of exploiting Medicare and Medicaid to the disadvantage of old people. Payments estimated at $100 million or more annually are made under Medicare for attending physicians' supervisory work with interns and residents at teaching hospitals. Hospitals have encouraged attending physicians to charge patients for this work. A supervisory physician is generally designated as the patient's attending physician at the time of admission, although patients are rarely advised of this. This practice has sprung up as a direct result of the availability of Medicare money. Private insurance companies like Blue Cross have never paid for such services. In view of the basic disinterest of teaching hospitals in the medical problems of the old, it is particularly ironic that they feel justified in adding this cost to patient fees. In a strongly worded 1970 report, Senate Finance Committee investigators called for an end to these payments, stating that it was questionable "whether the nation's aged should also be asked to subsidize medical education with many millions of dollars from their Part B premium payments. This latter subsidization takes place without the benefit of the ordinary procedure of justification and assignment of priorities, which are part and parcel of the regular appropriation process." Medicare payments to teaching hospitals should be tied to training and education, research and services to the elderly.

The Medicare program has perpetuated racial prejudice and segregation. Black elderly continue to be disadvantaged much as they were prior to Medicare. In fact, emergency provisions of Medicare law have helped some southern hospitals to avoid civil-rights requirements. Legally, a nonparticipating hospital may be paid for emergency treatment it gives a Medicare beneficiary when the patient is in danger and it is impractical to put him in a participating hospital. This provision was designed for real emergencies —cases in which the elderly patient might be risking death or impairment if treatment were delayed. However, more than two-thirds of such "emergencies" happened in the South. Over 50 percent originated in two states —Alabama and Mississippi.[48] It became clear that, rather than admitting black patients, hospitals were treating all of their elderly white patients as emergencies. Thus they were able to maintain segregation and still be paid Medicare money.

Presumably this loophole has been tightened by regulation (*Federal*

Register, November, 1968). In July, 1972, however, Representative Don Edwards (D.-Calif.) noted "a pattern of racial discrimination" existing in medical facilities receiving federal assistance under both the Medicare and Medicaid programs throughout the country and involving all kinds of admissions, not only emergencies. This view was supported by a report of the Congress's General Accounting Office based on studies in Detroit, Atlanta, Los Angeles, Birmingham and Wayne County, Michigan.

Another major cause of what some have called the "Medicare mess" has been the role of insurance companies as "fiscal intermediaries" in handling claims and administering the Medicare program. This was one of the prices the Johnson administration decided to pay to gain passage of Medicare. Medicare involves the use of some 130 insurance carriers to process claims, with Blue Cross–Blue Shield predominating. The thirty-five-year-old health-insurance "middleman" industry is an expensive addition to the health-care system. Many question whether the large number of people employed in this industry—its clerical, administrative and sales bureaucracy—is justi-fied or is less expensive than a government bureaucracy. Leonard Wood-cock, president of the United Auto Workers, said that private insurance has been a failure in providing comprehensive coverage and wasteful of $1.1 billion annually spent on administration. He also felt the health-insurance industry had not been innovative regarding delivery of care and had been inflationary in promoting high-cost institutional services.[49]

It can hardly be argued that insurance companies and insurance regu-latory agencies have done an outstanding job in control of quality and costs. In 1970 the Social Security Administration named eleven of fifty carriers as having insufficient data on fee control, including eight Blue Shield plans. The "Blues," fiscal intermediaries for most Medicare and much of Medic-aid, have a near monopoly; yet costs have soared. There are seventy-four Blue Cross plans in the United States, handling private and business as well as government coverage. In addition to administering the greater part of the Medicare program, they handle Medicaid in twenty states, health insurance for military dependents, and a health-insurance plan for five million government workers.

Blue Cross president Walter J. McNerney admitted before the Senate Antitrust and Monopoly Subcommittee in January, 1971, that Blue Cross was guilty of some inefficiency and was trying to improve its operations and save its subscribers money. He conceded that enough had not been done to hold down medical costs, but said the government, doctors, hospitals and even patients had to share the blame.

Without letting Blue Cross–Blue Shield off the hook, it must be admitted that the federal government has not shown an astute business sense in setting up Medicare. As an example, Medicare payments are usually significantly higher than Blue Shield payments for the same service. One would have assumed that if, for instance, Blue Shield paid an average of $220 for removal of a cataract (excision of lens), Medicare would have paid the same. But cataract surgery in 1970 cost $358 in Texas, $444 in Illinois, and $371 in New York Blue Shield–administered Medicare programs. Testimony of a representative of the National Association of Blue Shield Plans (May 6, 1965) before the U.S. Senate Finance Committee on the then pending Medicare legislation suggested payments be brought in line with those of Blue Shield. This did not occur, however, and as a result "Medicare payments do not mirror Blue Shield's reflection of prevailing fees. Medicare presents a distorted, much magnified and expensive image all its own. . . . No one can say for certain how much money has been overpaid as a result of the failure to apply the statutory limitations' 'reasonable charges.' . . . Medicare has spent many hundreds of millions of dollars more than would otherwise have been required had those same Blue Shield schedules served to limit reimbursement."[50]

But stranger things have happened. According to an HEW Audit Agency report of February, 1970, Blue Cross, Blue Shield and other fiscal intermediaries authorized federal payment of Medicare funds amounting to millions of dollars to help pay charges for hospital delivery rooms where young women have their babies.[51] Needless to say, it called forth unique stretchings of the imagination to justify the delivery rooms as a medical facility for the old.

The same HEW Audit Agency report challenged $1.1 million in costs charged by fifty-six insurers, including Blue Cross, for administering Medicare: $494,300 was recorded as "indirect costs" for items which benefited solely the intermediaries' non-Medicare business. A charge of $170,300 was uncovered for "personal services having nothing to do with Medicare activities." Twenty-six companies claimed $103,000 for "travel, meetings, entertainment and other expenses which, in our opinion, were greater than necessary, were not related to Medicare, or were of a personal nature."

Dealings in the health-care industry have led to suspicions regarding conflicts of interest. Looking at the "Blues" again, Blue Cross and the American Hospital Association had interlocking directorates until 1971. The Blue Cross symbol was AHA property. It seems obvious that this connection has influenced medicine's distinct emphasis upon institutional inpatient rather than preventive and ambulatory (outpatient) care.

The federal government has made some efforts to regulate the private insurance companies. In one case, it forced the Washington, D.C., Blue Cross and Blue Shield plans "to completely reorganize" before it renewed their Medicare contracts.[52] Included in the reorganization was the retirement of two of the plans' top officials and the computerization of Medicare billing procedures.* Former Senator John J. Williams (R.-Del.) had called the Washington plan "one of the poorest Medicare carriers in the country" before the reorganization. Besides its high administrative expenses for Medicare, it was accused by House investigators in May of 1970 of costing federal employees millions of dollars by depositing premiums in non-interest-bearing bank accounts. This practice has been discontinued.

Beginning efforts have been made elsewhere in the nation to slow down health-care costs and improve service. Well-publicized hearings were called in Philadelphia in March, 1971, to consider rate-increase requests totaling nearly $74 million by the Philadelphia Blue Cross.[54] Pennsylvania Insurance Commissioner Herbert S. Denenberg angered physicians, commercial insurance companies, trial lawyers, Blue Cross and hospital officials by ordering Blue Cross to cancel its contracts with participating hospitals and renegotiate to save costs. He also ordered Blue Cross to furnish him with the per-diem charges at each member hospital so that he could publish a "shopper's guide" for consumers, listing all the hospitals and their costs.† Further, he recommended that the Blue Cross board be reorganized to include consumers.‡ By January 1, 1974, all seventy-four Blue Cross plans were to have a majority of consumers on their governing boards. This was mandated by the board of governors of the Blue Cross Association.

As with various crucial issues, the 1971 White House Conference on Aging failed to consider the role of private insurance carriers, nor did it deal with specific questions about the "noncommercial" carriers, Blue Cross and Blue Shield, or the pros and cons of controlling doctors' fees. Elderly patients presently have little recourse but to acquiesce to the prevailing practices in health insurance. There are many "health organizations" that lobby in Washington.§ But missing is an established American Patients

---

* Texas millionaire H. Ross Perot's Electronic Data Systems, Inc., controls more than 90 percent of the subcontracted computer work on Medicare claims in the United States. The company received $72 million in gross payments between 1966 and 1971.[53]

† Denenberg's shopper's guides to hospitals and surgery (he has also produced useful guides to auto and life insurance) are an excellent start toward state-by-state guides for consumers.

‡ When board reorganization occurs that reflects greater consumer representation, struggles usually emerge. For example, in January, 1972, the Oklahoma State Medical Association withdrew its endorsement of the state's Blue Shield plan. This action followed reconstruction of the board to consist of twelve laymen and nine physicians rather than the previous equal balance. Doctors fear lay control.

§ Among them the American Medical Association, American Hospital Association, Association of American Medical Colleges, American Nursing Home Association, American Nurses Association, Health Insurance Institute, Health Insurance Association of America (which represents the three hundred companies that write about 80

Association, and most certainly there is no American Older Patients Association.

Medicare laws have brought modest advances, much confusion and a great deal of disillusionment. They nonetheless represent a step forward. Major revisions of these laws are yet to come. Ultimately we shall probably have to move beyond Medicare to a system of national health insurance.

MEDICINE TO FIT THE ELDERLY

SHOULD THERE BE A GERIATRIC MEDICINE?

Since 1969 the Gerontological Society has had a Committee on Post Graduate Medical Education in Geriatrics, chaired by Dr. Alfred H. Lawton of the University of South Florida.* It has tried to define the needs for undergraduate and postdoctoral training in clinical gerontology or geriatrics. There has been frustration and foot dragging in effecting curricular changes in medical schools. There have been discussions with the Veterans Administration and with the Academy of General Practice about introducing geriatrics into postgraduate education.

Lawton, a former president of the Gerontological Society, writes:

There is a special body of knowledge about the post-mature phase of the human life span which can be communicated as part of all education on health and medical care. This body of knowledge concerns the totality of man's individual and collective experience. It can be applied effectively to improve individual man's allotted life span if it is used as a common store of information to be taught to all future participants in the health disciplines, particularly from the social and natural sciences. Its application must include a very special ingredient—the loving kindness of man for men.

He sums up his committee's conclusions:

Our committee has tended to consider chronic diseases, aging and human development as a continuum and as a philosophical approach to medicine. The

---

percent of the nation's health insurance), national Blue Cross and Blue Shield organizations, American Public Health Association, Pharmaceutical Manufacturers Association, American Pharmaceutical Association. The AMA spent $1,155,935 in the 1965 Medicare fight. In 1969 it was fourteenth in lobby spending with $91,355. There are new groups to push specific legislation, such as the Committee for National Health Insurance. The AFL-CIO's Social Security Department handles organized labor's health operations.

* The members of the Gerontological Society are grouped in four sections: Biological Sciences, Clinical Medicine, Psychological and Social Sciences, and Social Research, Planning and Practice. The American Geriatrics Society is composed only of physicians. Since 1969 physicians have increasingly sought dual membership in field's understanding could arise from the basic sciences upwards throughout not only the whole medical school curriculum but also through the continuing education of the "lifetime of learning" we talk about for the physician.

Unfortunately, such an approach to medical education has not yet become widespread. Medical school students are, too often, still being taught in the mold of Oslerian medicine which usually approaches disease as acute illness with specific cause, treatment, and cure. The students are, therefore, too often frustrated by chronic and incurable disease, regard the aged as unpleasant "crocks" to be avoided, and cringe at discussions of death and dying.[55]

I am certain that many schools are making some effort to change their teachings about chronic diseases, aging and death. Probably much is occurring during the elective fourth year, internships, and residencies—particularly those latter aimed at preparing specialists for Family Medicine. The committee, however, is afraid that the progress in this direction is overly slow, with danger of being "too little and too late."[56]

On the other hand, organized medicine's view is to leave things as they are. Dr. Frederick C. Schwartz, chairman of the American Medical Association's Committee on Aging writes:

The concern you express about the little time spent in the medical school curriculum on diseases of aging was our concern too some 14 years ago when we began our work. We surveyed many medical school deans. The final consensus was that the oldster and his medical problems should not be segregated and that he would be best served in the mainstream of medicine.[57]

Unfortunately, in practice the AMA cannot provide assurance that the elderly will not, as previously, get lost in the larger medical picture.

Thus the United States remains ambivalent about taking a special interest in the medical problems of the old. The father of geriatrics, Ignaz Nascher, was an American, yet in the United States there are no great centers of geriatrics or chairs of geriatric medicine.* "Formal recognition of geriatrics and the special medical problems of old people by the Royal College of Physicians of London represents an important forward step in the history of gerontology and geriatrics," said N. W. Shock. Speaking of the United States, "There is more need for a specialty in geriatrics than pediatrics," says Dr. Russell Lee, a founder of California's Palo Alto Medical Clinic. He sees a geriatrician as part of a team working with

---

the two organizations. Since 1969 there has been growing cooperation between the Gerontological Society and the American Geriatrics Society.

* The English pioneers have been Trevor Howell, Marjorie Warren, Joseph Sheldon, Lord Amulree, Lionel Z. Cosin and W. Ferguson Anderson; the American pioneers, Nascher (who introduced the word geriatrics), Zeman and Stieglitz.

specialists on heart disease, stroke, fractures, perhaps most effectively in group practice.[58] The late Dr. Edward Henderson, editor of the *Journal of the American Geriatrics Society*, said in 1966, "some 40,000 specialists will soon be needed." There are now two American medical journals devoted solely to geriatrics.*

Whether the old eventually have their own medical specialty or not, physicians and other health personnel do require special training to work with the older age group. There are diseases that are more common with advancing age—pernicious anemia, atherosclerosis and diabetes are but a few. There are critically changing characteristics and circumstances with age that physicians should know. There are singular principles that apply to chronic care.

Every medical student should have experience working in chronic institutional-care facilities† and in home care of older patients. There should be continuing education and relicensing of American physicians.‡ Qualifications of physicians must be under regular scrutiny so that they are compelled to keep up with new developments in medicine for the old. Many need education for the first time in relating the epidemiology of illness to problems in society; and a greater social concern should become part of their medical repertoire. Physicians who elect to participate in Medicare should be required to complete educational levels in geriatrics until such time as geriatric medicine and chronic illness are adequately covered in medical curricula. How else can we even hope that they are rendering appropriate services?

Sensitive care of the dying must be part of the education of all health-care personnel. More than 50 percent of all deaths take place in hospitals. Many elderly also die in nursing homes. Doctors and institutions allow death to become a lonely and unnecessarily terrifying experience by concentrating on physical care and ignoring emotional needs. Doctors may overact by extravagant life-saving measures or underact by isolating the dying person. Dr. Melvin J. Krant, professor at Tufts University Medical School in Boston and director of a cancer unit, has written "The Organized

---

* The two major medical journals in geriatrics, the *Journal of the American Geriatrics Society* and *Geriatrics*, do not yet have high standards. Studies of drugs, for example, papaverine, without double blind evaluation comparing the agent with a placebo, are published. The *Journal of Gerontology* of the Gerontological Society is of higher quality in terms of standards.

† In 1974, the Chicago Medical School began offering its seniors a two-week elective course in geriatric total care at the Park View Home for the Aging.

‡ In 1967 the Oregon Medical Association became the first state medical society to require a minimum of formal continuing education (fifty hours per year) as a condition for continuing membership. In 1972 it became the first state to expel members for not fulfilling the conditions. The ages of those expelled ranged from 35 to 70.

Care of the Dying Patient,"[59] which contains ideas that could be adopted by other hospitals. He observed, "Helping someone die well should be conceived as a positive part of health care." His organization moves beyond the walls of the hospital, performing home visits as well. Fundamentally, Krant and his co-workers, and others such as Drs. Cicely Saunders and Elisabeth Kubler-Ross, who have contributed to work with the dying, concentrate on eliminating the denial of dying and death from their care. The right to die and the care of the dying will be discussed in greater detail in Chapter 12.

The Council for the Long-term Care of Geriatric Patients, formed in 1972,* is looking into specific areas of research that will result in better care for the aged. In addition to the American Geriatrics Society, which organized the council, six other organizations are involved: the Gerontological Society, the American Nurses Association, the American Nursing Home Association, the American College of Nursing Home Administrators and the American Association of Homes for the Aging.

Training and education of those in all the health professions—nursing, social work, medicine, occupational therapy, psychiatry, psychology—must cover both the phenomenon of aging and the nature of the elderly. Medical schools and universities could undertake to experiment with producing a range of health-skill groups, thereby clarifying functions and utilizing the time of teachers effectively. It is estimated that 125 different health-skill groups are currently being trained and are operating in America. University schools for health practitioners could be established to train staff in community medicine, health services in various medical environments, chronic diseases, and the coordinated team approach. Health professionals ranging from physicians to personal-care workers, including medical technologists, physical therapists, X-ray technicians and assistant physicians could be included.

The promotion of career ladders would be a vital part of the overall program of health training, for example, by including a New Careers component† in the establishment of a National Personal Care Corps. (The latter is a recognition of the need for broadly trained medical personnel who could fit into more than one of the 125 various health occupations.)

All of this would require more teachers. Why not recruit from the ranks of the retired themselves? Retired medical-school teachers could be offered

---

* Dr. Leslie S. Libow is chairman.

† "New Careers" is a concept whereby employees, with the help of their employers, are able to move from lower to higher job positions rather than be trapped in dead-end jobs.

opportunities to teach courses in geriatric health care. They have a natural interest and a valuable personal insight into the subject. "There are probably about 200 recently retired medical faculty professors in the New York area alone who would love the opportunity to go back into teaching," said Dr. Joseph Moldaver, former associate clinical professor of Columbia University's College of Physicians and Surgeons, himself 72 years old. In addition, retired medical men from the military (who are often quite young, usually in their fifties, when they retire) often do not want to enter private practice. They too might be a source for teaching and working in the field of aging.

To make up for the contemporary inadequacies in undergraduate and postgraduate medical education (and in the education of other health professionals), crash programs are called for. Because of the shortage of trained teacher experts (for example, there are fewer than twenty psychiatrists in the entire country who are expert in geriatric psychiatry), traveling teaching teams should be set up. The circuit riders should include an internist, psychiatrist, social worker, nurse, psychologist and physiatrist. Government or foundation funds should finance four-day workshops for various teaching institutions, which agree, in turn, to conduct similar workshops in other institutions in their geographic area. To test effectiveness there should be followup visits by the traveling group of specialists, and various forms of examinations.

MEDICARE IMPROVEMENTS

Pending adoption of a truly comprehensive health-care plan for all Americans, the major method of obtaining health care for the elderly must continue to be the Medicare system. There should be step-by-step improvements both in the benefits received and in financing.

The following are proposals that many, including myself, have made for revision of Medicare from a short-term financing system for acute illness to a program in keeping with the realities of old age:

1. Part B of the Medicare system—covering outpatient doctors' costs—should be automatic; and the monthly premium and the 20 percent co-insurance feature should be eliminated. Part B should be brought under Social Security through use of general-revenue funds.

2. There should be an end to the deductibles in Medicare that, in fact, deduct only from the care of the patient.

3. There should be expanded coverage for drugs* and prosthetics, so

---

* Senator Church said in 1972, "We could broaden Medicare coverage to include out-of-hospital prescription drugs for what we now spend for an aircraft carrier."

that those prescribed on an outpatient basis are included. Dentures, eyeglasses, hearing aids and foot care should be covered.

4. Medicare should be extended to cover all diagnostic and treatment services, both inside and outside the hospital. This would greatly reduce the incentive for unnecessary hospitalization, which has proved to be so expensive under the existing law. It would also encourage preventive-care practices by financing periodic checkups and multiphasic screening examinations.

5. Nearly five million people have no telephone or other communicative contact with the outside world. For many, a telephone to summon medical aid is a necessity. On the doctor's prescription the cost of a telephone should be an added Medicare benefit. A telephone can be both a more effective and a less expensive instrument to allay anxiety than a tranquilizer. We cannot underestimate the disruptive effects of loneliness and anxiety upon the physical and mental health of the isolated person.

6. There should be a realistic broadening of coverage of the "home health visit" to many additional forms of home care, as a means of reducing institutionalization. Thus escort, homemaker, and housekeeper services and other types of personal care would be covered.

7. At present Medicare coverage for psychiatric disorders is unrealistically limited. These limitations must be brought into line with those respecting physical illness.*

8. Social services should be covered.

9. Medicare should pay for blood transfusions. Medicare requires that the beneficiary pay for the cost of the first three pints of blood or provide replacement.† Old people don't have the money and all too frequently have no friends or family to call upon for replacement.

10. Medicare should operate wherever the beneficiary is living or traveling. Although travel is highly touted as one of the rewards of retirement, Medicare does not fully cover service outside the United States or its territories.

11. Medicare should cover advisory collateral visits to the doctor by family members when indicated, to offer a medical history and to aid in the treatment and care of the patient.

12. Dental care should be provided.‡

13. Expansion of coverage for rehabilitation, from physical medicine to occupational and activities therapy, is essential.

* See Chapter 8.
† Most blood in the United States comes from commercial rather than donated sources and must be paid for.
‡ Only about 2 percent of Americans have some form of insurance coverage for dental bills.

14. I might add quixotically that perhaps food should be a legislated Medicare prescription—until we have assured adequate income for all—so that the elderly are no longer poorly nourished owing to lack of funds.

15. A fixed percentage of Social Security and Medicare trust funds should be used in research and development studies that would improve income security and health delivery for the elderly. The National Institutes of Health should also be providing leadership and direction to programs designed to improve the health of the older people of the United States. Basic and clinical research and training in the causes, diagnosis, prevention and cure of diseases of old age are needed.

16. Physicians should have special training in geriatric medicine to be eligible for Medicare reimbursement.

BEYOND MEDICARE

Detractors have argued that too much purchasing power was placed in the hands of the medically needy too fast with the introduction of Medicare, thereby increasing demands on the medical establishment without its having the capacity to respond.[60] In addition, much of the money went into the pockets of providers of health services rather than to the "beneficiaries" themselves. Already many people are looking beyond Medicare to a national health-insurance plan. National health-care planning is in its early stages in the United States. The many health plans being proposed are basically oriented toward the financial aspects of care, and minimal attention is given to structural changes in the delivery of health care. None of the plans face squarely the need for chronic-disease prevention, care and treatment. Among major competing insurance approaches are Senator Jacob Javits's (R.-N.Y.) bill to expand Medicare to all ages, the American Medical Association's Medicredit system, the insurance scheme of Senators Russell Long (D.-La.) and Abraham Ribicoff (D.-Conn.) for catastrophic illnesses, health-care of the Health Insurance Association of America, the administration's Comprehensive Health Insurance Plan (CHIP), the Comprehensive Medical Reform Act of 1974, introduced by Ribicoff, Rep. Hugh Carey (D.-N.Y.) and Rep. Robert Steele (R.-Conn.), and the bill proposed by Senator Edward M. Kennedy (D.-Mass.), Representative Martha Griffiths (D.-Mich.), which is supported by labor,* and the 1974 compromise plan presented by Kennedy and Mills. The latter proposal

---

* Based on the Committee for National Health Insurance, composed of one hundred labor, business, government and medical leaders and chaired by the late Walter P. Reuther.

offered custodial nursing home care for the aged on a voluntary basis, but with high premiums. The Ameriplan of the American Hospital Association, which did call for the greatest structural change, has been laid aside.

Because the various national health schemes have essentially ignored long-term-care coverage, the American Nursing Home Association (ANHA) proposed a national health insurance for long-term coverage to provide for chronically ill persons under a federal tax-based prepayment system—Chronicare. However, the ANHA has never offered any specifics.

The most generally accepted "structural reform" being considered in both the Nixon/Ford and Kennedy bills is the introduction of prepaid group practice. The organizational unit in such practice is called the health maintenance organization (HMO). HMOs have a long history as prepaid group practices, among them the Kaiser-Permanente Plan* on the West Coast, the Health Insurance Plan of Greater New York, and the Group Health Association of Washington, D.C. There are also the medical-care foundations made up of medical-society membership suggested as an alternative to the closed-panel approach of Kaiser-Permanente. The first medical-care foundation was created by the San Joaquin County Medical Society in 1954. By 1971 there were forty-two in twenty states.

According to the Group Health Association of America some eight million people are served in part or in whole by various prepaid group plans. One major concern is whether the financial incentives involved in prepaid group practices might lead to the cutting of corners and a reduction of standards of medical care. Proponents argue that peer review and competition will offset such a possibility. Another serious question arises from the fact that these plans have been quite selective in their membership and it is not certain how they would function with representative groups of poor and elderly patients.

How to dovetail most effectively the contribution of the doctor, the non-medical systems experts, and the consumer is without a doubt very difficult. With respect to the situation of older people it is striking that there is practically no input from recognized specialists in the field of aging any more than from the elderly themselves.

It no longer seems radical to demand changes—including price controls in health-care delivery—when even *Fortune* Magazine (January, 1970) has editorialized that "much of U.S. medical care . . . is inferior in quality,

---

* Industrialist Henry J. Kaiser and surgeon Dr. Sidney Garfield began the program in 1933. The so-called Kaiser Plan was offered to the public for the first time in 1945. It had two million subscribers by 1970.

wastefully dispensed and inequitably financed," and when Thomas J. Watson, Jr., chairman of the board of International Business Machines, says:

> That brings us up against an old taboo, "socialized medicine." I completely believe in the American free enterprise system. But when the system fails to produce I think we should not flinch from looking to some sort of government intervention.
>
> That, in American medicine today, means some new form of national health insurance. . . .
>
> Twenty-one years ago President Truman urged a national health system. In 1949, as a dyed-in-the-wool free enterpriser, I accepted the argument that we didn't need it. But I cannot accept that argument in 1970.[61]

Even beyond national health insurance is the possibility that medicine may become a public utility. Upon taking office as president of the American Society of Internal Medicine in 1969 Dr. Clyde C. Greene, Jr., warned of this potential and stated: "The public has now placed health care alongside the other historic rights of all citizens—life, liberty, free education and the pursuit of happiness."

No political administration has written or filled an acceptable prescription for health care in America. There is no unified health philosophy and policy. This affects the elderly directly and, of course, all future elderly. By 1975 many feel the national health bill will go over the $100 billion mark and will employ 5½ million people, making it the largest industry in the United States! Levers for change toward effective programs with cost and quality control include the government and the unions, the two largest purchasers of health services in the United States. Together with training institutions, the medical and health professions and consumers, they will have the responsibility to exert the influence necessary to effect basic shifts in health-care philosophy, in the effort to make medicine fit the health needs of the elderly as well as the entire population.

Chapter 8

"THEY ARE ONLY SENILE"

EMOTIONAL PROBLEMS AND MENTAL ILLNESS IN OLD AGE

What is good mental health in old age? It means the capacity to thrive rather than simply survive. All of us meet older persons who are described as "full of life," "young for their years," "bright-eyed" and "zesty." Some older people appear serene and contented yet actively involved in life. Others delight in struggle or fighting for a cause. One sees in them the ongoing capacity for creativity, curiosity and surprise as well as a sense of consummation or fulfillment in life. Some may actively seek change and new knowledge while others concentrate on consolidating what they have built up over a lifetime. There are many ways to be emotionally healthy in old age, but several common themes emerge: the desire to be an active participant, to make one's own decisions, and to share mutual love and respect with others. Healthy older people experience many of the same feelings and responses as people of all ages, yet old age has its own unique flavor. The special qualities of late life come from having lived nearly an entire life span with all that this entails, and from facing the issues inherent in old age—time, aging and eventual death. Ultimately this means facing the meaning of one's own life.

Old age has the potential for being an immensely interesting and emotionally satisfying period of life. But this potential is endangered by many forces. Change and loss are predominant themes. Loss of physical health and the death of important persons—spouses, close friends, colleagues, relatives—are occurrences in late life which tend to place enormous stress on human emotions. Crises of all kinds must be met, sometimes one after another, sometimes simultaneously—retirement, widowhood, major and minor illnesses, changes in bodily appearance, sensory losses, a feeling of decreasing social status and, for many elderly, a drastically lowered standard of living. There is much energy expended as the old go through the processes of mourning for their losses, resolving grief, adjusting to the changes involved and recovering from the stresses. Multiple crises can leave people drained emotionally and weakened physically.

The age-related life crises, together with the stresses of daily living, produce a range of emotional problems from mild to severe, depending on the individual's personality and earlier life experiences, physical health and social and family supports. Finances, shelter, medical care and social roles are all intricately connected with emotional responses and capacities. Feelings of grief, guilt, loneliness, depression, despair, anxiety, helplessness, and rage are common and should not in themselves be considered mental disorders. If they remain unresolved, causing problems in necessary functioning or a great deal of emotional pain, outside assistance is advisable.

The point at which problems become severe enough to be called mental illnesses or disorders is difficult to establish. Serious problems in functioning, extraordinary emotional distress, and various observable symptoms of emotional and/or mental impairment are criteria by which behavior can begin to be evaluated. The mental disorders of old age are of two kinds: the organic disorders which have a physical cause, and the functional disorders which appear to be related to one's personality and life experiences. Organic disorders, also called organic brain syndromes, can be reversible or chronic. The reversible brain syndromes can often be successfully treated. Chronic brain syndromes, on the other hand, are the result of permanent damage to the brain, as in cerebral arteriosclerosis and senile brain disease. They can be treated symptomatically but not reversed. Functional disorders refer to psychotic disorders, neuroses of various kinds, personality disorders and psychophysiological disorders.

Acute reversible brain syndromes constitute major psychiatric–medical emergencies, as noted in Chapter 7, and are tragically important in the lives of many older persons. As Simon and Cahan wrote,

We found a large proportion (over half) of geriatric patients admitted for mental illness to be suffering from acute brain disorder and in urgent need of psychiatrically-oriented medical care. A gratifying proportion of them improved sufficiently, or recovered, to return to society.[1]

All too often, mentally confused older people are sent home untreated by doctors and hospitals when they are suffering from reversible confusional states—a surprising number of which are due to malnutrition, anemia, alcohol and unrecognized physical ailments including congestive heart failure, infections and even fecal impaction.[2] Sometimes these conditions are drug induced. For example doctors have created acute brain disorders through the use of tranquilizers.[3] Many workers, such as Cosin in Britain,[4] have demonstrated the treatability of confusional states in the elderly.*

The extent of mental disorders of all types can only be guessed at since so many of the elderly exist outside the purview of medical, psychiatric and social programs. A million persons over 65 are in institutions, primarily nursing homes, and well over 50 percent of these have evidence of some psychiatric symptomology and mental impairment.[6] About two million people living in the community have serious chronic disorders. A minority of these are primarily mental disorders, but while the majority are physically based, there are often associated emotional reactions requiring attention. Added to this are the elderly patients in mental hospitals (138,000 in 1968). The poverty conditions under which seven million elderly live are known to contribute to mental breakdown—among them malnutrition, stress and victimization through crime. And last, one must consider the emotional toll suffered as a result of lowered social status and loss of social roles.

Until recent pressures against admission, Americans 65 and older accounted for about 25 percent of the annual state-mental-hospital admissions. One study by the National Institute of Mental Health (reported by the World Health Organization in 1959),[7] shows the following occurrence of new cases of psychopathology of all types:

> 2.3 cases per 100,000 population   Under age 15
> 76.3 cases per 100,000 population   25–34
> 93.0 cases per 100,000 population   35–54
> 236.1 cases per 100,000 population   Over age 65

Clearly those over age 65 are the most susceptible to mental illness.

Suicides, too, increase with age (see Table 3) and it is surprising to learn that the rate of suicide is highest in elderly white men, probably the result of several causes: loss of status (in the largely white male-dominated society), desire to protect finances for a surviving wife, and a decision to avoid otherwise unavoidable physical helplessness and obdurate pain. For nonwhite women and men and for white women the curve of

---

* Unfortunately the American Psychiatric Association acquiesced to the makers of the international classification of medical diseases and dropped the clear distinction between acute and chronic brain disorders in its most recent edition of its diagnostic manual.[5] This simply compounds the confusion in many doctors' minds between reversible and chronic states. It is notable that no clinician specializing in the field of aging has ever served on the Committee on Nomenclature and Statistics of the American Psychiatric Association. Perhaps that accounts for such prejudicial and invalid statements as the following, given as part of the definition of "senile dementia": "Even mild cases will manifest some evidence of organic brain syndrome; self-centeredness, difficulty in assimilating new experiences, and childish emotionality."

suicide is bell-shaped, with the greatest peak during the earlier adult and middle years. Twenty-five percent of all known suicides take place in the over-65 population (that is, among 10 percent of the nation's population).

TABLE 3

Suicides per 100,000

Age	Male	Female
5–14	0.5	0.1
15–24	10.5	3.5
25–34	17.2	7.6
35–44	22.9	10.7
45–54	27.5	12.1
55–64	34.4	11.5
65–74	32.9	9.4
75–84	41.3	6.6
85 plus	50.9	5.5

SOURCE: "Vital Statistics of the United States," 1967, U.S. Public Health Service

More than that probably occur since families out of shame or guilt are frequently unwilling to report suicides.

When signs of emotional problems and mental disorders emerge in old age, immediate diagnosis and treatment are crucial, particularly in the case of the reversible brain disorders. Otherwise these conditions can become chronic and irreversible although still subject to palliation. Prompt care can be preventive in avoiding full-blown functional disorders if, for example, depression or anxiety can be alleviated. Older persons ordinarily face more stresses than the young and, given their declining reserves of strength, they may require swift attention in order to avoid being overwhelmed emotionally. Ideally, treatment should be a collaborative effort among the patient, his family if he has one, and mental-health personnel, with the patient or a family member making the initial request for services. Only in cases of legally established physical and mental incapacity or mortal danger to the patient or others can decision making be assumed by people acting on the patient's behalf. This issue will be discussed somewhat later.

Contrary to popular professional opinion, older persons can make effective use of the whole gamut of mental-health services, including psychotherapy, psychoanalysis, group psychotherapy, drug therapy, occupational, physical and recreational therapies, behavioral modification therapies, family and marital counseling, and last, but by all means not least, sex counseling and therapy. Because of the mental-health profession's disinterest in and prejudices against the old, and the overt and covert forms of discrimination on the part of agencies and institutions, most elderly persons never have a chance to obtain mental-health services. As one illustration, nursing homes seldom provide any form of psychiatric care, in spite of the fact that over 50 percent of their residents have been found to have psychiatric problems of sufficient magnitude to warrant professional attention. Numbers of older persons are transferred out of mental institutions directly into boarding homes,[8] welfare hotels and other cheap living quarters, with no follow-up psychiatric care or supportive services. Community mental health centers see only a tiny proportion of older persons. Private psychiatric services are too costly for most of them. In addition, the cost of transportation to public clinics may be prohibitive, and handicapped persons are usually unable to find a means of travel.

Other factors enter into the failure to obtain care: lack of the information necessary to recognize important symptoms on the part of patients and their families; shame or fear of mental illness; lack of knowledge regarding services; guilt in family members, who think they should be able to handle things; improper diagnoses by medical and mental-health personnel; and lack of services designed especially for the old.

When care is available, the general treatment principles for working with the elderly patient are similar to those with patients of all ages and diagnostic conditions. To paraphrase the American psychiatrist Harry Stack Sullivan, older people are more nearly human than otherwise. There are, of course, special qualities about the nature of mental problems in old age which demand special attention and training. Development of principles for the evaluation, care and treatment of mental disorders of the elderly is a continuing enterprise.[9]

Careful evaluation is imperative. In order to institute correct treatment, medical, social, psychiatric and personal information must be gathered together through a complete examination of the patient and a careful history taken from the patient or an informant. Moreover, the doctor and the staff must carefully observe the patient and be willing to use various forms of treatment to insure the accuracy of diagnosis. This is especially true in the reversible brain syndrome because the treatment itself may be necessary to clarify the diagnosis. A similar approach can also be useful in pinpointing mental disorders as functional rather than organic.

One important way in which mental-health professionals can become more effective is to become aware of their own feelings toward the elderly. For example, I have found it extraordinary in my consultative experience with a range of mental-health specialists, from psychiatrists to social workers, that they are so often impatient and irritable with their older patients for not responding swiftly to their ministrations. It would not occur to them to push for such rapid improvement in younger patients. In part, they fear the implacable clock: there will not be time enough in which to work. In part, they reflect the notion that old people cannot change. Ironically, part of the reason old people are eminently capable of change is that they stand so near to death. They have things to accomplish before it is too late.

Group as well as individual psychotherapy can be of benefit:

> A moment of silence that occurred in our psychotherapeutic group was ended by violinist John Powell quietly telling of his sense of oppression by the violin, accompanied by his great fear that his ability as a professional violinist would be ended by age and arthritis. He referred to a thought of Pablo Casals during an accident, "Thank God I will not have to play the cello again." The combination of love and hate of music and its discipline was familiar to the 64-year-old musician. He had been forced to take up the violin as a child of two years by his father. He was made to practice against his will and never learned any other occupation.
>
> He became an excellent musician and lived on call day and night, playing whenever he could. He only really felt good about himself when he was performing at his best. As John Powell explored his feelings, which leaped across nearly sixty years, his voice suddenly broke down into a long, profound, deeply sorrowing cry. He felt trapped by his father and the violin. The group was supportive but candidly and usefully questioned his sense of helplessness.

Group therapy is especially useful in late life because it helps overcome loneliness and offers the possibility of sharing common worries; and practically, it is less expensive than individual therapy for those with limited incomes.

One function of mental-health specialists which has direct application to work with older people is cultivation of the art of listening. The so-called garrulousness of old people and their wish to hold on so tenaciously to someone's attention is a social symptom related to their loneliness. Patience, listening and simply spending meaningful time with them are of great therapeutic value. Older people use reminiscence to review their lives and resolve problems, much as does classical psychoanalysis.

One of the great losses of old age is the loss of choice. Needs, interests and desires differ greatly. Choice, exercised as freely as possible, supports self-respect; when denied, it promotes helplessness. Symptoms such as anxiety, depression, dependency and anger rapidly develop when a person—of any age—has few options. Therapists should encourage a great variety of alternatives both in the emotional lives of old people and through changes in the social environment which touches their daily existence.

Irreversibility of emotional and mental disorders must never be casually assumed. Many conditions are subject to amelioration. Even people affected by the chronic brain syndromes or chronic physical illnesses have anxiety and depressive symptoms which are responsive to treatment. Depressive, paranoid and behavioral reactions present in the clinical course of organic brain damage can be helped. Depression may be masked as an organic state, showing itself as physical symptoms* and, if recognized, it can be treated. At the very least, intimate human responses are nearly always helpful.

Research evidence supports clinical impressions that older persons benefit from mental-health care. Studies in *private* mental hospitals show that as many as 75 percent of patients over 65 are returned improved to their own homes within two months.[10] Outpatient work in clinics and private offices also reveals capacities for change and recovery. Even severely brain-damaged patients respond in a prosthetic (artificial) milieu with well-planned programs for orientation, activities, socialization. Clearly, if there is a combination of resources and genuinely motivated interest on the part of professionals, older people, like patients of other age groups, respond to treatment.

PSYCHIATRY FAILS THE ELDERLY

All the various professional groups that work in mental-health settings —psychologists, psychiatrists, social workers, occupational therapists, nurses and others—give scant attention to the mental-health needs of older people. This mirrors what we have seen in every area of late life. As in the previous chapter I shall concentrate on describing my own profession— in this case psychiatry—keeping in mind that other professions could be scrutinized equally.† Psychiatry as a whole—in private practice, state institutions, community mental health centers, education, training and research—shares a sense of futility and therapeutic nihilism about old age. Part of this attitude represents familiar patterns of ageism or prejudice against the old, here disguised in professional trappings. A Group for the

---

* Diagnosis of organic brain disorders will be simplified in the near future by simple physiological measurements of cerebral blood flow and oxygen consumption.

† Of all the professions, nursing and social work are most involved in the social, medical and nursing care of the old, especially in home care. Yet even these disciplines do not address themselves to the specific mental-health needs of the old.

Advancement of Psychiatry report, "The Aged and Community Mental Health," in 1971 listed some of the reasons why therapists have such negative feeling: the old arouse therapists' apprehensiveness about their own old age; they arouse conflicts about the therapists' personal relationships with their own parents; therapists convince themselves that the old cannot change behavior; therapists believe it is a waste of valuable time and energy to treat people who may soon die; therapists are threatened by feelings of helplessness at the thought that patients may actually die while in treatment; and finally, therapists may be wary of the contempt of their colleagues if they show an interest in old age with its low social status.

"THEY ARE ONLY 'SENILE' "

Therapists use the term "senility" indiscriminately, tending to apply it to anyone over sixty with a problem who comes into their view. Having invoked the magic word, they need not undertake the kind of careful diagnostic assessment needed to determine a proper course of treatment. Indeed, if something is labeled "senility," no course of treatment is started.

To begin with, "senility" is not, properly speaking, a medical diagnosis at all but a wastebasket term for a range of symptoms that, minimally, includes some memory impairment or forgetfulness, difficulty in attention and concentration, decline in general intellectual grasp and ability, and reduction in emotional responsiveness to others. This condition, as studies at the National Institutes of Health[11] and elsewhere have made clear, is not an inevitable consequence of age *per se*. Rather, it is a reflection of any of a variety of different problems, including cerebrovascular disease, destruction of central-nervous-system cells, or emotional states such as severe depression. For example, the depression of an older person may be inner preoccupation and constriction manifesting itself as disturbed concentration, forgetfulness and withdrawal. The term "senility" should be discarded altogether in favor of "emotional and mental disorders in old age." More than semantics is involved here. Viewing disorders in this way would encourage a more careful diagnostic and treatment plan, as well as a broader perspective on the everyday problems and disorders of old age.

Another related problem is the view, shared increasingly by psychiatrists, lawyers and politicians, that the emotional and mental disorders of old age are not bona fide "mental illnesses." Therefore, diagnosis and treatment are not called for—only custodial care is necessary. The official nomenclature of the psychiatric diseases of old age include chronic brain disorders, but the inclination is to consider all of these "senile" and untreatable.

Most mental hospitals do not provide psychiatric treatment programs for the old. But they do offer more than patients are now receiving after transfer to nursing homes, boardinghouses and other so-called "community" facilities. At the very least, mental hospitals have a mixed age range, more physical space outdoors, theatres, churches, gymnasiums, larger and more varied staffs, social programs and a greater atmosphere of hustle and bustle, more like a community. All of this can provide some therapeutic effect. Ideally, of course, mental hospitals, nursing homes and all other care facilities should offer active treatment programs for both physical and mental illnesses and thus give patients alternatives in looking for proper care.

THE YAVIS SYNDROME OR HOW TO AVOID PSYCHOTHERAPY WITH THE OLD

William Schofield has described the YAVIS syndrome—the tendency for psychotherapists to treat young, attractive, verbal, intelligent and successful (which means well-paying) clientele.[12] The American Psychoanalytic Association study as reported by David Hamburg and others showed that 98 percent of psychoanalytic patients are white, 82 percent are under 45 and 78 percent are college educated.[13] (In contrast, only 6 percent of people over 65 are college graduates, and one-seventh are functionally illiterate.) Unlike state-hospital institutional personnel, both academic and privately practicing psychiatrists mainly see relatively wealthy, well-educated people from a narrow band of the American population.

Eighty-two percent of psychiatrists in a metropolitan area responded to a mail questionnaire survey concerning the quality and quantity of their contact with emotionally disturbed, community-resident elderly people defined as 65 years and over.[14] Fifty-five percent reported no contact with the elderly. The remaining 45 percent reported spending approximately 76 hours each per year with the aged. Based on the total number of psychiatrists responding, less than 2 percent of psychiatric time was spent with elderly patients, or less than one hour per week.

As a rule, elderly persons were seen by psychiatrists late in the course of their disturbances, when there was less opportunity to reverse the course of their illness. Active modes of treatment such as psychotherapy and electroconvulsive therapy were rarely utilized. Forty percent of the time spent with the aged was reported to have been in consultation, but referral for ongoing psychiatric treatment was found to be uncommon.

A report by the American Psychiatric Association, as noted by Karl Bowman in an annual review of psychiatric progress in geriatrics in 1959, pointed out that less than one percent of psychiatrists spend any major amount of time in geriatric practice and 40 percent treated no aged patients (compared with 55 percent in the independent survey referred to previously).

In a study by Anita Bahn, of psychiatric-clinic outpatients in the United States in 1959, it was found that "as in 1955 [at which time a similar study was conducted] the aged still comprise less than 2 percent of the outpatient population, in contrast to a high proportion among the inpatients." Bahn concluded that these findings ". . . suggest that mental-health clinics are not assuming a sufficiently important role in the care of geriatric patients."[15]

Since one finds limited contact between disturbed elderly people and psychiatrists in clinic settings as well as in private practice, it is obvious that medical, cultural and personal attitudes as well as financial limitations are causative. Psychiatrists and therapists in general take the view that they should work only with patients they want to work with, or whom they feel they can help, or who fall into certain areas of "interest." Medical-school or residency training programs never debate the ethics of such personal criteria in patient selection. And, of course, patient selection is seldom questioned once therapists enter upon their careers in practice or in academic or institutional psychiatry.

The general failure of mental-health practitioners to evaluate and treat older people is not entirely their own fault. Academia has much to account for because it offers psychologists, psychiatrists and social workers so little training and experience in working with older patients. Teachers whose professional interests are limited have furnished models for neglect and avoidance. Academic psychiatrists, for example, emphasize neuroses, functional psychoses and office practice in their teaching rather than organic disorders, community psychiatry and preventive psychiatry.

Students in training are not taught to make the diagnoses necessary to introduce treatment. Training programs often exclude older patients, so students do not become familiar with the extent of reversibility of mental and emotional disorders in this age group. Since they do not have experience in working with recoverable older patients, one can understand the ease with which their primitive, ambivalent and conflictual attitudes toward the aged are reinforced.

TERRITORIALITY

Psychiatry, while avoiding its own responsibilities, often battles with the related mental-health specialties when they attempt to provide psychiatric services. For example, in 1967–68 the local psychiatric society of Washington opposed the licensure of psychologists. There was concern about psychologists using the term "psychotherapy" and whether "medical supervision" should be mandatory. In New York State Dr. Alexander Levine, an officer on the Council of the New York District Branch of the American Psychiatric Association, wrote in the Council's bulletin that the "nefarious" encroachment by nonmedical persons into medical practice was "a spreading cancer in the field of psychiatry."[16] APA President Lawrence Kolb stated in 1968 that "only psychiatrists command the full depth of diagnostic knowledge and therapeutic skills."[17] There is a dog-in-the-manger element to this. Many psychiatrists know little beyond their own limited range of interests, and most of what needs to be known for proper psychotherapeutic treatment can be taught in other disciplines. Research offers strong evidence that the personality of the therapist is more crucial in producing positive therapeutic results than the method of training or school of thought involved.[18] Of course, even if personality factors did predominate in selection of therapists, training would still be necessary. The idea of training a new "fifth profession" was proposed by Henry, Sims and Spray in 1971:

Out of these four early professional routes (psychoanalysts, psychiatrists, psychologists and social workers) . . . there emerges . . . a fifth profession, the psychotherapist. . . . It is important to query the social utility of having four highly organized well-equipped, self-sufficient training pathways, each of which produces psychotherapists.[19]

Lawrence Kubie suggested creating a new profession called "medical psychology" to combine psychology, the humanities and pertinent aspects of medicine into one discipline.[20] Kubie proposed a curriculum that might serve as the means to implement the idea of a fifth profession.

It would be a major step forward in American health policy if national health insurance became national *service* insurance and expanded beyond the narrow medical model to include a comprehensive range of social and medical services provided by all the mental-health professions.

DRUG ABUSE

Psychiatrists are no less remiss than general physicians regarding drug use for older patients. Rather than offering psychotherapy, many psychiatrists "solve" the emotional and mental problems of old people through use of chemical strait-jacketing. While psychoactive agents can be of value when judiciously employed, they are too often a means for avoiding the long process required to help older people effectively through a crisis. Tranquilizers and antidepressants can induce and/or aggravate depression in those persons whose character structure requires a sense of activity and strength. The physical side effects of drugs can become so marked that the cure is certainly worse than the disease. Aspiration pneumonia, for example, can occur from the use of tranquilizers which impair the swallowing mechanism. Tardive dyskinesia is the most shocking drug-induced malady. It appears to be a more than occasional end result of prolonged treatment with one of the phenothiazine series—Thorazine or Mellaril—and tends to develop only after the reduction or withdrawal of the offending drug. It is characterized by slow, rhythmic and involuntary movement of the spine, face, and extremities. One may see chewing or gyrating of the jaws; grimacing, lip pursing, eyelid blinking, "fly catcher" tongue, swallowing difficulty and spastic neck stiffening. It seems to occur more frequently among brain-damaged individuals.[21]

Psychoactive drugs are essentially a means of dulling feeling. They can effectively quiet the patient and thus relieve the psychiatrist of his or her responsibility. But older persons deserve the opportunity to resolve their own emotional difficulties rather than to mask them with artificially induced calm and loss of sensation. Drugs should be one element in an overall treatment program, not an end in themselves. Sometimes the total elimination of drugs can be the first step toward recovery.

THE FAILURE OF COMMUNITY MENTAL HEALTH CENTERS

The federal community mental health centers program was enacted by Congress in 1963 to reform the system of delivery of mental-health services. Community mental health centers (CMHCs) were to be rationally distributed throughout the nation and to offer a minimum of five services, four of which are direct clinical activities: inpatient care, outpatient care, partial hospitalization (such as day care), and round-the-clock emergency service. The fifth required element is community education and consultation. Originally 2,000 centers were planned, but by 1973 only 325 were actively operating owing to limits in funding.

In general, community mental health centers have not been a great success in the United States, partly because of inadequate grants for construction and staffing and partly because their staffs do not have the perception, training and resources to deal with the inner-city poverty, racism and ageism that affect the patients who come to them. Location has also been a drawback because of poor linkage to the poverty areas in which many of the elderly reside. The problems have been compounded because many chronically mentally ill patients have been transferred from state hospitals to the community. The capacity of the CMHCs to respond has been limited by the strenuous demands of caring for both long-term mental patients and those with shorter-term acute emotional problems. Thus the patient with chronic problems may be seen several times and then dropped from the patient roster unless he develops a crisis.

A Nader-sponsored report, based on a two-year study,[22] concluded that the community mental health centers program of the National Institute of Mental Health failed to meet the needs of many Americans, especially the poor, the old and the chronically mentally ill. CMHCs are closed evenings and on weekends. The areas served by CMHCs rarely coincide with the organization of other public services, residences or the work patterns of patients.

Some CMHCs have refused to diagnose or treat older people, which is clearly against the law. Fewer than 18 percent of CMHCs have created any kind of special geriatrics program. Robert Dovenmuehle reported to the U.S. Senate Special Committee on Aging that the caseload of CMHCs have less than 5 percent of persons over 65, decidedly below known need.[23] CMHCs are not allowed to accept Medicare payments. Their personnel are not trained in the care of older patients. Few American-born physicians will work at CMHCs because of the low salaries. Therefore, one-half of the community mental health center psychiatrists are foreign born. Many have language problems, creating special difficulties in the field of mental health, which depends almost entirely upon verbal communication. They have limited perception of the cultural and familial traditions of the older patients. The Health Insurance Benefits Advisory Council (HIBAC)* has recommended that CMHCs be permitted to participate in the outpatient coverage of Medicare. Possibly private insurance, Medicare and Medicaid, and other third-party payments would increase participation of American-born physicians.

In spite of their poor record with regard to the elderly, the CMHCs have been presented to lawmakers and the public as a viable resource for the emotional illnesses of the old. President Nixon pocket-vetoed the 1972 Research on Aging Act, which would have created a National Institute on Aging† and would have authorized $20 million in fiscal 1973 for the construction and staffing of local facilities to provide mental-health care to the elderly. The President said: "I feel that both research and mental health programs for the aging should be carried out in the broader context of research on life span processes and comprehensive mental health treatment programs now under way." He stated further that the program "duplicates the more general and flexible authorities contained in the

---

* The official advisory committee created in conjunction with Medicare.
† Subsequently passed again and signed in 1974.

(1963) Community Mental Health Center Act." On the other hand, President Nixon tried to phase out federal support entirely for community mental health centers by 1980. Eventually they may be absorbed within the health maintenance organizations (HMOs) presently being built.

The activities of the community mental health centers programs together with the National Institute of Mental Health and its hospital-improvement grants do not begin to provide the range of services and facilities needed to meet the mental-health needs of the elderly. A national network of centers targeted for the elderly patient, with service, training and research components, should be located in general voluntary and municipal hospitals and nursing-home facilities. The establishment of such a network would require a major effort by the federal government.

MENTAL HOSPITALS

Hospitalization becomes necessary when older persons with mental symptoms and illnesses can no longer be adequately cared for at home by themselves or with their families or in community facilities. Organic brain damage is the major psychiatric admission diagnosis. Ideally, patients should have had access to a range of community services in order to live independently as long as possible before accepting institutional care. Realistically, however, many are forced into mental institutions because these services are not available in their homes and communities. Their mental conditions alone may not justify admission, but their medical, social and economic situations often leave no alternatives. Thus mental hospitals become inpatient collection centers for older people who really would not need to be there, as well as for those persons who legitimately can be considered proper candidates for mental-hospital care.

In 1968 (the last year for which figures are available) 120,000 persons over 65 were patients in state and county mental hospitals, with an additional 15,000 in private mental hospitals and 3,000 as mental patients in Veterans Administration hospitals. About two-thirds were first admitted at age 65 or older, and the remaining one-third were hospitalized at a younger age.

Private mental hospitals, both profit-making and voluntary, provide adequate to good care at high prices and thus are unavailable to most elderly. The Veterans Administration hospitals give reasonably good care but are restricted to veterans, predominantly males. They will become increasingly important as World War II veterans grow older.

State and county mental hospitals are the major resource for most older mental patients. The effectiveness of these hospitals is highly controversial and the subject of frequent exposés and investigations. Much of what Albert Deutsch described in *The Shame of the States* in 1948 is still applicable today to the 321 state and county hospitals. The physical plants and safety features within mental hospitals are far from ideal. The social climate is often abominable. "Institutionalitis" or "hospitalitis"—the development of a chronic state of psychological dependence and deterioration —is observed in substantial numbers of patients.

A 15-year-old girl who visited St. Elizabeths Hospital* observed:

> The halls and rooms reeked with awful odors. The whole place had a very depressed atmosphere. I felt apprehensive in there all of the time. The rooms and halls seemed like they had no lights. Everything was so dark and desolate. It was an experience I won't forget. Like I am sure most people do, I went away saying "Why doesn't someone do something?" I decided I don't want to live to be old.

Basic services like food are frequently inadequate. State hospital patients have been found to have pellagra, for example. Studies in one state, Maryland,[24] showed protein, iron and calcium as well as niacin deficiencies in the diets of their state hospitals. In Alabama, through 1970, only fifty cents per patient per day was spent for food.

Patients are treated by numbers of foreign-trained, unlicensed physicians—some 3,000—who form the bulk of the psychiatric staffs of state hospitals.[25] Hospital and ward attendants, orderlies or nursing assistants are usually underpaid and ill trained and hired with little consideration for their personal and emotional qualifications.

There are few hospital programs designed especially for older patients, and the old are often not included in occupational therapy, social and other existent rehabilitative programs open to younger patients. For too many the only activities available are the "work therapy" programs, in which patients may be required to work in the institution for little or no pay. This practice, which has been called "institutional peonage," has been ended by court actions in some states.[26]

An experiment frequently cited as one of the answers to some of these problems is the San Francisco Geriatrics Screening Project. This was initiated in 1963 with the support of the California Department of Mental Hygiene. It was an effort to reduce the number of "inappropriate" commitments to state mental hospitals, provide alternative plans by developing and utilizing community resources, and offer consultation and information

---

* St. Elizabeths Hospital is the federal mental hospital in Washington, D.C., under the jurisdiction of the National Institute of Mental Health.

to persons and agencies responsible for services to persons sixty years of age and over. The main goal of reducing the number of state-hospital placements was attained, the nursing home most often being substituted for the state hospital. But whether this has meant better treatment remains unclear. A follow-up study, although limited in its scope, produced findings indicating better orientation and self-maintenance among those in the control sample, namely state-hospital placements, than in the nursing-home group. The implication is that those "not needing" extensive services of state mental hospitals and referred to nursing-home care showed more mental and emotional decline after one year than those in state-hospital control groups.[27]

TRANSFERRING OLDER PATIENTS OUT OF MENTAL HOSPITALS

An article entitled "Mental Hospitalization of the Aged: Is It Being Overdone?"[28] expresses the prevailing mood in professional and public thinking regarding the old. It is certainly true that many older persons would not need to be in mental institutions if treatment in appropriate facilities were available. But much of the current massive transfer of patients back to the community is motivated by interests other than those of the patients.

The resident population of American mental hospitals declined from about 500,000 persons of all ages in 1955 to 337,000 persons in 1972. This drop is often erroneously attributed to the community mental health center movement; but the CMHCs did not get under way until approximately a decade after the hospital fall-off began. In fact, the trend was influenced by the introduction of tranquilizers, which enabled many people to live outside hospitals. But another lesser-known and very important reason for the decline is the recent trend toward exclusion from and mass transfer of old people out of mental institutions to save state and local money. The number of aged in state mental hospitals decreased by 40 percent between 1969 and 1973. Even patients who have been in an institution for decades may be transferred out. This is happening in many states, ranging from New York to Illinois and California. "Keep old people at home" and "Return patients to the community" are slogans which accompany these efforts. The financial incentive has been the enactment of Medicare and Medicaid amendments to the Social Security Act in 1965. State governors and legislators have been pleased to be relieved of much of the financial burden of care as a result of federal funds. State and county institutions have been able to transfer and discharge patients and reduce their costs because private profit and nonprofit care facilities for the old have proliferated to take advantage of monies from the federal government.

A social worker explains the transfer of patients, stating: "The cost of institutional care in a specialized mental hospital is high—much higher than a boarding home. . . . The per capita cost to the state mental institution is known. The cost of care in boarding homes is also known. It is easy to compute the financial savings to the State for each person who is removed from a State Hospital to community life."[29] The Washington *Post* in May, 1970, painted a happy picture for patients and institutions alike:

> More than 600 patients, senile, but not really mentally ill, were transferred from the hospital to less expensive and more comfortable foster homes. Among other economies, the Health Department saved $750,000 due to reduced patient load at St. Elizabeths Hospital.

Yet it was clear even at that time that many patients were being shifted to boardinghouse-type facilities that lacked adequate medical, nursing, social-service and psychiatric supervision. In many places welfare departments paid as little as $4 a day per patient to untrained operators of such facilities, and those operators had to obtain a profit for themselves out of the pittance. It is hard to imagine what necessities these foster homes could be offering, not to mention comforts.

In some states transfer has been precipitate, indiscriminate and whole-sale, despite knowledge that movement of older patients is often associated with increased deaths and illness. Numerous studies going back to 1945 demonstrate the dangers of transplantation for the very old and sick.[30] This is especially true for patients who have been hospitalized thirty, forty or even fifty years. Patients and their families often have little to say about transfers. Docile, withdrawn persons have a greater chance of being trans-ferred than obstreperous or active persons since they will cause less trouble in new locations.

Careful research studies of care in community facilities have been rare. Most follow-up studies of chronic mental patients transferred from hospitals have been short lived. There are almost no studies of the effects of foster-home care.* Nursing homes have been studied to some extent, but social-

---

* The otherwise excellent National Center of Health Statistics loses track of older mental patients since it does not include foster-care homes and boarding houses in its surveys. "Foster care" in this sense refers to community housing for the old rather than living with families as is the case with children's foster care.

behavior scales emphasizing "manageability" and other indications of do-
cility indicate a greater interest in measuring the control of patients than in
evaluating the results of active treatment.

Yet, despite the lack of specific research, it is abundantly clear from
observations by mental-health professionals and patients themselves that
present transfer policies are ill advised, untherapeutic and dangerous. The
complaints about the various community facilities to which mental patients
are being transferred mirror previously heard complaints about the mental
institutions themselves. Poor nursing and medical care, little or no psychiatric care, unhealthy and untherapeutic physical and social surroundings,
inadequate and unenforced safety regulations, and a host of other problems
abound in all of these treatment locations.

Senator Frank Moss held hearings on long-term care on December 17,
1970, during which Colonel William Hutton, executive director of the National Council of Senior Citizens and Claire Townsend and her group working under the direction of Ralph Nader gave reports on the poor conditions
in nursing homes across the country. I represented the Washington, D.C.,
Advisory Committee on Aging and testified to the fact that numerous older
people in community facilities live under even worse conditions than those
in typical nursing homes.[31]

In 1969 the Group for the Advancement of Psychiatry—composed of
much of the leadership of American psychiatry—expressed concern in their
report on the "Crisis in Psychiatric Hospitalization." GAP said that in the
effort to solve the long-standing problems of chronic hospitalization the
pendulum has now swung in the direction of rapid and premature discharge
of patients of all ages from the hospitals. These discharges frequently occur
before treatment is completed and prior to adequate preparation for the
patients' return to the community. The result has been a "revolving door"
phenomenon; in 1955, 30 percent of all persons entering mental hospitals
were readmissions, and in 1970 more than 70 percent were in this
category.

Influential psychiatric specialists in the field of aging, Alvin I. Goldfarb
of New York and Jack Weinberg of Illinois, have vigorously opposed indiscriminate transfers from state hospitals in their respective states.* In
Chicago, at hearings before Senators Charles Percy (R.-Ill.) and Adlai

---

* Although some psychiatrists and other interested citizens have voiced concern
over the rapid transfer of mentally ill patients into various types of unregulated
facilities, the organizations representing the elderly and the professional organizations involved with the mental-health care of older people have not protested in any
significant way.

Stevenson III (D.-Ill.) of the U.S. Senate Special Committee on Aging (1971), Weinberg testified:

I must state that I am one of those who criticized the program severely. I criticized it not because of its philosophical concept but rather because of the notion, the idea of transferring inordinately large numbers of people into nursing homes from mental hospitals.

I was amazed when, about two years ago, the new Governor of the State of Illinois, Governor Ogilvie, announced that he was going to release 7000 elderly patients into the community.

I didn't know who made the important clinical decision that these 7000 people were not mentally ill.

SENATOR PERCY: Don't you imagine that there is the possibility that the operators of these nursing homes organized into an association and an officer whom we will have before us in a few minutes put pressure on the state and other government officials to release patients so they want to fill beds?

They have got stockholders' reports to make and dividends to pay and profits to show. They have got empty beds and they are going to fill them with bodies and maybe those bodies are going to have to come out of the mental hospitals.

Don't you think that sets the pressure up then to fill those beds?

DR. WEINBERG: It certainly does. May I reveal something personally, that when I was asked to supervise this program and it was announced, someone in my family was approached by a nursing home operator, asking my brother, to be exact, to approach me to direct patients into his home and he would offer me a stipend of $100 per head.

This actually happened and appalled both my family and me.

Dr. Weinberg later continued:

. . . an individual who suffers from a chronic brain syndrome, which many define as senile, is suffering a mental illness . . . they are mentally ill people and often in need of protection and medical care.

I believe further that many of our mental institutions, even though some of them may be snake pits, are better places than some of the nursing homes in view of the fact that they, at least, have such necessary items of care as 24-hour coverage by a nurse, a fire alarm system and the food in the State hospitals is nutritionally adequate; and some facilities for some minimal activities is also present in most mental institutions of the States.[32]

Weinberg was commenting on the results of an Illinois state law which began the accelerated discharge of elderly patients from state mental hospitals in September, 1969.[33] Despite assurances from state officials that released patients would have suitable "aftercare" to help them in their return to the community, Chicago's local health officials were critical of the transfer program on several counts. They noted that about 50 percent of discharged patients were sent to nursing and residential-care homes in Chicago when it was well known that these facilities were already overcrowded. Others moved into rooming houses and converted lower-class hotels. Many of the transferred had grown old and dependent in state hospitals but after transfer were left almost entirely on their own. The City Health Commissioner, Dr. Murray C. Brown, described the north side of Chicago as a "psychiatric ghetto," in which between 12,000 and 15,000 mental patients were now residing in nursing homes and unlicensed halfway houses.

A New York State psychiatrist, Dr. Josephine Evarts, was in charge of a building to be closed at Harlem Valley State Hospital. She refused to participate in the transfer of 250 elderly women to community facilities. Specifically she refused an order to determine which of her patients would be able to endure a bus trip to a new location. She said:

These are the aged and infirm. Their ages range from 70 to 95. Many of them have been here 30 to 50 years. It is the only home they can remember, and the staff men and women who look after them are the only friends they have.

Now for the first time in 43 years in the practice of medicine I am being ordered to decide who shall go where. I am not trained in cruelty to the weak, aged and suffering, and now I am called on to cull the herd—ship out those who might possibly survive a trip to the Canadian border, keeping the weaker ones for a shorter trip to Utica.[34]

New York City Deputy Commissioner of Social Services Max Waldgeir discussed the lack of follow-up care after transfer:

Facilities here [in welfare hotels] are inadequate. And because there is no supervision for taking medication and no proper psychiatric care, the mentally ill often retrogress. What complicates the situation is that once a patient leaves the hospital, it's very difficult to get him back in, because of new, more stringent admission requirements.[35]

In Washington, D.C., criticisms were similar:

The Washington, D.C., Advisory Committee on Aging, the counterpart of State Commissions on Aging, issued a statement on June 5, 1970 regarding its grave concern over the ongoing and extensive transfer of elderly St. Elizabeths patients to foster homes with two to fifty patients each. It expressed fear the fiscal considerations have once again taken precedence over social and medical ones.

The Washington committee was interested in basic questions concerning the transfers: What kinds of evaluation are undertaken?* What tests? Are there psychiatric evaluations? How long do they take? What medical examinations are conducted? The committee wanted to see a study done of those who had been transferred: how long they remain on hospital rolls, how long they are followed, under what kind of supervision and by whom. What are the morbidity and mortality rates of such patients? The committee also wanted to know the names and addresses of community facilities, the training operators of the homes had had, details of the financial arrangements, how much profit, the character of the staffs, the staff-patient ratios, the kinds of nursing, social, medical and restorative activities and other services available, the quality of food, medical diets, fire and safety. Despite the committee's efforts over an extended period of time it never received satisfactory answers to its questions from St. Elizabeths Hospital.

It was learned from other sources that in the District of Columbia foster-care-home operators were given only six hours' training for their jobs. Only two of those hours were spent with clinical problems; four of the hours were related to the paperwork required for the welfare department, and with fire regulations and other administrative work. Foster-care sponsors frequently found ways to cut costs and earn more money. Many overloaded their homes, paying no attention to legal occupancy limits. Others did not buy first-aid kits or locks for medicine cabinets. There were often no medical records with progress notes, no reports of critical incidents, no doctors on call or responsible principal physicians. Sanitation and overall cleanliness were questionable. Fires had caused patient deaths.[36]

The struggle over transfer continues in many cities and states. Obviously the ideal solution is to base the decision for transfer on the best interests of the patient rather than primarily upon political and financial arrangements among states, the federal government and private enterprise. Thorough evaluation of patients selected for transfer is crucial, with consideration of their ability to tolerate a move. Careful preparation before and support dur-

---

* It was known that a patient "inventory" was made by a sociologist and psychiatrist at the direction of St. Elizabeths' leadership. Their study concluded that 68 percent of patients, mostly elderly, did not have to be in the hospital. Unfortunately this 1971 report was based on minimal evaluation of patients. Inexperienced first-year psychiatric residents admitted they gave little time to the work. One staff psychiatrist apparently filled out hundreds of forms with exactly the same data, including diagnoses, for each older patient.

ing a move would avoid much trauma.* Upgrading and consistent monitoring of the standards and care in nursing homes, foster homes and other community facilities are necessary. Home-care services should be available to those who move back to their families or live alone. The concept of care itself for older persons needs enlargement beyond provision of a place to sleep and something to eat. Care means providing a *home* in the best sense possible, whether for short or long periods of time; creating a socially stimulating environment; furnishing necessary medical, psychiatric and social services; giving personal care such as hair grooming, massage and attention to clothing; and supplying physical and occupational therapy, together with any necessary prosthetics and appliances (wheelchairs, hearing aids, glasses, canes, walkers, and other services). Religious activities and entertainment are essential. It is not impossible to achieve this. Some care facilities are already doing a good job. An example is the South Mountain Geriatric Center developed in Pennsylvania in 1959. Patients moved out of the state mental hospital into this facility, designed exclusively for older people, are reportedly showing favorable reactions.[39]

But even with ideal community facilities and services, hospitalization is useful or essential for numbers of older persons with mental symptoms. General and psychiatric hospitals could provide quality emergency care, overnight stays and short-term admissions in order to treat acute crises promptly. For longer-term care, the massive state and county mental hospitals need to be refurbished or, preferably, rebuilt in functional sizes in new locations closer to residential areas. Custodial care should be replaced by active treatment programs, with more elastic admission policies, periods of residence and discharges, and more flexible procedures aimed at integration of hospital care with family and community life.

PRESERVING PATIENT RIGHTS

THE RIGHT TO FREEDOM

The right of old people, like the right of all people, to refuse various types of care must be maintained. Concern about the railroading of patients into institutions has a particular importance to the aged, who, because of vulnerability and confusion (whether the confusion is a function of depression or an organic brain disorder), are especially subject to easy institu-

---

* Charles M. Gaitz[37] of the Texas Research Institute of Mental Sciences in Houston, Texas, as well as Bernard Stotsky[38] of Boston are among a few who have undertaken careful studies to try to advance our knowledge about the placement of older patients.

tional commitment. The older person may not want or really need care. Other elderly people are committed for social or medical reasons simply because there are no other appropriate facilities available.

Psychiatrist Thomas Szasz in his books *The Manufacture of Madness* (1970) and *The Myth of Mental Illness* (1961) discusses the question of psychiatric commitment. He maintains that the mental-health movement, and in particular institutional psychiatry (rather than freely contracted office psychiatry), is the modern counterpart of the Inquisition. "In open as well as in closed societies," he writes, "the institutional psychiatrist has long been in the business of putting under lock and key deviant citizens categorized as mentally ill."

He is interested in the dynamics of social control, of the relationship between the oppressor and the oppressed. Thus, he compares the concept of mental illness with the concept of witchcraft. He warns that as witches were created by witch hunters, madmen are created by psychiatrists. He is concerned that psychiatric stigmatization and persecution may be based on political belief, race, religion, socioeconomic status, or noncomformity.

Szasz is both gigantically right and gigantically wrong. The thread of truth in his fantasied ideal therapeutic state demands a greater tolerance and sensitivity toward nonconformity and aberrations, and even toward poor judgment. Unquestionably, there must be protection of basic human rights for all people. But the helpless and the troubled also require adequate services and, at times, institutionalization. Szasz is not as concerned with the oppression that results from failure to treat as he is with the direct abuse and possible conspiracy of psychiatry. There are people whose troubles have been manufactured by life itself and not by psychiatrists and their theories, as Szasz contends. In that sense mental illness, unfortunately, is not a myth. Since mental and emotional problems are real, people have a right to expect competent diagnosis and treatment. At present, institutional psychiatry is more often than not a confused mélange of nonservices, whose therapeutic effectiveness at times approaches absolute zero and, indeed, can do harm.

There has been a long history in American psychiatric institutions of diagnostic conferences where psychiatrists behave like medievalists discussing the number of angels who can stand on the head of a pin. They are more fascinated by diagnoses than by treatment, and patients have remained hospitalized for years under civil commitment. The very definitions of evaluation, care and treatment, discharge and recovery were, and often still are, Orwellian as well as just plain foggy. In fairness, society must share the blame since the manpower and facilities necessary for proper state and community mental-health programs have been lacking.

There have, however, been some humane developments in the care of troubled people of all ages, and these derive partly from landmark legal decisions that have offered the possibility for less punitive and more creative responses to damaged personalities and disordered behavior. This raises the difficult question of individual will and responsibility. If we eat, drink or smoke too much can we excuse ourselves on the basis of illness? If we have led lives that have been damaging to ourselves and others, whom shall we blame? Does our (mis)conduct reflect our own character and choice? Or determinism? Or some combination?[40] Are there special and legitimate categories of atypical behavior that are neither sickness nor sin? If so, how do we avoid returning to the moralizing and excessive punishment of the past?

Another legal issue is the question of whether mental illness is likely to lead to injury to the patient or to others if he is allowed to remain at liberty. For example, it is difficult to clarify the problem of the nonflamboyant, suicidal older person. Older people feeling powerless, humiliated, confused or depressed may be quietly suicidal over a long period of time, refusing medicine, eating little, overdrinking. Since they are not "obviously" homicidal or suicidal, the terminology of commitment laws may deny such people needed care.[41]

Other problems arise around the specifics of commitment procedures. In many jurisdictions, records of civil commitment hearings may not be kept at all.[42] Many psychiatrists give brief, inadequate mental-status examinations; they may not inform or prepare patients for hearings. It is imperative that the psychiatrist spell out in detail to the patient and his counsel the nature of the psychiatric evaluation. The patient must be informed of his rights, including his rights to decision, treatment and release. Too often the hospital psychiatrist may back down prior to a hearing and discharge the patient, not only as a "kindness" because court cases are "too disturbing to the older mental patients" but also because the patient decides to call for a jury trial which will take up the psychiatrist's time. Psychiatrists have tended to overestimate the fragility of their patients, especially their older patients, and such infantilization can be most destructive of civil rights. I know of no decisive studies whatsoever that show court trials to be dangerous. In fact, I have seen patients, particularly paranoid patients, become integrated under the stress of a trial.

It is also important to distinguish between civil commitment and competency, including contractual and testamentary capacities. In the District of Columbia and in some other jurisdictions the diagnosis of mental illness is separated from the adjudication of incompetency and thus, unless adjudication is made, the hospitalized individual does not lose his civil rights

—his right to vote, to drive a car, to make contracts and to conduct his own affairs. This policy should be nationwide.

The question of civil rights after discharge from institutions also becomes an issue. In some jurisdictions a patient is rapidly discharged from the state hospital and returned involuntarily to the state from which he originated, independent of medical and social considerations. Thus, one may see the indiscriminate return of older persons to their states of origin even though the only families they have reside near the hospital. States do this to spare themselves the costs of aftercare. This situation is similar to the residency requirement in welfare cases and should similarly be struck down by the courts. All states should join the Interstate Compact which provides cooperative and reciprocal agreements on funding.

THE RIGHT TO TREATMENT

What happens when commitment, voluntary or involuntary, becomes a necessary and unavoidable step? The elderly and chronically mentally ill patients in state and county hospitals do not receive care and treatment in keeping with available knowledge. One would hope they have a "right to treatment" equal to that given in private mental hospitals and private psychiatric wards of voluntary hospitals, yet this is not provided.

The "right to treatment" is not simply an idealistic dream. It is a novel yet sensible concept of great legal, social, political and fiscal importance. The term was originated in 1960 by physician-lawyer Morton Birnbaum,[43] who "addressed himself solely to the plight of the involuntarily hospitalized state hospital patient who was not receiving the same quality or quantity of care that was available to private psychiatric patients and who presumably therefore was being held for a longer period than those patients."[44]

The first significant "right to treatment" case was *Rouse* v. *Cameron*[45] in 1966, with Judge David Bazelon as presiding judge (U.S. Court of Appeals, District of Columbia). The patient was incarcerated in a mental hospital after he was found not guilty by reason of insanity of a charge of carrying a dangerous weapon. He was confined for four years, although had he been found guilty of a criminal charge he would have received no more than a year's sentence. The petitioner alleged that the confinement was unlawful since he was not receiving medical treatment for his illness during the incarceration. For the court, Judge Bazelon recognized that the petitioner did indeed have a right to be treated, pursuant to a D.C. mental-health statute. Birnbaum, earlier, expressed theoretical interest in the constitutional issues of denials of procedure and/or substantive due process (under the Fifth Amendment), denial of the equal protection of the law, and perhaps cruel and unusual punishment. Although the Bazelon-led court acknowledged that serious constitutional questions would have had to be raised if the D.C. statute had been absent, the court did not deal with the question of whether such an incarceration without treatment violates the U.S. Constitution.

The *Rouse* v. *Cameron* case was later remanded to the district court for an inquiry into the adequacy of treatment. The district court decided that the treatment was adequate; thus, the patient was not released nor has there been a court order to improve the quality of care. Nonetheless, the right to treatment received some judicial acceptance.

Birnbaum stated that constitutional due process of law "should allow the release of an institutionalized mentally ill person if he is not receiving adequate psychiatric treatment and medical care and treatment." The concept behind the "right to treatment" is that the purpose of hospitalization, and specifically involuntary hospitalization, must be for treatment and not for custodial care or punishment. From the constitutional standpoint that is the only justification allowing civil commitments to mental institutions. As Judge Bazelon has stated, "The need for an individualized treatment plan cannot be overemphasized. Without such a plan there can be no evidence that the hospital has singled out the patient for treatment and as an individual with his own unique problems."[46]

The *Wyatt* v. *Stickney* case* more closely fulfills Birnbaum's concept. This 1971 federal-court decision concerned treatment in Alabama's Bryce Hospital. As part of the decision Judge Frank M. Johnson, Jr. specified three criteria for adequacy of treatment—the provision of a humane psychological and physical environment, qualified staff in adequate numbers and individualized treatment plans.† The national impact of these criteria could be extraordinary—hopefully affecting favorably all patients regardless of age.

But how is the "right to treatment" to be financed? Will court decisions be subverted for lack of funds? On March 7, 1972, Judge Frank Johnson commandeered a list of landholdings of the Alabama Mental Health De-

---

* Incredibly, through 1973 the American Psychiatric Association did not support an enforceable right to treatment for any age or diagnostic group. It did not originally participate as a friend of the court in *Wyatt* v. *Stickney*, whereas many other professional organizations did—including the American Psychological Association, the American Orthopsychiatric Association, the National Legal Aid and Defenders Association, the American Civil Liberties Union and the Center for Law and Social Policy. In 1974 the American Psychiatric Association did become a plaintiff in a "right-to-treatment" suit against St. Elizabeths and the District of Columbia.

† In November, 1972, a federal-court jury awarded $38,500 damages to a former mental patient who charged he was locked up in a Florida state mental hospital for fifteen years but did not receive proper and individualized treatment.

partment and prepared a forced sale of the land in order to pay for the care of the mentally retarded in the department's Partlow School. The sale of land acreage held by the states and occupied by the 321 state hospitals of the nation could be a promising source of funds. New residential and out-patient treatment centers, strategically placed within reach of the population, could be built from the monies realized by this most unusual real-estate sale. However, federal and state tax dollars would still be required for the actual operation of the new facilities.

The mental-health professions have a role also. It is incumbent upon individual clinicians and their organized bodies, the American Psychological and Psychiatric Associations and the National Association of Social Workers, to develop objective standard guidelines that courts can apply to determine the adequacy of treatment provided.* It is necessary that the organizations and professionals be prepared to testify in "right to treatment" cases, as forthright advocates for substantial improvement in hospital care.†

THE RIGHT TO ALTERNATIVE COMMUNITY FACILITIES

The legal right to alternative community facilities was upheld in 1966 in a decision by the U.S. Court of Appeals for the District of Columbia, with Judge Bazelon presiding. In 1962, a 60-year-old woman, Catherine Lake, was picked up by the police and later committed to St. Elizabeths Hospital. The diagnosis was chronic brain syndrome with arteriosclerosis. Her sister instigated proceedings which led to the *Lake* v. *Cameron* case.[48] According to the judgment of the case, the patient was found not to need psychiatric services or to require total deprivation of her liberty. The patient, however, did not have the financial resources to find alternative community care. Judge Bazelon wrote:

Deprivation of liberty solely because of dangers to the ill persons themselves should not go beyond what is necessary for their protection. The court's duty to explore alternatives in such a case as this is related also to the obligation of the state to bear the burden of exploration of possible alternatives an indigent cannot bear.

---

* The American Psychiatric Association discarded its original staff personnel-patient ratios for mental hospitals as "meaningless as a general standard" in 1969.[47] In addition, the American Psychiatric Association has not fought to help state hospitals qualify for Medicare and Medicaid funds through Social Security Administration certification.

† The American Psychiatric Association finally became *amicus curiae* in appeal of the Wyatt case.

Such alternatives would include adequate outpatient treatment, foster care, halfway houses, day hospitals and nursing homes.

The *Lake* v. *Cameron* decision has great potential importance if it is applied and tested in various parts of the United States. However, this decision must not be misunderstood. It in no way should support the feeling current in some circles that any community facility, regardless of quality, may be more desirable than the mental hospital for any aged patient. Some civil libertarians, lawyers and psychiatrists who decry the authoritarianism and lack of patients' rights in mental hospitals overlook even more serious problems in improper alternative care facilities in the community. They should be concerned with the standards of such institutions, with the rights and protection of patients, the problem of private funds, the abuse of drugs in "management" of patients, and other issues which determine the quality of care.

FINANCING MENTAL HEALTH CARE

There is discrimination in present Medicare coverage for psychiatric disorders. Patients must pay 50 percent of the cost of outpatient psychiatric services rather than the 20 percent required for physical illnesses. There is an average annual limit on outpatient psychiatric care of $250. Since the average private psychiatric fee in various cities in the United States ranges from $35 to $50 per hour for individual sessions and $15 to $20 for group sessions, patients are restricted to about ten to twenty hours of outpatient care unless they can afford the fees themselves. This inadequate coverage makes hospitalization more likely as care within the community is priced out of the range of most people.

Another problem arises when patients are institutionalized. There is an unrealistic 190-day lifetime limitation in Medicare coverage for inpatient treatment in mental hospitals. Some persons require longer periods of care; others may need to be hospitalized the rest of their lives. Liberalization of the present restrictions on hospitalization has been called for by the Health Insurance Benefits Advisory Council. The American Medical Association has also supported this change. Dr. Robert W. Gibson, medical director of Sheppard and Enoch Pratt Hospital in Towson, Maryland, has frequently submitted testimony[49] on behalf of the American Psychiatric Association and the National Association of Private Psychiatric Hospitals calling for revisions in Medicare. Commenting on the overall cost of Medicare and Medicaid, Gibson[50] pointed out that in 1968 "based on claims made under Medicare, payments for psychiatric hospitalization represented only 0.7 percent of the total amount reimbursed, and the suggested changes would add little, if anything, to this."

The 190-day lifetime limit placed on treatment in a psychiatric hospital does not apply to treatment in a general hospital, even if that treatment is psychiatric. Consequently many old people must go to general hospitals in an attempt to find treatment for mental and emotional problems.

Medicaid has not served the elderly much better than Medicare. The state hospital systems which emerged following the pioneering efforts of Dorothea Dix have meant that the care and treatment of the mentally ill has been left to individual states. The National Mental Health Act of 1946 marked the occasion when the first federal assistance was offered to the states. The portion of the new Medicaid legislation with greatest significance in this area was sponsored by Senator Russell Long (D.-La.) in 1965. Federal financial participation and assistance for persons sixty-five years and older was permitted if they were patients in institutions for mental diseases. The Long amendment is the companion piece to the Title 18 legislation which provides—although in a severely limited manner—for those older persons with acute brain disorders and other mental illnesses who respond to relatively brief but intensive treatment in mental hospitals. The Long amendment also made provisions for the very many aged who are suffering from chronic disorders, either organic or functional, and who need long-term continued care from state mental-health facilities.

In implementing the Long amendment the Senate Committee on Finance expressed its desire to

ensure that the additional federal funds be made available to the states under the provisions of the bill [to] assist the over-all improvement of mental health services to the state . . . there is a great need for increased professional services in hospitals and for development of alternative methods of care outside of hospitals . . . the Committee bill provides that the *states will receive additional federal funds only to the extent that a showing is made to the satisfaction of the Secretary that total expenditures of the State or its political subdivision from their funds for mental health services are increased.* [Italics mine.]

Thirty-four jurisdictions serving Medicaid patients implemented the Long amendment and received $160 million by September 1, 1969. However, in most states the money designated by law for the improvement of care for the elderly mental-health patients in state hospitals had gone instead into the state general-revenue funds for uses of other kinds. In other words, there was a serious loophole in the legislation, allowing for misuse of funds. The 1972 Social Security Amendments failed to rectify this situation.

The Hospital Improvement Program (HIP) of the National Institute of Mental Health, created by Congress in 1963, has been of some limited help in providing mental-health care for the elderly, but again there are serious problems. The maximum per year to any individual hospital is a $100,000 grant. Many HIP projects tried to undo the "pernicious effects of chronic hospitalization" by transferring patients to nursing homes. Some older people were given active treatment leading to a return to their own homes. Many others were just moved from one inadequate facility to another.

MENTAL-HEALTH RESEARCH ON OLD AGE

Why should psychiatrists or any other of the mental-health disciplines study the old? There are practical, financial reasons—the cost to society for the care of old people would be greatly reduced by improving their health and extending their economic productivity. There are humanistic reasons —we all want a decent and dignified old age for ourselves and those we care about. There are broad social reasons—it is logical that study and understanding of one segment of the life cycle helps in the understanding of the other segments. There are philosophical reasons—if old age can become a substantial, satisfying period of life, people can lose some of their profound fear of growing old.

Studies of the nature of late life are necessary for the understanding of the whole of life—the life cycle. Old age has become increasingly visible ever since the seventeenth century. Longer life spans have "unfolded" the life cycle, making its stages or phases prominent. Aristotle, Cicero, Shakespeare, Rousseau and other philosophers and writers have considered the total life cycle as a concept and have proposed various methods of dividing and describing it. In the United States, in particular, social psychologists, sociologists and psychologists have shown some interest in studies of the life cycle. William James, George Mead, Charlotte Buhler, Robert Havighurst, Therese Benedek, Erik Erikson, Sidney Pressey, Raymond Kuhlen, Bernice Neugarten and Marjorie Fiske Lowenthal are among recent writers who have given attention to this subject, with some particular emphasis upon old age and the transitional middle-age period. The first major American book on the psychology of old age was that by G. Stanley Hall in 1922.

In the 1950s, lay child psychoanalyst and teacher Erik H. Erikson awakened psychoanalysts, psychiatrists and other mental-health workers to the fact of adulthood and the idea that humankind is not irrevocably molded in the first five years of childhood. Erikson's concepts of the life cycle[51] and his notions of crucial stages, which he sets up in antipodal form are arguable, and have been difficult to translate and test in the experimental situation.* However, Erikson's influence has been deserved and considerable, and it remains dismaying that, despite his work, the life cycle, and especially its later stages, has not received genuine attention. Rothschild, Gitelson, Grotjahn, Goldfarb, Weinberg, Linden, Busse, Simon, Greenleigh, Thompson and Berezin are among American psychiatrists whose work has begun to stimulate research into the psychodynamics of aging as well as the development of treatment approaches. But psychiatry as a whole has not developed its own theories of late life nor has it absorbed the studies of human development made by other professions.

The possibilities implicit in research on late life can increase our knowledge about many subjects which affect those who are younger. We might learn much, for example, about the nature of grief and depression, since both are so prevalent in the later years. The survival capacities of the old could provide clues as to the adaptiveness of various personality types throughout the life cycle. We need extensive basic and clinical research on the major organic brain disorders, particularly "senile brain disease," to understand why brain cells disintegrate. Studies of autoimmunity (the sensitivity of one's body to its own proteins) as a possible factor in the genesis of chronic brain syndromes[52] might both help the elderly and increase our understanding of autoimmune diseases in the young. The inherent features of late life—losses of loved ones, the implacable course of aging, the greater imminence of death—need to be better understood in terms of their emotional impact. Late life features such as sponsorship of the young and the desire to leave intellectual, spiritual, material and even physical legacies (many older people give their bodies for research after death) need exploration. The richness of research material is greater in the older age group than in any other simply because they have lived through more periods of life, a longer span of time and more historical events than anyone else. They are the most complicated and challenging of human beings.

Only 3 percent of the budget of the federal government's National Institute of Mental Health is devoted to the study of mental problems of old age. NIMH's program in aging has always been limited. A modest program headed by Dr. James E. Birren ended in 1964, and no specific research in aging has been done intramurally since that time. NIMH's extramural granting program in training, research and service maintains a modest program on Mental Health of the Aging. Grants for improvement of public mental hospitals as well as demonstration and research costs are funded, but

---

* His experience with the middle-aged and elderly is meager, and his popular conceptions of "generativity versus stagnation" and "ego-integrity versus despair" do not hold up well in my clinical and research experience with patients in middle and later life.

the overall amount of money involved was less than $3.4 million in 1971.[53]

NIMH directors have not taken major leadership in pressing for higher budgets within the Department of Health, Education, and Welfare or with Congress in proportion to the incidence, prevalence and costs of mental illnesses among the elderly. In 1972, under pressure from organizations interested in the elderly,* NIMH created the office of special assistant on aging, which has given the impression of activity and the illusion of change. There have been attempts to show that various training and research grants already involve the study of aging or aged persons.[54] Further, Dr. Bertram Brown, NIMH director, met with representatives of professional groups at their urging and appointed an intramural committee to develop a "mental health strategy for the aged in 1973." But no substantial increase in funds has appeared. The unofficial but anticipated priorities for the seventies proposed by NIMH do not include aging. They do include crime and law enforcement, drug use and abuse,[55] all more important politically as far as legislative support and funding are concerned.

NIMH is currently having difficulties maintaining the programs it now has, let alone expanding or creating new programs. In 1973 NIMH was reorganized into another HEW unit together with the federal units concerned with drug abuse and alcoholism. The NIMH budget has been held back and the community mental health center program has been threatened. This affords an understandable reason why NIMH may be reluctant to get involved with the elderly at this time. It does not, however, explain NIMH's neglect of the old when it was in its well-financed heyday in the late 1950s and 1960s, nor does it explain the unwillingness of NIMH leadership to re-examine its priorities and reallocate its present budget more in keeping with the prevalence of psychiatric problems. As matters stand, any hopes for expansion in the field of aging and mental health will probably have to come from congressional pressure.

TRAINING MENTAL-HEALTH PERSONNEL

The training of mental-health personnel to work with the elderly is still in its primitive stages. Duke University established a geropsychiatric training

---

* A committee, representing various organizations such as the American Psychiatric, Psychological and Sociological associations, asked for a budget for the elderly in the range of $10 million for the first year—$2.6 million for research, $2 million for training and $5 million for services. The remaining $400,000 would be operating funds for a center on aging. In retrospect it is clear that these objectives were extremely modest. The drug-addiction program alone in the District of Columbia was $5 million in 1971, half of what was being asked to help meet the mental-health needs of 10 percent of the nation's entire population!

program; members of the Boston Psychoanalytic Institute have helped build up a Society for Gerontological Psychiatry and publish a *Journal of Geriatric Psychiatry*; and a handful of psychiatrists have provided some individual education in the field. NIMH does not have a training committee on aging.*

It is self-evident that all personnel, including general practitioners of medicine, clergymen and others who have frequent contact with the older population, should be trained in early detection of mental-health problems, and the treatment of such problems or referral of troubled older people for appropriate care. An authentic community psychiatry would also include mental-health training courses for the police, given the number of occasions when the police encounter disturbed mental conditions in older people victimized by crime, or found wandering through the streets. The special realities of the elderly poor, of older women, and of minority-group elderly require understanding of the anthropological, sociological, cultural and economic aspects of mental illness. Psychiatrists are mostly white middle-class, middle-aged men, and the need for women and therapists who are members of minority groups is obvious.

In the preceding chapter I have discussed the special training required for medical care of the old. Mental-health components should be a basic part of every training program involving the old. In addition, the National Institute of Mental Health needs a funded, special training committee on aging, similar to the one for aging that operates with some success in the National Institute of Child Health and Human Development. That should increase the number of training programs in various mental-health disciplines, such as social work, psychology and psychiatric nursing.

NIMH-supported teams composed of mental-health specialists skilled in aging should be brought on a systematic basis to psychiatric training institutions, state mental hospitals, general hospitals, and community mental health centers to conduct intensive institutes with personnel.† Each organization visited should then build teams to continue in-service training programs and teach within the surrounding geographic area. The original teaching team would return for follow-up seminars and workshops on a regular schedule.

---

* "Geriatric programs" supported by NIMH exist only in fourteen schools of social work, one school of nursing and one medical school. There are also six in-service training grants at state hospitals and one continuing education grant (1971 figures).

† The Group for the Advancement of Psychiatry (GAP) and NIMH, under the direction of Robert D. Patterson, created a teaching guide of value to community mental-health centers and mental-health professionals.[56]

THE NEED FOR A COMMISSION ON MENTAL
HEALTH AND ILLNESS OF THE ELDERLY

The 1961 report of the Joint Commission on Mental Health and Illness, entitled *Action for Mental Health,* set the prevailing tone for presently objectionable public policies in mental-health care of the old. It called for the creation of a network of community mental health centers (described on pages 236–38) and the end of traditional dependence upon the massive state mental hospitals. Although many of the recommendations were sound for other age groups, the commission failed to consider the elderly mental patient. No organizations or agencies specifically concerned with the elderly participated in the commission's work; no psychiatrist, psychologist or social worker recognized as a specialist in the problems of the aged was included in the deliberations. As a result the Joint Commission supported ideas inimical to older people, such as the use of chronic disease hospitals for joint mental and physical care, largely for reasons of economy. The belief was perpetuated that chronic patients do not benefit from individualized, active forms of treatment. The commission recommended that "all existing state hospitals of more than 1,000 beds be gradually and progressively converted into centers for long-term and combined care of chronic diseases, including mental illnesses." The commission believed that many of the needs of mental patients requiring prolonged care are identical to those of patients with chronic physical illnesses needing prolonged care, though this is not the case. Indeed, "many chronic patients get along with minimal supervision in hospitals properly designed and the staffs trained in the care of long-term patients," the report said.

Only one commission member, Loula Dunn, dissented. Significantly, she stated that all the reasons that contraindicate effective care of patients in large mental hospitals apply equally to the care of patients with other chronic diseases. She pointed out that the institution caring for the long-term chronically ill patient not only must provide essential medical and related services but also must be a home for such patients, often for the remainder of their lives. It is unlikely that this can be achieved in an institution with more than a thousand beds. In addition, such institutions are often located at a considerable distance from urban areas, meaning that medical personnel and consultants as well as families and friends are not able to see patients easily.

Previously, the distinguished 1956 Commission on Chronic Illness, undertaking a thorough seven-year study, rejected the notion of the independent chronic-disease hospital. It was strongly recommended that chronic care systems be associated physically and administratively with general hospitals.

In order to ensure that the mental-health needs of older people are clarified and planned for, a Commission on Mental Health and Illness of the Elderly is necessary. This would afford an opportunity for various organizations, public and private, and for individuals in the field of aging, to prepare a body of major recommendations toward a public policy for the mental health of the aged. Certainly we already know more than is applied, and in that sense another commission would be redundant. Yet, in order to give national visibility to the mental-health problems of the aged and to build up a record for use in Congress, a commission is a valuable tool. Such a commission would study and evaluate the needs and resources of the elderly; specify the requirements for manpower, facilities and research; clarify for older people what they themselves could do to prevent mental illness; estimate the cost now and in the future to carry out necessary programs; and suggest methods of meeting these costs. Moreover, the commission would conduct feasibility studies on health-care delivery.

The commission should be nongovernmental and multidisciplinary, with inclusion of professional and lay groups interested in the old. Older people themselves should, of course, participate. There should be adequate funds under the joint administration of the National Institute of Mental Health and the Administration on Aging. Senator Edmund Muskie (D.-Me.), Chairman of the Subcommittee on Health of the Senate's Special Committee on Aging, first introduced a bill to establish such a commission in December, 1971. It has yet to be enacted.

At the 1971 White House Conference on Aging a variety of significant recommendations were made concerning the active care and treatment of the emotional and mental disorders of old age. The proposed Commission on Mental Illness of the Elderly was supported. A center on mental health of the aged within the National Institute of Mental Health was advocated. The right to treatment of older people in a variety of psychiatric settings was backed. The creation of a network of clinical and social services for the elderly throughout the country was endorsed. Medicare and Medicaid's bias against emotional illness compared to physical illness was criticized. In short, many solid recommendations were proposed. None have been implemented. Once again the tragedy of old age is reinforced by inaction.

Chapter 9

HOUSES OF DEATH
ARE A LIVELY BUSINESS

Unlike some primitive tribes, we do not kill off our aged and infirm. We bury them alive in institutions. To save our face, we call the institutions homes —a travesty on the word. I have seen dozens of such homes in the last six months—desolate places peopled with blank-faced men and women, one home so like the other that each visit seemed a recurrent nightmare.
—Edith M. Stern, "Buried Alive,"
Women's Home Companion, June, 1947

This famous exposé of institutions for the aged helped focus attention on a national problem. Yet, over twenty-five years later we have barely begun to solve the problem. In fact, we have new problems, for the elderly population has grown by leaps and bounds and the commercial-nursing-home business has evolved into a vast, largely unregulated industry. As nursing-home critic and former Congressman David A. Pryor* stated, the nursing-home industry has attracted the "fast-buck entrepreneur" and other fringe businessmen along with well-intentioned owners. Even the latter are rarely trained professionals. Only in America does such extensive "commercialization" of facilities for old people exist. Many facilities are described as "human junkyards" by Pryor, and "warehouses" by Senator Frank Moss (D.-Utah).

WHAT ARE NURSING HOMES LIKE?

Elderly people are quick to understand what life will be like in most homes for the old:

Almost all older people view the move to a home for the aged or to a nursing home with fear and hostility. . . . All old people—without exception—believe that the move to an institution is the prelude to death. . . . [The old person] sees the move to an institution as a decisive change in living arrangements, the last change he will experience before he dies. . . . Finally, no matter what the extenuating circumstances, the older person who has children interprets the move to an institution as rejection by his children.[1]

* Pryor was elected governor of Arkansas in 1974.

Families suffer guilt and ambivalence about the thought of moving an older family member into a nursing home. Yet there may be no alternative when elderly people become too mentally or physically ill to live at home. For many families the admission to a nursing home is so symbolic of death that they either openly or subtly mourn for the person as though he were already dead. Nursing homes are viewed as preburial storehouses where persons exist in isolation and excruciating boredom, with no possible hope for anything but their own demise.

How have nursing homes and other community facilities for the aged gotten such a grim reputation? Is this reputation deserved? To explore these questions one must begin by clarifying the term "nursing home." The dictionary definition is a "hospital for convalescent or aged people."[2] This is inaccurate, since there is little resemblance to hospitals in terms of medical, surgical, psychiatric or rehabilitative services. A nursing home is primarily a residential facility with a minimal level of nursing care, designed for the convalescence and long-term care of the seriously ill of all ages but primarily the aged.

HOMES FOR THE AGING

The public tends to include all residential community facilities for the old under the term "nursing home"; but the distinction must be made between commercial nursing homes and homes for the aging. Commercial nursing homes are operated for profit by anyone with enough funds to erect and maintain one. Homes for the aging are under the sponsorship of religious, fraternal (benevolent) and trust organizations, which are nonprofit and voluntary. A number of nonprofit homes are also run by federal, state, county and municipal governments. (See Table 4.)

The nonprofit homes for the aging and government homes, with some

TABLE 4

The Percent of All Old People
Living in Various Institutional Homes

Homes	*Percent*
1. Commercial nursing homes	79
2. Voluntary nonprofit homes for aging, nursing homes, "campus" complexes (religious, fraternal and trust)	14
3. Government homes (federal, state, county and municipal)	7

notable exceptions, tend to concentrate on residential and personal rather than nursing care. They are likely to offer medical and social services as long as their residents remain fairly healthy and independent. When a resident becomes seriously ill, he may have to move to a commercial nursing home.

These nonprofit homes account for only 21 percent of the nation's institutional homes and provide some 246,000 beds. (See Table 5.) They depend upon trusts, endowments, sustaining funds and Community Chest drives, as well as upon federal funds obtained through Medicare and Medicaid. They have received fewer federal tax dollars than the commercial homes although there is growing public support for diversion of public money to them.

Nongovernmental homes for the aging are often very selective in their admission policies. The overtly emotionally and mentally ill, the severely mentally impaired, the acutely or notably physically ill, and persons of minority racial backgrounds are often excluded from religious, fraternal and trust homes. This is due in part to economic limitations and in part to narrow definitions of social responsibility and sometimes outright prejudice. Some homes are excellent, with innovations like progressive, graduated care in campuslike facilities, and community social services such as meals on wheels and day-care centers. Others have emphasized racial

TABLE 5

Kinds of Nonprofit Homes for the Aging

Type	Number of Homes	Average Number of Beds	Total Number of Patients
Religious	1,500	84	117,180
Governmental (Municipal)	670	105	63,000
Others (Fraternal, Trust)	1,225	60	66,150
Summary:	3,395		246,330

SOURCE: Frank Zelenka, American Association of Homes for the Aging. From *Selected Institutional Characteristics of Long-Term Care Facilities*. Department of Health Care Administration, George Washington University, Long-term Care Monograph #4, January, 1970.

integration and have sought to provide care for the so-called senile patients. With increasing federal support, homes for the aging could become a vital resource for many more older persons. As of now, however, one cannot be assured of an adequate variety of services and high-quality care even at high prices.

COMMERCIAL NURSING HOMES

Commercial nursing homes* illustrate the conflict between profit and service in the care of the old. About 80 percent of older persons in institutionalized homes are in commercial nursing homes, and this represents almost a million people. One can find fine commercial homes where the elderly are well cared for. But the majority of homes can accurately be described as "halfway houses somewhere between society and the cemetery."³ A woman deeply despairing over the poor care of her mother in a nursing home wrote me:

My mother resolved her nursing home problem—she passed away the morning of March 11th—not knowing, of course, the newest impasse regarding her care. I was with her when she died—a great lady who brought up four kids alone and who had to spend her last years in anguish.

Since 1958, when I first began to look into commercial nursing homes, I have concluded that a nursing home is a facility that has few or no nurses and can hardly qualify as a home.† I continue to visit nursing homes regularly—sometimes disguising myself as though I were inquiring about a family member, sometimes visiting openly as a physician. I have seen patients lying in their own urine and feces. Food is frequently left untouched on plates. Boredom among patients and weariness among staff are common. I ask both the staff and patients similar questions in order to compare their answers: What is served for breakfast? How often are patients cleaned up? I am interested in whether the majority of patients are dressed in street clothes, or walk about in night clothes. I note the expressions on their faces. I listen to the way the patients are addressed by staff members. Are they patronizingly called by their first names or given the dignity due their years?

* The nursing-home industry prefers to call these "proprietary homes."
† In 1961 only 44 percent of nursing homes had a full-time registered nurse and 14 percent had no trained nurses.⁴

Much too often there are very few of the most basic elements of physical assistance necessary for survival, let alone special human courtesies and amenities. I always ask, for example, if fire drills have been conducted.* I run my hands over fire hoses and find some so flimsy and worn that they would never be strong enough to withstand water pressure. I observe floor hazards, inadequate illumination and corridors obstructed by storage and wheelchairs. I find stairways with fire doors left open, and hollow or paneled doors which clearly would not retard the progress of a fire for more than a few minutes. The National Fire Protection Association considers many homes to be firetraps, and overall it finds nursing homes to be the unsafest of all places in which to live.

One can also list a grim catalogue of the medical deficiencies of the nursing-home industry and related facilities. Nursing homes, however financed, do not provide well-organized, comprehensive medical care. Care must be obtained from family physicians or private physicians assigned by a welfare agency or the home itself. Many states do not even require a principal physician, let alone a medical director, for a nursing home, and when they do there is no assurance that the physician regards himself as responsible for the patients. Doctors seldom conduct regular rounds. Winter flu shots are often not given. There is minimal preventive care. Dental care is scarce. Public sanitation is questionable. Family doctors tend not to visit patients in nursing homes if they are too far away. Other doctors do "gang visits," seeing a number of patients quickly and submitting substantial bills to Medicare.† Those who thought Medicare would help bring better medical care to nursing homes have been disappointed. For example, the principle of continuity of care for patients, through the requirement of transfer agreements with hospitals, has not been fulfilled.

Frequently there is no emergency medical equipment. Medical records may be absent or misplaced. Routine lab tests are difficult to obtain. Individual treatment plans are uncommon. Rehabilitation is rare. Speech and occupational therapy are seldom offered. Physical therapy may be advertised, but it is often no more than a set of parallel bars alongside a massage table. There may be no physical therapists and none of the necessary equipment. Physical-therapy rooms are often used as storage closets.

---

* One may find that there is a fire evacuation procedure but that there has never been a fire drill. Or one may be told there have been fire drills, only to find that only the staff have gone through it—with simulated patients! In many instances, not even the lives of staff members are made any safer as a result. Evacuation, of course, should theoretically be a last resort since it is difficult to manage confused and disabled older people. After notifying the fire department, staff should make an effort to extinguish and contain the fire.

† One physician sent bills for 4,560 claimed visits to 54 patients in 1968. The same doctor received $42,000 for 8,275 injections of 149 patients.[5]

Many psychiatrically disturbed people end up in nursing homes without mental-health care of any kind. Other patients requiring basic medical attention may be misdiagnosed as psychiatric patients.*

Drug prescriptions may be administered incorrectly. Tranquilizers are frequently used as chemical strait-jackets. These tranquilizers are paid for out of Medicare money, and from a cost-benefit point of view one can reduce personnel expenses substantially if one "snows" or "zonks" patients on drugs.[6] Drug companies know this very well. The tranquilizer diazepam (Valium) has been advertised in professional journals as "useful in order to have a 'less complaining patient, less demanding patient, more coopera-tive patient.' "

Few medical students receive any training or work in nursing homes. Medical students, interns and residents, when and if they ever do get inside of nursing homes, are likely to learn by example to refer to the patients as "gooks" or "vegetables" or as "stroked out." There is little or no research going on in commercial nursing homes, and thus they make no contribution toward the further understanding of old people, aging and chronic disease. Autopsies are rarely performed.

Fundamental standards of hygiene are often neglected. For example the bedridden debilitated elderly are prone to bedsores. If the patient is not turned or if he or she is allowed to lie in urine-soaked bedding so that the skin macerates, the bedsores worsen and become infected. Malnutrition and anemia add to the problem. Infections resist recovery. Vitamin C deficiency and low protein (hypoproteinemia)—not rare in nursing homes —are most unfavorable to healing.

Often there is a pervasive, permeating odor of urinary and fecal inconti-nence. During heat waves old people die at a faster rate since air condition-ing is frequently absent in the hot, stench-filled homes. People may live in dingy, tiny cubicles, sharing community bathrooms that offer no privacy. In many places the old person or his family has to tip the attendants to get even simple personal care, such as shaving or combing hair, on a regular basis.

Food costs may be kept down to the point of malnourishment. The schedule of meals is sometimes compressed within seven to eight hours in order to reduce the culinary and serving staff. There is little recreation, social or religious activity. Occasionally there are books, shops and beauty parlors. Ironically, barbers and beauticians may have had more profes-sional training than either nursing aides or ambulance drivers.

---

* As a psychiatrist I was called to a nursing home to see an old woman who was showing signs of mental confusion. I observed ankle edema. Her mental confusion was due to congestive heart failure and not to any specific psychological state.

Senator Moss has said that "people off the street, paid the minimum wages, who have no training and who are grossly overworked, provide 90 percent of this work in U.S. nursing homes." It is important to emphasize the economic circumstances of nursing-home personnel. One wonders why nursing-home administrators are surprised at the high turnover among their employees when it seems obvious that staff are looking for higher pay and less difficult employment.* The hospital and nursing-home employees unions have not succeeded in unionization of individual nursing homes or nursing-home chains. Typically,† wages may be $1.80 per hour, $1.90 after three weeks, with scheduled increases up to $2.15 an hour, and then $2.40 an hour after a year or more. Two dollars and forty cents an hour is $96 a week or $4,992 a year.

Higher payrolls reduce profits, of course. *Time* magazine quoted Richard Rynd, a Baltimore nursing-home owner and Maryland state delegate (June 6, 1969, issue): "President Richard Rynd, 38, a onetime scrap metal dealer, openly scoffs at a competing home that employs registered nurses rather than aides. 'No wonder it loses money,' says Rynd."

Even certain arrangements originating from humanitarian motives have had damaging effects. In some places the amount of money provided by states to nursing homes is greater for the bedridden than for the non-bedridden patient. In addition it costs more, for example, to provide personnel to help guide physically impaired older persons to a common dining room than to have one staff member push a tray cart to each room. It is thus both easier and more economical to keep the patient in bed.

The rights of patients in nursing homes, living as they do under the most authoritarian circumstances, is another subject that is circumvented. These institutions are set up more for their own convenience than for the persons they serve. Institutional populations are controlled, regimented and often intimidated. Goffman has described "total institutions" vividly.[7] They resist change. They are impersonal. They lack the most ordinary pleasantries of life. As Dr. Prescott Thompson has observed, how often can the resident of a home go out freely and buy a hamburger or have a cocktail? What about keeping a small pet? Why not one's own furniture and some familiar personal possessions instead of institutional furnishings? What about privacy for sexual activities? What about one's money?‡

---

* In 1973 there were 53,235 registered nurses working in nursing homes (of 815,000 registered nurses in the United States), with a 71 percent turnover. In 1970 there were 40,000 licensed practical nurses, with a 35 percent turnover, and 215,000 aides and orderlies (43 percent of the staff), with a 75 percent turnover.

† Before the 1974 increases in minimum wages.

‡ Social Security checks are known to go to some home operators rather than to residents.

The poor have been pushed and crowded all their lives; but the middle-class patients are likely to be newly shocked by the loss of both choice and privacy that occurs in nursing homes, sectarian homes for the aged and related facilities.

WHO GOES TO A NURSING HOME?

Nursing-home residents are a highly specific group of people. Seventy percent are women simply because they live longer than men. Fifty percent of nursing-home residents either have no living relatives or have no direct relationship with even a distant relative. The average age of residents is seventy-eight. Ninety-six percent are white, a consequence of the shorter life expectancies and greater admissions difficulties of minority groups. Sixty to 80 percent are poor—though they may not have been poor when they entered old age—and have been on public assistance or the federalized Supplemental Security Income (SSI) program. Some 85 percent of persons who enter nursing homes die there, and the average length of stay is 1.1 years. One-third of all those who are admitted die within the first year; another third live up to three years in the institutions. The remaining third survive beyond three years.* The vast majority of nursing-home patients have more than one physical ailment. About 16 percent have serious hearing defects and a similar percentage suffer serious visual handicaps.

The problem of the black aged in nursing homes is a much-neglected topic. The primary difficulty for older blacks is in getting admitted at all. Both commercial and nonprofit nursing homes and homes for the aging remain largely segregated, even though segregation is usually not openly stated as a policy. Less than 3 percent of all nursing-home residents are black (not entirely explained by their lower life expectancy). Whites do not apply for admission to black homes, and white homes claim they have not received any "qualified" black applicants. Black-owned facilities having difficulty meeting health, fire and building standards may be closed rather than given guidance, financial assistance and encouragement. Community Chest organizations may refuse to allocate funds to black-owned facilities.† Many nonprofit, church-sponsored homes avoid integration by restricting admissions to their church's own parishioners—already a self-selected group in terms of race and social class.

---

* Studies have shown that a year or more of careful preparation before admission is associated with increased survival during the first six months in an institution.[8] Individual and group counseling of the person and his family should be part of the process of admission.

† To implement the Life Safety Code, for instance, is very expensive.[9]

The numbers of people in nursing homes with psychiatric disorders has been variously estimated; Alvin Goldfarb (1962) found that 87 percent of patients showed significant evidence of chronic brain syndrome. Psychiatric symptoms usually accompany such brain damage.

Disabling physical—and, recently, mental—conditions bring many elderly into nursing homes at the point where they and their families can no longer care for them. The most common physical problems are chronic congestive heart failure, stroke and cancer. Persons with mental impairments are now being sent to nursing homes rather than to mental hospitals. Urinary and fecal incontinence, disorientation and confusion, a tendency to wander away from home and the need for extensive nursing care are among the precipitating factors leading to admission.

Many who are admitted would be better cared for elsewhere or at home. Brandeis University's Levinson Gerontological Policy Institute made a study of nursing-home inhabitants in Massachusetts in 1971 that showed that of 100 patients:

37 needed full-time skilled nursing care;
26 needed minimal supervised "living";
23 could get along at home with periodic home visits by nurses;
14 needed nothing.

The Brandeis researchers concluded:

Large numbers of disabled are forced into nursing homes or mental hospitals at a very high charge to the public treasury simply because public programs could not give attention to alternative ways of meeting their needs outside of institutions.[10]

COSTS OF CARE

Care in most nonprofit institutions is very expensive for the average person. The well-to-do and their families have to give generously to these institutions to obtain admission and good continuous care. A certain number of the less affluent may receive "scholarships" but most religious, fraternal and trust homes are forced to limit the number of indigent they can serve. But the advent of Medicaid has helped considerably.

When an older person or his family must turn to the commercial nursing home, costs may be beyond their reach. The average monthly expense in a commercial "skilled nursing home" in 1971 was $420; in an "intermediate care facility," $270. These are averages only, and recent rampant inflation has undoubtedly increased them greatly; patients and their families may actually face basic monthly expenses that go as high as $600, $800, even $1,200, and a large number of additional charges as well. Supplementary bills can include charges for air mattresses, alcohol, drugs, baby oil, bedsore care, catheters, chest restraints, denture cups, disposable diapers, hand feedings, nasal catheters, Posey restraints, television, tissues, incontinent pants, *ad infinitum*. These items can be very expensive. In 1970, for example, one nursing home charged $45 per month for an air mattress, which, of course, could be used over and over again without replacement. Some institutions make additional charges for bedsore care and hand feeding, services that should be supplied as standard decent nursing care.

David Pryor, at the time a Congressman of 35, worked incognito on weekends for nursing homes as a nurse's aide. On February 23, 1970, he reported his experiences to Congress.* Referring to costs of care he stated:

I found two where I would be willing to put my mother if she needed this kind of care but I don't think I could afford either one on my $42,500 Congressional salary. . . . I have nothing against profit-making but I am against exploitation. Profits are booming, prices are rising, and services not improving.

In order to qualify for financial assistance in meeting costs, many states require the older person to be indigent, with no assets of his own. If he owns a house, it may have to be turned over to the state or county. The middle-income patient is often in the dilemma of having too much income to be eligible for assistance yet not enough to afford care on his own.

A number of financing mechanisms have been created to assist those who meet the financial eligibility requirements. These have resulted in classifying nursing homes in various categories. Here are the original categories, even though they no longer exist precisely in this form—and, as we shall see, there have been upgraded standards—since much of the literature and current language on aging still refers to these definitions:

- An *extended-care facility* (ECF) is more a function than a structure. (An ECF may be a separate institution such as a nursing home or part of other institutions such as a hospital or home for the aged.) It does not mean long-term care but care extended beyond hospitalization for a specific period of illness. The patient is expected to return to independent living

---

* When Representative Pryor made public his findings covering the inadequacies of nursing homes he worked in, he was treated to the same accusations other investigators have received. Dr. Matthew Tayback of the Department of Mental Health and Hygiene of Maryland said the Pryor report was "reckless and lacking humanity. Hundreds of people reading the report will be upset for months." He went on, "People are being treated well in nursing homes and there is no segment of business or industry which is 100 percent pure."[11]

after convalescence and/or rehabilitation. Thus an ECF is an extension of hospital care, with a probability of discharge. ECFs derive from Medicare legislation and are financed on a cost-reimbursement basis by the federal government.

   • A *skilled nursing home* (SNH) is a Medicaid-derived term and refers to long-term, unlimited nursing-home care without the requirement of previous hospitalization. Both long-term convalescent patients and those with terminal illnesses are eligible for admission. Financing is provided by a federal-state cost-sharing program administered by the states. In ECFs there have been retroactive denials of benefits; in SNHs loss of eligibility; in both cases leaving some patients and their families with unexpected, enormous bills to pay. The term "skilled nursing home" often suggests more skill than is actually present; there may be no registered nurse on duty. Moreover, the term implies that there are patients who may only need or can get along with "unskilled nursing" obtainable elsewhere. This is a questionable concept.

   • An *intermediate-care facility* (ICF) may best approximate what the public has in mind when it refers to a "nursing home." The ICF is designed for people who theoretically need "less than a skilled nursing home . . . but more than a custodial or residential home." Personal care, simple medical care and intermittent nursing care are the services under the jurisdiction of the ICFs. The care for those who cannot afford to pay was originally federally funded through state-administered public-assistance programs, but the ICFs are not subject to federal standards and are funded through Medicaid. Financially, the rates of both SNHs and ICFs may be negotiated with the states under the federal government's Medicaid provision, rather than based on costs (as in the case of ECFs).

These definitions have had little predictive value as to the actual services rendered in a particular home. Furthermore, the 1972 Social Security amendments created a single definition and set of standards for ECFs and SNFs, introducing a common name for both—the "skilled nursing facility" —which I will discuss later.

In addition, there are many other kinds of facilities where old people and the chronically ill are stowed away, which are neither "nursing homes" nor "homes for the aging." These go under a variety of names, some of which are euphemisms like "foster care" homes (not to be confused with foster family care), and "personal care homes." Old people are also found in boardinghouses and other facilities in which they are maintained under minimal funding from welfare departments.* The actual number of people in such living quarters is not known, but one could guess that perhaps 250,000 persons are living in this manner, under minimal care and without

* In most states, boardinghouses are not licensed. Many of those residing in boardinghouses need medical and nursing care. States should require medical evaluations of residents who have received welfare funding or now receive Supplemental Security Income.

amenities. In the following pages I will use the term "nursing home" loosely to include all of the institutional home facilities mentioned above as well as commercial nursing homes and homes for the aging, unless otherwise specified.

By 1975 there will be more patients in nursing homes than there are in hospitals. Expenditures for nursing-home care will probably rise faster than any other component of health care, with expenditures for hospital care running a close second.

The average age of entry into nursing homes is advancing—not so long ago it was 70, now it is approaching 84. The degree of illness at time of entry is worse. Nursing homes are receiving sicker people, and thus it becomes more and more imperative that a wide range of medical services be provided, in addition to residential and nursing care. Herbert Shore, an expert on institutional care, has observed:

It is the absence of a national policy for long-term care that has cast the institution into its present mold. It is the wholesale dumping of patients from state mental hospitals into nursing homes so that states can use the federal funds rather than their own that has contributed to the problem.

He further states:

Alternatives to institutional care are needed. A great host of services to aged in their own homes and in congregate care homes must be developed, but this will not in any way change the fact that at some point the aged need a complex of services available only in an institution. Yes, we need better utilization. I am also opposed to unnecessary institutionalization, but I am not opposed to the institution as a valid resource.[12]

Adequate home-care manpower (such as in a National Personal Care Corps), day hospitals, day-care centers, short-term and intermediate and long-term care centers would make it possible to institute definitive treatment and care programs[13] geared to individual needs and thus avoid unnecessary institutionalization. But residential nursing homes, homes for the aging and other care facilities will continue to be needed and used. The question is how we can ensure that they will be decent and humane places in which to live and receive treatment.

EARLY HISTORY OF NURSING HOMES

Nursing homes as we know them were almost nonexistent prior to 1935.* Instead, there were poor houses, poor farms, county infirmaries,

* For example, New York State had only 28 homes and 441 beds.

rest homes and even workhouses. Of course, homes for the aging sponsored by religious groups and benevolent associations have existed for centuries.* Municipal homes for the aged have evolved from the earlier county infirmaries. Many of these facilities were hidden away in the country. People who were admitted were thought of as having been "put away."

With the advent of the Social Security Act in the United States (comprising federal Old Age Assistance and old-age and survivors insurance) a new method of caring for the old began to develop in the 1930s. These programs put cash into the pockets of older people. More of them were able to avoid the county homes by buying care in private homes. Large old houses, often owned by widows living alone or by couples ("mom-and-pop" operations), were turned into boarding or nursing homes. Public assistance and Social Security checks from old people were a welcome source of income for the owners. Unfortunately, neither the houses nor the owners were equipped with facilities for often frail and sick older persons. Today, as more and more states tighten their licensing standards for nursing and boarding homes, this use of "leftover" housing has become unfeasible. In addition nursing homes are now becoming big business, so facilities specially designed for nursing-home care have sprung up.

THE NURSING-HOME BOOM

Business investors began to discover that there was "gold in geriatrics." Increasing numbers of older persons in the United States and the advent of Medicare and Medicaid in 1965 boosted the commercial nursing-home industry to a new position far beyond "mom-and-pop" operations. The original Medicare legislation provided that people over 65, after a stay of at least three days in a hospital, could receive coverage for up to one hundred days of convalescence in "an extended-care facility," if a physician so advised. The federal government reimbursed the facility for "reasonable costs" of care in a semiprivate room and allowed a return on equity tied to a prime interest rate of, say, 8½ percent. The return on equity is a formula based on the interest rate on Treasury bonds purchased by the Social Security trust fund.

Some 4,800 extended-care facilities or other nursing homes (ECFs) were receiving Medicare reimbursement by 1970.† As described earlier, the actual meaning of "extended care" is intensive, relatively short-term

---

* The first almshouse in Britain for the poor, usually the aged, was established in 1440.

† About 4,100 were separate nursing homes. The rest were units of hospitals, and a few were rehabilitation centers.

care rather than care extended over time. Some 7,000 skilled nursing homes (SNHs), which do provide extended nursing care over time, received Medicaid money under the cost-sharing program in the states. The intermediate-care facilities (ICFs) provided primarily personal care, originally financed through Old Age Assistance and aid to the infirm and the totally disabled, but since 1972 funded under Medicaid.

Disbursements for nursing-home care rose at an annual rate of 16 percent from 1955 to 1965, reaching $1.3 billion in 1965. Public sources had been expanding their percentage of participation from 21 percent in 1950 to 38 percent in 1965. With the 1965 enactments of Medicare and Medicaid amendments to the Social Security Act, dramatic changes occurred. The 1965–67 growth rate was 18.5 percent and by 1967 the public share of nursing-home expenditures had risen to 64 percent.

Nursing homes are highly profitable and relatively recession proof because there are steadily rising numbers of elderly to be served. At any one time there are one million people in some 24,000 nursing homes.* Five hundred thousand employees work in these homes. The federal government provides over 50 percent of the annual gross income of the nursing-home industry. Three hundred twenty million was paid to 4,500 homes under Medicare in 1969.† Some $1.17 billion was paid to 7,000 nursing homes under Medicaid in 1971. By 1972 the nursing-home-industry income was close to $3.5 billion, of which public (federal, state and county) funds represented almost 75 percent, and most of these homes, 80 percent, are run for profit.

Nursing-home issues burgeoned on the stock market. Some seventy chains of homes developed.‡

Chains of nursing homes are being established. The organizers are people like contractors, automobile dealers, farmers, bankers, real estate men as well as doctors. Certainly some of them are in it for quick profit. Stock in these establishments is doing very well on the securities market.[14]

Not all these chains have fared well. One spectacular example of the high stakes involved was the Four Seasons Company in Oklahoma City, operating fifty homes throughout the country and grossing more than $6

---

* Some 20 percent of the elderly population will require some institutional care (not hospitals) during the balance of their lives. This projection is based on our present health-care system, which offers little professional-level home care.

† However, by 1970 the Nixon administration had reduced the Medicare outlay to $180 million in an economizing effort at older people's expense.

‡ Everyone got in on the act, including the developers of Holiday Inns. Significantly, many nursing homes appear to be built so that easy conversion to motels would be possible if the nursing-home business proved unprofitable.

million in fiscal 1968. In 1970 Four Seasons filed bankruptcy proceedings because of financial fraud.*

The U.S. Senate Special Committee on Aging study (1973–74) found that 106 publicly held corporations controlled 18 percent of nursing-home beds and accounted for *one-third* of the industry's revenue.

Physicians were encouraged by entrepreneurs and by desire for profits to invest in the commercial nursing-home industry. The September, 1965, issue of *Physicians' Management*, for example, carried an article by C. Colburn Hardy entitled "Should You Put Your Money into Nursing Homes?"

Is building and operating a nursing home a profitable investment? Let's look at some pertinent facts. Nursing homes are being opened at the rate of nearly three a day, seven days a week. This means 169 new beds are being added every 24 hours to the 768,959 licensed nursing home beds in the United States. That's growth with a capital "G." . . .

There are profits to be made in owning and/or operating nursing homes. A passive owner who builds the home and leases it to an operator can make 13 to 15 percent on his investment plus the potential of capital gains when he sells. Some active owners, individually or in groups, are reporting profits as high as 25 percent, but the average earnings are lower and the greatest current attraction is the possibility of selling out to a publicly owned company. . . .

Needless to say, there is an ethical conflict-of-interest question about the propriety of doctors' owning nursing homes.

NURSING HOME STANDARDS

Given the huge contribution the public makes to the financing of care, is it getting its money's worth? Should a society permit a small number of businessmen to make money from the predicament of the infirm elderly? Is our definition of these care facilities too limited? Should we support the design and establishment of facilities which pay only minimal attention to nursing, diet, shelter, fire safety and sanitation, not to mention more comprehensive care features? These are the major questions, yet we are

---

* This was part of what became known in Ohio as the "statehouse mess," which involved loans from two sources—the School Employees Retirement System and the state treasury. Under Ohio law, short-term loans can be made to commercial firms from state funds that are not needed immediately for state spending. This was designed to provide the state with additional revenue from the interest. One loan of $4 million went to the Four Seasons Nursing Centers of Oklahoma City, Oklahoma, shortly before it went bankrupt.[15]

still so enmeshed in trying to establish adequate basic standards of physical safety and cleanliness, and to enforce these standards in the present often marginal facilities, that we have not been able to tackle them. The creation of a humane social environment is nowhere in sight in the majority of homes.

Here are two areas, fire and food safety, which demonstrate the kind of basic, elementary work that remains to be done.

FIRE SAFETY

News item:

Hearings before the United States Senate on February 26, 1970, brought out the fact that it was the carpeting in a Marietta, Ohio, hilltop nursing home that spread the flames in the January 9th fire that resulted in the deaths of 32 of 46 patients from asphyxiation from the acrid, deadly smoke.

Some 267 aged patients died in the decade ending October 19, 1971, in multiple-death nursing-home fires in the United States. (Statistics on single deaths in contrast to multiple deaths from fires are unavailable.) Yet there are still no uniform standards of fire safety under the different federal, state and local codes.

Carpeting is a vivid example. After the Marietta, Ohio, fire where smoke from the carpeting killed thirty-two old people, efforts to establish a uniform safety test for carpets began.[16] Social Security Administration bureaucrats argued over whether the "tunnel test" required by law should be used, rather than concentrating on enforcing it. They appeared more concerned with placating the carpet industry than saving the lives of elderly patients.*

The Marietta home had not merely failed to meet the state standards on carpet flammability. It did not have smoke doors to break up a long, drafty corridor. It had not held fire drills in ten months although Medicare requires twelve per year.[17]

While government officials, nursing-home representatives and business interests play out their roles and congressional committees hold hearings, patients continue to burn to death. In 1972, for example, the House Committee on Government Operations held hearings on a series of fires,

---

* The "tunnel test" is a rigidly controlled procedure. The test material is mounted at the top of a long cylinder. A gas jet is located at one end. It applies a controlled flame to the sample. An observation window makes it possible to track the process of the flame down the sample.

proceeded to endorse automatic sprinkler systems, and released still another report, *Saving Lives in Nursing Home Fires*. The chairman of the House committee, Representative Chet Holifield (D.-Cal.) announced that the committee recommended legislation to require the sprinklers as a condition for receiving federal funds under Medicaid, Medicare or Old Age Assistance.* Representative William Randall (D.-Mo.), chairman of the Special Studies Subcommittee, said: "The requirement to install complete automatic sprinkler systems with an alarm connection to the nearest fire department will do much to eliminate multiple deaths from fires in nursing homes, personal care homes, and boarding homes." Yet sprinklers may be more apt to save buildings, while smoke sensors may be more effective in saving human lives. One has to question either the priorities or the information available to the House committee in choosing to promote sprinklers alone.

The nursing-home industry's chief spokesman, Dr. Thomas G. Bell, has said the various state legislatures and the federal government should increase the payments they make for the care of patients, with the raises specifically earmarked for fire safety. He also suggested government-sponsored long-term, low-interest loans, a system of accelerated tax depreciation for fire-safety equipment, outright government grants or various combinations of these solutions.

He urged adoption of the 1967 Life Safety Code of the National Fire Protection Association by all jurisdictions as the standard for fire safety in nursing homes. The code specifies automatic sprinklers, but not in all types of buildings,† restrictions on spread of heat and smoke, more stringent flame-spread restrictions for interior finish materials, manually activated fire alarm systems, and emergency-exit lighting and signs. Some twenty-three states had adopted the Life Safety Code by 1972, but adoption and enforcement are not synonymous.

The staff is also a vital part of fire safety. There must be an adequate number of personnel for emergencies, particularly if smoking by patients is allowed, as it should be for habitual smokers. In case of fire, staff must know how to evacuate patients as well as detain those who may try to re-enter a burning building for possessions and keepsakes. Older persons have been saved from fires, only to be lost in this manner.

---

* Of the 4,400 homes approved by Medicare, some 200 are unprotected wooden buildings.

† The Life Safety Code does not require sprinklers in buildings that are fire resistant for two hours or in buildings of one story that are protected and noncombustible for one hour. One-hour protected combustible (that is, frame construction) buildings require sprinklers throughout. In all buildings, however, sprinklers are required in hazardous areas—kitchen, storage and trash rooms.

FOOD SAFETY

News item:

> Twenty-five residents of a commercial Baltimore nursing home died
> in a salmonella food poisoning epidemic in August, 1970 after delays
> in seeking medical help.*

As an illustration of poor food and sanitation standards in nursing homes,
the report of the investigation into the salmonella epidemic at Gould
Convalesarium in Baltimore by a board of inquiry appointed by the
Secretary of Health and Mental Hygiene in Maryland was an eye opener.†

The investigation indicates individual failures by physicians, by those who
run nursing homes, by state and city officials, by state and national government.
Collectively they add up to the failure of our society to properly concern itself
with the fate of its sick old people.[18]

When a tragedy like this occurs, people ask how such events can
possibly happen. What inspections were conducted? Why aren't licenses
ever withdrawn? Page 8 of the Gould report reads:

> In response to a request from this panel, Mr. John W. Debiak, director of
> nursing home licensing and certification for the state of Iowa and a recognized
> expert, conducted a survey of the inspection records of the Gould Nursing
> home . . . He states categorically he would not consider recommending this
> home for participation in either Medicare or Medicaid programs if that
> decision had to be made now. "But since the home is already certified for
> participation in these public programs," his report states, "it would be very
> difficult to de-certify because the inspection records maintained by the State
> Department of Health aren't adequate." Debiak points to "the difficulty of
> withdrawing certification from any home because the courts choose to view
> de-certification as depriving a nursing home operator of his livelihood." Debiak
> declares de-certification to be "a greater sin in the eyes of the judge" than
> depriving "an old person of his right to live in safety and good care."

Out of the salmonella tragedy came the decision of Dr. Neil Solomon,
the Maryland Secretary of Health and Mental Hygiene, to replace the

---

* Salmonellosis, a form of food poisoning due to the bacteria salmonella, is dangerous to infants, the debilitated and the aged. It is often transmitted by food handlers, particularly through meat, eggs, poultry and shellfish.
 † When twelve patients had died, the Washington *Post* stated that "in a telephone interview, Gould [the owner] complained about the focus of the news media on the 12 deaths over the weekend, saying 'is it really that big?' "

principal physicians of nursing homes with medical directors. The former were in effect physicians on call to nursing homes. Their responsibilities were either too loosely defined or not fulfilled. Medical directors, on the other hand, are responsible for organizing comprehensive care, supervising the staff and developing a program of preventive care.*

The board of inquiry recommended that an independent nursing-home inspection board be created in Maryland that would include physicians, members of the community, and, specifically, representatives of local citizens' groups.

The report also stated that

testimony suggested a very strong "nursing home lobby" exists in the Maryland State Legislature and that this lobby has had sufficient political power to prevent passage of legislation in Maryland that might set stricter standards for nursing homes. Our investigation disclosed evidence suggestive of political interference with a nursing home inspection. Witnesses testified that an unannounced inspection of the Harbor View Nursing and Convalescent Center in Baltimore was called off during the actual inspection. Explanations by the officials involved with the incident about the innocence of the cancellation remain singularly unconvincing.

The Board of Inquiry notes the Harbor View Nursing Home is owned by a corporation whose president and director is a member of the Maryland House of Delegates. We do not question that legislators are entitled to have business interests, we do, however, suggest that the possibility of conflict of interest should be examined. Given this kind of worrisome information, this Panel must raise the question as to how to control such powerful monetary interests. Have we opened our nursing homes to profiteering?

The report spelled out its concern over the failure of responsibility of the medical profession:

It also appears to this Board of Inquiry that the medical profession, as the group in society charged with rendering medical care and providing medical advice, has not, in the final analysis, shouldered its part of the responsibilities for nursing homes and possible abuses. . . . The Medical and Chirurgical Faculty of the State of Maryland, as spokesman for organized medicine in the State, should have insisted long ago on the stringent inspection of nursing

---

* It is important that compensation for medical directors should not be in the form of patient referral or consultation. The medical director should operate a nursing home as a hospital is operated—with records, rounds, comprehensive and emergency care. The AMA obtained a $172,000 cost-reimbursement contract with HEW to upgrade medical services in nursing homes by better preparing physicians working as medical directors. Strangely, the AMA did not support the concept of medical director until 1973.

homes by the State Health Department. Instead, the Faculty and its members have tolerated ineffectual inspection and has taken no action to assure that the quality of medicine practiced in nursing homes is consistent with the highest ideals of the medical profession.

The Gould salmonella tragedy in itself is unfortunately not all that unusual. What is unusual is that a thorough investigation was carried out which resulted in some state reforms.

FEDERAL AND STATE INVOLVEMENT IN STANDARDS

The federal government has not only contributed to making nursing-home care profitable to the owners, but failed to establish necessary comprehensive national standards until January, 1974. Their enforcement is another matter. As one example:

Under a 1966 law the federal government set—and still enforces—high standards for treatment of animals used for research or experimentation. Under a 1967 law the federal government set not-so-high standards for states to enforce in ICF institutions housing feeble or sick old people receiving public welfare payments. Theodor Schuchat observed: "Guinea pigs, hamsters and rabbits must be examined every other day. Humans in intermediate care facilities must be examined by a physician at least four times a year."[19]

Standards and enforcement are left to the fifty states. Since 1972, however, there has been some federal pressure to enforce the Moss amendments[20] to the Social Security Law passed in 1967, which were to take effect on January 1, 1969.[21]

The Moss amendments had the intent of raising standards in skilled nursing homes under Medicaid. One amendment required that at least one registered nurse be on duty on the day shift; another required compliance with the Life Safety Code of the National Fire Protection Association. A further amendment provided for disclosure of anyone owning a 10 percent or greater interest; still another called for medical review. Frank Frantz, the staff member of the Senate Special Committee on Aging's long-term-care subcommittee, helped shape the Moss amendments. In 1968 HEW Secretary Wilbur Cohen invited Frantz to HEW to help put the amendments into effect. The obstacles to his efforts have been massive. Federal regulations have been used to delay congressional laws, with the complicity of nursing-home interests. This continued to be the case in 1973, with still-weak regulations for skilled nursing homes and intermediate-care facilities.

Another amendment, the Kennedy amendment[22] (Section 236), was passed requiring all states to license nursing-home administrators by July 1, 1970, and to set up a state agency by that date to develop and apply licensure examinations for administrators in addition to the licensing of the homes themselves. Failure of the states to comply was to be penalized by denial of Medicaid funds.

In twenty-one of the first states to establish boards to advise on the licensing of nursing-home administrators, the boards were under the control of nursing-home administrators themselves. Nineteen seventy-two federal regulations required that no single interest group—consumers or nursing-home operators—could hold a majority of board membership. But the battle over control of the boards continues.

There is no up-to-date comprehensive booklet on state regulations and licensure of nursing homes.[23] Consumers need a detailed tabulation of such material in addition to data concerning specific institutions.

Abuses and the likelihood of fraud have been uncovered. Emerson Midyett, vice-president of the National Council of Senior Citizens, discusses the situation in California's state Medicaid plan:

MediCal's continuing deficiencies include illegal, under-the-table payments to enable Medicare beneficiaries to secure admission to a nursing home or other illegal charges for services paid for under MediCal. The cost of this abuse is high. In 1968, Deputy State Attorney General Charles A. O'Brien estimated that overpayments to providers of care under the MediCal program amounted to from $6 million to $8 million a year.

This abuse of the MediCal program was documented in the recent report of the Federal Government's General Accounting Office (GAO).[24]

Inspectors themselves are suspect. Congressman Pryor said in a speech before the House on February 24, 1970,

There are "some indications" we have received at this time that there might be a "cozy relationship" between some of the nursing home inspectors in this country and some of the owners of the profiteering firms.

Even if there were tougher laws to protect against bribery and influence, the problem would not be solved; there are not enough inspectors. Until 1972, only five people were involved in administering the entire HEW Medicaid program* and most of the time there were only three. In 1970 in Ohio there were twenty-three fire-safety inspectors in the entire state.

* In the Nursing Home Branch, originally the Office of Nursing Home Programs.

They not only had to check nursing homes but other institutions such as schools, hospitals, churches, theatres and libraries.

Nineteen sixty-five hearings in Indiana on the conditions and problems in the nation's nursing homes pointed up the fact that limited state budgets affect the allotment of inspectors in various types of programs. Senator Moss, for instance, found there were only twelve inspectors in the state fire marshal's office for the entire state of Indiana, and these twelve inspectors were to meet forty thousand requests for inspections. "A little arithmetic will show . . . that . . . the staff would have had to make a report of an inspection approximately every 40 minutes"—and that would have included travel time![25]

The public has been misled into false security (reinforced in part by the nursing-home industry* and the nonprofit homes) by such phrases as "Medicare-Approved." One of the most striking euphemisms in the language of Medicare is that a particular home is in "substantial compliance" with Medicare regulations. There is no legal basis for the notion of "substantial compliance" in certification. Section 1866 of the Medicare law deals with contracts rather than certification. The HEW Secretary may terminate contracts under this section when he finds nursing homes have "substantially" failed to comply. The Social Security Administration picked up this language from the statute and misapplied it to the appraisal of the status of nursing homes. People are thereby led to assume that nursing homes are under careful surveillance and are uniformly and universally licensed. This is simply not so. The Social Security Administration (SSA), for example, theoretically must approve nursing homes for participation as "extended care facilities" but the SSA has nothing to do with licensure. It is not in touch with individual homes. The studies are done on a state and county level, and the reports are sent to regional offices.

THE PUBLIC'S RIGHT TO KNOW

The confidential character of nursing-home inspection reports at the Department of Health, Education, and Welfare was challenged in April, 1972, when Malvin Schechter,[26] the Washington editor of *Hospital Practice* magazine, brought a freedom-of-information suit against the then HEW Secretary Elliot L. Richardson.

---

* There is a gradual effort on the part of the industry to police itself. Some nursing homes participate in voluntary standards programs; for instance, that of the Long Term Care Council of the Joint Commission on Accreditation of Hospitals. However, only 1,800 nursing homes have been accredited.

Specifically, Mr. Schechter asked the U.S. District Court to order Secretary Richardson to release copies of survey reports on several homes in the District of Columbia and Maryland. He also requested copies of reports on the nursing home in Marietta, Ohio, that had cost thirty-two lives.

When he asked HEW for a look at these reports he was refused. HEW personnel advised him that such reports were confidential under a 1937 provision (Section 1106) of the Social Security Act. Schechter pointed out that Medicare did not exist in 1937. HEW countered that the Freedom of Information Act of 1967 did not abrogate secrecy statutes existing before 1967 and therefore the 1937 provision was exempt. Schechter maintained that the provision cited by HEW was intended to deal with beneficiary and taxpayer records, but "the bureaucracy had extended the scope of the provision to include Medicare survey reports." Schechter did not contest the right of individuals to have their Social Security records kept confidential, but contended that information concerning facilities which voluntarily participate in a program financed by taxpayers is an entirely different matter. The public has a right to know.

His view was supported by U.S. District Court Judge Joseph C. Waddy, who so ruled in July, 1972. Through a clerical error, Judge Waddy's decision was not communicated to the litigants until several weeks after it was handed down. In the meantime, HEW Secretary Richardson proposed regulations to govern disclosure of certain Medicare reports and records. He did not intend to make old files available, but only those prepared after issuance of the new regulations, and he would include an institution's comments on the findings of a state inspector as well as a statement of any corrective action that might have been taken. Such reports as could be seen by inquiring citizens would be available at Social Security offices where the provider of services is located. The Richardson regulation was issued in advance of 1972 Social Security amendments enacted by Congress to require routine release of inspection reports or digests. However, the Social Security Administration dragged its feet in creating a workable system for doctors and the public to be able to obtain data covering nursing homes.

NURSING HOMES PROTECT THEMSELVES

The nursing-home industry becomes nervous at the thought of making inspection reports available to the public. Many homes do not welcome public inspection of their facilities by the press, public officials, families or older persons themselves. Some of the reasons cited for this reluctance are the following:

- It is unfair and disturbing to families to find fault and make it public.
- If you close down inadequate homes, where will the patients go but into the streets?
- Complaints about nursing homes derive from scapegoating by families who feel guilty over not keeping the older relative at home.
- Compared to hospitals, which can cost $100 per day, nursing homes are cheap at $30 per day, so how can you expect low prices and high standards at the same time?
- Nursing homes cannot meet standards because federal and state reimbursement levels are not sufficient.

To answer these arguments briefly: Blame of the family is one of the most transparent techniques of self-defense that nursing homes have invented and scarcely deserves rebuttal. Second, patients can be housed elsewhere on an emergency basis—for example, in hospitals, where, in 1971 twenty-three percent of beds were unoccupied. Third, nursing homes are cheaper precisely because they provide less; they should provide more and cost more, and be financed through insurance pooling of general-revenue tax dollars without further burdening of the individual patient and his family. Finally, studies have not supported the contention of nursing homes that they receive inadequate governmental support, but rather that they have shown excessive profits.[27]

Despite the deep commitments of Senator Moss and former Representative Pryor, of other elective and appointive officials on the federal and state level, of various medical and other journalists, geriatricians, gerontologists and social workers since the 1940s, the nursing-home industry remains powerful and relatively unregulated. It continues to fight investigations and complains bitterly of adverse publicity.

In December, 1970, consumer advocate Ralph Nader and his young Raiders reported their findings and recommendations before the Senate Subcommittee on Long-Term Care, which continually conducts hearings and issues reports on conditions in American nursing homes.[28] Six high-school seniors and one of their instructors comprised a Nader task force to study nursing-home conditions firsthand, as well as the role of the federal government. They conducted interviews with officials, studied letters of complaint, visited and worked in homes. Journals were kept of their observations and vivid accounts written about their experiences. The report issued by the Nader group called for strict accountability, education of health professionals, consumer protection and representation in policy making.[29] National attention was focused once again on the scandals in nursing homes. The nursing-home industry counterattacked by charging that young nonprofessionals conducted the study. Yet it was precisely the fact of young people viewing these conditions for the first time that gave the study its impact.

Some nursing homes have tried to don new public-relations images. In the Sunday edition of the Baltimore *Sun* on November 7, 1970, a full-page advertisement paid for by the Health Facilities Association of Maryland, Inc. (the Maryland affiliate of the American Nursing Home Association) included the following:

> For every reader of this page we sincerely and proudly extend an open invitation for you to visit any one of the nursing homes of the Health Facilities Association of Maryland. We invite you to see with your own eyes the accomplishments that have been made in the care and treatment of the people whom we call . . . our guests. Please telephone the nursing home you wish to visit for a mutually convenient appointment.

On November 14, however, the *Sun* reported:

> A reporter and photographer for the *Sun* were denied permission yesterday to accompany labor union officials in a tour of the Harbor View Nursing and Convalescence Center, 1213 Light Street.
>
> The nursing home is owned by Community Health Facilities, Inc. of which Delegate Richard Rynd (D.-Baltimore County) is a past president and a major stockholder.
>
> According to State records, the majority of the home's 300 patients are paid for out of State and Federal dollars. A total of 231 Harbor View patients are paid for under the State Medicaid program, according to State figures complete through October 30.
>
> George J. Comeaux, administrator of Harbor View, said the newspaper men needed permission from corporate headquarters before they could tour the facility. After telephoning corporate executives, Mr. Comeaux said this permission had been denied.
>
> In a telephone interview later, Erwin Brown, Executive Director of the nursing home chain, said all newsmen would be barred from the chain's facilities until they gained an "understanding" of what the corporation was trying to do for aged patients. Mr. Brown said, "the ban would stand until we feel you are qualified to make the objective appraisal you want to make." "Based on past history," he said, "the corporation has found that the press doesn't understand."

In the following Sunday issue of the *Sun,* November 15, 1970, Mr. Rynd is quoted as saying that newspapers "have been continually unfriendly to the nursing home industry." They only "want to sell newspapers," he said, "and they have been looking for the negatives only. . . . If the newspapers in the past had shown they were interested in showing the good side of nursing homes, there would have been no problem allowing anyone in."

The denial of full, free and unannounced access to nursing homes for the public and its representatives is paradoxical, given the fact that public money—tax money, federal, state and local—pays for over 70 percent of the care and, of course, the patients or their families pay for the remainder. A television documentary "When You Reach December," produced by Richard Hubert of Westinghouse Broadcasting Company, spoke to this issue. The documentary showed Colonel William R. Hutton, then chairman of the Maryland State Board of Examiners of Nursing Home Administrators,* accompanied by the author, then chairman of the Washington, D.C., Advisory Committee on Aging, discussing the cold reception they received on their unannounced visit to the above-mentioned Harbor View Nursing and Convalescence Center.

As Colonel Hutton explained:

Well, one of the functions and duties of the Board of Examiners of Nursing Home Administrators is, of course, to conduct a continuing investigation and study of nursing homes with regard to the administrators, the work of the administrators, etc. And so today, one of the days available to me . . . December 3, I decided to take . . . Dr. Robert Butler . . . along with me to help me get a feel of the situation in the Baltimore County nursing homes. And the first home I chose was the largest home—Harbor View.

Unfortunately, we weren't received with the kind of reception I had hoped to get. They objected to my not being there as an investigative member of the Board, they said that if other members of the Board had been there, and it had been voted by the Board, that would have been different, but just myself arriving on them unannounced, they said they didn't want it.

Now I feel that the nursing home is a public institution and I feel the best way that I can get to know what's really going on is by dropping in unannounced.

ASSOCIATIONS OF HOMES FOR CARE OF THE AGED

The defense of nursing homes has been buttressed by organizations which represent them. Two major associations for nursing homes and homes for the aging exist: the larger and older of the two is the American

* Also executive director of the National Council of Senior Citizens, with three million members.

Nursing Home Association (ANHA); the other being the American Association of Homes for the Aging (AAHA).* ANHA is a federation of state associations, founded in 1949, and represents 7,000 commercial and nonprofit homes with over half a million beds, but the bulk (some 85 percent) of its membership is composed of the profit-making homes. By its nature, ANHA is not a socially progressive organization since its primary purpose is to promote the interests of owners of homes. It maintains a lobby in Washington but spends most of its money in state rather than national political campaigns.† It has made modest reforms, but although professing interest in major reforms it has not yet instigated them.

Admission of member homes has been on a rather casual basis. Indeed, there are no standards of admission into ANHA. One of its member homes, operating without a license for fourteen years, was discussed by Congressman David Pryor:

> On the wall of this particular home, I think it's very interesting to note that they are a member of the American Nursing Home Association, which I think would hold out to the general public, or especially to relatives or to prospective patients looking over the home, that this home does represent the best in the standard of care inasmuch as they are a member of this American Nursing Home Association.[30]

Obviously, standards for admission to the association must be carefully formulated and adhered to if the association is to retain credibility in the public eye.‡

The ANHA has been self-protective in its approach to reforms:

- The ANHA backed adoption by the states of the 1967 Life Safety Code of the National Fire Protection Association. Following a 1972 Illinois nursing-home fire, ANHA president Don Barry expressed such support to "minimize the repetition of such tragedies." But ANHA wanted federal money to meet the life safety code rather than requiring that owners provide it. A law providing government-guaranteed loans for fire-safety equipment was passed in 1973.
- The ANHA endorsed public disclosure of Medicare inspection reports

---

* There is a third, the National Council of Health Care Services, which is the organization of the nursing-home chains.

† There are no uniform, effective laws requiring campaign monies to be reported within the states. To a state legislator campaigning for office $500 or $1,000 is a great deal of money.

‡ Interestingly, the ANHA approved a $1.4 million budget for 1973, including $211,000 for an expanded program of public relations! The public relations budget was even more greatly expanded in 1974. Also in 1974, ANHA changed its name to the American Health Care Association in a transparent effort to escape the stigma attached to the name "nursing home."

but called for exemption when a facility challenged the findings of an inspection.

- The ANHA supported strict enforcement of state standards, but wanted HEW to base its certification on "substantial," not "full," compliance.
- It conducted a nationwide training project for 10,000 activity directors, but only after obtaining a $139,000 HEW grant to do so.
- It regretted that all the national health insurance proposals ignored the chronically ill, and offered a limited and cautious program which it called Chronicare.*

The ANHA arrived at a joint agreement with HEW to promote volunteer services for Medicaid patients in nursing homes. The original idea was to utilize volunteers to complement, and not to supplant, the services and duties of paid personnel. But, however valid the concept, it draws attention away from the fact that the number of paid personnel presently available is too low. A staff of volunteers gives the false appearance of expanding services to patients and families.†

I wish the American Nursing Home Association would take leadership in cleaning up its own house, conducting research into such nursing-home operations as extent of tranquilizer use, experimenting with advanced technology and building bridges with medical schools. I do not understand why the American Nursing Home Association, with less than a third of nursing homes as its members, has felt the necessity to act in defense of all nursing homes in the industry, bad as well as good.

The second association, the American Association of Homes for the Aging (AAHA), comprises 1,200 nonprofit homes and was founded in 1961 through a Ford Foundation grant. AAHA has grown steadily in membership and in stature and since 1969 has made its national head-quarters in Washington, D.C. There are major differences in the goals of ANHA and AAHA. The latter is more oriented to the needs of the in-dividual patient and the public. In October, 1973, for instance, in con-junction with the National Council of Senior Citizens, it called upon Senator Moss to hold hearings on standards. AAHA has steadfastly sup-ported twenty-four-hour, seven-day coverage by registered nurses, despite the problems such a position causes some of its own membership.

Although it is generally more progressive than ANHA, AAHA con-

---

* Sponsored in the Senate by Senator Hubert H. Humphrey (D.-Minn.).

† Although volunteers can never be thought of as a solution to staffing shortages, with careful selection one can put together a loyal, conscientious group of volunteers who are a valuable adjunct to the quality of the institution.[31] Many providers of nursing-home care, however, are wary of volunteers because they don't want their weaknesses exposed. One volunteer group of Gray Ladies was so effective as advocates for patients that they were thrown out of a nursing home by the physician who owned it.

dones a number of questionable policies: AAHA includes sectarian homes that require the turning-over of all of one's life savings at entry, as well as plush life-care institutions that ask entrance fees as high as $40,000. Non-cancelable life contracts are still in existence. Admission criteria are strict, and difficult patients (i.e., people with psychiatric or severe medical problems), as well as the poor, the black and other minority groups, are frequently screened out.* Waiting lists can be very long, ranging from three months to three years, and many persons die before admission. Out of anxiety, some older persons apply too soon and are admitted prematurely when they would actually be better off in their own homes. There has been very little effort to provide interim service for those on the waiting lists, though some institutions such as the Philadelphia Geriatric Center have experimented along these lines.

Goldfarb has described "list hopping," wherein admission occurs for various reasons other than objectively determined need or order of application. VIPs, large financial contributors and other favored persons may receive preferential treatment.

In spite of these objectionable practices, the AAHA can be justly proud of some of its member homes. But the needs of the vast majority of old people have not been met by the nonprofit, municipal and voluntary homes because of their limited number and accessibility.

GOVERNMENT POLICY ON NURSING HOMES

Federal responsibility for nursing homes is divided among half a dozen government agencies and as many congressional committees as well as the health and welfare departments of fifty states.

In the House of Representatives the Committee on Ways and Means has jurisdiction over the Medicare and Medicaid programs. The Committee on Interstate and Foreign Commerce is concerned with health facilities, planning and funding for construction. The Banking and Currency Committee deals with the sections of the National Housing Act which provide mortgage insurance for various types of nursing homes and other facilities for the care of the aged. The Committee on Veterans Affairs is interested in providing nursing-home care for veterans in private nursing homes. The Committee on Government Operations is concerned with the quality of administration of nursing-home programs and the ef-

---

* Failure to comply with Title VI of the Civil Rights Act has left some nonprofit homes out of Medicare. Money-making institutions may end up less segregated than many religious-sponsored homes for the aging since the latter may not be as financially motivated to comply with Title VI.

fectiveness of federal and state government relationships in carrying out such programs.

At the executive-administrative level, too, there is not only the participation of the Department of Housing and Urban Development, and of Health, Education, and Welfare, but the Small Business Administration, which has its own criteria for making loans for nursing-home construction.

Moreover, the government has divided its responsibilities in nursing homes between housing and health. The Department of Housing and Urban Development provides monies through the Federal Housing Administration to build health facilities—for instance, insuring 90 percent mortgages. The Department of Health, Education, and Welfare provides the Medicare and Medicaid funds. This division leads to confusion in standards.

At the beginning of the 1970 congressional session, then Representative David Pryor led the fight for a resolution to create a Select Committee on Nursing Homes and Homes for the Aged. This was blocked by Representative William Colmer (D.-Miss.) who, ironically, was 80 years old himself. Later in the year Pryor broadened his conception and pressed for a Committee on Aging which would, in effect, be the counterpart of the Senate's Special Committee on Aging.* Congressman Pryor never did obtain his select committee. It was not until 1974 that the House voted to establish a Select Committee on Aging, through the efforts of Congressmen H. J. Heinz, III (R.-Pa.) and C. W. Bell Young (R.-Fla.).

POLICIES ON LONG-TERM CARE

The foundation-sponsored Commission on Chronic Illness in its report, *Care of the Long-Term Patient,* stated: "Since the people it serves are so much at its mercy, the institution which cares for long-term patients must go to great lengths to serve them in accordance with their needs."[32] This distinguished report was published in 1956 but its recommendations have yet to be realized.

Efforts were made by the Nixon administration to reduce federal support to long-term care; in 1970, Sections 225 a and b of House of Representatives Bill 17550 (the Social Security amendments of 1970) were just such an effort. These sections would have turned this responsibility over to the states, which could ill afford to pay for such care. The chairman

---

* Under the Senate committee Senator Frank Moss (D.-Utah) has chaired a Subcommittee on Long-Term Care since 1963. The author of substantial legislation aimed at improving standards of care in nursing homes and preventing abuses, he has been increasingly regretful that the amendments named after him were not being implemented to any substantial degree by the Department of Health, Education, and Welfare's Social and Rehabilitation Service.

of the House Ways and Means Committee, Wilbur Mills (D.-Ark.), called for these reductions to overcome any abuse caused by "overutilization."

> There is an extreme amount of overutilization of skilled nursing homes. In other words, the people will get along just as well in the intermediate care of domiciliary type nursing homes. They do not need the most expensive type of nursing care provided in the skilled nursing homes.

He wanted to cut back the federal matching percentage after ninety days of "skilled nursing home services" and declared:

> It is utterly impossible for me to believe medical science has not gotten to the point where most of these people will not be so improved at the end of 90 days they can get what it takes to care for their needs in less expensive types of nursing homes.[33]

Congressman Mills could not have been more wrong. Medical science has not gotten to that point, and won't as long as nursing homes remain outside the medical-care system and programs of education and research. Even under the best circumstances all individuals simply do not get well in precisely ninety days or less. A basic principle is that the level of care should be determined by the nature of the condition and of the individual, since individuals vary in their response to care and convalescence.

In addition to the efforts to reduce federal support of long-term care through Medicaid cutbacks by the administration and Congress, 1970 saw further emasculation of Medicare coverage of extended care. Part of the decimation of the Medicare program has taken the form of a rising volume of retroactive payment denials by Medicare.[34]

At one Senate hearing Dr. Frederick Offenkrantz, medical director of a nonprofit health facility, protested "on behalf of our patients . . . the number and method of Medicare cutoffs at our facility through our fiscal intermediary," and ultimately through Social Security Administration guidelines.[35] These cutoffs occurred despite the acuteness and severity of patients' conditions and the unanimous agreement of utilization review committees as to their potential for rehabilitation. One case cited was a patient with diabetes and arteriosclerotic hypertensive heart disease with pulmonary congestion and left lower-lobe pneumonia.

The rules have been inflexible, arbitrary and inconsistent. In response, many hospitals have discontinued extended-care facilities certified for Medicare, and many extended-care facilities have withdrawn from Medicare. This has very much damaged the concept of progressive care—that is, the use of the extended-care facilities after hospitalization.

Medicare patients are being denied extended-care benefits at a steadily increasing rate.* In 1971 the rate was about 8 percent; in 1972 it was 13 percent. While retroactive denials used to be the biggest problem, now the stringent guidelines for admission are closing the door on patients. On any given day in 1971 only 17 percent of Medicare-approved ECF beds were actually occupied by Medicare patients. The rest were occupied by persons of all other ages.

By December of 1971, 1,260 hospitals and 3,740† extended-care facilities had terminated their participation in Medicare. This represented about 30 percent of those participating in Medicare since its inception. Some withdrew because they had not met standards (and a number of them could not afford to meet them even if they had wished to), others to avoid being audited. Still others were frustrated and impatient with the bureaucratic confusion, the laborious and contradictory rules and regulations from the federal government, the retroactive denial of claims and other administrative difficulties. To make matters worse, new rules were announced retroactively, requiring that nursing-home operators pay back in 1969 some sums received from Medicare for patients served in 1968.

Patients were not informed of these changes, and they continued to expect Medicare to pay for one hundred days in an ECF as promised in the Medicare literature. Nursing-home operators found themselves having to explain these misconceptions to patients and families, and to suffer financial loss as well. They were caught in the middle—with claims disallowed and yet unable to collect from the patient or his family.

The cutback effort was successful only from the government's point of view. Medicare benefits dropped from $340 million in 1968 to $180 million in 1970.

The White House Conference on Aging special session on long-term care opposed cutbacks and urged provisions for all care and services for the aged to be removed from Title XIX (Medicaid) and XI of the Social Security law and put under an expanded and well-administered XVIII (Medicare). It also called for the federalization of Title XIX, meaning the full support of long-term care by federal general tax revenues. It recommended uniform national benefits and standards.

---

* Medicare patients and their families should have the opportunity for administrative and judicial review when claims are denied.[36] In general, consumer action is indicated to overcome nursing-home abuses and improve standards. There are excellent local groups, such as the Minneapolis Age and Opportunity Center (directed by Daphne H. Krause) and the National Council of Senior Citizens ombudsman programs located in a few cities.

† Since new facilities also entered the program, the actual net loss was about 700 facilities.

The conferees narrowly defeated "a proposed recommendation that the element of profit be eliminated from the care of persons and that the profit factor be confined to a limited return on equity capital, meaning a profit in the form of rental on land, buildings, improvements and furnishings, over and above the actual cost of the care and services provided."

Instead, they voted in the following by a hair's breadth: "It is recommended that the Secretary of Health, Education, and Welfare study the feasibility of health facilities (i.e., hospitals, nursing homes, extended care facilities, etc.), including long-term care facilities, becoming public utilities and that his report be submitted as part of the post–White House Conference on Aging report by December 21, 1972." No such report has been forthcoming.

FEDERAL REFORMS

As a result of a 1971 directive by President Nixon, the Health, Education, and Welfare Department established a new office to oversee all HEW programs relating to nursing homes. The Office of Nursing Home Affairs (ONHA) was to be responsible for coordinating efforts by different agencies in the department to upgrade standards nationwide for the benefit of nursing-home patients. Establishment of ONHA and the appointment of Mrs. Marie Callender as its head presumably meant that for the first time a single official was responsible for pulling together different HEW nursing-home efforts into a single coordinated program. Two hundred twenty-seven new personnel were added to federal enforcement. Furthermore, President Nixon formulated an eight-point nursing-home program, announced in 1971:

1. Training of 2,000 state nursing-home inspectors
2. Complete (100 percent) federal support of state inspections under Medicaid
3. Consolidation of enforcement activities
4. Strengthening of federal enforcement of standards
5. Short-term training for 41,000 professional and paraprofessional nursing-home personnel
6. Assistance for state investigative "Ombudsman" units
7. Comprehensive review of long-term care
8. Crackdown on substandard nursing homes: cutoff of federal funds to them*

This program, if fully implemented, would help meet the requirements of the present law, namely, the Moss amendments.

* Amplified in President Nixon's Message on Aging to Congress, March 23, 1972.

There are some 24,000 nursing homes in the United States, but the President's nursing-home plan concerned itself primarily with the 7,000 Medicaid skilled nursing homes and 4,339 Medicare extended-care facilities. By the government's own findings, as many as 70 percent of American nursing homes have basic deficiencies. Of the 4,339 Medicare-approved homes, some 3,199 or 74 percent have significant deficiencies.[37]

Five hundred seventy-nine nursing homes, 8 percent of the 7,000 facilities in the Medicaid program,* were decertified (327 principally for fire-safety failure) or voluntarily withdrew (252) from the program as of July, 1972. Over 4,700 skilled nursing homes (68 percent) were certified for only six months or less, during which time they were required to correct their deficiencies. But altogether only about 25,000 patients—of the one million in American nursing homes—were affected by these crackdowns.

HEW Secretary Richardson said at the 1971 White House Conference on Aging that thirty-eight of the forty-eight states in the Medicaid program had been found to have "substantial deficiencies" in the certification process. He gave the states until February 1, 1972, to correct these deficiencies. By July 1, 1972, the states were to show that they had inspected every facility eligible for the Medicaid benefit and that each institution had been certified through the state licensing authority as being in compliance with the regulations for skilled nursing homes. It is unclear how effectively and uniformly this has been accomplished.

Pressures from state governments, congressional delegations, nursing-home owners (including physicians, bankers, businessmen and legislators) raised questions as to the seriousness of the Nixon administration's commitment to reform—just as questions about the Johnson administration's commitment had been voiced previously. At best, the Nixon program represented minimal reform. Some of the problems include the fact that it is still the states that have the responsibility to close down homes. In some states the survey process is concerned with "paper analyses and procedures rather than people and patient care." Neither "peer review"—doctors directly checking medical services, nutritionists checking food services, etc.—nor consumer review occurs. The program covers less than a third of long-term care facilities. In 1973 Mrs. Callender was transferred within HEW. Federal regulations for the two categories of nursing homes were weakened. In short, the highly touted Nixon reform package seemed to have fallen by the wayside.

On another front, Congress voted reforms in the Social Security Amendments of 1972, eliminating separate requirements and separate certification

---

* There is overlap. There are 500 "Medicare *only*" homes. So some 3,500 Medicare extended-care facilities are among the 7,000 Medicaid homes.

procedures under Medicare and Medicaid for skilled nursing facilities and establishing a single set of requirements. The amendments created a single definition and set of standards for extended-care facilities under Medicare and for skilled-nursing homes under Medicaid. A new category was thereby introduced, the "skilled nursing facility," which would meet the prior definition of the extended-care facility. Mandatory and stricter requirements for admission prevailed. The result was that practically everybody was ineligible. Since few older people could get into skilled nursing facilities, the intermediate-care facility became all-important and potentially "the universal receptacle of the unwanted," to quote Val Halamandaris, staffer for Senator Moss's long-term-care subcommittee. Because the federal government pays the bill, the states accelerated the transfer of older state-mental-hospital patients into ICFs. For the same financial reasons, the intermediate-care facilities started to accept chronic alcoholic and tubercular patients. Unfortunately ICFs cannot give the kind of care these patients need. As an example, one requirement of intermediate-care facilities is the presence of one licensed practical nurse (LPN) for eight hours daily. Despite the fact that the statutory provisions exist for better nursing care, the writing of ICF regulations has been regressive.

By January, 1974, there was five-day registered-nursing coverage (but no medical director) and the intent of the 1967 Moss amendments and in theory the 1967 Kennedy amendment had finally been fulfilled insofar as the written regulations were concerned. But in practice nursing-home regulations continued to be inadequately enforced.

By December, 1974, came approval of significant regulations for skilled nursing facilities, including a "patient's bill of rights" (for example, including privacy for spouse's visits), a medical director (as of January 1, 1976), a registered nurse seven days a week and a discharge planning program. Obviously, though, the problem of enforcement remains.

Regrettably, the requirement for medical social services in ECFs and SNHs was eliminated by the Congress. The maintenance-of-effort clause applied to the states in the Long Amendment was repealed as well (see Chapter 8).

In another governmental move, more than half a million dollars in contracts to test ombudsman programs for patients in nursing homes were awarded by HEW in 1972. The contracts went to the National Council of Senior Citizens (NCSC) and covered the upper peninsula of Michigan and the states of Idaho, Pennsylvania, South Carolina and Wisconsin.

In sum, neither the Nixon program nor congressional action has gone far enough in securing quality nursing-home care.

IS THERE AN IDEAL FORM OF CARE OF THE OLD?

What would be an "ideal" nursing home?[38] One can quickly outline the basic elements. The home should truly be "homelike"—not sterile, antiseptic or reminiscent of a motel. It should be a lively place with many ties to the larger community, while simultaneously offering a quiet sanctuary for those who require it. It should have a trained administrator who understands old people and has a fundamental knowledge of aging as well as a business sense. There should be a medical director who is legally responsible for the health care of the residents and the sanitation of the institution. Social services should be available to both the older person and his family, along with a full complement of skilled rehabilitation personnel—from physical, occupational and speech therapists to doctors of physical medicine. Trained listeners—not necessarily professionals—should be available for the elderly to talk to. A nursing home should not be exclusively oriented to the care of its inpatients but rather should supply services beyond its walls. It should be the hub of many activities—day care, social dining, disease detection, intellectual and social programs, group and individual counseling and psychotherapy, outreach care, social services and health education. There should be a social and intellectual climate that makes it possible for the elderly who can and wish to do so to study, grow and enjoy themselves. There should be freedom of action and a sense of community with a minimum of authoritarianism and infantilization. Individual identity and dignity can be maintained through social contact, the presence of familiar possessions, and the exercise of personal freedom and choice. Where physical deficiencies exist, notably in ambulation, hearing and vision, a prosthetic milieu taking advantage of the latest technology must be created to compensate. There should be arrangements in the home or with a nearby hospital for prompt care of medical emergencies. And finally, fire and physical security must be assured.

Beyond this, we ideally should create new forms of care. The nursing-home industry alone cannot be blamed. Medical schools, medical associations, families, indeed society at large, all bear responsibility for what has been and what could be. The following points represent my ideas for the beginnings of a specific program for fundamental reforms to provide humane, decent and innovative care in a way that goes beyond our current experiences.* It would require a clear and enlightened national policy in

---

* To move in these necessary directions there must be a basic concern in our national sensibility for the old, the chronically ill and the helpless, which I shall discuss in Chapter 14.

place of the hodgepodge commercial mosaic in old-age and disability care.

1. Public monies, federal tax dollars, should be diverted from the commercial nursing-home industry to the creation of multipurpose centers or galaxies. These should be established as social utilities and given the opportunity to compete with the subsidized "free-enterprise" homes.* These galaxies may be set up as cooperatives, as the creations of religious organizations, unions and fraternal orders, as expansions of nonprofit hospitals and homes for the aging, as components of municipal care systems, or as public corporations. Consumers, especially old people within the geographic area, should participate in their control, serving as board members.

2. National health-insurance plans must be realistic and finance chronic care. With insurance in hand the individual has freedom of choice among competing social utilities and commercial businesses. All persons, regardless of income, would then be eligible to use social utilities.

3. Instead of having many different levels of care scattered in many types of institutions, it is sounder medically as well as financially to have comprehensive and continuous care available within the same multifunctional facility. There must be uniform standards of care, and care available independent of financial means. The present system of "skilled nursing facilities" and "intermediate-care facilities" represents fragmentation, and this fragmentation is now tied to the financing mechanisms.

4. Federal funds should be transmitted directly to the providers of services, excluding the expensive middleman realty and insurance industries.

5. Centers or galaxies could proceed from a vision of comprehensive planning that emphasizes social and personal care as well as medical care, on both a residential and outpatient basis. Because the medical profession has shown a disinclination to any involvement in long-term care, it is wise to move beyond medicine to the total care approach. The leadership of these galaxies should come from many professional groups, such as nurses, clergymen and social workers, in addition to physicians.

6. The galaxies should be interdependent with other components of the nation's care system—social agencies, hospitals, information and referral centers, community centers, health and mental-health centers. They must relate to a range of facilities and services in accordance with the reality of different levels of social, personal and medical need.

7. Land use and the right of eminent domain must be constructively used for the public's health. The galaxies should be geographically located in various neighborhoods with reference to the demographic and personal

---

* "Nonprofit" does not automatically mean good nor "profit" bad. However, competition is valuable and the profit-making homes do not actually operate in the free marketplace.

characteristics of the population. For those who must or choose to live in the inner city, downtown real estate should be made available. Some older people and other disabled people who require nursing homes are pleased to move to the suburbs where so many facilities are now built because of cheaper land costs. But many people would be much happier in the down-town city areas where they grew up or lived and where there are more activities.

8. Development of comprehensive diagnostic and treatment programs within these galaxies would avoid the common, tragic mistakes of failing to recognize and treat reversible disorders and misplacing people in incor-rect settings. Although the traditional nursing home is generally seen as "the last stop," the galaxy must be seen as a diagnostic-treatment-outpatient and residential center with emphasis upon discharge, home care, community care—as well as terminal care. It could supplement or be part of or be connected with the reception units in general hospitals recommended in Chapter 7 and the national network of mental-health programs recom-mended in Chapter 8.

9. There should be three parts to each galaxy—service, training and research. Research is now almost totally neglected in nursing homes, yet the enormity of the present and future problem of old age and chronic illness demands basic and applied clinical research.

10. A federal inspection system for surveillance and enforcement of standards of care, of administrators and personnel in all care programs for the aged must be established. This can only be done if institutions are tied to participation in a federally-funded program; otherwise, there are con-stitutional barriers to federal licensure. There must be adequate numbers of inspectors. Inspection records, whether federal, state or local, must be open to all—the press, the public, families. Unannounced inspections are an absolute. There should be round-the-clock visiting hours except upon individualized specific medical injunction. In my judgment older people and their family members must themselves become skilled at what to look for in institutions in order to act as monitors and "unofficial" inspectors.*

11. The establishment of quality home care through the creation of a National Personal Care Corps would be a critical component of the multi-purpose center. Such workers would perform many of the duties that are now inefficiently spread over the existing categories of visiting nurses, home-maker–home health aides, occupational therapists and others. They would be jacks-of-all-trades, performing some nurses' duties, escorting the patient to the doctor or to outside recreation, shopping for drugs or groceries,

---

* A new statewide organization called Friends and Relatives of Nursing Home Patients, Inc., was founded in Oregon in 1972.

teaching members of the family to change dressings, conducting active and passive exercises for stroke patients, listening and talking. They must be decently paid—at salary levels higher than those presently paid in our institutions—and there must be possibilities for career development.

The idea that families reject old people is an overworked notion—although, of course, sometimes valid. But many families struggle hard to keep their older people from being "put away." A corps of personal-care workers and other social services would make it possible for many more elderly to remain at home.

12. Among components of community services available through multi-purpose centers should be day care and weekend centers; the expansion of the Foster Grandparent and other programs so that centers or galaxies operate from a life-cycle perspective and give useful roles to old people; outreach programs modeled after Medicare Alert; and a national hot meals-on-wheels program.

13. Financial assistance should be available to help families maintain their older relatives at home when they wish to do so. There should be loans and funds for construction of additions to homes. There should be direct payments for care, for instance, when a family member is functioning as a homemaker or providing nursing services.*

14. Religious and other nursing homes should be encouraged to join together to share and pool their resources, in a practical ecumenism that moves beyond traditional institutional care to the provision of services in the community.[39]

15. When custodial care becomes inevitable, the meaning of the word "custodial" should signify the highest quality of personal, social and health care. Custodial care must continue despite the implacable time gradient of disease and dying. Thus personal care, from hair grooming to the passive exercise of limbs affected with residual paralysis, should be a daily occurrence. Advanced technology should be available to give handicapped patients as much direct control of their bodies as possible. (Some remarkably ingenious devices, such as wheelchairs that can be operated by eye movements, have been developed.) Social activities and occupational and physical therapies must always be available.

16. A strong, specific, legally enforceable "Bill of Rights" should protect the personal and property rights of institutionalized old people.

---

* In an excellent series of investigative articles on New York City nursing homes in 1974–75 in the *New York Times*, John L. Hess pointed out that in New York State, Medicaid pays the staggering sum of $10,000 per bed per year to a nursing home. If this money, which is $833 a month, were available to families maintaining a patient at home or for home care, it would be a sensible and humane step forward.

17. Above all, it is important that after institutionalization, family, social and personal relationships be maintained to the greatest extent possible. Some 80 percent of people do eventually end up dying in institutions (among them, of course, hospitals) rather than in their own homes. Nursing homes have the connotation of being "houses of death," and psychologically many older people consider themselves buried alive when they enter such a home. As John Updike wrote in *The Poorhouse Fair*, there is "death at their sides, the third guest at every meal." Families sometimes compound this sensation by their tendency to grieve when a person enters a nursing home, much as if the patient were already dead. There is a temptation to visit less and less frequently because visiting is a painful reminder of death. Guilt and shame over allowing a relative to live in a nursing home can be so intense that I have seen families ask newspapers not to mention the place of death in an obituary notice.

Families and older persons need help in dealing with their reactions to institutionalization. Individual and group therapy, seminars, readings and direct involvement in the institution are useful. Family members should be active in planning and preparing the older person psychologically for admission. It is helpful for them to know staff members personally. They should be encouraged to visit frequently, and provide extra amenities, attention and in some cases direct patient care to their relative. Grandchildren and other youngsters should be welcome. An atmosphere of liveliness would be a welcome relief to the dullness of so much of nursing-home life.

Facilities for the aged could become places where one goes to be rehabilitated to the greatest extent possible, nurturing the sense of hope and self-esteem which can make the last and often most difficult years of life worthwhile, up to the moment of death. Whether in the outside world or within an institution, the older person needs someone to talk to about his life, to review it, make sense of it, and come to terms with his dying.

Chapter 10

VICTIMIZATION OF THE ELDERLY

CRIMES OF VIOLENCE

Old people are victims of violent crime more than any other age group.* Indeed, people over 50—not only the old—are more vulnerable to violent crimes (particularly robbery). In Washington, D.C., in 1970, for instance, 25 percent of the city's population but some 35 percent of its crime victims were over 50.

Aside from the obvious physical dangers and property losses associated with crime, the elderly may become so fearful and cautious that they virtually become prisoners in their own homes. Social and personal isolation is difficult enough for old people, imposed as it often is by external forces like widowhood, the death of friends, mandatory retirement, poverty, physical and mental impairments and transportation difficulties. But added to these are the fear and the reality of crime, which locks many of them in their homes by day as well as by night. "Many elderly couples or single persons have told us they live almost entirely within their own walls, overwhelmed by illness, despair or fear of crime."[1] They are afraid to answer a knock on their door. Some keep lights burning all night or leave their TV's and radios running twenty-four hours a day. Many feel panic at any unknown sound and make a practice of sleeping lightly so as to be on guard at all times.

Yet such careful precautions can be futile. A significant part of violent crime against the old occurs within their own homes:

> In September, 1970, Charles and Flora Kurz, Sr., both 84, were robbed and beaten in the bedroom of their home. It took almost two days for Mrs. Kurz to climb down to the porch seeking help. Mr. Kurz died in the hospital two weeks later. His skull had been fractured.

---

* Older people themselves commit very little crime. Violent crime declines with age. Embezzlement rises on the job during the middle years until retirement. Most of the crime committed by the old is petty thievery to supplement inadequate pension or welfare checks.

She recovered. They had just completed arrangements to move because their home had been broken into several times.*

Sexual violence against older women is not uncommon:

> The morning newspaper remained outside Mrs. Jones's apartment all day. The manager investigated. The 82-year-old woman had been sexually molested. A pillow case was over her head, her underclothing was stuffed in her mouth. She had died of suffocation. Her deafness had contributed to her vulnerability. Her apartment showed evidence of having been searched but not ransacked.

Eccentric or unusual behavior can become known in a neighborhood or community and lead to exploitation. Distrust, of recent development or lifelong duration, may prove dangerous.

> An elderly woman in Philadelphia hid $100,000 in life savings in her basement in two canvas bags stacked near the heater. She did not trust banks. When she aired her beliefs to neighbors her money was quickly stolen.

Vandalism is common in low-income areas, and older people in their homes may be subjected to terrorism. Stones are thrown through windows. Clothes are stolen off clotheslines. Vegetable and flower gardens are pilfered or stamped on. Threatening or mysterious phone calls and letters upset them. When a crime occurs, especially a crime associated with violence or continued harassment, the psychological consequences may require a longer recovery period than actual physical injury. For some elderly people "things are never the same again." Their emotional resources are stretched to the breaking point.

Poor vision, hearing loss, slowed motor and mental response, decreased coordination and a host of other physical and mental impairments increase their vulnerability. They simply are no match for younger, stronger victimizers. Frequently the crime becomes more serious than was intended by the perpetrators:

> Seventy-one-year-old Harriet Brown was pronounced dead of head injuries. She never regained consciousness from the moment she was struck down by two 15-year-old youths. The boys had been sitting idly on a cemetery wall on June 4, 1968, when they saw the elderly woman carrying a blue plastic purse. She stepped off a bus and walked toward her home. They crossed the street to follow her. One of them darted

* Charles Kurz had been a volunteer in our NIH studies of healthy older men.

toward her and grabbed her purse. She struggled momentarily. With the snatching of the purse, the woman pitched forward to the ground, striking her head on the curb. She died two weeks later. Robbery, not first-degree murder, had been the intention.

Old people are systematically preyed upon. During the first days of the month, when Social Security, pension, public-assistance and other checks arrive, robberies, burglaries and assaults escalate. Nearly twenty thousand Social Security checks are stolen each year, usually by direct looting of mailboxes. This becomes a crisis to someone who has no other income for rent and food. It may mean the loss of income altogether or a long delay resulting from the need to prove the loss before another check is sent in replacement. Fortunately, the 1972 Social Security Amendments now make it possible for beneficiaries to have their checks directly deposited in a bank, credit union or building and loan association, with the Social Security number functioning as the identifying control. This has been the practice for some years now with federal civilian and military retirees' pension checks.

The setting for much crime against the elderly is in the inner city.* Those living in both private and public housing are affected, though persons living in more expensive apartments are, of course, often better protected by means of doormen, buzzer systems, TV monitors, special locks and grillwork. Apartment dwellers and roomers in private tenements and public housing often have little security. Senator Harrison Williams (D.-N.J.) reports: "We have been told—and with ample heart-breaking documentation—that elderly tenants in private and public housing in many of our big cities are the most vulnerable victims of theft, violence, rowdyism, and outright terrorism."[2]

There are approximately three thousand public-housing projects across the United States. Nearly 20 percent of the people who live in such lower-income housing are 65 years old or more. As one might expect, urban public housing is the most dangerous (for example, there has been a consistent increase in such crime in New York City†) whereas crime in country or rural public housing is not nearly so high.

Public housing has become so identified with crime that it is becoming more and more difficult to find locations for such housing. Fear of crime affected the reactions of Forest Hills, New York, residents to a new project.[4] The fact that 60 percent of the project inhabitants were to be white and

---

* Although recently crime in the suburbs has begun to rise dramatically.
† For instance in the Jacob Riis, Bernard Baruch and Lillian Wald houses.[3]

40 percent elderly was of little importance in the reactions of this white middle-class community. The constant theme running through the discussions was the association between public housing and crime.

Other public programs have led to equally difficult results. A social policy presumed to serve a useful purpose can lead to the creation or reinforcement of other problems, at great personal and social cost. The current policy to reduce the hospitalization of mental patients of all ages through rapid discharge and transfer to the "community" is illustrative. Former patients may have little experience in protecting themselves or may be incapacitated mentally to the extent that they are vulnerable victims. Their income usually limits them to undesirable, high-crime areas of cities. Increased crime is the natural result. In New York City, for example, discharged mental patients are housed in welfare hotels along with drug addicts and persons with criminal records. These welfare hotels, largely concentrated on Manhattan's Upper West Side, are centers of crime, serving as bases of operation for pimps and prostitutes, drug pushers and users. More than thirty hotels provide single-room occupancy at rents within the range allowed by New York City's Department of Social Services.[5]

Black, white, Spanish-speaking and other elderly are all subject to the dangers of crime. At times this leads them to band together to protect themselves and each other from the young. But more often crime encourages the spread of racial unrest and prejudice. This is clearly demonstrated in the case of elderly Jewish merchants with businesses in all-black neighborhoods. Black-white antagonisms are deeply rooted, with both blacks and Jews reacting to long histories of exploitation. Such merchants become prime targets for robbery as racial tensions have increased and their own aging has made them more susceptible.

Cultural factors can also be responsible for the presence of Jewish elderly in the inner city. In 1972 a three-man special commission of the Union of Orthodox Jewish Congregations of America expressed its concern about the elderly Jews who will not move out of their inner-city neighborhood because there are no orthodox synagogues elsewhere near enough for them to be able to walk to services. It is estimated that in the New York metropolitan area alone there are at least fifty thousand elderly Jews who feel unable to move for various reasons.

The elderly of all groups and races tend to become trapped in high-crime centers because of their low incomes or their reluctance to move to unfamiliar locations. The fear of change can be even greater than the fear of crime. But the most significant factor is probably the fact that many elderly simply cannot afford to move anywhere else.

Who commits crimes of violence against old people? Troubled, desperate people, those in need of money for drugs, robbers of various types, sociopaths and people with sex problems; but also caretakers, acquaintances, even relatives:

> In 1971 a seventy-four-year-old resident of a nursing home (having been there for five years) was taken by her caretakers, the operator and an assistant, to a bridge over a local river and thrown to her death. They stated that they killed her because she was so crippled by arthritis that she had become a burden to them.

Armed robbers, gangs and muggers are often youthful. Most violent crime is committed by persons between 15 and 24. The main victims are in fact blacks, although white victims generally receive more publicity.

Much crime is never reported by the elderly. There is too much fear of retaliation, particularly when crime occurs within a family (one family member against another) or among neighborhood residents. In addition, it is expensive to participate in the pursuit of justice—to get to and from the courthouse, to eat lunch out, to hire a lawyer. Many have no telephone on which to call police. When crimes *are* reported (by people of all ages) only 12 percent end in arrests, only 6 percent in convictions, and 1 percent in imprisonment—figures that give some idea of the extent to which crime is "successful."

If a person resists crime, the chances of injury and death are increased. In general, 10 percent of robbery victims are badly injured and 10 percent are killed, but reliable statistics categorized by age are not available. Indeed, the victims and their characteristics have not been nearly as well studied as the characteristics of the perpetrators of crime. This is true of the FBI's Uniform Crime Reports as well as local police records.

One of the few studies of elderly crime victims has been a 1970 demonstration study called Project Assist conducted in Washington, D.C., which developed a useful model for establishing a program of police-community relations to benefit old people.[6] This eight-month $24,000 project (funded through the Older Americans Act) examined the extent of victimization and the kinds of social and health problems which result, as well as the circumstances under which older people come to the attention of the police whether or not a crime has been committed.

The mean age of the elderly served by Project Assist was 70. Robbery was the number-one crime. Physical illness topped the list of non-crime-related problems which were brought to the attention of the police. About 20 percent of the sample had multiple social problems. Women were more victimized than men; 63 percent of the clientele were women, 37 percent men. Blacks were more frequent victims than whites. Many of the sample were physically and/or mentally impaired in some serious way, adding to their vulnerability to crime and social problems. A substantial percentage of the sample were poor, and more were on Old Age Assistance (OAA) than in the city's population as a whole. Widowed and single people were also disproportionately represented in the sample. One-third had no phone. To be old and poor, widowed and female increases the chances for police contact. One can surmise that this is true not just for Washington, D.C., but for the nation at large.

Project Assist had the blessing of the Metropolitan Police Department and the cooperation of the Third Police District, which made available the names of older persons reporting crimes they had suffered, or who became known to the police because of social crises. The report of Project Assist pointed to "a large group of old people . . . a depressed under-class . . . who are particularly vulnerable to crime, easy victims of street robbery, unable to move out of high crime neighborhoods . . . and likely to have no other community resources to turn to other than the police if trouble occurs." Police, of course, are one of the community agencies that are immediately identifiable and are called upon to provide social service as well as protection. Because of this it was one of the aims of Project Assist to develop appropriate means of liaison and referral through and by the police. A social worker with training in community organization was especially useful in helping coordinate police contacts with community social-service agencies and resources. It became clear that programs and services must be designed categorically to respond rapidly and effectively to older people who have contact with the police either as a result of criminal activity or social problems. Follow-up by the social worker–director[7] and/or her case aide resulted in dramatic, even life-saving assistance, along with practical solutions to many everyday problems. In the eight-month study some 220 persons received direct help, such as emergency money, replacement of food stamps, medical assistance and sheltered care. Project Assist found help for many who were simply unaware of available services—although it was abundantly clear that both private and public agencies were very limited in their capacities to meet fully the community-wide needs of older people.

The report included extensive computerized statistical analysis on a city-wide basis (beyond the locale of the project) to probe the scope and characteristics of the burden of crime carried by the elderly and the degree to which the police are the first line of defense turned to by older people and their neighbors in the inner city. In addition, the report provided numerous case descriptions and an analysis of the role conflicts of police personnel when confronted with social problems as well as crime. It also tried to offer guidance to social workers in constructing effective liaison with police officers.

One of the most serious consequences of crime is the unwillingness of service groups* to make home visits in inner cities. Public-health and visiting nurses, homemakers and some social workers are notable exceptions. Physicians have become increasingly reluctant to practice in high-crime areas.

On the other hand, Dr. Charles Goodrich of New York's Mount Sinai School of Medicine observed, after six years of experience working in East Harlem, "Security is a factor, but it's a minor one and is more of a problem for ghetto residents themselves than for health personnel. Among the more than 100 medical people working in East Harlem there haven't been any problems."[8] And Myrna Lewis, a psychiatric social worker functioning in Washington, D.C.'s, inner city has noted:

In our own experience (with a staff of 12 community workers) of over three years work in one of the highest crime areas in Washington, D.C., we have had only one close call, and during the episode no one was injured. It would appear that the terrified attitudes of most professionals toward community work may be covering a more profound reluctance to care for the poor, the elderly, the minorities and others living in the inner city.[9]

Undoubtedly fear has at times outdistanced reality, but fear becomes its own pervasive reality with untoward effects.

What should be done about crime in America, particularly as it affects old people? There are those who take the hard line—more crime fighting and more law and order. According to a 1973 Gallup Poll, the public considers crime to be the worst urban problem, and public support for the death penalty has risen to its highest point in twenty years.[10] The personal fear of criminal assault, both realistic and exaggerated, has led to the massive revenue-sharing program of the Department of Justice through which millions of dollars have passed. But the Law Enforcement Assistance Administration, authorized under the Safe Street Act, remains caught up in politics, bureaucracy and gadgetry. The war on crime, like the war on poverty, has hardly been a notable success.

Others insist that crime be considered a symptom of poverty and racial inequality, that to eliminate it successfully requires a major commitment

---

* This includes the TV repairman, who, by not coming, further compounds isolation, and the grocery store that will no longer deliver, which may necessitate the institutionalization of the housebound and chairfast.

to overall social progress. Efforts to deepen our cultural sensibility toward old people and to inaugurate fundamental reforms to get to the root of poverty for all age groups would mean increasing standard income-maintenance programs and adequate social services.

Nonetheless, specific programs to reduce crime against the elderly and to assist them after a crime has been committed are in order as long as crime remains a major threat to their well-being. The following protective measures are illustrative of what could be done at this time:

1. Emergency shelter for elderly crime victims when immediate care is needed and while decision making takes place as to what to do next.

2. Twenty-four-hour social services, including protective services and public guardianships (described in Chapter 5).

3. Compensation of elderly victims for medical expenses resulting from a crime and for costs associated with court cases, such as travel and food.

4. Protection against reprisals through increased police observation and notification of neighbors, friends, and relations who can take protective measures. Perpetrators are less likely to carry out criminal actions in a social network which increases their visibility and chance of being apprehended.

5. Expansion of arrangements for direct banking of pension and Social Security checks and the familiarizing of older people with these procedures.

6. Self-defense and survival education.

7. Provision for security in the home through buzzer systems to announce visitors, sturdy locks, adequate illumination and locked mailboxes. A small dog, where this is allowed, is often an excellent alarm system. Guards, doormen or TV monitors, usually provided in higher-income apartments, should be available in public-housing developments. Specific danger spots in residences for older people are similar to dangerous areas of all age groups— basement laundry rooms, where there is often noise because machines are running, elevators, dark halls and back doors. All of these require protective measures.

8. Improved street lighting.

9. Community escort service. In public housing in urban areas, for example, elderly residents are frightened of the prospect of living near families with adolescents because they are understandably afraid of young people. In some cities youth patrols have been organized to escort older people to stores and to provide other protective services for them. Practiced more widely, this could also help overcome their fear of younger people.

10. Self-help. Older people can help protect themselves through voluntary action when adequate security is not available. The Cuyahoga (Ohio) Metropolitan Housing Authority began a program in twenty high-rise buildings housing more than three thousand elderly and disabled persons. Five hundred older residents, mostly women, were trained as volunteer guides. They operated on a two-hour-per-day basis, monitoring buildings, reporting the presence of strangers, checking the functioning of security devices such as buzzers, locks and alarms, and sending for ambulances or police as needed.

Contacts between the police and the elderly could be greatly improved. The police are subject to much scrutiny and criticism, which can be extremely useful and sometimes necessary to reduce corruption and excessive "politicization" under the banner of "law and order." But the police are also unfairly abused. Theirs is a very high-risk occupation. The excellent motion-picture documentary *Law and Order* by Frederick Wiseman records the way in which police work itself will blunt human sensibility if there are not forces such as continuing education to counter it. In some cities, too, the police lack adequate insurance protection against liability. If they are sued for acts performed on duty—such as false arrest, or assault and battery—they must pay the damages themselves if they lose the case. Understandably, then, the police are reluctant to undertake certain procedures. In Washington, for instance, the police are uneasy about potential lawsuits if they take possible commitment cases to the local mental hospital, St. Elizabeths.

The average policeman is underpaid, undereducated and unprepared to deal with the range of social problems he encounters and about which he is rarely taught. Physicians, social workers, public officials and others have not joined forces with the police in effecting better techniques to protect various age groups, from children to old people, and to become more cognizant of the variety of aspects of human behavior they may encounter, including mental disorders and their symptoms.

Some specific recommendations on police functioning are as follows:

1. Greater emphasis on training of police about the sociology of crime, the roots of criminal activity and the recognition of the vulnerable (for example, the mentally ill and aged).

2. Liaison between police and social services (e.g., the model of Project Assist).

3. Collective liability insurance for the police (in addition to the more obvious need for better pay and fringe benefits).

4. Police training of youth "courtesy" patrols and use of police reserves in high-crime areas to escort older people to shops, services and recreation.

5. Provision of police or police-trained escort services for physicians, social workers and other health personnel as well as service and repair personnel (TV repairmen, grocery delivery men) in high-crime areas.

6. Special policing where older people are concentrated, in certain private and public housing, and at public transportation sites such as subway stations and bus stops.

7. Easy-to-remember emergency police telephone numbers.

8. Police-led education for community resident elderly on techniques of self-protection, residential security and street safety. In some locations the police are willing to make on-site inspection of homes for security checks.

A speedier and less complicated judicial system and the provision of legal counsel for those who cannot afford their own would be of obvious benefit to the elderly.

FRAUD

Old people are victimized in many ways other than through violent crime. They are pursued by fortune hunters anxious to separate them from their pension checks. Door-to-door salesmen offer persuasive "bargains" bolstered by "free" gifts and prizes. Those with visual handicaps are cheated when change is made in stores. At a time of loss and grief, first the funeral directors and then all kinds of salesmen—dealing with real estate, investments and the like—may exploit them. Cosmetic firms make them feel they are ugly and extract their money in exchange for "youth-restoring" beauty aids. Quack doctors, appliances and drugs give them false hope. Pharmaceutical firms realize high profits from unnecessary sales to the elderly. Many of the starker varieties of victimization are exploitative rather than illegal; and all of them occur in a general cultural framework that denigrates older people.

According to the 1966 report of the Senate Subcommittee on Frauds and Misrepresentation Affecting the Elderly, the American people "are now paying the greatest price they ever paid for worthless nostrums, ineffectual and potentially dangerous devices, treatments given by unqualified practitioners, food fads and unneeded diet supplements, and other alluring products or services that make misleading promises to cure or to end pain." The report continues, "It is shameful that the elderly of the United States are now the major victims of the hugely organized, high-pressure techniques of the modern medicine man. But this is clearly the case, and it was verified as woeful fact by witnesses who addressed the subcommittee."[11]

Not all older people are victims of fraud, of course. But an important minority are highly susceptible and the magnitude of this minority is not yet known. Collectively, the elderly constitute a significant source of income, given their $60 billion of annual aggregate income, and with their own frailties and vulnerabilities, this makes them tempting prey.[12]

Medical frauds and misrepresentations are perhaps the single most widespread area of fraud. The loss to the public during fiscal year 1973 has been estimated to be $10 billion and the majority of losers were the elderly. Cancer cures, arthritis remedies and "medicines" of all kinds are offered. As just one example, for every dollar spent on research on arthritis as much as $25 is spent on fraudulent nostrums. This is an annual waste of $400 million. If the arthritis victim has a temporary remission by coincidence, it is a special boon to the quack. Very often the chief ingredient of these expensive remedies is the old inexpensive standby, aspirin.

Inoperative or ineffective medical devices such as respirators, heart pacemakers and catheters are sold and used. Some of the appliances are hazardous to others as well as the patient. For example, improperly made oxygen cylinders may leak and cause fires.

Hearing impairments affect as many as five million elderly Americans and thus hearing aids of questionable quality have become a high-profit industry. Many elderly bypass the audiologists, who are trained specialists in programs accredited by the American Speech and Hearing Association, and otolaryngologists or otologists, who are physicians specifically trained to treat ear disorders. Instead they depend upon high-pressure door-to-door salesmen whose "tests" are likely to lead to sales. Such salesmen offer low prices, installment payments and easy accessibility to hearing aids. The Nader Retired Professional Action Group conducted a study that compared the tests of hearing-aid dealers and clinical audiologists.[13] Tests by the former are not performed in soundproof rooms, essential for valid examinations. In addition, dealers and salesmen test air conduction but not nerve conduction.* The hearing aids themselves are often therapeutically deficient and do not live up to their promise, either in terms of cost or performance. Senator Charles H. Percy (R.-Ill.), himself hard of hearing, submitted legislation calling for drastic reforms in the hearing-aid industry in 1974.

Closely related to medical frauds are anti-aging schemes. Rich and poor alike are susceptible to their promises.[14] Men worry about their potency, women about their attractiveness. There are people ready to assist—for a price! There was Professor Paul Niehans—who died at eighty-eight—purveyor of cellular therapy with "Live Lamb Embryo." He selected his wealthy patients carefully, gave them rest, good care and good food, and barred liquor and tobacco. Many felt much better after their "cures" in spite of the fact that scientific studies have found little value in cellular therapy as such. Dr. Ivan Popov, the founder of Renaissance Center in Nassau, Bahamas, specializes in "revitalization" treatments.[15] Dr. Ana Aslan's Gerovital H_3—based on simple procaine, the painkiller used by dentists—has attracted world-wide attention and many visitors to Rumania. The rich can afford to seek out the "youth doctors," but the everyday citizen depends on the less-costly do-it-yourself anti-aging fads. Special

---

* Hearing impairments are of three kinds, due to defective conduction by air or nerve or both.

jellies, creams, lotions, powders, mechanical devices, masks, clothing, exercises and the like purport to ward off the great offender, aging, and improve attractiveness and potency.

Lonely old people may be easy marks for the fast-talking or friendly-sounding representatives of the "loneliness industry," which sells everything from computerized dating services to "lifetime" dance lessions:

> As a psychiatrist I examined 69-year-old Miss Parker for her attorney to find if there was a psychiatric basis for an incapacity to make contracts that would hold up in court. She had been lonely, and in an effort to find social contacts she had made contracts totaling over $10,000 with a dancing studio, not only for dancing lessons—with instructors who flattered her—but for special trips to Puerto Rico and Acapulco (paying her teacher-escorts' expenses). She won medals in phony contests, was "tested" and "awarded" new contracts for progress from simple lessons to more complex dancing techniques. She finally belonged to the "300 Club" named for the number of lessons she had had. She had paid for 270 unused dancing lessons when illness caused her to become bedridden. She tried to terminate the contracts and sought a refund of her money. The studio refused. My medical opinion was that she was indeed susceptible to fraud. Psychologically it was a prima-facie case, but legally it was not. None of the legally accepted bases—for instance, organic brain disease—was present, and Miss P. was unable to recover her money.

Get-rich-quick schemes have special appeal for the elderly, given their generally marginal incomes. These schemes invariably earn money for the promoter and little or nothing for the investor, who has been beguiled by spectacular promises of big profits. A current example: franchise rights to vending machines are sold for territories that are poor, are unlikely to have good sales, or already belong to other franchised operators. The machines themselves may be falling apart. Another common get-rich-quick-at-home scheme: promoters charge a fee ($2 to $10 in advance) for mailing lists of companies that will supposedly buy a person's services—for example, addressing or stuffing envelopes. But these lists often turn out to be stale or the companies are not interested in services at all.

Franchises and distributorships of many kinds promise large potential profits. Franchising is the system by which a large national business organization contracts with an individual to represent it in a specified territory. "You are your own boss," they say. "You can be independent." One presumably benefits from the national company's advertising, volume buying and advance operations, and naturally one must be willing to invest sizable capital. Franchising is big business, legitimate and profitable for many, but illegitimate and disastrous for others. Dubious franchise operations are now under investigation in some states.

"Work at home . . . no experience needed" is a great come-on that lures the elderly into financial ventures. Fly-by-night deals which take their money and vanish have become the Postal Service's number-one mail-fraud offender.[16]

Retirement-home and land sales are a high-pressure business. Inducements, such as gifts, free gasoline, and dinner parties where "shills" are hired to start the sales pitch, gather in potential customers. Deceptive sales practices are commonplace in the $6 billion (1973) business of land sales. Overpriced, underdeveloped and often worthless land is bought unseen by many people about to move or in retirement, who give in to the pressure of the fast-buck salesmen. Land is sold as "ready for building" when, in fact, there are no sewer mains or water supply. Money goes into the hands of developers describing golf courses and marinas that are never built. The developers try to conceal the true state of the properties they are hawking. Prospective buyers are not given full certified financial statements and property reports. Land has been sold where the only available water is a thousand feet straight down or when the land itself is under water.* Whether desert or swamp land, it is usually a far cry from the paradise in Florida, New Mexico or Mexico that had been promised.

Condominium buying, now popular, carries special risks for the elderly. It offers the tax advantages of ownership, with maintenance work and other amenities as part of the package. But the residence may be ready for occupancy long before the promised swimming pool and garden, and buyers are forced to accept it as it is or lose part or all of their deposit. Costs of maintenance and utilities go up, but older buyers have been encouraged to think they will remain fixed and have not calculated these costs into their budgets.

Insurance provides another possibility for misrepresentation and outright fraud. The elderly, quite reasonably, try to protect themselves through health insurance. But mail-order health insurance has been very misleading

---

* Even the most venerated older retired person cannot walk on water, but the Gulf-American Corporation sold "thousands of acres of water in the Big Cypress Swamp," according to John Hunter in "Selling Land in Florida" (*The New Republic*, 157:20, 1967). The GAC Corporation took over the Gulf-American Corporation in 1969. In 1974, the Federal Trade Commission (FTC) made a pioneering settlement with the GAC Corporation in a major land-sales case, granting buyers $17 million in refunds in cash and in land for unfair and deceptive practices in Florida and Arizona.

to the public—and most lucrative to the companies. These policies are usually sold as supplements to Medicare or group coverage. There are innumerable exclusions (such as preexistent conditions, a foregone conclusion for the elderly), limitations and deductibles. The policies are hardly worth the premiums they cost. Though Senate hearings exposed these practices in 1964[17] there has been very little improvement in methods of sales. The U.S. Special Committee on Aging also investigated "pre-need burial insurance" in 1964 and found that victims were usually elderly persons who sought to make certain that they themselves, rather than their survivors, would absorb the costs of burial.

Attempts to get money out of the accounts of elderly people in banks, credit unions, and savings and loan associations are a unique category of fraud. These are all variations of the confidence game. Lonely old people are prey to the spiel of the con artist as well as the ordinary huckster and solicitor who comes to the door or operates by phone. One typical way the con man finds out about well-to-do elderly, often widows who have acquired money through the sale of their homes or other property, is through advertisements of the property in the newspaper. Another popular technique is the "bank examiner" swindle.[18] The crook calls a widow and tells her that shortages have been found in a number of accounts and that the bank wants her help—indeed is willing to pay a substantial bonus for her help—in uncovering the dishonest employee. She only need withdraw a large sum of money and wait at home for a further call. Then the "examiner" calls and tells her a "bank messenger" will pick up the money as "evidence" and give her a "receipt." She never sees her money again.

There are numerous variations on this same theme:

> Mrs. Y. was a 65-year-old widow who had just retired from a government job and was living alone. Project Assist called to offer help after notification by the police of a purse robbery. Mrs. Y. felt she did not need assistance at the time; but several mornings later she called the case aide to report that she had been approached two days before by two men who identified themselves as police officers. They showed her photographs, and she identified the men who had taken her purse. Then they told her that to catch the men she would have to give them $5,000 (all of her savings) as a decoy. She agreed and went to her bank. The teller insisted on giving her a cashier's check. The men told her to meet them and they would arrange to help her cash the check. She became suspicious and called Project Assist, which in turn immediately called the police, giving the descriptions of the men. They were apprehended and the check not cashed.

Why are the elderly so susceptible to fraud? It is not age *per se*. People do not automatically lose their intelligence and judgment as they grow older. We are all susceptible to the personality of others, the factor of charisma. The attractive door-to-door salesman or the medicine man may mesmerize unsuspecting people through sheer weight of personality. But a variety of factors can contribute toward making an older person especially vulnerable: current medical status, the presence of organic brain damage, loneliness, grief and depression, the fear of aging and death, pain and anxiety, educational level, personality, cultural characteristics and poverty.* Psychological reactions to physical changes are complex and varied. Judgment, the ability to reason, can be further affected by both cognitive and emotional changes. Cognitive judgment is impaired by organic brain damage through intellectual confusion, memory loss and disorientation. Emotional judgment is influenced by states of mood and systems of thinking, particularly depression, anger and loneliness. Paranoid systems of thinking, such as feelings of persecution or of grandiosity, may also seriously affect judgment.

Desperately lonely individuals, as the elderly often are, are easily persuaded by the ostensible warmth of friendly-sounding salespeople, by telephone as well as in person. Grief is another frequent companion of late life. Part of the process of recovery from grief includes the renewal of hope that the bereaved person may be able in some way to find a substitute for the loved one he has lost. This deep longing often makes for special vulnerability. When grief is complicated by hostility over being bereft, or when frank, overt depressions occur, the extent of vulnerability increases still further. Depression, for example, can involve guilt, and the tendency to self-punishment may manifest itself in spending one's money uselessly— a perfect setup for fraudulent financial schemes.

Simple factors which can influence susceptibility—for example, visual impairments—must not be underestimated. Older people often report being cheated in the process of receiving change in stores, because they cannot see properly. The print in contracts may be too small to read. Individuals with hearing problems can be too embarrassed to ask for written explanations and thus are subject to exploitation.

In the face of illness and intractable pain people may turn desperately to quack "cures" for cancer, arthritis, heart disease and other common diseases of old age. The possibility of death can induce a frantic search for help. Human credulity is usually defined as the readiness to believe something without sufficient evidence. Some people will persist in their beliefs even

* Viola Bernard has emphasized many of these in explaining why people of all ages, not just the elderly, become victims of medical quackery.[19]

in the face of the most overwhelming contrary evidence. One such belief is that of personal invulnerability. For people with such beliefs any person or magic promise that supports their sense of invulnerability is likely to have appeal. It is wrong to explain this phenomenon simply on the basis of "weakness" or "ignorance." In some instances this kind of unshakable credulity reflects necessary illusions they must maintain in order to survive as long as possible.

Old age can sometimes produce a hedonism that encourages risk taking in the hope of some pleasurable return. This is the philosophy that "you can't take it with you." Unfortunately the elderly are not in a position to recoup any financial losses should their ventures fail before they themselves do. Others feel pressured by the reality of death. Time is running out, and if they are going to make a move to a sunny state, buy a retirement home or make other crucial decisions, they must act promptly. This often means hasty decisions based on unsound evaluation.

Useful activity or purpose or meaning in life may be wanting in old age because the elderly are so often outside the mainstream of human activity. Their isolation tends to make them responsive to the charlatan who helps them feel less useless because he is paying attention to them.

Finally, one must take into account lifelong personality features. Some people who are vulnerable to fraud are no more or less susceptible in late life than when they were younger.

An informed elderly population is important in decreasing susceptibility to deception. The present average educational level of the population 65 and older is about eight years of public schooling, but we must consider also the impact of experience and self-learning. In our studies at the National Institute of Mental Health one of the subjects with a limited education said: "It came to my mind that I am getting older and my mind slower. Suppose someone would come to me and sell me on an idea on how to invest money. . . . But this idea would not be worth two cents. . . . So, I made a trust fund." This is the self-responsibility of which many older people are capable. But others fall prey to fraudulent practices because they are ill informed and inexperienced or naïve.

Much could be done to protect the elderly against fraud. Consumer educational campaigns are obviously of importance. Although the communication media—television, radio, newspapers and magazines—presently do little in the elderly public interest, they could certainly help to alert and educate the elderly to the tactics of fraud and the hazards of high-pressure selling. "Senior citizen" clubs, multipurpose senior centers and counseling centers offer opportunities for direct consumer education.

Better Business Bureaus and Chambers of Commerce should be developing ethical business practices with specific reference to the elderly. Older people need representation in organizations such as the Consumer Federation of America, the Consumer League, the Consumers Union, the American Automobile Association, and many others.

Professional persons—physicians, ministers, lawyers, nurses, social workers and others—have a responsibility in the education of the elderly. For example, the minister could play a much more important part in advising survivors about the practical aspects of funeral arrangements as well as caring for the spiritual and psychological aspects of grief. Doctors could do much more to warn older patients and their relatives about fake medical remedies and nostrums.*

The American Medical Association, the Food and Drug Administration and other organizations publish valuable pamphlets on quackery which ought to be displayed in doctors' waiting rooms and clinics. Moreover, pamphlets are available describing various diseases which commonly affect the elderly. If the doctor would take time to explain to the patient the nature of his illness, its likely course, and the valuelessness of quack procedures and drugs, older people could be saved considerable expense, disappointment and further risks to their health.

But in many instances the physician treating an elderly patient leaves no hope, throws up his hands, and refers only to the limitations of age, leaving an open doorway to quack cures and quick remedies. The following is an example of the importance of physicians' attitudes in maintaining effective and humane contact with patients:

> An 81-year-old woman with a severely painful arthritic destructive process of the head of the femur (the hip bone) sought help. Her physician of long standing told her there was nothing he could do and that he could not advise surgery. Her son, an engineer, pressed for a referral to an orthopedist, who was equally discouraging. Both the internist and the orthopedist told the son privately, "She's too old. Nothing can be done." The son became frantic and began looking for anyone or anything that could help his mother. Finally by luck he contacted a second orthopedist, who explained the pathological process to the son in greater detail. This orthopedist talked at length to both the patient and the son. He reviewed the use of analgesics, indicated his

---

* The Food and Drug Administration reported in October, 1972, upon the ignorance of the American public concerning health. Four out of ten would not be convinced that a cancer cure was worthless. Less than 50 percent felt cures judged to be useless should be banned by law. Two-thirds believe in the need for a daily bowel movement. One-third seek special methods of weight reduction which are medically questionable.

willingness to be available at times of greatest discomfort, and described the likely course of events in realistic terms. Both the patient and her son felt confidence in this orthopedist, appreciated his openness and his activist attitude, and maintained their contact with him.

It is surprising how much a physician can accomplish by taking a realistic, active approach rather than the easier common alternatives—false optimism and false reassurance on the one hand, or therapeutic nihilism on the other.

Public education campaigns, professional counseling and improved patient care will never be enough, however, to stop fraudulent practices. The responsiveness to quacks and cures often stems from unconscious and powerful psychological needs or from brain damage. Too many unscrupulous operators are at work looking for opportunities. Specific legal protections are necessary.

The question of mental competence may be an issue. Every person of legal age is presumed to be mentally competent and to have the mental capacity to carry on his everyday affairs. The burden of proof of incompetence is upon others. To determine that a person is incompetent it must be shown that he not only has a mental disorder but that this mental disorder causes a defect in judgment which renders him incapable of managing his property and other affairs. The psychiatric diagnosis itself (describing the *kind* of mental disorder) is not as critical as determining the degree to which judgment is actually impaired (which requires evaluation of day-to-day functioning).

Like the concept of partial responsibility, with respect to criminal acts, that has developed under the law, we need a new concept of partial competency. Impairments of judgment are not uniform and complete; there are degrees. Unfortunately, at times, older people are deprived of *all* their opportunities to make decisions, even though they are still competent in certain areas. The results can be disastrous psychologically and even physically:

> Eighty-seven-year-old Martha Wilson wanted to die in her own home. Her wishes were not honored. She was pressured to enter a nursing facility "for her own good." Her spirit gone, her beloved possessions unavailable, she died quietly nine days after admission.

Community programs providing protective services for the aged may further our understanding of older people and their range of capacity in decision making. The goal must be to preserve for the older person his civil rights—including the right to make what others might regard as a "mistake"—and yet provide protection when it is obvious that his judgment renders him helpless to exploitation and other dangers.

A variety of types of legal services are, of course, important as preventive measures against various forms of pressure, intimidation, and outright crimes like embezzlement. Protective services and public guardianships are illustrative.*

Moreover, the consumer-protection movement has accelerated in the 1960s and consumer-protection laws have been helpful. Class-action suits, a powerful legal weapon in which one person can sue both for himself and as representative of a larger class of similarly affected persons, have for a time made it economically feasible to go to court against small and big-time swindlers and merchandising organizations.† The "little man" was able to fight poorly made products and deceptive selling. *Caveat emptor* ("Let the buyer beware") became at least a trifle balanced. Liberalized class-action legislation would improve the situation even further, but the Supreme Court severely limited class-action suits in mid-1974 by its decision in *Eisen* v. *Carlisle & Jacquelin*, seriously impairing their effectiveness.

We urgently need a federal Consumer Protection Agency with strong advocacy powers, one along the lines envisioned by Ralph Nader and supported by the AFL-CIO and the Consumer Federation of America. This would institutionalize a consumer lobby within the executive branch and hopefully solve an old problem, the natural tendency of regulatory agencies to be dominated by the very industries they are supposed to regulate. But this attempt to establish a legal place for the consumer has been voted down since 1970.

The role and influence of the Office of Consumer Affairs should expand, and it should be a central repository for information on various products and services. The government regularly tests air conditioners, typewriters, floor polishers, automobiles and other equipment. As former HEW Secretary Wilbur J. Cohen has recommended, these data should be made available to the public under the Freedom of Information Act. Representative Benjamin S. Rosenthal (D.-N.Y.) and other consumer spokesmen have long argued for the release of such information. In 1969 there was a breakthrough of sorts when the Veterans Administration published its important data on hearing aids.[20]

---

* In fact, legal services are not readily available for older people. Private counsel is too expensive. Legal-aid societies generally have not given special attention to the needs of the elderly. Moreover, fly-by-night lawyers often find it easy to exploit older people.

† In the usual lawsuit individuals or corporations assert only their own legal claims.

The Flammable Fabrics Act of 1953 (amended in 1967, 1971 and 1973) needs to be strengthened again and enforced. Children and old people[21] are particular victims of serious and fatal burns from fabrics, although fire-retardant techniques are available to manufacturers.

There should be a model law regulating pre-market and post-market testing of hearing aids, physical therapeutic devices and medical appliances by the Food and Drug Administration or a potent consumer agency.

Strong legislation and enforcement by the appropriate municipal, state and federal agencies are mandatory if we are to control various kinds of quackery. The Federal Trade Commission, the Securities and Exchange Commission, the Food and Drug Administration, and the Postal Inspection Service are pertinent federal agencies. The Senate report referred to earlier has recommended the establishment of a Federal Anti-Quackery Bureau which would endeavor to coordinate various programs.

We also need more effective organization of paramedical as well as social services in the community. Even though a health manpower shortage exists —for example, grossly inadequate numbers of occupational therapists, physical therapists, and other health personnel—better utilization of existing personnel should be attempted. Experimenting with various nostrums would be reduced if older people had appropriate resources to which to turn for help when they need it. Psychological and physical rehabilitative efforts could at least compete with, if not "outsell," fake gadgets.

Improvement and enforcement of the Interstate Land Sales Full Disclosure Act of 1968* and expansion of the scope of the Office of Interstate Land Sales Registration of the Department of Housing and Urban Development would benefit elderly investors. Federal regulations should be supported by state buyer-protection laws and public-education campaigns.

There should be expansion and enforcement of the "truth-in-packaging" and "truth-in-lending" laws, passed by Congress in 1966 and 1968 respectively. "Truth-in-warranties" and "truth-in-insurance" laws need to be adopted and enforced immediately. Full descriptions of all articles and preparations sold, from medicines to real-estate plots, should be required in writing and made available to the buyer before sale.

Unit pricing, in easily read print, and special packaging in quantities suitable for people living alone would make shopping easier for the old. Older people themselves could and should organize to protect themselves by pressuring for education programs, new legislation and better marketing

---

* This act only covers developers who sell fifty or more unimproved lots across state lines.

and sales.* Control of advertising claims within the advertising agencies themselves and through legal enforcement is necessary.†

Perhaps most important, if older people have social roles of purpose and substance and a secure life, their need to believe in quick cures and extravagant promises will be minimized.

* "Social Security pamphlets explaining Medicare generally use small type and complicated language and are hard for the elderly to read and understand," complains William Hutton, executive director, National Council of Senior Citizens.

† The government has not done a distinguished job. The Federal Trade Commission, like most regulatory agencies, has "tired blood." After a ten-year enforcement battle, the FTC again gave the makers of Geritol another chance to stop "misrepresenting" the effects of their "medication." It was a 3-2 decision this time; Commissioner Philip Elman dissented. Elman wrote: "Respondents have advertised and continue to advertise the product Geritol as a generally effective remedy for tiredness when in fact it is not. This iron and vitamin preparation has become the largest selling product of its kind primarily because of the respondents' extensive use of national television advertising."[22] In August, 1971, Elman, then departing from the FTC, outlined a proposal for changes in the structure of regulatory agencies, most notably to reduce them from multimember commissions to single administrators. Finally in 1973 Federal Court Judge Constance Baker Motley denounced the defendants' "bad faith," "gross negligence" and "recklessness" and assessed $812,000 in fines. This is believed to be the largest civil judgment ever made for ignoring FTC orders. The case is under appeal, however.

Chapter 11

PACIFICATION
AND THE POLITICS OF AGING

THE PACIFICATION OF OLD PEOPLE

Powerlessness is a condition considered by many to be synonymous with old age in America. All too many old people have been brainwashed and pacified into believing they are powerless. In part this is a result of their acceptance of the culture's stereotyping of them as helpless. They have been patronized and infantilized. They are treated like children and insulted by labels referring to old age as "second childhood." The physical diseases and chronic health problems which beset so many of them encourage their acquiescence to this attitude. They have been subdued into apathy and depression by the crushing social circumstances of old age, which add unnecessary burdens to their daily lives and waste their vitality. Token service programs and other half measures deceive them into thinking their problems are being attended to.

This has truly terrible consequences. Many of the old hate themselves and their age group, seeing nothing useful or interesting in late life. They believe they are decrepit and burdensome to their families and society. They have no appropriate outlets for aggression and anger in work, protest or other creative endeavors. No one wants to listen to their complaints.

Dependency is reinforced when the elderly must depend on others or the state for financial help. They are made cautious by the continuing threat of further dependency, poverty, illness and placement in nursing homes or other institutions. They are intimidated by crime, dangerous living conditions and inaccessible transportation. They are often treated discourteously in public and even at home. Frequently they have been pacified by drugs. Medical personnel in and out of institutions overmedicate them, quieting their body movements and their emotional reactions.

Numbers of older people resist identifying with others of their own age group because of the powerlessness that age implies. The strongest and most fortunate can avoid some of the impact of stereotypes by denying that they are old. The affluent are particularly disinclined to identify with the economically disadvantaged. The result of this is the fragmentation of the elderly into isolated groupings.

With the notable exception of the Townsend movement in the depth of the Great Depression, the elderly have been relatively quiescent and undemanding, politically as well as in every other way. This generation of older persons has experienced such tremendous changes during its lifetime that for many there is only a desire for the status quo. Social, demographic, economic and technological changes have occurred rapidly, with profound consequences. The old are inclined to roll with the punches and not make waves, hoping only to "get by" in their struggle to survive.

But things seem to be slowly changing. The elderly are becoming more aware of their fate and more sophisticated about political action, and it has been instructive for them to watch the protests of the civil rights, peace and women's movements of the 1960s and '70s. Moreover, they are remaining healthier and "younger," are experiencing extended middle age and are living longer. They have more and more years of formal education, combined with their more varied life experiences. As older people continue to increase in absolute numbers and relative proportion (especially with zero population growth), they will become an even more vital and powerful potential in American political life.

All politics contains therapeutic elements: the opportunity for catharsis, the struggle for control over one's destiny, the advantages of self-confidence and respect, the hope and actuality of gaining one's goals. Old people need to become alive to the possibilities for change. To do so they must overcome apathy, self-hatred and fatalism. Self-confidence and self-respect follow the assertion of one's rights and legitimate needs. Cicero spoke to this point:

> Old age is respectable just as long as it asserts itself, maintains its proper rights and is not enslaved to anyone. . . . The great affairs of life are not performed by physical strength, activity or nimbleness of body, but by deliberation, character, expression of opinion. Of these old age is not only not deprived; but, as a rule, has these in a greater degree. . . . Old men retain their intellects well enough if they only keep their minds active and fully employed. . . . The crowning grace of old age is influence.[1]

If an old people's liberation really gets under way, one by-product might be an improvement in the emotional energy level available to them. In work at the National Institute of Mental Health we observed the critical significance of the surrounding social environment upon mental health. The struggle for sheer survival needs, along with loneliness, idleness and depression, absorb and bind considerable energy. Effective commitment to something outside oneself and the ability to act on one's own behalf are energizing.

Some people already worry that the old will gain too much for themselves at the expense of others; a few even fear a gerontocracy; others feel threatened by the possibility that a young charismatic agitator will unite and exploit the numerous elderly. But nothing to date indicates that any of these alternatives is likely; indeed, the elderly have been somewhat reluctant to organize and vote as a bloc for their own self-interest. Available evidence shows they are more apt to work for the common good and espouse a variety of goals of value to all ages. They are neither power-hungry nor even sufficiently self-serving. Nor can they be easily labeled as conservative, moderate or liberal.

One unhappy aspect of the politics of aging is the pitting of one age group against another in the quest for scarce social resources. For example, Social Security increases mean higher payroll taxes and therefore smaller take-home pay for workers. The consequent resentment of the younger age groups can boomerang against old people.[2] Most younger adults do not realize that they themselves benefit greatly from Social Security since their current deductions are insurance for the present as well as the future. If they are disabled or die, their wives and children will be protected. Income will be provided. Their children will be educated up to the age of 22. It has been estimated that a young person has the equivalent of a $225,000 insurance policy under his Social Security coverage. Very few could afford the premiums for such a policy in the private marketplace. Social Security is actually weighted in favor of the young rather than the retired. One-fourth of the Social Security beneficiaries are under 60. In 1970, for example, there were 2.5 million disabled workers and their dependents receiving monthly payments. Nonetheless, new ways of financing Social Security could be found to avoid burdening the young and the middle and lower classes disproportionately.* (See Chapter 2.)

What are the most effective political actions in which the elderly can engage? How can they use their potential power effectively? Some believe the electoral process alone can gain the ends they seek. There is some evidence in a number of communities and states that the elderly vote can be decisive. Others believe that old people, through mass membership organizations, must concentrate on developing power at the local, state and federal levels in order to implement passage of legislation. Still others feel the long, steady route of legal activism, with special emphasis on class-action suits, is the most reliable approach. But there is no reason to think

* In the 91st Congress alone 1,460 Social Security bills and 166 related bills were introduced.[3]

that old people—any more than any other group—can achieve their goals in American society through any single route. They must be prepared to use all available means—the ballot box, lobbying, legislation and litigation. In addition, I shall be proposing a broad range of activities which I have called an "Agenda for Activism."

THE ELDERLY VOTE

Those directly involved in the political process are beginning to take the vote of the elderly quite seriously. Older people constitute 10 percent of the population, but they represent 15 percent of eligible voters. In addition, they have a better voting record than do almost any other age groups. Ninety percent are registered to vote, and over 65 percent of these vote regularly.

The elderly are a diversified group in terms of issues which they support, but various trends manifest themselves in public-opinion polls. For example, the old were more inclined than even the young to view the war in Southeast Asia as a mistake.[4] Though many of them never participated in demonstrations and peace marches, the Gallup polls from 1965 on show they tended to feel "we should pull out of Vietnam entirely," rather than recommending that "we take a stronger stand."

On the other hand, when compared to younger age groups, white people over sixty-five are less in favor of federal action in support of fair employment, desegregation of schools or open housing.

The elderly represent the whole political spectrum from radical to liberal, moderate to conservative, though as we have noted earlier, much of the reputed political conservatism of the old comes from a need to protect their small resources.*

Political analysts like Richard Scammon feel the elderly are an influential "swing" vote in elections.[5] He believes Republican presidential candidate Barry Goldwater lost significant numbers of elderly votes when he spoke out against compulsory Social Security in 1964. Political journalists and politicians themselves now study the elderly vote as a serious force. In the 1972 Florida Democratic party primary, for instance, James Reston

---

* Old people can be useful tools in politics because of their often precarious financial status. Governor George Wallace cut back the Alabama welfare rolls in 1971. Blacks were the chief victims. There was speculation that this would enable Wallace to increase payments the following year to the state's 115,000 Old Age Assistance recipients, who were, of course, mostly white and thus more likely to vote for him than would indigent blacks. This probably led some white elderly Alabamians into voting for Wallace.

of the *New York Times* regarded Humphrey and Wallace as having the greater opportunity for securing the elderly vote.[6] In the 1972 Pennsylvania primary, Humphrey aimed his campaign at constituencies he had worked for in over thirty years in public life—older people, of whom there were 1.2 million in Pennsylvania, blacks (1 million) and Jews (500,000)—and he won. In the 1972 primaries Humphrey did better than McGovern among the old. In another example, *Business Week* pointed out that in 1970 in Florida, "Older voters were the deciding factor in electing two political unknowns to major office: Democrats Lawton M. Chiles, Jr. to the U.S. Senate and Reubin Askew to the governorship."

Some scholars, such as Robert Binstock of Brandeis University, question the power attributed to the vote of older people and observe the absence of hard data. For instance, President Lyndon B. Johnson's open espousal of Medicare presumably helped him win in 1964. Richard Harris states: "An analysis of the election returns showed that 22 percent of the vote had been cast by people over the age of sixty, two million of whom had switched from the Republican column to the Democratic. And although seven of the ten states with the highest percentage of elderly voters were traditionally Republican, all ten went to the Democrats."[7] But Binstock says, "Even for this election, however, no one has produced an analysis to show a shift to Johnson and Democratic congressional candidates among normally Republican voters that was greater among the aged than among younger segments of the population."[8]

Political observers have noted that the National Council of Senior Citizens' (NCSC) efforts on behalf of political candidates have been usually, but not exclusively, Democratic. Two recruits from the union movement, James O'Brien and Charles Odell, led the Citizens for Kennedy in the 1960 presidential campaign. In that election John F. Kennedy did not carry Pinellas County, Florida, which has the highest concentration of the elderly in the nation, but Lyndon B. Johnson did in 1964. By then the Social Security Medicare issue had become more sharply defined. When the Democratic National Committee completed its analysis of the 1960 election, it claimed that elderly votes contributed significantly, and in some key districts decisively, to Kennedy's victory.

The early membership of NCSC came largely from auto, steel and railroad workers and machinists. Nelson Cruikshank, its current articulate and knowledgeable president, feels that the victory of Democratic Senator John V. Tunney in California was helped by the NCSC. NCSC strength is located in New York, New England, Illinois, Kentucky, Idaho, Wisconsin, California, Washington, Arizona and Missouri. The late Republican

Senator Winston Prouty of Vermont got help from the NCSC along with various veterans' groups and felt that the elderly helped him in his victories. In 1970 the NCSC worked very hard for Senator Harrison Williams (D.-N.J.), who won, and for Senator Albert Gore (D.-Tenn.), who lost.

The most populous states, California, New York, Pennsylvania, Illinois, Ohio and Texas, have 40.4 percent of the older population and 40.8 percent of the total United States population. These six states have 189 electoral votes, a substantial contribution to a presidential election, since 270 of 538 electoral votes are necessary for victory. Each of four crucial electoral-vote states has over a million older people—New York (with 1.9 million), California, Pennsylvania and Illinois. Areas with the largest concentrations of older persons (at least 11 percent of the population) are in the agricultural Midwest, New England and Florida.

If the elderly do prove to be a crucial factor in elections, it is still no assurance that their own age-group problems will be dealt with. As Binstock warns, "It is one thing for a group to be able to influence the outcome of an election. It is quite another for the outcome to have an important bearing on the solution of the group's problems." The old must learn the difficult task of representing their own interests.

THE 1972 PRESIDENTIAL CAMPAIGN

The elderly were unquestionably a target in the 1972 presidential campaign. For the first time a major and sophisticated effort to corner the elderly vote was made. The Republican party actively sought their support. In fact, the Republican National Committee, in an effort to switch the Italian-American vote from the Democratic column, directed a major direct-mail campaign to 40,000 to 60,000 retired Italian-Americans living in Italy on Social Security and other United States benefits, asking them to write back to friends and relatives in the United States to vote for the President.

The White House and the President's men tried to "politicize" the federal bureaucracy, with resultant abuse of governmental power and the misuse of agencies and funds, including possible violation of criminal and civil laws.

Some of the abuses:

• An effort was made to purchase support of voter blocs with public money through the White House creation (on March 29, 1972) of the Federation of Experienced Americans. In a memorandum of November 17, 1972, Irven M. Eitreim (himself in his 60s), the unintimidated Chief of OEO's Older Persons Programs, questioned a $400,000 grant to the Federation of Experienced Americans, "an outfit of which I had never heard despite my intimate familiarity with all recognized national organizations in the aging field." He found the Federation to be not only inexperienced but "totally unqualified to do the job." The Government Accounting Office reported that "the grant and contract awards were processed outside normal procedures." "Never in my long experience in the federal government have I experienced anything approaching the impropriety of this grant," said Eitreim. Another grant of $1.5 million was made by the Department of Labor to the Federation. This affected the funding of outstanding organizations for the aged with excellent track records as government contractors. Indeed, the esteemed National Council on the Aging went through a shaky period which required it to reduce its staff by one-third.

• The Federation of Experienced Americans prepared radio spots advertising administration programs favorable to the President. These were sent to radio stations in states considered crucial to the President's re-election.

• The National Council of Senior Citizens, a mass organization for the elderly, was placed on the "enemies list." Moreover, according to a deposition filed in U.S. District Court in Washington, Charles W. Colson, the former special counsel to the President, sought the names of contributors to the National Council from the Internal Revenue Service because "this outfit is giving us trouble."

• Federal agencies mailed out millions of pieces of pro-Nixon literature to the elderly in the guise of official government publications during the final weeks of the campaign. These were distributed under White House instruction at taxpayers' expense[9] and were sent out using federal agency lists and preprinted mailing labels. There were also bulk mailings to senior citizen centers, elderly housing projects and nursing homes. The 3,400 delegates to 1971 White House Conference on Aging received copies. Five of the six pamphlets began with a quotation from President Nixon, filled with exaggerated claims of what the administration "did" or would do for the elderly.

Social Security checks mailed out to twenty-eight million recipients on October 3, 1972, included a printed note giving President Nixon the credit for the 20 percent boost in benefits that was included in these checks. It read: "Your Social Security payment has been increased by 20 percent, starting with this month's check, by a new statute enacted by the Congress and signed into law by President Richard M. Nixon on July 1, 1972." This was particularly hypocritical in view of the fact that the administration had actively opposed the 20 percent rise, favoring instead a 5 percent increase. The National Council of Senior Citizens complained:

If the White House Social Security policies had prevailed over the past three years, nearly 1.5 million more older Americans would be on the poverty rolls and the elderly would have lost $10 billion in benefits!

These stark facts have not prevented those responsible for the multi-million-dollar propaganda campaign to re-elect the President from implying that the recent Social Security gains could be credited to the White House incumbent.[10]

The Social Security Administration defended itself, saying the use of such notes was traditional, nonpartisan and not intended to boost one presidential candidate over another.

In other less questionable efforts the President sent four Cabinet officers and other top administrative officials to the 1971 White House Conference on Aging to explain his programs. He addressed the conference himself; he included the aged in his 1972 State of the Union address; he sent a special message to Congress on the aging; and Mrs. Nixon and their daughters appeared at "senior citizens" rallies.

Shrewd strategy included a five-minute 1972 Nixon campaign film on older Americans, which opened with various older people discussing their problems and then dissolved to the President's address at the 1971 White House Conference on Aging. He is saying, "Any action which enhances the dignity of older Americans enhances the dignity of all Americans, for unless the American dream comes true for our older generation, it cannot be complete for any generation." Interestingly, eight days before the election he vetoed significant bills affecting the elderly, the Older Americans Act amendments and the National Institute on Aging.

The Democrats took a less vigorous and much more traditional approach to the elderly vote, as when Democratic vice-presidential candidate Sargent Shriver observed the ninetieth birthday of his mother in an elaborate television celebration before fifteen hundred elderly persons bused in for the occasion. Other than supporting Social Security legislation, one gets the distinct impression that Democrats take the elderly for granted and assume that they are easily placated. Despite the reform efforts for an open convention with appropriate representation of minorities, the 1972 Democratic national convention had fewer than 4 percent of delegates over sixty-five. This is not a serious effort to include the elderly in party decision making.

GOVERNMENTAL SUPPORT OF POLITICAL GOALS FOR THE ELDERLY

THE OLDER AMERICANS ACT

The Older Americans Act, passed in 1965, explicitly outlined a national policy on aging, and listed "Objectives for Older Americans": *

1. An adequate income
2. The best possible physical and mental health
3. Suitable housing
4. Full restorative services
5. Opportunity for employment without age discrimination
6. Retirement in health, honor and dignity
7. Pursuit of meaningful activity
8. Efficient community services when needed
9. Immediate benefit from proven research knowledge
10. Freedom, independence and the free exercise of individual initiative

Many hoped that at last the elderly would be represented within the government itself through the Administration on Aging, the agency which this act established. But by 1971 the Administration on Aging had been decimated and submerged in Social and Rehabilitation Services, a larger HEW agency. Along with other organizations and individuals, the National Association of State Units on Aging (NASUA)† expressed grave concern at the weakening of the Administration on Aging and cutbacks in AOA funds. A bill strengthening AOA was finally passed, but vetoed by the President. A section of this bill called for a direct line of responsibility between the Commissioner on Aging and the office of the HEW Secretary. It would also have required all federal agencies proposing to establish programs affecting the elderly to consult with AOA before initiating such programs.‡

* The late Senator Pat McNamara (D.-Mich.) and Congressman John E. Fogarty (D.-R.I.) were the principal architects of the Older Americans Act and the Administration on Aging.

† NASUA is made up of the chairman and staff directors of state advisory bodies on aging. Generally speaking the state bodies on aging have not been very powerful. This is all the sadder given the struggle since 1972 for revenue-sharing money. By 1973 only Massachusetts had a separate cabinet-level department representing old people.

‡ The Older Americans Comprehensive Services Amendments of 1973 established a Federal Council on the Aging composed of fifteen members appointed by the President with the advice and consent of the Senate for three-year terms. At least five members must be older persons. The HEW Secretary and the Commissioner on Aging are ex officio members.

In 1974 the NCSC advocated an independent department with a Secretary of Elder Affairs.

By 1972, through its entire seven-year life, the AOA had reached only an estimated 1.1 million—far less than 5 percent—of the nation's elderly. There had been one thousand small programs averaging about $14,000 each. The Administration on Aging is the one agency of government really dealing with the integrated problems of income, health, housing and social needs, but it is hampered by lack of funds and authority.

THE CONGRESS AND AGING

In 1959 a significant series of Senate hearings took place on "The Aged and the Aging in the United States (The Community Viewpoint)."* In 1961 the U.S. Senate Special Committee on Aging was formed.[11] It has been useful but, with no power to initiate legislation, it is reduced to holding hearings and issuing reports. Still, the Senate Committee on Aging is popular among Senators because of its political significance. One out of every five Senators serves on this committee.

Former Congressman David Pryor (D.-Ark.) led the call for creation of a Special Committee on Aging in the U.S. House of Representatives, to be a counterpart to the Senate committee. A majority of the House, 235 Congressmen, co-sponsored the Pryor resolution, but it was blocked by 81-year-old Rules Committee Chairman William Colmer (D.-Miss.) who refused to give the proposal a hearing.†

Recognizing the fragmentation of congressional efforts to deal with the problems of aging, Senator J. Glenn Beall, Jr. (R.-Md.), introduced a resolution to establish a Joint House-Senate Committee on the Aging. Congressman Albert H. Quie (R.-Minn.) joined him in this effort in 1971, but it was not passed. The House committee was set up in 1975.

In anticipation of the 1971 White House Conference on Aging, Senator Church (D.-Ida.) formed a series of advisory councils and committees

---

* These were held in many cities, including Boston, San Francisco, Grand Rapids and Miami by the Subcommittee on Problems of the Aged and Aging of the Committee on Labor and Public Welfare, Senator Pat McNamara (D.-Mich.), chairman; Sidney Spector, staff director; and Harold L. Sheppard, research director.

† Age is a convenient scapegoat for a variety of problems productive of stagnation in Congress. It is easier to deal with the issue of seniority than with the deeper institutional problems that Congress might be too fearful and perhaps cynical to deal with, such as corruption or the lack of educational and occupational diversity of its body. In any case the seniority system has been largely a function of the one-party system in the South.[12]

to deal with the needs of elderly minorities such as blacks and American Indians.

OTHER GOVERNMENTAL UNITS' INVOLVEMENT IN AGING

Former New York Mayor John B. Lindsay organized an Urban Elderly Coalition in the fall of 1972 to persuade Congress to pay more attention to city poverty. More than 5 million older people live in large cities. Ninety cities, all with populations over 100,000, responded favorably to Lindsay's invitation to join. Mayors of 24 cities with populations of 500,000 or more were represented at the first meeting of the coalition. The chairman of the steering committee was Alice Brophy, director of New York's Office for the Aging. The immediate aim of the coalition was to mandate funding for cities for planning and coordination.

In another state effort, then Republican Governor Francis Sargent of Massachusetts signed a law creating a cabinet-level Department of Elder Affairs to oversee all programs for the elderly, including income maintenance, licensing of nursing homes, construction and administration of housing, and transportation services for the elderly. The budget rose from $750,000 to $3.3 million in one year, 1972.

THE WHITE HOUSE CONFERENCE ON AGING

The years 1961 and 1971 saw White House Conferences on Aging. Efforts to recognize, define and measure the problems of the old and to recommend solutions created shelves of reports which are now gathering dust. The 1961 conference, of course, had the excitement of the Medicare fight. But nothing dramatic, compelling, innovative or surprising emerged from the 1971 conference.

The purpose of the second White House Conference on Aging (November 28–December 1, 1971) was to build a national policy for the elderly in America. It turned out to be a bland, well-organized and well-orchestrated conference. It gave some short-term psychotherapeutic benefits to the 3,400 delegates but offered little that was substantial and immediate for older people. At best, the conference may have enlightened some Americans on the problems of older people and thus contributed to an enhanced sensibility concerning the elderly.

There was considerable patronization of the elderly. In preparation for the conference, issues were handed down from above, by way of technical advisory committees appointed by HEW Secretary Richardson, to community forums and state White House Conferences on Aging. Moreover, the technical advisory committees were partisan, with their representation of Republicans and Democrats five to one. Independents did not rate at all. There was considerable complaint about the degree of representativeness, which was answered by some improvement in the allocation of delegates. Roughly two-thirds of the conferees were over 55 and one-third over 65, with minorities comprising about 20 percent of the total. In addition, there were 112 youth delegates aged 17 to 24 attending, in order to develop what was hoped would be an awareness of the plight of older people. The government provided transportation expenses and $25 daily to about 2,500 elderly delegates to encourage their participation despite low income. But the poor were still underrepresented, as were women, especially widows. There was also inadequate representation according to the concentration of the elderly among states. New York and California, which together have nearly 20 percent or 4 million of the nation's elderly, had only seven-tenths of one percent of all the delegates. National professional and social-welfare organizations, which have consistently failed to make significant contributions on behalf of the elderly, were overrepresented.* The two mass organizations directly representing old people —the American Association of Retired Persons (combined with the National Retired Teachers Association) and the National Council of Senior Citizens—were given only 14 delegates each. The conference cost $2 million in federal taxpayer money.

The various organizations for the elderly were naïve and too optimistic in accepting the basic ground rules of the White House Conference on Aging.† Partly this was because the techniques of cooptation and the politics of intimidation were at work. During the conference itself, little effective representation of the full interests of the old occurred. For example, Cruikshank and the National Council of Senior Citizens pushed the Kennedy national health plan although it affords grossly inadequate coverage of chronic long-term nursing-home and mental-health care, and depends upon largely regressive tax support.

The conferees made liberal but not fundamental recommendations in the nine areas into which the conference had been divided: income, health, housing, education, employment, nutrition, retirement roles and activities, transportation and spiritual well-being. Delegates wended their way through

* Neither the Chamber of Commerce of the United States nor the National Association of Manufacturers accepted a request to participate in the Conference.

† The six major organizations are the American Association of Retired Persons, the National Retired Teachers Association, the National Council of Senior Citizens, the National Association of Retired Federal Employees, the National Council on the Aging and the National Caucus on the Black Aged.

unimaginative "issues" developed initially through the technical advisory committees. The following is illustrative:

Issue: "Should a system of coordinated personal-health services of both the short- and long-term care of the physically and mentally aging be developed, legislated and financed? Or, should the uncoordinated, generally fragmented health services as now provided be continued?"

They did not detail what would be mandatory to achieve the elimination of poverty, the production of adequate housing, and the provision of quality health care for older Americans. One would have hoped that at a minimum principles, policies, programs and "costing out" would have been carefully completed on these three key issues.

The National Caucus on the Black Aged had conducted a special conference a month previous to the conference, at which time seventy-five elderly demonstrators had picketed the White House, singing "We Shall Overcome." One 72-year-old woman was arrested for "disorderly conduct." The caucus held a "Special Concerns" session at the White House Conference and recommended a minimum guaranteed annual income of $6,500 for a single aged person and $9,000 for an aged couple. It also urged that the minimum-age eligibility requirement for primary beneficiaries of Social Security be reduced by seven years for black males, to reduce inequities based on lower black life expectancy.

President Nixon gave a conference speech in which he was very careful in his "promises."* He noted, "These proposals involve very difficult budgetary problems for the government." He promised to "*propose* to the Congress a new program to reform our private pension system . . . *recommend* new laws requiring the vesting of pensions . . ." (Italics mine.) Under HR 1, the President claimed, the Nixon welfare package would "provide some $5.5 billion in additional benefits to older Americans."

Nelson Cruikshank, president of the National Council of Senior Citizens, welcomed President Nixon's speech at the White House Conference on Aging as a "complete turn around in the administration's philosophical approach to the problems of the aged."† In the political arena, philosophical generalities should rarely be taken as promises of policy. He said, prematurely, that the President was now endorsing "categorical programs" for

---

* This conference may have been especially important to the President since many feel the elderly voters gave the presidency to the late John F. Kennedy in 1960 when Nixon did not support Medicare.

† Some thought that Cruikshank and the National Council (which is essentially union-related and closely tied to the Democratic party) were holding back at the time of the White House Conference to be ready for a confrontation later as the 1972 presidential campaign heated up.

the elderly. The President's later 1972 veto of the Older Americans Act amendments demonstrated how wishful that hope was.

The respected Dr. Arthur S. Flemming, chairman of the White House Conference on Aging, put himself on the line: "We will speak out in no uncertain terms when action does not keep pace with rhetoric." The politics and the realities of presidential vetoes since the conference have made Flemming's job a difficult one.

The conference's purpose of establishing a national priority for the old was not achieved. The conferees, hard-working and serious beyond question, simply did not develop the blueprint necessary to do what needs to be done. Their modest proposals, even if implemented, would only perpetuate the patchwork of token, piecemeal and ineffective income and service programs currently in operation.

The President, in his careful, nonspecific speech at the White House Conference on Aging, offered far, far less than the delegates recommended. Since the power of decision of course lies with the President and with Congress and not with the conferees, it had to be concluded that still less would be legislated than even the Chief Executive touched upon. Moreover, it was extremely difficult to maintain the momentum for change in the critical postconference period. Nineteen seventy-two presidential politics might have done this, but in fact issues concerning old age were not prominent. Despite their number and voting power the elderly had little impact upon the election, partly because of the wide margin of victory of the incumbent President.

The problem, however, is not a partisan one. Senator Church called for a broad coalition by members of both parties to improve the conditions of America's elderly. "I believe that the recent Democratic Administration— despite Medicare and the Older Americans Act—failed to go far enough and must share their part in the responsibility for today's inadequacies," he said. "This nation is ready to question and discard many sacred cows that have already lived too long. We have questioned a foolish, futile war. . . . Our treatment of the elderly certainly tells us . . . that if we are indifferent toward the latter years of life, we diminish the dreams of all our people."

GROWTH OF ORGANIZATIONS FOR OLDER PEOPLE

Life magazine in 1936 took note of the beginning activities of older persons on their own behalf:

As individuals, most old people are . . . pleasant and undemanding . . . but in today's frightened and uncertain world, the old folks of America have become fearful and insecure. Urged on by pension leaders like Dr. C. A. Ellis of Colorado, they have banded together to demand government pensions. In sheer numbers and singleness of purpose, they have become a great political force and a grave economic menace. . . . Dr. Townsend's plan, or California's $30-every-Thursday proposal, would bankrupt the nation just as Dr. Ellis' $45-a-month law is now bankrupting Colorado. This autumn, candidates in 18 states are paying lip service to the pension demands of the old. Already their pressure has forced the U.S. to set up the huge Social Security system which, however, is largely planned to take better care of the old of tomorrow than the old of today.

Many of the early political movements and organizations on behalf of the elderly developed in California. EPIC (End Poverty in California), Upton Sinclair's gubernatorial campaign program, contained an old-age pension plan. The Ham and Eggs movement to end poverty in old age flourished between about 1938 and 1950. George H. McLain's pension movement was established in 1941 and faded out following his death in 1965. The Townsend movement began in 1933, peaked in 1936, and was more or less out of business by 1948, with club membership declining 98 percent between 1936 and 1951. But at its height even conservative Maine elected Townsendites to Congress. The Townsend movement proposed pensions of $200 per month to everyone over sixty, financed through a 2 percent tax on the sale of goods.*

The *National Association of Retired Federal Employees* (NARFE) is a fifty-year-old nonprofit organization composed exclusively of former federal employees and their survivors, with national headquarters in Washington, D.C. Its primary purpose is to improve pension benefits. As of 1971 there were more than 153,000 members and over 1,100 chapters in all 50 states, Puerto Rico, the Philippines and the Canal Zone.

The two largest organizations for older persons are the *National Council of Senior Citizens* (3 million members) and the combined *American Association of Retired Persons and the National Retired Teachers Association* (about 4.5 million members). In the early years after the National Retired Teachers Association (NRTA) was organized in 1946, an organizational objective, as enunciated by its president, Ethel Percy Andrus, was the establishment of a nationwide health-insurance program to serve retired teachers. Dr. Andrus had been frustrated by unproductive contacts

---

* Nelson Cruikshank, of the National Council of Senior Citizens, commented: "The Townsend people back in the 1930s were wildly irresponsible. If they had had their way the United States would have been bankrupt inside of a year. I was afraid we might create a sort of gerontocracy that would plague the government for one handout after another."[13]

with forty insurance-company officials who indicated disinterest in providing group health insurance for retired teachers through a group health policy. She wanted a reasonably priced policy that would be noncancelable and would not require a physical examination. In 1955 Dr. Andrus's efforts bore fruit. An insurance broker in Poughkeepsie, New York, Leonard Davis, set up a group insurance program to serve the retired teachers in New York State through the Continental Casualty Insurance Company. Dr. Andrus and Mr. Davis received this insurer's approval to launch the program nationally, with hospital-insurance coverage, to all members of the National Retired Teachers Association.* Their efforts led to a variety of related programs. In 1958, when the American Association of Retired Persons (AARP) was also organized by Dr. Andrus similar services were extended to all members of that association.

AARP was created to open up membership to persons other than teachers in an organization similar to NRTA. AARP/NRTA share the same offices and staff but keep their separate identities. AARP members must be fifty-five years of age or over and need not be retired. The organization has also begun to develop a movement of the middle-aged under the name Aid for Independent Maturity, or AIM.† AARP has legislative representatives at the federal and state levels. AARP/NRTA has especially emphasized the state and local levels of politics and has issued state legislative guidelines.

By 1974 AARP/NRTA had over 7 million claimed members in over 2,500 local units. (Spouses are counted in AARP, not in NRTA, which has some 450,000 members.) More than 300 companies have been persuaded to donate memberships to retiring employees. Over 3,000 new members per day was the 1972 rate of growth. AARP/NRTA publishes two magazines, *Modern Maturity* and the *NRTA Journal*.

The *National Council of Senior Citizens* (NCSC) was first organized by some of the conferees attending the 1961 White House Conference on Aging. It developed, in part, through labor leader Walter Reuther's support of Medicare. The long-range goal of the NCSC, which was to be nonpartisan, was to represent "the views of older persons on major issues confronting the nation"; but in the past it was supported largely by labor and is still strongly Democratic. NCSC was first led by Amie J. Forand (D.-R.I.), who gave up his congressional seat in order to run NCSC effectively and to lead the fight for Medicare. Its second president, until 1969, was John Edelmen, long associated with the trade-union movement.

* AARP/NRTA was against Medicare when it was first proposed.
† The emergence of the American Indian Movement might lead to a change in name.

He was followed by Nelson Cruikshank. Its present executive director is William Hutton. Another early figure in NCSC was Zalman Lichtenstein, director of the Council of the Golden Ring, a colorful man remembered for his capacity to organize busloads of older people to appear at strategic places on behalf of the fight for Medicare.

By 1973 the NCSC had some 3 million members, mainly from the ranks of organized labor, in 3,500 affiliated clubs across the United States. Many of its members are poor, and anybody of any age can join. There are no mandatory dues, and it gains no financial benefits from its services, which include supplemental insurance for Medicare, low-cost travel and discount drugs. Nonetheless it has been increasingly more able to be self-sustaining through its growth in membership, and accepts less and less funding from the labor unions.

The NCSC publishes a monthly newspaper, the *Senior Citizen News*, which is both informative and highly political. One of the offshoots of NCSC is the Concerned Seniors for Better Government, begun in 1968. It was chaired by Matthew DeMore* and served to encourage Senior Citizens clubs to become active in presidential and congressional primary elections. In 1968 it was active in Senate election campaigns in eighteen states. It supplied information to retired citizens on the voting records of various candidates for national and state offices. Senior Citizen Club leaders were urged by the organization to seek delegate positions to their political-party conventions.

The union movement, so strong in NCSC, has grown reluctant about Social Security reforms, since it must also protect its younger workers from the increasing Social Security payroll taxes. A farsighted union approach would be to oppose increased payroll taxes in favor of the use of general revenues. The NCSC is beginning to move gingerly in that direction. The wariness has at its base the view that the trust funds do protect against congressional whim. There is also concern about older workers remaining in the labor force, as revealed in the NCSC's position against dropping the retirement means tests. The NCSC position states: "We recommend that the basic principles of the [means] test be retained, not eliminated" for "elimination would place unfair higher tax burdens on younger workers for the purpose of paying full retirement benefits to the comparative few who continue to work at full earnings."[14]

The NCSC advertises that it "seeks a better life for *all* Americans," and emphasizes the fact that it is "more than a special interest group for the elderly, having backed the test ban treaty, the Peace Corps, the war on

---

* DeMore is a vice president of the NCSC and a former general secretary-treasurer of the International Association of Machinists and Aerospace Workers.

poverty, clean air and clean water legislation, legal protection for the consumer, and similar measures of general concern."

NCSC's goals for the elderly are quite modest:

- Social Security benefits at a meaningful level
- Medicare improvements, low-cost modern housing for the elderly poor
- A nationwide senior-citizens service corps to employ seniors who want to work in socially useful employment not normally available to them
- Property-tax relief for elderly home owners with limited incomes
- Reduced fares for the elderly during nonrush periods on national and local transportation systems

Following the Nixon 1974 budget-cut announcement, the National Council reacted in horror. Cruikshank and Hutton began to speak out strongly against the administration's cutbacks. They helped mobilize mass meetings on the steps of state houses in cities such as Sacramento and Albany. In June, 1973, ten thousand persons marched to the National Capitol steps to protest.

Each of the national mass organizations for older people has its limitations. The National Council of Senior Citizens, as we have seen, is deeply enmeshed with the trade unions and Democratic party politics. There is a kind of schizophrenia in the NCSC. As an organization representing retirees, but linked to the union movement, it finds itself struggling to take into account the needs of younger workers. In a sense this is valuable, providing a kind of in-house laboratory for working out issues between the young and old. On the other hand, it means that neither of the two mass organizations, NCSC and AARP/NRTA, has the interests of older people as its exclusive goal.

The American Association of Retired Persons/National Retired Teachers Association must be questioned as to its fundamental allegiance to the cause of the elderly. Leonard Davis, the insurance broker who set up the insurance program for Dr. Andrus's NRTA, became a multimillionaire, according to the Washington *Post*,[15] through his investments in the insurance company Colonial Penn Group, Inc., of Philadelphia and New York, and in associated travel and employment enterprises. These have close relationships with the nonprofit AARP/NRTA. In its February, 1972, story the Washington *Post* asserted that Davis and his wife owned 28.6 percent of the common stock of Colonial Penn. This stock was worth $183.7 million on the over-the-counter market at the close of business February 11, 1972. The value of Davis's principal stockholding increased $60 million in 1971, and from the beginning of 1972 to the date of the *Post*'s account had risen $52.3 million more. The major portion of Colonial Penn's business was attributed to its relationship with the two older people's organizations, as stated by Colonial Penn in a prospectus filed with the Securities and Exchange Commission in November of 1971. Colonial Penn has access to the AARP/NRTA publications and the organizations' mailing lists. Competition is not allowed. Davis told the Washington *Post* that his position was "very fair" because the company "has gone out of its way, and invested fortunes of money, to develop new programs that were never available to these people."[16]

An added problem is the fact that both the NCSC and the AARP/ NRTA are tax-exempt organizations. Arthur Flemming has said, "Tax exempt organizations play according to the rules of the Internal Revenue Service, and non-tax groups play by the same rules as political parties."[17] Thus these organizations are not free to be openly political in their efforts on behalf of the old. Most observers regard the individual members of the NCSC and AARP/NRTA as informally linked to the Democratic and Republican parties respectively. They do not jeopardize their tax-free status with the Internal Revenue Service by endorsing candidates or officially campaigning for them.

An added limitation in the mass organizations is that women and minority groups are not proportionately represented in the leadership of either the NCSC* or the AARP/NRTA. Women make up 20 percent of union membership but have little participation in union leadership.

The mass organizations should be more than service organizations† or legislative lobbyists. They have to become action oriented. In some respects they have begun to do this. With the advent of revenue sharing, organizations concerned with the aging wanted to be certain that money be allocated for the aging on a local and state level. Bernard Nash, executive director of the National Retired Teachers Association and of the American Association of Retired Persons, sponsored a National Forum of State Legislators on Older Americans in December, 1972. The importance of revenue sharing was emphasized during this novel effort to inform state legislators about the problems of aging. Each state had four representatives, two Republicans and two Democrats, most of whom were selected because they had no previous familiarity with aging.

---

* Of the fifty members of the NCSC board about 8 percent are women.

† Providing low-cost travel, drugs, health-insurance supplements to Medicare, etc. The AARP/NRTA pledged $2 million to the University of Southern California for the construction of the Ethel Percy Andrus Gerontology Center. This research institution, under the directorship of Dr. James E. Birren, was dedicated in 1973.

The *National Council on the Aging* (NCOA) is an organization made up of other organizations involved with aging, and some individual memberships. With the help of the Ford Foundation the National Council was founded as a private, nonprofit, tax-exempt corporation. It grew out of the National Assembly of Social Welfare. As an organization of organizations, NCOA has always played a kind of convener role. Its functions include providing technical assistance, publications and training materials for public and private agencies in the field of aging at national, regional, state and local levels. It has been concerned with employment and retirement, housing, health, protective services, institutional care, community organization, community services, senior centers, education, leisure and public policy. NCOA's membership includes about 1,400 organizational facilities, mostly public and private health, social-work and community-action agencies. Industry and organized labor are also involved.

It began as a modest operation, with a staff of one volunteer in 1950. By 1972 NCOA had 106 employees, ten regional offices and a budget close to $3.5 million. Its progress was largely attributable to the dedicated work of people well known in the field of aging, such as Ollie Randall, Geneva Mathiasen, Edwin Shelley and Juanita Kreps. In 1973 Jack Ossofsky, NCOA's director, identified the serious problem that 97 percent of NCOA's budget comes from projects performed under contract for the federal government. Other sources of income are essential in order to reduce the dependency of NCOA on federal government funds and influence. Indeed, because of its ties to the government, by 1973 it was necessary for NCOA to cut its staff by one-third. To survive, it chose, perhaps wrongly, to reduce its field staff in order to maintain its central Washington headquarters.

The professional societies which are concerned with the elderly include the *Gerontological Society* (founded in 1945) with some 2,800 members and the *American Geriatrics Society* (founded in 1942) with some 18,000 members. Neither has much political impact except indirectly. The Gerontological Society has an active public-policy committee to contribute professional knowledge to the legislative process. Professional and scientific organizations can and probably should form political-action components or give up their tax-free status and fight for their objectives by paying their own way.

One group which has captured the fancy of the press and public is the *"Gray Panthers."*

We did not select our name; the name selected us. It describes who we are: 1) We are older persons in retirement; 2) we are aware of the revolutionary nature of our time; 3) although we differ with the strategy and tactics of some militant groups in our society we share with them many of the goals of human freedom, dignity and self development; and 4) we have a sense of humor.

Our purpose is to celebrate the bonus years of retirement as a time for new contributions to the new age of liberation and self determination. As older persons we will unite with others to use our time, experience, skills and other resources for social initiative, for freedom, justice and peace for all persons everywhere.

The Gray Panthers' official name is Consultation of Older and Younger Adults. They hope to "radicalize a growing number of the elderly." This group of perhaps six thousand or more people of all ages was started in 1970 by sixty-seven-year-old Margaret (Maggie) E. Kuhn, a retired Presbyterian Church worker. She disdains the activities of golden-age clubs as "playpens for the old" and declares, "We are not mellow, sweet old people. We have got to effect change and we have nothing to lose."[18]

The *Retired Professional Action Group* (PRAG) was established by Ralph Nader to "provide older people opportunities to help solve society's problems," including those of old age. By 1973, some seven hundred people from all over the United States were participating. Its purpose was not to establish a national organization with local affiliates "but to promote a mechanism . . . for action. . . ." PRAG was funded by Public Citizens, Inc., an organization also formed by Nader. PRAG has been associated with the Gray Panthers and by 1973 they were producing a joint newsletter.

The newest of the organizations for the aging active in national politics is the *National Caucus on the Black Aged* (NCBA), which evolved in 1970 in anticipation of the 1971 White House Conference on Aging. Most of its membership is black. Its chairman and secretary, Hobart Jackson and Jacqueline Johnson Jackson respectively, have devoted enormous amounts of energy and voluntary time to the cause. NCBA was formed because the largely white organizations for the aged were not giving significant attention to the problems of blacks and other minority aged. Even in existing black organizations, only the National Urban League took much note of the plight of the elderly blacks.[19] In 1974 a National Center on Black Aged was established by NCBA. It offers technical assistance and consultative services in programs for older black Americans.

The *International Senior Citizens Association* (ISCA) was founded in 1963 in Copenhagen, Denmark, and now has headquarters in Los Angeles, California.* It is nonpolitical, nonprofit and noncommercial. Its president,

---

* The problems of the elderly are, of course, international. The United Nations is studying the problems of old age on a world-wide basis. Senator Church has proposed a World Assembly on Aging for 1975.

Mrs. Marjorie Borchardt, says, "We emphasize noncommercial because commercialism corrupts the development of a subculture of age." The purpose is to

provide coordination on an international level, safeguard the interests and needs of senior citizens of the world, establish means of friendly communication between older persons throughout the world for educational and cultural purposes, and enhance the prestige of older persons in world affairs through the utilization of their wisdom and experience.

Likely to prove more effective than ISCA is the *International Federation on Aging,* formed in 1973. Headquarters for the federation is the Washington, D.C., home of AARP/NRTA. IFA members include Age Concern, London; Panhellenic Federation of Civil Service Pensioners, Athens; AARP/NRTA; Federation of Bank Employee Pensioners, Athens; Center for Liaison, Study, Information and Research on Problems of the Elderly, Paris; National Federation of Associations of the Elderly, Paris; National Interfederal Union of Private Health and Social Organizations, Paris; Australian Council on Aging, Melbourne; Elderly and Pensioners Association of the Catholic Employees Movement, Cologne; Pensioners United, Copenhagen; and The Third Age, Brussels.

In order to combine the strength of all these organizations I would recommend the formation of a council of the national organizations for the elderly and retired similar to the Council of National Organizations for Children and Youth. The council should include any group with a legitimate and *tested* concern for older people and encourage the interest of those who may not yet have come to recognize the validity of the needs of older people. Thus, for example, the poverty of retired household workers and the poverty of the rural elderly would mean that the National Household Workers Union, the United Farm Workers Union and the National Farmers Organization should be involved.

Among the organizations for the elderly, only the National Caucus on the Black Aged, the National Association of Retired Federal Employees and the National Council on the Aging have focused almost exclusively on the problems of the elderly. They do not have a hidden agenda representing other interests. The larger mass organizations (NCSC and AARP/NRTA) suffer from a variety of pulls that affect their independence, primarily because of union and business interests. As we have noted earlier, to be more effective, organizations for the elderly should avoid tax-deductible status and thus free themselves for partisan political work. They should be financially independent—much more work could be done for much less money. Government and private grants are no less a problem than business or union involvement in limiting freedom of movement for an organization. Finally, leadership should derive more directly from the ranks of the elderly themselves.

AN AGENDA FOR ACTIVISM

Older people are already showing signs of increasing activism, even occasional militancy. But much more could be done.

The following agenda for activism is a summary of the many activities which older people should conduct under their own leadership:

Agenda For Activism

Basic Activities
Consciousness raising: age awareness and acknowledgment
Conscience raising
Political education and organizing

*Political Activity**
1. Voting as a bloc on issues of concern to the elderly
2. Running for office; running own candidate
3. Becoming delegates to political party conventions
4. Political campaign work for local, state and federal officials and legislators who support the elderly's interests. Raising money. Telephoning. Transportation on election day. Registering nursing-home and old-age-home residents as absentee voters.
5. Lobbying
6. Petition drives
7. Demanding, attending and participating in public hearings. Giving written and oral testimony.
8. Political education of the older population
9. Visiting elective and appointive officials to present grievances
10. Forming coalitions with other organizations sharing common interests
11. Training older persons in political and social advocacy†

---

* The National Council of Senior Citizens published *A Handbook of Grassroots Politics* and a *Voting Record of Congressmen* for the first time in 1974.
† Advocacy is being taught to older people in some locations.[20]

Community Activity

1. Membership by the elderly on boards of trustees, advisory
   councils, committees on all levels of community activity:
   for example, public housing, Model Cities commissions,
   nursing and old-age homes, hospitals, voluntary agencies,
   health and welfare councils, community mental health
   centers, zoning agencies, company pension boards,
   pharmacies, city and state committees and commissions,
   federal councils such as the Health Insurance Benefits
   Advisory Council (HIBAC), educational institutions
2. Controls over providers of services through licensing and
   other forms of accountability
3. Involvement in police-community relations
4. Pressure for general revenue-sharing monies
5. Full utilization of Internal Revenue Service offices
   for help with income taxes

Legal Activity

1. Class-action lawsuits against organizations and institutions which
   discriminate against or do not properly serve the elderly* (a
   1974 Supreme Court decision [*Eisen* v. *Carlisle & Jacquelin*] sets
   up requirements that will restrict such suits considerably):
   a. Hospitals and other medical facilities (the right-
      to-treatment suits)
   b. Educational institutions
   c. Employment and personnel departments and agencies
      (age discrimination in employment and right-to-work suits)
   d. Nursing homes, old-age homes and other homes for the aging
   e. Organizations providing legal services (issues of
      legal representation, guardianship, conservatorship)
   f. Transportation facilities, housing, architectural barriers, etc.
   g. Air and water pollution
   h. Zoning regulations
   i. Boards of philanthropic institutions
   j. Enforcement of existent Freedom of Information Act[22]
      to obtain information related to legal suits

---

* An example of what can be done in the way of class-action cases is the instance
in which a retired Federal Aviation Administration administrator brought class
action on behalf of 1.5 million persons enrolled in Blue Cross and Blue Shield
against Washington banks in 1970. Premium funds were being deposited in non-
interest-bearing accounts, resulting in money lost to federal employees.[21] The practice
was stopped.

2. Individual lawsuits:
   a. Small claims and tax suits*
   b. Malpractice suits
   c. Fraud suits

Registration Drives

Registering all those elderly eligible for:
   a. National Supplemental Security Income for the Aged, Blind and Disabled
   b. Medicaid
   c. Food stamps, meals on wheels, group dining, food commodities
   d. Public housing
   e. Employment programs
   f. Recreation and leisure activities, e.g., specially priced tickets, special use of community facilities
   g. Transportation benefits (reduced fares)
   h. Free (mobile) health testing

Grievance Activity

1. Using grievance procedures of Social Security, welfare departments and local medical societies
2. Presenting grievances to medical, social-work, nursing and other professional schools which fail to teach courses relevant to the older population; calling for teaching positions in geriatrics
3. Harassing local Environmental Protection Agencies for failure to maintain quality of air, so deadly to the elderly with respiratory diseases such as emphysema
4. Pressing physicians to prescribe drugs by generic (scientific) rather than more expensive brand name

Collective Activity

1. Organizing societies and associations to meet and represent the unmet needs of the elderly; revamping and renaming Golden Age Clubs
2. Membership drives, participation and taking leadership in already existing organizations for the elderly, and in organizations with many elderly members, such as veterans' groups†

* The small tax case division of the U.S. Tax Court was created by Congress in 1968 to let the individual taxpayer whose claim involves $1,500 or less in taxes have his day in court for a $10 fee. The jurist has a lifetime appointment and no ties to the Internal Revenue Service.

† There are, for example, 70,000 Florida members of the Veterans of World War I.

3. Marches, sit-ins and demonstrations by and on behalf of the elderly where a dramatic appeal to the public is indicated. Focusing on evicted old people, nursing-home residents. Passive resistance. Politics of confrontation.

For example:

   a. Mass loading of buses and subways to show need for reduced fares
   b. Mass visits to facilities serving the elderly, such as nursing homes,* hospital emergency rooms
   c. Mass public meetings and marches in streets and parks to emphasize need for recreation and freedom from crime
   d. Mass visits to elective and appointive officials to present grievances
   e. Squatting in abandoned buildings to dramatize housing shortages
   f. Monitoring courts (e.g., tenant-landlord) in cases involving older people

Resistance Activity

1. Mass resistance to paying regressive property taxes
2. Appealing the assessments for property taxes
3. Voting against bond issues
4. Consumer boycotts at stores—selective food (e.g., meat) boycotts regarding pricing, quality, packaging and variety
5. Rent strikes
6. Use of squatters' rights
7. Declaring bankruptcy
8. Refusal to let banks deduct property taxes with mortgage payments
9. Refusal to leave jobs on compulsory retirement; sit-ins on jobs
10. Wheelchair sit-ins as indicated

Protective Activity

1. Organizing escort services for the elderly in high-crime areas
2. Actively exploring and fighting fraud against the elderly (bogus dance lessons, hearing aids, insurance, work-at-home schemes)
3. Consumer education of the elderly

---

* There is a new statewide organization called Friends and Relatives of Nursing Home Patients, Inc., founded in Oregon in 1972. Detroit, Michigan, has a somewhat similar activistic organization called Citizens for Better Care.

4. Teaching the elderly how best to protect themselves from crime on the streets and in their homes

Surveillance Activity
1. Citizen surveillance of nursing homes and other facilities (announced and unannounced individual, group and mass visits, reviewing financial records, visiting with residents and relatives). Construction of a checklist.
2. Surveillance of inspections records (especially in Social Security offices) for institutional standards and enforcements. Studying incident reports in institutions for evidence of patient abuse.
3. Monitoring public and private pension funds; how invested?
4. Attending advisory committees on local, state and federal level
5. Enforcement of American Hospital Association's twelve-point "Patient's Bill of Rights"
6. Use of the Freedom of Information Acts (federal and in some states) to obtain information about governmental functions of all types

Cooperative Activity
1. Organizing food, drug, insurance, travel and other volume-purchasing cooperatives
2. Communes and housing cooperatives
3. Low-cost repair services utilizing the skills of retired persons
4. Organizing employment services especially for the elderly
5. Credit loans
6. Craft shops
7. Comparative shopping
8. Blood collection
9. Memorial societies (versus expensive funerals)
10. Common gardens, windowbox gardens and urban green-houses on roofs
11. Purchase of legal advice on trusts, wills, probate, etc. One mechanism is prepaid legal services.
12. Mutual assistance agreements within apartment buildings and neighborhoods

Communications and Education
1. Campaigns to obtain regular TV, radio and newspaper time and space devoted to the interests of the elderly (e.g., national and locally syndicated columns on the

elderly, educational programs, more representation of
the elderly as actors, actresses, news commentators,
etc., a more positive presentation of old age)

2. Suits against the Federal Communications Commission
to obtain appropriate programming
3. Use of radio and TV talk shows to air problems, concerns
and also the positive aspects of old age (Elderly can call
in to talk shows which have audience participation.)
4. Writing letters to the editors of newspapers and magazines
5. Demanding a "Hyde Park Corner" on radio and television
where the elderly (and others) can speak their minds
6. Use of cable TV to educate, entertain, inform and
involve the elderly, especially shut-ins in homes and
institutions; "Colleges of the Air"
7. Obtaining a communications ombudsman locally and nationally
to guard the interests of the elderly; demand time for
counter editorials on radio and television
8. Establishing speakers' bureaus, to focus on the problems
of older people
9. Pressing public schools, colleges and universities to
open doors to middle-aged or older students; establishing
special colleges utilizing skills of older people, with
student bodies of all ages
10. News releases
11. Publication and dissemination of public-interest documents:
e.g., nursing home surveys, government publications with
useful information for the elderly
12. Setting up clearinghouses for information and referral systems

Whistle Blowing

The French writer Montaigne said, "I speak truth, not so much as I
would, but as much as I dare; and I dare more as I grow older." When one
is on the verge of retirement, strange new stirrings of independence and
public-spiritedness have been known to appear. Freed from the necessity of
having to keep one's job, the newly retiring person may find himself or
herself liberated from old prudent feelings of "don't make waves," "don't
rock the boat," "be careful what you say," "tread softly," "don't go over-
board," "follow the rules," "it's always been that way," "things won't
change." One of the activist techniques older people can use is that of
"whistle blowing." As they are retiring they may decide to "tell all" about

their jobs or their employer—telling it to the public, the press, legislators, congressional investigators or any other persons or organizations which can use such information in the public interest. To minimize the risk, Ralph Nader has set up a permanent clearinghouse for whistle blowers, which serves to "provide information to inquiring professionals and . . . receive in confidence information considered in the public interest."

There are many examples of individual older activists:

> Miss Vivien Kellems, a Connecticut manufacturer, was 78 when she died in January, 1975. To the very end she continued to fight for fair tax treatment for single individuals. This is not, strictly speaking, part of the politics of the aging. Yet many of the elderly are single. There is extensive research that shows that some 30 million single women and men, whether unmarried, divorced or widowed were "being flagrantly discriminated against" by the income-tax code.
>
> "There is absolutely nothing in the Constitution that says that you can tax a single person more than a married person. If you can tax me more because I am single, then you can tax me more because my eyes are gray or because I am 75 years old," Miss Kellems said in 1971. Her previous lobbying paid off somewhat when Congress passed the 1969 Tax Reform Act which reduced the average difference between married and single rates from 43 percent to 20 percent.

> January, 1972, found Jeannette Rankin of Missoula, Montana, 91, lifelong pacifist and activist, still struggling for her causes. She was the first woman to win membership in the U.S. House of Representatives. She was now living in a house with a dirt floor in her living room. She had been donating her money to the peace movement. She demonstrated what Emerson said of Thoreau, that he had made himself rich by making his wants few. In 1968 at 87 she had led the Jeannette Rankin brigade of 5,000 women to Washington to protest the Vietnam war. A year before she died, she was quoted (*New York Times*, January, 1972) as saying that if she had her life to relive, "I'd be nastier."

> Eighty-six years old in 1972, Josephine Roche played a major role in the labor movement, working for the United Mine Workers with John L. Lewis. She was fighting against the 1972 re-election of W. A. (Tony) Boyle. She particularly tried to reach the 292 locals of the United Mine Workers which were composed largely of 70,000 retired pensioners who were afraid to vote against Boyle.

It is possible that the elderly will not only begin to fight more openly for their own interests but will begin to join forces with other groups. Natural alliances with other age groups, particularly the late-middle-aged (55 to 65 years of age)* and with youth might occur. It would be useful to build appropriate bridges with groups that could represent their interests, such as the National Tenants Organization, the National Welfare Rights Organization, or the new National Coordination Movement for Economic Justice that Dr. George Wiley endeavored to form. They might secure the interest of the various elements of the Women's Liberation movement, which should be more concerned than it has been about the impoverishment and loneliness of nearly six million elderly widows. It is time for widows themselves to unite and to shape new life styles.

TOWARD A NATIONAL POLICY ON AGING

The 1960s and '70s saw a crisis of awareness in the United States, increasing the recognition of the inequities based upon race, sex, class and, to a lesser extent, age. Nineteen seventy-six marks the two hundredth anniversary of the United States. It also marks another campaign for the presidency. Thus 1976 is an appropriate occasion to press once again the needs of the elderly.

I would like to see a citizens' committee of inquiry—with open-ended membership—that would convene a special conference on the elderly in Washington, D.C., in June of 1976 for: (1) a post-mortem audit of the administrations' and the Congress's implementation of the 1971 White House Conference on Aging recommendations; (2) a revision of those recommendations toward the fundamental resolution of the problems of old age; (3) a review of the 1976 and 1977 federal fiscal budgets to obtain a picture of the incumbent Republican administration's commitment to the old; and (4) the presentation of programs on behalf of the elderly by all 1976 presidential aspirants of all parties.

I have briefly summarized here the major, immediate goals to be included in a national policy on aging:

GOAL 1. REORDERING OF PRIORITIES

At the risk of emphasizing the obvious, it remains necessary to state the importance of reordering national priorities toward human needs, including appropriate provision for all high-risk groups—children, the disabled, the

* The late-middle-aged comprise 18 million Americans. If they joined the 20 million over 65, a formidable force could result.

sick and the elderly. In a more dramatic way, Senator Church has said, "We could abolish poverty among the elderly for what it cost to run the war in Southeast Asia for just three months."[23]

GOAL 2. CREATION OF A WHITE HOUSE OFFICE ON AGING

To represent the case of the elderly and to build and implement a national policy on aging effectively, a White House Office on Aging is required. Governmental programs for the old are too diffuse and too low in priority to gain access to the President and his staff. The President's Task Force on Aging in 1970 and the Senate Advisory Committee of 1971 both called for such an office. Senator Church introduced an Action Office on Aging Act in 1973 which would have established a White House–level office, directed by a Presidential Assistant on Aging. An alternative is a Secretary of Aging heading a separate cabinet department. The post of Assistant Secretary of Aging should be established in the Cabinet departments having concern with human resources, such as HEW, HUD, DOT and Labor.* In addition, there should be cooperation between the new Committee on Aging in the House and its Senate counterpart.

At the state level, governmental bodies created to deal with the elderly (commissions, advisory committees, and the like) should be given authority similar to that of the federal Administration on Aging. Creation of offices of Secretary of Aging in state government cabinets would keep the needs of the elderly before the governors.

GOAL 3. ELIMINATION OF MALNUTRITION AND POVERTY AMONG THE ELDERLY

In order for older Americans to live somewhere near the average American standard of living, poverty must be redefined in realistic terms, more nearly like the deprivation index proposed by economist Leon Keyserling. (See Chapter 2.) The federal floor on income for the elderly[24] should be elevated to that of the highest of the budgets for elderly couples, prepared by the Bureau of Labor Statistics.

Financing of Social Security through the payroll plan now falls most heavily upon the low-income groups. This may soon incur a counterreaction of workers against the elderly, which ultimately means against their future selves. Payroll taxes are the fastest-growing taxes, contributing 4 percent of the revenue dollar in 1949 but 23 percent in 1971. Instead,

---

* The American Academy of Pediatrics (AAP) has called for an HEW deputy assistant secretary for children and youth. Thus the idea of different age groups having their special advocates is not confined to the elderly.

a compulsory national Social Security system financed through general revenues, utilizing a graduated income tax, could become one component of a three-part retirement system which would also include private pension plans and voluntary pension plans. Such a national Social Security system should have two built-in escalators—one related to the cost of living, which now exists; and the second tied to the general economic productivity.

There should be a supplementary, voluntary, national Personal Security System that is individually financed but subject to federal standards and protection of its investments. This would be similar to the present self-employed individuals' retirement plan under the Keogh Act and the "Individual Retirement Accounts" (IRAs) created by the 1974 Pension Reform Act.

The 1974 private pension reform law should be vastly improved. Thus both collective and individual providence could characterize income provision in old age.

Blacks and other minority groups have higher mortality rates and therefore often do not live long enough to receive Social Security benefits. Computational arrangements must be made so that these groups can be assured of Social Security benefits in accordance with their life expectancies and greater degrees of disability.

GOAL 4. PROVISION OF CHOICE IN HOUSING

Six million older Americans need better shelter, and varieties of living arrangements should be created to provide options for them. Such choices should be facilitated by adequate income maintenance and, as necessary, through the interim steps of housing vouchers or allowances.

Property taxes need to be drastically reduced to make home ownership possible. Federally collected general revenue funds rather than local property taxes would better enable states to support quality education. (President Nixon called for federal relief for elderly home owners at the 1971 White House Conference and during his 1972 campaign.)

Zoning laws on the local level need revision in accordance with human needs.

There should be a refund of that part of rent payments which is allotted to property taxes, to provide relief for elderly renters.

GOAL 5. THE RIGHT TO WORK

Arbitrary retirement and age discrimination in public and private employment at all ages must be ended. The Social Security penalty that forces older persons to lie about their income and discourages them from working must be eliminated. A public policy of full employment with the government as the employer of first resort rather than last resort is necessary for the old.

GOAL 6. THE RIGHT TO SOCIAL ROLES

A wide range of roles of substance and purpose should be available for those elderly who choose to retire. Part of this could be accomplished through a National Senior Service Corps, encompassing Foster Grandparent and other programs, and a national service program that matches skills and needs for persons of all ages.

Greater flexibility could be encouraged through reallocating work, education and leisure throughout the life cycle so that people of all ages have more choices.

GOAL 7. PROVISION OF CONTINUING AND LIFE CYCLE EDUCATION

Public and private schools and universities should extend their responsibility beyond youth to provide both continuing education and education concerning the nature of the life cycle. Provision could be made for periodical sabbaticals for all workers, with opportunities to advance and to switch jobs and careers and thus reduce unnecessary human obsolescence.

There are two aspects of lifetime education: continuing education throughout life to maintain and/or build new skills and to support flexible choice, and education that is tailored to fit the changing characteristics of the life cycle. Such life-cycle education would deal with childhood, courtship and marriage, career, leisure, grief, death—all the major occasions and processes of life.

GOAL 8. FREEDOM OF MOBILITY

There should be a balanced mass-transit system. Transportation systems must be redesigned to fit the needs of the elderly, ill, handicapped, pregnant women, and children, with elimination of architectural barriers. These systems must be public utilities with control of fares.

GOAL 9. PROTECTION FROM CRIME

Protection from crime is essential. Old people are disproportionately vulnerable to violent crime, such as robbery and assault; to fraud, shady land deals, quick remedies and other schemes. Old people should learn protective skills. In addition, protective services, public guardianship, legal assistance as well as police protection and service should be available. There should also be specific emergency funds to help crime victims meet their daily needs when these have been jeopardized.

GOAL 10. SUPPLY OF COMPREHENSIVE SERVICES

Old people do not have time to wait. Appropriate services must be made rapidly available to help them remain in their own homes when they wish to do so, through expansion of such manpower services as case aides, homemakers and home health aides, and visiting nurses. A National Personal Care Corps would overcome jurisdictional disputes among the different vocations and help provide comprehensive care. A fully established national nutrition program should include meals on wheels for the homebound, as well as group dining. While every effort should be made to help maintain older people in the community, if institutionalization becomes necessary it must be skillfully arranged, beginning with a careful transition from home.

Services *must* be categorical at first, targeted directly to the needs of the elderly group until such time as older people are no longer placed at the bottom of the barrel in the allocation of personnel and monies. Services should be available without humiliating means tests and special stigmatizing arrangements. Ideally they should be offered in the form of noncommercial social utilities. Financing of services could come through a national human-services plan, of which national health care would be one major component.

GOAL 11. CREATION OF DECENT HEALTH AND SOCIAL CARE

Structural reform of the health-delivery system is required as well as changes in its financing. A comprehensive social-care program in the nation would include health, social and other services. Particular attention must be given to chronic illness. Geriatric medicine must be developed within medical schools, and special training in the field of aging should be given to allied health professionals, social workers, nurses. Pending adoption of a major reform in the structure and financing of national health care, revision in Medicare is mandatory. Deductibles, co-payments and other features that *deduct* from the care of the patient need to be eliminated. Outpatient medications should be provided for, home health services must be expanded. Prevention of illness must become a major focus.

GOAL 12. SUPPORT OF SOCIAL UTILITIES IN PLACE OF COMMERCIAL NURSING HOMES

The nursing-home industry is already a subsidized rather than a free-enterprise industry. Monies provided by the federal government in such subsidization, in both construction and patient care, should be diverted to nonprofit organizations which would establish care programs that emphasize home care and outpatient care as well as institutional care. Nonprofit social utilities should be created that would control profits and maintain standards.

GOAL 13. THE RIGHT TO MENTAL-HEALTH CARE

The mental-health specialties, including psychiatry, must assume their responsibilities in research and the provision of service for the emotional and mental disorders of late life. Community mental-health centers, hospitals and other facilities must provide a network of quality programs for the diagnosis, treatment and care of both acute and long-term emotionally and mentally ill patients. Medicare revision and ultimately a national social and health-care program should finance such services. Class-action legal cases must be undertaken to reinforce the right to treatment of emotional problems and mental illnesses. If the psychiatric, social-work, psychological and other mental-health professions do not appropriately meet the mental-health needs of the elderly, a new profession should be supported. In order to set national policy with respect to the mental-health care of the elderly, a Commission on Mental Illness of the Elderly should be established by Congress. The National Institute of Mental Health should have a center on aging and a network of training, research and other programs throughout the nation.

GOAL 14. BASIC AND APPLIED RESEARCH

A National Institute on Aging has been established to plan and coordinate studies in the biomedical, social and the behavioral aspects of the aging process and to conduct and support education and training in both research and service in the field of aging. HEW has been dragging its feet in getting the Institute started and "moving." Studies should be as concerned with the quality of life as with the extension of it.

There are three major focuses in the politics of building an appropriate and dignified old age for Americans: first, a positive change in cultural sensibility toward the needs of the old; second, the allocation of national resources in this direction; and third, the creation of effective political representation and activist outlets for the old and their supporters.

Chapter 12

THE GIFT OF LIFE

Vanity is to wish a long life and take but little pains about a good life.

THOMAS À KEMPIS,
Imitation of Christ

Wish not so much to live long as to live well.

BENJAMIN FRANKLIN,
Poor Richard's Almanac

By the year 2000—the magic year that commentators and planners so often refer to—there will be some 33 million retired persons. Actually, between now and that year some 65 million Americans will attain the age of 65, not all of them, of course, surviving to the year 2000. Should our nation maintain zero population growth, some 15 percent of the population will be 65 and above.* If heart disease, cancer and some of the other major killers are conquered, these figures will be much larger.†

Major social changes are taking place, reflecting the impact of enhanced survival.[1] But they are occurring slowly, tentatively and in piecemeal fashion. We are ill prepared for the increased survival of large numbers of older people. We have been unable to provide adequately even for the elderly alive today.‡ To extend the quantity of life but not its quality is a macabre joke. It is not enough to have more and more people simply surviving; they have to be a vigorous, involved, contributory, self-respecting group of people who are still a vital part of their society.

---

* With zero population growth the median age of the population would rise from 27.7 years to 37.2 years by the year 2000.

† It has been said that eliminating cancer would add about 2.3 years to the life expectancy at birth in the United States; and eliminating cardiovascular-renal diseases would add 10.9 years.

‡ Doom sayers who ponder the impact of increasing numbers of people include Professor J. W. Forrester at the Massachusetts Institute of Technology with his world modeling system. In his computer work he considers five major world factors: population, pollution, resources, food supply and industrial output, and he predicts doom will descend by A.D. 2100.[2]

If in the past scientists have been reluctant to spend their careers in the field of growth and aging because of insufficient theoretical and technical knowledge, today some scientists may be equally reluctant because of the awesome social consequences of major breakthroughs in aging. Given significant research developments in biochemistry, in molecular biology and in genetics, the possibilities of understanding such diverse phenomena as "wild" growth (cancer) and aging have been enhanced. But how can we handle the enormous impact and the long-term consequences of such accomplishments?

One alternative would be to adopt an antiscientific attitude right now—to call off all medical and gerontological research, to regulate death and birth rates in order to restrain population growth. This radical view has been proposed to buy the time we need to deal with the many other factors that now contribute to the worsening quality of life around us, our sulfurized cities, contaminated waters and depleted energy. Some, like the retired chairman of the Atomic Energy Commission, Glenn Seaborg, hold that "knowledge is born without moral properties." But others, including Professor Jerome Wiesner of the Massachusetts Institute of Technology, believe that the scientist is responsible for the knowledge he gains because he decides what kind of knowledge to seek. Perhaps governments, consciously or unconsciously, do not provide generous support for medical and gerontological investigations for fear that success will create burdensome numbers of older persons.

Actually, in the Western nations where the risk of infectious disease has become negligible, we have begun to see mortality rates reach an irreducible minimum.* Only major medical breakthroughs could reduce it further in any significant way. Mankind has progressively eliminated the causes of premature death but has done little as yet to add to basic longevity. Thus the greatest result of medical advances has been to allow many more people to reach old age rather than to extend old age itself. We are seeing more physically "younger" older persons, while at the same time we are also accumulating a greater number of severely sick and disabled elderly. It is here that an appropriate research aim should be focused—not simply on the extension of life but on the creation of a healthy, vigorous, self-productive old age, with a much briefer and shorter period of disability prior to death. This would help reduce the present crushing burden on the middle-aged to support and care for the sick elderly.

In this chapter I shall discuss public policy in relation to increased survival, along with the improvement of the quality of survival itself

* Seventy percent of all deaths in the United States occurred after 65 in 1970, compared to 15 percent in 1900.

through a broadened conception of preventive medicine. I shall also consider the point in time when life is no longer a gift, when it is a burden to oneself and to others, when it is time to consider the right to die.

PUBLIC POLICY ON THE GIFT OF LIFE

What kinds of public-policy proposals need to be considered as part of an appropriate national response to the challenge of increased survival?

First we need to know how major breakthroughs in medical science and technology will affect our lives. An orderly, scientific investigation into the consequences on human living has yet to be undertaken. To meet the need, a flexible pool of federal and foundation research funds should be established and tailored to specific medical development. For example, perhaps 5 percent of the medical research grant for heart transplants, or for tracking down an aging deterrent, should be removed from the research itself and set aside for the study of probable demographic, ecological, economic and personal results of the particular development. An additional percentage (perhaps also 5 percent) should be set aside for educating the public about the development and its consequences.

In this manner a social form of preventive medicine may be brought to bear on many potentially disruptive changes. It will be more economical and humane to plan for the consequences of change than to have to make a tardy diagnosis and offer emergency treatment in a crisis atmosphere. We must make major commitments to the social and behavioral sciences if we are to react appropriately to the effects of major medical and health progress on the social and economic aspects of the life cycle. At present only 3 percent of the funds spent for science in America is devoted to these human sciences.

Second, comprehensive multidisciplinary research on the process of aging ought to be fostered through the National Institute on Aging, and regional institutions. Such research should aim toward the enhancement of late life and not just its extension.

Third, as will be developed in Chapter 13, education, work and leisure ought to be distributed throughout the life span rather than concentrated at the three distinct periods of childhood, middle life and later life. If through inadequacies of education we fail to make people productive, thus isolating specific groups (for example, racial minorities), or if we automatically retire older people and make them unproductive, we make them parasitical, they feel parasitical, and they are seen as parasitical. Clearly such social policies are abhorrent.

We must deal with the fact that the steadily increasing numbers of older people must be financially supported, but not solely through increasing the responsibilities of the middle-aged. A variety of approaches are necessary as we move toward a service society where we must reorder our conception of work, widening it to include the provision of all kinds of human services. Medical and scientific discoveries as well as the improved delivery of health care will help to ensure an extended middle age and therefore produce a healthier and more vigorous body of older people who can work as well as take better care of themselves. The expansion of work opportunities for older people will become mandatory.

Fourth, we should be building a new kind of education, one that will prepare people for survival and leisure. To be able to live alone, to experience human solidarity beyond the family, to learn to live fully and joyfully and not lose the free play of imagination—these should be considered critically important educational goals. W. E. B. Du Bois, the black writer and leader, reflected on his life at age seventy-three:

> I am especially glad of the divine gift of laughter; it has made the world human and lovable, despite all its pain and wrong. I am glad that the partial Puritanism of my upbringing has never made me afraid of life. I have lived completely, testing every normal appetite, feasting on sunset, sea and hill, and enjoying wine, women and song. . . . Perhaps above all I am proud of a straightforward clearness of reason, in part a gift of the gods, but also to no little degree due to scientific training and inner discipline. By means of this I have met life face to face. I have loved a fight and I have realized that Love is God and Work is his prophet; that his ministers are Age and Death.[3]

Enrichment of life and self-education should be stressed. Students of all ages should not only be "taught" but should be encouraged to extract from within themselves what they have already learned from life.

Fifth, it is not enough to give consideration only to a person's direct participation in the present. We need a sense of national commitment to the future. Values change in the course of life, and subjective interest in the future becomes most pronounced in later life. How much do we guide public policy on the basis of this concern? There is no major government agency for the long-range, coordinated planning that would demonstrate our commitment to future generations. We operate on annual budgets and tend not to project beyond the year 2000. Yet the pollution of the environment, the poor utilization of our resources are symbols of our mindless failure to consider those who follow us. There should be a major agency or department considering what the world will be like several generations from now and determining what we ought to be doing now to prepare for it.

Bertrand Russell, writing in his autobiography, comments on how far we have to go:

Three passions, simple but overwhelmingly strong, have governed my life: the longing for love, the search for knowledge, and the unbearable pity for the suffering of mankind. . . . Children in famine, victims tortured by oppressors, helpless old people, a hated burden to their sons, and the whole world of loneliness, poverty and pain make a mockery of what human life should be.[4]

PREVENTIVE MEDICINE

PREVENTION OF ILLNESS

In spite of advances in the field of medicine and increases in the numbers of persons living to old age, life expectancy in the United States is still less than in many other nations. In 1971 Americans were fortieth in life expectancy from birth for men and tenth for women. Overall health, especially in old age, is far from what it could be. This is a function of inadequate health care, an unsupportive socioeconomic system, and poor health and dietary education. Prevention of illness and early treatment to prevent exacerbation of existing illnesses are underemphasized.* For example, patients may be untrained in responding to the warning signals of serious illness. One study found that as many as half of the persons who die of heart attacks outside of hospitals do so because they have waited at least five and one-half hours before seeking medical care. That would mean that at least 250,000 of the 400,000 Americans who die annually from heart attacks do not have the advantage of any kind of medical effort.[7] Intensive coronary-care units that provide constant electrical and personal monitoring in hospitals are proving useful if heart attacks are treated early enough. Deaths which used to be caused by bradycardia (slow heartbeat) and paroxysmal tachycardia (fast heartbeat) can now be prevented.

Emergency medical care for all types of illnesses "is one of the weakest links in the delivery of health care in our nation" according to the National Academy of Sciences in 1972. A Health, Education, and Welfare Depart-

---

* As a society, only four cents out of every health dollar is spent in the United States on preventive health care, to consider just one ingredient in the quality of life. For example, of some 200 million persons alive in America today 50 million will develop cancer and 34 million will die of it. Half of these deaths will occur before age 65.[5] In 1969 we spent $410 per American citizen on defense, $125 on the Vietnam war, $19 on the space program, $19 on foreign aid, and 89 cents on cancer research.[6]

ment study in 1972 reported that some 60,000 persons of all ages who died from accidents, heart attacks and other sudden illnesses could have been saved through proper emergency care. Poor ambulances, slow service, untrained attendants and inadequate equipment were all part of the problem.

Of the ten leading causes of death, the diseases of the heart, malignancies and cerebrovascular disease (mostly stroke) account for about 70 percent of annual deaths for older people. These causes of death—along with accidents, ranking fourth; cirrhosis, fifth; suicide, ninth; and homicide, tenth—all present some potential for control and prevention.* The generalization that to be long-lived one must have long-lived ancestors is increasingly less valid as we learn how to prevent and control disease. (Indeed, there is some evidence that the effect of heredity upon life expectancy has been exaggerated.)

A 1971 governmental Task Force on Arteriosclerosis† called for a major national effort against the "natural epidemic" of heart diseases, mainly due to arteriosclerosis. More than one million die annually from arteriosclerosis or its effects, and many more are disabled.‡ Successful efforts against this disease would alter the picture of old age as we know it today—alleviating some of the wrinkling, slowing and other physical features associated with old age that are undoubtedly due to reduced blood supply following "hardening of the arteries."

Arteriosclerosis begins early, progresses slowly, is chronic and more common and devastating as the years go by. Blood vessels have three layers. In arteriosclerosis proper, the vessel hardens as a result of fibrous and mineral deposits in the middle layer of the vessel wall. The more critical associated condition is atherosclerosis. Fatty substances collect on the inside vessel wall, forming atheromas (pulpy, fat-laden deposits), narrowing the passage and impeding the blood flow. The heart, brain, kidneys

---

* We at present have the least control over neoplasms (malignancies) except for those that relate to air and water pollution and cigarette smoking. There is a massive public-health problem as a result of food contamination with pathogens and chemicals (including carcinogens), and environmental pollution (sulfurized air, insecticides, etc.). It has been estimated (for example, by a study done for the Environmental Protection Agency) that in 1972 pollution levels cost the United States $1 billion to $3 billion in added health care! The elderly have a particular reason to fight pollution, especially air pollution, for they are very susceptible. To give one illustration, of the twenty persons who died in the famous Donora, Pennsylvania, smog in 1948, most were old men. They would be gripped in a paroxysmal cough, try to catch their breath and topple over dead.

† Appointed by Dr. Theodore Cooper, director of the National Heart and Lung Institute.

‡ Heart disease is the most common affliction among more than one-half million persons under 65 receiving Social Security disability benefits. Clearly, prevention would provide large economic savings for all.

and other organs are impaired by the diminished supply of food and oxygen that reaches them because of the impaired blood circulation. Heart attacks and strokes result from the impairment and clots that form.* Arteriosclerosis and atheromata are not distributed uniformly throughout the circulatory system of the body. Consequently there may be discrete, local lesions, causing damage in specific organs in the absence of ill effects elsewhere.

Because the development of arteriosclerosis begins in childhood, prevention must begin early. Dr. Sidney Blumenthal, University of Miami professor of pediatric cardiology, has offered guidelines for the early recognition of the high-risk child. He looks for primary hyperlipemia, hypertension, diabetes and obesity. He urges taking careful, complete family histories. In the absence of family history of physical indications, the disease may develop silently. Prevention and treatment are still controversial since much remains to be learned, but diet is an important factor.

The Task Force on Arteriosclerosis sharply criticized current federal efforts in arteriosclerosis research as "totally inadequate" because of "sparse and discontinuous funding, a dearth of long-range planning, and uncoordinated programming." The group proposed a permanent national commission to monitor progress against heart disease and to help direct future efforts to combat it.

At present, despite the lack of a complete answer to the diet-disease controversy surrounding arteriosclerosis, the Task Force recommended dietary changes for the general public as a preventive measure. "Pending confirmation by appropriate diet or drug trials, it . . . would appear prudent for the American people to follow a diet aimed at lowering serum lipid concentrations. For most individuals, this can be achieved by lowering intake of calories, cholesterol, and saturated fats." This is the first time that the National Heart and Lung Institute has ever endorsed a recommendation for changing the United States diet.

Hypertension, or high blood pressure, afflicts an estimated 23 million Americans, playing a direct role in the deaths of at least 60,000 men and women yearly, the majority in their fifties. Black people are more frequently affected than white. Government figures show that one in seven blacks has high blood pressure. Former HEW Secretary Elliot Richardson reported, "hypertension kills more than 13,000 blacks every year compared with sickle cell's toll of 340.† The death rate points up the racial

---

* Strokes also follow "blowouts" with hemorrhage, due to hypertension.

† Sickle-cell anemia is a hereditary anemia found among black people, characterized by oxygen-deficient sickle-shaped red blood cells, episodic pain and leg ulcers.

disparity even more sharply; the nonwhite death rate for hypertension is 58.4 per 100,000, more than twice the 27.1 per 100,000 rate for whites." There are data showing that those blacks who live in the highest urban stress areas have the highest blood pressure of all. Stress and inhibition in the freedom to express anger seem clearly related to rising blood pressure. Here we see social conditions that affect both life style and bodily adjustments.

Atherosclerosis is aggravated and accelerated by hypertension, but there is no established evidence that reducing blood pressure reduces the incidence of myocardial infarctions (the medical name for heart attacks). A Veterans Administration Cooperative Study has indicated that antihypertensive drugs do prevent hemorrhagic stroke, congestive heart decompensation, renal failure and accelerated hypertension. The National Heart and Lung Institute began a nationwide campaign against hypertension in 1972, aimed at educating both the medical profession and the general public. Since antihypertensive medication is effective, it is all the more irresponsible to allow people to go untreated.

Alcoholism is the fourth leading killer in the United States, producing more than 85,000 deaths annually through liver diseases, highway and other accidents, and crime. Is drinking a disease, or is it much more than that? Acculturation has persuaded many people that drinking is manly or daring, sexually useful,* fun, relaxing, sophisticated or helpful in solving problems.[8] Actually, alcohol is a depressant, rather than a stimulant, of the central nervous system. In some measure drinking is within societal and individual control. The conspicuous public use of alcohol in governmental, entertainment, fashion, industry and professional circles reinforces the public feeling that drinking is harmless and acceptable.†

More patients with histories of alcoholism survive into old age than in the past, as a result of more effective treatments (nutrition, antibiotics). In addition, late-life alcoholism can develop for the first time in a person's life in the wake of grief and the presence of loneliness. I am of the opinion that alcoholism and concomitant malnutrition are causes of significant portions of the memory impairment in old age erroneously attributed to "hardening of the arteries." There are also dangers in the casual prescription of alcohol for older people to help them sleep, improve their appetite and add to their sociability. Alcohol blunts reaction time, impairs coordination and fuzzes mental abilities, especially memory. Serious falls and misjudgments can result.

---

* In fact, alcohol has a detrimental effect upon sexual ability.
† In 1973 it was clear that alcohol was becoming popular again among young people.

We badly need continued research on alcoholism. In 1972 the American Hospital Association reported the astounding fact that 25–30 percent of all adult medical-surgical patients in metropolitan hospitals, regardless of diagnosis, had alcoholism.* As many as nine million Americans may be alcoholics. It ranks very high among the country's major health and social problems.

SENSIBLE LIFE STYLES

Seneca, the Roman philosopher, said, "Man does not die, he kills himself." There is no question but that much of our behavior over which we can exercise some degree of control is influential both in the quality and length of our lives. Yet we do not take personal responsibility either for ourselves individually or collectively as a society by shaping our lives into the kind of regimen that would enhance both the character and length of life.

With due respect to Seneca, the rights of human beings over their own lives must be preserved—including the rights to gourmandize, to smoke, to drink, to be physically indolent.† These are defensible individual rights as long as they do not impinge on others, but they should be freely chosen. Advertising on behalf of tobacco and alcohol exerts undue influence on people from childhood on. The excessive emphasis of the American diet upon meat and dairy products remains basically unchallenged in the public eye. There is little serious public discussion, education and encouragement regarding the merits of physical exercise, prevention of illness and recognition of health danger signals.

Poor diets, overeating, smoking, physical inactivity, excessive drinking, the overuse and misuse of drugs, accidents, stress and life-endangering life styles‡ are all targets of preventive medicine. One can see interrelations between these elements and many physical conditions. A graphic example is found in the work being done on the influence of personality and life styles on heart attacks. The great physician Sir William Osler was among

---

* The seven thousand voluntary hospitals of the United States are reluctant to admit acutely ill alcoholics, many of whom are addicts and old people. The AHA president, Alex McMahon, said, "Many professionals still believe the alcoholic is a nuisance, not a sick person." On the other hand, the admission of alcoholic patients to hospitals may be disguised as something else to protect patients and their families.

† There are always, of course, exceptional individuals who live long lives in spite of heavy drinking, smoking or inactivity.

‡ For example, contrary to popular belief some studies have shown that when there is less organization and complexity in the daily activities of life, mortality is more likely.[9]

the first to suspect that emotional factors contribute to coronary heart disease. In 1955 a San Francisco cardiologist at the Mount Zion Hospital and Medical Center, Dr. Meyer Friedman,[10] described a behavioral pattern he called the Type A personality, characterized by "an overwhelming sense of time urgency and competitive drive." The Type A personality "usually confidently advances to grapple with his challenges; the subject with a true anxiety neurosis despondently retreats before his." As important as diet, inactivity, smoking, and other factors may be in the genesis of heart attacks, Friedman believes the Type A behavioral pattern may be more significant.*

A Type A man insists upon being on time, eats rapidly, "wastes" no time with hobbies, does several things simultaneously, like reading while eating or listening to the radio while shaving, and is materialistic, quantitative, punctilious and impatient. He even tends not to take a vacation unless he can organize it around a business trip. While the Type A may link his drive with his creativity, the truth is that he is no more creative than the less frantic Type B personality which Friedman also describes.

Friedman recommends the establishment of counter habits, a new regimen and behavior pattern. He suggests that people discontinue their simultaneous thinking and working, and begin to listen without interrupting, read books that demand concentration, learn to enjoy good food and relaxation, find a way of retreating at home, take trips and vacations unrelated to business, and *plan to waste time.* There should be joy, the fulfillment of personal qualities and the lowering of daily stress.

In contrast to Friedman's results and theory, Jules B. Quint and Bianca R. Cody[11] noted that "their findings contradict the beliefs in some quarters that the mercilessness by which men drive themselves during their forties to outstanding careers was reflected in broken health during their fifties." They reported a twelve-year study of men listed in the 1951–52 edition of *Who's Who in America.* All men of high achievement, they live longer than the average citizen. The situation is complex indeed and obviously more study is indicated.

Nutrition is a vital element in preventive medicine. One's food habits may serve one well or badly in old age. Quite apart from malnutrition due to limited incomes, one sees nutritional inadequacy in the diets of older people resulting from poor habits, misinformation, grief and loneliness.

The Venetian nobleman, pioneer gerontologist Count Ludovico Carnaro (1467–1566), wrote in his eighty-third year in his *Discourses of the Healthy Life,* "He who would eat much, must eat little," and overweight is indeed dangerous to health in later life. Food habits are part of one's life

---

* Friedman himself suffered a heart attack at fifty-six and diagnosed himself as a Type A.

style, and overeaters pay for their habits by earlier deaths. Most Americans eat too many calories,* fats, sugar and salt,† not to mention foods contaminated with chemicals. Red meats and dairy products make up too large a portion of the average daily diet. Almost 25 percent of the money Americans spend on food is for meals outside the house, and these are too often the nutritionally dubious specialties of the fast-food franchises, such as fried chicken, hamburgers, hot dogs and soft drinks. Children acquire poor food habits very early, and these habits tend to persist throughout life.

Dr. Jean Mayer, Harvard nutritionist, said, "In the 1930s and 1940s nutrition was taught as part of biochemistry. Now, if you can call it an improvement, I give one lecture in the first year of medical school and one in the fourth, and nutrition also appears in some courses in social medicine." It is amazing how few medical schools have courses in applied nutrition dealing with the basic relationship between nutrition and health. A family physician should be well trained in preventive medicine and health education, including nutritional education.‡ An essential part of medical care is advising people of all ages on maintaining healthy dietary habits.§

Older persons need help in planning diets which promote vigor and well-being. Many, of course, need financial assistance in obtaining such diets. Food packaging for one- or two-person families, menus for persons on special diets and help in preparing meals should be available. Meals on wheels and group dining are essential for some. Perhaps more than any other life-style element, good nutrition is critical for well-being in later life.

Just as with nutrition, accident prevention and safety training should begin early in life. Many of the injuries and disabilities of middle and later life could thereby be avoided. In old age, people especially need training in avoidance of home accidents and pedestrian travel mishaps. Special precautions may be necessary to compensate for physical and mental changes.

"Exercise is the closest thing to an anti-aging pill now available. It acts like a miracle drug, and it's free for the doing," writes researcher Josef P.

---

* In 1932, Dr. Clive M. McKay of Cornell demonstrated that he could prolong the lives of rats by one-third by reducing calories in their diets.

† It has been estimated that Americans consume twenty times as much salt as the body needs or can use. Such excess of salt intake contributes to high blood pressure and arteriosclerosis, obesity and tooth decay. The dangers of "soul food" with its excessive salt has been expressed as a specific problem.

‡ The American Heart Association has published a *Cookbook*, New York: David McKay Company, 1973. It offers the "Prudent Diet."

§ The White House Conference on Aging took no position on the nation's dietary habits.

Hrachovec.[12] Yet about 45 percent of adult Americans—49 million of 109 million men and women—are sedentary, not engaging in physical exercise.[13]

Substantial evidence supports the value of exercise in maintaining health, improved circulation and respiration, better sleep and diminished stress. Exercise reduces the risk of heart attack and enhances survival following an attack. Swimming, walking, running and bicycling are especially good and inexpensive forms of exercise, since they actively strengthen the circulatory and respiratory systems.

Age need not be an impediment to bicycling and other forms of exercise. Tolstoy learned to ride a bike at age sixty-seven. Paul Dudley White, President Eisenhower's physician, urged bicycling as a preventive and curative exercise. Nineteen seventy-two saw the sale of 13 million bicycles in the United States, exceeding the sale of American and foreign automobiles by some 2.4 million. It is estimated that about 18 million Americans now ride bicycles, both as recreation and as a form of transportation. By 1973 there were at least five bills before Congress to appropriate money or land or both to provide safe and separate bicycle paths, special lanes in traffic, shelters, parking facilities and traffic control devices. Bicycles with side wheels can be used by older people who worry about balancing but want the exercise. A basket on the back makes it easy to carry packages, and the bicycle can be used for going distances too long to walk.

Spectator sports hold a large place in American life, with college and professional sports centering upon a few well-exercised athletes.* The same money might better be spent on programs and facilities that encourage physical exercise for the population as a whole. Health clubs and the YMCA and the YWCA could offer programs tailored to older people. The large amounts of public park space presently gobbled up by golfers could be more equitably divided among hikers, swimmers and other sports enthusiasts.

Exercise must be planned on a routine daily basis. One simply must make time for it. In addition, advantage must be taken of spontaneous opportunities for physical activity. Emptying the trash, mowing the lawn and walking upstairs instead of taking the elevator should follow a redefinition of what is called drudgery and what is exercise. So-called labor- and time-saving devices may reduce physical fitness. Gardening is a fine hobby as well as an attraction that gives pleasure to others. It saves money to garden, cut the grass, pull weeds, do household chores. Purchase of a

---

* Ironically, athletes may have shorter life spans than average. See, for example, "Longevity and Cause of Death Among Harvard College Athletes and Their Classmates," *Geriatrics*, October, 1972.

handyman guide for work around the house can lead to exercise and save repair costs too.

Dancing is an activity that combines social, interpersonal and physical pleasure. Folk dancing, square dancing and ballroom dancing should be part of the available repertoire. The rugged outdoor life—hiking and trail blazing—is also valuable for older people.

Medical monitoring of exercise is important in later life. Regular physical exams and discussions of appropriate exercise with a doctor can lessen the chance of overdoing or miscalculating one's abilities. Treadmill electrocardiac surveillance (including testing under stress) is very valuable. Education around common dangers is another imperative. For example, in 1970 the Federal Trade Commission warned the elderly and infirm to be careful about sauna and steam baths because of adverse effects of rising body temperature, blood pressure and pulse rates. There is evidence also to suggest that isometric, static or overly sustained exercises may elevate blood pressure to the point of provoking a heart attack.

Sexual activity is a useful form of exercise for the relief of tension, mild tuning-up of circulation and muscles and for emotional well-being. Massage is another very helpful technique, especially crucial for the bedridden, but relaxing and stimulating for all.

STUDIES OF HEALTHY OLD AGE

If the child was "discovered" in the seventeenth century (before that, children were not thought of as a separate category with special capacities and needs), old age has been "discovered" in the twentieth. But the discovery is new and much remains to be learned about health in old age.

In the study of things, our attention seems always to turn first to disorder before it is directed to order, to disease before health, to problems before successes. Yet we need to study order, health and successes for several reasons—not the least of which is to prevent problems to whatever degree possible.

Though the over-75 age group is the fastest growing of American population groups (between 1960 and 1970 it increased 37.1 percent compared to 13 percent for the group between 65 and 75), studies of people this age are still rare and this is even truer of women and of minority groups. There have been a few intensive, longitudinal studies of healthy, community-resident elderly: at Duke University; in Baltimore under Nathan Shock; at the National Institute of Mental Health and the Philadelphia Geriatric Center; at the Lovelace Foundation in Albuquerque, New Mexico; in

Framingham, Massachusetts (the Heart Study); and in the Veterans Administration Normative Study (the Boston Outpatient Clinic).

Daniel Offer and Melvin Sabshin, two psychiatrists, have tried to consider that old conundrum normality in terms of people of all ages, and have offered four perspectives through which to view it—health, utopia, statistical average and process.[14] Health can be seen as the absence of pathology, an antonym. It can also be viewed in a utopian perspective as the World Health Organization defines it: positive, optimal functioning above and beyond the absence of disease, as well as the psychoanalytic perspective of ideal functioning (for instance, the ego in the "average expectable environment"). Statistics offer a measure of the typical or average. Process emphasizes change, the constantly altering outcome which is a function of individual maturation and cultural difference. Process has some kinship, it would seem, with social philosophers' ideas of progress. The truth is there may indeed be many kinds of normality and many possible normal channels of development and maturation. We need far more comprehensive data on multiple populations, varying groups, categories, classes and races.

It is important to remember that normality is not forced conformity. It is and must be an elastic concept. Creativity, for instance, cannot easily be bound by our definitions of normality; it is a kind of leap in nature. American anthropologist Ruth Benedict's concepts of cultural relativism remind us that what may be regarded as neurotic, or even psychotic, behavior in one culture may be regarded as creative and constructive in still another.

In order to gain a realistic picture of aging and of the elderly some investigators in the late 1950s and the early 1960s began to study healthy, community-resident, socially autonomous old people by a wide spectrum of research procedures. Some of the first studies began at the University of Colorado under the auspices of Dr. Ewald W. Busse. These studies of community-resident old people were carried on at the Duke University Medical Center after Busse moved there. This continuing work has been recently summarized by Busse in a 1967 monograph. The many articles of the Duke group have been collected in a 1970 volume *Normal Aging*.

To look anew at some of the prevailing ideas and previously reported findings concerning both the processes of human aging and the nature of aging persons, some of us at the National Institute of Mental Health, representing a number of separate academic disciplines and medical specialties, undertook a series of collaborative studies in 1955.*

* Leadership and coordination of this project was originally undertaken by Dr. James E. Birren and later by me. My own interest was a broad, multidisciplinary one. Dr. Louis Sokoloff and Dr. Seymour Kety (co-developer of the Kety-Schmidt

We selected medically healthy, community-dwelling aged so that we might maximize the opportunity of studying the effects of time, of chronological aging itself, and minimize the effects of sickness, institutionalization and social adversity.

Among some of the specific questions in mind were:

- Are the changes in cerebral blood flow and metabolic rate described in the literature a result of aging of the nervous system, or are they the result of disease?
- To what extent is the postulated slowing in speed of reaction time with age the result of a general process of change in the central nervous system?
- What personality factors contribute to the adaptation and maladaptation of the community-resident, healthy individual to the crises of late life?
- How do environmental factors of cultural background and of immediate circumstances contribute to adaptation and maladaptation of the aged?

To our general surprise we found that psychological flexibility, resourcefulness and optimism characterized the group we studied rather than the stereotype of rigidity. Many of the manifestations heretofore attributed to aging *per se* clearly reflected medical illness, personality factors and social-cultural effects. Not confirmed was the previous belief that cerebral (brain) blood flow and oxygen consumption necessarily decrease as a result of chronological aging. It was found rather that when such changes did occur they were the probable result of vascular disease, which the public calls "hardening of the arteries." The nearly 50 elderly men in our sample who were over 65 (who had an average age of 71) were found to have brain physiological and intellectual functions that compared favorably with those of a young control group. Intellectual abilities did not decline as a consequence of the mysterious process of aging but as the result of specific diseases. Therefore "senility" is not an inevitable outcome of aging. Studies at Duke and elsewhere point in the same direction. All the usual psychiatric disorders found among the elderly seemed to be similar in their genesis and structure to those affecting the young.

There was evidence of slowing of speed and response which was found

---

method of measuring the flow of blood to the brain and its consumption of oxygen and sugar) had a particular interest in examining and exploring interrelationships between cerebral and intellectual functioning in relationship to age. Dr. Seymour Perlin, who had combined research and clinical experiences at the Home for Aged and Infirm Hebrews in New York City, wanted to understand better how organic brain disorders might be explained. Dr. Marion Radke Yarrow, a social psychologist, was interested in the cultural impact on aging, while Dr. Samuel Greenhouse, a biostatistician, demonstrated methods for integrating various disciplines in the study of aging.

to be a function of aging. However, such slowing—which on the surface appears so characteristic of old age—was also found to relate statistically to environmental deprivation and depression as well as to decreasing health.

The importance of the immediate environment for adaptation was repeatedly observed. For example, education, occupation and other lifelong social factors were not as decisive to adaptation as was the degree of current environmental deprivation.

This work was originally published in 1963 by the government under the title *Human Aging: A Biological and Behavioral Study*.[15] It was republished for the occasion of the White House Conference on Aging in 1971 along with a second volume reporting the eleven-year follow-up.

Over the eleven years from 1955 to 1966 the original NIH sample was followed.[16] The group was readmitted and re-evaluated at the end of five years. Much of the report of the five-year follow-up centered upon aspects of survival and adaptation. Nonsurvivors, compared to the survivors, showed statistically significant differences in the following: greater incidence of arteriosclerosis (i.e., hardening of the arteries) and a greater percentage of chronic cigarette smoking. Nonsurvivors also tended toward other statistically significant differences: they had not adapted as well psychologically, had suffered widowhood and were more dissatisfied with their current living situations. They also had less clearly defined goals. Thus survival was associated with the individual's self-view and a sense of continued usefulness, in addition to good physical health. At the end of eleven years, as at the end of five years, good physical status and absence of cigarette smoking were related to survival. Structured, planned, varied new contacts and self-initiated activities and involvement (referred to as "organization of behavior") were found associated with survival. The fact that organization of behavior was so strongly a statistical predictor of survival runs counter to the disengagement theory.

Much more work of this kind needs to be done. In addition, specific areas demand research attention because they represent such an integral part of aging as we know it today. For example, the sex differential in mortality between men and women has been widening and is mainly a function of heart disease, chronic respiratory diseases and lung cancer.* The government and academia have shown little concern for this important phemonenon. It would be in the interest of both women and men to establish widows' funds or endowments for research into differential sex mortality. Male death rates in the United States have changed little since

---

* With increasing cigarette smoking among women we find the differential with respect to lung cancer changing. Women are smoking more and dying more. They are catching up with men.

the mid-1950s and female death rates, on the other hand, have continued to decline.* Men are subject to greater mortality than females at every stage of life. White men in 1968, for example, died at double the rate of white women between 45 and 64 years of age. Heart disease is responsible for three-fifths of this difference. As men and women pass beyond 65, men still die more rapidly from malignant neoplasms, pneumonia and influenza, and heart diseases. Mortality from cerebrovascular disease in old age begins to equalize between the sexes.

Studies of death are important too.† George Engel has presented valuable anecdotal material on "sudden and rapid death during psychological stress."[17] Over a six-year period Engel collected 170 items from newspapers. Fear, rage, grief, humiliation and even joy were the settings in which sudden death occurred: specifically, the actual or threatened death of someone close, acute grief, an occasion of mourning or an anniversary, loss of status or self-esteem, personal danger or threat of injury with death usually occurring after such danger is over; and, finally, reunion, triumph or happy ending. He felt the psychological mechanisms in such intense settings were conducive to cardiac death, especially in the presence of cardiovascular disease.

Cross-cultural studies could be useful in clarifying the elements of life which enhance survival for the old. There are certain cultures that seem to have created conditions that are favorable to both a fulfilling as well as an extended old age. Three that are frequently cited are the land of Hunza in the Karakoram Range in Pakistani-controlled Kashmir, the Soviet Republic of Georgia's Abkhasia in the Caucasus, and the Andean village of Vilcabamba in Ecuador. In these regions, people over one hundred years of age who are healthy both physically and mentally have been reported. However, longevity is exceedingly difficult to document.

Sula Benet has described the Abkhasian older people as the *long-living people* of the Caucasus.[18] This term has much to recommend it. It is direct and empirical, describing the fact of increased life expectancy rather than the decline we associate with terms like "aged" and "elderly." Work, diet and a meaningful social structure are believed to be the key elements in the long living of the Abkhasians. They work actively far into late life. They eat slowly, have low caloric intake and consume relatively little meat, eggs and salt. Few of them smoke. Benet was impressed by the social

---

* This is true in most nations. See: *United Nations Department of Economics and Social Affairs Statistical Yearbook*, 1971.

† Only 30 percent of United States deaths are followed by autopsies, yet this is a crucial source of continuing education for the doctor. There are all too often tragic discrepancies between pre- and post-mortem diagnoses. Less than 50 percent of cases of pulmonary embolism are recognized, for example, before death.

integration of the old into the larger community. She describes the "high degree of integration in their lives, the sense of group identity that gives each individual an unshaken feeling of personal security and continuity . . . a sense of continuity in both their personal and national lives is what anthropologists would call their spatial and temporal integration. . . . Their spatial integration is in their kinship structure." The Abkhasians, then, can expect a long and useful life, look forward to it and know they are valued. We have yet to learn the wisdom of these simple but profound life styles.

A word of caution needs to be added to the general call for more research on aging and the elderly. Any human experimentation must be strictly monitored. This is especially true in studies of those who are ill or incapacitated. Old people in institutions who are without living or involved relatives are especially vulnerable. One of the twelve points in the Patient's Bill of Rights the American Hospital Association announced in 1973 reads: "The patient has the right to obtain from his physician complete information concerning his diagnosis [and] . . . any proposal to engage in or perform new experiments on the patient affecting his care or treatment." Federal legislation to tighten the rules for clinical research theoretically affected some 85 percent of biomedical research conducted in the United States. But enforcement is not simple.*

The public has become aware only recently of the degree to which experimentation is performed. In 1959 Pulitzer prize-winning journalist Jack Nelson wrote a series of articles charging Milledgeville (Georgia) Central State Hospital with using experimental drugs on mental patients (including older patients) without the permission or knowledge of relatives. In the course of a government funded study in New York, live cancer cells have been injected into older patients at a chronic-disease hospital without their knowledge and consent. The U.S. Public Health Service's forty-year Tuskegee syphilis study has recently been exposed; in it participants (all of whom were black) were not adequately informed of the nature of the study at the outset or at any point during the forty-year experiment. In the late 1940s the successful treatment of syphilis with penicillin became possible in all stages of the disease, including late latent syphilis and tertiary syphilis, but this treatment was not given to the Tuskegee subjects. A class-action suit was initiated on their behalf in 1973.

Many older people want the opportunity to contribute to others through participation in research studies. But they should have the choice and not be misled or abused.

---

* There has been great resistance among American hospitals to abiding by the Bill of Rights articulated by their association. They are fearful of lawsuits.

The National Institute on Aging should study national habits and cultural and behavioral patterns as well as biomedical questions concerning old age.* Advantage should be taken of "natural experiments"—society's and nature's. Careful observation of early widowhood and military retirement, for example, can give insights into experiences common to old people but occurring in isolation from the other events of old age. In medicine, progeria and Werner's syndrome offer compressed motion pictures of accelerated "aging," and intensive study might be very instructive indeed.

Brandeis University's Max Levinson Gerontological Policy Institute, directed by Professor Robert Morris, deals, among other matters, with the impact of social and institutional changes on aging citizens.

Nathan W. Shock's Gerontological Research Center in Baltimore City Hospitals (part of the National Institutes of Health) is pursuing its multiphasic studies of man and animal. Dr. Charles H. Barrows, a staff biochemist, has found in his studies of the minuscule multicellular aquatic animals called rotifers that the lowering of environmental temperature extends their life expectancy. Perhaps, as Bernard Strehler has suggested, temperature-reducing drugs will extend the life of man up to twenty years.

Whether one or several contemporary theories of aging—or none of these—turns out to be true, man's struggle to discover continues. Collagen cross-linking? Errors in protein synthesis? Autoimmunity? Gradual loss of information in the deoxyribonucleic-acid molecule? Decline in cell division? Free radical disruption of cell membrane structure and enzyme activity with resulting formation of lipofuscin ("the age pigment")? Amyloidosis? Failure of hypothalamus in regulation of normal body rhythms and functions? We don't know. Barely one percent of the National Institutes of Health budget was spent to find the answers to such questions, and the greatest killer of all, cardiovascular disease, is insufficiently funded.

Beginning with the Johnson administration and continuing in the Nixon administration there was a shift in emphasis in national science and health policy from medical research to practical application and the provision of care. This sounds good, it sounds humane; but the truth is that it is the adventitious discovery in research—serendipity—that often leads to the

---

* The NIA should support various regional institutes on aging throughout the nation. It is often said that students have very little interest in the process of aging, but in my experience this is not so. Studied from the life-cycle perspective, its relevance becomes apparent. Some older people themselves turn to the study of old age. V. Korenchevsky, a Russian-born physician and physiologist, devoted himself to advancing gerontological research throughout the world after his retirement. He was the organizing force behind the first International Gerontological Congress held in 1950 and has been called the father of gerontology.

greatest of conquests. No better example exists than Sir Alexander Fleming's accidental discovery of penicillin through his keen observation of pathogenic bacteria killed by mold. Unquestionably the delivery of medical care must be improved, but basic research studies have to continue.

By not conducting sufficient studies of cellular aging, for example, we may be making it more difficult to understand the impact of diseases which seem to be related to, or indeed dependent upon, age but not a direct function of age.* Age-associated diseases may only be understood as we understand the aging process.

Great and original ideas in research cannot literally be bought by money, but favorable supporting conditions encourage the entry of creative persons into the field. Cutbacks in training and research can therefore have profound long-term consequences. One must be wary of policies which may dismantle the base upon which future research depends.

There is a microscopic Adult Development in Aging Branch in the National Institute of Child Health and Human Development (NICHHD). This has been the federal unit responsible for the support of research and research training in the biological, psychological, medical and social aspects of aging. The amounts of money that have been made available to it are minuscule. The umbrella institute (NICHHD) was established in 1962, only partly influenced by the 1961 White House Conference on Aging and more directly influenced by the interest of the Kennedys in mental retardation. President Kennedy, in signing the act creating the National Institute of Child Health and Human Development, said, "This legislation will encourage imaginative research in the complex processes of human development from conception to old age."

One of the pioneer gerontologists, Nathan W. Shock, had urged the establishment of a National Institute of Gerontology for years.[19] Indeed, the need for a free-standing National Institute on Aging (or Gerontology) has been voiced by many. Legislation to establish it passed Congress in 1972 and 1974. President Nixon vetoed it the first time and signed it the second.

THE RIGHT TO DIE

"Passive" euthanasia† refers to permitting a patient to die naturally, rather than exercising heroic means to keep him "alive" when such life leads to a vegetative existence or unmitigated suffering. "Active" euthanasia

* For example, malignant cell lines keep dividing, whereas normal cells age. (Cited by Leonard Hayflick.)
† Literally meaning "a good death."

is the active killing of those presumed to be hopelessly sick or disabled. Both lend themselves to abuses of all kinds, including the possible use by the state to rid itself of expensive helpless victims (not to mention political "undesirables"). But passive euthanasia is beginning to be cautiously considered as a viable social and medical practice under carefully controlled circumstances. This is because we have begun to take seriously the individual's right to die.

As a result of medical advances, persons with previously fatal illness can be maintained at minimal functioning even though they can no longer experience life in any meaningful way. Others are kept alive to suffer interminably through long, costly, painful illnesses.* Heart-lung machines, intravenous feedings, organ transplants, artificial kidneys, auxiliary heart defibrillators, pacemakers, respirators, life-sustaining drugs can sustain people indefinitely with minimal-to-no conscious activity. These are the living dead, the extreme examples in the passive euthanasia controversy. They breathe, their hearts beat, but they are incapable of any of the functioning we call "human."

The modern definition of death itself is gradually being revised to mean the irreversible destruction of the brain.† Two states, Kansas and Maryland, have adopted laws allowing medical efforts to cease when the brain is declared dead. However, it is not an easy matter emotionally, morally or even scientifically. Present clinical criteria are unacceptable and the electroencephalogram is not infallible. With the increased use of organ transplants, a more acceptable and reliable definition of death has become even more urgent.

In the absence of arrangements for passive euthanasia, do we force some suffering people to commit suicide, or their loved ones to consider killing the sufferers? How far can we go in giving individuals the right to decide when they no longer wish to live?‡ It would all be so much

---

* Indeed, "passive euthanasia" has been supported on fiscal grounds. Dr. Walter W. Sackett states that in Florida alone it would cost $5 billion to allow "1,500 individuals retarded to the point where they are bedridden, diapered, tube-fed and completely unaware, to live out artificial lives prolonged by the marvels of science. The money could better be used on persons that could be cured." I believe this is dangerous thinking.

† In 1968 Henry K. Beecher described total brain death as no reflexes, no spontaneous respiration, and no electroencephalographic activity for twenty-four hours.

‡ Dr. Elisabeth Kubler-Ross testified at U.S. Senate hearings: "My own mother wanted to die very badly. She is kept now alive two years in the hospital, and cannot possibly sign herself out. She is totally paralyzed. She cannot say one word. She lies there like a body and stares at you, fully conscious, and would very much love to die, but she is kept alive with tubes through her nose, and begging (with her eyes) to let her die, and you cannot find a place that would let her die with peace and dignity, and she lies there for two years like that."[20]

easier if loss of the will to live and the natural time of death would coincide nicely. It is essential, of course, that we consider the right to die from the ethical perspective. It is healthy that it should always be a lively, open and controversial subject.

The medical profession is increasingly criticized for maintaining life irresponsibly. Doctors are seen as espousing "the vitalistic urge of the medical profession, which makes biological continuance the absolute good even when the price is the loss of dignity of the individual."[21] Yet doctors should not be given the sole power to end life. I strongly feel that the medical profession should be primarily concerned with the prolongation of life, and must share with others any decisions concerning dying.* Indeed, as a physician I would not trust doctors any more than any other persons acting on their own with the power to make decisions about death.† In 1967 in a London hospital the initials N.T.B.R. (Not to Be Resuscitated) were found marked on the treatment cards of over sixty-five patients with chronic chest or kidney diseases or malignancies. An English physician, Dr. Kenneth A. O. Vickery, also suggested that a specific age, 80, be the limit after which there would be no resuscitation. Arbitrariness based on specific diseases or ages leaves totally out of account the unique qualities and characteristics of an individual, his family and their needs. Today, in point of fact, it is all too often left to doctors to make decisions about death. They decide out of their own personal biases, incomplete information concerning the wishes and needs of the patient and his family, and as a result of cultural attitudes. Self-appointed "skillful neglect" is an illustra-

---

* As an admittedly extreme example, doctors have been known to be the fortunate beneficiaries of patients' wills and consciously or unconsciously precipitate patients' deaths. A British physician was acquitted in 1957 of charges of murdering an 81-year-old patient who had remembered him in her will. He was expelled from Britain's Medical Register for fourteen violations of prescription, dangerous drug and cremation regulations.

In addition, doctors are as ill trained concerning age and death as they are about sex and nutrition. Present-day medical students are receiving *somewhat* better training in these subjects, with the possible exception of aging. But they have a long history to overcome. In Osler's farewell address at Johns Hopkins in 1905 he spoke of "the comparative uselessness of man over forty years of age." He recalled Trollope's novel *The Fixed Period* in which "the plot hinges upon the admirable scheme of a college where at the age of sixty men are retired for a year of contemplation before a peaceful departure by chloroform." He was being ironic, but this giant in medicine helped to contribute, however unwittingly, to the negative attitudes within medicine toward old people.

† The New York State Medical Society declared in a policy statement in 1973 that "the use of euthanasia is not in the province of the physician." "The right to die with dignity; or the cessation of the employment of extraordinary means to prolong the life of the body when there is irrefutable evidence that biological death is inevitable, is the decision of the patient and/or the immediate family with the approval of the family physician." The American Medical Association adopted a similar position in 1973.

tive attitude of some doctors. From hearsay and observation it is known that the majority of doctors probably do practice passive euthanasia. They should not be left to their own devices.

How can the individual's right to die be clarified and provided for satisfactorily with maximum safeguards? The right to obtain a full explanation of one's medical condition in clear, concise terms and to choose death by rejecting medical therapy were affirmed in the "Bill of Rights" issued by the American Hospital Association in 1973. For some time numbers of people have been signing living wills—documents which state that if there is "no reasonable expectation of my recovering from physical or mental disability I . . . request that I be allowed to die. I do not want to be kept alive by 'artificial means or heroic measures.' " It asks that one's wish be honored if one is not in a position to make such a decision in the future. It is addressed to a patient's family, physician, clergyman and lawyer. This document is not legally binding. As of 1972 some fifty thousand copies had been distributed through the Euthanasia Education Fund.*

Old people—all people—fear and dislike pain, dependency, deterioration, indignity. Physician-legislator Walter W. Sackett of Florida has tried unsuccessfully each year since 1967 to gain approval for a proposal to allow every person to "have the right to die with dignity; that his life shall not be prolonged beyond the point of meaningful existence."

If we are to have legislation to provide for the "right to die," I suggest there be a panel in each case composed of the patient, family members (if any), two independent doctors (and the doctor in charge of the case), an attorney, a social worker, a clergyman (if desired) and a representative of the state. The panel would participate in the decision as to whether to honor the patient's expressed wish to die, made in the present or in the past through a living will. The panel, for instance, would consider the contemporary activity level of research into the patient's particular disease; how imminent is an advance or a cure? The entire family's emotional and financial health would be evaluated. A dying younger father, for example, needs all the meaningful time he can have with his sons and daughters.

Older persons may want to effect reconciliations or finish other uncompleted work. Individual wishes and needs must be respected.[22]

Laws allowing passive euthanasia must be cautiously worded, fastidiously applied and subject to continuing review. Once the patient is not able to signify his wishes and is helpless—as in coma—there should be a third party involved, whose interests must also be evaluated. I agree with

* There are two major euthanasia groups in the United States—the Euthanasia Educational Fund and the Euthanasia Society of America. The first finances studies and seminars. The second is an action organization seeking political change.

Dr. Angelo D'Agostino, both a Jesuit priest and a psychiatrist, who said, "Laws have to be very carefully written, otherwise you end up with human guinea pigs. Remember Nazi Germany."

In 1957 Pope Pius XII said that a doctor is not required to employ "extraordinary means" to keep alive a patient in a coma and beyond recovery. Death—in the abstract—is the enemy of medicine; it must never be regarded as casual. On the other hand, dying persons are not abstractions and should never be treated in dehumanized fashion.

THE HANDLING OF DEATH

And is not the awareness of death the chief distinction between animals and ourselves: Has not the awareness of death and timor mortis been the chief preoccupation of fully self-conscious mankind, and the fountain spring of most of its thinking and planning, from the first endeavors to preserve the corpse, to Christian Scientists who deny death? How few face it even now?[23]

DYING

Death is a powerful psychological fact of life, helping motivate people to action for both positive and negative change. The idea of death can also be paralyzing. Clinical experience leads me to share the impression of other observers that some of what is so casually termed "senility" is a defense against death: certain older people simply regress in the face of eternity.[24] But this, obviously, is not a theory susceptible of experimental corroboration.

On the other hand, older persons tend to fear death less than the young, and many can accept the idea of personal death with equanimity. At times it represents a welcome relief from the pain of a terminal illness. In other situations older persons feel they are ready, they have lived out their lives and are able to let go. Strong religious or philosophical convictions can be of immense comfort in the process of dying. Attitudes toward death give clues as to the life that has been lived, reflecting the problems, resolutions, fears and hopes faced by each person during the course of his life.

Historical circumstances, too, influence personal attitudes toward death. As the plague stalked Europe and Asia in the fourteenth century, death was a pre-eminent literary, musical and artistic theme, preoccupying entire nations of people. In this era of the atomic bomb, children have discovered the fear of death in a new way at an early age. Yet, with most people dying in hospitals rather than in their homes, there is little personal experience with the death process. One seldom sees the last moments of death. Every-thing is taken care of swiftly and silently with no opportunity for the experience to sink in visually or tactilely. At the very least, children (and adults for that matter) should visit their dying relatives in institutions, attend funerals and discuss openly what dying means to them and to others.

In philosophy and religion, death is depicted from every conceivable vantage point: as punishment, as a step to eternal reward, as a period of penance, as separation, as reunion. Ludwig A. Feuerbach (1804–72), a German philosopher, believed that death was bound up with life from the beginning. He saw the anticipation of death as an instrument for gaining knowledge of being. The German philosophers Georg Simmel and Martin Heidegger held similar views. Indeed, Heidegger saw the real meaning of existence in the fact of death, in that we perceive time only because we know that we have to die. J. M. A. Munnichs, who has studied attitudes toward death in the older person, has used the word "finitude" to mean "knowing and realizing that one's life will come to an end."[25]

Dr. Gerald J. Gruman, a physician and historian, has summarized man's constant search for a prolongation of life.[26] The impulse to permanence can reach catastrophic proportions, for example, in what is called the Hero-strates complex. In ancient Greece, Herostrates burned himself and a public building down in an effort to be remembered. In a more modern example, the Cryonics Society deep-freezes bodies at death, preserving them in liquid nitrogen indefinitely for "resurrection" at such time as science will be able to treat the disease which was the cause of death. The bodies are kept in aluminum capsules. Between 1967 and 1972 fifteen people were frozen in "Cryonic suspension." The idea came from a professor of physics, Robert C. W. Ettinger, and is an extreme example of how painful it is for many persons to face death and nothingness.[27]

A survey by *Geriatrics* magazine, reported in July, 1970, found that fewer than one in five physicians voluntarily tells a patient that he is going to die. Researchers on death have urged more open disclosure regarding death, thereby giving people an opportunity to work through the process of their dying. Dr. Elisabeth Kubler-Ross vividly describes dying. She finds there are five stages through which people pass: denial and isolation, anger, bargaining, depression and finally acceptance. If persons have sufficient time and support they can reach a peaceful resolution of the fight against inevitable death.

When death becomes imminent it must be handled openly. Every per-son has the right to know when he is dying. It gives him some control over his own life, if not his death. He can make arrangements for any bequests and order his relationships with friends and loved ones as well as prepare himself psychologically and spiritually. Perhaps most important, death should be shared with people close to the dying person. The fear of dying alone is an unnecessary and cruel fear to add to the burden of death. The living have the capacity to comfort the dying and to learn more about life in the process. Dr. Cicely Saunders' work at St. Christopher's Hospice in London is concerned with affirmation of life until its termination.

LEGACY

Human beings tend to feel a sense of completion and accomplishment if they can arrange to leave a legacy behind after their death. These legacies can be personal possessions or money to children, friends, relatives, churches and charities. Children and grandchildren are themselves gifts to the "future." Some persons create lasting works of art or perform acts that will be remembered afterwards. The donation of one's body or parts of the body to science or a medical school is a further example of legacy.* Since 1968 the Uniform Anatomical Gift Act, adopted by fifty states and the District of Columbia, has made it possible for people to donate their body parts for transplantation or their body for anatomical study. One may carry the Uniform Donor Card as a "pocket will."

Of course not everyone feels the urge to leave legacies. Man's relation to the future and to posterity has been emphasized throughout time, but a variety of responses are called forth. Consider the following four illustrative attitudes toward death and personal legacy.

1. Nihilism—"Let the world end with me!"
2. Cynical indifference—exemplified by Mark Twain, who said, "The future does not worry about us, so why should we worry about the future?"
3. Leaving a trace—concern with a legacy to the future and to the later generations, the wish to teach or support the young or the culture, to write a memoir, or to influence grandchildren.
4. Preservation—efforts to conserve what is valuable in the present for the future, but in some necessarily new form. An example would be an art collector who arranges to have his collection housed in modern, climatically controlled surroundings for the future.

* With changing religious attitudes and the desire to spare survivors soaring funeral costs, there are now more donated bodies than needed by medical schools in some parts of the country. (Some people—status-conscious to the end—want to leave their bodies only to prestige schools like Harvard.)

These several attitudes delineate different ways of handling one's grief over the loss of oneself. All have their individual adaptive value. The last two have social adaptive value as well because they make contributions to others.

MEMORIAL AND FUNERAL SERVICES

The high cost of dying can be a serious financial burden to families at a time when they are most vulnerable and least able to judge what would be appropriate. See Table 6 for sample expenses of typical funeral and burial services in 1972. Expenses can go much higher as arrangements become more elaborate. Consequently, the funeral business has been under attack, and nonprofit memorial societies have evolved to provide less ostentatious, more economical funerals. "In a funeral the center of attention is the dead body; the emphasis is on death. In a memorial service the center of concern is the personality of the individual who has died."

Memorial societies enable persons to "obtain simplicity, dignity and economy in funeral arrangements through advance planning."[28] These 120

TABLE 6

Sample Expenses of Funeral and Burial Services in 1972 for What Undertakers Describe as "Simple" Arrangements

Funeral	
Professional services	$ 578.00
Casket (metal; tailored cream-colored interior)	1,154.00
Vault	360.00
Dress	42.50
Slippers	4.95
Limousine	40.00
Obituaries (two papers)	33.60
Death certificates (4) @ $1 each	4.00
Sales taxes	48.00
	$2,265.05

At the Cemetery	
Lot itself	$ 300.00
Open and close ($30 more on Saturday)	170.00
Headstone (actually a flat stone)	210.00
Pallbearers (6) @ $10 each	60.00
Limousine	40.00
	$ 780.00

societies are organized as nonprofit organizations that are democratically controlled by their 600,000 members.*

In addition to educating the public about alternative services, the tendency toward elaborate showy funerals can be minimized by encouraging the open expression of grief, guilt and remorse toward the dead—thus eliminating some of the psychological motivation for compensatory, lavish funerals. Finally, in a society which has become increasingly secular, there may be a need to establish social rituals around death to replace religious ones.

MOURNING

Geoffrey Gorer observed that the majority of people today are "without adequate guidance as to how to treat death and bereavement, without social help in coming to terms with grief and mourning." He describes three distinct stages of mourning. The first is a short period of shock lasting a few days; the second, a time of intense grief during which the mourner suffers psychological changes, such as listlessness, disturbed sleep, failure of appetite and loss of weight; and third, a gradual reawakening of interest in life.† Gorer emphasizes that during the second phase, lasting from six to eight weeks, "the mourner is more in need of social support and assistance than at any time since infancy and early childhood." Open grieving, alone and in the presence of others, is a crucial outlet. If grief is denied expression, depression is a possible reaction. Another is an insulation against feeling that may border on callousness. Denial of grief is not the sole cause of depression, of course; ambivalence toward the deceased, anger and conflict can complicate the usual course of grief. It is the task of therapy to help open up the grief process. It is the goal of prevention to see that grief is not bottled up to begin with.

Simultaneous lengthening and invigoration of life may make it possible to create a strikingly different kind of old age, freed from most of the present physical incapacity and suffering. Death, when it does come, may eventually be preceded by a gentle, predictable decline. Sensitivity to the psychological meaning of death will contribute toward making the last crisis of the life cycle a time for potential meaning and summation. We actually have within our grasp the chance to live the gift of life fully and completely up to the moment of death itself.

---

* A number of these memorial societies form the Continental Association of Funeral and Memorial Societies, 59 East Van Buren St., Chicago, Illinois, 60605.
† It is some measure of the impact of personal losses of spouses that the death rate of the bereaved themselves rises after such a loss.[29]

Chapter 13

LOOSENING UP LIFE

All too many Americans become burned out, bored or angry before old age, living out their noisy or quiet lives in a desperation marked by disillusionment in their marital and family relationships and obsolescence of their work and educational skills. Is this all necessary? Are personal freedom and growth possible in the midst of family and economic responsibilities? What elements might give support to the full development of human potential? René Dubos has written, "Each human being is unique, unprecedented and unpredictable," but to make that elegant expression meaningful, society must be so organized that people can continue to grow to the very end of life. Obviously the attainment of that objective is a tremendously complex undertaking, but its complexity in no way diminishes its urgency.

Social and individual forces today lean heavily in the direction of rigidification, with political, educational, economic, cultural and other constraints. From early childhood the life of the modern American is programmed. First comes a block of education continuing at least into his late adolescence and, increasingly often, into his twenties, offering an extended but basically "one chance" educational opportunity. He then faces a massive block of work for forty years—in the foundry, on the assembly line or in the office—followed by retirement and "leisure."

This fixed design is stultifying not only to the individual but to society. By retirement, people may be too exhausted to enjoy their leisure or they may want or need to continue working. Even if they do wish to relax and enjoy themselves, their forty years of consecutive work have given them little preparation for the creative use of leisure.

At the other end of the life cycle the adolescent may be thrust into a system of higher education before he is ready for it.* He may want to work, to try his hand at various kinds of jobs. He may need to dream, travel or

---

* Barely 50 percent of college entrants actually complete college, according to a 1971 study of the Carnegie Commission on Higher Education.

simply enjoy life before making major and possibly binding decisions.*

Both ends of the life cycle press upon the middle generation.† It is they who must support the education and care of the young and the retirement of the old. They have the heaviest responsibilities and expenses. Some are angry, not only at the young and old but at those in better financial condition or those "on welfare," because they see these groups "getting all the benefits" while they, hard pressed, pay all the bills. Furthermore, they fear, with reason, technological obsolescence and their own loss of employability. A few attempt escape—some take to drink, others "drop out" and literally disappear. But the vast majority continue in their jobs, in their marriages, in their established molds. Even when they would like to change their life styles, shift their interests or simply have the leisure to catch their breath, they are likely to lack the resources to finance time off for education, a long vacation or a complete change of career. And when such resources exist a person may be afraid to shift gears in a society which seems to regard drastic career changes as bizarre.

WORK RUTS

For many Americans their forty years of work are forty years of tedious routine, their plight not unlike that of the worker in Charlie Chaplin's *Modern Times* (1936). (Remember the little man turning and twisting an invisible wrench as he walked to the men's room?) There is little to stimulate them. Workers show their boredom through absenteeism, high turnover, shoddy work, even sabotage, or drinking or smoking pot on the job.[1] Still other Americans, particularly in the professional-managerial class, operate under nearly constant pressure. If some workers tend to sleep on the job, others may find it difficult to sleep at all. Instead of slowly drying up, they literally burn out. The middle-aged smell retirement ahead and are tailgated by youth. Competition threatens them. Sometimes they retreat from the firing line and seek the kind of administrative jobs that conceal their growing incapacity, their dimming creativity or their fears. It is little wonder then that beyond a possibly benevolent motive in our compulsory retirement policies there is in addition a cruel elimination of the "obsolete" from the American work force. No one wants to take on the person who has been burned out in a pressure job or fossilized in a

* The Grand Tour originated in the seventeenth century as an aristocratic custom, but it has evolved into an educational tradition for many American youngsters from a variety of economic backgrounds.

† Workers between roughly 25 and 60 bear the weight of economic productivity. The middle-aged group, conventionally defined as 40 to 60, bear additional pressures that are filial, social and cultural.

tedious one. Compulsory retirement is often accompanied by unofficial personnel policies that discourage the hiring of people in their forties and fifties.*

Fundamental changes are needed if we are to reverse the unfortunate trends toward compartmentalization of education, work and retirement. We must free ourselves from seeing these as three separate periods of life and begin thinking of them as running concurrently and continuously throughout life. Existing financial supports—private and public funds for education, unemployment insurance, in-service training funds, Social Security and pensions—would, of course, have to be reallocated to support such a basic change.

Youth could then feel free to work or travel as well as to attend college. The 40-year-old would be encouraged to take time off to study, change directions or relax. The 70-year-old, in part because he would have had these refreshing experiences throughout life, would be as prepared for work and study as he would be for the true enjoyment of leisure if he chose it. To do this we would have to challenge the whole complex of laws, customs, union and management rules that discourage adolescent work and encourage compulsory retirement. We would need to reappraise the supposed "social" advances of job tenure, career ladders and seniority rights that tend to lock people into forty years of work, and to devise new ways of stimulating men and women to use more of these years for learning and leisure.[3]

In some measure, mid-career clinics, sabbaticals and shorter work weeks are small experiments in this direction. Unfortunately, organized labor, which might be a nucleus for innovation, is no longer in the vanguard of social conscience and social development. The federal government with three million employees would, however, be a place to conduct a variety of useful social experiments of this kind.

---

* Perhaps we need a system to cover "human depletion." In 1972 Senators Mike Mansfield (D.-Mont.) and George Aiken (R.-Vt.) introduced a bill calling for a personal depletion-allowance deduction for individuals. They wrote, "The emphasis that we as a nation have placed on things over people—on economic growth over social good, on the protection of tangible assets—could lead one who was not blinded by the obvious to ask whether our emphasis is misplaced." They noted: "The man and woman who are made old before their time—the man who stoked the fires of the steel mill, who digs the minerals from the bowels of the earth and the woman who likewise engages in difficult work should be considered. Their bodies and spirits can be exhausted long before the age of general retirement." The Senators set their figure at a minimum deduction of 10 percent, which can rise to 23 percent. They selected that particular figure because it is one percent higher than the highest depletion allowance then provided in the Tax Code (that being for oil).

One physician and his wife filed a 1971 tax form stating that their physical skills were eligible for a depletion deduction. However, the court of appeals agreed that the body does not come under the capital code of a definition of "natural deposits."[2]

Professor Juanita Kreps projected the possibility that by 1985 the gross national product might exceed $1.5 trillion or the per-capita GNP might move from the 1970 figure of $3,000 per annum to an 1985 figure of $6,000 per annum. Were this to happen, society would have the following choices with respect to work: there could be a 22-hour work week, a 27-week work year, retirement at 38, or the placement of one-half of the total labor force in retraining programs. Finally, as Kreps herself has advocated, the choice could be made to distribute work and leisure better throughout the life span.

Experiments in redistributing and decreasing the work week are already taking place. We forget that only since about the 1940s has the forty-hour five-day week been the "traditional" way of work. It is possible that there will be difficult adjustment reactions as people learn how to make use of more leisure time just as there have been such difficulties with retirement.

One of the reasons older people have so much trouble adjusting to not working in late life is that they have had very little experience with actual leisure. The definitions of the word "leisure" vary, ranging from nonworking time to contemplative time, from passive reception to active searching. The idea of increased leisure in America has had the character of a myth, as Sebastian de Grazia has shown.[4] In the working force, that is, largely those who are pre-65, the economic conditions in our country have led to the reduction of hours of work on a specific job while at the same time "moonlighting" has increased. The Bureau of Labor Statistics reports that one of four jobholders works 49 to 60 hours per week. Moreover, American housewives have increasingly gone to work while still having many of the responsibilities of child and home care. The chaos and the time involved in transportation to and from work reduce further the leisure we are said to have gained from shorter work hours. The decreased quality and the increased cost of services have driven Americans to the "do-it-yourself" movement. Thus, when de Grazia adds it all up he finds that the actual "free" time gained in the last hundred years is no more than two or three hours per week. This free time is the "leisure" everyone is talking about. It is little wonder that the elderly and their younger counterparts find themselves at a loss when they first encounter a large block of free, nonwork time. Education and training are in order here as in every other learned activity.

EDUCATION THROUGHOUT LIFE

Charles E. Silberman's book *Crisis in the Classroom* followed the books of John Holt, Edgar Z. Friedenberg, Paul Goodman, Jonathan Kozol and Herbert Kohl, all of whom write about the need for major educational reforms. Much human behavior is maladaptive rather than adaptive, and our educational programs are out of synchronization with what people need to learn. No one tells the child that his life is the one and only life he has, that it is tender and short and must be carefully nurtured, that it is easy to "blow it." No one tells the child that he is a unique person and has a unique range of possibilities before him. No one prepares him to be continually growing for a lifetime. People enter upon courses of action and decision which reside in the self, but they are not given models of flexibility. People enter friendships, marriages and work often unguided, and once entered into, these courses tend to become fixed. Yet one's behavior need not be ordained by unconsidered decisions and traced out with an indelible pencil.

Beginning very early, young people should be involved in a myriad of enterprises, investigating specific activities of history, government, professions; collecting information to be reviewed as part of the practicum of continuing courses in civics and humanities, psychology and sociology. The concept of citizenship should certainly be an important part of their learning, and that citizenship should include the workings of democracy in its broadest forms, including social organization, the elective process and legal remedies. Apprentice systems could be reintroduced to give youngsters a taste of future careers.

I would urge basic changes in the attitude toward the so-called "minor" subjects in schools. Music and the arts should become major subjects,* for they lend zest and pleasure to human life. They draw upon the imagination, which now tends to atrophy with time and disuse. The expansion of the minor subjects to major subjects, with proper economic support, would do much to prepare people for leisure through the entire course of life and in retirement.

Physical education should also be a major subject. It can make a crucial contribution to physical and emotional well-being. Spectator sports, interschool games and professionalism should be de-emphasized and a greater stress placed upon participatory sports, group and individual, in which all students could develop certain basic skills. Bicycling, swimming, hiking and camping are as much physical education as the school competitions that turn so many young people away from the healthy use of their physical skills.

True education for survival is also indicated: how to take care of oneself, the kinds of foods one should eat, how to conduct mouth-to-mouth resuscitation, how to induce a heartbeat, how to apply first aid, how to

* We need more public high schools specializing in music and the arts, as in New York City.

provide home care to a sick child or an older person—all of these are elements of health education in the broadest sense.

Family education, in which children, parents and grandparents within the entire family could be learning together, is another aspect of education that has scarcely been touched. Of course parents should not be doing homework for their children, but they should be involved with them in a continuing sense of an educative process throughout life. School buildings and facilities could become multipurposed, used by all ages at different times of the day and evening.

Continuing education should be part of life, not the prerogative of youth alone. Public schools, colleges and universities should expand their responsibility to the entire span of adult development. This is necessary to offset intellectual and skill obsolescence, to make retraining programs possible and to redesign individual skills to fit with work, just as in many instances work could be redesigned to fit the special skills of the individual.

Distinctly different from continuing or adult education is what can best be called life-cycle education, in which different psychological, personal, familial, occupational and other tasks related to specific processes and stages of life are taught. We need to understand the general processes of life and the various rites of passage which come along—sex, marital choice, early marriage, parenthood—and how to handle disability, illness and finally death.

These notions concerning the broadening and deepening of education cannot be adequately developed within the confines of this book, but are mentioned here as adding to the richness of life. Saint-Exupéry once said, in describing poor French children on a train, "I saw Mozart murdered in their faces." Resignation and the destruction of imaginative and creative possibilities begin in earliest life. The echoes of that destruction can reverberate through every phase of the life cycle, including old age.

MONEY DOES MATTER

American society and institutions have grown fixed, inflexible and class oriented despite the continued existence of "social mobility," the social scientist's term for "getting ahead." There are now hard-core rich as well as hard-core poor; military, technological and social classes; public and private bureaucracies; tedious tenure in academia; seniority in unions and Congress; and a variety of other nearly overwhelming constraints. Some of our values, such as material success and security, are among the limiting features of the national landscape. The Protestant ethic, the dread of death, the worship of technology, efficiency and productivity—all for their own sake—contribute still further to the already-described compartmentalization of life's activities. America has arrived at middle age, one might say, and as F. Scott Fitzgerald once said, "There are no second acts in American lives."

It has been argued that financial security reduces the excitement of challenging growth. That is simply not true. Indeed, security probably promotes growth rather than impedes it. The poor *per se* are not usual sources of change, as the behavior of the peasant classes of the world demonstrate. Poverty requires too much in the way of the brutish struggle simply to exist and survive. Thus some measure of security must frame creative growth.

If we look at life from the perspective of the life cycle, what would be necessary financially to provide underpinnings for the right to live? One might want life-cycle credit systems and the availability of money more directly related to occasions of need. When young people are starting out, for example, they may need money to establish their homes and purchase their furniture. In the middle years they may need collective systems to provide college education for their children or perhaps to support the family through the destructive features of divorce. To take just one aspect of our present system, Social Security is available to a female divorcee if there have been twenty years of marriage and if at the time of the ex-husband's death the wife depended on him for more than half her support. Thus Social Security is already somewhat tied to divorce and should be tied more closely. The amounts of money involved could be related by formula to the number of years of marriage. It need not be tied to other sources of income because if there were truly an adequate, progressive income tax then the individual would be paying any excessive income back in the form of taxes anyway. It can be seen that revisions in Social Security could greatly enhance flexibility in the course of the life cycle in a variety of ways: in terms of marriage, education, replacement of earnings upon disability, retirement and providing for survivors. What employers now call fringe benefits could be incorporated more effectively into a broad Social Security program. Such a program should provide a minimum income without destroying incentive. It cannot and should not provide for all that would be possible. But it should meet the requirements for security and thus open up the doors to further growth and development.

LOOSENING UP MARRIAGE

There are several general issues that currently shape marital and other forms of intimate relationships. First is the socioeconomic and cultural framework that has created inequalities which lead to frustrations and rage. Each partner can become angry at the other, feel taken advantage of, at times to the point of exploitation. Dominance and subordination result in power struggles. Each blames the other for insensitivity and callousness. Another issue in marriage is the participants' capacity for intimacy, mutuality, give and take. We can call this the individual equation. The third element is the interrelationship between two different personalities, the interpersonal interplay, whether complementary or adversary. In other words, how well do they "fit" together?

With the increased survivorship there are now greater numbers of couples who remain together longer. Thus a fourth issue has emerged. It was always present even when relationships were made brief owing to the realities of disease and death, but it is now a greater problem with the extended survival of people to their middle and later years. This is the problem of fidelity and infidelity in human relationships, and in the broadest sense, the nature of trust and distrust, the durability of human feeling and the intrusion of boredom.

The twentieth century has seen changes in all four aspects of intimate relationships. There is a demand for a greater equality, a cry for a deeper internal growth and possibility for intimacy, a wish and expectation for greater depth and possibilities in the interpersonal relationship, and finally, the relatively novel problem of wrestling with continuity and time. Thus have emerged issues and movements, among them the feminist movement, increased rates of divorce, proposals for divorce insurance, the advent of marital counseling and the emergence of late-life divorce, marriage and remarriage.

The National Organization of Women (NOW) adopted the following statement at their organizing conference in Washington, D.C., in 1966:

We reject the current assumptions that a man must carry the sole burden of supporting himself, his wife and family, and that a woman is automatically entitled to lifelong support by a man upon her marriage, or that marriage, home and family are primarily woman's world and responsibility—hers, to dominate —his, to support. We believe that a true partnership between the sexes demands a different concept of marriage, an equitable sharing of the responsibilities of home and children and of the economic burdens of their support. We believe that proper recognition should be given to the economic and social values of homemaking and child care. To these ends we will seek to open a re-examination of laws and mores concerning marriage and divorce, for we believe that the current state of "half-equality" between the sexes discriminates against both men and women and is a cause of much unnecessary hostility between the sexes.

American men have yet to realize the openness and decency of the purposes of Women's Liberation at its most serious. It is not simply an expression of women's rights, but an expression of the rights of men and women to share equally and together in common goals. In short, in its best sense, Women's Liberation is concerned with human liberation. The inflexibility of men and women as they live out their lives together, but often on separate tracks, contributes to resentment. The situation of the woman is especially complex. The facts are all too compelling; examination of pay levels, educational and occupational job opportunities all demonstrate the unequal status in which women of all ages are placed. The older woman ordinarily cares for her spouse after retirement, is his deathbed nurse, and then, because of a longer life span, must face difficult years as a widow.

Simone de Beauvoir, Betty Friedan and others have written effectively of the political and economic requirements essential to build toward an equality between women and men and have also dealt with the "feminine mystique and sensibility in regard to women."[5] But neither they nor the "movement" has yet begun to deal with the inequalities of longevity and the destitution that faces so many older women as widows.[6]

Looking at marriage as a whole, the problem of the individual's capacity for intimacy and mutuality and of marital choice have not been thoroughly explored. There are, of course, books on the history of marriage. There is also quite a body of material that has come from the consulting chambers of psychiatrists and marriage counselors. There are philosophic works, largely existential, concerning human interactions and their expression, such as Martin Buber's *I and Thou* concerning mutuality. But in the main, given the enormous import of marital choice and intimacy upon human happiness, it is difficult for persons to find guidance.

The significance of this is not just for the marital couple alone but for their children. The family has been conceived as an economic unit and has been fundamentally a protection for children. (It has proven to be less of a protection for older family members.) Because the family is created more by chance than by wisdom, the old matchmakers may not have been any less successful than those who have made a choice based on romantic love. It seems sadly true that, as Bertrand Russell said, "A marriage is likely to be what is called happy if neither party expected to get much happiness out of it."[7]

What draws people together? Often physical attraction and sexual pressure. Often great expectations of romantic love. Sometimes shyness and loneliness, the fear of being alone. In many instances a marriage choice is based on the struggle to resolve one's childhood, one's relations toward one's parents and the relations between one's parents. One can act out in marriage the conflicts of childhood, and even resolve these, yet still be unable to handle the other conflicts intrinsic in the marriage.

The individual's capacity for intimacy and mutuality can be aided and abetted by the education system but will be affected most by family life during childhood, the quality and nature of the relationship between one's own parents. The woman who has never really had a father or has had a cruel or an indifferent and passive father may be deeply and adversely affected in her own growth. She may be nonorgasmic, she may be full of hatred and revenge, and she may be frightened and disturbed. The man whose mother was overwhelming and powerful may move in diverse ways in his own sexual orientation to protect himself against the possibilities of deep and close but seemingly dangerous personal relationships. The capacity for intimacy, however, need not be unalterably fixed in relationship to one's father and mother. If possibilities for important experiences exist with other adults and fellow members of the same generation as one's parents or grandparents, particularly in an open community that includes the open classroom or an open church, then it is often possible to act out or re-enact and resolve some of the stumbling blocks in the family experience.

It may be said that all human relationships are eventually disappointing. People need and expect much more than they can realistically receive. People are also limited in what they can give. Disillusionment is therefore inevitable, and part of the resolution of the question of intimacy is to be able to accept its imperfections. Finally, one must be prepared to accept the loss of every intimate relationship, if not through circumstance, then certainly through the death of one of the participants. The romantic concept "I can't live without you" must be faced with pain and grief. This is the way it must be. The human paradox is to be able to live without each other, to be able to accept the inevitability of separation and yet to desire and wholly participate in intimacy when it is obtainable.

The importance of intimacy and mutuality cannot be overestimated. D. H. Lawrence wrote, "All the literature of the world shows how profound is the instinct of fidelity in both men and women, how both men and women hanker restlessly after the satisfaction of this instinct, and fret at their own inability to find the real mode of fidelity." A capacity for intimacy is the real goal of most people. Without it, lives which are otherwise successful will seem wanting. With intimacy, even the most difficult lives can be judged worthwhile and satisfying.

Beyond the capacity for intimacy is the problem of the match between two people. A man who is aggressive, work-oriented and highly sensitive to personal hurt may find himself in a deteriorating marriage to a woman who is timid and easily intimidated, frightened, inhibited, and therefore angry in a sabotaging style. For all the genuine idealism and hope that began their marriage, each may be unable to find in the other what each so much desires. It is often the underlying similarities between partners and not the differences which precipitate marital difficulties. Because of the essential identity in their psychodynamics—the underlying forces—neither party possesses the detachment necessary to help the other to overcome the disruptive, usually grim, angry, dependent form of relationship which appears to be the most common source of marital conflict. True intimacy, mutuality and interpersonal tolerance become impossible. In my experience, however, many marriages contain the possibility of success and resolution because the features the partners share also represent the strengths of the marriage. Moreover, actual differences stimulate excitement, interest and respect when and if the obstructions of seemingly irreconcilable similarities are removed.

Marriage counseling has boomed as a business. More and more marriage counselors are beginning to agree with psychiatrists that it is not alone the marriage that must be helped, but the individual participants. They must learn about themselves. The focus of counseling must be upon the elements which have contributed to the failure of the marriage, so that people can build anew, whether separately or as a couple.

The problem of sexual inhibition in intimacy is a heritage of Victorian attitudes and repressive religious thinking,[8] and it continues to affect many people, including the elderly. In the twentieth century Sigmund Freud, Havelock Ellis, Margaret Sanger, Bertrand Russell, Alfred Kinsey, and Masters and Johnson have made serious efforts and great contributions toward freeing humankind from sexual inhibition through liberalization of attitudes toward sex, marriage and abortion. In part, the facts—when exposed—spoke for themselves, indicating a greater amount and greater diversity of sexual activity than had been realized.[9] But be wary of generalizations; the present generation of the elderly, now in their seventies, were among the early experimenters in the flapper age of the 1920s.

There are concrete issues of sexuality in late life: the varying aging rates of sexual partners, which influence sexuality; the unavailability of sexual partners for widows; unexpressed homosexuality, which leads to needless inhibitions; and a general lack of adequate information about sexuality in late life. A sex manual geared to the elderly is as important as one for the young and middle-aged.

Continuity of the marital relationship over time is a further issue that is little understood. Our National Institute of Mental Health study[10] showed deterioration in up to a third of marriages in the late years. Mutuality may be reinforced, however, through the social and medical aspects of late life, when the couple unites in fighting the outside enemies—illness, loneliness and death—to survive. The specter of death tends to keep people married, each to nurse the other during the final days. It is more often the woman, of course, because of the differential in life expectancy, who has the task of nursing her spouse and then faces years of loneliness. In later years, then, dependency may hold people together, but irritation and anger may supervene, especially in the face of crisis. A woman, for example, often feels it morally incumbent on her to take total and complete care of her slowly dying husband. All efforts to get her to obtain help to relieve some of the pressures may fail. Ultimately she may become quite resentful, and what might have been a reasonably good marriage may end, sadly, with considerable anger and subsequent guilt, prolonged grief and possible depression in the survivor.

Women also experience what Bernice Neugarten has called a "rehearsal for widowhood," by realistically taking into account the fact of the sex differential in mortality and utilizing the human capacity for anticipatory grief in order to weaken the powerful impact of the likely death of a husband. Paradoxically, in those relationships that had been the most firm and sound, the survivors are generally not as disrupted by loss, and eventually feel freer to move on to other relationships. But where the relationship has been grim and complicated by dependency or anger, unresolved and often unarticulated, the grief may be intense and the possibilities of picking up the pieces and renewing oneself are vastly reduced. Thus the tranquil widow or widower must not be seen as a callous survivor relieved by the death of a spouse, but rather as a compliment to the marriage itself.

The specter of death plays a part in the re-evaluation of the middle years that people go through. Taking an inventory and taking stock are necessary functions of the middle years, as one begins to count the time left until death rather than counting forward from birth. Birthdays take on a very different meaning. Death lurks in the background of mid-life; it says that if one is going to make a different life, it must be made now. There is, then, a sense of urgency; one may be reduced in a foreseeable future to helplessness and illness, to lack of choice. Under this hard scrutiny marriages are vulnerable.

But marriages do not invariably deteriorate after middle age. There may be growing affection and acceptance, growing tolerance for each other's idiosyncrasies, tensions and sources of tension, and evolving mutuality.

The question of fidelity over a period of many years can become an issue in itself. People seem to have an effervescent and constantly resurging need for excitement and adventure. Sexual affairs, to the extent that they reflect this need, may represent the desire for freedom to explore and experience anew.

Society, to be stable, does require control of human impulses, aggressiveness and sexuality. In that sense stable marital and family life is in some measure a foundation of society, but that foundation can only serve adequately if there is room for growth, excitement, and new levels of intimacy. The vast majority of Americans stay married "until death do us part" but often with great pain and dour consequences. "They lived together but had been in a state of emotional divorce for many years," said one daughter of her parents. Other marriages are disrupted violently, or even needlessly, by divorce.

A more general flexibility in all of life's roles—wage earner, parent, spouse, community member, student—would help to reduce the pressure on marriages. In addition, rather than being automatically destructive, infidelity in some instances may help a marriage. There can be a therapeutic advantage to affairs.* It may help the man or the woman to see that the grass is or is not greener on the other side of the fence, to work out some of his own sexual inhibitions, and to learn to know and grow with another person.† Whether this should be generalized into such catchy concepts as "open marriage"[11] is questionable. Whether "affairs" should be handled privately or openly by the married couple is not resolved by generalized edicts; it requires individualized appraisal and perhaps skilled counseling.

There have been experiments around marriage, with various forms of realtionships, from time immemorial. Even today some families live in polygamy. There are long, enduring, successful and happy homosexual relationships, and recently some of these have been formalized by marriage. There have been communal forms of relations that date back centuries. The 1960s and 1970s have seen growing movements toward communal and group marriages.

Collective marriages and unmarried couples who elect to have children are found currently in situations where the people involved can afford the social hazards—in the wealthy upper classes, bohemian circles or among celebrities. But not too many people are able to brave the severe social

---

* Universities, foundations, the National Institute of Mental Health and other institutions cannot easily support studies of love affairs, which are so common in practice and which, as a clinician, one sees so frequently. This is an instance of one of the real issues of human life that is not subjected to study because it is so freighted with societal mores, conflicting feelings and repressive tendencies.

† I have known wives who have urged their impotent husbands to have affairs in hopes that it would cure them, and husbands who want frigid wives to do the same.

criticism and ostracism that can follow if their lives are lived in conventional towns and work situations.

To add both to the freedom and flexibility of marriage itself and to the seriousness with which the participants perceive and evaluate each other, their children and their life together, there have been a variety of suggestions, including the periodic renewal of marriage contracts that includes proving the wisdom of renewal or having the freedom to decide to leave each other.

With liberalization of abortion laws and the advent of the contraceptive pill, young people are living together more freely and there are fewer shotgun marriages. This has, in effect, provided a physiologically supported basis for the trial-marriage concepts of Bertrand Russell in the 1920s. (There are, of course, dangers to the pill. Serious side reactions and the possibility of long-term time-bomb effects cannot be ruled out.)

In the broader sense there ought to be more tests before marriage than the Wassermann, including counseling and review of the circumstances leading to the marriage. There might be a trial of living together when it is not destructive to the religious or moral upbringing of the persons in question. Written contracts around issues of real or anticipated disagreement could be considered.

It remains essential that the right to live include the right to open and honorable intimacies between persons in love where that love is an informed love—a love that accepts growth and development and is not based upon false or exaggerated expectations. It remains essential that such love and the establishment of relationships not be constricted by locking partners in a bond that stops being meaningful. For those who came together for reasons that no longer hold, or for inappropriate or merely erotic reasons to begin with, freedom should be given to part without destructiveness and with a choice for learning and further growth. But while it is important that personal relationships be given greater choice, greater flexibility and greater freedom for coming together and for parting, it does not follow that the concepts of commitment of marriage and family are dead, or that orgiastic and irresponsible sexuality should replace intimate, informed, creative, supportive, growth-producing personal relationships.

Many question the right of the state to become involved in the intimate affairs of people. In *Griswold* v. *Connecticut*, the state was limited in its right to restrict the dissemination of birth-control information. In *Loving* v. *Virginia,* miscegenation was protected; in *Stanley* v. *Georgia*, personal sexual tastes. In Illinois the elimination of sanctions against homosexual acts between consenting adults represents another example of personal and individual rights transcending the state. Liberalization of abortion is probably the most far-reaching of these changes. The trend to no-fault divorces is another. This does not mean, obviously, that the state can totally sacrifice its interests. But necessary monitoring should not be achieved through repressive and punitive laws. It may evolve more appropriately through a wise balancing of the state's needs against the needs of individuals in the state—the protection of children, for example, through child support; the protection of divorced women through job counseling and insurance; the nurture of children from the earliest years by quality education—the state taking responsibility as never before to ensure the basic fundaments of human living.

Marital and other forms of interpersonal relationships cannot be discussed in a vacuum any more than I could earlier discuss education, work, leisure or retirement without drawing on their interconnections. Marriage and divorce are profoundly tied to social and economic circumstances. The poor find the costs of divorce extremely cruel and may remain married. The National Center of Health Statistics does not even contain data related to common-law marriage, which is one way by which the poor, especially the black poor, traditionally maintained privacy and lived together economically.

IDENTITY CRISES CAN BE HEALTHY

So many lives, lived as a result of fixed decisions, victims of the inequalities and failures of education, employment, economic support, and marriage, are wasteful in comparison to what they might have been.

When journalists put the familiar question to older people, "Would you like to live your life over?" many of them say no. Is it because, as H. L. Mencken said, "No show is so good that it should last forever"? Not entirely. At 83 years of age Benjamin Franklin, for example, said, "Hitherto this long life has been tolerably happy, so that if I were allowed to live it over again I should make no objection, only wishing for leave to do, as authors do in a second edition of their works, correct some of my *errata*."[12]

And W. E. B. Du Bois wrote of the sense and reality of life and death to him. He found:

It is incomprehensible for me to see persons quite panic-stricken at the approach of their 30th birthday and prepared for disillusion at forty. . . . Of course, one sees some reasons: the disappointment of meager accomplishment which all of us to some extent share; the haunting shadow of possible decline; the fear of death. . . . I have never shared what seems to me the essentially childish desire to live forever. Life has its pain and evil—its bitter disappointments; but I like a good novel and in healthy length of days, there is infinite joy in seeing the World, the most interesting of continued stories, unfold, even though one misses The End.[13]

In my experience as a clinician, I find that people seem to regret most what they did not do rather than what they did. When older people tell of their lives, those who have led open, evolving and changing lives, those with open personalities and the capacity to change, prove to be relatively few.

All too many have allowed themselves the kind of forced identity which has led them to several modes of coping.[14] Many lives have an infrastructure; infralives are hidden, secret, parallel lives often maintained with vast expenditures of energy. Underground living may be seen in the everyday bourgeois who becomes a weekend hippie and the statistician who experiences his greatest joy in collecting rare books. Some people hold close a secret self which, because it is revealed to no one, often leads to the elaboration of rich fantasies and daydreams. For some, an extramarital relationship may be more crucial than their marriage. The avocation may be more salient than the vocation, the lives of one's children may be more highly valued than one's own.

Second are the pseudo lives lived as whole lives—barren, stark, empty —which basically retreat from danger. They suggest the fraudulent identity. They are involved in acting and role playing. The homosexual who denies his impulses, the person who continues to do what he no longer believes in, those who pretend socially in order to preserve status and income are examples of pseudo lives.

Third are others who lead "lives of quiet desperation." They usually do not have infralives and may be too honest or aware to allow themselves pseudo lives. Thus they live desperate, immobile existences, feeling miserable but doing nothing about it.

Fourth are those who simply disappear, though not all of them permanently. Some may try to start completely anew, changing their names, leaving their families and friends; some simply drop out for a time to a new style of life, a new community or country.

To obviate the necessity for all of these often less than satisfying methods of coping, it is essential that there be greater freedom over and against fixed identity, with freedom to rebel against that which no longer "fits." But, despite some radical changes in attitudes and personal relationships, especially among the young, our culture may actually be moving in the opposite direction. With the threat of so many social and technological changes, instead of an unfreezing of roles and loosening of identities, there has been a greater intensification in many respects.

Some behavior is "on time" in terms of both individual and social perspectives. Some is quite outdated and anachronistic. Some is ahead of time, which could be called proleptic. There are experimenters, individuals who play with change, who may influence life styles of the future. But it is surprising how punitive society can be toward those individuals who endeavor to try out such new life styles.

Continuity of personality over the life span is, of course, fundamental and, though it is not to be misconstrued that I favor complete and continued diffusion of personality, I am dubious of the wisdom of an excessive preoccupation with the maintenance of identity. Much of this preoccupation only amounts to a rather systematic renunciation of ourselves and our possibilities.

I deem identity to be a potentially regressive concept, implying the consolidation of one's past identifications as to "who" one is. As applied to the adolescent, identity as described by Erikson has, I believe, too many of the connotations of passivity, acceptance and resignation. The so-called adolescent turmoil or "identity diffusion" or "identity crisis" is seen as problematic. Erikson does spell out the occurrence of what he calls "selective repudiation" of the past in the development of one's identity, but he still favors the importance of consolidating one's identity and sticking with it as a healthy sign throughout life. He writes in "The Problem of Ego Identity":

. . . for the young individual must learn to be most himself where he means most to others—those others, to be sure, who have come to mean most to him. The term identity expresses such a mutual relation in that it connotes both a persistent sameness within one's self (selfsameness) and a persistent sharing of some kind of essential character with others. . . .

These new identifications are no longer characterized by the playfulness of childhood and experimental zest of youth: with dire urgency they force the young individual into choices and decisions which will, with increasing immediacy, lead to a more final self-definition, to irreversible role pattern and thus to commitments "for life."[15]

Integrity is the acceptance of one's one and only life cycle as something that had to be, and that, by necessity, permitted of no substitution. It is a comradeship with the ordering ways of different times and different pursuits. Although aware of the relativity of all the various life styles which have given meaning to human striving, the possessor of integrity is ready to defend the dignity of his own life style against all physical and economic threats, for he knows that an individual life is the accidental coincidence of but one life cycle with but one cycle of history, and that for him all human integrity stands or falls with the one style of integrity of which he partakes.[16]*

People are locked in by such a theory. They have made their "commitment." They have fulfilled Erikson's definitions of health based upon identity, and they suffer from such so-called health based on identity all their lives—locked into work, marital choices and life styles.

Interestingly, Tolstoy at age 81 predated Erikson in stressing the consciousness of the self that is called identity.

I remember very vividly that I am conscious of myself in exactly the same way now, at 81, as I was conscious of myself, my "I," at five or six years of age. Consciousness is immovable. Due to this alone there is a movement which we call "time." If time moves on, then there must be something that stands still, the consciousness of my "I" stands still.[17]

But it is important to know that, while there is that firm root of sense of oneself, there can also be continuing possibilities, as Tolstoy demonstrated beautifully in his own life. Art historian Bernard Berenson at 83 found room for change and expansion:

I for one have never touched bottom in self, nor even struck against the surface, the outlines, the boundaries of this self. On the contrary, I feel the self as an energy only which expands and contracts.[18]

Can we find ways to create diversification within ourselves and our institutions? Excessive or exaggerated identity seems clearly to be an obstacle to continued growth and development throughout life and to appreciation of the future. I would go so far as to say that *a continuing lifelong concern with one's identity is a sign of good health,* and the *right to have such a concern is one of the important rights of life.* Human beings need the freedom to live with change, to invent and reinvent themselves a number of times throughout their lives. By loosening up life we enlarge the value of the gift of life.

---

* But I cannot accept Erikson's passive view of life. His claim that Integrity versus Despair is *the* psychosocial issue of old age does not fit my experience with older people, whose anger, despair and other evidence of not accepting one's fate are healthy.

Chapter 14

GROWING OLD ABSURD

Ladies and gentlemen, in certain instances death
Is preceded by old age.[1]

HOW WE GOT THAT WAY

The American poet Ralph Robin gently reminds us of something we would like to forget, namely, that old age must be reckoned with psychologically. Our sensibility concerning later life has been dulled and diminished by fear and denial, by distaste and bitterness. We view aging as little more than decline, with no redeeming personal or social value. Old age has become an absurdity, a time of life with virtually nothing to recommend it.

In Chapter 1 I sketched the contemporary devalued view of the older person, calling it "ageism"—the prejudice against those who are old. Negative attitudes toward the old range from pity and infantilization to avoidance or direct hostility. The old are forced into—and for the most part accept—a narrow definition of appropriate behavior, usually quiet and passive. Yet some among them manage in spite of obstacles to create a life for themselves which allows room for decision making, self-esteem and involvement. How do they do it? What inner and outer resources do they draw on? Are there positive psychological qualities inherent in old age which belie the popular image of decline and decay? And why have we become insensitive to these possibilities? A number of forces combine to make old age a relatively meaningless marking of time before death, rather than a valuable final segment of the life cycle.

Some of the forces behind ageism in America are ancient legacies handed down through the generations. Others are unique to our culture and those other cultures sharing similar psychological and social orientations. Still others are a consequence of the time in which we live, the result of industrial and technological changes, medical progress and changes in the standard of living.

On the personal level, negative attitudes toward aging go beyond the obvious elements of pain, disease, fears of helplessness and fears of ruin.

Perhaps the most primitive aspect of the psychology of ageism is the problem of grief over the changes and diminishing functions perceived in one's own body with age. Our bodies are "us," and grief can easily be aroused over signs of the ultimate loss of one's self.

The philosophic conviction that death is tragic—an outrageous affront —reflects Western civilization's strong emphasis on the importance of the individual self. Religion has offered an answer to this problem by postulating the idea of a continuance of the self after death of the body. This lessens fear and makes death more acceptable, either as "sleep" or as a transitional step. But those who do not hold religious views are forced to deal directly with the question of the dissolution of the self. Recently there has been an active scientific and psychological literature on attitudes toward death in the United States. We may indeed be moving toward a more open and candid relation to the inevitability of dying.

Many also view aging as chastisement. To cite one example, people's feelings about aging skin can be profoundly negative. They are ashamed of wrinkles and "age spots." I recall one man who told me the skin blemishes which appeared on his scalp with age were God's subpoenas—indictments for his many "crimes and follies." This is an exaggerated reaction, but it reflects the melancholy depiction of aging as punishment. Such a view may derive from personal feelings of guilt over the past or fears about helplessness; but it also can be a reaction to feeling "punished" by societal attitudes. The biblical proverb "The hoary head is a crown of glory" portrays the old age of legend and fairy tales rather than current reality.

Old age can invite aesthetic reactions such as distaste. How does one deal with the bad sights, smells and sounds surrounding old people who are sick? Many of the late-life body changes, especially those associated with disease, cause revulsion. There is little that is beautiful about a sick body. Illness and pain can ravage one physically. Even psychologically there can be unattractive aspects to old age—depression, stagnation, isolation and loneliness are not inspiring emotional states. Many old people present a picture of dejection, diffidence, a lack of change and growth, a dearth of exhilaration in being alive that are certainly unappealing to those who are younger. Older people are often acutely aware of others' reactions and at times will exaggerate their physical and psychological symptoms to gain favors, services, sympathy, pity or a sense of revenge, by instilling fear in the young. Through a lowered self-esteem, scant economic resources or lack of energy, some elderly neglect their appearance even when they are not actually ill.

The issue here is one of learning to change the unattractiveness that can and should be changed while at the same time becoming humane and accepting of those things that are inevitably unpleasant to the senses. To allow particular aesthetic sensibilities to stand in the way of full participation in the life cycle is to rob ourselves and others of profound and worthwhile experiences. The temporary suspension of certain sensitivities may be required in order to encourage the larger goal of offering aid and comfort, learning about illnesses and death, sharing in the human drama.

Age segregation is a significant element in the negative feelings toward the old. There is an increasing segregation of different age groups in America, paralleling separations by social class, marital status, income, race, ethnicity and religion. People of the same age group are encouraged to believe they have little in common with other ages. Youngsters are wary of those over thirty; old people are led to feel they have nothing to teach or learn from those who are younger. The tendency of the old to be kept out of sight in their homes, in institutions, or in retirement communities contributes to the attitude of out of sight, out of mind. We pay a price for these attitudes. What are children, youth and the middle-aged to do for models if they have no contact with the old? They lose the opportunity to learn by word and deed the nature of the entire life experience, of survival to old age. They lose their sense of ancestry, history and roots, and so lose a valuable understanding of themselves. They begin to fear the natural process within themselves of growing and maturing to old age because late life represents unfamiliar and forbidding territory.

Urie Bronfenbrenner, in comparing the United States and Russia in *Two Worlds of Children*, points out:

> . . . it is our view that the phenomenon of segregation by age and its consequences for human behavior and development pose problems of the greatest magnitude for the Western world in general and for American society in particular. . . . [W]e cannot escape the conclusion that if the current trend persists, if the institutions of our society continue to remove parents, other adults, and older youth from active participation in the lives of children, and if the resulting vacuum is filled by the age-segregated peer groups we can anticipate increased alienation, indifference, antagonism, and violence on the part of the younger generation in all segments of our society—middle-class children as well as the disadvantaged.[2]

As a result of ageism and resultant age segregation the elderly have developed many of the characteristics of a minority group.[3] When they are subjected to prejudice, derogation, discrimination and stereotyping by younger groups they react with hypersensitivity and defensiveness about their status. Oppressed groups develop their own subculture in which values and behavior patterns are shared.[4] This is seen in the tendency of the old to want to live and socialize primarily with their own contemporaries. Obviously old people, like any age group, legitimately have much to share with their peers. Up to a point it is healthy and functional for persons to help one another solve the problems that are peculiar to their period of life. But the present extreme degree of age segregation is non-functional.

Because of concern over the psychological impact of age segregation, a social-worker colleague, Myrna I. Lewis, and I have experimented with age integration in psychotherapy groups as one way to combat the effects of segregation:

Since 1970, Lewis and I have conducted four age-integrated psychotherapy groups (8 to 10 members each) with one contrasting middle-aged group. We have integrated persons ranging from age 15 years to age 80 and above in each of the four groups, based on the belief that age segregation as practiced in our society leaves very little opportunity for rich exchange of feeling, experience and support possible between the generations. The groups are oriented toward persons experiencing a crisis in their life, varying from near-normal to pathological reactions to adolescence, education, marriage or single life, divorce, parenthood, work and retirement, widowhood, illness and impending death. Thus, such groups are concerned not only with intrinsic psychiatric disorders but also with preventive and remedial treatment of people as they pass through the usual vicissitudes of the life cycle. Criteria for membership include absence of active psychosis and presence of a life crisis (acute, subacute or chronic). Reactions to life crises follow traditional diagnostic categories, of course, including depression, anxiety states, hysterical reactions, obsessive-compulsive and passive-aggressive reactions, hypochondriasis, alcoholism and mild drug use. Groups are formed balanced for age, sex and personality dynamics. They meet once a week for one and a half hours. We have found it useful to have male and female co-therapists. Individual membership in a group averages about two years, and new group members are asked to participate for a minimum of three months.

The life cycle crisis approach to group therapy needs to be neither strictly an encounter approach nor strictly psychoanalytic. Rather it can be equally concerned with the interaction among and between group members as determined by reality and the past histories of each member, and with the individual problems of each member. The goal is the amelioration of suffering, the overcoming of disability and the opportunity for new experience of intimacy and self-fulfillment.

Regarding the elderly, some of the phenomena we have observed include: pseudo-"senility," a "Peter Pan" syndrome (refusal to grow up), and leadership pre-empted by the middle aged, with neglect or "mascoting" of elderly and young (necessitating therapeutic intervention). Unique contributions of the elderly include models for growing older, solutions for loss and grief, the creative use of reminiscence, historic empathy and a sense of entire life cycle. We are convinced that possibilities for psychological growth continue to the end of life.[5]

Age segregation and ageism erode family life and perpetuate ambivalence over responsibility to one's elders. Filial responsibility—the obligation of children to their parents—refers not only to law and custom but to general attitudes. Medieval church law held children accountable for the care of their parents. The Elizabethan poor law established for the first time the idea that the community would assist the elderly person after the children had done what could be done, but it did not fully clarify the extent of what was to be expected of children.

The issue of family responsibility for older family members has varied throughout history and from culture to culture.[6] In general, the middle-aged and younger family members have been expected to provide for their elders. This was often reinforced in the past by the fact that elders held the power and influence in a community. Our own society is caught up in controversy between individual and societal responsibility. State laws on the question of "family responsibility" are a maze of inconsistencies. Part of this is explained by serious practical problems. Costs of care may be exorbitant. Families may not be able to secure necessary services. Furthermore, with increasing numbers of people living longer life spans, a family may have responsibility for four living grandparents and even great grandparents.*

In addition, problems in relationships between parents and children affect filial attitudes. Conflicted emotional feelings can make people reluctant to assume responsibility for parents. Guilt, resentment and other unresolved emotional ties affect judgment and generosity. Some overcompensate and do too much; others become resentful and do too little. Some "pay their parents back" for the wrongs done to them in childhood by neglecting them. The resolution of long-standing family conflicts is often a first step in helping adult children decide on an appropriate role with respect to their elders.[8]

Social Security is of course based on the concept of intergenerational

---

* Studies show that in 1920 only 4 out of 5 children at the age of 10 were apt to have one living grandparent whereas 50 years later 19 out of 20 were apt to. In 1920 the chance of a 10-year-old child having at least two grandparents alive was 2 in 5. In 1970 it was 3 in 4. The chance of a 10-year-old having at least three living grandparents has risen from 1 in 10 to 3 in 8. The chance of having all four has gone from 1 in 90 to 1 in 14. (These figures pertain to white children.)[7]

support as a society-wide filial responsibility. Kenneth E. Boulding has summarized its nature as follows:

One of the things we know for certain about any age group is that it has no future. The young become middle-aged, and the middle-aged become old, and the old die. Consequently, the support which the middle-aged give to the young can be regarded as the first part of a deferred exchange, which will be consummated when those who are now young become middle-aged and support those who are now middle-aged who will then be old. Similarly, the support which the middle-aged give to the old can be regarded as the consummation of a bargain entered into a generation ago.[9]

Social Security has freed families from some of the burden of full financial support, but financial assistance is still a frequent necessity, particularly when long-term nursing care is needed. Families are also called upon to provide a variety of services which are currently unavailable to the old from other sources. And, finally, families can provide the warmth, affection, personal support and social network which are so important in old age. Persons without families are sometimes able to find such support in closely knit neighborhoods or social groups.*

The contention that many American families preserve a complex pattern of supportive relationships with older members is verified by a number of studies. Shanas refutes the "myth of alienation" by observing:

The physical separation of older people and their children in the United States is more apparent than real. Despite extensive internal migration in that country, older people and at least one of their children still maintain a close physical relationship. Four of every ten older unmarried people with children live in the same household with at least one child and an additional three of every ten are ten minutes or less distant from their nearest child. In all, 82 percent of all unmarried old persons in the U.S. who have children are less than 30 minutes distant from at least one of these children. In time of illness, older parents turn to their adult children for help. Parents expect that their children will be available to help them, children on their part expect to give whatever assistance is needed.[10]

Litwak refers to the American family as a "modified and extended" system in which the nuclear family is not isolated but is part of "an extended kin family system, highly integrated within a network of social relationships and mutual assistance that operates along bi-lateral kin lines and vertically over several generations."[11]

* Some older persons have been maintained for years in their own homes through the help of a network of neighbors and friends. These are usually persons who have lived in a particular community for a number of years and have strong roots there.

A MORE BALANCED VIEW OF OLD AGE

What would we find if we swept away ageism with its stereotypes and saw the elderly more realistically? On the basis of present knowledge I have constructed an image of aging which portrays the following view:

> Older people are as diverse as people in other periods of life, and their patterns of aging vary according to the range they show from health to sickness, from maturity to immaturity, activity to apathy, useful constructive participation to disinterest, from the prevailing stereotype of aging to rich forms of creativity.
>
> Ninety-five percent of older people live in the community and are not institutionalized or in protective settings. Physical illnesses are frequent and often chronic and limiting. This period of life is characterized by complex changes that are multiple, occur rapidly and have profound effects. Some people are overwhelmed. Others can come to accept or substitute for the loss of loved ones, prestige, social status and adverse physiological changes.
>
> "Old age" and "brain damage" alone do not account for the changes seen or the modes of adaptation of older people. Diseases, life experience, socioeconomic and other forces along with the subjective experience of growing old and approaching death, all interweave to contribute to the picture of old age.
>
> Older people are apt to be reflective rather than impulsive. Having experienced a great deal and having been "burned often," they think before acting. Under suitable circumstances, the present remains very much alive and exciting to them; but they also turn to a review of their past, searching for purpose, reconciliation of relationships and resolution of conflicts and regrets. They may become self-centered or altruistic, angry or contrite, triumphant or depressed.
>
> Those old people who are optimistic and resourceful may at the same time be painfully aware of the brevity of life and its tragedies. Optimism is tempered by a more balanced view of the joys and sadnesses of life. The old continue to learn and change in response to their experiences and to human relationships. They are not often overwhelmed by new ideas for they recognize how few of them there are. Many are employable, productive and creative. Many wish to leave their mark through sponsoring the young as well as through ideas and institutions.

It is extremely important to recognize that old people are not a homogenous group. There are wider deviations from the mean of many physiological measurements in the elderly than in other age groups. Similarly there is much variation in the character of the old. Massive brain disease, illiteracy or abject poverty has a leveling or homogenizing effect, but when those variables are not operating it is obvious that human personality is unique, and the manifestations of this are particularly striking in later life when personality reaches fullest development.

SOME CHARACTERISTICS OF OLDER PERSONS

With the fact of diversity safely established, it becomes possible to talk of special characteristics of late life without placing the old once again in prescribed roles. Late-life characteristics are *tendencies* frequently observed in older persons. *They are not inevitable* nor are they found to the same degree in each person who manifests them. But they do show themselves regularly enough to be considered typical of people who have lived a long time and are viewing the world from the special vantage point of old age.

1. Change in the Sense of Time

Old age is the only period of life with no future; therefore, a major task in late life is learning *not* to think in terms of a future. Children are extremely future oriented and look forward to each birthday as a sign of growing up. The middle-aged, as Schopenhauer said, begin to count the number of years they have left rather than the number of years since birth. In old age one's time perspective is shortened even further as the end of life (and one's time) approaches. Some avoid confronting this fact by retreating to the past. (This is not to be confused with the useful review of one's past which I shall discuss later.) Others deny their age and continue to be future oriented. The latter are people who fail to make wills, who leave important relationships unresolved, who put off enjoyments, who experience the boredom and frustration that can come from never fully experiencing the present.

A more satisfying resolution is found among those elderly who begin to emphasize the quality of the present time remaining rather than the quantity. When death becomes imminent there tends to be a sense of immediacy, of here and now, of living in the moment.*

This emphasis on quality runs counter to the culture. Americans are fascinated with speed and the quantitative aspects of time, related to the production-oriented ethos; they are less cognizant of time's qualitative

---

* There is little to support the assertion of many, including the great American psychologist William James, that time "moves faster" when we grow older. Rather it is the quality of life, the way one "fills" time, that determines the subjective appreciation of the duration of time.[12]

aspects. The historical depiction of time has been dominated by the theme of destruction. Father Time stands waiting with his scythe and Kronos eats his children. Modern views are less passionate and more mechanistic, with time seen as a commodity. Industry is interested in time-and-motion studies. Science explores periodicity and biological clocks. The gerontological literature emphasizes speed of reactions rather than the power of mental processes. Cost-benefit analysis is applied not only to products but also to human services, like the Foster Grandparent Program.[13]

The French philosopher Henri Bergson* helped formulate the differences between objective and subjective time. *Le temps humain* is a concept that the value and meaning of time does not correspond with either a period of life or with the quantitative amount of time available. The significance of the quality of time is illustrated by Bernard Berenson's description of "life-enhancing experiences," often characterized as spontaneous, elusive, natural and simple rather than artificial and elaborate.[15]

Old age, because of its time perspective, can be a period of emotional and sensory awareness and enjoyment. Under favorable personal conditions, older people may resolve fears about time running out, end the impulse to time panics and to boredom, and develop a more appropriate valuation of time. The elemental things of life—children, plants, nature, human touching (physical and emotional), color, shape—assume greater significance as people sort out the more important from the less important. This can be called a sense of presentness or elementality. Such a characterization is true of a significant minority of present-day elderly. It is likely to be more common among those with good health and adequate financial means. I have seen these factors most frequently in stable persons who have a lifelong history of inner resources and a currently supportive environment, and who have come to personal terms with the idea of death.

Some elderly persons seem to transcend the sense of time altogether. T. S. Eliot describes this beautifully:

> Home is where one starts from. As we grow older
> The world becomes stranger, the pattern more complicated . . .
> There is a time for the evening under starlight,
> A time for the evening under lamplight . . .
> Love is most nearly itself
> When here and now cease to matter.
> Old men ought to be explorers
> Here and there does not matter

---

* Bergson, Proust and Meyerhoff,[14] among others, have been interested in the nature of subjective time.

We must be still and still moving
Into another intensity
For a further union, a deeper communion
Through the dark cold and the empty desolation,
The wave cry, the wind cry, the vast waters
Of the petrel and the porpoise. In my end is my beginning.[16]

2. Sense of the Life Cycle

Only in old age can one experience a personal sense of the entire life cycle.[17] There are at least six psychological elements contributing to this understanding, with the subjective *awareness of death* in the forefront. The knowledge of death is a powerful motivating factor in human behavior, underlying much creativity, as well as despair, through the sense of urgency it produces.*

The sense of the life cycle as an *unfolding process of change* is a second element. It expresses a sense of historic interconnectedness between the generations. It is revealed by an interest in sponsoring or teaching young people and in contributing in other ways to the future. I have used the phrase "average expectable life cycle" as the counterpart to the psychoanalytic theoretician Heinz Hartman's phrase "average expectable environment."[18] The "average expectable life cycle" refers to the typical possibility of the way one's life will unfold.

A third aspect is the *experiencing of a sense of time*—human time, as Bergson distinguished it from scientific or objective time. Subjective time is made possible by the human capacity for memory.

Next is the *sense of life experience*. This is marked by a broadening perspective and by personal growth. One comes, in part at least, to know what life is all about.

There is an *accumulation of factual knowledge* of what is to be expected at particular points in the life cycle.

Finally, there is the *idea of stages or phases*. Stage theories connote a progressive, universal and purposive sequence of changes in psychological

---

* Existential philosophers have placed death at the center of their thinking since death is seen as determining the very boundaries of life. Religion itself has been called the great psychotherapy of death by the American psychologist G. Stanley Hall. In addition to orthodox religious beliefs I have observed idiosyncratic beliefs evolve in some persons as they age. Various versions of reunion and reincarnation are found.

Religion in old age should, of course, be seen both in terms of its social significance, that is, the seeking-out of social and personal relationships, and in terms of its interior sense of the need to acquire meanings about the nature of human existence and death. Older people are by no means doctrinaire in their religious beliefs. Some are deeply religious, some agnostic; most are somewhere in between.

development. For one to move to the next stage one must have successfully passed through a preceding one. All people go through the same stages. Certain significant goals are fulfilled. Freud, Piaget and Erikson have offered schedules of stages in childhood development. But no stage theory, including Erikson's, offers an adequate account of life from conception to death. There is a question as to the legitimacy of the concept of stages. Certainly it becomes more difficult to delineate stages after the achievement of adolescence. What kind of changes occur? Are they superficial variations in personality and mental content, or are they basic structural changes in personality? Are there partial changes that do not refute the idea of a fundamental immutability of character?

A sense of life and the concepts of the life cycle are not nearly well enough developed in the social and psychological sciences, particularly as applied to the postmeridian period of life. We need many more studies, such as those at the University of Chicago (Havighurst, Neugarten) and the University of California (Lowenthal) which focus on adult development. We need studies across the generations, including historical approaches.[19] The idea of bringing together psychology and history, while not new, has been underdeveloped, and there are few people with dual training in these fields.[20]

When the inner experiences of old age are being studied, the universal experiences can be put into relief by comparisons with older cultures. Thus anthropological studies directed toward looking for universal phenomena, such as the denial of aging and death and ideas of rejuvenation and reincarnation, rather than for exotic differences, could be fruitful.[21]

3. Tendency Toward Life Review

Old age inaugurates the process I have called the life review, promoted by the realization of approaching dissolution and death.[22] It is characterized by the progressive return to consciousness of past experiences, in particular the resurgence of unresolved conflicts which can now be surveyed and reintegrated. The old are not only taking stock of themselves as they review their lives, they are trying to think and feel through what they will do with the time that is left and with whatever emotional and material legacies they may have to give to others. During this time they frequently experience grief. The death of others, often more than their own death, concerns them. Perplexed, frightened at being alone and increasingly depressed, they at times become wary or cautious to the point of suspicion about the motivations of others. They are more apt to feel saddened, anxious and angered at the realities of their own contemporary lot, as reinforced by past psychological conflicts. They are particularly apt to be influenced by a sense of impotence and powerlessness because their fate depends upon so many elements over which they have little control. Other researchers have pursued the concept of the life review and found that increased and intense introspection occurs in early late life and tends to wane again in later late life, leading to a more serene and tranquil disposition.

If unresolved conflicts and fears are successfully reintegrated they can give new significance and meaning to an individual's life and help prepare him for death, mitigating his fears. I have used the concept of the life review in my psychotherapeutic work with older persons.

Life-review therapy includes the taking of an extensive autobiography from the older person and from other family members as indicated. (Such memoirs can also be preserved by means of tape recordings.) Use of family albums, scrapbooks and other memorabilia, the searching-out of genealogies, and pilgrimages back to places of import evoke crucial memories, responses and understanding in patients. A summation of one's life work by some means is useful. The consequences of these steps include expiation of guilt, exorcism of problematic childhood identifications, the resolution of intrapsychic conflicts, the reconciliation of family relationships, the transmission of knowledge and values to those who follow and the renewal of ideals of citizenship.[23] Such life-review therapy can be conducted in a variety of settings from senior centers to nursing homes. Even relatively untrained persons can function as therapists by becoming "listeners" as older persons recount their lives.

Reminiscence of the old has often been devalued; it is regarded as a symptom, usually of organic dysfunction, and is felt to bespeak "aimless wandering of mind" or "living in the past." The value of reminiscence is seen in the great memoirs composed in old age which not only have provided fascinating accounts of unusual and gifted people but are of great historical value: Casanova, Goethe, Franklin, Chateaubriand, Clemenceau, Steffens, Stravinsky. Indeed, in 1938 Allan Nevins, the distinguished American historian, not wishing to leave the writing of memoirs to chance, conceived the Oral History Collection at Columbia University, wherein men and women of varied fields are invited to reminisce in taped interviews.

The life review may be seen in film and fiction. Ingmar Bergman's beautiful 1957 motion picture *Wild Strawberries* shows an elderly physician whose dreams and visions concerned his past as he changed from remoteness and selfishness to closeness and love. Literature is replete with examples of the life review: Joyce Cary's *To Be a Pilgrim*; Ernest Hemingway's "The Snows of Kilimanjaro"; Henry James's "The Beast in the Jungle"; Giuseppe di Lampedusa's *The Leopard*; Muriel Spark's *Memento Mori*; Samuel Beckett's *Krapp's Last Tape*; Leo Tolstoy's *The Death of Ivan Ilyich*.

4. Reparation and Resolution

Older people are constantly writing and rewriting the scenarios of their lives. Sometimes chased by the furies of guilt, they try to resurrect and come to terms with regretted actions of commission and of omission out of their past. There are those who refuse to admit that old people, like all people, suffer from past guilt and acquire new guilt for their deeds and misdeeds. They pretend that old age is as innocent as childhood. This is wholly invalid. Old people have made—and continue to make—their own contribution to their own fate. I am quite certain that I have never seen anyone at any age who did not have a sense of guilt, and, in some measure, a legitimate basis for it. The old are not served by dismissing the reality of human greed and cruelty in their lives or the variegated fabric of their past. This attitude denigrates their humanness. They often make reparations to resolve their sense of guilt and are more inclined to expiatory behavior than other age groups. The impulse to atone is more common in those who sense that time is running out.

An added element in today's old people is that they tend to act as though they had total free will and self-responsibility rather than that their behavior is in any way determined. This belief is clearly related to the socio-psychological beliefs prevalent in their early lives. Thus they rely heavily upon independence, self-reliance, pride, industry, prudence and thrift and are likely to hold themselves highly responsible for their feelings and actions.

5. Attachment to the Familiar

A nostalgic, memorial attachment to familiar objects—home, pets, heirlooms, keepsakes, photo albums, scrapbooks, old letters—is common in old age.* This relates to and facilitates the life review, for the mind is jogged and encouraged to remember both the immediate and the distant past. Familiar objects provide a sense of continuity, comfort, security and satisfaction. They contribute to a maintenance of orientation, especially if one's world is quickly changing.

---

* This should not be confused with an excessive and pathologic mania to collect or hoard. The latter may be seen throughout life and can be accentuated in old age when one may be afraid of loss and ruin.

6. *Conservation of Continuity*

Although traditionally (and inaccurately) conservatism is assumed to increase with age, there are three periods of life when conservatism is salient. First comes the conservatism of childhood, the most conservative period of all. I call this the conservatism of survival. Children cannot tolerate change, are bound to ritual, are dependent upon the figures and structures of their milieu. This begins to change significantly only after pubescence with the growth of independence.

Second, there is the conservatism of obligation or responsibility which peaks in middle age. Hard pressed by responsibilities toward both ends of the life cycle (education and care of the young; care of the elderly), the middle-aged have the greatest income and the largest demands upon them. In earlier times, interestingly, middle age was called the period of gravity.

Finally, there is a conservatism of continuity, the potentially consummatory opportunity for the old to appraise, extract and pass on that which is worthy. I have called this the "elder" function.

In differing societies the various kinds of conservatism become intensified. For example, in old China and some African societies the oral tradition of teaching, counseling and other aspects of continuity are common activities of older people. In our own society, the elderly are forced into a conservatism of survival as well as continuity. Indeed, continuity is reduced because so many of the elderly in America must struggle for their very existence, leaving them little time and energy to pass on knowledge to younger generations—who may, in turn, be reluctant to accept such knowledge.

7. *Desire to Leave a Legacy*

I have used the term "legacy" to refer to that desire, so profound in older people, to leave something behind when they die. This may be children and grandchildren, lasting work or art, or even memories in the minds of others. There may be a preoccupation with succession (who will follow) and with bequeathing intellectual and spiritual knowledge. The sense of legacy can also be gained by donating one's organs or body parts at the time of death. There is often an involvement in material legacy— to whom to leave money, jewelry, furniture. There may be pleasure in anticipating the willing of some possession to someone the older person cares for; the old may also manipulate their inheritors, change their wills, cajole, threaten. Some older persons develop an interest in husbandry of the earth and conservation of resources for future generations.

The older person who does show social knowledge of and personal concern about "leaving traces" and preserving a heritage for the future tends to reveal greater psychological health. Motivations for a tendency toward legacy may be several—wanting to be remembered; wanting to give magnanimously to those who survive; wishing to remain in control in some way even after death; rewarding or punishing those who survive by giving or withholding bequests; tidying up responsibility before death.

8. Transmission of Power

One of the psychological issues of old age is when (or when not) to give over one's power and authority to others. This is true in the public as well as the private sphere. In all societies, including our own, older people (usually men) are often active in the determination of public policy and the carrying-out of executive, administrative and judicial responsibilities.* Over 85 percent of the service on the United States Supreme Court has been rendered by men over 65. Political, religious and business leadership has often been in the hands of the old.†

Power transmissions take place in many ways. Giving over property or businesses to one's children, allowing a son or daughter to make certain decisions for the older person, and playing a supportive rather than a disciplinary role with grandchildren are some examples in private life.

An important task in late years is knowing when to give up power. Sometimes it is given over too quickly while the person still has much to contribute. At other times people cling to power long after they can no longer exercise it in their own interest or the interest of others. A businessman, for example, may find it difficult to "let go" and retire despite increasingly incapacitating physical and mental changes. Counsel should be available to enable him to acknowledge these changes and to collaborate in setting up appropriate succession within his firm. To continue to deny his declining capacities and persist in a willful, angry insistence upon running the firm himself, even if it means running it into the ground, will harm him and what he has built over the years. A sense of continuity following the successful development of the mechanism of succession is infinitely more desirable than bringing oneself to a humiliating end.

Too often the elderly, especially the economically disadvantaged elderly,

---

* There have been societies in the form of gerontocracies—that is, governed by old men or, occasionally, old women. Ancient Sparta created councils of aged called Gerousia.

† Admittedly, these positions are open to very limited numbers of older men, and many if not most such positions were already obtained in middle age.

are deprived of their power without their consent. Institutionalized patients are particularly vulnerable. There are, of course, times when medical-legal intervention is necessary for the mentally or physically ill. But in most cases the elderly are capable of making their own decisions, including the decision to let someone else decide for them.

9. *Sense of Consummation or Fulfillment in Life*

A sense of satisfaction with one's life is more common than recognized but not as common as possible. It is a quality of "serenity" and "wisdom" derived from resolving personal conflicts, reviewing one's life and finding it acceptable and gratifying, and viewing death with equanimity. One's life does not have to have been a "success" in the popular sense of that word in order to be gratifying. People take pride in a feeling of having done their best, of having met challenge and difficulty and sometimes from simply having survived against terrible odds.

10. *Capacity for Growth*

The capacity for curiosity, creativity, surprise and change* do not invariably decline with age. To maintain a sense of wonder and expectation is to counter the possibility of disillusionment and cynicism. Goethe at age 80 said he was still capable of being surprised. The sense of perspective is related to this: the capacity for evaluation, giving appropriate importance to elements of one's life.

Creativity can often be found in older persons, not only in the famous, but also in the daily lives of ordinary people. A person may in fact first become creative in late life when previous burdens and responsibilities lessen. The desire to change and grow can be heightened by the realization of life drawing to a close. Personality and behavior changes can occur up to the moment of death.

AGE-RELATED LIFE CRISES

The special characteristics of older persons which I have just outlined are psychological traits commonly found in late life. They must be differentiated from emotional reactions to what I call "age-related life crises"— events which occur as part of the current aging experience in the United

---

* The possibility for all kinds of change in old age is indeed remarkable. As an example, Havelock Ellis, who contributed so much to our understanding of sexuality, suffered from lifelong impotence, which was cured in his old age.[24]

States. Widowhood, late-life marital and sexual problems, retirement, sensory loss, aging, disease, pain, hospitalization, surgery, institutionalization and dying are among the major crises of old age. They are difficult to face, especially if several occur simultaneously or closely following one upon another. Grief, guilt, loneliness, depression, anxiety, rage and a sense of helplessness are frequent reactions to these events, particularly in initial stages. The elderly may shield themselves by denial, rigidity or any of the other defenses through which people of all ages protect themselves and attempt to solve their problems.

Rather than assuming their situation is hopeless, the elderly need help in recognizing their feelings and correctly identifying psychological symptoms. Wherever possible, age-related problems need to be differentiated from environmental problems, disease from aging, characteristics inherent in old age from characteristics related to a devalued status. Recovery from and compensation for deeply felt losses requires encouragement of a restitutional capacity. Some things must be lived with, others can be changed. The old need the opportunity for growth and renewal, for striking out in new directions, especially if previous capacities and possibilities are lost or altered. Human contact and warmth, support and challenge, and the teaching and learning of new roles, outlooks and directions are all vital in old age. Not every fight can be won, but each can be fought creatively and bravely, with a sense of self-esteem, dignity and a sharing in the human struggle.

THE DEVELOPMENT OF A NEW SENSIBILITY

In each of the previous chapters I have outlined ideas for confronting ageism and developing new ways of looking at and reacting to old age. I have addressed both interior ageism—the ways in which each of us views aging—and the institutionalization of views toward the old in social practice and custom. The young and middle generations must examine and resolve their conflicted feelings toward old age and ultimately toward themselves as they grow older. The old must assert themselves in a self-respecting and effective manner. Perhaps even a new name is in order. All our terms for old age conjure up negative images—some more, some less. Few people are willing to be identified as "aged," aging," "elderly," "retired," "old-timer," "gramps," "granny" or even "old" itself. "Senior citizens" or "golden ager" are sugary euphemisms. "Old fogy," "old biddy," "old gal," "crock" and "geezer" are putdowns. We can either rehabilitate the least objectionable of these names (perhaps "elderly" and "old") to a new and respected status, or we can come up with a new name altogether. The

Abkhasians in the Soviet Union solve this problem in a unique manner by describing their elders as "long living" rather than "old." The connotation is one of continuing life rather than approaching death.

The arts are an important way of illuminating old age yet there are relatively few novels, poems, movies or other art forms in Western civilization that deal with older persons as central subjects. Elderly heroes, heroines and even villains are rather rare. The old, if depicted at all, usually play supporting and highly stereotyped roles.

Certain writers are exceptions. Cervantes, Balzac, Proust, Joyce and Mann showed special understanding of the entire span of life. Tolstoy's intensely autobiographical work makes him the novelist par excellence of the life cycle. He wrote continuously throughout his long life, examining the issues and values which predominated in each phase. His first writings were the autobiographical trilogy of novels, *Childhood*, *Boyhood* and *Youth*. Then, as a young man, he wrote the *Sevastopol Sketches* and the great *War and Peace*. *Anna Karenina*, written in his late forties, deals with middle age in terms of the problem of fidelity—not only the marital fidelity of Anna but also the social fidelity of the spiritually torn Levin. Then came *The Death of Ivan Ilyich*, completed in his fifties. In his *Confession* he recounts the "conversion of his middle years." He was soon to call for a radical Christianity of nonviolence, brotherhood and communal property ("property is theft") and he became more famous for this mission than for his literature. During the last decade of his life he was perhaps the most venerated man in the world. He composed a fine novel, *Resurrection*, which detailed the brutality and injustice of religious and social institutions. The subject reflects his own attempt to search out an ultimate meaning for his life.

Tolstoy also illustrates the continuance of creativity into old age. "Tolstoy is not a fixed point; he is constantly on the move, carrying us with him," wrote John Bayley in *Tolstoy and the Novel* (1967). He was stalked by thoughts of death and fought them with all possible passion. He was protean and contradictory. All of his life he invented and reinvented himself, an autodidactic quality which becomes highly adaptive in old age.

Artists and photographers have always been fascinated by different age groups, finding old faces, lined and expressive, of striking interest; such faces may be seen in many galleries. The fine charcoal "The Portrait of an Old Man" by Minerva Chapman (1858–1947) and Goya's self-portrait in his own old age are illustrative.

Films are another form in which sensibility toward old age can be promoted. The physician in Bergman's *Wild Strawberries* reshapes his being in the light of the past following a dream in which he sees himself dead. Upon awakening, "I uttered words of realities against my dream. . . . My name is Isak Borg. I am still alive. I am 76 years old. I really feel quite well." His daughter-in-law, Marianne, speaks for others in describing him as he has been, "You are an egoist, father, you are completely inconsiderate and you have never listened to anyone but yourself. All this is well hidden behind your mask of old-fashioned charm and your friendliness, but you are as hard as nails even though everyone depicts you as a great humanitarian. We who have seen you at close range, we know what you really are." Dr. Borg muses, "I have found that during the last four years I glided rather easily into a blue light world of memory and dreams which are highly personal. I have often wondered if this is a sign of increasing senility. Sometimes I have asked myself if it is a harbinger of approaching death." But Dr. Borg is "punished" for a life of indifference, for his intellectualism and his emotional withholding. His egoism is described as "loneliness" and/or "deadliness." "The last few months I have had the most peculiar dreams . . . it's as if I'm trying to say something to myself which I don't want to hear when I'm awake . . . that I am dead although I live." And he said, "Whenever I am restless or sad I usually try to recall memories from my childhood to calm down." In this unusual film the change that occurs in this man in the face of death is remarkable; he becomes more compassionate and sensitive to love.

Television, radio and the newspapers largely ignore the elderly. When news coverage deals with older people at all, it tends to focus on extraordinary happenings: old persons performing rare feats of strength or endurance, "cute" items on late-life romances and marriage, or creative people who function "in spite of" old age. Since 1970 there have been some "plight of the elderly" articles but no systematic reports or practical solutions. The old are the butt of jokes for comedians and situation comedies. "The old people come stumbling in and are portrayed as witless and senile," complains one older woman. "They ridicule old people . . . they pretend that old age is something to laugh at," observes another.

In 1972 the Clark Foundation awarded a grant to the National Council on the Aging to explore ways for the media to meet the needs of middle-aged and older persons more effectively and to project them more positively and accurately.* Also in 1972 a Ford Foundation–sponsored panel on the

---

* The participation of private foundations in the problem of aging has been rare. The Foundation Grants Data Bank reported in November, 1973, that only 0.3 percent of monies given by philanthropic foundations was directed toward the old, and less than one-eighth of this small amount involved research.

representation of minorities on public television proposed wide-ranging changes in coverage (including coverage of the elderly), TV employment practices and board membership.*[25]

LIFE AS A WORK OF ART

> Do not yearn after immortality.
> But exhaust the limits of the possible.

So sang the Greek lyric poet Pindar in the fifth century B.C., in the *Olympiads*. And the aged Sophocles wrote the closing lines of *Oedipus Tyrannus* "Of no mortal say 'That man is happy,' till vexed by no grievous ill he pass life's goal." But what is life's goal? Bernard Berenson at eighty-two declared: "After nihilism the only impulsion that is reasonable is to take life as a fine art of which we are the practitioners, all engaged upon producing a masterpiece and a completely humanized mankind."

Berenson spoke of his own aspiration as "getting out of myself all that goes to turn an animal into a human being, a work of art." The simultaneous lengthening and invigoration of life may make it possible to re-emphasize the human personality as a work of art, balancing irrationality, muting greed, containing rapacity and violence, and encouraging compassion, creativity and a responsible inclination toward legacy and future generations.

None of us know whether we have already had the best years of our lives or whether the best are yet to come. But the greatest of human possibilities remain to the very end of life—the possibilities for love and feeling, reconciliation and resolution.

What can be done about humankind's uneasy knowledge that life is brief and death inevitable? There is no way to avoid our ultimate destiny. But we can struggle to give each human being the chance to be born safely, to be loved and cared for in childhood, to taste everything the life cycle has to offer, including adolescence, middle age, perhaps parenthood and certainly a secure old age; to learn to balance love and sex and aggression in a way that is satisfying to the person and those around him; to push outward without a sense of limits; to explore the possibilities of human existence through the senses, intelligence and creativity; and most of all, to be healthy enough to enjoy the love of others and a love for oneself.

---

* Information and entertainment can be conveyed while simultaneously challenging stereotypes. In 1974, Peter Weaver, nationally syndicated consumer expert, and I created for public television *Lifetime Magazine of the Air*, intended for older viewers, their families and others interested in their own future. The "magazine" comprised four departments: Lifestyles, Money, Health and Personalities.

After one has lived a life of meaning, death may lose much of its terror. For what we fear most is not really death but a meaningless and absurd life. I believe most human beings can accept the basic fairness of each generation's taking its turn on the face of the planet if they are not cheated out of the full measure of their own turn. The tragedy of old age in America is that we have made absurdity all but inevitable. We have cheated ourselves. But we still have the possibility of making life a work of art.

APPENDIXES

APPENDIX A. SOURCES OF GERONTOLOGICAL AND GERIATRIC LITERATURE*

1. Bibliographies

National Council on the Aging: *Current Literature on Aging,* published quarterly, Washington, D.C.

Shock, N. W.: *A Classified Bibliography of Gerontology and Geriatrics,* Vol. I, 1900–1948; Vol. II, 1949–1955; Vol. III, 1956–1961, Stanford University Press, Stanford, Calif., 1951, 1957, and 1963, respectively.

———. "Index to Current Periodical Literature," published quarterly in the *Journal of Gerontology.*

2. Periodicals

Administration on Aging, Department of Health, Education, and Welfare: *Aging,* Washington, D.C.

American Association of Retired Persons: *Modern Maturity.*

American College of Nursing Home Administrators: *Journal of Longterm Care Administration,* Silver Spring, Md.

American Geriatrics Society: *Journal of the American Geriatrics Society,* New York.

American Nursing Association Company: *American Journal of Nursing,* New York.

American Nursing Home Association: *Modern Health Care* (formerly *Modern Nursing Homes*), Hightstown, N.J.

———: *Nursing Homes,* Lake Forest, Ill.

American Public Health Association: *American Journal of Public Health,* Washington, D.C.

* From Robert N. Butler and Myrna I. Lewis, *Aging and Mental Health*, St. Louis, 1973, The C. V. Mosby Co.

Baywood Journals, *International Journal of Aging and Human Development,* Farmingdale, N.Y.

British Geriatrics Society and the British Society for Research in Ageing: *Age and Ageing,* Williams and Wilkins, Baltimore, Md.

Gerontological Society: *The Gerontologist,* St. Louis, Mo.

————. *Journal of Gerontology,* St. Louis, Mo.

Institute of Gerontology, The University of Michigan-Wayne State University: *Occasional Papers in Gerontology,* Ann Arbor, Mich.

International Universities Press: *Journal of Geriatric Psychiatry,* New York.

Lancet Publications, Inc.: *Geriatrics,* Minneapolis, Minn.

National Association of Retired Federal Employees: *Retirement Life,* Washington, D.C.

National Association of Social Workers: *Social Work,* New York.

National Council of Senior Citizens (NCSC): *Senior Citizen News,* Washington, D.C.

National Council on the Aging: *Perspectives in Aging,* Washington, D.C.

National Retired Teachers Association (NRTA): *National Retired Teachers Association Journal.*

National Therapeutic Society (a branch of the National Recreation and Park Association): *Therapeutic Recreation Journal,* Washington, D.C.

3. *Pamphlets, bulletins, reports, etc.*

Ciompi, L.: *A Comprehensive Review of Geronto-Psychiatric Literature in the Postwar Period: A Review of the Literature to January 1, 1965,* U.S. Public Health Publication No. 1811, National Clearinghouse for Mental Health Information, Washington, D.C., 1969.

National Institute of Child Health and Human Development: *International Directory of Gerontology,* U.S. Government Printing Office, Washington, D.C., 1968. (Includes a list of persons specializing in geriatrics and gerontology by geographical area.)

Social Security Administration: *Social Security Bulletin,* Washington, D.C.

United States Senate Special Committee on Aging: Hearings and task force reports, Washington, D.C.

United States Health, Education, and Welfare Department: *Directory, Medicare Providers and Suppliers of Service,* Government Printing Office, Washington, D.C.

APPENDIX B. ORGANIZATIONS PERTAINING TO THE ELDERLY*

American Aging Association
University of Nebraska Medical Center
Omaha, Neb.
Made up of scientists, it seeks to promote research in aging.

American Association of Homes for the Aging
529 14th St., N.W.
Washington, D.C. 20004
AAHA represents the nonprofit homes for the aging—religious, municipal, trust, fraternal.

American Association of Retired Persons
1909 K St., N.W.
Washington, D.C. 20006
Age 55 or above, retired to still-employed.

The American Geriatrics Society
10 Columbus Circle
New York, N.Y. 10019
The American Geriatrics Society, made up of physicians, has an annual meeting.

American Nurses Association, Inc.
10 Columbus Circle
New York, N.Y. 10019

American Nursing Home Association (American Health Care Association)
1025 Connecticut Ave., N.W.
Washington, D.C. 20036
ANHA represents the commercial-nursing-home industry.

American Occupational Therapy Association
251 Park Ave. South
New York, N.Y. 10010

American Physical Therapy Association
1740 Broadway
New York, N.Y. 10019

Division of Adult Development and Aging
American Psychological Association
1200 17th St., N.W.
Washington, D.C. 20036

The Forum for Professionals and Executives
c/o The Washington School of Psychiatry
1610 New Hampshire Ave., N.W.
Washington, D.C. 20009
The interests of this group have ranged from contemplation to active examination of public issues, including those affecting the elderly.

---

* From Robert N. Butler and Myrna I. Lewis, *Aging and Mental Health*, St. Louis, 1973, The C. V. Mosby Co.

The Gerontological Society
1 Dupont Circle
Washington, D.C. 20036
This professional society has an annual meeting and an international meeting every three years. It is made up of four components — Biological Sciences, Clinical Medicine, Psychological and Social Sciences and Social Research, Planning and Practice.

Gray Panthers
6342 Greene St.
Philadelphia, Pa. 19144
Activistic group of old and young people who resent "stereotyping."

The Institute for Retired Professionals
The New School of Social
Research
60 West 12th St.
New York, N.Y.
This pioneering school also led the way in providing intellectual activities for retired professional people.

The Institutes of Lifetime Learning
These are educational services of the National Retired Teachers Association and the American Association of Retired Persons.

The International Federation on Aging
1909 K St., N.W.
Washington, D.C. 20006
Confederation of aging organizations of various nations.

International Senior Citizens Association, Inc.
11753 Wilshire Blvd.
Los Angeles, Calif. 90025
Endeavors to reflect old people of many nations.

National Association of Retired Federal Employees
1909 Q St., N.W.
Washington, D.C. 20009
Represents and lobbies for needs of retired civil servants.

National Association of Social Workers
2 Park Ave.
New York, N.Y. 10016

The National Association of State Units on Aging
Because this address shifts as the presidency of the Association changes, write your local State Office on Aging (see Appendix D) for the current address.
Information resources on state policies on aging. Represents and lobbies for state agencies at the federal level.

The National Caucus on the Black Aged
1725 DeSales Street, N.W.
Washington, D.C. 20036
Advocates improving quality of life of the black aged.

The National Center on Black Aged
1725 DeSales Street, N.W.
Washington, D.C. 20036
Provides comprehensive program of coordination, information, and consultative services to meet needs of aged blacks.

National Council on the Aging
1828 L St., N.W., Suite 504
Washington, D.C. 20036
Research and services regarding the elderly.

National Council of Health Care Services

407 N St., S.W., Washington, D.C.

Represents commercial nursing home chains.

National Council for Homemaker Services

1790 Broadway
New York, N.Y. 10019

National Council of Senior Citizens

1911 K St., N.W., Room 202
Washington, D.C. 20005

Represents and lobbies for needs of the elderly.

Membership at any age.

National Federation of Licensed Practical Nurses

250 W. 57th St.
New York, N.Y.

Educational foundation.

National Retired Teachers Association

1909 K St., N.W.
Washington, D.C. 20006

Members once active in an educational system, public or private.

National Tenants Organization, Inc.

Suite 548
425 13th St., N.W.
Washington, D.C. 20004

Represents old people, among others, in public housing.

The Oliver Wendell Holmes Association

381 Park Ave. South
New York, N.Y. 10016

This group is interested in the expansion of the intellectual horizons of older people.

Retired Professional Action Group

Suite 711
200 P St., N.W.
Washington, D.C.

This action group was organized through Nader. Its efforts include investigative reports and class-action cases.

Urban Elderly Coalition

c/o Office of Aging of New York City
250 Broadway, New York, N.Y.

Effort of municipal authorities to obtain funds for the urban elderly poor.

APPENDIX C. GOVERNMENT PROGRAMS
FOR THE ELDERLY*

VOLUNTEER/ EMPLOYMENT PROGRAMS	SPONSOR	PURPOSE	ADDRESS
RSVP (Retired Senior Volunteer Program)	ACTION	Funds for volunteer programs in public and nonprofit institutions; volunteers reimbursed for travel and meal expenses	ACTION Washington, D.C. 20525
SCORE (Service Corps of Retired Executives)	ACTION, administered by Small Business Administration	Retired businessmen advising novices in business	ACTION Washington, D.C. 20525
VISTA (Volunteers in Service to America)	ACTION	Volunteers for one to two years in community projects in United States, with small salary to cover living expenses	ACTION Washington, D.C. 20525
Peace Corps	ACTION	Overseas service	ACTION Washington, D.C. 20525
IESC (International Executive Service Corps)	An independent organization supported by government and nongovernment funds	Overseas service by executives	International Executive Service Corps 545 Madison Ave. New York, N.Y. 10022

* From Robert N. Butler and Myrna I. Lewis, *Aging and Mental Health*, St. Louis, 1973, The C. V. Mosby Co.

LOW-INCOME ELDERLY PROGRAMS*	SPONSOR	PURPOSE	ADDRESS
Foster Grand-parents	ACTION	Provide relationship and care to orphans and mentally retarded children in institutions for 20 hours per week at $1.60 per hour	ACTION Washington, D.C. 20525
SOS (Senior Opportunities for Service programs)	OEO	Service in programs to meet needs of older people: nutrition, consumer education, outreach service	Office of Economic Opportunity, Office of Program Review, Washington, D.C.
Operation Mainstream programs			
1. Green Thumb (men) Green Light (women)	National Farmers Union Green Thumb/ Green Light 1012 14th St., N.W. Washington, D.C. 20005	Conservation and landscape (men) Community service (women)	Write sponsor or Manpower Administration, Operation Mainstream, Department of Labor, Washington, D.C.
2. Senior AIDES	National Council of Senior Citizens 1511 K St., N.W. Washington, D.C. 20005	Community service	Write sponsor
3. Senior Community Service Programs	National Council on the Aging 1828 L St., N.W. Washington, D.C. 20036	Community service	Write sponsor
4. Senior Community Service Aides	National Retired Teachers Association Senior Community Service Aides Project 1225 Connecticut Ave., N.W. Washington, D.C. 20036	Community service	Write sponsor

* Only persons over 60 with incomes below OEO (Office of Economic Opportunity) guidelines are eligible.

APPENDIX D. GOVERNMENT AGENCIES
FOR THE ELDERLY

National

U.S. Administration on Aging
330 C St., S.W.
HEW South
Washington, D.C. 20201

Regional Offices

Region I (Conn., Maine, Mass., N.H., R.I., Vt.)
J. F. Kennedy Federal Bldg.
Government Center
Boston, Mass. 02203

Region II (N.J., N.Y., Puerto Rico, Virgin Islands)
26 Federal Plaza, SRS, AoA
New York, N.Y. 10007

Region III (Del., D.C., Md., Pa., Va., W. Va.)
P.O. Box 12900
Philadelphia, Pa. 12900

Region IV (Ala., Fla., Ga., Ky., Miss., N.C., S.C., Tenn.)
50 Seventh St., N.E., Rm. 404
Atlanta, Ga. 30323

Region V (Ill., Ind., Mich., Minn., Ohio, Wis.)
433 West Van Buren, Rm. 712
New Post Office Bldg.
Chicago, Ill. 60607

Region VI (Ark., La., N. Mex., Okla., Tex.)
1114 Commerce St.
Dallas, Tex. 75202

Region VII (Iowa, Kans., Mo., Nebr.)
601 East 12th St.
Kansas City, Mo. 64106

Region VIII (Colo., Mont., N. Dak., S. Dak., Utah, Wyo.)
19th and Stout Sts., Rm. 9017
Federal Office Bldg.
Denver, Colo. 80202

Region IX (Ariz., Calif., Hawaii, Nev., Samoa, Guam, T.T.)
50 Fulton St., Rm. 406
Federal Office Bldg.
San Francisco, Calif. 94102

Region X (Alaska, Idaho, Oreg., Wash.)
1319 2nd Ave. Mezzanine Floor
Arcade Bldg.
Seattle, Wash. 98101

State Offices on Aging

Alabama
Commission on Aging
740 Madison Avenue
Montgomery 36104

Alaska

Office on Aging
Department of Health and
Social Services
Pouch H
Juneau 99801

Arizona

Bureau on Aging
Department of Economic
   Security
2721 North Central, Suite 800,
South Tower
Phoenix 85004

Arkansas

Office on Aging
Department of Social and
Rehabilitation Services
4313 West Markham
Hendrix Hall
P.O. Box 2179
Little Rock 72203

California

Office on Aging
Health and Welfare Agency
455 Capitol Mall, Suite 500
Sacramento 95814

Colorado

Division of Services for
the Aging
Department of Social Services
1575 Sherman Street
Denver 80203

Connecticut

Department on Aging
90 Washington Street
Room 312
Hartford 06115

Delaware

Division of Aging
Department of Health and
Social Services
2407 Lancaster Avenue
Wilmington 19805

District of Columbia

Division of Services to the Aged
Department of Human Resources
1329 E Street, N.W.
Munsey Building, 10th Floor
Washington, D.C. 20004

Florida

Division on Aging
Department of Health and
Rehabilitative Services
1323 Winewood Boulevard
Tallahassee 32301

Georgia

Office of Aging
Department of Human Resources
618 Ponce de Leon
Suite 301
Atlanta 30308

Guam

Office of Aging
Social Service Administration
Government of Guam
Post Office Box 2816
Agana 96910

Hawaii

Commission on Aging
1149 Bethel Street, Room 311
Honolulu 96813

Idaho

Office on Aging
Department of Special Services
Capital Annex #7
509 North 5th Street
Boise 83720

Illinois

Department on Aging
2401 West Jefferson
Springfield 62762

Indiana

Commission on Aging
and Aged
Graphic Arts Building
215 North Senate Avenue
Indianapolis 46202

Iowa

Commission on the Aging
415 West 10th Street
Jewett Building
Des Moines 50319

Kansas

Division of Social Services
Services for the Aging Section
Department of Social and
Rehabilitation Services
State Office Building
Topeka 66612

Kentucky

Aging Program Unit
Department for Human Resources
403 Wapping Street
Frankfort 40601

Louisiana

Bureau of Aging Services
Division of Human Resources
Health and Social and
Rehabilitation Services
Administration
P.O. Box 44282, Capital Station
Baton Rouge 70804

Maine

Services for Aging
Community Services Unit
Department of Health & Welfare
State House
Augusta 04330

Maryland

Commission on Aging
State Office Building
1123 North Eutaw Street
Baltimore 21201

Massachusetts

Executive Office of Elder Affairs
State Office Building
18 Tremont Street
Boston 02109

Michigan

Office of Services to the Aging
1026 E. Michigan
Lansing 48912

Minnesota

Governor's Citizens Council
on Aging
690 North Robert Street
St. Paul 55101

Mississippi

Council on Aging
P.O. Box 5136
Fondren Station
Jackson 39216

Missouri

Office of Aging
Department of Community Affairs
505 Missouri Boulevard
Jefferson City 65101

Montana

Aging Services Bureau
Department of Social and
Rehabilitation Services
P.O. Box 1723
Helena 59601

Nebraska

Commission on Aging
State House Station 94784
300 South 17th Street
Lincoln 68509

Nevada
Division of Aging
Department of Human Resources
201 S. Fall Street, Room 300,
Nye Bldg.
Carson City 89701

New Hampshire
Council on Aging
P.O. Box 786
14 Depot Street
Concord 03301

New Jersey
Office on Aging
Department of Community
Affairs
P.O. Box 2768
363 West State Street
Trenton 08625

New Mexico
Commission on Aging
408 Galisteo–Villagra Building
Santa Fe 87501

New York
Office for the Aging
New York State Executive
Department
855 Central Avenue
Albany 12206

North Carolina
Governor's Coordinating
Council on Aging
Department of Human Resources
Administration Building
213 Hillsborough Street
Raleigh 27603

North Dakota
Aging Services
Social Services Board
Department of Social Services
State Capitol Building
Bismarck 58501

Ohio
Commission on Aging
34 North High Street, 3rd Floor
Columbus 43215

Oklahoma
Special Unit on Aging
Department of Institutions,
Social and Rehabilitative Services
Box 25352, Capitol Station
Oklahoma City 73125

Oregon
Program on Aging
Human Resources Department
315 Public Service Building
Salem 97310

Pennsylvania
Office for the Aging
Department of Public Welfare
Capitol Associates Building
7th and Forster Streets
Harrisburg 17120

Puerto Rico
Gericulture Commission
Department of Social Services
Apartado 11697
Santurce 00910

Rhode Island
Division on Aging
Department of Community
Affairs
150 Washington Street
Providence 02903

Samoa
Government of American Samoa
Office of the Governor
Pago Pago, American Samoa
96920

South Carolina
Commission on Aging
915 Main Street
Columbia 29201

South Dakota
Program on Aging
Department of Social Services
St. Charles Hotel
Pierre 57501

Tennessee
Commission on Aging
510 Gay Street
Capital Towers, Fl B–3,
Suite B–1
Nashville 37319

Texas
Governor's Committee
on Aging
P.O. Box 12786
Capitol Station
Austin 78711

Trust Territory of the Pacific
Office of Aging
Community Development
Division
Government of the Trust
Territory of the Pacific Islands
Saipan, Mariana Islands 96950

Utah
Division of Aging
345 South 6th East,
Dept. of Social Services
Salt Lake City 84102

Vermont
Office on Aging
Department of Human Services
126 Main Street
Montpelier 05602

Virginia
Office on Aging
Division of State Planning
and Community Affairs
9 North 12th Street
Richmond 23219

Virgin Islands
Commission on Aging
P.O. Box 539
Charlotte Amalie
St. Thomas 00801

Washington
Office on Aging
Department of Social
and Health Services
P.O. Box 1788—M.S. 45–2
410 W. Fifth
Olympia 98504

West Virginia
Commission on Aging
State Capitol
Charleston 25305

Wisconsin
Division on Aging
Department of Health and
Social Services
1 West Wilson Street
Room 686
Madison 53702

Wyoming
Aging Services
Department of Health and
Social Services
Division of Public Assistance
and Social Services
State Office Building
Cheyenne 82002

APPENDIX E. OTHER NATIONAL ORGANIZATIONS WITH PROGRAMS IN THE FIELD OF AGING

Forty-six national organizations have been selected out of 284 organizations listed in:

National Council on the Aging. *Directory: National Organizations with Programs in the Field of Aging.* Washington, D.C., The Council, 1971.

These particular organizations have been selected because they, or their local affiliates, maintain programs directly available to elderly persons. Many of the service organizations listed carry out programs for the elderly in some, but not all, chapters. Because the willingness and capability are expressed nationally, a demonstration of desire and need can often stimulate a local chapter to institute such programs.

Adult Education Association of the U.S.A., 1225 19th Street, Washington, D.C. 22036
Special interest section on Education for the Aging, holds annual meetings to provide information, orientation and leadership opportunities for the membership. The programs of education for adults in the middle years contribute to successful aging. Sponsors many pre-retirement programs through local units.

Altrusa International, Inc., 332 South Michigan Avenue, Chicago, Illinois 60604
Altrusa Clubs sponsor meals-on-wheels programs, senior centers, "adopt" the elderly in nursing homes, provide sales outlets for senior craftsmen, stage hobby fairs, develop job opportunities, take the elderly on outings, single out accomplished elders for honor awards, sponsor home-manager training programs to prepare women to go into homes where elderly live with relatives and free relatives for their own jobs.

American Association of Workers for the Blind, Inc., 1511 K Street, N.W., Suite 637, Washington, D.C. 20005
Promotes various programs dealing with the blind, such as rehabilitation, social service work, physical restoration or prevention of blindness.

American Federation of Labor and Congress of Industrial Organizations, 815 Sixteenth Street, N.W., Washington, D.C. 20006

Provides assistance to older members and affiliates ranging from social security legislation to individual counseling on the local level. However, the role of the AFL-CIO in direct programs in these areas is to primarily assist affiliated unions in these tasks by providing supplementary manpower and guidance. Generally available only to members but cooperative efforts with other groups are frequent.

American Foundation for the Blind, Inc., 15 West 16th Street, New York, New York 10011

Draws attention to needs and stimulates research and action nationally and locally in behalf of the elderly blind person via meetings, conferences, publicity, consultation. Serves as a catalyst for program development and planning with other disciplines.

American Home Economics Association, 1600 20th Street, N.W., Washington, D.C. 20009

There is an AHEA Coordinator on the Aging who encourages and assists State home economics associations in expanding their services to older persons. Leadership in the State programs is provided by a State coordinator on aging. The State home economics associations work with the official State agencies on Aging and assist organizations with programs for older persons on food and nutrition and consumer education. They may train homemaker-home health aides, develop menus and recipes adopted to needs of older persons, give

consultation on feeding in institutions for the aged. Units on Aging have been developed for high schools and college home economics curricula to increase understanding of aging and the aged and to encourage services to older persons.

The **American Legion,** 1608 K Street, N.W., Washington, D.C. 20006

Promotes programs for the aging war veteran through a joint Economic-Rehabilitation Subcommittee on the Problems of the Aged and Aging. The staff deals with federal legislation and Administrative procedures, with the Veterans Administration, U.S. Department of Labor, U.S. Civil Service Commission, etc. which involves cash benefits, medical care, employment, veteran preference affecting veterans of all ages, as well as the aging war veteran.

The **American Lutheran Church— Division of Social Service,** 422 South 5th Street, Minneapolis, Minnesota 55415

Primarily—institutional care of the elderly—including health care. Non-institutional care is increasing. At present they have about 60 to 70 community centers for the elderly, a number of home-delivered meals programs, Home Visitation Programs, etc. Programs are available to all, regardless of membership or other conditions. Also provides consultation services to congregations of the Church and assists them in development of programs for the care of the elderly—

involving corporate structure, design of buildings, finance, accounting procedures, and program development. These services are provided without charge to the congregations of The American Lutheran Church.

The American Woman's Auxiliary Medical Association, 535 North Dearborn Street, Chicago, Illinois 60610

Establishment of Homemaker Services; programs to help meet nutritional and recreational needs of the aged; programs on safety in the home for the aged; support and promotion of American Medical Association's six major objectives to positive health program for the aged. Home Center Health Care Program makes visits to homes of the aged and to nursing homes and hospitals when they are confined. Tele-Care, a community information and referral service for the aging through an emergency answering service.

American National Red Cross, 17th and D Streets, N.W., Washington, D.C. 20006

The American Red Cross has few programs directed specifically to the needs of the aged. However, many programs help the aged as well as other age groups. Health education courses such as First Aid and Home Nursing enable family members to give better care to the aged.

American Public Welfare Association, 1313 East 60th Street, Chicago, Illinois 60637

The Division on Administration's Section on Administration of Programs for Older Adults is organized on a regional basis. Regional chairmen, together with state representatives involved in aging and any individual member interested in the field, comprise the Section. It provides leadership in emphasizing and encouraging interest in older adults in the scheme of society's and agencies' priorities.

American Veterans Committee, 1333 Connecticut Avenue, N.W., Washington, D.C. 20036

Provides such financial, medical, vocational, and educational assistance to all veterans as is necessary for complete readjustment to civilian life; to resist and defeat all attempts to create strife between veterans and non-veterans.

Association of the Junior Leagues of America, 825 Third Avenue, New York, New York 10022

The individual leagues sponsor various programs such as hobby shows, recreation, senior centers, television programs, studies and research in the field of aging.

B'nai B'rith, 1640 Rhode Island Avenue, N.W., Washington, D.C. 20036

Volunteer programs for the aging such as participation in the Golden Age Clubs, individual recreation programs, sectarian and nonsectarian. Have a home for the aged in Memphis, Tennessee. The first B'nai B'rith Senior Citizen's Housing Project, a $3,000,-000, 12-story, 173-unit high-rise open to persons 62 and older whose moderate incomes make them ineligible for public housing, constructed in Wilkes-Barre, Pa.

Board of Christian Social Concerns of the United Methodist Church, 100 Maryland Avenue, N.E., Washington, D.C. 20002

The Board does not maintain programs of direct services for the aging. Other agencies of The United Methodist Church do. The Board's functions and focus centers on the process of national policy formation on many issues of primary importance to the aging.

Boy Scouts of America, National Council, North Brunswick, New Jersey 08902; National Representative, 1010 Vermont Ave., N.W., Washington, D.C. 20005

Older people work with boys in local troops and also assist in district and council responsibilities. Individual troops have programs of various kinds to provide services for elderly people.

Committee on Retired Workers, United Steelworkers of America, 1500 Commonwealth Avenue, Pittsburgh, Pennsylvania 15222

Present services include pre-retirement, post-retirement, counseling and establishment of day centers—setting up programs for cultural, educational and recreational assistance to retirees; contacting individual senior steelworkers, as well as organized groups through publications; research and exploration of new techniques; and testifying before congressional committees.

Episcopal Society for Ministry to the Aging, Inc., c/o The Bishop Penick Home, East Rhode Island Avenue Ext., Southern Pines, North Carolina 28387

An organization which unites Episcopalians with the common purpose of provision of care services to the elderly. *Professional educational services offered to Episcopalians beginning this ministry.* To strengthen an awareness of the necessity of this, Programs and Services to the Aging.

Family Service Association of America, 44 East 23rd Street, New York, New York 10010

Counseling in relation to family, local specialized programs such as homemaker services and other help to aging; special projects. National project: Social Work Team with Aging Family Service Clients—5 local Family Services Agencies participating in project financed by NIMH; objectives are to enrich and extend service to elderly clients and their families, and to test the efficacy of a team approach consisting of a professionally educated case worker, supervising and collaborating with an agency-trained assistant; a new pattern of service. Family Service Agencies are available to nonmembers and are supported locally by the United Way and serve people of all income levels. Fees are on graduated basis for those able to pay.

General Federation of Women's Clubs, 1734 N Street, N.W., Washington, D.C. 20036

Part-time employment for healthy older women, newspaper columns, such as an "ideas exchange" for new skills for the aged, recreational facilities, and especially "Keep Well Clinics," emphasizing education and prevention.

Girl Scouts of the U.S.A., 830 Third Avenue, New York, N.Y. 10022 Girl Scouts "adopt" older persons as troop grandmothers and grandfathers, organize shopping and delivery services for the homebound, and help in programs to deliver meals to shut-ins. They visit people in hospitals and nursing homes, write letters, play games, assist in recreation and rehabilitation. Older Americans use their skills to enrich the lives of Girl Scouts by serving as teachers and consultants in creative arts, camping, sports and games, ecology, homemaking, citizenship and health and safety programs. They volunteer for jobs in Girl Scout councils, help in finance campaigns, make uniforms, assist in the leadership training program.

Golden Ring Council of Senior Citizens, 22 West 38th Street, New York, New York 10018 Entertainment and educational programs in the clubs and senior citizens gatherings to promote social action and to improve legislation for the elderly.

Greek Orthodox Archdiocese, 10 East 79th Street, New York, N.Y. 10021 Local senior citizen clubs, and a home for the aged (St. Michael's Home for the Aged of The Greek Orthodox Church, Inc., at 3 Lehman Terrace, Yonkers, New York 10705). Each group has its own policies, which vary.

International Union, United Automobile, Aerospace and Agricultural Implement Workers of America, UAW (Retired Workers Program), 8731 E. Jefferson, Detroit, Michigan 48214 A retired worker chapter is organized in every local union which has 25 or more retired members, and in additional areas where numbers of UAW retirees reside. The chapters send delegates to councils at the area, regional and international levels which provide leadership to the retired workers movement. Retired worker chapters meet monthly and function with leadership from their own officers and committees, in cooperation with the local unions.

Kiwanis International, 101 East Erie Street, Chicago, Illinois 60611 Under club committees on Public and Business Affairs, Support of Churches, and Vocational Guidance, Kiwanis Clubs conduct a variety of local projects designed to assist the elderly and the retired. Do not have "international" or "national" programs, but all clubs select their service projects based on the needs of their particular community and area. There are no special programs for members only. Any Kiwanis owned and operated retirement home, for example, is open to anyone.

The Little Sisters of the Poor, 601 Maiden Choice Land, Baltimore, Maryland 21228

The work of the Little Sisters is entirely dedicated to the aging. The Programs within the homes offer a wide range of services and activities—rehabilitation; physical, occupational and recreational therapy; medical care, including dental and podiatric services; "Work Therapy" which includes some of the residents who participate in housekeeping tasks, etc. —all of which is integrated into a religious environment.

Loyal Order of Moose, Supreme Lodge, Mooseheart, Illinois 60539

Founded and built Moosehaven in 1922 on the banks of the St. Johns River in Florida as a complete home for the dependent aged members of the Order, and their wives. More than 3,000 aged men and women have been served at Moosehaven, which is now a complete community with a current population of nearly 500.

National Association of Jewish Homes for the Aged, 2525 Centerville Road, Dallas, Texas 75228

Represents the best interests of aged residents served in these homes; advance standards of care; exchange information, provide leadership. Spokesman for Jewish Homes representation with government.

National Association of State Units on Aging. Address can be obtained by writing your local State Office on Aging.

Improves the status of older people in our society and provides an organized channel for officially designed state leadership to exchange information and mutual experience and join together for appropriate action.

National Board of the Young Women's Christian Association of the U.S.A., 600 Lexington Avenue, New York, N.Y. 10022

Some community associations sponsor senior citizen clubs, adult education classes in art, writing, etc., as well as participation in health, physical education and recreation programs. The possibilities in homemaking services as related to the needs of older people are explored. Determines areas where national legislation is needed and interprets functions of national agencies. Local chapters give employment counseling which gives women insight into employment possibilities. Some loan facilities to groups meeting recreational needs of older persons. Senior citizens fill many volunteer roles.

National Council for Homemaker Services, Inc., 1740 Broadway, New York, N.Y. 10019

Many of the almost 400 member agencies of the National Council provide homemaker-home health aide services to older persons as part of their program. The presence of a homemaker-home health aide, who is a trained, mature woman (sometimes a man) working under the supervision of a nurse or social worker, enables people to remain in their own homes much longer than they would be able to without this help. Also, the quality of life of many older couples or older individuals is substantially enhanced through the services a few hours a day, or a few hours a week, of a homemaker-home health aide.

National Council of Jewish Women, Inc., 1 West 47th Street, New York, New York 10036

Initiated Golden Age Clubs many years ago. These continue. A few sections serve in meals-on-wheels programs. Sections have set up employment services for older adults. Senior Services Corps program opened volunteer services for senior citizens, and sparked interest in legislation. Make "out-of-pocket" expenses available to them in the course of their voluntary services. Apartment houses for older adults have been established by sections. They have facilities for serving food and engaging in recreational and educational activities. Volunteers assist in these activities. Distribution of surplus government foods to the elderly poor is the newest service.

National Council of Young Men's Christian Associations, New York, N.Y. 10007

Educational and recreational programs for individuals and groups. A National Committee develops guidelines and suggestions for local YMCA's.

National Easter Seal Society for Crippled Children and Adults, 2023 West Ogden Avenue, Chicago, Illinois 60612

Operates comprehensive rehabilitation centers, treatment centers, home therapy programs, "friendly visitor" programs for the homebound, provision of special equipment, etc., all of which provide services which are applicable to the needs of aged persons with physical handicaps.

National Federation of Grandmother Clubs of America, 203 North Wabash Avenue, Chicago, Illinois 60601

Its objects are to honor Grandmotherhood through the observance of the second Sunday of October as National Grandmothers' Day, and to work to have it so established by legislation throughout the United States. To further the social and educational interests of its Members. To promote better understanding of the privileges and obligations of American citizenship. To contribute to the research for cause and cure of children's diseases.

National Federation of Licensed Practical Nurses, Inc., 250 West 57th Street, New York, N.Y. 10019

National, regional, state and local institutes, and seminars, in specialized clinical areas including geriatrics and rehabilitative nursing. Under contract with the Department of Health, Education and Welfare, an Instructor's Guide and Textbook has been completed to prepare licensed practical nurses for Charge Nurse positions in nursing homes, extended care and related facilities.

National Society of the Volunteers of America, 340 West 85th Street, New York, New York 10024

A multiple-service agency providing a wide range of services for people of all ages. Family counseling services, rehabilitation and sheltered workshop programs, emergency care services, housing for low and moderate income individuals and families are services for people of all ages, including the aging. Developed specifically for the aging are: Homes for the Aging, Sunset Clubs providing a wide range of activities and services; visitation programs for shut-ins; meals-on-wheels; special services tailored to meet individual needs are available to all.

National Therapeutic Recreation Society, 1700 Pennsylvania Avenue, N.W., Washington, D.C. 20006

Developing closer working relationships with the Gerontological Society, the National Council on the Aging, Inc., and Nursing Home Division of PHS. Assisting in the development of therapeutic recreation programs in Nursing Homes, Homes for the Aged, Senior Citizen Centers and other agencies providing services to the aged. Assisting in the development of community awareness to meet the needs and interests of the aged. Programs and services are available to members and non-members as follows: Consultation to individuals and organizations regarding conferences and workshops, personnel standards, salaries, certification, awards and citations, legislation, ethical practices, internships, research and publications.

Pilot Club International, 244 College Street, P.O. Box 4844, Macon, Georgia 31208

Sponsor senior citizen groups. "Adopt" the aged as "special" friends and provide services such as visits, gifts, remembrances on special occasions, etc.

The Salvation Army, 120 West 14th Street, New York, New York 10011

Programs and Services for adults are open to all ages, including employment, counseling, special work situations, hospitals, casework, institutional housing, recreation, camping, drop-in centers, other stimulating and challenging programs to make life meaningful and as complete as possible for those in this special category, and programs and services are available to all.

Seventh-Day Adventist Welfare Service, 6840 Eastern Avenue, N.W., Washington, D.C. 20012

Provides material assistance made possible through church assisted funds; counseling services provided by pastors, assisting pastoral staff, health and welfare center directors; volunteer service opportunities, through Dorcas-welfare and other societies; Home for the Aging; pension benefits;

medical assistance and other benefits for retired employees; medical assistance through sanitariums and hospitals; occupational therapy in sanitariums and private nursing homes.

Sex Information and Education Council of the United States (SIECUS), 1855 Broadway, New York, N.Y. 10023

Education of professionals in all helping disciplines to recognize that sexuality is a valid component of being human at all age levels, and that the sexuality of the aging, as now being studied, has its own characteristics that need to be understood if the individual over 60 is to be helped to continue to live fulfilled interpersonal relationships.

Superior Council of the United States, Society of St. Vincent De Paul, 611 Olive Street, Suite 1893, St. Louis, Missouri 63101

Friendly visitation and informal counseling are the typical volunteer contributions. Autonomous local Councils may provide social services and care facilities or sponsor recreational clubs in accord with community need and available Vincentian resources at the local level. Parish units usually offer emergency financial assistance. Programs and services are provided without racial or religious discrimination to those who apply.

Synagogue Council of America, 432 Park Avenue South, New York, N.Y. 10016

The constituent agencies conduct religious, educational, cultural, and recreational programs for Jewish senior citizens through their affiliated synagogues. Congregational affiliates—men's clubs, sisterhoods, young married couples groups—include in their programs visits to homes for the aged, nursing homes, etc. The national agencies provide materials, sponsor workshops and conferences to guide the activities of their local affiliates.

The Townsend Plan National Lobby, 5500 Quincy Street, Hyattsville, Maryland 20784

"To establish an equitably financed system of social security insurance which will assure older people, who have no other resources, freedom from poverty and full participation in the benefits of our national economy and in the prevailing standards of living." The bulk of the Townsend program is to assure a "financial floor beyond which we will not allow people to live."

Travelers Aid Association of America, 44 East 23rd Street, New York, N.Y. 10010

Casework counseling, information and direction services to elderly persons in trouble away from home, available to all.

ACKNOWLEDGMENTS

I am grateful to the many older people with whom I have worked over the years. Those active themselves in the effort to improve the final period of life have taught me much about old age. I have also learned from my collaboration with older people in research and in treatment: and in this book all descriptions of older persons (though fictitious names are used) are taken from actual lives.

I am especially indebted to Myrna I. Lewis, psychotherapist and social worker. Mrs. Lewis, who was co-author with me of the book *Aging and Mental Health*, provided professional and editorial criticism of this work from its earliest forms through its many revisions.

Special thanks go to the following critical readers of various chapters: Constance Beaumont, Roberta B. Brown, Frank Frantz, Val Halamandaris, Stuart Knoop, M. Powell Lawton, David Marlin, Robert C. Maynard, Jack Ossofsky, George Roby, Malvin Schechter, Theodor Schuchat, Harold Sheppard and Peter Weaver.

I wish to acknowledge Ollie Randall's personal support and long-term efforts in public policy on behalf of the elderly. I am also grateful to my colleagues in the studies of human aging (*Human Aging*, Volumes I and II) at the National Institute of Mental Health, to members of the Committee on Aging of the Group for the Advancement of Psychiatry, and to the Washington School of Psychiatry, which has given generous professional support to my work for many years. The staff of the U.S. Senate Special Committee on Aging has been most generous in its help.

The Frederick and Amelia Schimper Foundation of New York (Mr. William E. Friedman, president) provided financial support. Mr. and Mrs. George Wolfe have aided me in completing a variety of tasks in the field of aging, including this book.

I appreciate the research assistance of Jean Jones, librarian of the American Psychiatric Association, John Balkema, Librarian of the National Council on the Aging, Marc Moskowitz, Victoria Fries and Joy Rabin, and thank Monte Vanness and Cindy Hamilton, who typed the manuscript.

Finally, my deep appreciation to Ann Harris, senior editor at Harper & Row, for her sensitivity and her understanding of the objectives of this book.

NOTES

CHAPTER 1. THE TRAGEDY OF OLD AGE IN AMERICA

1. Carl Bernstein, "Age and Race Fears Seen in Housing Opposition," Washington *Post*, March 7, 1969.

2. Robert N. Butler, "The Effects of Medical and Health Progress on the Social and Economic Aspects of the Life Cycle," *Industrial Gerontology*, 2 (1969), pp. 1–9. Presented at National Institute of Industrial Gerontology, March 13, 1969.

3. See Erdman Palmore, "Gerontophobia Versus Ageism," *The Gerontologist*, 12 (1972), p. 213.

4. Robert N. Butler and Myrna I. Lewis, *Aging and Mental Health: Positive Psychosocial Approaches* (St. Louis: C. V. Mosby, 1973).

5. Memorandum RM—5115–TAB, prepared for Technical Analysis Branch, United States Atomic Energy Commission, the Rand Corporation, Santa Monica, California, December, 1966.

6. *Ibid.*, p. 122.

7. *Ibid.*, p. 123.

8. Mrs. Mae B. Phillips, president, Senior Citizens Clearinghouse Committee, Washington, D.C. Hearings on Needs of Senior Citizens, D.C. City Council, October 15, 1968.

9. Marvin J. Taves and G. O. Hansen, "1,700 Elderly Citizens," in Arnold M. Rose (ed.), *Aging in Minnesota* (Minneapolis: University of Minnesota Press, 1963), pp. 73–181.

10. Jacob Tuckman and Irving Lorge, "Classification of the Self as Young, Middle-aged or Old," *Geriatrics*, 9 (1954), pp. 534–36.

11. See, for example, Talcott Parsons, "Age and Sex of the Social Structure of the United States," in *Essays in Sociological Theory* (Glencoe Illinois: Free Press, 1954), especially pp. 89–103.

12. James E. Birren, Robert N. Butler, Samuel W. Greenhouse, Louis Sokoloff and Marion R. Yarrow, *Human Aging: A Biological and Behavioral Study*, U.S. Public Health Service Publication No. 986 (Washington, DC.: U.S. Government Printing Office, 1963, reprinted 1971, 1974).

13. Herbert Spencer, *Social Statics, or The Conditions Essential to Human Happiness Specified*, 1851.

CHAPTER 2. HOW TO GROW OLD AND POOR
IN AN AFFLUENT SOCIETY

1. *The Golden Years: A Tarnished Myth.* A report prepared for the Office of Economic Opportunity by the National Council on the Aging on the Results of Project FIND (1970), p. 4.

2. The 30-day emergency food budget, or Economy Food Plan for emergency use, derives from Department of Agriculture data refined by Social Security Administration staff economists. See specifically Mollie Orshansky, "Consumption, Work and Poverty," in Ben B. Seligman (ed.), *Poverty as a Public Issue* (New York: The Free Press, 1965).

3. Anthony Downs, "Who Are the Urban Poor?," Committee for Economic Development Supplementary Paper. November 26, 1969; revised edition, September, 1970.

4. Herman Brotman, "Income Resources of the Elderly, 1967," *Aging* (May, 1970), p. 25. (Brotman is Chief of Statistics and Program Development, Aging Section, Department of Health, Education, and Welfare.)

5. Herman Brotman, "The Older Population: Some Facts We Should Know," Administration on Aging, mimeographed, 1970.

6. See Sidney Goldstein, "Consumer Patterns of Older Spending Units," *Journal of Gerontology*, 332 (1959). See also Harold L. Sheppard, "The Poverty of Aging," in Seligman, *op. cit.*, pp. 98–99.

7. Leon Keyserling, *Progress or Poverty* (Washington, D.C.: Conference on Economic Progress, 1964).

8. Juanita Kreps, cited in *Developments in Aging*, Report (1970) U.S. Senate Special Committee on Aging, p. 5.

9. National Urban Coalition, *Counterbudget: A Blueprint for Changing National Priorities 1971–1976*, R. Benson and H. Wolman (eds.) (New York: Praeger, 1971), p. 289.

10. U.S. Senate Special Committee on Aging, *The Multiple Hazards of Age and Race: The Situation of Aged Blacks in the United States*, a working paper prepared by Dr. Inabel B. Lindsay, September, 1971.

11. *Ibid.*

12. National Urban Coalition, *op. cit.*, p. 294.

13. U.S. Senate Special Committee on Aging, *Future Directions in Social Security* (1973).

14. Sargent Shriver's testimony at hearings before the Senate Special Committee on Aging, June 16–17, 1965.

15. Personal communication, March 1, 1971, Cleonice Tavani.

CHAPTER 3. WHAT ABOUT MY PENSION?

1. Ben B. Seligman, "The Poverty of Aging," in *Permanent Poverty: An American Syndrome* (Chicago: Quadrangle Books, 1968).

2. Milton Friedman, "Social Security: the Poor Man's Welfare Payment to the Middle Class," *The Washington Monthly*, 4:8–11, 18 (1972).

3. *Ibid.* See also Vincent J. Burke, " '72 Social Security Dividend Eyed," Washington *Post*, October 31, 1971.

4. Congressional testimony of Thomas R. Donahue, a former Labor Department Assistant Secretary, 1969. Quoted in the Washington *Post*, November 24, 1970.

5. For further detail (beyond the *New York Times*) see testimony, Senate Labor Subcommittee of Committee on Labor and Public Welfare, hearings on company retirement plans, July 27–29, 1971. *Private Welfare and Pension Plan Study* (1971). Part I (Washington, D.C.: U.S. Government Printing Office, 1971).

6. James Graham, *The Enemies of the Poor* (New York: Random House, 1970).

7. Ronald Kessler, Washington *Post*, November 24, 1970.

8. Fred J. Cooke, "The Case of the Disappearing Pension," *New York Times Magazine*, March 19, 1972.

9. Paul F. Harbrecht, *Pension Funds and Economic Power* (Millwood, New York: Kraus Reprint Company, 1959).

10. Herman Brotman, "Income Resources of the Elderly, 1967," *Aging* (May, 1970), p. 25.

11. *Time* magazine, August 23, 1971.

12. From hearings on an initial sample study of 87 pension plans around the country, Senate Labor Committee. Washington *Post*, April, 1971.

13. U.S. Senate, 90th Congress, Second Session. On S3421, S1024, S1103, S1255. *Pension and Welfare Plans,* hearings before the Subcommittee on Labor of the Committee on Labor and Public Welfare (Washington, D.C.: U.S. Government Printing Office, 1971).

14. Ralph Nader, *The Company State* (New York: Grossman, 1971).

15. National Council of Senior Citizens. Dockets Nos. 910 and 161. Motion for leave to file brief as *amicus curiae*. In the Supreme Court of the United States, October term, 1970.

16. These figures are from an HEW survey, January, 1971.

17. See generally law review journals: Comment 39NYUL Rev S58 (1964) and Mandelker, "Family Responsibility Under the American Poor Laws," *Michigan University Review*, 54 (1956), p. 497.

18. Personal communication, James Kraus, Deputy Director, Center on Social Welfare Policy and Law. Columbia University, March 10, 1971.

19. Sir William Henry Beveridge, *Full Employment in a Free Society* (New York: W. W. Norton, 1945). Second edition (New York: Hillary House, 1960).

20. Robert Heilbroner, "Benign Neglect in the United States," *Trans-Action,* 17 (October, 1970), p. 16.

21. Ralph Nader and Kate Blackwell, *You and Your Pension* (New York: Grossman, 1973).

22. President's Task Force on Aging, *Toward a Brighter Future for the Elderly* (April, 1970), pp. 19–20.

23. Estimate of Isadore Goodman, Chief of the IRS Pension Fund Branch. See the Washington *Post*, November 24, 1970.

24. Gilbert Burck, "That Ever-Expanding Pension Balloon," *Fortune,* October, 1971, p. 116.

CHAPTER 4. THE RIGHT TO WORK

1. Interview with author, 1970.

2. Paul Weiss, "Age Is Not a Number," *New York Times*, January 1, 1971.

3. Terry S. Kaplan, "Too Old to Work: The Constitutionality of Mandatory Retirement Plans," *Southern California Law Review*, 44 (1971), pp. 150–80.

4. U.S. Census Bureau, *Current Population Report, Population Estimates and Projections,* Projections of the Population of the United States by Age and Sex (Interim Revisions): 1970 to 2020 (Series P-25, No. 448, August 6, 1970), p. 34.

5. See, for example, *Employment Aspects of the Economics of Aging,* U.S. Congress, Senate Special Committee on Aging, Committee Print, 91st Congress, 1st Session, December, 1968, p. 10.

6. Manpower Administration of the Department of Labor, *Back to Work After Retirement* (1972).

7. Elizabeth M. Heidbreder, "Cancelled Careers: the Impact of Reduction-in-Force Policies on Middle-Aged Federal Employees," a report to the Senate Special Committee on Aging, Institute of Industrial Gerontology. The National Council on Aging, May, 1972.

8. See June 30 and August 25, 1971, issues of *Legislative Supplement of Industrial Gerontology.*

9. See, for example, Gordon F. Streib and Clement J. Schneider, *Retirement in American Society in Fact and Process* (Ithaca, New York: Cornell University Press, 1971).

10. An example is the July, 1970, issue of *Fortune,* which detailed the hatred Detroit automobile workers feel toward their work. See especially Harold L. Sheppard and Neal Q. Henrick, *Where Have All the Robots Gone: Worker Dissatisfaction in the 70's* (New York: Macmillan, 1972). See also Studs Terkel, *Working* (New York: Pantheon, 1974).

11. Ethel Shanas *et al., Old People in Three Industrial Societies* (New York and London: Atherton and Routledge and Kegan Paul, 1968).

12. Frances M. Carp, "Differences Among Older Workers, Volunteers, and Persons Who Are Neither," *Journal of Gerontology*, 23 (1968), pp. 497–501.

13. Sigmund Freud, *Civilization and Its Discontents* (1929), in the Standard Edition of the *Complete Psychological Works,* Vol. 21 (London: The Hogarth Press, 1961).

14. Bernardino Ramazzini, *De morbis artificum* (Modeno, Italy: 1700). *Disease of Workers,* trans. W. Wright (Chicago: University of Chicago Press, 1940).

15. Oka Taskashi, *New York Times,* February 27, 1971.

16. See Allen Bernard, *Geriatric Focus,* 11 (September, 1972).

17. See the National Council on the Aging, *Utilization of Older Professional and Scientific Workers,* May, 1961. Nathan W. Shock, "Older People and Their Potentialities for Gainful Employment," *Journal of Gerontology*, 2 (1947), pp. 92–102. Ross A. McFarland, "The Older Worker in Industry," *Harvard Business Review,* Summer, 1943, pp. 505–10.

18. Harvey C. Lehman, *Age and Achievement* (Princeton, N.J.: Princeton University Press, 1953), pp. 200–201.

19. Interview with author, July, 1966.

20. Robert N. Butler, "Age: The Life Review," *Psychology Today*, 5:49–51 (1971).

21. See for interview guide, Robert N. Butler, *Living History: Program for the Acquisition of Tape-recorded Memoirs of History*, Commission on History of the American Psychiatric Association, October, 1970.

22. D. E. Snodgrass, "The Sixty-five Club," *Journal of the Michigan State Medical Society*, 59 (1960), pp. 774–76.

23. Margaret J. Rioch, "A Training Program in Mental Health Counseling for Middle Aged Women," *Journal of the American Association of University Women*, May, 1962.

24. "From Work Discrimination to the Possibility of Work Abuse," *Wall Street Journal*, November 2, 1970.

25. See Peter Weaver, *You, Inc.* (New York: Doubleday, 1973).

26. *Parade*, June 20, 1971.

27. U.S. Department of Labor, *The Older American Worker: Age Discrimination in Employment* (Washington, D.C.: U.S. Government Printing Office, 1965).

28. V. L. Senders, "The Minnesota Plan for Women's Continuing Education: A Progress Report," *The Educational Record*, October, 1961. See also Mary D. Bunting, "The Radcliffe Institute for Independent Study," *The Educational Record*, October, 1960; E. Raushenbush, "Unfinished Business: Continuing Education for Women," *The Educational Record*, October, 1961; T. A. Van-Sant, "Responsibility of Education to the Older Adults," in Wilma Donahue and Clark Tibbetts (eds.), *Growing in the Older Years* (Ann Arbor: University of Michigan Press, 1951), pp. 15–26.

29. To be found in *The Insecurity of Freedom* (New York: Farrar, Straus and Giroux, 1966).

30. E. Belbin, *Training the Adult Worker: Problems of Progress in the Industry*, No. 15 (London: Her Majesty's Stationery Office, 1964). See also R. M. Belbin, *Employment of Older Workers II: Training Methods* (Paris: Organization for Economic Cooperation and Development, 1965); S. Barkin, "Retraining and Job Redesign: Positive Approaches to the Continued Employment of Older Persons," Chapter 3 in Sheppard, Harold E. (ed.) *Toward an Industrial Gerontology* (Cambridge, Mass.: Shenckman Publishing Co., 1971); National Institute of Industrial Gerontology of the National Council on the Aging, *Employment of the Middle-aged Worker*, 1969.

31. Ross A. McFarland and F. H. Philbrook, "Job Placement and Adjustment for Older Workers," *Geriatrics*, 13 (1958), pp. 802–807.

32. A concept that runs through *Work in America*, a report prepared for the HEW Secretary by the Upjohn Institute for Employment Research, 1972.

33. Ginzberg used personal memoirs to study labor. See Eli Ginzberg, *The American Worker in the Twentieth Century: A History Through Autobiography*, 1963.

34. United Community Service of St. Joseph County, Inc. Project ABLE (Ability Based on Long Experience). Final Report Contract No. MDS37-64, Older Worker Employment, South Bend, Indiana, December, 1965.

35. Statement of Lester J. Fox, executive director, Real Services and United

Health Foundation, St. Joseph's County, Indiana, Hearings before the Subcommittee on Employment and Retirement Incomes of the United States Senate, Special Committee on Aging, June 4, 1971 (Washington, D.C.: U.S. Government Printing Office, 1971).

36. Quoted by H. Johnson and N. Kotz, Washington *Post,* April 9, 1972.

37. J. E. Frankel, "Removal of Judges: California Tackles an Old Problem," *American Bar Association Journal,* 49 (1963), pp. 166–71.

38. B. Harrison, H. L. Sheppard and W. J. Spring, "Government as the Employer of First Resort. Public Jobs, Public Needs," *The New Republic,* November 4, 1972.

39. See review of program funds and personnel. Report of ACTION in Appendix, *Developments in Aging,* 1971 and January-March, 1972. Report of the U.S. Senate Special Committee on Aging (Washington, D.C.: U.S. Government Printing Office, 1972).

40. Hearings, Subcommittee on Aging of the Senate Committee on Labor and Public Welfare (Washington, D.C.: U.S. Government Printing Office, 1967).

41. R. K. Baker, "The Peace Corps Matures," Washington *Post,* October 5, 1969.

42. C. Rosenfeld and Elizabeth Waldman, "Work Demonstrations and Chronic Health Problems," *Monthly Labor Review,* January, 1967.

CHAPTER 5. NO PLACE TO LIVE

1. There are a few recent impressive studies conducted in the State of Delaware. See Jerome R. Lewis *et al., Housing Delaware's Elderly, Findings and Recommendations* (Newark, Delaware: University of Delaware, 1972); Jerome R. Lewis and Rebecca L. Pott, *Programs to Aid Housing for the Elderly* (Newark, Delaware: University of Delaware, 1972); Robert A. Wilson and Bernard L. Dworsky, *Social Indicators for Delaware's Aged* (Newark, Delaware: University of Delaware, 1971).

2. U.S. Senate Special Committee on Aging, *The Multiple Hazards of Age and Race: The Situation of Aged Blacks in the United States,* a working paper (prepared by Dr. Inabel B. Lindsay), September, 1971.

3. U.S. Senate Special Committee on Aging, Subcommittee on Housing for the Elderly, *Homeowner Aspects of the Economics of Aging,* 1969.

4. Mason Gaffney, "In Praise of the Property Tax," *The Washington Monthly,* 4 (1973), pp. 2–6.

5. James L. Rowe, Jr., "Mortgage Roles Held Biased Against Minority, Elderly, Women," Washington *Post,* October 5, 1971.

6. See Marjorie Cantor, Karen Rosenthal and Mary Mayer, "The Elderly in the Rental Market of New York City," *Facts for Action,* New York City Office for the Aging, April, 1970.

7. Sanford J. Ungar, "Elderly Strike Luxury Units," Washington *Post,* March 31, 1970.

8. Peter Marcuse, "The Rise of Tenant Organizations," *The Nation,* 213 (1971), pp. 50–53.

9. Frances M. Carp, *A Future for the Aged. Victoria Plaza and Its Residents* (Austin, Texas: University of Texas Press, 1966).

10. Interview by Myrna I. Lewis, June 19, 1971.

11. Calvin L. Bealle, Chief Demographer, Department of Agriculture, Interview, *New York Times,* March 23, 1969.

12. See, for example, Irving Rosow, *Social Integration of the Aged* (New York: The Free Press, 1967); Lewis Mumford, "For Older People, Not Segregation but Integration," *Architectural Record,* 119 (1956), pp. 91–94.

13. M. B. Hamovitch and J. E. Peterson, "Housing Needs and Satisfactions of the Elderly," *The Gerontologist,* 9 (1969), pp. 30–32.

14. Lawrence E. Davies, "Retirement Villages: A New Life Style," *New York Times,* January 18, 1970.

15. "Wake Up and Live, A Reporter at Large," *The New Yorker,* 1964, pp. 120–77.

16. Washington *Post,* April, 24, 1966.

17. Washington *Star,* November 5, 1970.

18. Comments in symposium entitled "Death Education: Preparation for Living," Hamline University, St. Paul, Minnesota, February 15, 1970.

19. Robert J. Samuelson, "Mobile Homes Counted to Meet Housing Aim," Washington *Post,* April 2, 1970.

20. John Deck, *Rancho Paradise* (New York: Harcourt Brace Jovanovich, 1972). Rancho Paradise is a mobile-home park, a trailer camp in Yucaipa, California, behind Los Angeles, made up largely of retired older people. See also Sheila K. Johnson, *Idlehaven Community Building Among the Working-Class Retired* (Berkeley: The University of California Press, 1971).

21. Carlton Smith, "Mobile Home Costs Add Up," Washington *Star-News,* August 3, 1973.

22. Martin Waldron, "Trailer Parks Accused of Rent Gouging," *New York Times,* October 19, 1972.

23. See Hearings, "Fire Safety in Highrise Buildings for the Elderly," U.S. Senate Special Committee on Aging, Subcommittee on Housing for the Elderly, Washington, D.C., February 27–28, 1973 (Washington, D.C.: U.S. Government Printing Office, 1973).

24. Leonard Downie, Jr., and Jim Hoagland, "Mortgaging the Ghetto," Washington *Post,* series, January 5–14, 1969; and Leonard Downie, Jr., *Mortgage on America* (New York: Praeger, 1974).

25. Frank C. Porter, "Romney-Meany Argument May Set Tone of Housing Debate," Washington *Post,* January 21, 1969.

26. Robert N. Butler, "Ageism: Another Form of Bigotry," *The Gerontologist,* 9 (1969), pp. 243–46.

27. Personal communication from James Frush, Jr., vice president of Retirement Residence Incorporated, San Francisco, California, 1969.

28. Michael Harrington, "Urban Renewal," Washington *Star,* November 8, 1970.

29. Jane Jacobs, *The Death and Life of Great American Cities* (New York: Random House, 1961).

30. Joan Colebrook, "A Reporter at Large. The Renewal," *The New Yorker,* January 1, 1966.

31. Paul L. Niebank and Mark R. Yessian, *Relocation and Urban Planning from Obstacle to Opportunity* (Philadelphia: University of Pennsylvania Press, 1968).

32. Hearings, U.S. Senate Special Committee on Aging, August 4, 1971 (Washington, D.C.: U.S. Government Printing Office, 1972).

33. *Aging,* February-March, 1970, pp. 184–85.

34. See series of hearings "Usefulness of the Model Cities Program to the Elderly," U.S. Senate Special Committee on Aging (Washington, D.C.: U.S. Government Printing Office, 1968).

35. *A Position Paper for the Development of the W. Seton Belt "Home Farm" Property,* Washington Episcopal Diocese, 1971. This is the first formulation of this projected new town. Undoubtedly there would be changes in many of these plans as the problems of implementation become apparent. See also "Seton Belt Village," editorial, Washington *Post,* August 4, 1974.

36. Interview with Myrna I. Lewis, June 29, 1971.

37. Specifications are available at United States of America Standards Institute (U.S.A.S.I.) Specification A-117–61.

38. Alexander Kira, *The Bathroom: Criteria for Design* (Ithaca, N.Y.: Cornell University Center for Housing and Environmental Studies, 1966).

39. Edward T. Hall, *The Hidden Dimension* (New York: Doubleday, 1966).

40. M. Powell Lawton, Kermit K. Schooler, Leon A. Pastalem and Louis Gelwicks are among some who have worked in this field. For example, K. K. Schooler, "The Relationship Between Social Interaction and Morale of the Elderly as a Function of Environmental Characteristics," *The Gerontologist,* 9 (1960), pp. 25–29.

CHAPTER 6. NO TIME TO WAIT

1. Robert N. Butler and Myrna I. Lewis, *Aging and Mental Health: Positive Psychosocial Approaches* (St. Louis: C. V. Mosby, 1973).

2. Ethel Shanas *et al., Old People in Three Industrial Societies* (New York: Atherton Press, 1968).

3. Ethel Shanas, "Measuring the Home Health Needs of the Aged in Five Countries," *Journal of Gerontology,* 26 (1971), pp. 37–40.

4. Nick Kotz, *Let Them Eat Promises: Politics of Hunger in America* (Englewood Cliffs, N.J.: Prentice-Hall, 1969).

5. *Toward a Brighter Future for the Elderly,* report of the President's Task Force on Aging, April 1970, p. 48.

6. Sandra Howell, testimony before the Select Subcommittee on Education, the House Committee on Education and Labor, Washington, D.C., September 17, 1970.

7. Department of Health, Education and Welfare, Administration on Aging, *Increased Mobility Among Isolated Older People,* 1970.

8. A. O. Mowbray, *Road to Ruin* (Philadelphia: J. B. Lippincott, 1961).

9. S. G. Finesilver, *The Older Driver: A Statistical Evaluation of Licensing and Accident Involvement in Thirty States and the District of Columbia* (College of Law, University of Denver), January, 1969.

10. Legal Research and Services for the Elderly, *A Handbook of Model*

State Institutes (Washington, D.C.: National Council of Senior Citizens, 1971).

11. See United States Senate Special Committee on Aging, *Hearings on Income Tax Overpayments by the Elderly* (Washington, D.C.: U.S. Government Printing Office, 1970). In 1974 the committee published a pamphlet, *Protecting Older Americans Against Overpayment of Income Taxes (A Checklist of Itemized Deductions).* This is available from the Government Printing Office.

12. Interview with James L. Rowe, Jr., Washington *Post,* July 15, 1972.

13. Annual meeting, D.C. Advisory Committee on Aging, Washington, D.C., May 27, 1970.

14. Personal communication from Ollie A. Randall, September 10, 1972.

15. Jodie Allen, "Backdoor Revenue Sharing—and on a Big Scale," Washington *Post,* August 8, 1972.

16. See Wilbur J. Cohen and Robert N. Ball, "Public Welfare Amendments of 1962 and Proposals for Health Insurance for the Aged," *Social Security Bulletin,* 25, No. 10, October, 1962.

17. Jane E. Bloom and R. H. Cohen, *Funding Social Services in Model Cities: A Guide to Title IV, Part A of the Social Security Act,* 1971. Also, National Council on the Aging, *Social Services for the Elderly, Funding Projects and Model Cities Through Titles I and XVI of the Social Security Act,* 1972.

18. Washington *Post,* August 11, 1972.

19. See a how-to manual to help public and private agencies serving the elderly get their fair share of revenue-sharing funds: Jane E. Bloom, *Revenue-Sharing and the Elderly: How to Play and Win* (Washington, D.C.: The National Council on the Aging, Inc., 1973).

20. See Helen H. Lamale, "Changes in Concepts of Income Adequacy over the Last Century," *Journal of the American Economic Association,* May, 1958, pp. 291–97. Lamale compares "actual levels of living in the United States and the goals of standards of living which have been accepted in different historical periods and for different purposes."

21. From White House Conference on Aging, 1971, *Report on Special Concerns,* p. 61.

22. Elinor Horwitz, "Jewish Poverty Hurts in Miami's South Beach," *The National Jewish Monthly,* 86 (1972), pp. 32–40.

23. United States Department of Health, Education, and Welfare Administration on Aging, *Objectives, Priorities and Activities on Aging's Research and Development Grants Program,* 1970.

24. The National Council on the Aging, "Plight of Elderly Among Minorities Detailed," *NCOA Journal,* 3 (1967), p. 7. See also Frances M. Carp, "Factors in Utilization of Services by the Mexican-American Elderly," Final Report by American Institutes for Research, Palo Alto, California, for the U.S. Department of Health, Education, and Welfare Administration on Aging, May, 1968.

25. See David Hapgood, *Diplomaism* (New York: Donald W. Brown, 1971).

26. Dr. Miguel Cerrolaza, Queen Elizabeth Hospital, Montreal, Canada, quoted in "Nonmedical Workers Cause Serious Threat to Psychiatry," *Psychiatric News,* August 2, 1972.

27. Speech before the Republican Governors Conference, Williamsburg, Virginia, April, 1971.

28. Margaret Blenkner, M. Bloom, Edna Wasser and Margaret Nielson, "Protective Services for Old People; Findings from the Benjamin Rose Institute Study," *Social Casework*, 52 (1971), pp. 483–522.

29. Robert N. Butler, "Toward Practical Ecumenism," *Bulletin of the American Protestant Hospital Association*, 34 (1970), pp. 6–12, and Butler, *Hospital Progress, Journal of the Catholic Hospital Association*, 51 (1970), pp. 94–98.

30. See Nancy M. Anderson, *Senior Centers: Information from a National Survey* (Minneapolis: Institute for Interdisciplinary Studies, American Rehabilitation Foundation, 1969).

31. See "Comprehensive HEW Simplification and Reform Plan" and "Report on the HEW Potential for the Seventies," Department of Health, Education, and Welfare, January, 1973.

32. John B. Martin, statement to Technical Committee on Training, White House Conference on Aging, Washington, D.C., December 22, 1970. He referred to studies by both the Administration on Aging and the Advisory Council for the National Institute of Child Health and Human Development.

CHAPTER 7. THE UNFULFILLED PRESCRIPTION

1. Leslie S. Libow, "Pseudosenility: Acute and Reversible Organic Brain Syndromes," *Journal of the American Geriatrics Society*, 21 (1973), pp. 112–120.

2. H. E. Clow and E. B. Allen, "A Study of Depressive States in the Aging," *Geriatrics*, 4 (1949), pp. 11–17.

3. See M. S. Pathy, "Clinical Presentation of Myocardial Infarction in the Elderly," *British Medical Journal*, 29 (1967), p. 190; P. G. Cohen, "Hyperosmolar Coma: A Geriatric Medical Emergency," *Geriatrics*, 25 (1970), pp. 102–106.

4. See Ruth Bier, "The Nurse's Management of the Aged Dependent Patient," *ANA Regional Clinic Conference*, VI (1965), pp. 16–23; *Strike Back at Stroke*, U.S. Department of Health, Education and Welfare, Public Health Service Publication Number 596 (Washington, D.C.: U.S. Government Printing Office, 1958).

5. William H. Masters and Virginia Johnson, *Human Sexual Inadequacy* (London: J. and A. Churchill, 1970), p. 316.

6. George Winokur, "Depression in the Menopause," *The American Journal of Psychiatry*, 130 (1973), pp. 92–93. He also has found no greater risk of developing depression during the menopause than during other times of the life span.

7. R. Ruben, "Aging and Hearing," in *Clinical Geriatrics* (Philadelphia: J. B. Lippincott, 1971).

8. H. B. Moorehead *et al.*, "Causes of Blindness in 4965 Persons Whom It Stated Were Added to Their MRA Registers in 1966," in *Proceedings of 1960 Conference of Model Reporting Area for Blindness* (Washington, D.C.: U.S. Public Health Service, 1969).

9. R. G. Harlin, "Estimated Prevalence of Blindness in the United States, 1952," *Social Security Bulletin*, 16 (1953), pp. 8–11.

10. David Sudnow, *Passing On: The Social Organization of Dying* (Englewood Cliffs, N. J.: Prentice-Hall, 1967).

11. The work of Meyersburg, Sudnow and others has delineated the hostile attitudes toward the so-called "crock."

12. Quoted in Washington *Post*, November 30, 1970.

13. Donald C. Spence, Elliot M. Feigenbaum, Faith Fitzgerald, and Janet Roth, "Medical Student Attitudes Toward the Geriatric Patient," *Journal of the American Geriatrics Society*, 16 (1968), pp. 976–83.

14. Joseph T. Freeman, "A Survey of Geriatric Education: Catalogues of United States Medical Schools," *Journal of the American Geriatrics Society*, 19 (1971), pp. 746–62.

15. Quotations are from *New York Times*, November, 1970.

16. Carnegie Foundation for the Advancement of Teaching (Clark Kerr) *Higher Education and the Nation's Health* (New York: McGraw-Hill, 1970).

17. Rashi Fein, *The Doctor Shortage: An Economic Diagnosis* (Washington, D.C.: The Brookings Institution, 1967). Fein emphasized the need for physicians' services which might be accomplished by subordinates rather than simply increasing the number of physicians.

18. *Medical Economics,* August 30, 1971.

19. R. R. McGee, "Let's Stop Kidding Ourselves About Peer Review," *Medical Economics*, September 11, 1972.

20. Washington *Post*, November 30, 1970.

21. *Medical World News*, February 5, 1971.

22. Washington *Post*, November 30, 1970.

23. Karlyn Barker, "Patient Put on Shuttle While Doctors Argue," Washington *Post*, September 28, 1972.

24. Sudnow, *op. cit.*

25. *Medical World News*, November 5, 1971, p. 19.

26. Ronald Kessler, "The Hospital Business," Washington *Post*, October 29–November 3, 1972.

27. *Medical World News*, March 24, 1972.

28. Dr. Philip R. Lee, chairman, HEW Task Force on Prescription Drugs, *The Drug Users*, 1968. Also see Milton Silverman and Philip R. Lee, *Pills, Profits and Politics* (Berkeley: University of California Press, 1974).

29. Washington *Post,* February 16, 1969.

30. *Time* magazine, April 3, 1964, p. 79.

31. See Richard Harris, *The Real Voice* (New York: Macmillan, 1964) and Morton Mintz, *The Therapeutic Nightmare* (Boston: Houghton Mifflin, 1965). Mintz gives full details of the MER/29 case.

32. Morton Mintz, "FDA's Revolving Door Spins On," Washington *Post*, March 18, 1968.

33. *Medical World News*, February 1, 1971.

34. *Geriatrics*, February, 1971.

35. Barry Commoner, *The Closing Circle: Nature, Man and Technology* (New York: Alfred A. Knopf, 1971).

36. R. H. Moser, "Diseases of Medical Progress," *The New England Journal of Medicine,* 255 (1956), pp. 606–14.

37. Morton Mintz, "Students Veto Gift of Drug Firm," Washington *Post,* February 1, 1969.

38. Samuel W. Greenhouse and Donald F. Morrison, "Statistical Methodology," in J. E. Birren, R. N. Butler, S. W. Greenhouse, L. Sokoloff and Marion R. Yarrow, *Human Aging: A Biological and Behavioral Study,* 1963. Reprinted as Publication No. (HSM) 71–9051, 1971. K. W. Schaie, "A General Model for the Study of Developmental Problems," *Psychological Bulletin,* 64 (1965), pp. 92–107.

39. From William B. Kannel, "Framingham Study and Chronic Disease Prevention," *Hospital Practice,* 5 (1970), p. 78.

40. "Recent Mortality from Cerebral Vascular Diseases," *Statistical Bulletin,* Metropolitan Life, September, 1970.

41. Thomas R. Dawber, "The Framingham Study: A Need to Continue," Current Opinion, *Medical Tribune,* October 12, 1970.

42. "Medical Care Spending for Three Age Groups," *Social Security Bulletin,* May, 1972.

43. Dorothy P. Rice, statement before the Subcommittee on Health of the Elderly of the U.S. Senate Special Committee on Aging, September 30, 1966.

44. William A. Nolen, "Are Doctors Profiteering on Medicare?," *Medical Economics,* February 20, 1967; "Doctors, Money and Medicare," *Medical Economics,* October 16, 1967; "Look What Medicare's Doing to Medical Ethics," *Medical Economics,* February 15, 1971.

45. Group for the Advancement of Psychiatry, *Toward a Public Policy for Mental Health Care of the Elderly,* Report No. 79, 1970.

46. See Marjorie Cantor and Mary Mayer, *The Health Crisis of Older New Yorkers. Facts for Action* (New York: New York City Office for the Aging, 1972).

47. See Barbara and John Ehrenreich, "The Medical-Industrial Complex," *The New York Review,* December 17, 1970.

48. See Mal Schechter, " 'Emergency' Medicare and Desegregation: A Special Report," *Hospital Practice,* July, 1968, and Schechter, "Faith, Home, and Medicare," *The New Republic,* 159 (1968), pp. 20–21, and Harold M. Schmeck, Jr., "Medicare Abuse in South Hinted," *New York Times,* July 15, 1972.

49. Hearings, U.S. Senate Finance Committee, September 27, 1970.

50. *Medical Economics,* April 13, 1970.

51. See Morton Mintz, "Health Plans Found Billing Barred Fees to Medicare," Washington *Post,* May 20, 1971.

52. See Stuart Auerbach, "U.S. Forces Shakeup of Blue Cross," Washington *Post,* July 16, 1970.

53. See Stuart Auerbach, "Perot Medicare Bonanza Revealed," Washington *Post,* August 29, 1971.

54. See *American Medical News,* January 10, 1972.

55. *Journal of the American Geriatrics Society,* 17 (1969), pp. 30–34.

56. Committee correspondence, February 17, 1970.

57. Committee correspondence, February 19, 1969.

58. See account of Lee's views in "New Specialty for Old Patients," *Medical World News*, May 5, 1967.

59.. Melvin J. Krant, "The Organized Care of the Dying Patient," *Hospital Practice*, 7 (1972), pp. 101–108.

60. See Sidney R. Garfield, "A Health Plan to 'Cure' the Well," *Scientific American*, 222 (1970), pp. 15–23.

61. Excerpted from a speech delivered at the Mayo Foundation, *New York Times*, December 19, 1970.

CHAPTER 8. THEY ARE ONLY SENILE

1. Alexander Simon and Robert B. Cahan, "The Acute Brain Syndrome in Geriatric Patients," in Werner M. Mendel and Leon J. Epstein (eds.), *Acute Psychotic Reaction*, Psychiatric Research Reports, No. 16, American Psychiatric Association, Washington, D.C., 1966.

2. See David Rothschild, "Pathological Changes in Senile Psychoses and Psychological Significance," *American Journal of Psychiatry*, 93 (1937), pp. 757–88; Martin Roth, "The Natural History of Mental Disorders in Old Age," *Journal of Mental Science*, 19 (1955), pp. 281–301; and Robert N. Butler, Darab Dastur, and Seymour Perlin, "Relationships of Senile Manifestations and Chronic Brain Syndrome to Cerebral Circulation and Metabolism," *Journal of Psychiatric Research*, 3 (1965), pp. 229–38.

3. See F. J. Kane, Jr. and J. A. Ewing, "Iatrogenic Brain Syndrome," *Southern Medical Journal*, 58 (1965), pp. 875–77.

4. Lionel Z. Cosin, Margaret Mort, Felix Post, Celia Westrapp and Moyra Williams, "Experimental Treatment of Persistent Senile Confusion," *The International Journal of Social Psychiatry*, 4 (1958), pp. 24–42.

5. See World Health Organization, *Eighth Revision of the International Classification of Disease* (ICD–8), 1967, 1968, and American Psychiatric Association, *Diagnostic and Statistical Manual of Mental Disorders*, 2nd Edition (DSM–II) (Washington, D.C., 1968).

6. See Alvin I. Goldfarb, "Prevalence of Psychiatric Disorders in Metropolitan Old Age and Nursing Homes," *Journal of the American Geriatrics Society*, 10 (1962), pp. 77–84.

7. Similar findings are reported by E. Gartley Jaco, *The Social Epidemiology of Mental Disorders* (New York: The Russell Sage Foundation, 1960), Table 1, p. 32.

8. For example, see "The Boarding House Racket," Philadelphia *Bulletin*, March 23, 1971.

9. See Robert N. Butler and Myrna I. Lewis, *Aging and Mental Health: Positive Psychosocial Approaches* (St. Louis: C. V. Mosby, 1973).

10. Robert W. Gibson, "Medicare and the Psychiatric Patient," *Psychiatric Opinion*, 7 (1970), pp. 17–22. His sample included some 6,400 patients admitted to 49 private psychiatric hospitals between 1960 and 1964.

11. National Institutes of Health, *Human Aging: A Biological and Behavioral Study*, 1963. (Reprinted 1971.)

12. William Schofield, *Psychotherapy: Purchase of Friendship* (Englewood Cliffs, N.J.: Prentice-Hall, 1964, 1974).

13. David Hamburg *et al.*, "Report of Ad Hoc Committee on Central Fact Finding Data of the American Psychoanalytic Association," *Journal of the American Psychoanalytic Association*, 15 (1967), pp. 841–61.

14. See Robert N. Butler and Lillian G. Sulliman, "Psychiatric Contact with the Community-Resident, Emotionally Disturbed Elderly," *Journal of Nervous and Mental Disease*, 137 (1963), pp. 180–86.

15. Anita K. Bahn, *Outpatient Population of Psychiatric Clinics, Maryland 1958–59*, Public Health Monograph No. 65, U.S. Department of Health, Education, and Welfare.

16. *Psychiatric News*, American Psychiatric Association, December, 1967.

17. Quoted in *Psychiatric News*, November, 1968, pp. 1, 5.

18. See Jerome Frank, *Persuasion and Healing* (Baltimore: Johns Hopkins Press, 1961); F. Sobey, *The Non-Professional Revolution in Mental Health* (New York: Columbia University Press, 1970); E. Fuller Torrey, *The Mind Game: Witchdoctors and Psychiatrists* (New York: Emerson Hall Publishers, 1972); and John C. Whitehorn and Barbara J. Betz, "A Study of Psychotherapeutic Relationships Between Physicians and Schizophrenic Patients," *American Journal of Psychiatry*, 111 (1954), pp. 321–31. Whitehorn and Betz correlated patient improvement with personal characteristics of therapists who had comparable clinical experience. "Group A physicians" emphasized active doctor-patient personal interaction and a rational nonauthoritarian approach. "Group B physicians" were less personal, more passive and permissive and oriented to illness.

19. William E. Henry, J. H. Sims, and S. L. Spray, *The Fifth Profession* (San Francisco: Jossey Bass, 1971).

20. Lawrence S. Kubie, "Need for a New Subdiscipline in the Medical Profession," *Archives of Neurology and Psychiatry*, 78 (1957), pp. 283–93.

21. See George E. Crane, "Tardive Dyskinesia in Patients Treated with Major Neuroleptics," *American Journal of Psychiatry*, 125 (Suppl.) (1968), pp. 40–48, and "Persistence of Neurological Symptoms Due to Neuroleptic Drugs," *American Journal of Psychiatry*, 127 (1971), pp. 1407–1410.

22. Franklin D. Chu and Sharland Trotter, *The Madness Establishment* (New York: Grossman, 1974).

23. Robert H. Dovenmuehle, "A Review of the Impact on the Community Mental Health Center Movement on Psychiatric Services to Senior Citizens," Appendix 2, Item 4, in *Mental Health Care and the Elderly: Shortcomings in Public Policy*, a report by the U.S. Senate Special Committee on Aging (Washington, D.C.: U.S. Government Printing Office, 1971).

24. "Pellagra Found in Maryland State Hospitals," *Psychiatric News*, May 5, 1971, p. 18.

25. See E. Fuller Torrey and Robert S. Taylor, "Cheap Labor from Poor Nations," presented at 125th Annual Meeting of the American Psychiatric Association, May 1, 1972, and F. L. Bartlett, "Present-day Requirements for State Hospitals Joining the Community," *New England Journal of Medicine*, 276 (1967), pp. 90–94.

26. F. L. Bartlett, "Institutional Peonage," *Atlantic*, 215 (1964), pp. 116–19.

27. Leon J. Epstein and Alexander Simon, "Alternatives to State Hospitalization for the Geriatric Mentally Ill," *American Journal of Psychiatry,* 124 (1968), pp. 955–61.

28. Lawrence Kolb, Sr., "Mental Hospitalization of the Aged: Is It Being Overdone?" *American Journal of Psychiatry,* 112 (1956), pp. 627–36.

29. Annie Mae Pemberton, *Helping Older People Who Have Been in Mental Hospitals,* second in a series of reports for public welfare departments on how public welfare serves aged people. (Chicago: American Public Welfare Association, 1954).

30. The dangers of transfer have been widely documented. See David Camargo and George Preston, "What Happened to Patients Who Are Hospitalized for the First Time When Over Sixty-four?" *American Journal of Psychiatry,* 102 (1945), pp. 168–73; C. Knight Aldrich and E. Mendkoff, "Relocation of the Aged and Disabled: A Mortality Study," *Journal of the American Geriatric Society,* 11 (1963), pp. 185–95; and Margaret Blenkner, "Environmental Changes and the Aging Individual," 7 (1967), p. 2.

31. "Trends in Long-term Care," hearings before Subcommittee on Long-term Care of the United States Senate Special Committee on Aging, Washington, D.C., December 17, 1970. Part II. (Washington, D.C.: U.S. Government Printing Office, 1971).

32. *Ibid.,* April 2–3, 1971.

33. See account in *Mental Health Care and the Elderly: Shortcomings in Public Policy, op cit.,* pp. 13–14.

34. John Sibley, "Budget Cuts Sow Despair at a State Mental Hospital," *New York Times,* May 19, 1971.

35. Quoted by M. Siegel, "Wide Community Crime Traced to 'Singles' in Welfare Hotels," *New York Times,* November 16, 1972.

36. See Alfred E. Lewis and Claudia Levy, "Fire Kills Two Mental Patients. Chief Orders Foster Care Curbs," Washington *Post,* December 8, 1971.

37. Charles M. Gaitz and P. E. Baer, "Placement of Elderly Psychiatric Patients," *Journal of the American Geriatrics Society,* 19 (1971), pp. 601–13.

38. Bernard A. Stotsky, "A Controlled Study of Factors in the Successful Adjustment of Mental Patients to Nursing Homes," *American Journal of Psychiatry,* 123 (1967), pp. 1234–51.

39. See Elias S. Cohen and A. C. Kraft, "The Restorative Potential of Elderly Long-Term Residents of Mental Hospitals," *The Gerontologist,* 8, pp. 264–68.

40. See René Dubos, *A God Within* (New York: Scribner, 1972).

41. For example, as in the D.C. Hospitalization for the Mentally Ill Act, D.C. Code 1967 edition, Title 21, Sections 21–501 to 591.

42. See "Judges Urge Transcripts of D.C. Mental Hearings," Washington *Post,* June 3, 1969.

43. Morton Birnbaum, "The Right to Treatment," *American Bar Association Journal,* 46 (1960), pp. 498–505.

44. J. Robitscher, "Courts, State Hospitals and Right to Treatment," *The American Journal of Psychiatry,* 129 (1972), pp. 298–304.

45. *Rouse v. Cameron,* 373F 2nd 451 (D.C. Cir. 1966).

46. David Bazelon, "Implementing the Right to Treatment," *University of Chicago Law Review,* 742, 746 (1969).

47. F. DeMarneffe, "The New APA Standards for Psychiatric Facilities," *The American Journal of Psychiatry*, 122 (1969), p. 879.

48. U.S. Court of Appeals, District of Columbia Circuit, 364 F. 2nd 657, 1966. Dr. Dale C. Cameron was then superintendent of St. Elizabeths Hospital.

49. One example: Testimony, U.S. Senate Finance Committee, September 16, 1970.

50. *Ibid.*

51. Erik H. Erikson, "Identity and the Life Cycle," Monograph No. 7, Volume 1, *Psychological Issues* (New York: International Universities Press, 1959).

52. J. R. Tkach and Y. Hokama, "Autoimmunity in Chronic Brain Syndrome: Preliminary Report," *Archives of General Psychiatry*, 23 (1970), pp. 61–64.

53. According to Marie L. Blank, social-work consultant.

54. An "Inventory of Training Projects in Aging Supported by the Division of Manpower and Training Programs, FY1971," March, 1972, a mimeographed document, illustrates the lengths to which NIMH went to stretch their meager point.

55. *Psychiatric News*, official newspaper of the American Psychiatric Association, September 1, 1971.

56. Group for the Advancement of Psychiatry, *The Aged and Community Mental Health: A Guide to Program Development*, Report No. 80, 1971.

CHAPTER 9. HOUSES OF DEATH ARE A LIVELY BUSINESS

1. Ethel Shanas, *The Health of Older People: A Social Survey* (Cambridge, Mass.: Harvard University Press, 1962).

2. *The American Heritage Dictionary of the English Language* (New York: American Heritage Publishing Co., 1969).

3. David A. Pryor, "Somewhere Between Society and the Cemetery: Where We Put the Aged," *The New Republic*, April 25, 1970.

4. J. A. Solon, "Nursing Home and Medical Care," in L. J. DeGroot (ed.), *Medical Care: Social and Organization Aspects* (Springfield: C. C. Thomas, 1966) p. 198.

5. See Morton Mintz, "Rules Issued to Halt Fraud in Medicaid," Washington *Post*, March 28, 1971.

6. Patricia M. Wald and P. B. Hutt, *Dealing with Drug Abuse. A Report to the Ford Foundation* (New York: Praeger, 1972).

7. Erving Goffman, *Asylums* (New York: Anchor Books, 1961).

8. Morton A. Lieberman, "Psychological Effects of Institutionalization," *Journal of Gerontology*, 23 (1968), pp. 343–53.

9. Carol Honsa, "Stoddard Baptist Home for Elderly Lacks Funds to Give Full Services," Washington *Post*, April 25, 1971.

10. *Alternatives to Nursing Home Care: A Proposal*, U.S. Senate Special Committee on Aging. Prepared by Levinson Gerontological Policy Institute, Brandeis University, Waltham, Massachusetts, October, 1971 (Washington, D.C.: U.S. Government Printing Office, 1971).

11. Washington *Star*, February 24, 1970.

12. Herbert Shore, "Institutional Care for the Aged. Letter to HEW Secretary Elliot Richardson," *The Gerontologist*, 12 (1972), pp. 7, 109.

13. See Jerome Kaplan, "An Editorial: Alternatives to Nursing Home Care: Fact or Fiction," *The Gerontologist*, 12 (1972), p. 114.

14. Former Congressman David Pryor, *New York Times*, February 24, 1970.

15. See "Ohio GOP Hurt by Scandal," Washington *Star*, July 26, 1970, and "Four Seasons Scandal Biggest Stock Fraud in Modern Times," Washington *Post*, December 12, 1972.

16. Mal Schechter, "Nursing Home Fire: The Anatomy of a Tragedy," *Hospital Practice*, 7 (1972), p. 139. See also *Senior Citizen News*, January, 1973, p. 26. Between 1952 and 1973, 779 lives were lost in 60 nursing-home fires.

17. For full and absorbing details see Mal Schechter, "Of Carpets, Patient Safety and Decision Making at HEW," *Hospital Practice*, 3 (1971), p. 33.

18. Board of Inquiry Appointed by Dr. Neil Solomon, the Secretary of Health and Mental Hygiene of Maryland (Father Joseph Sellinger, S.J., Dr. David Rogers and John Moxley), *Report of an Investigation into the Salmonella Epidemic at Gould Convalesarium in Baltimore in July, 1970*. (Because of its excellence and coverage this report is quoted at length.)

19. Theodor Schuchat, "Animals' Protection Better than Humans'," Washington *Star*, July 15, 1969.

20. Named after Senator Frank Moss (D.-Utah).

21. Public Law 90–248, Sections 224 and 234.

22. Named after Senator Edward M. Kennedy (D.-Mass.).

23. Jordan Braverman, a research associate in the office of the executive director of the American Pharmaceutical Association, composed a booklet, *Nursing Home Standards: A Tragic Dilemma in American Health, An Analysis by States of Nursing Home Standards Under Federal Medicare and State Licensure Programs* (American Pharmaceutical Association, Washington, D.C., 1970). It is quite comprehensive but outdated.

24. Presented at a forum conducted by former Representative David Pryor (D.-Ark.) on "Urgent Needs to Improve Standards of Care in U.S. Nursing Homes," Washington, D.C., October 20, 1970.

25. Senator Frank Moss (D.-Utah), opening statement, hearings on *Conditions and Problems in the Nation's Nursing Homes* (Washington, D.C.: U.S. Government Printing Office, 1965).

26. Mal Schechter, "Medicare's Secret Data," Washington *Post*, September 26, 1971.

27. See, for example, Report by Federation for Community Planning, Cleveland, Ohio, December, 1972.

28. Hearings, Subcommittee on Long-term Care, U.S. Senate Special Committee on Aging, *Trends in Long-term Care*, Part II, December 17, 1970 (Washington, D.C.: U.S. Government Printing Office, 1971).

29. Later published: Ralph Nader's Study Group Report on Nursing Homes (Claire Townsend, project director), *Old Age: The Last Segregation* (New York: Grossman, 1971).

30. On 1970 TV documentary, "When You Reach December."

31. Herbert Shore, "How to Get Better Results with Volunteers," *Professional Nursing Home*, March, 1963.

32. Commission on Chronic Illness, *Care of the Long-Term Patient*, Commonwealth Fund, Volume II (Harvard University Press, 1956).

33. Speech, House of Representatives, May 21, 1970.

34. See R. M. Thurlow, "Extended Medicare: A New Disappearing Act," *Medical Economics*, June 5, 1972.

35. See hearings on *Trends in Long-term Care, op. cit.*

36. See the Health Law Project directed by Edward V. Sparer who teaches at the University of Pennsylvania.

37. See Senator Abraham Ribicoff (D.-Conn.), *Congressional Record* S2791, February 29, 1972. Report, Social Security Administration, March, 1971.

38. See Chapter 11 of Robert N. Butler and Myrna I. Lewis, *Aging and Mental Health: Positive Psychosocial Approaches* (St. Louis: C. V. Mosby, 1973).

39. R. N. Butler, "Toward Practical Ecumenism," *Bulletin of the American Protestant Hospital Association*, 34 (1970), pp. 6–12, and *Hospital Progress: Journal of the Catholic Hospital Association*, 51 (1970), pp. 94–98.

CHAPTER 10. VICTIMIZATION OF THE ELDERLY

1. U.S. Senate Special Committee on Aging, *Older Americans and Transportation: "Crisis in Mobility"* (Washington, D.C.: The U.S. Government Printing Office, 1970).

2. Opening statement, hearings, *Adequacy of Federal Response to Housing Needs of Older Americans*, August 2, 1972 (Washington, D.C.: U.S. Government Printing Office, 1972).

3. See Eric Pace, "Patterns Seen in Theft Killings of the Lower East Side Elderly," *New York Times*, September 11, 1971.

4. Stephen Isaacs, "Fear in Forest Hills: A Crisis of Public Housing," Washington *Post*, November 26, 1971.

5. M. Siegel, "Wide Community Crime Traced to 'Singles' in Welfare Hotels," *New York Times*, November 16, 1972.

6. See Phyllis Mensh Brostoff, *Metropolitan Police Contacts with the Elderly*, Appendix II, District of Columbia. The Washington School of Psychiatry (sponsor), report to the 1971 White House Conference on Aging, 1971. See also Phyllis Mensh Brostoff, Roberta B. Brown, and Robert N. Butler, " 'Beating Up' on the Elderly: Police, Social Work and Crime," *The Public Interest*, Report No. 6. *Aging and Human Development*, 3 (1972), pp. 319–22.

7. The director was Phyllis Mensh Brostoff, MSW. The project was made possible through the efforts of Roberta B. Brown, then Chief, Office of Services to the Aged, D.C. Department of Human Resources.

8. Quoted in *Medical World News*, December 18, 1972.

9. Symposium: Delivery of Geriatric Community Care—Balancing Professional Responsibilities. 25th Annual Scientific Meeting, The Gerontological Society. San Juan, Puerto Rico, December 20, 1972.

10. The reader should compare the humanitarian views Karl Menninger expressed in his *The Crime of Punishment* (New York: Viking Press, 1968).

11. U.S. Senate Report of the Subcommittee on Frauds and Misrepresentations Affecting the Elderly of the Special Committee on Aging, 1966.

12. See Amram Ducovny, *The Billion $ Swindle* (New York: Fleet Press Corporation, 1969).

13. See hearings on *Hearing Aids and the Older American* before the U.S. Senate Special Committee on Aging, September 10, 1973.

14. See Patrick M. McGrady, Jr., *The Youth Doctors* (New York: Coward-McCann, 1968).

15. See Judith Ramsey, "Ponce de Leon Is Alive and Well in Nassau," *Medical Opinion*, August, 1971.

16. See Peter Weaver, "Promises, Promises: Gyps by Mail," *Washington Post*, June 23, 1972. Weaver's consumer column details many of the problems facing older people in the marketplace.

17. See *Deceptive or Misleading Methods in Health Insurance Sales*, hearings before the Subcommittee on Frauds and Misrepresentations Affecting the Elderly of the U.S. Senate Special Committee on Aging, May 4, 1964 (Washington, D.C.: U.S. Government Printing Office, 1964).

18. See Mirian Ottenberg, "Con Men vs. Aged. Loneliness Opens Doors," Washington *Star*, September 16, 1973.

19. Viola W. Bernard, "Why People Become the Victims of Medical Quackery," *American Journal of Public Health*, 55 (1965), p. 1142.

20. Victor Cohn, "VA Releases Test Data on Hearing Aids," Washington *Post*, April 13, 1969.

21. U.S. Senate Committee on Aging, Hearings, *Flammable Fabrics and Other Fire Hazards to Older Americans* (Washington, D.C.: U.S. Government Printing Office, 1972).

22. Philip Elman, dissenting statement, June 25, 1969.

CHAPTER 11. PACIFICATION AND THE POLITICS OF AGING

1. Marcus Tullius Cicero, *De Senectute*, trans. by F. O. Copley (Ann Arbor: University of Michigan Press, 1967).

2. Two respected and liberal journalists note the problem without fully clarifying: Nick Kotz, "Social Security Bill Making Life Worse for Nation's Poor," Washington *Post*, October 11, 1972, and David S. Broder, "Budget Funds for Elderly Grow Rapidly," Washington *Post*, January 31, 1973.

3. U.S. Social Security Administration, "Listing of Bills Relating to the Social Security Program and Other Selected Bills of Interest Introduced During the 91st Congress," January 3, 1969, January 2, 1971. Washington, D.C.

4. See Hazel Erskine, "Polls: Is War a Mistake?" *Public Opinion Quarterly*, 34 (1970), pp. 134–50, and Angus Campbell, "Politics Through the Life Cycle," *The Gerontologist*, 11 (1971), pp. 12–17.

5. Richard Scammon, address, Forum for State Legislators, Washington, D.C., December 5, 1972. See also Richard J. Scammon and Ben J. Wattenberg, *The Real Majority* (New York: Coward-McCann, 1970).

6. James Reston, "The Over 65 Vote," *New York Times*, January 26, 1972.

7. Richard Harris, *A Sacred Trust* (New York: New American Library, 1966), p. 74.

8. Robert Binstock, "Interest-Group Liberalism and the Politics of Aging," *The Gerontologist*, 12 (1972), p. 267.

9. "Taxpayers Stuck with the Cost of Nixon's Campaign Literature?" *Senior Citizen News*, November, 1972.

10. *Senior Citizen News*, November, 1972.

11. Established by Senate Resolution 33, 87th Congress; agreed to on February 13, 1961.

12. Robert N. Butler, "Fighting Seniority with Bigotry," *The Washington Monthly*, 3 (1971), pp. 37–42.

13. See Richard Harris, *A Sacred Trust* (New York: Pelican, 1966), p. 136.

14. The National Council of Senior Citizens, *A Platform for the Seventies for All Older Americans*, November, 1971.

15. Morton Mintz, "Serving the Elderly Proves Profitable. Golden Days of Retirement," Washington *Post,* February 13, 1972. See also Robert C. Maynard, "Investigative Reporters: A First Amendment Test," Washington *Post,* January 10, 1974, regarding investigation of Leonard Davis by journalist Theodor Schuchat.

16. Morton Mintz, *op. cit.*

17. Address before the American Aging Association, October 27, 1971.

18. Quoted in *Time* magazine, June 3, 1972.

19. See Hobart Jackson, "The Black Elderly: Jeopardized by Racism and Neglect," interview, *Geriatrics*, June, 1972.

20. California Rural Legal Assistance Senior Citizens Project, *Training Older Americans in Advocacy* (San Francisco: The Project, 1971).

21. Timothy Hutchens, "U.S. May Take Action on Blue Cross Interest," Washington *Star*, July 2, 1972.

22. "The Freedom of Information Act: What It Is and How to Use It" (Freedom of Information Clearinghouse, P.O. Box 19367, Washington, D.C. 20036).

23. "State of the Aging" address in the U.S. Senate, February 7, 1972.

24. The National Supplemental Security Income, 1972 Social Security Amendments.

CHAPTER 12. THE GIFT OF LIFE

1. Robert N. Butler, "The Effect of Medical and Health Progress on the Social and Economic Aspects of the Life Cycle," *Industrial Gerontology*, 1 (1969), pp. 1–9.

2. See Donnella H. Meadows, Dennis L. Meadows, J. Randers, Jr., and W. W. Behrens III, *The Limits to Growth* (Potomac Associates, 1972).

3. W. E. B. Du Bois, *Dusk at Dawn* (New York: Harcourt, Brace, 1940).

4. Bertrand Russell, *The Autobiography of Bertrand Russell: 1872–1914*, Volume I (Boston: Little, Brown, 1967).

5. National Program for the Conquest of Cancer, *Report of the National Panel of Consultants on the Conquest of Cancer* (Washington, D.C.: U.S. Government Printing Office, 1971).

6. Editorial, *The Medical Tribune*, July 5, 1972.

7. Manning Feinleib and Michael J. Davidson, "Coronary Disease Mortality.

A Community Perspective," *The Journal of the American Medical Association*, 222 (1972), pp. 1129–34.

8. Don Calahan, *Problem Drinkers: A National Survey* (San Francisco: Jossey-Bass, 1971).

9. Robert D. Patterson, Lee Freeman and Robert N. Butler, "Psychiatric Aspects of Adaptation, Survival and Death," in S. Granick and R. D. Patterson (eds.), *Human Aging II* (Washington, D.C.: U.S. Government Printing Office, 1971). See also John Bartko, Robert D. Patterson, and Robert N. Butler, "Biomedical and Behavioral Predictors of Life Span Among Normal Aged Men," in E. Palmore (ed.), *Prediction of Life Span* (Lexington, Mass.: D.C. Heath, 1971).

10. Meyer Friedman and R. H. Rosenman, "Type A Behavior Pattern: Its Association with Coronary Heart Disease," *Annals of Clinical Research*, 3 (1971), pp. 300–12. See also *Type A Behavior and Your Heart* (New York: Alfred A. Knopf, 1974).

11. Jules V. Quint and Bianca R. Cody, "Preeminence and Mortality: Longevity of Prominent Men." Paper presented before the American Public Health Association, November 13, 1968. Summary published in *Statistical Bulletin* of the Metropolitan Life Insurance Company, January, 1968, pp. 2–5.

12. J. Hrachovec, *Keeping Young and Living Longer* (Los Angeles: Sherbourne Press, 1973).

13. Report, President's Council on Physical Fitness and Sports, 1973.

14. Daniel Offer and Melvin Sabshin, *Normality: Theoretical and Clinical Concepts of Mental Health* (New York: Basic Books, 1966).

15. James E. Birren, Robert N. Butler, Samuel W. Greenhouse, Louis Sokoloff, and Marian R. Yarrow, *Human Aging: A Biological and Behavioral Study*, Public Health Service Publication (Washington, D.C.: U.S. Government Printing Office, 1963). Reprinted in 1971, 1974.

16. Samuel Granick and Robert D. Patterson, *Human Aging II: An Eleven-year Follow-up Biomedical and Behavioral Study*, Public Health Service Publication (Washington, D.C.: U.S. Government Printing Office, 1971).

17. George L. Engel, *Archives of Internal Medicine*, 74 (1971), p. 74.

18. Sula Benet, "Why They Live to be 100, or Even Older, in Abkhasia," *New York Times Magazine*, December 26, 1971, p. 3.

19. Nathan W. Shock, *Trends in Gerontology* (Stanford, Cal.: Stanford University Press, 1951).

20. U. S. Senate Special Committee on Aging, Hearings on *Death with Dignity: An Inquiry into Related Public Issues* (Washington, D.C.: U.S. Government Printing Office, 1972), p. 42.

21. T. Reich Warren, senior researcher, the Kennedy Center for Bioethics, testimony, U.S. Senate Special Committee on Aging, 1972.

22. See Kurt W. Back and Kenneth J. Gergen, "Individual Orientation and Morale of the Aged," Chapter 19 in Ida H. Simpson and J. C. McKinney (eds.), *Social Aspects of Aging* (Durham, N.C.: Duke University Press, 1966).

23. Bernard Berenson, *Sunset and Twilight: From the Diaries of 1947–1958* (New York: Harcourt, Brace and World, 1963).

24. W. H. Gillespie, "Some Regressive Phenomena in Old Age," *British Journal of Medical Psychology*, 56 (1962), pp. 303–309.

25. J. M. A. Munnichs, *Old Age and Finitude: A Contribution to Psychogerontology* (Basel, Switzerland: S. Karger, 1966).

26. Gerald J. Gruman, *A History of Ideas About the Prolongation of Life*, Transactions of the American Philosophical Society, December, 1966.

27. Robert C. W. Ettinger, *The Prospect of Immortality* (New York: MacFadden Books, 1964).

28. Ernest Morgan, *A Manual of Death Education and Simple Burial* (Chicago: The Celo Press, 1973).

29. R. D. Rees and S. G. Lutkins, "Mortality of Bereavement," *British Medical Journal*, 4 (1967), pp. 13–16.

CHAPTER 13. LOOSENING UP LIFE

1. There are many who are writing on this subject, among them Harold Sheppard, Judson Gooding ("Blue Collar Blues on the Assembly Line," *Fortune*, July, 1970) and Studs Terkel.

2. Franklin Wallick, *The American Worker: An Endangered Species* (New York: Ballantine, 1972).

3. Robert N. Butler, "The Burnt Out and the Bored," *The Washington Monthly*, 1 (1969), pp. 58–60. See also: Testimony, U.S. Senate Special Committee on Aging, Subcommittee on Retirement and the Individual, Chairman, Senator Walter Mondale (D.-Minn.), July 15, 1969 (Washington, D.C.: U.S. Government Printing Office, 1970).

4. Sebastian de Grazia, *Of Time, Work and Leisure* (Garden City, N.Y.: Anchor Books 1964).

5. Simone de Beauvoir, *The Second Sex* (New York: Alfred A. Knopf, 1952). Betty Friedan, *The Feminine Mystique* (New York: W. W. Norton, 1963).

6. Myrna I. Lewis and Robert N. Butler, "Neglected by Women's Lib. Why Elderly Females Need Help Against Discrimination," *The National Observer*, July 29, 1972.

7. Bertrand Russell, *Marriage and Morals* (New York: Liveright, 1929).

8. A most interesting book on the problem of romantic love is Denis de Rougemont's *Love in the Western World* (New York: Harcourt, Brace, 1940).

9. R. R. Bell, *Premarital Sex in a Changing Society* (Englewood Cliffs, N.J.: Prentice-Hall, 1966).

10. James E. Birren, Robert N. Butler, Samuel W. Greenhouse, Louis Sokoloff and Marion R. Yarrow, *Human Aging*, 1963; reprinted 1971, 1974.

11. Nena O'Neill and George O'Neill, *Open Marriage* (New York: Avon Books, 1972).

12. See Thomas Flemming (ed.), *Benjamin Franklin: A Biography in His Own Words* (New York: Newsweek–Harper & Row, 1972).

13. W. E. B. Du Bois, *Dusk at Dawn* (New York: Harcourt, Brace, 1940).

14. See Robert N. Butler, "Looking Forward to What? The Life Review, Legacy and Excessive Identity Versus Change," *American Behavioral Scientist*, 14 (1970), pp. 121–28, and Robert N. Butler, "Psychology and Psychiatry of Middle Life," chapter 34 in A. M. Freedman, H. I. Kaplan and B. J. Sadock (eds.), *Comprehensive Textbook of Psychiatry*, 2nd ed., 1975.

15. Erik H. Erikson, "The Problem of Ego Identity," in *Identity and the*

Life Cycle: Psychological Issues, Volume I, Number 1 (New York: International Universities Press, 1959), pp. 110–11.

16. Erik H. Erikson, *Childhood and Society*, 2nd ed. (New York: W. W. Norton, 1963), p. 268.

17. Leo Tolstoy, *Last Diaries*, trans. by Leon Stilman (New York: Putnam-Capricorn, 1960), p. 43.

18. Bernard Berenson, *op. cit.*, p. 64.

CHAPTER 14. GROWING OLD ABSURD

1. From the poem "The Nursing Home" by Ralph Robin, *The Southern Humanities Review*, 7 (1973), p. 421.

2. Urie Bronfenbrenner, *Two Worlds of Children: U.S. and U.S.S.R.* (New York: Russell Sage Foundation, 1970), pp. 116–17.

3. M. L. Barron, "Minority Group Characteristics of the Aged in American Society," *Journal of Gerontology*, 8 (1958), pp. 477–81.

4. See Arnold M. Rose, "The Subculture of Aging: A Topic for Sociological Research," in Bernice L. Neugarten (ed.), *Middle Age and Aging: A Reader in Social Psychology* (Chicago: University of Chicago Press, 1968), pp. 29–34.

5. See Robert N. Butler and Myrna I. Lewis, *Aging and Mental Health: Positive Psychosocial Approaches* (St. Louis: C. V. Mosby, 1973).

6. See Alvin L. Shorr, *Filial Responsibility in the Modern American Family* (U.S. Department of Health, Education, and Welfare, 1960).

7. Source: the Statistical Bureau of the Metropolitan Life Insurance Company. See "Statistical Bulletin," *Metropolitan Life Statistical Bulletin*, 53 (1972), pp. 8–10.

8. See Margaret Blenkner, "Social Work and Family Relationships in Later Life with Some Thoughts on Filial Maturity," in Ethel Shanas and Gordon F. Streib (eds.), *Social Structure and the Family: Generational Relations* (Englewood Cliffs, N.J.: Prentice-Hall, 1965).

9. Kenneth E. Boulding, "Reflections on Poverty," in *The Social Welfare Forum: 1961*, published for the National Conference on Social Welfare by Columbia University Press, New York, 1961, pp. 45–58.

10. Ethel Shanas, "The Unmarried Old Person in the United States: Living Arrangements and Care in Illness, Myth and Fact," paper prepared for the International Social Science Research Seminar in Gerontology, Markaryd, Sweden, August, 1963.

11. Eugene Litwak, "Occupational Mobility and Extended Family Cohesion," *American Sociological Review*, 25 (1960), p. 10.

12. See Herman Feifel, "Judgment of Time in Younger and Older Persons," *Journal of Gerontology*, 12 (1957), pp. 71–74.

13. See Martin Kraskowski, *Cost-Benefit Analysis of the Foster Grandparent Program* (Washington, D.C.: Office of the Assistant Secretary for Planning and Evaluation, Department of Health, Education, and Welfare, January 14, 1971).

14. Hans Meyerhoff, *Time in Literature* (Berkeley: University of California Press, 1955).

15. Bernard Berenson, *Sunset and Twilight: From the Diaries of 1947–1958* (New York: Harcourt, Brace and World, 1963).

16. From "East Coker," in T. S. Eliot, *Four Quartets* (New York: Harcourt, Brace, 1943).

17. See Robert N. Butler, "Toward a Psychiatry of the Life Cycle," in Alexander Simon and Leon J. Epstein (eds.), *Aging in Modern Society* (Washington, D.C.: American Psychiatric Association, 1968), and "A Life-cycle Perspective: Public Policies for Later Life," Chapter 5 in Frances Carp (ed.), *Retirement* (New York: Behavioral Publications, 1972).

18. Heinz Hartman, *Essays on Ego Psychology* (New York: International Universities Press, 1958).

19. See David Hunt, *Parents and Children in History. Family Life in Early Modern France* (New York: Basic Books, 1970).

20. David Musto is one of the rare scholars trained in both psychology and history. For an example of his work see *The American Disease: Origins of Narcotic Control* (New Haven: Yale University Press, 1973).

21. See Leo W. Simmons, *The Role of the Aged in Primitive Society* (New Haven: Yale University Press, 1945).

22. See Robert N. Butler, "Re-Awakening Interests," *Nursing Home, Journal of the American Nursing Home Association*, 10 (1961), pp. 8–19, and "The Life Review," *Psychiatry*, 26 (1963), pp. 65–76.

23. Myrna I. Lewis and Robert N. Butler, "Life Review Therapy," *Geriatrics*, 29 (1974), pp. 165–173.

24. See Arthur Calder-Marshall, *The Sage of Sex: A Life of Havelock Ellis* (New York: G. P. Putnam's Sons, 1959).

25. This study panel, chaired by Robert C. Maynard, issued its report in the fall of 1973.

BIBLIOGRAPHY

Abraham, Karl. "The Applicability of Psychoanalytic Treatment to Patients at an Advanced Age," in *Selected Papers of Psychoanalysis*. London: Hogarth Press, 1949, pp. 312–17.

Advisory Commission on Intergovernmental Relations. *Urban and Rural America: Policies for Future Growth*. Washington, D.C., 1968.

Albrecht, Ruth. "Social Roles in the Prevention of Senility," *Journal of Gerontology* 6:380, 1951.

Allen, Frederick Lewis. *The Big Change: America Transforms Itself, 1900–1950*. New York: Harper & Brothers, 1952.

Altmeyer, Arthur J. *The Formative Years of Social Security*. Madison: University of Wisconsin Press, 1966.

American Heart Association. *The National Diet-Heart Study*, Monograph Number 18. New York, 1968.

American Institute of Architects. Report of the National Policy Taskforce, *A Plan for Urban Growth*, 1972.

American Nursing Home Association. *Thinking About a Nursing Home?* Washington, D.C.: American Nursing Home Association, 1973.

American Psychiatric Association. "Position Statement on the Question of Adequacy of Treatment," *American Journal of Psychiatry* 123:1458–60, 1967.

———. *Diagnostic and Statistical Manual of Mental Disorders*. 2nd ed. (DSM-II), Washington, D.C., 1968.

Aries, Philippe. *Centuries of Childhood: A Social History of Family Life*. Trans. by R. Haldick. New York: Alfred A. Knopf, 1962.

Bartko, John J.; Patterson, Robert D.; and Butler, Robert N. "Biomedical and Behavioral Predictors of Survival: A Multivariant Analysis," in E. Palmore (ed.), *Prediction of the Life Span*. Lexington, Mass.: Heath Lexington Books, 1971.

Bauer, Catherine. *Modern Housing*. New York: Houghton Mifflin, 1934.

Bazelon, David. "Lake v. Cameron," in R. C. Allen; Ferster, Elyce Zenoff; and Rubin, J. G. (eds.). *Readings in Law and Psychiatry*. Baltimore: Johns Hopkins Press, 1968, pp. 196–210.

Beard, Bella Boone. *Social Competence of Centenarians*. Athens, Georgia: University of Georgia Printing Department, 1967.

Beyer, Glenn H. *Housing and Society*. New York: Macmillan, 1965.

Birnbaum, M. "Some Comments on the Right to Treatment," *Archives of General Psychiatry* 13:33–45, 1965.

Birren, James E.; Butler, Robert N.; Greenhouse, Samuel W.; Sokoloff, Louis;

and Yarrow, Marion R. *Human Aging: A Biological and Behavioral Study.* U.S. Public Health Service Publication No. 986. Washington, D.C.: U.S. Government Printing Office, 1963. Reprinted 1971, 1974.

Blenkner, Margaret; Bloom, M.; Wasser, Edna; and Nielson, Margaret. "Protective Services for Old People: Findings from the Benjamin Rose Institute Study," *Social Casework* 52:483–522, 1971.

Brenner, Harvey. *Mental Illness and the Economy.* Cambridge, Mass.: Harvard University Press, 1973.

Brewster, Agnes W., and McCamman, Dorothy. *Health Costs of the Aged.* Report No. 20, Social Security Administration, Bureau of Research and Statistics. Washington, D.C.: U.S. Government Printing Office, 1956.

Brody, Elaine M., and Spark, G. M. "Institutionalization of the Aged: A Family Crisis," *Family Process* 5:76–90, 1966.

Brotman, Herman B., Assistant to the Commissioner for Statistics and Analysis, Department of Health, Education, and Welfare. Numerous reports: Series *Facts and Figures on Older Americans,* 1971, especially No. 3, *Income and Poverty in 1970—Advance Report,* June, 1971.

———. "One in Ten: A Statistical Portrait," Geriatrics issue of *Medical World News,* Winter, 1972, pp. 51–53.

Brown, J. Douglas. *An American Philosophy of Social Security: Evaluation and Issues.* Princeton: Princeton University Press, 1972.

Buhler, Charlotte. "The Course of Human Life as a Psychological Problem," *Human Development* II: 184–200, 1968. (Original formulation: *Der Menschliche Lebenslauf als psychologisches Problem.* 1st ed. Leipzig, Germany: S. Hirzel, 1933.)

Burgess, Ernest W. *Retirement Villages: New Living Patterns for the Later Years.* Ann Arbor: University of Michigan, 1961.

Burns, Eveline M. *Social Security and Public Policy.* New York: McGraw-Hill, 1956.

———. *Analysis of Selected Current Health Insurance Bills.* Community Service Society of New York, January, 1972.

Busse, Ewald W. *Therapeutic Implications of Basic Research with the Aged.* Philadelphia: The Institute of Pennsylvania Hospital, Strecker Monograph, Series No. IV. 1967.

Butler, Robert N. "The Façade of Chronological Age," *American Journal of Psychiatry* 119:721–28, 1963.

———. "The Life Review: An Interpretation of Reminiscence in the Aged," *Psychiatry* 26:65–76, 1963.

———. "Man's Heritage: Studies of Constructive Healthy Old Age and the Transmission of Knowledge," *Proceedings,* Seventh Congress of the International Association of Gerontology, June 26, 1966–July 2, 1966. Vienna Academy of Medicine, Publishing Department, 1966.

———. "Studies of Creative People and the Creative Process After Middle Life," in Levin, S., and Kahana, R. J. (eds.), *Psychodynamic Studies on Aging: Creativity, Reminiscing and Dying.* New York: International Universities Press, 1967.

———. "Patterns of Psychological Health and Psychiatric Illness in Retirement," in Frances Carp (ed.), *The Retirement Process.* Public Health Service Publication. No. 1778, 1968.

————."Toward a Psychiatry of the Life Cycle," in Epstein, L. J., and Simon, A. (eds.), *Aging and Modern Society.* Washington, D.C.: American Psychiatric Association, 1968.

————. "Why Are Older Consumers So Susceptible?," *Geriatrics* 23:83–88, 1968.

————. "Age-ism: Another Form of Bigotry," *The Gerontologist* 9:243–46, 1969.

————. "Immediate and Long-Range Dangers to Transfer of Elderly Patients from State Hospitals to Community Facilities," guest editorial, *The Gerontologist* 10:259–60, 1970.

————. "Old Age Dividends for Lifetime Investments in America," *Aging and Human Development* 1:175–85, 1970.

————. "Should There Be a Geriatric Psychiatry?," *Psychiatric Opinion* 7:27–32, 1970.

————. "A Life Cycle Perspective in Public Policies of Retirement," chapter 5 in Carp, Frances (ed.), *Retirement.* New York: Behavioral Publications, 1971.

————, and Lewis, Myrna I. *Aging and Mental Health: Positive Psychosocial Approaches.* St. Louis: C. V. Mosby, 1973.

Camus, Albert. *The Myth of Sisyphus and Other Essays.* Trans. Justin O'Brien. New York: Vintage Books, 1959.

Cantor, Marjorie, and Mayer, Mary. *The Health Care Crisis of Older New Yorkers: Facts for Action.* New York: New York Office for the Aging, 1972.

Carley, Michael. "The Politics of Age: Interest Group or Social Movement," *The Gerontologist* 9:259–63, 1969.

Carp, Frances M. *A Future for the Aged: Victoria Plaza and Its Residents.* Austin: University of Texas Press, 1966.

———— (ed.). *The Retirement Process.* Public Health Service Publication No. 1778. Washington, D.C.: U.S. Government Printing Office, 1968.

Chandler, A. R. "Aristotle on Mental Aging," *Journal of Gerontology* 3:220–24, 1948.

Choron, Jacques. *Death and Western Thought.* New York: Collier Publishers, 1963.

Clark, Ramsey. *Crime in America.* New York: Simon & Schuster, 1970.

Comfort, Alex. *The Process of Aging.* New York: New American Library, 1961.

————. *The Joy of Sex: A Cordon Bleu Guide to Love Making.* New York: Crown, 1972.

Commission on Chronic Illness. *Chronic Illness in the United States.* Vol. 2, *Care of the Long-term Patient.* Cambridge, Mass.: published for The Commonwealth Fund by Harvard University Press, 1956.

Committee on the Costs of Medical Care. *Medical Care for the American People: The Final Report of the Committee.* Chicago: University of Chicago Press, 1932.

Committee on Research and Development. "Goals in Social Gerontology of the Gerontological Society." Chapter II, "Living Arrangements of Older People," "Ecology," *The Gerontologist* 9:37–54, 1969.

Committee on Ways and Means, U.S. House of Representatives. Summary of Provisions of H.R.I. "The Social Security Amendments of 1971" as amended

May 12, 1971. Washington, D.C.: U.S. Government Printing Office.

Cosin, Lionel Z.; Mort, Margaret; Post, F.; Westropp, Celia; and Williams, Moyra. "Experimental Treatment of Persistent Senile Confusion," *The International Journal of Social Psychiatry* 4:24–42, 1958.

Cowdry, Edmund U., and Steinberg, Franz V. *The Care of the Geriatric Patient*. St. Louis: C. V. Mosby, 1971.

Crowly, Frances J. "The Social Security Retirement Test; Earnings Test." Library of Congress Legislative Reference, February 20, 1969. Revised.

Cumming, Elaine, and Henry, William E. *Growing Old: The Process of Disengagement*. New York: Basic Books, 1961.

Curtin, Sharon. *Nobody Ever Died of Old Age*. Boston, Little, Brown, 1973.

Davis, Donald. "Growing Old Black," in *Employment Prospects of Aged Blacks, Chicanos and Indians*. Washington, D.C.: National Council on the Aging, 1971, pp. 27–53.

de Beauvoir, Simone. *A Very Easy Death*. New York: Putnam, 1966.

de Grazia, Sebastian. *Of Time, Work and Leisure*. Garden City, N.Y.: Anchor Books, 1964.

Donahue, Wilma, and Tibbits, Clark (eds.). *Politics of Age*. Ann Arbor: University of Michigan, 1962.

Ehrenreich, Barbara and John. *The American Health Empire: Power, Profits and Politics. A Report from the Health Policy Advisory Center* (Health-PAC). New York: Random House, 1971.

Eissler, Kurt. *The Psychiatrist and the Dying Patient*. New York: International Universities Press, 1955.

Epstein, Lenore S. "Income of the Aged in 1962: First Findings of the 1963 Survey of the Aged," *Social Security Bulletin,* March, 1964.

Erikson, Erik H. *Identity and the Life Cycle. Psychological Issues*, Vol. I, No. 1. New York: International Universities Press, 1959.

Evans, Rowland, and Novak, Robert. *Lyndon B. Johnson: The Exercise of Power*. New York: New American Library, 1966.

Executive Office of the President. Program fact sheet, *OEO Older Persons*. Office of Economic Opportunity, Washington, D.C., November 23, 1970. Mimeographed.

Feifel, Herman. *The Meaning of Death*. New York: McGraw-Hill, 1959.

Fox, Renée C. *Experiment Perilous*. Glencoe, Illinois: Free Press, 1959.

Frankl, Viktor E. *Man's Search for Meaning: An Introduction to Logotherapy*. Originally *From Death-camp to Existentialism*. New York: Washington Square Press, 1959.

Freeman, Joseph T. "Medical Education in Geriatrics," in *Research and Training in Gerontology*. A working paper. Prepared for the U.S. Senate Special Committee on Aging. Washington, D.C.: U.S. Government Printing Office, 1971.

Friedman, Milton, and Cohen, Wilbur J. *A Debate: Social Security: Universal or Selective?* Washington, D.C.: American Enterprise Institute for Public Policy Research, 1972.

Friedmann, E. A., and Havighurst, Robert J. *The Meaning of Work and Retirement*. Chicago: University of Chicago Press, 1954.

Gerber, Alex. *The Gerber Report*. New York: David McKay Company, 1971.

Gibson, Robert W. "National Health Insurance: Will Psychiatry Be Dragged

Screaming into the 1970s?," "Psychiatric Forum" in *Psychiatric Digest* 31:11–14, 1970.

Glaser, Barney G., and Strauss, Anselm L. *Awareness of Dying.* Chicago: Aldine Publishing Company, 1965.

Goldfarb, Alvin I. "Institutional Care of the Aged," Chapter 14 in Busse, E. W., and Pfeiffer, E. (eds.), *Behavior and Adaptation in Late Life.* Boston: Little, Brown, 1969, pp. 289–312.

Gorer, Geoffrey. *Death, Grief and Mourning in Contemporary Britain.* London: Grosset Press, 1965.

Granick, Samuel, and Patterson, Robert D. *Human Aging II: An Eleven-Year Biomedical and Behavioral Study.* Washington, D.C.: U.S. Public Service Monograph, 1971.

Group for the Advancement of Psychiatry. *Crisis in Psychiatric Hospitalization.* Report No. 72, New York, 1969.

———. *Toward a Public Policy on Mental Health Care of the Elderly.* Report No. 79, New York, November, 1970.

———. *The Aged and Community Mental Health: A Guide to Program Development.* Report No. 81, New York, November, 1971.

———. Symposium No. 12. *The Right to Die: Decision and Decision-makers.* New York, 1973.

Gunther, John. *Death Be Not Proud.* New York: Harper & Brothers, 1949.

Guttman, David C. "The Country of Old Men: Cross-Cultural Studies of the Psychology of Later Life," in *Occasional Papers in Gerontology, 5.* Institute of Gerontology, Ann Arbor: University of Michigan Press, 1969.

Halpern, Charles. "A Practicing Lawyer Views the Right to Treatment," *The Georgetown Law Journal* 57:782–817, 1969.

Harmer, Ruth Mulvey. *The High Cost of Dying.* New York: Crowell-Collier Press, 1963.

Harris, Richard. *A Sacred Trust* (1966). Rev. ed. Baltimore: Pelican Paperback, 1969.

Hayflick, Leonard. "Current Theories of Biological Aging," *The Gerontologist* 14:352, 1974.

———. "The Strategy of Senescence," *The Gerontologist* 14:37–45, 1974.

Heschel, Abraham J. *The Insecurity of Freedom: Essays on Human Existence.* New York: Farrar, Straus and Giroux, 1966.

Heusinkveld, Helen, and Musson, Noverre (eds.). *Best Places to Live When You Retire: A Directory of Retirement Residences.* New York: Frederick Hill, 1968.

Hill, Robert B. "A Profile of the Black Aged," in *Occasional Papers in Gerontology.* Ann Arbor: University of Michigan-Wayne State University, 1971.

Hinton, John M. *Dying.* London: Penguin, 1967.

Hodgins, Eric. *Episode: Report on the Accident Inside My Skull.* New York: Atheneum, 1964.

Hollingshead, August B., and Redlich, Frederick C. *Social Class and Mental Illness.* New York: John Wiley and Sons, 1958.

Holtzman, Abraham. *The Townsend Movement.* New York: Bookman Associates, 1963.

Howard, Sir Ebenezer. *Garden Cities of Tomorrow.* London: Faber and Faber, 1946.

Howe, Irving. *The World of the Blue Collar Worker.* Chicago: Quadrangle Books, 1972.

Howes, Mary H. "Measuring Retired Couples' Living Costs in Urban Areas," *Monthly Labor Review*, Bureau of Labor Statistics, U.S. Department of Labor, November, 1969.

Jackson, Jacqueline J. "The Blacklands of Gerontology," *Aging and Human Development* 2:156–71, 1971.

Jaco, E. Gartley. *The Social Epidemiology of Mental Disorders.* New York: Russell Sage Foundation, 1960.

Jacobs, Jane. *The Death and Life of Great American Cities.* New York: Random House, 1961.

Jaffe, A. J. "The Retirement Dilemma," *Industrial Gerontology*, No. 14, Summer, 1972.

Joint Commission on Mental Illness and Health. *Action for Mental Health.* Final Report of the Commission. New York: Basic Books, 1968.

Joint Economic Committee of the Congress of the United States. *The Economics of Federal Subsidy Programs.* Staff study by Jerry J. Jasinowski, Washington, D.C.: U.S. Government Printing Office, 1972.

Joint Publication of the Committee on Finance of the U.S. Senate and the Committee on Ways and Means of the U.S. House of Representatives. *Summary of Social Security Amendments of 1972.* Public Law 92-603 (HRI). Washington, D.C.: U.S. Government Printing Office, 1972.

Kahana, Eva, and Kahana, B. Boaz. "Therapeutic Potential of Age Integration: Effects of Age-Integrated Hospital Environments of Elderly Psychiatric Patients," *Archives of General Psychiatry* 23:20–29, 1970.

Kaplan, Oscar J. (ed.). *Mental Disorders in Later Life.* 2nd ed. Stanford: Stanford University Press, 1956.

Kastenbaum, Robert, and Candy, Sandra E. "The 4% Fallacy: A Methodological and Empirical Critique of Extended Care Facility Population Statistics," *International Journal of Aging and Human Development* 4:15–21, 1973.

Keith, Nathaniel S. *Politics and the Housing Crisis Since 1930.* New York: Universe Books, 1973.

Keyserling, Leon H. *Progress or Poverty: The U.S. at the Crossroads.* Washington, D.C.: Conference on Economic Progress, 1964.

Kreps, Juanita. *Lifetime Allocation of Work and Income: Essays in the Economics of Aging.* Durham, N. C.: Duke University Press, 1971.

Kubler-Ross, Elisabeth. *On Dying and Death: What the Dying Have to Teach Doctors, Nurses, Clergy and Their Own Families.* London: Macmillan, 1969.

Lawton, Alfred H. "Continuing Postgraduate Medical Education in Geriatrics," *Journal of the American Geriatrics Society* 19:97–101, 1971.

Lederberg, Joshua. "The Dilemma of Tainted Blood," Washington *Post,* August 1, 1971.

Legal Research and Services for the Elderly. *A Handbook of Model State Institutes.* Washington, D.C.: National Council of Senior Citizens, 1971.

Lehman, Harvey C. *Age and Achievement.* Princeton: Princeton University Press, 1953.

Lehman, Virginia, and Mathiasen, Geneva. *Guardianship and Protective Services for Older People.* New York: National Council on Aging Press, 1963.

Lewis, Myrna I., and Butler, Robert N. "Life Review Therapy," *Geriatrics* 29:165–173, 1974.

Libow, Leslie S. "Old People's Medical and Physiological Characteristics: Some Implications for Transportation," in Cantilli, E. J., and Schmelser, June L. (eds.), *Transportation and the Aged: Selected Issues*. Washington, D.C.: U.S. Government Printing Office, 1970.

Lieberman, Morton B. "Some Preliminary Observations on Death and Dying," *The Gerontologist* 6:70–72, 1966.

Lowenthal, Marjorie Fiske; Berkman, Paul C.; and Associates. *Aging and Mental Disorders in San Francisco*. San Francisco: Jossey-Bass, 1967.

Lowenthal, Marjorie Fiske, and Chiriboga, D. "Transition to the Empty Nest: Crisis, Challenge or Relief?," *Archives of General Psychiatry* 26:8–14, 1972.

McGuire, Marie C. "The Status of Housing for the Elderly," *The Gerontologist* 9:10–14, 1969.

McNeil, J. S., and Giffen, M. B. "Military Retirement: Some Basic Observations and Concepts," *Aerospace Medicine* 36:25–29, 1965.

Marris, Peter. *Widows and Other Families*. London: Routledge and Kegan Paul, 1958.

Martin, Alexander R. "Urgent Need for a Philosophy of Leisure in an Aging Population," *Journal of the American Geriatrics Society* 10:215–24, 1962.

Mathiasen, Geneva (ed.). *Flexible Retirement: Evolving Policies and Programs for Industry and Labor*. New York: G. P. Putnam's Sons, 1957.

Mayer, Jean. *Overweight: Causes, Cost and Control*. Originally published 1968. Mt. Vernon, N. Y.: Consumers Union edition, 1969.

Mendelsohn, Mary Adelaide. *Tender Loving Greed*. New York: Alfred A. Knopf, 1974.

Miller, Arthur. *The Death of a Salesman*. New York: Viking Press, 1949.

Mitford, Jessica. *The American Way of Death*. New York: Simon & Schuster, 1963.

Moore, Jean E. "Relocation of People: A Challenging Aspect of Urban Renewal and Redevelopment," *Social Casework* 47:657–662, 1966.

Morgan, James N., *et al. Income and Welfare in the United States*. New York: McGraw-Hill, 1962.

Moser, Robert H. (ed.). *Diseases of Medical Progress: A Study of Iatrogenic Disease; A Contemporary Analysis of Illness Produced by Drugs and Other Therapeutic Procedures*. 3rd ed. Springfield, Illinois: Charles C. Thomas, 1969.

Mumford, Lewis. *The Urban Prospect*. New York: Harcourt Brace Jovanovich, 1968.

Nader, Ralph. *Old Age: The Last Segregation*. (Claire Townsend, project director) New York: Grossman Publishing Company, 1971.

National Advisory Commission on Civil Disorders. Report of the National Advisory Commission on Civil Disorders, *The Kerner Report*. New York: Bantam Books, 1968.

National Commission on the Causes and Prevention of Violence, to Establish Justice, to Insure Domestic Tranquility. (Dr. Milton Eisenhower, chairman) New York: Award Books, 1969.

National Commission on Urban Problems. The Douglas Report of former

Senator Paul Douglas, its chairman, 1966; *Building the American City.* New York: Praeger, 1969.

National Committee on Aging. *Standards of Care for Older People in Institutions* (3 volumes). No. 1. *Suggested Standards for Homes for the Aged and Nursing Homes*; No. 2. *Methods of Establishing and Maintaining Standards in Homes*; No. 3. *Bridging the Gap between Existing Practices and Desirable Goals.* New York: 1953 and 1954.

National Council on the Aging. *A National Directory of Housing for Older People Including a Guide for Selection.* New York: 1969.

———. *Resources for the Aging: An Action Handbook.* New York, 1969.

———. *The Golden Years: A Tarnished Myth.* A report prepared for the Office of Economic Opportunity on the results of Project FIND. Washington, D.C.: 1970.

———, in cooperation with the U.S. Department of Labor. *Employment of the Middle-aged Worker.* Washington, D.C.: 1969.

———. *Employment Prospects of Aged Blacks, Chicanos, and Indians.* Washington, D.C.: 1971.

Neugarten, Bernice L. *Personality in Middle and Late Life: Empirical Studies.* New York: Atherton Press, 1964.

Neugarten, Bernice L. (ed.). *Middle Age and Aging.* Chicago: University of Chicago Press, 1968.

Nevins, Allan. Preface, *The Gateway to History.* New York: D. C. Heath, 1938.

Nicholson, Edna E. *Planning New Institutional Facilities for Long-term Care.* New York: G. P. Putnam, 1956.

Office of Research and Statistics, Social Security Administration. *Financing and Mental Health Care Under Medicare and Medicaid.* Research Report No. 37. Washington, D.C.: U.S. Government Printing Office, 1971.

Orshansky, Mollie. "Counting the Poor: Another Look at the Poverty Profile," *Social Security Bulletin* 28:3–29, 1965.

Ossofsky, Jack. "Foundations Are Failing the Aged," *Foundation News* 15:30–39, 1974.

Palmore, Erdman. *Normal Aging.* Durham, North Carolina: Duke University Press, 1970.

———, and Jeffers, Frances (eds.). *Prediction of Life Span.* Lexington, Mass.: Heath Lexington Books, 1971.

Pinner, Frank A.; Jacobs, Paul; and Selznick, Philip. *Old Age and Political Behavior.* Berkeley: University of California Press, 1959.

Porter, Katherine Anne. "The Jilting of Granny Weatherall," from *Flowering Judas.* New York: Harcourt and Brace, 1930.

Post-White House Conference on Aging Reports, 1973. Towards a New Attitude on Aging—April, 1973. A Report on the Administration's continuing response to the recommendations of the Delegates to the 1971 White House Conference on Aging. Together with: *Final Report of the Post-Conference Board of the 1971 White House Conference on Aging—June 1973.* Prepared for the Subcommittee on Aging of the Committee on Labor and Public Welfare and the Special Committee on Aging, U.S. Senate, September, 1973. Washington, D.C.: U.S. Government Printing Office, 1973.

Pound, Louise. "American Euphemisms for Dying, Death and Burial," *American Speech* 11:3:195–202, 1936.

President's Task Force on Aging. *Toward a Brighter Future for the Elderly.* Washington, D.C.: U.S. Government Printing Office, April, 1970.

Querido, Arne. "Experiment in Public Health," *Bulletin of World Federation of Mental Health* 6:203–16, 1952.

Quint, Jules V., and Cody, Bianca R., "Preeminence and Mortality: Longevity of Prominent Men," *American Journal of Public Health* 60:1118–24, 1970.

Randall, Ollie A. *A 20th Century Philosophy for Homes for the Aged.* New York: National Social Welfare Assembly, 1949.

Reed, Louis; Myers, Evelyn; and Scheidemandel, Patricia. *Health Insurance and Psychiatric Care: Utilization and Costs.* Washington, D.C.: American Psychiatric Association, 1972.

Rennie, Thomas A. C., and Woodward, L. E. *Mental Health in Modern Society.* New York: Commonwealth Fund, 1948.

Rice, Dorothy P., and Cooper, Barbara S. "National Health Expenditures, 1920–1970." *Social Security Bulletin,* January, 1971.

Riley, Matilda W., and Foner, Ann. *Aging and Society.* Vol. I: *An Inventory of Research Findings* (1968); Vol. II: *Aging and the Professions* (1969); Vol. III: *A Sociology of Age Certification* (1972); New York: Russell Sage Foundation.

Rosow, Irving. "Old Age: One Moral Dilemma of an Affluent Society," *The Gerontologist* 2:182–91, 1962.

————. *Social Integration of the Aged.* New York: The Free Press, 1967.

Rossman, Isadore (ed.). *Clinical Geriatrics.* Philadelphia: J. B. Lippincott, 1971.

Rutstein, David D. *The Coming Revolution in Medicine.* Cambridge, Mass.: The M.I.T. Press, 1968.

Sadler, Alfred M., Jr., and Sadler, Blair L. "Recent Developments in the Legal Aspects of Transplantation in the United States," *Transplantation Proceedings* 3:293–97, 1971.

Sander, Kenneth G. "The Retirement Test: Its Effect on Older Workers' Earnings," *Social Security Bulletin* 31:3, 1968.

Saunders, Cicely. *Care of the Dying.* London: Macmillan, 1959.

Saveth, Edward N. *Utilization of Older Professional and Scientific Workers.* The National Council on the Aging, May, 1961.

Schlesinger, Arthur G., Jr. *The Politics of Upheaval.* Boston: Houghton, Mifflin, 1960.

Schoenberg, Bernard; Carr, Arthur C.; Peretz, David; and Kutscher, Austin (eds.). *Loss and Grief: Psychological Management in Medical Practice.* New York: Columbia University Press, 1970.

Schulz, James H. *Providing Adequate Retirement Income.* Hanover, N.H.: University Press of New England, 1974.

Seligman, Ben B. "The Poverty of Aging" in Larner, J., and Howe, I. (eds.), *Poverty: Views from the Left.* New York: The Free Press, 1965.

Shanas, Ethel, and Streib, Gordon F. *Social Structure and the Family: Generational Relations.* Englewood Cliffs, N.J.: Prentice-Hall, 1965.

Shanas, Ethel; Townsend, Peter; Wedderburn, Dorothy; Friis, H.; Milji, P.; and

Stehouwer, W. *Old People in Three Industrial Societies.* Chicago: Aldine Publishing Company, 1968.

Sheppard, Harold L. "The Poverty of the Aging" in Seligman, Ben B. (ed.), *Poverty as a Public Issue.* New York: The Free Press, 1965.

————, and Herrick, Neal Q. *Where Have All the Robots Gone? Worker Dissatisfaction in the 70s.* New York: The Free Press, Macmillan, 1972.

Slote, Alfred. *Termination: The Closing at Baker Plant.* Indianapolis: Bobbs-Merrill, 1969.

Stieglitz, Edward J. (ed.). *Geriatric Medicine: Medical Care of Later Maturity.* Philadelphia: J. B. Lippincott, 1954.

Stotsky, Bernard A. *The Elderly Patient.* New York: Grune and Stratton, 1968.

Strehler, Bernard C. *Time, Cells and Aging.* New York: Academic Press, 1962.

Time Magazine. Cover story, "Growing Old in America: The Unwanted Generation," August 3, 1970, pp. 49–54.

Tolstoy, Leo. *The Death of Ivan Ilyich* (1886). New York: Signet Classics, 1960.

Townsend, Peter. *The Family Life of Old People.* London: Routledge and Kegan Paul, 1957.

Tuchman, Barbara W. *The Proud Tower: A Portrait of the World Before the War: 1890–1914.* New York: Macmillan, 1966.

U.S. Committee on Finance. Prepared by the staff. *Staff Data Relating to Medicaid-Medicare Study.* Washington, D.C.: U.S. Government Printing Office, 1969.

U.S. Department of Health, Education and Welfare, Social Security Administration. *A Budget for an Elderly Couple.* Social Security Bulletin, February, 1948, pp. 4–12.

U.S. Department of Health, Education and Welfare, Special Staff on Aging. Report of 1961 White House Conference on Aging, *The Nation and Its Older People.* Washington, D.C.: U.S. Government Printing Office, 1961.

U.S. Department of Health, Education and Welfare. *U.S. Task Force on Prescription Drugs. Final Report.* Washington, D.C.: U.S. Government Printing Office, 1969.

U.S. Department of Labor. *The Older American Worker—Age Discrimination in Employment.* Washington, D.C.: U.S. Government Printing Office, 1965.

————. *Retired Couple's Budget for Moderate Living Standard, Autumn, 1966.* Bulletin 1570–4. Washington, D.C.: U.S. Government Printing Office, 1966.

————. *Three Budgets for a Retired Couple in Urban Areas of the United States 1967–68.* Bulletin 1570–6. Washington, D.C.: U.S. Government Printing Office, May, 1970.

U.S. Senate. 90th Congress, Second Session. On S3421, S1024, S1103, S1255. *Pension and Welfare Plans,* hearings before the Subcommittee on Labor of the Committee on Labor and Public Welfare. Washington, D.C.: U.S. Government Printing Office, 1971.

U.S. Senate Committee on Finance. Report of the staff. *Medicare and Medicaid Problems, Issues and Alternatives.* Washington, D.C.: U.S. Government Printing Office, 1970.

U.S. Senate Special Committee on Aging. *Relocation of Elderly People,* hearings before the Subcommittee on Involuntary Relocation of the Elderly, 87th Congress, 2nd Session. Six volumes. Washington, D.C.: U.S. Government Printing Office, 1962–63.

————. Subcommittee on Long-term Care. *Long-term Institutional Care for the Aged,* hearings, Washington, D.C., 1963. *Nursing Homes and Related Long-term Care Services,* hearings in various cities, 1964. *Conditions and Problems in the Nation's Nursing Homes,* hearings in various cities, 1965. *Trends in Long-term Care,* hearings in various cities, 1970–71. Washington, D.C.: U.S. Government Printing Office, 1963, 1964, 1965, 1970, 1971 and 1972.

————. Subcommittee on Long-term Care. *Nursing Home Care in the United States: Failure in Public Policy.* Washington, D.C.: U.S. Government Printing Office, 1974.

————. *Frauds and Deceptions Affecting the Elderly—Investigations, Findings and Recommendations.* Washington, D.C.: U.S. Government Printing Office, December, 1964.

————. Report of Subcommittee, *Frauds and Misrepresentations Affecting the Elderly.* Washington, D.C.: U.S. Government Printing Office, 1966.

————. *War on Poverty as It Affects the Elderly*, Report No. 1287. Washington, D.C.: U.S. Government Printing Office, January, 1966.

————. *Reduction of Retirement Benefits Due to Social Security Increases.* Washington, D.C.: U.S. Government Printing Office, August 21, 1967.

————. Hearings, *The Usefulness of the Model Cities Program to the Elderly.* Washington, D.C.: U.S. Government Printing Office, 1968.

————. Hearings, *Hearing Loss, Hearing Aids and the Elderly.* Washington, D.C.: U.S. Government Printing Office, 1968.

————. *Health Aspects of the Economics of Aging.* Washington, D.C.: U.S. Government Printing Office, July, 1969.

————. Report prepared by Dr. Robert Morris, Levinson Gerontological Policy Institute, Brandeis University. *Alternatives to Nursing Home Care: A Proposal.* Washington, D.C.: U.S. Government Printing Office, 1971.

————. Report prepared by Dr. Ethel Shanas, *Making Services for the Elderly Work: Some Lessons from the British Experience.* Washington, D.C.: U.S. Government Printing Office, 1971.

————. U.S. Senate Hearings, *Cutbacks in Medicare and Medicaid.* Washington, D.C.: U.S. Government Printing Office, 1971.

————. Report, *Mental Health Care and the Elderly: Shortcomings in Public Policy.* (Consultant, Robert N. Butler, M.D.) Washington, D.C.: U.S. Government Printing Office, 1971.

————. Annual Reports, *Developments in Aging.* Washington, D.C.: U.S. Government Printing Office.

————. *Action on Aging Legislation in 92nd Congress.* Washington, D.C.: U.S. Government Printing Office, October, 1972.

————. *Home Health Services in the United States.* Prepared by Brahna Trager, Home Health Consultant. Washington, D.C.: U.S. Government Printing Office, 1972.

————. *Death with Dignity: An Inquiry into Related Public Issues.* Washington, D.C.: U.S. Government Printing Office, 1972.

————. Hearings, *Future Directions in Social Security,* Parts 1, 2, 3. Washington, D.C.: U.S. Government Printing Office, 1973.

————. *Hearings of Subcommittee on Health of the Elderly, Part 3: Health Aspects.* Washington, D.C.: U.S. Government Printing Office, July 17-18, 1969.

————. A working paper prepared for a hearing on *Social Security for the Aged: International Perspectives on the Economics of Aging*. Washington, D.C.: U.S. Government Printing Office, August 25, 1969.

————. *Legal Problems Affecting Older Americans*. Prepared by Legal Research and Services for the Elderly, National Council of Senior Citizens. Washington, D.C.: U.S. Government Printing Office, 1970.

————. *Older Americans and Transportation. A Crisis in Mobility*. Washington, D.C.: U.S. Government Printing Office, 1970.

————. *Economics of Aging: Toward a Full Share in Abundance*. Report. Washington, D.C., U.S. Government Printing Office, December, 1970.

————. *Income Tax Overpayments by the Elderly*. Report No. 91–1464. Washington, D.C.: U.S. Government Printing Office, December, 1970.

————. *The Multiple Hazards of Age and Race: The Situation of Aged Blacks in the United States*. A working paper, preliminary survey prepared by Dr. Inabel B. Lindsay. Washington, D.C.: U.S. Government Printing Office, September, 1971.

————. *A Pre–White House Conference on Aging. Summary of Development and Data*. Report. Washington, D.C.: U.S. Government Printing Office, November, 1971.

————. *Home Health Services in the United States: A Working Paper on Current Status*. Washington, D.C.: U.S. Government Printing Office, 1973.

————. Subcommittee on Federal, State and Community Services. *The Rise and Threatened Fall of Service Programs for the Elderly*. Washington, D.C.: U.S. Government Printing Office, 1973.

U.S. Senate Special Subcommittee on Aging of the Committee on Labor and Public Welfare. Hearings, *Older Americans Community Service Program*. Washington, D.C.: U.S. Government Printing Office, 1967.

U.S. Senate Subcommittee on Aging of the Committee on Labor and Public Welfare and the Special Committee on Aging of the U.S. Senate. *Legislative History of the Older Americans Comprehensive Services Amendments of 1972*. H.R. 15657—not approved. Pocket-vetoed by President, October 28, 1972. Washington, D.C.: U.S. Government Printing Office, 1972.

Veterans Administration. *The Veteran Age 65 and Over: A Profile,* March, 1968.

Walkley, Rosabelle P.; Mangum, Wiley P., Jr.; Sherman, Susan R.; Dodds, Suzanne; and Wilner, Daniel M. *Retirement Housing in California*. San Francisco: Diablo Press, 1966.

Weisman, Adrian D., and Kastenbaum, Robert. *The Psychological Autopsy: A Study of the Terminal Phase of Life*. Community Mental Health Journal, Monograph No. 4. New York: Behavioral Publications, 1968.

White House Conference on Aging, 1971. Report of the Delegates from the Conference Sections and Special Concerns Sessions. Washington, D.C., December, 1971.

————. *Toward a National Policy on Aging*. Final report. Volumes I and II, 1973.

Worcester, Alfred. *Care of the Aged, the Dying and the Dead*. 2nd ed. Springfield, Ill.: Charles C. Thomas Company, 1961.

World Health Organization. *Mental Health Problems of the Aging and Aged*. Technical Report Series, No. 171. Geneva: World Health Organization, 1959.

INDEX

ABOUT THE AUTHOR

Dr. Robert N. Butler was born in New York City in 1927, was graduated from Columbia College, and received his medical degree from the Columbia University College of Physicians and Surgeons. He is a practicing psychiatrist and psychoanalyst as well as a research psychiatrist and gerontologist at the Washington School of Psychiatry. He is also on the faculties of the Washington Psychoanalytic Institute and the Howard and George Washington University Schools of Medicine in Washington, D.C.

Dr. Butler has written extensively for professional journals and for lay publications as well, and is co-author of *Human Aging* and *Aging and Mental Health.* His broad professional and personal commitment to the elderly includes service as a consultant to the U.S. Senate Committee on Aging and the chairmanship of the Group for the Advancement of Psychiatry's Committee on Aging. His activities over the past twenty years encompass research and observation, clinical practice, writing, muckraking and public advocacy.